Edited by Michael Haralambos and Peter Langley

Written by
Michael Haralambos, Andrew Pilkington and Alan Yeo

CP

Picture research by Louise Edgeworth

Cartoons
Unless otherwise credited, the cartoons in this book have been specially drawn by BRICK www.brickbats.co.uk

Cover picture
The End of the Greeks, 1964 by Hundertwasser, © Hundertwasser Archive, Vienna

British Library Cataloguing in Publication Data
A Catalogue record for this book is available from the British Library.

ISBN: 978-1-4058-9669-6

First Impression 2004, Third impression 2006
Second Edition First impression 2009

Printed and bound in Great Britain by Scotprint, Haddington, East Lothian.

Contents

1 Beliefs in society

Introduction

A belief is something that a person holds to be true. It may be a conviction that the world is flat *or* that the world is round. It may be a conviction that human beings were created by a supernatural power *or* that they evolved from other organisms by a process of natural selection.

This chapter looks at sociological explanations for beliefs. It is concerned with beliefs held by large numbers of people – hence the title *Beliefs in society*. It starts from a standard sociological approach that many beliefs are shared, they are learned as part of society's culture, and just as culture varies from society to society, so do beliefs.

Religious beliefs form the main focus of the chapter. Beliefs based on science and ideology are also considered. In each case, sociologists argue that beliefs are formed in social contexts, that they are socially constructed.

Over two million Muslim pilgrims gather in Mecca to perform the annual hajj ceremony. Islam is now the world's second largest and fastest growing religion.

chaptersummary

▶ **Unit 1** looks at the social construction of science.

▶ **Unit 2** outlines theories of ideology.

▶ **Unit 3** examines sociological theories of religion.

▶ **Unit 4** assesses the role of religion, both as a conservative force which maintains things the way they are and as a radical force which encourages social change.

▶ **Unit 5** discusses different types of religious organisation, including churches, denominations, sects, cults and New Religious Movements.

▶ **Unit 6** looks at explanations of the relationship between religious beliefs, religious organisations and social groups.

▶ **Unit 7** investigates the secularisation debate – whether or not societies are becoming increasingly secular or non-religious.

▶ **Unit 8** examines contemporary religion from a global perspective.

Unit 1 Science and society

keyissues

1 How are belief systems constructed?

2 How are scientific beliefs constructed?

1.1 The social construction of reality

In an influential work entitled *The Social Construction of Reality* (1967), Peter Berger and Thomas Luckmann argue that human beings construct their beliefs in a social context. They manufacture *universes of meaning* which organise their experiences and make sense of their lives. They construct their own social worlds and work to maintain them against the threat of uncertainty and disruption.

A universe of meaning requires constant *legitimation*. It needs repeated reinforcement and justification. Members of society must be told and re-told that their universe of meaning is legitimate – right, true and correct. Without this support, a universe of meaning would tend to crumble, life would become meaningless and the stability of society would be threatened.

Belief systems are socially constructed. They form the basis of universes of meaning. And they feed back and reinforce the society that constructed them. This applies to the whole spectrum of beliefs. In this respect, there is little difference between scientific theories, political beliefs and religious doctrines. They are all socially constructed, they all help to make sense of the world and they all form a part of and legitimate universes of meaning. Here are some examples.

Religious beliefs provide answers to basic questions such as the meaning of life, the origin of the human species and what happens after death. They also provide justification for the legal system. For example, many laws are based on religious beliefs about right and wrong. Religion provides ultimate support for universes of meaning – it places them within a supernatural reality which believers do not question. By comparison, science offers support for universes of meaning by grounding them in reason and evidence. For example, the origin and evolution of the human species is explained in terms of Darwin's theory of evolution which is based on evidence from the fossil record.

Berger and Luckmann argue that the certainty provided by universes of meaning has a precarious foundation. Universes of meaning are real because people believe they are real. Life is meaningful because of the meaning people give to it. However, there is no universal standard or yardstick against which reality can be shown to be real, that beliefs can be shown to be true. One society's truth may be another society's falsehood. Common sense in one society may be nonsense in another. Universes of meaning are insecure and easily shattered.

key terms

Universe of meaning A socially constructed belief system which gives meaning to people's lives.
Legitimation To make right, true, correct.

activity1 *science and the construction of reality*

Item A *Galileo's telescope*

The centre of the Milky Way galaxy taken from NASA's Chandra X-ray Observatory

The telescope built in 1609 by Galileo had the magnifying power of a cheap pair of binoculars. Yet it opened up a new world. Galileo could see that Jupiter had four moons and the Sun had spots – which led him to conclude that the Sun was rotating. His telescope provided evidence that the Sun rather than the Earth was the centre of the solar system. As more powerful telescopes were built, people became aware of a vast universe in which they were inhabitants of an insignificant dot, part of a galaxy of billions of stars, each carrying their own solar systems.

Source: *Lederman*, 2008

Item B *The Large Hadron Collider*

Part of the Large Hadron Collider

The Large Hadron Collider was completed in 2008 at a cost of $10 billion. It is built in a 17 mile circular tunnel, 100 metres below ground near Geneva, Switzerland. It is a particle collider – it will crash subatomic particles together.

The aim of the Large Hadron Collider is to re-create the conditions that existed one trillionth of a second after the Big Bang which many scientists believe created our universe 13.7 billion years ago. Scientists hope that this will reveal the origins of the forces of nature and unlock the secrets of time and space.

Source: *The Guardian*, 11.9.2008

questions

1 How has Galileo's telescope helped to produce a new universe of meaning?

2 How might the Large Hadron Collider help to produce a new reality?

1.2 The social construction of science

In today's society, many of our beliefs are based on the observations and theories of science. Modern genetics has unravelled the human genome and Darwin's theory of evolution has provided an explanation for the origin and evolution of the human race. In 2008, the Large Hadron Collider, a particle collider, was built near Geneva, 100 metres beneath fields in a 17 mile circular tunnel. It aims to reveal the origins of the universe and the forces of nature by simulating aspects of the Big Bang.

The origins of modern science

Researchers have placed the origins of modern science in 18th century Europe during a period known as the Enlightenment. Scholars from a number of countries contributed to a publication know as the *Encyclopédie*. It was based on two principles. First, the belief that reason could provide an understanding of the world. And second, the belief that this understanding could be used to improve the lives of human beings. Knowledge was based on reason and observation. This formed the guidelines for the *scientific method* – the procedure for 'doing science'.

These beliefs directly challenged the view of the world provided by the Roman Catholic Church. According to the Church, knowledge was based on divine revelation – eternal truths revealed by the word of God. In contrast, science claimed that reason and observation formed the basis for knowledge and the foundation for many beliefs. (See pages 257-259 for further discussion of science and the Enlightenment.)

The traditional view of science

The traditional view of science in modern society is fairly straightforward. Science is based on systematic observation and measurement. Ideas about the behaviour of matter in the natural world can be tested and shown to be true or untrue. In the laboratory, for example, the scientist observes the behaviour of matter under various conditions, measuring variables such as temperature and pressure. These observations are objective – they are not influenced by the values or religious beliefs of the scientist. They can be shown to be accurate by *replication* – by the repetition of the experiment under the same conditions. If the results are the same, then the observations are seen to be accurate.

Theories are then constructed to explain the behaviour observed. If later observations show that behaviour differs from that predicted by the theory, then the theory is modified or changed. In this way science progresses – it provides an increasingly accurate and comprehensive understanding of the behaviour of matter.

In modern society scientists have had high status. Their findings have generally been accepted and seen as beneficial to humankind. For example, scientific advances in medicine have been welcomed and seen as a major factor in improving health and increasing life expectancy.

However, the view of science described above is overly simple. And the belief that science brings benefits to humankind has been increasingly questioned.

Science and falsification

How do we know that scientific theories provide accurate explanations? According to Karl Popper in his influential book *The Logic of Scientific Discovery* (1959), theories can be tested through observation and experiment. In this respect, they are superior to 'everyday' knowledge and beliefs. However, Popper argues, we can never know with certainty that a theory is true. All we can say is that so far the theory has not been shown to be false. For example, many scientists accept the Big Bang theory of the origin of the universe – it is supported by a range of observational data. However, evidence yet to be discovered may disprove or *falsify* this theory. Scientists therefore accept theories 'for the time being' because there is general agreement that to date they are supported by observations. As a result, 'science does not rest upon a solid bedrock' (Popper, 1959).

According to Popper, science is based on the systematic testing of theories in an attempt to disprove them. If theories withstand this attempt, then they gain acceptance. However, they can never be finally proven. In practice, theories are eventually modified or overturned by new theories. (For further discussion of Popper, see page 230.)

The fabrication of facts

Popper argued that scientific theories 'do not rest on a solid bedrock'. Karin Knorr-Centina, in an article entitled *The Fabrication of Facts* (2005), makes a similar point about the 'facts' used to test scientific theories. In her words, 'facts are not something we can take for granted or think of as the solid rock upon which knowledge is built'. She argues that the systematic observations and measurements made by scientists are not the objective 'facts' they are often seen to be.

So-called 'facts' are *fabricated* – they are constructed by scientists. The 'facts' they observe in the laboratory or the natural world are shaped by their theories and by their measuring instruments. Theories direct scientists what to look for and how to see it. For example, the theory of evolution directs scientists to examine fossils to see how they fit into an evolutionary sequence and to look for 'missing links' in order to fill gaps in that sequence. And measuring instruments construct the 'facts' available to scientists. For example, Galileo's telescope was essential to provide the observations that supported his theory that the Earth went round the Sun. As new measuring instruments are invented, new observations are possible and new 'facts' can be manufactured. In this respect, science is based on the fabrication of facts.

The social construction of scientific knowledge

Thomas Kuhn's book *The Structure of Scientific Revolutions* (1962) challenged the traditional view of science. He saw science as socially constructed within scientific communities. This rejects the view that science is based solely on rationality and objectivity.

According to Kuhn, scientists work in communities centred on particular branches of science and particular research projects. They operate in terms of shared *paradigms*. A paradigm is a framework stating which theories should be developed, what kinds of data should be collected and which research methods are appropriate. Scientists tend to look for data which supports the paradigm and refine theories contained within the paradigm. The paradigm shapes the way they see the world. This outlook is supported by communities of scientists. In this respect, the paradigm is socially constructed and socially legitimated.

Kuhn argues that for most of the time scientists conduct *normal science*, that is within the framework of the current paradigm. Normal science develops and refines the paradigm rather than challenging it. Most scientists are committed to the existing paradigm – their career has been based upon it, their reputation has been built in terms of it and they find it difficult to see the world in any other way. There is a tendency to ignore or explain away contradictory evidence which challenges the paradigm of the day.

According to Kuhn, significant changes – *scientific revolutions* – occur when sufficient evidence accumulates which cannot be explained in terms of the existing paradigm. A new paradigm which appears to explain this evidence then develops. However, there is often considerable resistance to a new paradigm. For example, Newton's theories, which formed the basis of a new paradigm in physics, took over 50 years to become established. Once accepted, a revolutionary paradigm becomes the order of the day and normal science is then conducted within its framework.

key terms

Scientific method The accepted method for conducting scientific research.
Replication The repetition of a piece of research using the same methods.
Falsification Showing a theory to be incorrect.
Fabrication of facts The social construction of things seen to be true.
Paradigm A framework within which scientists work which states what kinds of theories, methods and data are acceptable.
Normal science Science conducted within the framework of the existing paradigm.
Scientific revolution The overthrow of an existing paradigm by a new paradigm.

activity2 scientific revolutions

Item A Galileo (1564-1642)

Galileo demonstrating his telescope to the nobles of Venice

Galileo, an Italian mathematician and astronomer, challenged the accepted view that the Earth was the centre of the universe. Based on mathematical calculations and observations using an advanced telescope, which he designed, Galileo argued that the Earth went round the Sun. This was in direct conflict with the views of astronomers, mathematicians and philosophers of the day, and with the teachings of the Roman Catholic Church. Galileo was put on trial in a church court, found guilty of heresy – going against the word of God – and punished with house arrest. He continued his work and his book had to be smuggled out of Italy and taken to Holland for publication.

Item B Charles Darwin (1809-1882)

The British naturalist Charles Darwin published his theory of evolution in *The Origin of Species* in 1859. Today, his idea of natural selection forms the basis of the biological sciences. However, it was condemned by many of the leading scientists of his day. Darwin's tutors at Cambridge University rejected his theory, as did Richard Owen who headed the Victorian scientific establishment.

Darwin was ridiculed by the popular press who poked fun at the idea that human beings, apes and monkeys were descended from a common ancestor.

This cartoon shows Darwin (on the left) with an ape's body.

question

What support do Items A and B provide for Kuhn's views on scientific revolutions?

1.3 Science in late modern and postmodern society

A number of sociologists argue that societies like the UK have moved from the *modern era* to the *postmodern era* during the last quarter of the 20th century. Other sociologists see this change as less dramatic, arguing that we have entered *late modernity*, an extension of the modern era. However, both groups agree that this has involved important changes in attitudes towards science.

Anthony Giddens – science in late modern society

Giddens (1991) argues that people in late modern society have serious doubts over Enlightenment beliefs about the promise and potential of science. No longer is science seen as bringing certainty and 'securely founded knowledge'.

This change of outlook is based on the realisation that no matter how well established a scientific theory, it will probably be revised or discarded in the light of new ideas and findings. Many people find this uncertainty troubling.

The Enlightenment view that science will improve the human condition is now treated with increasing scepticism. Science may bring benefits to humankind but it also brings risk and danger – for example, the dangers of nuclear energy as revealed by the explosion of the nuclear power station at Chernobyl in the former Soviet Union in 1986 (see Activity 3, Item C).

According to Giddens, these negative views of science are balanced by more positive ones. In late modern society, science is seen as creating risk and danger but also as promising benefits for humankind. Attitudes towards science are often contradictory – 'approval and disquiet, enthusiasm and antipathy'.

Ulrich Beck – risk and globalisation

According to Ulrich Beck (1992), late modern society is characterised by uncertainty and risk. Risk is magnified by the process of globalisation – the increasing interconnectedness of parts of the world. This can be seen by the global nature of financial crises, terrorism and nuclear accidents, all of which cross national boundaries.

Many of the risks and uncertainties of late modern society are seen to be associated with science and technology. This has led people to be suspicious of so-called 'scientific advances' such as genetically modified (GM) food crops and stem cell research. Their suspicion has been heightened by disagreements between scientists – for example, about the advantages and disadvantages of GM food (see Activity 3). As a result, the credibility of beliefs based on scientific research has been reduced.

Jean-Francois Lyotard – science in postmodern society

According to the French writer Lyotard (1984), people in postmodern society have lost faith in the *metanarratives* of modern society. A metanarrative is a 'big story' like the Enlightenment view of progress, Christianity's view of life and Marx's view of history. In postmodern society, metanarratives no longer inspire, they no longer direct action, they no longer form the basis for beliefs. Science is a metanarrative – a big story about the origin of the universe, behaviour in the natural world, and the evolution of species.

Lyotard believes there is widespread disillusionment with science in postmodern society. Science has failed to deliver on the Enlightenment promise of progress. People no longer trust scientists and have lost faith in the grand claims of science.

Rather than being concerned with human betterment, science is becoming the servant of industry and commerce. Scientists are increasingly concerned with technology, focusing their attention on producing goods for sale. This can be seen from the rapid advances in electronic goods. From this point of view, science is becoming *technoscience*, concerned with producing commodities for the global marketplace (Irwin & Michael, 2003).

summary

1. Berger and Luckmann argue that beliefs are socially constructed.

2. Science can be seen as a social construction.

3. Many of today's beliefs are based on theories produced by scientists.

4. The Enlightenment view of science was based on two principles:
   - The belief that reason could provide an understanding of the world.
   - The view that this understanding could be used for the betterment of humankind.

5. Traditionally, in modern society, science was seen to be based on objective observation and measurement.

6. According to Popper, scientific theories can be falsified but cannot be proved.

7. So-called facts can be seen as fabricated or socially constructed. As such, they are not objective.

8. According to Kuhn, science is directed by paradigms constructed within communities of scientists.

9. Giddens argues that in late modern society there are serious doubts about the objectivity and value of science.

10. According to Beck, late modern society is characterised by uncertainty and risk. He sees science as contributing to this situation.

11. Lyotard sees science as one of the metanarratives which are increasingly dismissed in postmodern society.

key terms

Metanarratives The 'grand' explanations or 'big stories' of modern society provided by science, religion and political ideas.
Technoscience The application of science to technical commodities.

activity3 *science in late modern society*

Item A Monsanto

Monsanto are the world's leading producer of GM crops. 'We're excited about the potential for genetically modified food to contribute to a better environment and a sustainable, plentiful and healthy food supply.' Here are some of the benefits of GM crops.

- They produce more food on less land at lower cost.

- This helps farmers by increasing profits and helps consumers by reducing prices.

- Genetic engineering can produce food plants that are resistant to pests and drought and require fewer fertilisers.

- Insecticides and chemical fertilisers can harm the environment. Almost all GM crops reduce the need for these.

Source: www.monsanto.com

Harvesting genetically modified corn in California

Item B Greenpeace

Greenpeace are an environmental pressure group. 'Our goal is to protect the environment and biodiversity – the many different varieties of plant life on the planet.' GM crops can threaten this goal in the following ways.

- They can reproduce and interbreed with natural crops and spread to new environments in an unpredictable and uncontrollable way.

- They can threaten biodiversity if they replace the variety of existing crop plants.

- If we become dependent on one type of GM crop – for example, GM maize or soya beans – and it is attacked by a new disease, then widespread starvation may result.

- Crop diversity is essential to resist new pests, diseases and changing climatic and environmental conditions.

- Farmers can become dependent on biotech companies. They must buy fresh seeds from them each year. They are likely to be prosecuted if they save seeds from the previous year's crop for re-planting.

- We do not know the long-term effects of GM foods on people's health.

Source: www.greenpeace.org.uk

Greenpeace activists in Italy attempt to prevent the unloading of GM soya (GMOs are genetically modified organisms).

Item C Chernobyl

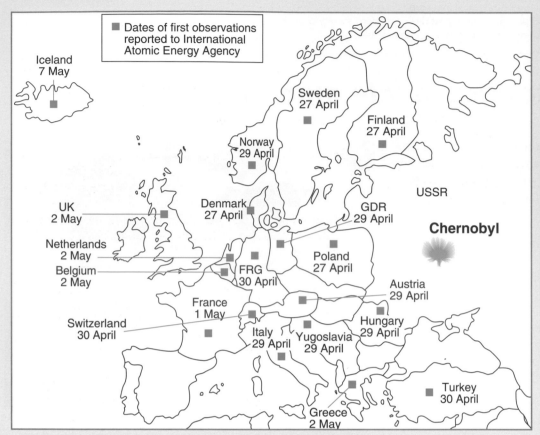

■ Dates of first observations reported to International Atomic Energy Agency

Iceland
7 May

Sweden
27 April

Finland
27 April

Norway
29 April

USSR

UK
2 May

Denmark
27 April

GDR
29 April

Chernobyl

Netherlands
2 May

Belgium
2 May

FRG
30 April

Poland
27 April

Austria
29 April

France
1 May

Switzerland
30 April

Italy
29 April

Yugoslavia
29 April

Hungary
29 April

Greece
2 May

Turkey
30 April

FRG = Federal Republic of Germany (the former West Germany)

GDR = German Democratic Republic (the former East Germany)

Dates of first measurement of radiation fallout from Chernobyl in various countries, 27 April to 7 May 1986. Map based on information from the International Atomic Energy Agency.

On 26th April 1986, the nuclear power station at Chernobyl in the former Soviet Union exploded as a result of human error. Thirty-one workers and firefighters died within days (of radiation burns) and 50,000 square kilometres of surrounding land was contaminated. The nuclear fallout reached 20 countries, including Britain. Scientists have estimated that between 280,000 and 500,000 deaths will result worldwide from this accident.

Source: Greenpeace, *Nuclear Power*, 1992

question

What support do the items in this activity provide for the views of Giddens and Beck?

Unit 2 Ideology

keyissues

1 What is ideology?
2 What are the main political ideologies?

2.1 What is ideology?

The term ideology has many meanings. This section gives a brief outline of some of the more common usages of the term.

A closed system of thought The philosopher Karl Popper (1959) saw ideology as a closed system of thought. By this he means that ideologies are closed to evidence which challenges their beliefs. Ideologies reject alternative views, they do not tolerate opposing ideas. They are immune to rational argument. Their version of the truth has an answer for everything.

Popper's view of ideology was largely based on his analysis of systems of fascist and communist totalitarian regimes in the 20th century. As a result, he also saw ideology as an instrument of social control and oppression.

A distortion of reality Ideology is often used in a negative sense to describe a set of ideas which distort reality. Marxists use the term in this way. When they refer to *ruling class ideology*, they are talking about beliefs which produce a *false consciousness*, a picture of the world which is false and distorted. Some feminists use ideology in this way when they talk about *patriarchal ideology*.

A justification for inequality From this perspective, ideology not only distorts reality, it also provides a justification for inequality. Thus ruling class ideology justifies the position of the ruling class and supports its dominance. And it blinds members of the subject class to the truth about their situation. For example, the emphasis on freedom in capitalist society – the free market, free democratic societies, individual freedoms – projects an illusion which disguises the oppression and exploitation of the subject class.

The term patriarchal ideology is used in a similar way. It presents a false picture of the characteristics of males and females. And this picture serves to justify and maintain gender inequality.

Neutral views of ideology

The views of ideology outlined above are all negative. Ideology seen as bad, false and oppressive. Neutral views see ideology as neither good nor bad, true nor false, liberating nor oppressive.

The term 'political ideology' is often used in a neutral way. It refers to viewpoints such as liberalism, conservatism, and socialism.

The various types of ideology outlined in this section will now be examined in more detail.

2.2 Marxism and ideology

Karl Marx (1818-1883)

Marx saw society as a structure divided into two major parts. The first and most important part is the economic base of *infrastructure*. The second major part, known as the *superstructure*, consists of the rest of society – the political, legal and educational systems, religion, the mass media and beliefs and ideas.

Marx claimed that the infrastructure shapes the superstructure – in other words, the economic system shapes the rest of society. For example, from a Marxist viewpoint, the education system in modern industrial society has been shaped by the requirements of a capitalist economy for a literate and well-disciplined workforce.

Social classes Marx saw conflict between social classes as the basic characteristic of all known human societies. Every society has two main social groups, a *ruling class* and a *subject class*. The power of the ruling class comes from its ownership of what Marx called the *means of production*. This includes the land, raw materials, machinery, tools and buildings used to produce goods. Thus in Western industrial society, *capitalists* – those who own private industry – form the ruling class. The subject class – the *proletariat* in capitalist society – is made up of workers who sell their labour in return for wages.

There is a basic conflict of interest between capitalists and the proletariat. Workers produce wealth in the form of goods yet a large part of that wealth is taken in the form of profits by the capitalist class. Thus one group gains at the expense of the other.

Marx believed that this conflict could not be resolved within the framework of capitalist society. It would eventually result in the overthrow of the capitalist class. A workers' revolution would lead to a communist society in which the means of production would be owned by everyone, classes would disappear, and exploitation and oppression would end.

Ruling class ideology This, however, would only happen when workers became fully aware of their exploitation. But this awareness will not occur overnight because of the way society is structured. Since the infrastructure largely shapes the superstructure, the relationship of dominance and subordination between the ruling class and subject class will be reflected in the superstructure. Thus, the political and legal systems will support ruling class power – for example, laws will protect the rights of capitalists to own industry and take profits. In the same way, the beliefs and values of society will support ruling class domination. Thus, capitalism will be seen as reasonable and just, rather than exploitative and oppressive. In this way, beliefs and values will disguise and distort the true nature of society.

In Marxist terms, beliefs and values form a ruling class ideology. This produces a false consciousness which prevents people from seeing the reality of their situation. However, Marx believed that ruling class ideology can only slow down the eventual overthrow of capitalism. The conflicts of interest within the capitalist system will inevitably lead to its downfall. In the classless society that will follow, there will be no ideology. (See pages 23-24 for further discussion of Marx's views.)

key terms

Infrastructure In Marxist theory, the economic base of society which shapes the superstructure.

Superstructure The rest of society – the political, legal and educational systems, the family, religion, beliefs and ideas.

Means of production This includes the land, raw materials, machinery and buildings used to produce goods.

Ruling class Those who own the means of production.

Subject class Those who do not own the means of production and are subject to the power of the ruling class.

Capitalists The ruling class in capitalist society who own and control the means of production.

Proletariat The subject class in capitalist society who sell their labour for wages.

Ruling class ideology A set of beliefs which support the position of the ruling class by distorting reality.

False consciousness A false view which prevents people from seeing the reality of their situation.

Patriarchal ideology A set of beliefs which support male domination by distorting reality.

activity4 pictures of Marxism

Item A

This Russian cartoon from 1900 shows a social pyramid from the Tsar (monarch) at the top to the proletariat (workers and peasants) at the base. The text from the top downwards reads:

- We reign over you (the Tsar)
- We rule you (the nobles)
- We fool you (the priests)
- We shoot you (the army)
- We eat for you (the middle class)

The banner held by members of the proletariat reads: 'To live in freedom, to die in struggle'.

Item B

A Soviet poster of 1919 showing a bloated capitalist.

question

What aspects of Marxist theory are illustrated by the cartoons?

Antonio Gramsci (1891-1937)

According to the Italian Marxist Antonio Gramsci, beliefs and ideas can change society. They are not simply a reflection of the infrastructure – to some extent they have a life of their own.

Gramsci used the term *hegemony* to describe what he called the 'intellectual and moral' dominance of the ruling class. Hegemony is maintained partly by force – for example, the army and police – and partly by ideology – by persuading the subject or working class that the dominance of the ruling class is in everybody's interest and therefore justified.

Ideological persuasion could not be total and, as a result, hegemony could never be complete. This is because the

key terms

Hegemony The intellectual and moral dominance of the ruling class.
Dual consciousness A set of contradictory beliefs.

working class have a *dual consciousness* – a set of contradictory beliefs. Some of their beliefs are shaped by ruling class ideology and some are shaped by their own experience of work in a capitalist economy – in particular, their experience of low wages and poor working conditions. To a limited extent, this allows them to see through the smokescreen of ruling class ideology. Gramsci believed that capitalism could only be overthrown by working-class intellectuals who must sweep aside the false consciousness produced by ruling class ideology. To do this they must produce a general awareness of exploitation and oppression and lead the working class to revolution.

The dominant ideology thesis

In a study entitled *The Dominant Ideology Thesis* (1980), Abercrombie, Hill and Turner reject the view that there is a ruling class ideology that dominates capitalist society. They surveyed a variety of studies and found little evidence of acceptance of the beliefs that Marxists see as forming this ideology – for example, that capitalism was a just system and that wealth and income were fairly distributed.

Instead, Abercrombie et al. argue that the working class are 'kept in their place' primarily by economic necessity – they have to work to survive. The alternative for most is unemployment and poverty.

Evaluation

Marxism has been criticised in term of both theory and evidence. Abercrombie et al. argue that there is little evidence of widespread acceptance of a ruling class ideology. And Marxist predictions of a workers' revolution and the end of capitalism have been rejected as wishful thinking, especially since the downfall of communism in Eastern Europe and the former Soviet Union.

Despite these criticisms, some of the key elements of Marxist views on ideology remain influential. Many researchers agree that in certain places at certain times ideology can distort, it can broadcast false beliefs, it can disguise oppression and exploitation, and it can justify and legitimate inequality.

2.3 Feminism and ideology

Marxists see the class system as the main source of oppression and inequality. For many feminists, the gender system – the social divisions between women and men – are just as, if not more, oppressive. There are many versions of feminism. The account which follows is brief and partial.

Feminists often start from the following observations. In practically every known human society there is a division of labour based on gender – there are men's jobs and women's jobs. And in most cases, men's jobs bring higher rewards – in terms of status or prestige, in terms of power, and in terms of pay. Even when men and women have the same jobs, men still tend to receive the highest rewards. As a result, there is a system of social inequality which benefits men at the expense of women.

This system of gender inequality tends to permeate the whole of society – it is not simply limited to occupational roles. For example, it may be reflected in religious beliefs which see men as superior to women, or in marriage vows which state that the duty of a wife is to serve her husband. It may be reflected in the education system if parents support their sons at the expense of their daughters. It may

be seen in top jobs such as MPs, judges, barristers and surgeons, where despite equal opportunity laws, men still predominate. And it may be seen in family life if boys and girls are socialised to expect and accept male dominance.

The term *patriarchy* is sometimes used to describe a social system based on gender inequality. It describes a system in which male dominance is present in people's working and family lives, and is reflected in social norms and values, roles and institutions. In this sense, patriarchy has been defined as 'the combination of economic and cultural systems which ensures male supremacy' (Coote & Campbell, 1982).

Patriarchal ideology

Some feminists use the term patriarchal ideology to describe the beliefs which justify and support male domination and disguise and maintain female subordination. According to Kate Millett in *Sexual Politics* (1970), it is 'the most pervasive ideology of our culture'.

Here are some examples of patriarchal ideology.
- A woman's place is in the home.
- Men should be head of the family.
- Women should be primarily responsible for housework and childcare.
- Part-time employment is suitable for women because of their domestic responsibilities.

According to many feminists, beliefs such as these make male domination appear normal and natural and obscure women's position as second-class citizens, both at home and in the workplace.

key term

Patriarchy A social system based on male dominance.

2.4 Political ideologies

Definitions

Researchers who use the term political ideologies do not necessarily see ideologies as a justification for inequality or as a false view of reality. Here are some definitions of political ideologies.
- They 'map the political and social worlds for us'. They are 'aimed at the political arena' and seek to shape 'public policy' (Freeden, 2003).
- They are 'interrelated sets of ideas that in some way guide or inspire political action' (Heywood, 2002).
- They are 'reasonably coherent structures of thought shared by groups of people'. They are 'a means of explaining how society works and how it ought to work' (Dobson, 1992).

This section looks at three major political ideologies – liberalism, conservatism and socialism. There are many versions of these ideologies. This section focuses on the key ideas of each.

activity5 happy housewives

question

How might these advertisements be seen as examples of patriarchal ideology?

Liberalism

In its broadest sense, liberalism is the ideology of modern Western democracies. The following are some of the key ideas of liberalism.

Individual freedom The aim of liberalism is to create a society in which every individual is free to develop their own unique talents. Individual freedom is central to liberal thinking. Each person should be able to act as they please, so long as they don't threaten the freedom of others to do likewise.

Equality of opportunity Each individual should have an equal opportunity to develop their talents to the full. This does not mean that everybody should be equal in terms of wealth, income and social status, only that they should have an equal chance to attain positions of power and status.

Liberals believe in equal rights – for example, equality under the law and political equality in the sense of one person, one vote.

Government by consent Government should be based on the consent of the governed – a representative democracy translates this ideal into practice. One of the main tasks of government is to protect individual freedom. Many liberals believe in a form of limited government that protects but does not infringe on the rights and liberties of the individual.

Conservatism

Conservative ideas emerged in the late 18th and early 19th centuries. They have been seen as a reaction to the rapid economic, social and political changes brought about by industrialisation (Heywood, 2002).

Edmund Burke's *Reflections on the Revolution in France*, published in 1790, provides an early illustration of conservative views. Burke saw the French Revolution as a threat to order and stability. Change should not be sudden, it should not be based on a brand new model which swept away the past. Instead, it should be gradual, built on institutions which have stood the test of time, and based on the accumulated wisdom of the past. In Burke's words, the way forward is 'change in order to conserve'.

Tradition Burke's views illustrate the key theme of conservative thought – the importance of tradition, of tried and tested ideas, experience and institutions. What has been shown to work in the past should be conserved for the present and the future.

Change It follows that change should be built on the best of the past. It should not be based on a brand new blueprint which sweeps away everything that went before. Change should proceed gradually and be approached with caution.

Human nature Conservatives tend to see human beings as imperfect and flawed. They can be selfish as well as unselfish, irrational as well as rational, greedy as well as generous.

The state In view of the imperfections of human nature, society needs a strong state to maintain law and order and ensure social stability. People need leadership and guidance from above.

Society Where liberalism tends to focus on the individual, conservative thought stresses the importance of the family and the nation. The family is seen as the cornerstone of society, transmitting shared values and contributing to social stability. The nation provides people with a common identity and a collective purpose. Symbols of the nation such as the flag, the national anthem and the monarchy help to make individuals feel part of something greater than themselves.

Socialism

Socialism emerged in the early years of the 19th century in response to the development of capitalist industrial society. Some of the key ideas of socialism are outlined below.

Collectivism The ideal society is based on collectivism, where everybody works for the common good rather than individual self-interest. To this end, private property should be abolished and economic resources used for the benefit of the whole community.

Equality This is a guiding principle of socialism. The extremes of wealth and income between the rich and poor are seen as evil. Equality brings out the best in human nature. And it brings cooperation, stability and cohesion in human society.

Capitalism Capitalism exploits and dehumanises wage earners. It generates widespread social inequalities, and a range of social problems including poverty, unemployment and crime.

Social class Socialists see social class as the main division in society – for example, the capitalist ruling class who own and control private industry and the subject or working class who sell their labour in return for wages. Socialists tend to support the working class who they see as exploited and oppressed.

Human nature Socialists, as their name suggests, see humans as social beings. They see people as shaped by their social situation rather than being essentially good or bad, generous or selfish. They look forward to a society based on cooperation rather than competition, on collectivism rather than individualism. This will bring out the best in people (Heywood, 2002).

summary

1. The term ideology has many meanings.

2. According to Popper, ideology is a closed system of thought which rejects alternative views.

3. According to Marx, ruling class ideology.
   - Distorts reality
   - Produces a false consciousness
   - Justifies inequality
   - Supports the position of the ruling class
   - Reflects the economic relationships in the infrastructure.

4. Gramsci argues that beliefs and ideas can change society – they are not simply a reflection of the infrastructure.

5. Gramsci claims that the working class have a dual consciousness which allows them a limited view through the smokescreen of ruling class ideology.

6. According to Abercrombie et al., there is little evidence that the working class accept the dominant ideology.

7. Despite the rejection of many aspects of Marxism, Marx's views on ideology remain influential.

8. Some feminists claim that patriarchal ideology justifies and maintains male dominance and makes it appear normal and natural.

9. Political ideologies are sets of beliefs which guide political action and seek to shape public policy.

10. Liberalism emphasises individual freedom, equality of opportunity and government by consent.

11. Conservatism emphasises tradition, a strong state and the family as the cornerstone of society.

12. Socialism emphasises collectivism, equality and cooperation.

activity6 socialism

question

How does this cartoon illustrate socialist ideas?

Unit 3 *Theories of religion*

keyissues

1 What is religion?
2 What are the main theoretical approaches to religion?

3.1 Defining religion

Religion has been defined in many ways:

- As a belief in some kind of supernatural power
- As an expression of this belief in collective worship
- As a set of moral values which guide action
- As a force which brings people together and unifies society.

These definitions let in a variety of activities under the heading of religion. For example, people talk about football as 'the new religion'. Many fans are devoted to the game. They are united in support of their team and, in some ways, a football match can be seen as a religious ritual.

There are many activities which can be seen as supernatural – astrology, palmistry, fortune telling, witchcraft and a belief in ghosts. Should these be regarded as religious?

As a starting point, most sociologists would probably agree that religions typically involve:

- an organised collectivity of individuals, with
- a shared system of beliefs and
- a set of approved activities and practices.

There are, of course, serious questions about the extent to which members of any of the world's religions agree with fellow members' beliefs and practices. Indeed, Judaism, Christianity, Islam, Hinduism, Buddhism and Sikhism all experience divisions into often rival groupings. There are even questions about how organised a collectivity of individuals has to be to constitute a religion – especially since the advent of the internet.

Most sociological definitions of religion focus on what religion is – *substantive* definitions – or the roles religions play in society – *functional* definitions.

Substantive definitions of religion

Belief in the supernatural Sociologists adopting substantive definitions have tried to identify what is distinctive about religious *beliefs*. For example, Max Weber saw religion as involving a belief in the *supernatural*, that is some power above the forces of nature. This suggests a belief in a being or beings, powers or forces, which are in some ways superior to humans, and which cannot be verified or explained by Western science.

Relating to the sacred An alternative substantive definition is provided by Emile Durkheim. For him, the key to

religious beliefs is not that they relate to a supernatural power or being, but that they relate to things which a society's members perceive as *sacred*.

Durkheim argued that, in all societies, people divide the world about them into things which are regarded as sacred and those which are considered *profane* – non-sacred, worldly, ordinary. Sacred things are 'things set apart and forbidden'. Things, or people, seen as sacred evoke strong emotions of awe, respect and deference. For instance, in some societies, the monarch has inspired a sense of what Durkheim calls 'the sacred'. Things regarded as sacred both draw the believer towards them while at the same time maintaining their distance. Part of the appeal of Princess Diana was that she was seen by many admirers both as someone 'ordinary' and as someone who was 'very special' (Jones, 1998).

In practice, a supernatural being (such as a god) is likely to be regarded as sacred. However, it seems as though anything could be regarded as sacred, however ordinary and mundane it may appear to outsiders – the Black Hills of South Dakota to the Dakota Sioux, the bone of a saint to medieval Christians, a cow to a Hindu. People or things regarded as sacred do not, therefore, have to be supernatural.

Functional definitions of religion

Functional definitions stress the ways religions contribute to societies. They focus on the *role* or *function* of religion in society. For Durkheim, as we have seen, religion refers to beliefs and practices concerning sacred things. These religious beliefs and practices 'unite into one single moral community ... all those who adhere to them'. Thus, a key component of religion, he suggests, is that it encourages *social solidarity* or *social unity* between the fellow-believers who make up a society.

That, of course, isn't the only function that religion may perform in society. Other suggested functions are discussed shortly. Nevertheless, in Durkheim's view, it is because religion plays this crucial role of strengthening social solidarity that it occurs in all societies.

Definitions of religion – some criticisms

Supernatural beings or forces One criticism made of the widely-held view that religion involves belief in the supernatural is the recognition that not all cultures see a distinction between the 'natural' and the 'supernatural'. Angels, spirits and gods can be a 'real', 'lived' and 'natural' part of people's experience. Indeed, it can be argued that what is meant by supernatural may be nothing more than what is currently beyond Western scientific understanding.

Also, if religion always involves belief in the supernatural, is every supernatural belief, by definition, religious? For example, are astrology, fortune telling and witchcraft religious?

The sacred Durkheim's notion of the sacred has also been challenged as not universally applicable – that is, not present in every society. For example, anthropologists found that no distinction was made between the sacred and non-sacred amongst the Azande of southern Sudan and in some West African societies (Hamilton, 2001).

It has also been pointed out that what people regard as sacred does not always command respect and awe. For instance, as Hamilton (2001) notes, 'In Southern Italy, a saint who does not respond in the desired manner after long and repeated prayers may be severely admonished, the statue turned upside down, even whipped or discarded and replaced with that of another saint'.

Durkheim's view of the sacred has been criticised for being too broad and including too much. It allows other belief systems, such as nationalism or communism, to be seen as religious. For example, a nation's flag can be defined as 'sacred' when it is regarded with respect, deference and devotion. Even sport can be seen as 'sacred' – for example, the hallowed turf of certain football and cricket grounds and the respect and devotion given to the team's colours.

Functional definitions – a criticism Functional definitions have also been criticised on precisely the same grounds as Durkheim's focus on the sacred. Such definitions would again include belief systems such as communism and nationalism, and even activities such as sports, where shared beliefs and rituals also encourage unity among 'believers'.

key terms

Supernatural A being or beings, power or force beyond the laws of nature.
Sacred According to Durkheim, things which are 'set apart and forbidden', things which evoke feelings of awe, respect and deference.
Social solidarity Social unity which results from the bonds that draw members of society together.

3.2 Functionalist interpretations of religion

Functionalists see society as a system – a set of parts which work together to form a whole. These parts are the institutions of society – for example, the family, the religious system and the political system.

Functionalists assume that society has certain basic needs which must be met if it is to survive. First and foremost is the need for social order. It is assumed that social order requires a certain degree of cooperation and social solidarity. This is made possible by shared norms and values – a consensus or agreement about society's norms and values. Without this consensus, people would be pulling in different directions and conflict and disorder would result. Because of this emphasis on consensus, functionalism is also known as *consensus theory*.

When analysing any part of society, functionalists often ask, 'What is its function?' By function, they mean what is its contribution to the maintenance and wellbeing of the social system.

The functionalist approach can be seen clearly in the French sociologist Emile Durkheim's analysis of religion *The Elementary Forms of the Religious Life*, first published in 1912.

Emile Durkheim – religion and the worship of society

As noted earlier, Durkheim recognised that things held 'sacred', which often appear 'ordinary' to non-believers, evoke in believers powerful emotions of awe, deference and respect. Therefore, he inferred, it seems their significance is as symbols – they must represent something. And what they represent, he concluded, is the *collective consciousness* – the basic set of shared beliefs, values, traditions and norms which makes social life possible. And in worshipping a society's sacred symbols, its members are unwittingly worshipping the society of which they are a part.

Durkheim's analysis was largely drawn from studies of the religion of Australian Aborigines, which he called *totemism*. Aboriginal society was divided into clans, whose members shared various duties and obligations towards each other. Each clan had a totem – a symbol, usually either an animal or plant – by which it distinguished itself from other clans. The totem was regarded as sacred and was carved on the bullroarer, the most sacred of Aboriginal objects. According to Durkheim, the totem was both the symbol of the Aborigines' god and of the clan. Though the Aborigines consciously worshipped their god, the society was the real object of their veneration. And, Durkheim surmised, 'Primitive man comes to view society as something sacred because he is utterly dependent on it'.

Reinforcing the collective consciousness Without a collective consciousness, a society cannot survive. And for Durkheim, regular acts of collective worship and shared ritual play a crucial role in ensuring society's survival. In effect, the society's members are repeatedly re-affirming their support for their shared values and beliefs.

Strengthening social solidarity Durkheim also claimed that the shared experience of the community's oft-repeated rituals further functions to unify and bind together a society's members. Whether celebrating the group's myths or history in commemorative rites, or coming together in marriage or mourning rituals, society's members are renewing their sense of membership and unity. The very act of communal worship and the practice of rituals raises people's awareness of their common situation and strengthens the bonds between them.

Although participants in societal rituals are unlikely to be consciously aware of it, Durkheim claimed that they are also expressing their sense that the society, the collective, is of supreme importance. The shared, ritualised

activity7 defining religion

Item A Taking the oath

Barack Obama taking the oath to become President of the USA.

Item B A Christian saint

Catholics carry a statue of their neighbourhood's patron saint in Havana, Cuba.

Item C A clairvoyant

A clairvoyant and spiritualist in Whitby, Yorkshire.

Item D Witchcraft

A white witch conducts a ceremony at the Long Man of Wilmington, Sussex.

Item E Remembrance Sunday

Remembrance Sunday service at the Cenotaph, London to remember Britain's war dead.

Item F The World Cup

England soccer team supporters at a World Cup 2006 match between England and Paraguay.

questions

1 How can the activities illustrated in Items A and B be seen as religious? Refer to the definitions of religion outlined in the text.

2 Briefly criticise the view that all of the activities pictured above should be seen as religious.

experiences encourage an awareness that they, as individuals, are relatively insignificant and dependent. But together they are strong. In this respect, one of the main functions of religion is to strengthen social solidarity.

Supporting individuals' adaptations Though he saw the social functions of religion as of primary importance, Durkheim was not blind to its importance for individuals. Hence, he recognised that religious belief and practice can provide individuals with a sense of renewed strength, confidence, serenity and enthusiasm, and help them 'either to endure the trials of existence, or to conquer them' (Durkheim, 1968).

Conclusion In Durkheim's view, therefore, all religions fulfil certain functions for the individual and for society. For the individual, religion provides continuing motivation to face up to life, and social support based upon a sense of belonging. For society, religion unifies members around the shared values, norms, meanings and traditions of the collective consciousness and thereby encourages social integration and social solidarity. The symbols which members of the group worship may or may not be regarded as supernatural. But, to committed believers, they inspire the devotion and awe appropriate to sacred things.

Bronislaw Malinowski – religion and situations of emotional stress

Malinowski was one of the first anthropologists to live for a long period in a small-scale society. His interpretation of religion placed more emphasis on its psychological functions for the individual. He accepted that religion played a central role in promoting social solidarity, but argued that it had developed as a response to the psychological needs of individuals in specific situations of emotional stress. Situations which provoke anxiety, uncertainty and tension threaten social life and it is with such potentially disruptive situations that religion is

activity8 the functions of religion

Item A The Promise Keepers

A Promise Keepers' rally in Denver, Colorado. The Promise Keepers are dedicated to introducing men to Jesus Christ.

Item C Bar Mitzvah

A Jewish boy carries the Torah, a scroll containing God's laws, during his Bar Mitzvah (initiation ceremony) at the Wailing Wall in Jerusalem.

Item B Christmas blessing

The Pope gives his annual Christmas blessing in St Peter's Square.

question

How might the activities shown in Items A, B and C reinforce the collective consciousness and strengthen social solidarity?

typically concerned. In particular, Malinowski identified two types of event with which religion is characteristically involved.

In all societies – but perhaps most acutely in small-scale societies with few members – *life crises* such as birth, puberty, marriage and death are potentially disruptive and typically involve religious ritual. In particular, religion minimises the potential disruption of death by creating 'valuable mental attitudes' towards it. Religion's forceful assertion of immortality comforts the bereaved, and the religious rituals of the funeral ceremony bind together the survivors and counteract the sense of meaninglessness which might otherwise undermine social life.

The second type of event which Malinowski identified as creating anxiety and involving religion concerns activities whose outcome is important but uncertain and uncontrollable. In his study of the Trobriand Islanders in the western Pacific, Malinowski noted that when they fished in the calm, safe waters of the lagoon, where they used the reliable method of poisoning the fish, they felt no need for religious ritual. But, when they fished beyond the barrier reef in the open sea, where success and even survival were much less certain, fishing was preceded by rituals. Again, Malinowski suggested the use of religious ritual increases people's sense of control, diminishes anxiety and unifies the group (Malinowski, 1954).

Talcott Parsons – religion and 'problems of meaning'

Another influential interpretation of religion in the functionalist tradition was developed by Talcott Parsons (1965). In his view, religion is the primary source of meaning for members of a society. In addition, it provides and legitimises the *core values* of a culture and thereby promotes social solidarity and stability.

Religion provides meaning by furnishing answers to the 'eternal' questions about humanity and the world, such as those concerning suffering, justice and death. Why do people suffer? Why do villains prosper? Why do some people die at an early age? Often there appears no justice in such happenings. As a result, they threaten to undermine people's sense that life has meaning. Yet religion offers answers. Suffering tests a person's faith, punishes them for their sins and gives dignity to those who struggle on in the face of adversity. Villains get their just desserts in the afterlife, and so on. By providing explanations of events – particularly those which threaten our sense of meaning – religion makes sense of the apparently meaningless, helps people adjust to their situation, and promotes social stability.

Religion also provides core values and norms, which it sacralises (makes sacred) and legitimises. For instance, Parsons argues that Protestantism in the United States encouraged and sacralised values such as individualism, democracy, self-discipline and equality of opportunity. Religion also sacralises and supports the web of norms which are derived from such values – norms such as universal access to legal rights and life-chances and the

formal separation of the state and religion. So, by establishing and legitimising values and social norms, religion further promotes the social consensus which Parsons argues is essential for order and stability in society.

key terms

Core values The central values of society.
Life crises Events which are common to most people, which can disrupt both their lives and the wider society – for example, birth, puberty, marriage and death.

Robert Bellah – civil religion

Durkheim's interpretation of religion's traditional function – to bind together members of a society by encouraging awareness of their common membership of an entity greater then themselves – was largely based on an analysis of small-scale, pre-industrial societies. However, it may still provide a powerful insight into the collective rituals of people in modern societies.

The concept of *civil religion* was popularised in sociology by the American Robert Bellah (1967), who drew upon the ideas of both Durkheim and Parsons. Parsons had argued that Americans were unified by values and orientations derived from Protestantism, such as individualism and self-discipline. Durkheim's insight – that any human group may be unified by a shared system of 'sacred' beliefs and practices – led Bellah to conclude that, despite America's social divisions, what largely unified them was an overarching 'civil' religion: a faith in Americanism. Unlike the 'conventional' religions of Catholicism, Protestantism and Judaism, which are unable to claim the allegiance of all Americans, civil religion generates widespread loyalty to the nation state. And, though a nation's civil religion would not necessarily involve supernatural beliefs, in American civil religion, Bellah argues, it does.

God and Americanism appear to walk hand in hand. American coins tell the world 'In God We Trust', American presidents swear an oath of allegiance before God, and the phrase 'God Bless America' ends speeches given by dignitaries across the USA. This is not the particular God of Catholics, Protestants or Jews – it has a more general application as 'America's God'. In this respect, the faith in Americanism helps to unite the American people.

Does the UK have a civil religion?

According to Gerald Parsons (2002), 'the most widespread and visible expression of British civil religion' is probably the events and ceremonies which annually surround Remembrance Sunday – the Sunday closest to November 11th, on which day, in 1918, the armistice ended the appallingly bloody First World War. On that Sunday, in thousands of communities across the country, people gather to remember and honour those killed in all of Britain's wars since that 'Great War'. And at the Cenotaph in Whitehall,

activity9 further functions of religion

Item A Individual and social stress

Soldiers of the Irish Guards praying during the Gulf War, 2003

Funeral of Princess Diana, 1997

Item B The problem of meaning

Buddhism

'Bad human beings think it is to their advantage to prevail over their fellow men, to use any method which seems expedient, no matter how cruel, in order to achieve this advantage. The advantage will not last – the methods used only create more problems, more suffering, more mistrust, more resentment, more division. The result is not good for anyone.'

'Better it were to swallow a ball of iron, red-hot and flaming, than to lead a wicked and unrestrained life eating the food of the people!'

Christianity

'You who oppress the poor and crush the destitute, the Lord has sworn by his holiness that your time is coming.'

Judaism

'The righteous suffer for the sins of their generation.'

Hinduism

'Great souls who have become one with Me have reached the highest goal. They do not undergo re-birth, a condition which is impermanent and full of pain and suffering.'

Islam

'Or do you think that you shall enter the Garden (paradise) without such trials as came to those who passed away before you?'

'For those nearest to God will come rest and satisfaction and a garden of delights, and peace. But if you are one of those who have gone wrong, then your entertainment will be boiling water and hellfire. Truly, this is the absolute truth and certain.'

Source: Cole, 1991

questions

1 Malinowski argued that certain situations threaten psychological and social stability. Using the examples in Item A, show how religion might function to reduce this threat.

2 According to Talcott Parsons there are situations which can make life appear meaningless. Using Item B,

   a) Give examples of these situations.

   b) Show how religion addresses them.

   c) Suggest how, in doing so, religion contributes to the wellbeing of the individual and society.

London, the royal family leads the nation's official, nationally broadcast, act of remembrance. The previous evening, there is a now-traditional Festival of Remembrance at the Royal Albert Hall, also televised, 'culminating in the emotional intensity of the descent of a million poppy petals on the heads of a new generation of young servicemen and women' (Parsons, 2002). Millions wear red or white poppies and observe a short period of silence at 11am. Taken together, such rituals and symbols function 'as a means of transcending divisions and unifying what might otherwise be a deeply divided national community' (Parsons, 2002).

Clearly, in the UK, the monarchy has provided a focus for sentiments of what may be called civil religion. This has perhaps been most evident at times of war and national threat – for example, when King George VI and Queen Elizabeth the Queen Mother went walkabout in bomb-blasted, Second World War London. However, changes in attitude towards the royal family raise questions about the extent to which the monarchy is now capable of playing such a role.

James Beckford (2003) recognises that there are occasions when the nation is drawn together by rituals and observances such as the funeral of Princess Diana in 1997 and the Queen's Golden Jubilee in 2002. However, he believes 'it is doubtful that these occasions can compensate for the UK's deep social divisions and high rate of religious diversity and indifference. If the country has a civil religion, it is at best occasional – and at worst weak.'

activity10 civil religion in America

Item A Symbols of Americanism

A modern commemoration of a wagon train heading West

In the 19th century there was a vast migration to new lands in the West. Many migrants travelled in wagon trains, pushing back the American frontier and opening up new land to White settlement. These 'heroic treks' are pictured in books, paintings and on postage stamps, featured in films and commemorated in statues. Sometimes the 'virgin territory' of the West is pictured as the 'promised land' and the settlers as the 'chosen people'.

The Lincoln Memorial, Washington DC

Every American knows the story of Abraham Lincoln who was born in a log cabin and rose from these humble origins to live in the White House as President of the United States before dying from an assassin's bullet in 1865. Pictured on coins, sculpted in marble in the Lincoln Memorial, he has become an almost mythical figure.

Item B America's national faith

While some have argued that Christianity is America's national faith, few have realised that there actually exists alongside the churches and synagogues an elaborate and well-institutionalised civil religion in America – a collection of beliefs, symbols and rituals with respect to sacred things which are an established part of American society. This religion – there seems no other word for it – while not opposed to, and indeed sharing much in common with, Christianity, is not in any specific sense Christian.

Behind this civil religion at every point lie Biblical models – the Exodus, Chosen People, Promised Land and New Jerusalem, Death and Rebirth. But it is also genuinely American and genuinely new. It has its own prophets and its own martyrs, its own sacred events and sacred places, its own solemn rituals and symbols.

Source: O'Toole, 1984

Item C Shrines, saints and ceremonies

Many American civil ceremonies have a marked religious quality. Memorial Day, which remembers Americans killed in war, the Fourth of July, which commemorates the American Declaration of Independence from Britain, and the anniversary of presidential inaugurations, all celebrate national values and national unity. There are national shrines such as the Lincoln Memorial in Washington DC, the birthplaces of key presidents, war memorials and other 'special' places. It is not their age or even historical significance that inspires awe and reverence, but their ability to symbolise the nation as a 'people'.

Likewise, there are sacred objects of the civil religion – especially the flag. The extent to which these ceremonies, shrines and objects are set apart as sacred can be seen in the intensity of outrage at inappropriate behaviour or 'desecration'. Some people were arrested during the 1960s for wearing or displaying a copy of the American flag improperly, for example, on the seat of their pants.

American civil religion also has its myths and saints. Lincoln is an historical figure who particularly symbolises the civil religion, and his life from humble birth to martyrdom, typifies its values. Other 'saints' include key presidents such as Washington and Kennedy, folk heroes such as Davy Crockett, who died in 1836 fighting for Texan independence from Mexico, and military heroes such as Eisenhower, commander-in-chief of the Allied Armies in the Second World War, who defended democracy and freedom against the fascist governments of Germany and Italy. Similarly, there are stories that enshrine American values such as individual achievement and upward social mobility. Lincoln's story of log cabin to White House is one. So is Davy Crockett's earlier history when, after years of hunting bears and fighting Indians on the frontier, he was elected to Congress where he was known as the 'Coonskin Congressman'. Socially important myths include America as the land of plenty, unlimited social mobility, economic consumption and achievement.

While these shrines, saints and ceremonies are not religious in the same sense as, for example, Greek Orthodox shrines, saints and ceremonies, they are still set apart as special and not to be profaned.

Source: McGuire, 1981

questions

1 Read Items A and B.

   a) How are the symbols of Americanism linked to Biblical models? Why might this make them more effective?

   b) Why have the wagon train and Abraham Lincoln become symbols of Americanism?

2 How can the symbols of Americanism in Item C be seen as 'religious'?

3 What are the social functions of civil religion in America?

Functionalist views – an evaluation

Positive functions From a functionalist perspective, religion is good for society and good for individuals. It performs positive functions for society – reinforcing social solidarity and value consensus – and for the individual – reducing anxiety and stress. This emphasis on positive functions ignores the many examples of religion as a negative force – as an instrument of oppression – and as a divisive force – conflict between Catholics and Protestants in Northern Ireland being a case in point.

The origins of religion Functionalism fails to explain the origins of social institutions. Where does religion come from, how did it arise in the first place? Identifying the functions of religion does not necessarily tell us anything about its origins.

Religion today Durkheim examined religion in small-scale, non-literate societies. Today's large-scale, complex societies usually contain a variety of different religions – a situation known as *religious pluralism*. It is difficult to see how religion can perform its traditional functions of reinforcing social solidarity and value consensus in modern societies with a plurality of religions.

The idea of civil religion gets round this problem. Robert Bellah (1967) makes a strong case for civil religion providing social unity and integration in societies characterised by religious pluralism. But is civil religion really religion? Does it involve worship and the supernatural? Can Abraham Lincoln and Davy Crockett be compared to saints in the Catholic Church? This brings us back to the problems of defining religion outlined in Section 3.1.

3.3 Marxist views of religion

In contrast to consensus or functionalist perspectives, Marxist theories are sometimes known as *conflict theories*. This is because they see a basic conflict of interest between the two main classes in industrial society – the capitalist or ruling class, and proletariat or subject class. From a Marxist perspective, religion is one of the institutions which maintains capitalist rule – it is an instrument of domination and oppression which keeps the proletariat in its place.

For Marx, people's religious beliefs reflect their *alienation*. In pre-communist societies, people are alienated or cut off from their work, from the products of their work and from each other. For example, in capitalist societies, they work for capitalists rather than for themselves. They do not own the products of their labour, and they work as individual wage earners rather than with each other for the benefit of the community. They have little control over their work and are exploited and oppressed by the capitalist ruling class.

Religious beliefs and practices arise in response to, and as a protest against, people's lack of control of their destiny and their dehumanisation and oppression. In a much-quoted passage, Marx argues that religion is both 'the expression of real distress and the protest against real distress. It is the sigh of the oppressed creature, the heart of a heartless world, just as it is the spirit of a spiritless situation. It is the opium of the people.'

In Marx's view, 'Man makes religion, religion does not make man. In other words, religion is the self-consciousness and self-feeling of man who has either not yet found himself or has already lost himself again.' Truly liberated individuals have no need of religion. Thus, if the alienation and exploitation associated with classes are eradicated, and people are freed to develop their human potential and 'find themselves', religion will no longer be needed and will cease to exist.

Religion and ideology Although religion represents a protest against a dehumanising social world and human alienation, it leads people in a false direction – the hopes and 'solutions' it promises are illusory. Religion, for Marx, is part of *ideology* – a pattern of beliefs which obscures and distorts the true nature of reality in ways which benefit the ruling class. Insofar as members of subject classes accept religious ideas, they suffer *false consciousness*. Thus, although religious ideas appear to express social consensus, those ideas are essentially tools in the domination of one class by another.

Religion and social control The argument that religion functions to maintain ruling class domination may be developed in a number of ways. First, religion distorts reality by encouraging the belief that people are dependent upon supernatural beings or sacred powers. For example, the belief that events are controlled by supernatural powers means there is little people can do to change their situation, apart from trying to influence the supernatural powers by prayer, sacrifice or some other means. In this way, religion obscures the human authorship of, and responsibility for, social inequality and thereby discourages the realisation that working for social change may be possible and desirable.

Second, religion often appears to lend sacred support to the current social order, and in so doing reinforces prohibitions against actions which would challenge those in power. Thus, in his letter to Christians in Rome, St Paul wrote:

'Let every soul be subject unto the higher powers. For there is no power but of God: the powers that be are ordained of God.'

'Whosoever therefore resisteth the power, resisteth the ordinance of God: and they that resist shall receive to themselves damnation.'

(*Romans*, Ch13, vs 1-2)

Likewise, in medieval Europe, the Church taught that the various unequal 'estates of the realm' – monarch, barons and bishops, knights, freemen and serfs – were God's creation. This meant that attempts to change the social order would not only be acts of treason against the monarch, but also a rejection of God's plan, punishable by eternal damnation.

In modern capitalist societies, however, in which change, innovation and high rates of social mobility are required for the success of capitalist enterprises, such religious teachings have been largely abandoned. Nevertheless, it can still be argued that mainstream religion continues to legitimise privilege and inequality – by giving its blessing to rituals involving royalty, such as the Coronation, and by the continuing presence in the House of Lords of the Archbishops and Bishops of the Church of England. Indeed, the relationship between the supernatural, inequality and national wellbeing may be neatly summarised in the phrase 'God, Queen and Country'.

Religion as compensation While religion operates primarily as a means of social control for the exploiters, for the exploited it has psychological functions as a source of solace and compensation for the misery of their alienation. So, where Durkheim sees religion as an expression and celebration of people's solidarity, Marx sees it as a consolation for experience which lacks the genuine solidarity of which people are capable.

The specific compensations religion offers vary. In Christianity, Judaism and Islam, for example, religion offers the fantasy escape of heavenly rewards – and, in Christianity, the intriguing promise that the poor would have less difficulty gaining access to heaven than the wealthy. In Hinduism and Buddhism, followers are taught that life may be better in later incarnations.

Many religions offer their followers hope by promising supernatural intervention into human affairs. In the religious history of the Jews, for instance, God is believed to have intervened many times to assist or protect his chosen people – as in parting the Red Sea to allow the Jews to escape their Egyptian pursuers.

According to Marx, religion promises happiness, but the happiness it promises is an illusion. True happiness and fulfilment are possible only when the exploited shake off the chains of their oppression and seize and practise their freedom.

key term

Alienation A key Marxist idea which states that the nature of work in capitalist society cuts the worker off from themselves, from others, from their work and what they produce.

3.4 Neo-Marxist interpretations of religion

For Marx, religion, as part of the superstructure of society, is largely shaped by the infrastructure or economic base. As such, it reflects the interests of those who own and control the economy – the ruling class. Some neo-Marxists ('new' Marxists) have modified this view.

Antonio Gramsci

One of the most influential figures in the neo-Marxist reassessment of religion is the Italian, Antonio Gramsci. He rejected the traditional Marxist view that the cultural superstructure merely reflected society's economic base. In his view, the superstructure is more autonomous and independent than Marx acknowledged, and beliefs are no less real or important than economic forces.

For Gramsci, if the communist age were to come, it would require proletarian (working-class) action. But this action must be guided by theoretical ideas. And, just as intellectuals of the Roman Catholic Church had shaped the minds of its followers over centuries, so must the industrial working class produce its own intellectuals who can articulate working-class experience and help shape working-class consciousness.

As an Italian, Gramsci was well aware of the control over consciousness which the Catholic Church had traditionally exercised over its members. This control he referred to as

activity11 monarch and God

Item A *The divine right of monarchy*

Henry IV at his coronation in 1399 receiving a blessing from archbishops

'Kings are called Gods by the prophet David because they sit on God's throne on earth. Kings exercise divine power on earth. They have the power of life and death, they are judges over all their subjects and yet are accountable to none but God only.'
James 1, King of England from 1603-1625

Medieval monarchs ruled by divine right – they were seen to have a God-given right to rule. Although modern British monarchs no longer claim divine right, Elizabeth II's coronation in 1953 was in many ways similar to that of Henry IV. She too was crowned and blessed by archbishops.

questions

1 Analyse the information in Item A from a Marxist view.

2 Why does Birnbaum (Item B) argue that it is 'the very absence of shared values in Great Britain' which accounted for the attention paid to the Coronation?

3 How and why, in Birnbaum's view, did the press encourage false class consciousness through their coverage of the Coronation?

Item B *The Coronation of Queen Elizabeth II*

Queen Elizabeth II shortly after she was crowned by the Archbishop of Canterbury in Westminster Abbey, 1953

Although it is often assumed that there is a moral consensus in society, and that this consensus is personified in the person of the monarch, our evidence shows that societies like our own are arenas for conflicts of belief and moral standards unmatched in history.

I would argue that it was the very absence of shared values in Great Britain which accounts for some of the attention paid to the Coronation. The Coronation provided, for some sections of the populace, some measure of respite and relief from that condition of conflict which is more or less permanent for complex societies of a capitalist type.

From this viewpoint, the role of the press in stirring up popular enthusiasm for the Coronation is understandable. In response to the class interests it generally represents, the press continually seeks to minimise awareness of the real conflicts characteristic of British society. In this context, the personality of the Queen and her family functioned as the object of various fantasies and identifications in a way not much more 'sacred' than the cult of adulation built up around certain film stars. But the tawdry baubles of the Coronation celebration constitute no adequate substitute for the lost faith of millions.

Source: Birnbaum, 1955

---

hegemony. He was highly critical of what he regarded as the Church's characteristic subservience to the state and ruling-class interests. Nevertheless, he did not assume that religion must inevitably play such a role. He argued that, at different historical times, popular forms of religion had emerged which expressed and supported the interests of oppressed classes. Thus, he accepted the possibility that religious beliefs and practices could develop and be popularised, particularly by working-class intellectuals, to challenge the dominant ruling class ideology and support working-class consciousness and liberation.

Otto Maduro

The possibility that religion may play a progressive role in the political struggles of oppressed classes has been taken up by a number of modern Marxists, including Otto Maduro (1982). Writing about developing countries, Maduro argues that, in societies in which religion remains a dominant and conservative institution, social liberation can only be achieved if significant change occurs within the churches. This could occur if the oppressed, finding that all possible forms of protest are blocked by the central power, take their discontent to the churches – as in certain

Latin American societies, in South Africa, and in Poland before the abandonment of communism. In this situation, Maduro argues, the anguish and aspirations of the oppressed may be reflected and voiced by members of the clergy. Thus, the clergy may then fulfil the functions of Gramsci's proletarian intellectuals, by expressing the discontents of the oppressed, by shaping their consciousness of the situation, and by working with them to devise strategies of action. Evidence to support this view is given in Activity 12.

Marxist views – an evaluation

Religion as ideology Marx saw religion as a form of ideology which helped to maintain ruling class power. Critics agree there is evidence to support this view from certain times and places. However, they reject the claim that this is the primary role of religion.

To some extent, neo-Marxists avoid this criticism by admitting the possibility that religion can open the eyes of the oppressed to the reality of their situation. And this, in turn, can encourage them to take action to end their oppression.

Religion as compensation Is religion simply a compensation for oppression, a crutch which helps people to live with their situation, a balm for their wounds and a drug to give them false happiness? Again, there is plenty of evidence that can be used to support this view.

But, critics argue that this is a very one-sided view – that there is a lot more to religion than compensation. For example, as Parsons states, religion can give meaning to and make sense of birth and death – events which affect *all* people in *all* societies.

Marxism and values To some extent, the reader must 'buy into' Marxist value judgements to fully accept Marxist views. Capitalism, and the class societies which went before, are seen as unjust and evil. Communism is the ideal society – a society in which social classes disappear, oppression ends and, as a result, religion disappears. However, there are plenty of examples of religion thriving in the communist societies of the 20th century – for instance, Poland under communism was a strongly Roman Catholic country.

Advantages of Marxism Despite these criticisms, Marxism has provided important insights. Religion has often supported the interests of the powerful. It has often provided solace and comfort for the oppressed. It has often been influenced by economic factors. And Marxism has provided a useful balance for functionalist perspectives which have tended to take a one-sided view of religion as a positive force in society.

3.5 Feminist views of religion

There are several versions of feminism, but they have a number of things in common. Most use *patriarchy* as a key idea. This refers to a social system which is organised for the benefit of males, a system in which male dominance is supported by beliefs, values and norms.

Many feminists claim that religion is a patriarchal institution. Teachings and practices from a range of religions suggest that they systematically benefit males over females.

*activity*12 *liberation theology*

Item A **Liberating the poor**

Liberation theology is a religious justification for the liberation of oppressed peoples. It developed in Latin America in the 1950s and 60s as an alternative to the standard view of the West's duties towards the Third World. It criticised the view that the West could end the poverty of the Third World by transferring economic resources from one to the other. The theology of liberation said that, far from being the passive objects of aid, it was essential that the poor take control of their situation and accept the responsibility for ending their poverty.

That meant understanding their own condition and the reasons for it, and responding accordingly. In liberation theology's purest form, the sort the Vatican was most worried about, those conditions and the reasons for them are analysed in Marxist terms, and so is the remedy.

What the theology of liberation has to say is that the only escape from poverty which does justice to human dignity is that engineered and struggled for by the poor themselves.

Source: Longley, 1986

Item B **Father Camilo Torres**

Father Camilo Torres was a Roman Catholic priest in Colombia in South America. The vast majority of Colombian people are desperately poor. Sixty-five per cent of the land is owned by a handful of powerful families. Father Torres believed this was unjust – his solution was a Christian revolution. In his words: 'Revolution is necessary to feed the hungry, give drink to the thirsty, clothe the naked and procure a life of wellbeing for the needy majority of our people. I believe that the revolutionary struggle is appropriate for the Christian and the priest. Only by revolution, by changing the concrete conditions of our country, can we enable men to practise love for each other.'

The Catholic Church did not support Torres. Believing that the government would crush peaceful protest, he joined a guerrilla movement. Torres was killed fighting government forces in 1966. The peasants saw him as a martyr and in 1968 many priests followed his example and pledged their support for revolutionary struggle against the state.

Source: Jenkins, 1987

Item C *Archbishop Romero*

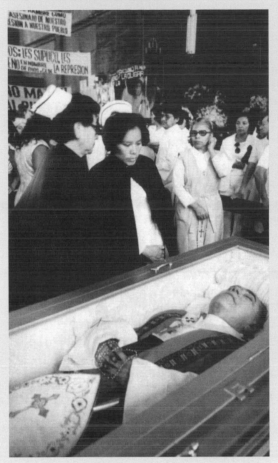

Item D *Father Rogelio Cruz*

Father Rogelio Cruz, a Catholic priest, leads 200 families, left homeless in December when police bulldozed a squatters' village, in a nightly protest mass at a temporary tent camp in Santo Domingo, Dominican Republic, 2000.

Mourners in El Salvador gather round the corpse of Archbishop Romero. He was shot dead in his cathedral in 1980 by four gunmen, allegedly members of a right-wing death squad. Archbishop Romero was a champion of social and economic reforms to improve the lot of the poor.

questions

1 'Liberation theology sounds like a Christian version of Marxism.' Comment on this statement.

2 Use the information in this activity to assess the differing views of Marx and Maduro on the role of religion in society. Does the information disprove Marx's view?

Here are some of the main feminist concerns.

The sacred texts

● In almost all the world religions, the gods are male. Hinduism comes closest to being an exception, with its female goddesses.

● The sacred texts overwhelmingly feature males and male activity.

● They were also written, and have been interpreted, by males. They incorporate many traditional male stereotypes and biases. For instance:

1) In the creation story (shared by Judaism and Christianity) God created Adam and then 'the fowl of the air' and 'the beasts of the field'. Only later did he decide to create Eve, as a 'helpmate' for Adam, observing that 'It is not good that the man should be alone'. And, as is well known, Eve was created out of one of Adam's ribs.

2) Having been commanded by God not to eat the fruit from the 'tree of the knowledge of good and evil', it was Eve whom the serpent persuaded to disregard God's command. Having also fed it to Adam, Eve and he both then experienced sin and shame and covered their naked bodies (*Genesis*, Ch.2, v.15-Ch.3 v.7).

3) In the Christian tradition, the two central women – the Virgin Mary and Mary Magdalene – are typical female stereotypes. The 'Holy Mother' Mary is chaste (a virgin), giving, caring, self-sacrificing, suffering. Mary Magdalene, a prostitute who became one of the few women very close to Jesus, represents woman as temptress and seductress.

Religious professionals In all world religions, the majority of religious professionals are male. In Christianity, females are not eligible to become priests in the Roman Catholic, Greek or Russian Orthodox churches, and only became eligible since 1992 in the Church of England. Nor can they become rabbis in Orthodox Judaism.

Worship In most religions, women are likely to be the main attendees. Yet their role tends to be secondary – they don't often participate actively in the service. Orthodox Jewish women, for instance, can't read from the Torah scroll or participate in symbolic actions at festivals.

Limitations and exclusions In many religions, females are limited in where they may go, both at home, and outside the home, and in centres of worship. In Orthodox Judaism, the women sit in the balconies at the back of, and above, the main space, or behind screens, so as not to distract the males. Sometimes they can't see or hear properly (Swale, 2000).

In everyday life, too, female followers of world religions are often significantly more limited than males with regards to where they can go, and with whom they may associate.

Differential treatment In a number of religions, or in cultures heavily influenced by religion, women have fewer options or receive less favourable treatment than men in daily life.

● In Western Christianity, for a significant part of its history, a wife was the property of her husband. She lost her property to him on marriage, was required to promise him life-long obedience, and was unable to divorce him.

● In some versions of Islam, the male is allowed up to four wives. In some Islamic countries, a male may divorce a wife by declaring so three times, though the female may not divorce her husband.

● In Islamic Iran, though such practices have significantly diminished since Ayatollah Khomeini was in power, females may still be flogged for dress-code violations and stoned to death for adultery. In Afghanistan, 'girls are still given away in marriage against their will, women who "dishonour" their families are routinely murdered and, although rape is widespread, offenders usually go unpunished as few women dare speak out' (Amnesty International, 2003).

● However, such inequalities are by no means found solely in some Islamic countries. They exist, too, in some predominantly Christian and Hindu cultures. For instance, in parts of (Christian) South America, (Hindu) India and the (Muslim) Middle East, sexual norms are more strict for females. Also, the transgression of such norms results in more frequent, and more severe, punishment for females than males. Moreover, such punishment is often applied unofficially – not infrequently physically, sometimes fatally – by males, who are often family members.

Feminist views – an evaluation

Goddesses According to many feminists, religion has been a major institutional means for controlling women – perhaps, for much of history, *the* major means. Yet, in many ancient and folk religions, females have had key positions. In ancient Greek and Roman religion, for example, goddesses were neither uncommon nor unimportant. The Greek goddess Athena, for instance, was god of war, wisdom and the arts. Goddesses remain important in Hinduism. And modern followers of pagan Wicca (witchcraft) worship a goddess of the moon and of the woodlands, whom they claim was worshipped throughout Celtic Europe.

Leadership roles Religion has also been a means through which some women have developed leadership roles. In Christianity, a few have created religious faiths and organisations, some of which now number millions of followers around the world. In 19th century America, Ellen White founded the still-flourishing Seventh Day Adventist Church, and Mary Baker Eddy, the Church of Christ, Scientist (Christian Science).

Today, thousands of women around the world have assumed positions of leadership in the fast-growing Christian Pentecostal movement and in other apparently patriarchal and conservative religious movements. Moreover, these important roles – at least within the Pentecostal movement – often lead on to leadership roles in the wider community (Martin, 2003).

Freedom within religion In all religions, there are those who argue that freedom and fulfilment for women can only be found *within* a religious tradition. Evidence which may provide support for this view is provided in Activity 13.

Advantages of feminism Feminists have often been criticised for being preoccupied with gender inequality and ignoring other aspects of society. While there is some truth in this, the sharp focus of feminism does have some advantages. In terms of religion, it highlights those aspects of belief and practice which support male dominance and keep women in their place.

key term

Patriarchy A social system which systematically benefits males over females.

3.6 Weber's views on religion

Marx paid little attention to the specific religious beliefs of different groups and cultures. Durkheim based his general statements about religion on a small number of examples. The German sociologist Max Weber's studies, however, involved an ambitious series of detailed analyses of major religions – Confucianism and Taoism (in China), Hinduism and Buddhism (in India) and ancient Judaism (in Palestine). Additionally, in his most famous work, *The Protestant Ethic and the Spirit of Capitalism* first published in 1904, he analysed the influential Calvinist tradition within Christianity.

activity13 women and religion

Item A *Religious leaders*

Pope Benedict XVI

Rev. Sun Myung Moon, founder of the Unification Church (the 'Moonies')

Former Iranian leader Ayatollah Khomeini

Item B *Gender roles and Orthodox Jews*

Instead of the feminist programme of broader gender definitions and options, sexual liberation, an emphasis on careers, and the acceptance of a variety of family patterns, Orthodox Judaism proposed clear and firm gender norms, the control of sexuality, assistance in finding partners, and explicit guidelines for nuclear family life.

In the USA, many women were converted to Orthodox Judaism because it supported and legitimated their desires for the 'traditional' identity of wives and mothers in nuclear families. The rabbis told the recruits that women's role was highly valued in Orthodoxy and that women's primary place in the home, where a majority of the rituals took place, gave her special status within the Jewish religious world. In addition, women gained an extra benefit – strong support for a view of men's roles that placed great stress on men's involvement in the home and with their families.

Source: Davidman, 1991

Item C *The veil*

Increasing numbers of women in Islamic countries are wearing the veil in public places. At the same time, growing numbers of women are entering university and the professions and participating in life outside the home.

The veil can be seen as a restriction on their freedom. On the other hand, it can be seen as a way of making the transition into the public sphere more comfortable. From this perspective, Islamic dress can be seen as the uniform of transition.

Source: Ahmed, 2000

An Afghan woman in Kabul

questions

1 What support do the pictures in Item A provide for feminist views on religion?

2 How can Items B and C be used to a) support and b) criticise feminist views?

Although Weber accepted that religion often functioned to justify social inequality, as Marx had argued, he was also concerned to show that religion did not inevitably function in this conservative manner. Religion existed, he believed, because people everywhere needed a system of basic beliefs to make sense of their existence and to have a sense of their identity. Religion provided people with *meaning*. However, Weber's major argument was that societies developed differently partly because the religious beliefs and ideas about the ethical conduct of their members were different. In other words, religious beliefs and religious movements *can* help shape social change.

Calvinism and the 'spirit of capitalism'

The major question which Weber addressed in much of his writing about religion was why the capitalism which had developed in some Western countries had not also emerged in the East. He concluded that while Eastern religions, for example Hinduism and Buddhism, embodied certain key teachings and values which had discouraged the development of capitalism, Judaism and Christianity, and especially the Calvinist and Puritan varieties of Christianity, had encouraged it.

Protestantism and capitalism Weber argued that although individual greed and the pursuit of gain may be found in all societies, only in the West did entire societies develop, and come to accept, *rational capitalism* – a system which encouraged the methodical pursuit of profit by legal means, involving calculation, book-keeping and long-term planning, and which relied on the creation of free markets and a free labour force. In Weber's view, modern capitalism had been able to develop in the West, and particularly in predominantly Protestant areas, because it was compatible with the Calvinist teachings which guided many of the early Protestant movements such as the Puritans, Presbyterians, Baptists and Quakers. And it was among these movements, he argued, that capitalism flourished. It was much less compatible with religions such as Hinduism which taught that if believers accept their lot in this life and act in accordance with tradition, they will gain the reward of a higher caste position in the next life. Such beliefs discourage rational calculation and innovation and therefore the development of capitalism.

A question of salvation The most significant teaching of John Calvin (1509-64) was that of *predestination*. According to this doctrine, even before their birth, God has selected some for *salvation* and others for eternal damnation. Neither the saved nor the damned could influence the decision, either by the strength of their faith or by their earthly actions. And moreover, no-one could be sure whether he or she had been pre-selected for heaven or for hell.

Such terrifying beliefs could well have driven followers into an attitude of helpless fatalism, resignation and inactivity. Instead, Weber argued, the 'salvation anxiety' with which they were plagued, provoked the opposite response. Despite Calvin's teaching that people's behaviour could not influence God's decision, some followers developed doctrines which held out a measure of hope that individuals could discover reassuring 'signs' that they were among those chosen for salvation.

Work as a 'calling' While none could be sure of their salvation, all were required to pursue an intensely active life of labour. Work was a 'calling', and God was most effectively worshipped through a rigorously disciplined life of work, and a denial of indulgence. Any activity which unnecessarily detracted from work was evil. Mere socialising, sleeping longer than strictly necessary, or even religious contemplation if it interfered with a person's daily labours, were regarded as sins, for they detracted from the active performance of God's will. But if a person's work was rewarded with material success, this may be a sign of God's grace and indicate that they were among the elect – that they had been chosen by God for salvation.

Thus, to cope with the chronic anxiety of damnation, Calvinists energetically threw themselves into highly disciplined economic activity and a lifetime of 'good works'. Those in business pursued profit and wealth, not as ends in themselves, but as Christian obligations to make the best use of their God-given gifts and talents and as indications of God's favour. And, because they were limited in how they could spend their wealth – they could not 'waste' it on expensive 'luxuries' – they tended to save and reinvest in their businesses.

According to Weber, the Calvinist idea of the calling affected not just the employer but also the worker. For capitalism to take root, drastic changes were needed in the attitudes of workers who traditionally were concerned merely to earn the wage necessary to meet their modest expectations and otherwise to spend their time in leisure. The Calvinist notion of the calling transformed the traditional, easy-going, undisciplined workforce into 'sober, conscientious, and unusually industrious workmen, who clung to their work as to a life purpose willed by God' (Weber, 1958). Thus, the Protestant ethic encouraged not merely the 'spirit of capitalism' but a new 'spirit of labour' as well, without which the spirit of capitalism could not have been translated into action.

Religion and rationality In these ways, Weber concluded, Calvin's influential religious teachings, popularised and interpreted by generations of Puritan successors, had significant, though unintended, consequences for the economic system of capitalism. For, alone among the teachings of the world's major religions, they encouraged among believers a rational, calculating, efficient and highly committed approach to work which provided capitalism with a fertile soil in which to take root. And it is the growth of *rationality* which provides a key, perhaps *the* key, to understanding the nature of modern societies.

In developing his argument about the significance of Calvinist teachings for the development of capitalism, Weber believed that he had successfully challenged Marx's somewhat deterministic view that religious ideas merely reflect a society's economic base. Weber was careful to make clear that he was not claiming that Calvinism was the sole cause of capitalism – he acknowledged that, even in countries with a significant Calvinist population, such as Scotland or Switzerland, capitalism would not develop if economic conditions were not right (for example, if there was a shortage of skilled labour or investment capital, as was the case in Scotland). Nevertheless, he could reasonably claim to have demonstrated that religious beliefs can have a significant role in influencing a society's economic system and development.

Evaluation of Weber's argument

Which came first, Calvinism or capitalism? There are a number of challenges to Weber's argument. The most central is the challenge to Weber's claim that Calvinism preceded capitalism. Eisenstadt (1967) argues that the first great upsurges of capitalism occurred in Catholic Europe – in Italy, Belgium and Germany – *before* the Protestant Reformation. The historian Tawney (1938) claims that society had already changed radically, in a capitalist direction, before the advent of Calvinism. New technologies had been invented and introduced, a capitalist class had emerged and new ways of viewing society had developed. In this view, as Calvinism emerged, it was adopted by the rising capitalist class and, with some changes in emphasis, provided a religious justification for a rational capitalism which was already established and developing.

Other religions and capitalism Another important criticism, voiced by some writers on Hinduism and Islam, is that Weber misunderstood those religions and failed to recognise the many elements in them which could have been supportive of rational economic action. Weber has also been criticised for underestimating the capitalist spirit of the Jews. Because they were openly interested in profit, would trade in anything, would compete and try to undercut the competition, and would lend money at interest, Jews proved formidable business competitors, and were probably more capitalist than Weber suggested.

Interpreting Calvinism Doubt has also been cast on Weber's interpretation of the attitudes of influential Calvinists to wealth and the pursuit of gain. As Weber himself recognised, many Calvinist preachers taught that wealth was a great danger, providing unending temptations, and that its acquisition was morally suspect. Moreover, it is not clear why Calvinists should come to regard economic success as the major benchmark which God might use to indicate his favour. Nor is it clear why Calvinists should have had to reinvest the profits they accumulated. Could they not have been given away to the poor (for which practice there seems some scriptural support) or used to boost employees' wages?

There is also the puzzling question of why and how Calvinism was able to attract converts – or, even more baffling, succeed as a major religious movement. As depicted by Weber, Calvinism had little to offer its followers. It did not promise them salvation and made it disconcertingly clear that membership made not the slightest difference to their prospects either in this life or the next.

Conclusion The debate about the relationship between Calvinism and capitalism still continues. It will probably never be settled. The historical documents tell us little about the way Calvinist teachings 'were received, understood and interpreted by ordinary believers', or how they were translated into behaviour (Hamilton, 2001).

key terms

Predestination The idea that people's destination after death is predetermined by God.
Salvation The saving of the soul and its admission to heaven.
Protestant ethic Moral beliefs based on Protestantism which led to self-denying, self-disciplined lives of labour which, in turn, encouraged the development of capitalism.
Rationality Action directed by reason rather than emotion or tradition.

3.7 An interpretivist view of religion

Peter Berger – religion, rationalisation and 'the problem of modernity'

Rationalisation Weber's analysis of Calvinist Protestantism forms an important part of a broader argument. Weber believed that the modern world was characterised by a process of *rationalisation*. This involved systematically working towards a clearly defined goal by precisely calculating the way to reach that goal. This can be seen in the rise of capitalism which emphasised rational calculation in business activity and rationally organised work practices in order to maximise efficiency and profit. In particular, it can be seen in the spread of bureaucracy, the characteristic institution of modern society. Bureaucratic institutions are rational – they systematically and efficiently organise people in order to attain particular goals.

Weber believed that rationalisation has its costs. Reason replaces faith, and the support which faith provides disappears. This leads to disillusionment, to *disenchantment*. The world is 'demystified', its richness, mystery and magic taken away. It now appears cold. And social relationships, particularly in bureaucratic settings, become increasingly impersonal.

These themes have been taken up since the 1960s by the Austrian-born American sociologist Peter Berger. Berger's main concern has been with what he calls 'modernity' – in particular, with questions of how changes in social structure and social interaction in modern society are experienced by individuals, and how they strive to create a meaningful reality. He takes an interpretivist approach, seeking to discover the meanings which people impose upon the world in order to make sense of it.

activity14 the protestant ethic

Item A A pre-capitalist view

It is much sweeter to spend money than to earn it. I think that I have done more by having spent money well than by having earned it. Spending gave me a deeper satisfaction, especially the money I spent on my house in Florence.

(An example, from a medieval Florentine, of a pre-capitalist attitude towards money.)

Item B The Protestant ethic

From a pamphlet published in 1653. Father Christmas is driven out of town by a Puritan (on the left).

A Puritan family meal in the early 17th century. Their dress is simple and their food is plain. The children are standing at the table to eat their food. This was considered good discipline by Puritan parents.

The Godly and hardworking man shall have prosperity, but he that follows pleasures shall have much sorrow. Don't be too concerned about being popular and sociable – it can waste a lot of valuable time.

(John Browne, a 16th century Protestant)

Even if you are called to the poorest labouring job, do not complain because it is wearisome, nor imagine that God thinks any the less of you. But cheerfully follow it, and make it your pleasure and joy that you are still in your heavenly master's services, though it be the lowest thing.

(Richard Baxter, a prominent 17th century English Puritan)

Items A and B quoted in Kitch, 1967

Religion must necessarily produce hard work and discourage the wasting of money. We must encourage all Christians to gain what they can and to save all they can – that is, in effect, to grow rich.

(John Wesley, 1703-1791, English founder of Methodism)

Quoted in Weber, 1958

questions

1 Read Item A. How does this view differ from Calvinist attitudes?

2 a) What attitudes, identified by Weber as characteristic of Calvinism, are expressed in Item B?

   b) Using Weber's argument, show how these attitudes could encourage the growth of capitalism.

Berger begins by elaborating on Weber's argument that Protestantism has played a unique role in rationalising attitudes and social structures, particularly in the spread of bureaucracy. And, like Weber, he believes that the process of rationalisation, encouraged by Protestantism, has tended to 'demystify' the modern world and has led to modern people's 'disenchantment of the world'.

Plurality of life-worlds The spread of rationalisation – and associated disenchantment – Berger argues, has been accompanied by other changes in the conditions and experiences of people in modern societies. Significantly, the high levels of social and geographical mobility, combined with widespread exposure to the electronic media, have given people an unprecedented awareness of alternative social worlds, lifestyles and belief systems. As a result, each person's life-world has become pluralised. It is no longer a single, unified and integrated world. Instead it is fragmented and diverse.

Homelessness In this situation, traditional religion is plunged into a crisis of credibility as individuals are faced with any number of competing belief systems and ways of living. In today's pluralistic and multicultural societies, each religion becomes one among many. It becomes increasingly difficult to maintain that *any* religion has a monopoly of truth. And all religions have to compete with a rapidly growing diversity of secular belief systems. This undermines traditional religious teachings, it erodes past certainties about morality and people's identity, it encourages a sense of meaninglessness. The result is *anomie* or loss of confidence in the norms, whereby people lack direction and guides to action. Using Berger's

term, people are 'homeless', cut off from traditional supports and comfort and sense of self, all of which made them feel 'at home'. And religion – whose main function, Berger believes, has been as a shield against anomie – has been rendered largely impotent. It no longer has the power to give meaning to life.

activity15 *problems of modernity*

Item A *Social diversity*

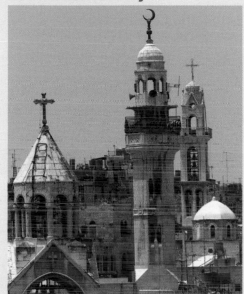

Christian belltowers and a Muslim mosque in Bethlehem

People at Respect Festival, 2001

Item B *Homelessness*

Many of the discontents of modern society stem from the pluralisation of social life-worlds. These discontents can be characterised as 'homelessness'. The pluralistic structures of modern society have made the life of more and more individuals migratory, ever-changing, mobile. Not only are an increasing number of individuals in a modern society uprooted from their original social settings, but, in addition, no subsequent setting succeeds in becoming truly 'home' either. A world in which everything is in constant motion is a world in which certainties of any kind are hard to come by. The age-old function of religion – to provide ultimate certainty – has been severely shaken.

The problem becomes most clearly apparent when one looks at that ancient religious function which Weber called 'theodicy'. This means any explanation of human events that gives meaning to the experiences of suffering and evil. Modern society has threatened the plausibility of religious theodicies, but it has not removed the experiences that call for them. Human beings continue to be stricken by sickness and death. They continue to experience social injustice and deprivation. What modernity has accomplished is to seriously weaken those definitions of reality that previously made the human condition easier to bear. This has produced an anguish all its own.

Source: Berger, Berger & Kellner, 1974

questions

1 a) With reference to Items A and B, explain what you understand by the 'pluralisation of social life-worlds'.

   b) What sort of 'discontents' may pluralisation encourage?

2 How might the pluralisation of social life-worlds undermine religion?

3.8 Postmodernism and religion

A number of sociologists have tried to identify the main developments in human society. Some distinguish between *premodern society* and today's *modern society*. Others believe we have moved beyond modernity and are now living in *postmodern society*.

Sociologists who take this view are known as *postmodernists* and the theory they have developed is known as *postmodernism*.

Postmodern society

Sociologists have identified various characteristics of postmodern society. They include:

ICT The development and spread of information and communication technology (ICT), including television and the internet. As a result of this development, people are increasingly exposed to images, ideas and information from around the world.

Consumerism The growth of consumerism – buying goods and services is becoming increasingly central to people's lives. What we buy says who we are. A range of branded goods from Nike trainers to Gucci sunglasses and Armani fragrance allows us to select items to fit our chosen identities.

Movement of people Mass travel and migration – people are increasingly exposed to different societies and different ways of life. Countries are becoming more and more multicultural.

Risk and uncertainty A sense of growing social and environmental risk. People's lives are increasingly insecure. Few can look forward to a job for life. Relationships are more at risk as the rise in divorce indicates. And with global warming and worldwide pollution, the environment we live in appears increasingly dangerous and uncertain.

Globalisation We live in an increasingly global society. The boundaries between nation states are breaking down with transnational organisations, such as the European Union, and transnational companies, like the Ford Motor Company, Nestlé and Coca-Cola. Interaction between nation states becomes more frequent and intense as goods, capital, people, brands, images, fashions and beliefs flow across national boundaries.

The cultural impact

Postmodernists believe that the changes outlined above have had a major impact on the culture of societies in the postmodern age. According to David Lyon (2000), this involves changes in people's attitude to *authority*, to their sense of *identity*, and to their ideas of *time* and *space*.

Authority According to Lyotard (1984), postmodern culture is characterised by a widespread loss of confidence in the grand explanations – the 'big stories' or *metanarratives* – traditionally provided by science, religion and politics. People are less likely to accept that there are absolute truths, whether religious, scientific or political. And, along with an increased pessimism that science and reason will provide solutions, comes a declining confidence in the inevitability of *progress*. Thus, sources previously regarded as authoritative, such as the scientific community, the clergy and politicians, are regarded with increasing scepticism.

To some extent, these developments are consequences of the global spread of information, which exposes growing numbers to competing interpretations of 'reality', and claims to the truth. As diverse worldviews – religious, ethnic, political, scientific – penetrate societies around the globe, knowledge in postmodern society comes to be seen as *relative*. There is no longer a single truth. It has been replaced by a multitude of truths which are relative to particular times and places.

Identity In modern society, people's identities are largely shaped by their occupation, gender, social class and nationality. In postmodern society, their identities are constructed more by personal choice. As a result, they are more fluid and flexible. However, they are also more under threat.

According to Manuel Castells (1996), this is primarily a result of the information technology revolution and globalisation. Individuals' destinies and their sense of themselves are largely at the mercy of a dynamic, globalised capitalism, which can rapidly create and destroy jobs and change communities in ways beyond political control. In this insecure, postmodern world of sudden flows of power, employment, and wealth, trying to construct an identity, either as an individual or a community, becomes of central importance (Castells, 1996).

And increasingly, according to Zygmunt Bauman (1992), individuals in postmodern societies are constructing their identities primarily through what they choose to *consume*. As David Lyon (2000) puts it, 'self-esteem and our recognition by others may be purchased over the counter'.

Time and space Postmodern society has seen a restructuring of time and space. Distance no longer provides a barrier to communication – people can talk to or email each other almost instantly across the world. This provides immediate access to cultures, practices, ideas and belief systems which were once remote and inaccessible.

Postmodernity and religion

Postmodern society has resulted in:

● A decline of previously dominant religious organisations
● A growth of fundamentalism in all world religions
● The spread of new types of religious organisations, movements and networks.

The decline of dominant religious organisations Modernity is associated with authoritative institutions which provide a metanarrative in which to believe. In modernity, the metanarratives of the world religions were transmitted via sacred texts and interpreted by highly-regarded religious authorities.

However, globalisation – in particular, the spread of people and ideas around the world – has resulted in a greatly increased exposure to rival metanarratives, including a wide range of contradictory religions and philosophies. Repeated exposure to alternative versions of the truth may undermine people's confidence in them all, and encourage a view of truth as relative. Hence, one consequence of postmodernity may be a decline in the authority of both established religious institutions and religious metanarratives. (This suggestion is discussed further on page 69.)

The rise of fundamentalism While postmodern *relativism* may undermine some religious institutions and diminish their support, it may at the same time encourage a counter-response. The last few decades have witnessed a rise in religious *fundamentalism* in all major world religions. For example, the worldwide membership of the Jehovah's Witnesses grew from 44,080 in 1928 to over six million in 2000. This is expected to at least double by 2020.

Fundamentalism is seen by its followers as a return to the basics or fundamentals of religion. It often involves a literal interpretation of religious texts and strict moral codes of behaviour. People tend to look to the past, to a 'golden age' of religion, and use this as a template for the present and the future.

One interpretation of the growth of fundamentalist movements such as Jehovah's Witnesses is that they offer hope, direction and certainty in a world which seems increasingly insecure, confusing and morally lost (Holden, 2002).

In poorer societies, whose traditional cultures and religions are subjected to the forces of Westernisation and globalisation, fundamentalism can also provide a defence against cultural and religious dominance. Perceiving a threat to their faith and identity, people may respond by looking backward to traditional truths. Thus, for Bauman (1992), 'fundamentalist tendencies' may 'reflect and

articulate the experience of people on the receiving end of globalisation'. Similarly, Castells (1996) sees fundamentalism as a way in which people construct 'resistance identities', as globalisation undermines their traditional sense of self.

However, although fundamentalism may reject aspects of globalisation, it is not necessarily against science and technological progress. For instance, in Egypt and other Islamic societies, while conservative Islam has grown in influence in politics, law, education, and on the street, it has nevertheless embraced modern science and technology. It has stressed the 'complementary' relationship between science and Islam in its education system and in its literature (Herbert, 2001). Similarly, as Starrett (1998) notes, it has accepted many modern medical technologies (including in-vitro fertilisation, plastic surgery and birth control), as long as they are applied within certain limits. And, as Castells (1996) shows with regards to Christian, Hindu and Islamic fundamentalism, such groups are highly dependent on ICT to mobilise ideas, money and social links.

The spread of new religious movements As noted earlier, personal identity in postmodern society is increasingly constructed by individuals rather than shaped by the groups to which they belong. And identity is increasingly reflected by personal consumption – the goods and services a person chooses to buy. This emphasis on identity and consumption can be seen in people's choice of religion and the uses they make of it.

Postmodern society encourages people to select religious beliefs and practices to suit their chosen identities. Traditional religious metanarratives have lost much of their authority. As a result of travel, migration and the 'information explosion' from the new electronic media, people are exposed to a vast array of religions. Postmodern consumers are already well-prepared to select those items which appeal to them. This freedom of, and desire for, choice has led to a spread of new religious movements.

Those interested can dip in and select a 'pick and mix' assortment from the beliefs and practices on offer at the 'spiritual supermarket'. These can then be tested out to see if they 'work' for the consumer. If the experience proves rewarding, the beliefs and practices can be incorporated into the individual's identity. If not, they can be dropped.

Postmodernism – an evaluation

While accepting some of the trends identified by postmodernists, many sociologists argue that they have gone too far. Have we really entered a brand new age of postmodernity? Are all truths relative? Is fundamentalism a response to postmodern society?

The relativisation of truth Steve Bruce (2002) rejects the view that faith in science and reason is dead and all truths carry equal weight.

Although people nowadays are much more cautious about the consequences of science, for example, genetic modification and nuclear power, Bruce denies that this amounts to a wholesale rejection of the metanarrative of science and to the relativisation of thought. Not all the ways of viewing the world have become equally plausible. For instance, most still see 'a difference in kind between astronomy and astrology, or between surgery and aura healing'. And 'most practitioners of spiritual medicine defer to conventional doctors for more serious ailments' (Bruce, 2002).

Consumption and individualism Bruce (2002) accepts that greater wealth and consumer choice have allowed people to create what they see as their own particular identities. However, he criticises postmodernists for ignoring the possibility that consumers may be manipulated by advertising to purchase items of mass consumption and to see this as an expression of their individuality.

Postmodernists present a picture of individuality based on consumption – of the individual constructing their identity based on personal choice. Bruce argues that this view underestimates the power of *group* identities. For

key terms

Fundamentalism Movements within established religions which seek a return to the basic texts or beliefs – the 'fundamentals' – of religion.
Relativism The idea that there is no single or absolute truth. Truth is therefore relative.

instance, social class, ethnicity, gender and age all continue to shape our identities in important ways.

Fundamentalism Is the growth of religious fundamentalism a response to the particular changes brought about by postmodern society? This may be the case. But fundamentalism has a long history. For example, Abdullahi An-Na'im (2003) identifies many instances of Islamic fundamentalism over the past thousand years. He sees them as a response to social, political and economic crises. As such, there is nothing particularly new about today's Islamic fundamentalism.

summary

1. Substantive definitions ask what religion is. For example, religion is a belief in the supernatural.

2. Functional definitions ask what are the functions or roles of religion in society. For example, religion strengthens social solidarity.

3. Durkheim's functionalist analysis states that religion reinforces the collective consciousness and strengthens social solidarity.

4. Malinowski argues that religion reduces the disruption caused by life crises and the anxiety produced by activities whose outcome is uncontrollable and uncertain.

5. Parsons claims that religion deals with the 'problem of meaning' by providing answers to universal questions such as why do people die unjustly. Religion also sacralises and legitimates core values which, in turn, strengthens social consensus.

6. Bellah argues that civil religion – a faith in Americanism – unites American society.

7. For Marx, religion reflects the alienation and exploitation of class-based society. It acts as a system of social control, it justifies social inequality, it produces false consciousness, and provides compensation for alienation and oppression. In doing so, religion discourages political action by the subject class to improve their situation.

8. Some neo-Marxists argue that religion can challenge ruling class dominance – for example, liberation theology in Latin America.

9. Many feminists claim that religion is a patriarchal institution. Supernatural beings and religious professionals are overwhelmingly male. And in many religions, women play a secondary role in worship. In strongly religious societies, women tend to have fewer options and less favourable treatment.

10. Weber argues that at certain times and places religion can be a force for social change. He claims that early forms of Protestantism, particularly Calvinism, encouraged the rise of capitalism. The Protestant ethic, with its emphasis on hard work, self-discipline and self-denial, provided the basis for the spirit of capitalism.

11. Weber's views have been widely criticised. For example, some critics argue that capitalism preceded early forms of Protestantism.

12. Peter Berger agrees with Weber's view that rationalisation has led to disenchantment. He argues that the pluralisation of people's life-worlds has produced an unprecedented awareness of different belief systems. This undermines traditional religious teachings. The result is anomie. Religion no longer has the power to give meaning to life.

13. According to postmodernists, the metanarratives of modern society have been undermined in postmodern society. As a result, knowledge and beliefs are increasingly seen as relative. This has led to a decline in traditional religion which can no longer claim a monopoly of the truth.

14. Some researchers have seen the rise of religious fundamentalism as a response to this development. They see people going 'back to basics' in an age of uncertainty.

15. People are seen to increasingly construct their own identities in postmodern society – largely on the basis of what they consume. The growth of new religious movements reflects this – people can select a mix of beliefs and practices to suit their desired identity.

activity 16 religion in postmodern society

Item A Mixing to taste

Glenn Hoddle

Glenn Hoddle, the former England football coach, is a controversial figure. He made no secret of his strong Christian beliefs. He used a faith healer for counselling his team. And he was forced to resign in 1999 as a result of his statement about karma which was seen as offensive to people with disabilities. In Hoddle's words, 'You and I have been given two hands and two legs and half-decent brains. Some people have not been born like that for a reason. The karma is working from another lifetime. I have nothing to hide about that. It is not only people with disabilities. What you sow, you have to reap.'

Statements of mixed religious belief are becoming more commonplace. Hoddle's apparent Hinduism (belief in karma) is hitched to a (Christian or Jewish) Biblical phrase about reaping what you sow. And how does this square with his consulting a New Age faith healer? The evidence shows that more and more people can both claim some fairly conventional religious positions and cheerfully add on other elements – Feng Shui, yoga, mysticism, astrology, Shiatsu, Reiki and the rest. It has been likened to cocktail mixing – mixing divine drinks to individual taste.

Source: Lyon, 2000

Item B What works for me

In postmodern religion, truth is relative to what people imagine will satisfy their requirements. People have what they take to be 'spiritual' *experiences* without having to hold religious *beliefs*. Instead of authoritative texts providing truth, 'truth' is seen in terms of 'what works for me'.

Source: Heelas, 2000

Item C Religious shopping mall

Item D Islamic fundamentalism

Today, *Sharia* law – a legal system based on Islamic teachings – has been adopted in a number of Islamic countries – for example, parts of Pakistan and Islamic areas of Nigeria. This is often seen as a recent development and as an example of fundamentalism. However, there is nothing new about this. For example, it occurred in 10th century Morocco and 11th century Moorish Spain.

Fundamentalist *jihad* movements developed in Islamic areas of West Africa in the 17th, 18th and 19th centuries. Some of these resulted in the creation of Islamic states – for example, Ivory Coast and Guinea.

Source: An-Na'im, 2003

questions

1 How do Items A, B and C illustrate postmodernists' claims about the nature of religion in postmodern society?

2 How can Item D be used to criticise postmodernists' views?

Unit 4 Religion and social change

key issues

1 Is religion a conservative force?

2 Is religion a radical force?

One of the major debates in the sociology of religion concerns the relationship between religion and social change. Is religion a conservative force? Does it maintain things the way they are and discourage social change? Or is religion a *radical force*? Does it initiate social change, does it encourage new ideas and new ways of behaving? Or does it do both at certain times and places? Is religion sometimes a conservative force discouraging social change and sometimes a radical force encouraging social change?

Some of the main sociological theories of religion deal with these questions. The answers they provide will now be examined.

4.1 Social change and theories of religion

Marxism

From a traditional Marxist view, religion is a conservative force. According to Karl Marx, it justifies the dominance of the ruling class and provides consolation for the subject class. As a result, religion discourages social change.

Religion and the ruling class Religion often legitimates – defines as right – the position of the ruling class. For example, monarchs in medieval Europe ruled by divine right. How can human beings change what is ordained by God? To do so would be punishable by eternal damnation. Justifying ruling-class domination as God-given discourages attempts to change the situation.

Religion and the subject class According to Marx, religion is 'the opium of the people'. It provides consolation for the misery of oppression by offering the false promise of eternal happiness in the next life. This illusion of happiness makes life appear bearable and therefore discourages attempts by the subject class to change their situation. Again, religion acts as a conservative force which maintains things they way they are.

Alternative Marxist views Marx's friend and co-writer Friedrich Engels saw glimmers of a demand for change in some religious movements which looked forward to change in the here-and-now rather than in the afterlife. For example, he saw aspects of communism in early Christianity. However, because of religion's emphasis on the supernatural, Engels felt that these movements were doomed to failure – they would not lead to political revolution.

As noted in Unit 3, some Marxists argue that religion can contribute to radical change. For example, Antonio Gramsci and Otto Maduro claim that, at certain times and places, religion can directly support the liberation of the subject class and help them to become aware of their true situation.

Evaluation As outlined in Unit 3, there is evidence to support the standard Marxist view that religion is a conservative force – that it supports the powerful and helps to keep the masses in their place. However, there is plenty of evidence which suggests that religion can sometimes encourage social change. For example, Roman Catholicism in Eastern Europe in the 1970s and 80s supported resistance to the domination of the Soviet Union (Hunt, 1992).

Feminism

A number of feminists have seen religion as a conservative force. Where Marxists have seen religion as maintaining the power of the ruling class, feminists have seen it as maintaining patriarchy – the domination of women by men.

Christianity provides evidence to support this view.

- The Christian God – 'our father' – has traditionally been seen as male.
- Eve was created as a 'helpmate' for Adam.
- Christianity traditionally defined a wife as the property of her husband. She owed him life-long obedience.
- Until recently, women could not become clergy in Christian churches. This changed in 1992 in the Church of England. But women are still barred from becoming religious professionals in the Roman Catholic Church.

These examples support the view that religion serves to keep women in their traditional place – subordinate to men.

Evaluation There is plenty of evidence to support the view that religion reinforces patriarchy and discourages change. As such, religion is a conservative rather than a radical force. However, there is evidence to question this view. As noted in Unit 3, goddesses played a significant part in ancient Greek and Roman religion. And today, thousands of women have positions of leadership in the rapidly growing Christian Pentecostal movement.

Functionalism

In general, functionalist theories have seen religion as a force for stability rather than change. It reinforces value consensus, it strengthens social solidarity, it deals with life crises which threaten to disrupt society. As such, religion is seen as a conservative force which maintains the status quo – keeping things the way things are.

Emile Durkheim According to Durkheim, religion reinforces the collective conscience – the norms and values of society. Religious rituals strengthen social solidarity by binding together members of society. In these respects, religion is a force for stability rather than change.

Bronislaw Malinowski According to Malinowski, religion serves to reduce the anxiety and tension which result from events which threaten to disrupt social life. Such events

activity 17 religion in Black America

Item A Gospel music

Throughout the USA, Black churches have resounded with the sound of gospel music. In Detroit, the Reverend C.L. Franklin, father of the famous soul singer Aretha Franklin and pastor of the Bethel Baptist church, has raised congregations to fever pitch with his preaching and gospel singing. So intense is the feeling that he arouses that nurses are regularly on hand to tend members of his flock overcome with emotion. People leave the church feeling cleansed, their burdens lifted, recharged and ready to face the problems of a new week.

Gospel singers

At a Madison Square Garden gospel concert in New York City, Mahalia Jackson, the Queen of Gospel, sings *Just Over The Hill*, a song about going to heaven. As she sinks to her knees, singing with intensity and jubilation, women in the audience shriek and faint. Gospel music, in the words of one of its singers, 'stirs the emotions'.

A member of the Ward Sisters, a famous Black gospel group states, 'For people who work hard and make little money, gospel music offers a promise that things will be better in the life to come'. According to Thomas A. Dorsey, one of the founders of modern gospel music, 'Make it anything other than good news and it ceases to be gospel'. Many gospel songs ring with joy, excitement, anticipation and conviction about reaching the 'blessed homeland' and 'waking up in glory'. Life on earth might be hard and painful with little hope for improvement, but life after death is nothing but good news.

God not only promises eternal salvation and perfect happiness, he also provides support and direction for life on earth. Typical lines from gospel songs include, 'Take your burdens to the Lord and leave them there', 'God will carry you through', 'Since I gave to Jesus my poor broken heart, he has never left me alone', and 'What would I do if it wasn't for the Lord?'

Source: Heilbut, 1971 and Haralambos, 1995

Martin Luther King giving his 'I Have a Dream' speech during the March on Washington in 1963.

Item B Protest

In the late 1950s and early 1960s, some Black preachers came out of their churches and onto the streets. Led by the Reverend Martin Luther King, the Southern Christian Leadership Council, an organisation of Black churches in the southern states of the USA, directed mass protest against racial discrimination. Partly due to their campaign, the American government passed civil rights laws which declared discrimination on the basis of skin colour to be illegal.

Source: Franklin and Starr, 1967

questions

1 How does Item A support the traditional Marxist view of religion as a conservative force?

2 How does Item B question this view?

include life crises – birth, puberty, marriage and death. For example, a funeral ceremony checks the disruptive emotions which follow the death of a loved one. It promises life after death and brings together family and friends to support the bereaved. In doing so it reintegrates society.

Again, religion is seen to bring social stability rather than change.

Talcott Parsons Like Durkheim, Parsons sees religion as reinforcing value consensus – for example, the Christian Ten Commandments back up the norms and values of Western societies. In addition, he sees religion as giving meaning to and making sense of life. This helps people to adjust to and accept their situation which, in turn, promotes social stability. Again, the emphasis is on stability rather than change.

Evaluation Functionalists have been criticised for presenting what many see as a one-sided view of religion – for their emphasis on religion promoting social solidarity and value consensus and for neglecting instances of religion as a force for social change. This criticism is not entirely fair. For example, Talcott Parsons (1951) argued that Christianity not only reinforced, it also helped to produce, the norms and values which shaped modern societies and were essential to their economic development.

Max Weber

From a Marxist view, religion is largely shaped by economic factors. As part of the superstructure of society, religion reflects the infrastructure or economic base. Max Weber argued that in certain cases, the opposite was true – religion can help to shape entire economic systems and bring radical changes to society as a whole.

Weber argued that human action is directed by meanings. As a result, social change can result from a change in meanings, from a change in world view – the way people see the world. And these new meanings can be generated by religion.

This was the argument Weber used in his most famous work, *The Protestant Ethic and the Spirit of Capitalism* (see pages 28, 30-31). He claimed that a number of Protestant religions which developed in 16th century Europe produced the ideas which were essential for the development of capitalism.

As outlined in Unit 3, these ideas included self-discipline, rational thinking, a 'calling' in life which the individual must follow in a determined and single-minded way, and a condemnation of time-wasting, laziness, luxuries and entertainment. From these ideas developed the 'spirit of capitalism' which was a major factor in the creation of the capitalist system.

Evaluation If Weber is correct, religion can sometimes be a significant force for social change. However, as noted in Unit 3, a number of researchers claim that early forms of capitalism preceded the new Protestant religions. In terms of their argument, Weber got it the wrong way round – capitalism came first and helped to produce Protestantism.

4.2 Religious fundamentalism

In recent years, there has been a rise in religious fundamentalism – in particular, Christian fundamentalism in the USA and Islamic fundamentalism in North Africa, the Middle East and the Far East.

Religious fundamentalism is seen by its followers as a return to the basics or fundamentals of religion. It usually involves a literal interpretation of religious texts and strict moral codes of behaviour. Its followers often see it as turning the clock back to true religion, to a time when religion was not watered down, tarnished and corrupted by the evils of modern society.

Some researchers see fundamentalism as a particularly conservative form of religion – it looks backward, it rejects many of the changes in modern society, it tries to return to a former time.

This is a somewhat different view of religion as a conservative force. Rather than maintaining things the way they are, fundamentalists aim to make things the way they were. In one respect they are conservative, in another respect they are not because they seek to change the existing society.

Christian fundamentalism in the USA

In the 1970s, there was a revival of Christian fundamentalism in the United States. In 1979, Jerry Falwell and a small group of preachers founded the Moral Majority – a conservative political movement which aimed to return to traditional values. Basing their views on a literal interpretation of the Bible, their goal was to restore God to the centre of American society. In his book *Listen America*, Jerry Falwell urged Americans to come 'back to God, back to the Bible, back to reality'.

The Moral Majority pointed out what they saw as the ills of American society – high divorce rates, widespread juvenile delinquency, pornography on the internet, adultery in the White House, abortion on demand and increasing tolerance of homosexuality. This, in their view, was not God's way (Ammerman, 2003).

The election of Ronald Reagan as President of the United States has been seen by some as an indication of the Moral Majority's power. Reagan shared many of their views. However, by the 1990s, many members felt that the movement had failed. Two prominent members published *Blinded by Might* stating that, 'Today, very little that we set out to do has gotten done. In fact, the moral landscape of America has become worse' (quoted in Ammerman, 2003).

Despite this apparent failure, there is evidence that Christian fundamentalism had a significant influence on the election of George Bush in 2000 and on his policies from then on. Bush himself is a fundamentalist, born-again Christian. Shortly after his election, he created the Office of

Faith-Based Programs which encourages religious groups to take over welfare services for the homeless, unemployed, drug addicts and alcoholics. This is part of Bush's 'compassionate conservatism', a phrase borrowed from his close advisor, the fundamentalist Christian Marvin Olasky, who wrote a book entitled *Compassionate Conservatism*. Olasky's message for dealing with the poor is summed up by his statement: 'What we've found is the most useful kind of poverty-fighting is spiritual. And we forgot that in the 20th century' (quoted in Saunders, 2001).

Islamic fundamentalism

Although Islamic fundamentalist movements vary due to local history and circumstances, they have certain things in common. Islamic fundamentalists see themselves as the saviours and moral guardians of their societies. They are the chosen few who must restore true religion in an immoral and decadent society which has abandoned God's design for living. They have a duty to translate God's will into practice in line with a literal reading of the Qur'an – the Muslim bible (An-Na'im, 2003).

The Iranian revolution The following case study on the revolution in Iran in 1979 highlights some of the main features of Islamic fundamentalism.

In the 1920s and 30s, the Shah (ruler) of Iran felt that traditional Islamic culture was holding back the modernisation of his country. He introduced a Western curriculum into schools, secular (non-religious) laws into courts and invited Western companies into Iran to develop agriculture and industry. The development of the oil industry brought considerable wealth to a small elite, while leaving the mass of the population in poverty.

By the 1970s, parts of Iran, particularly the capital Tehran, were becoming increasingly Westernised with bars, cinemas, discos, night clubs, and Western dress, food, music and films. Many people resented both the wealthy

activity18 *fundamentalism in the USA*

Item A *Pat Robertson*

One of the leaders of the Moral Majority, TV evangelist and former presidential candidate Reverend Pat Robertson outlines his vision of America after fundamentalist Christians have taken control. 'When the Christian majority takes over this country, there will be no satanic churches, no more free distribution of pornography, no more abortion on demand, and no more talk of rights for homosexuals.'

Pat Robertson at an anti-abortion demonstration in Wichita, Kansas

Item B *President Bush*

According to George Bush, the greatest hope for the poor is not a reform of government welfare services but 'redemption' – in other words, religious belief. Welfare is a poor alternative to the power of religion. Like all fundamentalists, Bush takes the Bible literally as the word of God. He sees the world in religious terms. When he talks about the 'axis of evil', referring to states like Iraq under Saddam Hussein, he is identifying his enemies as literally satanic, as possessed by the devil.

Source: Saunders, 2001 and James, 2003

George Bush in the pulpit in New Orleans, claiming that the 'miracle of salvation' is the answer to many of society's problems.

question

With some reference to Items A and B, how can Christian fundamentalism be seen both as conservative and as a movement for social change?

elite and the influence of the West.

The ayatollahs – religious leaders – blamed the poverty of the masses on the decline of Islam and on Western influence. They saw the solution as a return to a truly Islamic society based on the Qur'an and a rejection of Western capitalism and Western ways. This would cure the disease of 'westoxicifation' and restore God's design for living (Bruce, 2001).

In 1979, the people overthrew the Shah and an Islamic state was established under the leadership of Ayatollah Khomeini. Bars were looted and burned, cinemas destroyed, casinos and nightclubs closed down, and alcohol and Western music banned. Women were encouraged to stay at home and study the Qur'an, and in public they were required to cover themselves with the *chador* – veil. Islamic law – the *sharia* – was reinstated, and schoolchildren now recited the Qur'an rather than singing the national anthem.

Religious fundamentalism – conclusion

In one respect, fundamentalist movements are conservative forces. They look backwards for their inspiration for the future, they attempt to turn the clock back to a time of true religion. But no movement can hope to completely restore the past. And there are often many new features in fundamentalist movements. Steve Bruce (2001) gives the following picture of fundamentalism in Iran. 'Although Islamic fundamentalists typically portray their task as a return to the past, the Islam they promote is not the traditional rather easy-going rural religion of a nomadic tribal people who gave a high place to the magical powers of the cults of local saints. It is a puritanical "reformed" Islam that places unusually strict requirements on individuals and replaces the magic of the saint cult with rigorous self-discipline.'

Although the aim of religious fundamentalists is a return to the past, they also aim to change existing society.

activity 19 fundamentalism in Iran

Item A Westoxification

In the words of an Iranian ayatollah:

'Islam was defeated by its own rulers, who ignored Divine Law, in the name of Western-style secularism. The West captured the imagination of large sections of our people. And that conquest was far more disastrous for Islam than any loss of territory. It is not for the loss of Andalusia (a reference to the Moors being driven out of Spain) that we ought to weep every evening – although that remains a bleeding wound. Far greater is the loss of sections of our youth to Western ideology, dress, music and food.'

Quoted in Taheri, 1987

Item B An Iranian woman

'Once we thought that Western society had all the answers for successful, fruitful living. If we followed the lead of the West we would have progress. Now we see that this isn't true. They are sick societies, even their material prosperity is breaking down. America is full of crime and promiscuity. Russia is worse. Who wants to be like that? We have to remember God. Look how God has blessed Saudi Arabia. That is because they have tried to follow the (Islamic) Law. And America, with all its loose society, is all problems.'

Quoted in *History of the 20th Century*, Vol. 8, 1994

Item C Anti-American demonstration

Anti-US demonstration outside the American Embassy in Tehran, 1979. The poster on the right shows a picture of the religious leader, Ayatollah Khomeini.

question

In what ways do the items illustrate Islamic fundamentalism?

Christian fundamentalism in the USA aims to change the moral landscape of America. Fundamentalism in Iran aimed to rid the country of Western influence and create an Islamic society. These are radical aims. And sometimes they can lead to radical social change – in the case of Iran, they led to a revolution.

4.3 Religion and social change – conclusion

The first section in this unit looked at theories of religion. Most theories see religion as a conservative force, as a force which maintains the status quo. Weber, however, argued that at certain times and places, religion could be a radical force, helping to change society in significant ways.

The second section looked at religious fundamentalism arguing that though conservative in their outlook, fundamentalist movements can sometimes lead to radical change in the wider society.

This section examines further evidence and ideas about the relationship of religion and social change.

Religion as a force for change

Geoffrey K. Nelson (1986) argues that there are many instances in history when social change and even revolution have been directed by religious beliefs. He gives the following examples.

- One of the leaders of the Peasants' Revolt in England in 1381 was a priest called John Ball. He claimed that God had given the land to all men equally, and that the peasants should rise up against the lords who had stolen the land from them.

- Churches played an important part in the civil rights movement in the USA during the 1960s. Protests led by the Reverend Martin Luther King influenced the government to pass civil rights laws which banned segregation on the basis of skin colour.

- From the 1960s, a number of radical individuals and groups have emerged from the Roman Catholic Church in Latin America. They argued that Christians have a duty to help liberate the poor and oppressed. They developed a set of teachings known as *liberation theology* and sometimes joined movements to overthrow oppressive regimes. For example, in 1979 Catholic revolutionaries played a part in the overthrow of the right-wing government in Nicaragua.

Nelson argues that examples such as these indicate how religion 'can spearhead resistance and revolution'. However, he also notes that in each case there are examples of religion encouraging the opposite response. During the Peasants' Revolt, many churchmen supported the lords and condemned the rebellion. In the USA, some Black religious groups discouraged civil rights protest. And in Latin America, many Roman Catholic churchmen supported the position of the ruling groups.

Nelson's point is that in certain times and places, religion can be either a conservative or a radical force.

Stability and change

Nelson's research suggests that the question should not be, 'Is religion a conservative or a radical force?' Instead, it should be, 'Under what circumstances does religion encourage or discourage change?' This is the approach taken by Meredith McGuire (1981) who asks, 'In what way and under what conditions does religion promote rather than inhibit change?' She answers this question in the following way.

Beliefs Religions with strong moral codes are more likely to be critical of the wider society. As a result, their members are more likely to demand changes in society. Religions which focus on the social conduct of their members in this world are more likely to produce change than religions which focus on spirituality or other-worldly concerns. In terms of this view, Protestantism is more likely to produce change than Buddhism with its spiritual goal of eliminating the self and earthly desires.

Culture Where religious beliefs are central to the culture of society, they are more likely to be used to justify or legitimate demands for stability or change. This can be seen in Central and South American countries with a strongly Roman Catholic tradition.

Social location If religious institutions are closely integrated with other parts of the social structure – for example, the political and economic systems – they have greater power to produce stability or change. For example, the Roman Catholic Church in Poland was closely linked to Solidarity, a trade union organisation which played an important role in the overthrow of communism.

Internal organisation Religious institutions with a strong, centralised authority will have more power to affect stability or change. For example, the Roman Catholic Church has a powerful centralised authority and a strict hierarchy of religious professionals. They tend to speak with one voice. And when they don't, they are disciplined from on high and even expelled from the church. This happened to some Latin American churchmen who supported liberation theology.

Evaluation McGuire has outlined factors which influence whether religion acts as a force for stability or change. In many cases, however, she does not indicate *why* the same religion with the same beliefs, the same relationship to culture and the same social location and internal organisation, sometimes promotes change and sometimes inhibits change. Why, for example, after years of emphasising the joys of the afterlife, did Black congregations in the USA take to the streets in protest under the leadership of Martin Luther King? Answers to this question require an examination of the social context and circumstances which led to this change of direction.

summary

1. Marx saw religion as a conservative force which justified the position of the ruling class and provided consolation for the subject class. As a result, it tended to keep the subject class in its place, so discouraging social change.

2. Some neo-Marxists argue that religion can sometimes help to make the subject class aware of their situation and support their liberation. In this respect, religion can sometimes act as a radical force.

3. Some feminists have argued that religion is a conservative force, seeing it as maintaining patriarchy – keeping women in their traditional place as subordinate to men.

4. In general, functionalists have seen religion as a force for stability rather than change. By reinforcing value consensus and strengthening social solidarity, religion tends to maintain society the way it is.

5. On the basis of his analysis of the relationship between early Protestantism and capitalism, Weber argued that religion can sometimes be a significant force for social change. In his view, early Protestantism provided the meanings and guides for action which were an important factor in the rise of capitalism.

6. Some researchers see fundamentalism as a particularly conservative form of religion – it looks backwards, it rejects many of the changes in modern society and tries to return to a former time.

7. Despite this, fundamentalism can be seen as a force for change – fundamentalists do try to change society even though their model for change is based on the past.

8. There is evidence that religion can act in some circumstances as a conservative force and in others as a radical force.

9. In view of this, some researchers argue that the question should not be, 'Is religion a conservative or a radical force?' Instead, it should be, 'Under what circumstances does religion encourage or discourage change?'

10. Meredith McGuire has attempted to answer this last question. She has outlined factors which influence whether religion acts as a force for stability or change.

Unit 5 Religious organisations and movements

keyissues

1 What are churches, sects, denominations and cults?

2 What are New Religious Movements?

3 What is the New Age movement?

Religious organisations differ in many ways. Some are organised in terms of a rigid hierarchy – for example, the Roman Catholic church with the Pope at its head and a chain of officials leading down to local priests. Others lack a clearly defined hierarchy and official positions.

Religious organisations also differ in terms of their relationship to the wider society. Some generally accept society's norms and values, others reject them.

Sociologists have used such differences to classify religious organisations into types. This unit looks at the main types they have identified. It begins with four concepts – church, sect, denomination and cult. It is important to note that these are *ideal types* – they are models of 'pure types' of religious organisations. In the messy real world, no organisation will exactly fit an ideal type – it will only tend to fit one type better than others.

5.1 Church and sect

Max Weber introduced the distinction between *church* and *sect* in the early 20th century. His friend, Ernst Troeltsch (1931) developed this idea, seeing churches and sects as very different types of organisation.

Church

Membership A church aims to be the 'spiritual home' of everybody in society. Membership is open to all and easily obtained. The church is the dominant religious organisation in a society and people qualify for membership simply by being born into that society – though there are formal rituals such as baptism which officially signify membership.

In its most developed form, a church seeks to be universal and all-inclusive – to include members of all social groups in all societies.

Organisation Churches have a complex, formal hierarchy made up of professional clergy. In the Roman Catholic church, for example, the Pope heads an organisational pyramid of cardinals, archbishops, bishops and priests.

Worship and ritual Worship in churches tends to be restrained. Rather than being spontaneous, it is often based on traditional ritual – for example, a fixed order of service, standing for hymns, and regular repetition of prayers.

Sense of legitimacy This refers to the legitimacy or 'rightness' of religious beliefs. Churches claim to have a monopoly of truth – only their teachings offer the truth, they provide the only legitimate religion.

Relationship to the wider society Churches generally accept the norms and values of the wider society. They are often closely linked with society's major institutions – for example, church and state were closely linked in medieval Europe.

Involvement and commitment Although churches encourage members to play an active role – to regularly attend services and participate in church functions – there is no compulsion to do so. Those who show low levels of involvement and commitment are still regarded as members.

Sect

Membership Unlike churches, the attitude of sects to the world outside is highly exclusive – they erect strong boundaries between themselves and the wider society and exclude people considered 'unworthy'. Gaining membership is not a right, but has to be earned by personal merit. This might be indicated by a knowledge of doctrine, a conversion experience, or the recommendation of existing members. There is therefore a clear distinction between members and non-members. Jehovah's Witnesses, Seventh Day Adventists, Christadelphians and the Amish of the United States are examples of sects.

Organisation Sects generally lack a professional clergy and a complex hierarchy. Instead, they depend for leadership upon the special, God-given talents of members.

Worship and ritual There is little use of ritual, and worship is typically emotional, expressive and spontaneous. For example, members of Christian sects often cry out phrases such as 'Hallelujah' and 'Praise the Lord' as the spirit takes them.

Sense of legitimacy Historically, church and sect have seen the other as rivals and, often, as dangerous enemies. Significantly, both claim that they have a monopoly of the truth and that they are the only true religion.

Sects often look forward to an event of great significance – for example, the second coming of Jesus, the anticipated battle of Armageddon between God's forces and Satan's, the Day of Judgement, and 'life' in heaven or hell. Members are encouraged to think of themselves as an elite who possess special enlightenment or spiritual insight, with salvation reserved for them alone, while non-believers are rejected.

Relationship to the wider society Sects are generally critical of the wider society and expect members to stand apart from it. Contact with non-members is generally discouraged except in an attempt to convert them. Sects are also critical of the mainstream religious bodies – whom they regard as too worldly – and distance themselves from them.

Involvement and commitment of members Sects demand high standards of behaviour from their members and high levels of commitment. Much of the members' spare time is spent in sectarian activities – for example, in Bible study, trying to gain converts, or socialising with sect members. However, if members fail to meet the sect's high standards, they may be punished, and even expelled – a powerful sanction when their whole way of life has been built around the group.

activity20 church and sect

Item A The Roman Catholic Church

The Roman Catholic Church is the largest Christian grouping. Its followers accept the authority of the Pope – the Vicar of Christ – as Christ's representative on earth. When he defines matters of faith or morals, the Pope's statements are regarded as infallible (incapable of error) and binding on all Catholics.

The Pope stands at the head of a complex hierarchy. Below him are the cardinals, who are responsible for electing and advising the Pope. Next come the 'greater' patriarchs (eg of Jerusalem), and 'minor' patriarchs (eg of Lisbon). Then come archbishops and bishops followed by priests, deacons and subdeacons.

Worship is based on traditional rituals. It is governed by detailed rules and regulations, including strict dress codes for the various religious professionals. Here are part of the instructions for the Roman Catholic Mass.

Bishops in purple robes and cardinals in red robes attend a Mass inside St Peter's Basilica at the Vatican.

The procession comes to the altar. The procession consists of the incense bearer, attendants, master of ceremonies, subdeacon, deacon, and officiating priest, all dressed in the appropriate vestments. First, the preparatory prayers are said at the foot of the altar. The altar is 'incensed'. The officiating priest reads – and the choir sing – the *Introit* and *Kyrie*. The priest, the deacon and subdeacon recite the *Gloria in Excelsis* (Glory in the Highest) which is also sung by the choir.

Source: *Catholic Encyclopaedia*

Item B Jehovah's Witnesses

The following was reviewed for this book by The Watch Tower Bible and Tract Society of Pennsylvania.

Jehovah's Witnesses are an international Christian religious organisation that currently has over 7 million members. They view the Bible to be inspired by God and inerrant, identifying the true God as Jehovah and his first created Son as Jesus Christ, whom God uses to redeem sinful mankind. They do not believe in the Trinity, immortality of the human soul, or universal salvation. In the words of their official publication *The Watchtower*, Witnesses 'do not share in the divisive politics of this world although they subject themselves to human governments as long as God allows these to function. Instead, they patiently await the Day of Judgement and the unfolding of God's purpose for men on Earth'.

Witnesses are not anti-social but separate themselves morally from wider society. They view being law-abiding citizens as a Christian duty. They disagree doctrinally with other religions, particularly mainstream Christianity, which they see as heretical – contrary to God's teachings in the Bible. Witnesses' lives revolve around Bible study, meetings, social activities and door-to-door visits with the aim of gaining converts.

A Jehovah's Witness passes out the 'Watchtower' magazine.

Their organisation, based in New York, together with branch facilities worldwide, prints a variety of Bibles and Bible study aids in some 450 languages. *The Watchtower* is published in more than 170 languages and *Awake!* in more than 80. Personal Bible study and frequent classroom-style meetings often convince students that Bible knowledge is the basis for religious truth.

The few members who persistently spread contrary doctrinal views or live immorally are no longer accepted as Jehovah's Witnesses and are shunned. In this way, they maintain a high level of doctrinal and moral purity, which they believe is required to be saved on the Day of Judgement when God will overturn the existing social order and his Kingdom rule by Christ will bring mankind peace, health and everlasting life.

Source: *The Watch Tower Bible and Tract Society of Pennsylvania, 2008*

question

With reference to Items A and B, why is Roman Catholicism defined as a church and Jehovah's Witnesses as a sect?

5.2 Denomination and cult

Denomination

The concept of *denomination* was introduced to sociology by the American Richard Niebuhr in 1925. Denominations are usually described as part-way between church and sect. Though widely seen as conventional, respectable and mainstream, they often have a history of challenging authority. Unlike the sect, they tend to be tolerant of others' beliefs. Examples of denominations in the UK include Methodists, Baptists and United Reformed.

Membership Unlike the church, the denomination is not 'universalistic' in that it does not seek to make members of the whole population. Although membership is open to all, there is no sect-like test of merit. Denominations tend to be disproportionately middle class.

Organisation Denominations have a professional clergy but their organisational hierarchy is much less complex than that of a church. They have no bishops, archbishops, patriarchs or popes. But the hierarchy is more developed than that of a sect, which typically has no professional clergy. Laypeople play a more direct role than in a church – as non-professional lay-preachers, for instance – but less than in a sect.

Worship and ritual Worship is relatively formal, with less ritual than a church but less spontaneity than in a sect. Though most stand to sing and sit to pray, there is no crossing oneself, incense or bells, as at a church service, nor cries of 'Hallelujah' or 'Praise the Lord' as in a sect. Most sociologists would agree that in the USA, the so-called churches are closer to denominations.

Sense of legitimacy Unlike churches and sects, denominations do not claim an exclusive monopoly of the truth. As a result, they are more tolerant of alternative beliefs and less demanding of their members. And, because they accept that there are other paths to salvation, they will more readily cooperate with other religious organisations.

Relationship to the wider society While churches tend to be closely associated with the state, denominations are explicitly separate from the state. However, unlike many sects, they do not reject the state or the wider society. Hence, in Britain, clergy of such denominations as the

United Reformed and the Methodists appear at national occasions, such as Remembrance Sunday, alongside Church of England clergy who usually officiate as representatives of the national church.

Involvement and commitment Although denominations wish to increase their members, they put relatively little pressure on potential recruits to commit themselves to a particular set of beliefs, to regular attendance, or to membership. In part, this reflects a fundamental value of *individualism*. The right of individuals to interpret the scriptures themselves, without priests as intermediaries, has been central to the 'non-conformist' Protestant traditions such as Methodism, Baptism, Presbyterianism and Unitarianism.

Cult

In everyday language, the terms *cult* and sect are often used interchangeably to refer to relatively small religious groups whose beliefs and practices deviate from those of mainstream religions and appear strange to most people. However, some sociologists make a distinction between sects and cults.

According to Roland Robertson (1970), the key difference between cults and sects is as follows. Sects believe they have a monopoly of the truth, while cults believe their teachings are just one of many paths to the truth. Cults are therefore more tolerant of the beliefs of others and of the behaviour of their members.

Roy Wallis (1974) developed this distinction between sects and cults. Where sects are exclusive, closed, tightly-knit organisations, cults are more loosely organised and open to the outside world. Where sects demand membership tests and strict codes of behaviour which apply to all their members, cults have none of these restrictions. Cults are more individualistic in that they allow individual members to decide what they will or will not accept.

While sect members usually believe in a God who is external to human beings, many cults emphasise the 'power', 'divinity' or 'real self' which is said to reside within individuals. A main aim of such cults is to help people experience their 'inner power' or 'inner divinity'.

Membership Cults are usually open to all and welcome those with a sympathetic interest. There may be no concept of membership – people may simply join in or drop out as they wish.

Organisation Cult organisation is likely to be loose. There may be a charismatic leader, but hierarchies and ideas of seniority are usually discouraged.

Sense of legitimacy Unlike sects, cults do not claim to have a monopoly of the truth. As a result, cults are relatively tolerant – sometimes even welcoming – of followers' involvement with other groups.

Relationship to the wider society Because of the wide range of cults, there is no common orientation to the wider society. Followers generally expect to live 'in the world' and cult-related activity is likely to be part-time.

Involvement and commitment Many cults do not demand high levels of commitment from their followers. Nor do they demand acceptance of their teachings. They simply ask that people be open to the experiences they offer. If people find these experiences rewarding, then they will be likely to learn more about the cult's teachings and increase their involvement

activity21 cults

Item A *Dianetics*

In early 1950, L. Ron Hubbard published an article which developed a psychological theory claiming that there were two sectors of the mind – the analytical and the reactive mind. The analytical mind was the basis of intelligent reasoning, and when its functioning was not constrained, it had much greater power than normally available. When a person was fully 'cleared' of 'engrams' – the recordings of traumatic incidents suffered by an individual – they would be completely free of any psychological problems or psychosomatic illnesses and would have a vastly increased IQ. Following a best-selling book which elaborated these ideas, thousands tried out the technique and hundreds enrolled for short courses of 'auditing' (Dianetic therapy), or training.

L. Ron Hubbard

The movement, known as Dianetics and later as Scientology, developed rapidly all over America. Local enthusiasts formed groups to pursue the study and practice of Dianetics and recruited others. However, Hubbard's work was seen as a starting point, to be developed further by others. The view that many held was that Dianetics was a science to which any individual could contribute. One editor of a Dianetics newsletter emphasised this individualistic orientation: 'There is no reason to take what I say as the "truth", as the "right way". Your way is the best for you.' And Dianetics practitioners claimed: 'There are many, many roads to a higher state of existence. No man can say "This is the route for all to follow".'

Source: Wallis, 1975

Item B 'Is there anybody out there?'

The Raelians were founded in 1973 after a young Frenchman, out walking in wild countryside, came upon a flying saucer from which emerged a benign, 4ft tall, humanoid alien. Over a few afternoons, the extraterrestrial (ET), who could speak any human language, dictated his messages to Rael, messages which provide humanity with a revolutionary account of its origins, and offer guidance and hope for our future. In a nutshell, long ago a group of ETs had settled Earth and perfected their ability to create life in forms like their own. We Earthlings were the result. Thereafter, they withdrew, but kept a kindly eye on us and sent periodic messengers, such as Buddha, Christ and Joseph Smith of the Mormons, to inform us of our origins and – with limited success – to try to guide us. Although they created us, we mistook them for gods.

However, suddenly aware of the scale of our ability for destruction at Hiroshima (where the first atomic bomb was dropped), they became very alarmed and felt an urgent, and perhaps final, urge to help before we ran out of time. Unsurprisingly, however, they are not entirely confident of their likely reception by the Earthlings. Our reactions to Rael and the messages he conveys are the litmus test. Rael is the messenger for this 'Age of Revelation'. But he also comes bearing a set of meditative techniques taught him by his ET contact which can remove the root causes of most of our earthly ills. It's called 'Sensual Meditation' and proposes to 'awaken the mind by awakening the body'.

Though humanity is not perhaps inevitably doomed to self-destruct without their guidance, Rael's task is to persuade us to ponder our unexpected origins, practice the meditative

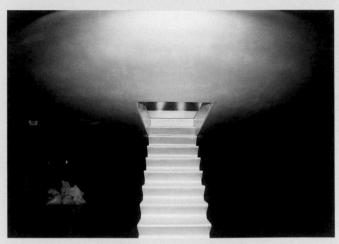

The spacecraft which brought the ETs to Earth to speak to Rael.

techniques taught to him, and demonstrate that we are capable of wisdom and benevolence by building the aliens a home, an embassy, in which to welcome them. Then they will return.

Worldwide, the Raelians claim between 15,000 and 25,000 followers. In Britain there are about 300 names on the mailing list but only a dozen or so whom the British representative regards as really committed. Enquiries are welcome and no commitment is required.

Source: Yeo, 1988

Using Items A and B, show how a cult differs from a sect.

5.3 Church, sect, denomination and cult – an evaluation

Problems of classification As noted at the start of this unit, the categories or concepts used to classify religious organisations are ideal types or 'pure' types. Their fit with real organisations will not therefore be exact. But is the fit close enough to be useful? Some researchers have their doubts. For example, Stark and Bainbridge (1987) argue that the long list of characteristics used to define each type of religious organisation can be a recipe for confusion. When a researcher looks at an actual religious organisation in the real world, they may find that some of its characteristics fit a sect, others a cult and yet others, a denomination. Clearly this makes classification extremely difficult.

A possible solution is to limit the defining characteristics of religious organisations to a relatively few essential or key characteristics. For example, Stark and Bainbridge (1987) define sects as breakaways from established religious organisations and cults as entirely new movements.

Problems of general application Can the classification of church, sect, cult and denomination be applied universally to all religious organisations and movements? Troeltsch's classification of church and sect indicates some of the problems of general application. It was based on the history of sects within Christianity. While it may offer insights into some religious traditions – perhaps Judaism and Islam – it is doubtful whether it can be applied to others such as Hinduism and Buddhism.

In addition, Troeltsch's classification may only be applicable to a particular time period and place. Churches may well be a thing of the past – in particular, medieval Europe. Steve Bruce (1995) argues that today's so-called churches, such as the Church of England, are more like denominations.

Problems of stigma As Hadden (2003) points out, the terms sect and cult are problematic for research because of their associations in everyday thought. They are often seen as 'weird', 'freaky', and sometimes as 'threatening' and 'dangerous'. No member of an unconventional religious organisation would want to be labelled by such terms.

5.4 New Religious Movements

Sociological interest in unconventional religious movements increased dramatically throughout the West in the 1960s and 1970s. As more and more groups emerged, sociologists increasingly found the terms sect and cult inadequate to describe, categorise and analyse the new movements. For instance, although some, such as the meditative, Hindu-based Siddha Yoga movement, appeared to be cult-type religions – emphasising inner experience and the divine within – they quickly developed complex organisational structures quite untypical of cults. Gradually, in addition to the still useful concepts of sect and cult, a new concept was introduced – the *New Religious Movement* (NRM).

One influential attempt to identify types of NRM was made by Roy Wallis (1985). Wallis noted that they mainly drew upon Christian traditions (such as the Jesus People), on non-Western religions (usually Hindu, Buddhist or Muslim), or from Western psychology and psychotherapy, as in organisations such as the Ehrhard Seminars Training (Est).

His main point, however, was that NRMs also differed significantly in how they are 'orientated to the world'. He proposed that NRMs are either primarily *world-affirming*, *world-rejecting* or *world-accommodating*.

World-affirming NRMs broadly accept the world. Many do not appear conventionally religious at all and their language may be much more akin to business. What they offer their members or 'clients' are techniques to enable them to live more satisfactorily or successfully in the world.

In Transcendental Meditation, for instance, each person is assured that they will relax and cope better with life if they meditate on a secret mantra (chant), or sacred word, given to them personally during initiation to the movement.

World-accommodating NRMs encourage their members to remain within the wider society, though they are dissatisfied with and critical of the secular (non-religious) nature of society. They try to help their followers cultivate their awareness of their inner power or inner divinity. However, like the denomination, they claim to be merely one of a variety of paths to truth or salvation. In Siddha Yoga, for instance, meditation and chanting are practised regularly, not primarily to help people cope with or succeed in life, but as a spiritual experience in which they come into contact with their own spiritual core or inner self. The churches and denominations are seen not as corrupt, but as failing to help people have such spiritual experiences.

World-rejecting NRMs are sect-like organisations, often founded by a charismatic leader. They are critical of or even hostile to the wider society – they keep their distance from it and often from other religious organisations. Like sects, they are seen by their members as uniquely legitimate – as the sole means of access to truth or salvation. They therefore draw clear boundaries between members and non-members, set strict conditions for entry and continuing membership, and require a high level of commitment. For instance, the Jesus People lived in group houses, sometimes on the land in agricultural communes, and abandoned in their thousands the drugs, drinking and promiscuous sex of their former lives to devote themselves to bringing others to Jesus.

activity22 New Religious Movements

Item A Scientology and Transcendental Meditation

Psychologically-based movements such as Scientology typically place little emphasis on collective ritual or worship but focus instead on the problems of individuals. They market themselves as a service which individuals can purchase and consume at their convenience. Their practices are directed more to reducing the problems of this life than to achieving salvation in the next. Such movements often draw upon ideas from the fringes of modern psychology or from Eastern thought.

Even some of the new religions which draw more directly from an existing religious tradition, such as Transcendental Meditation, also appear to be orientated to enabling people to achieve the conventional goals of this life – such as better jobs, a higher IQ, or greater success in personal relationships. These movements seem to form a type, sharing the common characteristics of accepting most of the goals and values of the wider society but providing new means to achieve them. Their organisational form is also distinct from traditional religion.

John Travolta, a follower of Scientology, attending an exhibition of the works of its founder, L. Ron Hubbard.

Rather than organising as churches or chapels, they typically organise themselves in the form of multinational business corporations and employ the techniques of modern marketing and advertising.

Source: Wallis, 1985

Item B Neo-Pentecostalism and Charismatic Renewal

Some religious movements neither fully accept the norms and values of the surrounding society, nor entirely reject them by cutting themselves off in communities of the like-minded. Rather, they feel that the secular world and even many religious bodies have slipped away from God's design for human life. However, individuals can overcome this problem in their own lives without separating entirely from the secular world. Believers will normally continue in conventional jobs and family life, their religious practice reinvigorating and re-equipping them to face a degenerating secular world. This group includes Evangelical Christian movements such as Neo-Pentecostalism and the Charismatic Renewal. They claim that the Holy Spirit is still alive in the world and can be experienced through various divine 'gifts' – for example, through the gift of 'speaking in tongues'.

An Evangelical prayer meeting

Such groups are essentially a protest against the loss of vitality in existing religious institutions and their abandonment of a living spirituality. The new movement restores this spirituality and returns to traditional certainties in a world where religious institutions have become colder, more bureaucratic and less certain of their role and even of their fundamental beliefs.

Source: Wallis, 1985

Item C ISKCON and the Children of God

Some religious movements reject the world around them, seeing it as utterly corrupt. The world has to be abandoned or totally transformed. Such movements separate themselves from the wider society in communities of the faithful. Some look forward to a spiritual revolution. Members of the International Society for Krishna Consciousness (ISKCON) spend much of their lives in ritual prayers and chants, seeking spiritual truth to escape the illusion and corruption of the outside world.

Other movements look forward to a supernatural intervention. The Children of God live in a state of high expectation, awaiting the imminent return of Christ who will transform the world around them.

Source: Wallis, 1985

Hare Krishna festival, London

question

Each of the items provides an example of one of Wallis' types of NRM – world-affirming, world-accommodating, world-rejecting. Match each item to one of these 'orientations to the world'. Give reasons for your choices.

NRMs – an evaluation

Nothing new Critics have argued that there is nothing particularly new about so-called New Religious Movements. They've been regularly appearing over the last 200 years (Hunt, 1992). The only difference over the past 50 years has been an acceleration in their rate of growth – the data bank of NRMs at the London School of Economics estimates that there are now nearly 2600 'new religions' (Barker, 1999).

Former terms OK Many sociologists feel that the term New Religious Movement adds little or nothing to the existing classification of religious organisations. For example, Hadden (2003) doubts that it adds anything of importance to existing terms such as sect and cult.

Some NRMs are 'new' Other sociologists claim that some of the new movements are sufficiently different from existing religious organisations to justify the term NRM. They point to movements like the Unification Church, often known as the Moonies, which draw from a variety of belief systems and are difficult to classify in terms of the existing types. The founder of the Unification Church, Sun Myung Moon, has integrated aspects of Christianity, Taoism and Confucianism along with a liberal sprinkling of new ideas which he has concocted (Hunt, 1992).

Orientations to the world Wallis' claim that NRMs have distinctive orientations to the world has been criticised. The same movement may have a different character and orientation to the world at different organisational levels or when facing different publics. Thus, a movement's elite may be living largely world-rejecting lives in a sect-like refuge, while ordinary followers may be living world-accommodating or even world-affirming lives in the community. We cannot therefore assume that each movement has only one distinctive orientation to the world.

5.5 The New Age movement

Alongside the variety of religious organisations discussed above, new movements have emerged which seem to lack even the degree of coherence and organisational structure of many cults. Although cults are often precarious and short-lived, they at least have some organisational structure and common belief system. That does not seem to be the case with the so-called 'New Age movement'.

The New Age movement has certain things in common with cults. It draws together people who are engaged in an individualistic quest for spiritual experience. However, even sociologists who describe it as a movement, acknowledge that it has few of the attributes normally associated with social or religious movements (Sutcliffe, 2003). And few of those interviewed by researchers use the term New Age movement to describe the groups or ideas in which they are interested.

Why is it so difficult to characterise the New Age movement? First, because the groupings which are commonly identified with the New Age are so diverse, it is difficult to identify common characteristics. Indeed, there is no agreement about which groups are part of New Age. So, while Hunt (1992) identifies neo-Pagans as a strand 'of major importance', Sutcliffe's detailed study of British New Agers includes very few references to pagan groups (Sutcliffe, 2003).

Second, as Sutcliffe points out, the so-called New Age movement lacks a leader, headquarters, a prescribed text, organisational boundaries, a public policy and common goals. Nor has it common doctrines or beliefs. In short, it lacks precisely the qualities one would expect of religious or other movements. Yet sociologists commonly refer to it as if it is a movement (Sutcliffe, 2003).

Rather than New Age being a movement, Sutcliffe argues, it is more a collection of individuals, most of whom gather, when they choose, in loose and egalitarian groups. These individuals and groups commonly link into wider networks of people – in the region, in other regions, in other countries – who share similar spiritual interests. And,

as Sutcliffe points out, people will 'seek' along different paths at the same time – what he calls *multiple seeking*. Those interested, for instance, in 'holistic healing' may dip into any number of practices – 'astral projection, guided visualisation, iridology, reflexology, chromotherapy, rebirthing, shiatsu, pyramids and crystals (Sutcliffe, 2003). Each of these attract enthusiasts, and through them individuals are able, if they wish, to contact other groups and networks of people with complementary or related interests. And the internet has, of course, facilitated such individualistic contacts between seekers.

Membership Interested individuals can attend and participate in any activities. There is no concept of membership. What unifies seekers – insofar as they feel they have anything in common – is the quest for spiritual experience or growth, though each will take their own individual paths.

Organisation Like the cult, the primary concern of those interested in New Age groupings is highly individualistic – often, some form of mystical or spiritual personal experience. The most important organisational form is the network, whereby individuals or couples come into contact with like-minded people in small groups and learn the groups' beliefs, norms, values and practices. People are likely to meet in private houses or rented premises and come together for special 'workshops' or more regular contact.

Worship and ritual Although individual New Agers may believe in some kind of God, the sacred is likely to be seen as within. As a result, there is unlikely to be worship as such, though there may be some ritual behaviour – such as chanting, incense burning or sitting in the lotus position – to assist the 'inner quest'.

Sense of legitimacy Whereas churches and sects believe that there is one truth, which they alone have access to, those involved in New Age believe that there are many truths which may come from a whole range of sources. People should be open to truth whatever its source. In an important sense, the source of legitimacy for New Age groupings is located within individuals. What is important is what 'works' for the individual in their spiritual quest. However, New Age seekers tend to be critical of 'religion' which they see in terms of dogma, organised belief and church control. As such, it discourages genuine spirituality (Sutcliffe, 2003).

Relationship to the wider society New Age seekers live 'in the world'. In Britain, the most significant exceptions are those who live or stay at Findhorn in Scotland, Britain's only New Age settled 'colony'. Ecological and environmental concerns are widespread throughout New Age, in line with the concept of the Earth as Gaia, a living – and perhaps dying – organism. Many are, therefore, active in 'Green' campaigns.

Involvement and commitment The commitment of New Age seekers is primarily to their own spiritual growth or progress. Groups usually stay together only as long as they satisfy the needs of participants, for the group is essentially just a convenient source of support and encouragement. However, Heelas (1996) identifies three levels of commitment among seekers.

- 'The fully engaged' who have given up conventional lifestyles for a spiritual quest – for example, residents of Findhorn and some New Age travellers.
- 'Serious part-timers' who lead otherwise conventional lives but devote serious time and effort to spiritual concerns.
- 'Casual part-timers' who experiment with 'exotic' things as consumers.

Evaluation – the New Age movement

The New Age and religion This chapter began with a review of definitions of religion. For example, religion has been defined as:

- A belief in some kind of supernatural power
- An expression of this belief in collective worship
- A set of moral values which guide action
- A force which brings people together and unifies society.

In terms of each of these definitions, it can be argued that New Age spirituality falls short of religion. In many cases, there is no evidence of a supernatural power. For example, what have herbalism, crystal healing, meditation, Tarot cards and shiatsu massage got to do with the supernatural?

Nor is there much evidence of collective worship or common values which guide action. And apart from the Findhorn Community – around 200 people – and a visit to the annual Festival for Mind-Body-Spirit, there is little evidence that New Age beliefs and practices bring people together and unify society. In fact, the opposite seems the case – the 'movement' is individualistic rather than social, self-centred rather than group-centred. According to Steve Bruce (2002), its social impact is insignificant.

It can therefore be argued that the New Age movement fits none of the definitions of religion outlined above.

A movement? As noted earlier, critics have argued that New Age groupings are so diverse and loosely organised that they cannot be said to be a movement. In addition, those identified by sociologists as New Agers rarely see themselves as part of a movement, nor label themselves as such.

Spirituality Despite these criticisms, it would be unwise to dismiss the whole idea of New Age spirituality. Since the late 1960s, there has been a growth in self-orientated, spiritually-concerned groups which don't seem to fit the existing typologies of church, sect, denomination and cult, or even New Religious Movement. It appears that increasing numbers of people in the West are seeking their inner self, are searching for their true nature, for spirituality, vitality, wisdom, tranquillity, love and creativity, all of which are to be found and developed in their inner life (Heelas, 1996). But whether this spiritual seeking can be called religion is another question.

summary

1. In their analysis of religious organisations, sociologists have used four main ideal types – church, sect, denomination and cult.

2. Churches and sects are seen as opposite ends of the religious spectrum. Churches are open to all members of society, accept the state and the political and economic systems, are hierarchical and have a professional clergy. Limited demands are made on members and worship is ritualised and restrained. Both churches and sects are likely to claim a monopoly of the truth.

3. Sects, however, are widely perceived as unconventional and deviant. They distance themselves from – and are critical of – the wider society. They generally lack a professional clergy and place high demands on members. Worship lacks formal rituals, and emphasises spontaneity.

4. Denominations tend to be seen as conventional and respectable. Unlike churches and sects, they do not claim a monopoly of the truth. They place fewer demands on their members compared to sects. Denominations are separate from the state and tolerant of the wider society. They have a professional clergy but a less complex hierarchy than a church. Worship is less ritualised than a church but less spontaneous than a sect.

5. Cults, like sects, are often regarded as deviant by the wider society. Unlike sects however, they claim no monopoly of the truth and are therefore more tolerant of other paths. Many emphasise an 'inner divinity' or 'power within', and try to help seekers to experience and develop it. They make few demands – they simply ask people to be 'open' to their teachings.

6. With the emergence in the West of large numbers of new movements that did not fit existing classifications, the term New Religious Movement (NRM) was coined. NRMs mainly draw on Christian or other world faith traditions or Western psychotherapy. Wallis identified world-affirming, world-accommodating and world-rejecting NRMs.

7. The New Age movement is not a religious organisation as such. It is more like a loose network of more-or-less like-minded 'seekers' who dip into a variety of beliefs and practices. Insofar as followers share a common characteristic, it is a quest for spiritual experience and personal growth.

8. It can be argued that New Age spirituality falls short of religion. For example, in many cases there is no evidence of a supernatural power.

activity23 *the New Age movement*

Item A *The Emissaries of Divine Light*

'Emissaries of Divine Light is a global network of people who share the understanding that at our core we are Creator Beings, and that it is because of spiritual amnesia that humanity has lost connection to this essential reality. We offer programs and activities that assist people to awaken more fully to what is most true about them, and to let that be real for them. An emissary of divine light lives and acts from his or her authentic spiritual core, opening up new possibilities for creative living, and for offering leadership at all levels of human experience.

We see this era in the history of Planet Earth as a time of global transformation, filled with risk and opportunity. Human consciousness is clearly a critical factor in our collective future. Through all we do, we seek to model a new relationship with the earth, with each other, and most importantly with the Invisible Source of all life, which has been called God.

We see the potential of a global body of awake people – the potential to bring a new state of consciousness into the world.'

Source: www.emissaries.org, 2008

Item C *Getting through the day*

Ellen was a member of a spiritual healing group. She used mini-meditations during her hectic moments at the office, applied acupressure and visualisation to counter a headache and employed breathing techniques and visualisation at each stoplight to handle the stress of a difficult commute home. At home, she used a mantra (chant), crystal and visualisation to 'centre' herself during and after an argument. Most days, she spent one hour on exercise followed by stress-reducing visualisations in the sauna. Later, she had a cup of herbal tea and meditated for half an hour.

Source: McGuire, 2003

Item B *Smudging*

Eleni Santoro is a New Age practitioner. She offers a 'smudging service' to New York estate agents which removes 'bad vibes' by 'balancing energies'.

The tools of her trade include objects from all over the world – silver Tibetan bells, a statue of Ganesh (the Hindu God of prudence and wisdom), an antique Chinese bell, an African necklace of yellow, red and green beads and a silver bowl containing three limes.

Having meditated for several minutes, shuffling a slim pack of 'angel cards', she picks three. Or rather, as she later explains, it is the angels who pick the cards – Light, Release, Humour – best suited to this interior. The smudging session also has a soundtrack – sounds of mountain streams or Japanese drums.

Source: Fowler, 1997

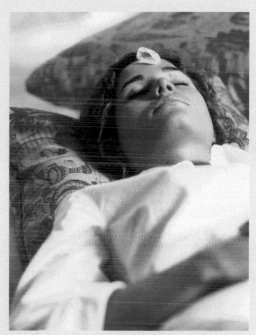

A crystal after work

Item D *Picking and mixing*

The New Age ransacks myths, legends, rituals and symbols from different times, places and cultures – from Celtic Christianity, from Eastern religions, from ancient Norse and Germanic religions, from Australian Aborigines and Native Americans.

The 'movement' uses a wide range of practices and techniques picked up from all over the world – meditation, aromatherapy, crystals, mantras, self-hypnosis, reflexology, herbalism, spiritual healing.

Followers pick and mix from this cornucopia of beliefs and practices, concocting a DIY 'religion' which fits their individual requirements.

Source: Bruce, 2002 and Hunt, 1992

Spirituality & Health, a New Age magazine

questions

1 With reference to the items, how would you evaluate the claim that the New Age is:

   a) a movement

   b) a religion?

2 How can the items be used to support the claim that the New Age reflects postmodern society?

Unit 6 *Explaining religious movements*

key issues

1 What explanations have been given for the origins of sects, cults, denominations, New Religious Movements and the New Age movement?

2 What explanations have been given for their development?

As the key issues state, this unit is concerned with explanations. It focuses on the relationship between religious beliefs, religious organisations, social groups and social contexts. Why, for example, do members of certain social groups join particular types of religious organisations? What is it about their social situation that attracts them to certain religious beliefs?

6.1 Sects

As noted in the previous unit, sects are close-knit religious groups whose members claim to have a monopoly of the truth. Life often revolves around the sect – high standards of behaviour and levels of commitment are demanded. Members tend to cut themselves off from the outside world and exclude those considered 'unworthy'. This section examines various explanations for sects – how they arise, why they appeal to particular groups, and what social situations encourage their growth.

Social marginality

According to Max Weber (1963), those on the margins of society are most likely to join sects. They are on the outside looking in – for example, the poor and members of some ethnic minority groups. Many feel they have been denied the prestige, the occupational status, income and opportunities which they deserve.

Sect membership can address this problem. In Weber's terms it can offer members a *theodicy of disprivilege* – a religious explanation for their situation and a promise of a 'sense of honour' either in this life or the next. Sect members now become the 'chosen few' rather than outsiders relegated to the margins of society.

The Black Muslims, an African-American sect which rose to prominence in the 1960s, illustrates these points. Its objective was to recruit 'the Negro in the mud' – the unemployed, the homeless and the destitute. It stated that Blacks are 'by nature divine', and that Whites are inferior and evil. It prophesied that Whites and their religion will be destroyed and that Blacks will then rule forever under Allah's guidance. Members claim that belonging to the sect gave them self-respect and hope for the future.

Relative deprivation

Deprivation refers to a lack of something – for example, a lack of prestige, employment, income or decent housing. From the point of view of the individual concerned, deprivation is *relative* – it is relative to an expectation that is not fulfilled, to a position they feel they deserve but have been unable to attain, to a comparison between themselves and other members of society which leaves them wanting. Relative deprivation refers to the deprivation or loss that people perceive or feel (Glock, 1964).

Sects offer a religious solution to relative deprivation. As one of the chosen few, sect members are no longer deprived. Following the strict code of behaviour laid down by the sect, and provided with the support of fellow members, they may gain self-respect and a sense of community. And the self-discipline demanded by many sects may improve their material situation – for example, they may find a job or get a better paid job (Hamilton, 2001).

Again, the Black Muslims provide an illustration. In most large cities, they operate small businesses – barber's shops, clothing stores and restaurants. Their *Economic Blueprint for the Blackman* advocates economic independence from White America. They are encouraged to work hard, save and abstain from luxuries. A strict moral code forbids the use of alcohol, tobacco and narcotics, sexual intercourse outside of marriage, dancing, dating and many forms of sport. In particular, the responsibilities of the man as husband, father and breadwinner are emphasised. Members take courses on self-improvement and look after the welfare of their fellow members.

The idea of relative deprivation does not just apply to those at the bottom of the class system or to those who experience racial discrimination. It can also apply, for example, to members of the White middle class – for instance, those who feel disillusioned with the materialism of Western society and the teachings of mainstream religion can sometimes find what they're looking for in the beliefs and community of a sect (Wallis, 1984).

Social change and relative deprivation The experience of relative deprivation may become more intense as circumstances change. For example, the Black Muslims came to prominence in the 1960s. This was a period which promised change and improvement for African Americans – for example, laws were passed banning discrimination and segregation in many areas of public life. As a result, expectations rose rapidly. However, for many, particularly those in low-income, inner-city areas, those expectations were not met – things were as bad as ever. As a result, the experience of relative deprivation became more intense.

For some, the Black Muslims offered a means of translating rising expectations into reality. Statements by members indicate that the sect gave them purpose, direction, pride and hope.

The relationship between social change and the development of sects is examined in detail in the following section.

Social change and social dislocation

Sects tend to emerge during periods of rapid social change. Such circumstances can lead to *social dislocation*, to a feeling of being uprooted. This can result in *anomie* – a sense of normlessness, a feeling that traditional norms have broken down and that guidelines for action are no longer in place.

Sects with their clearly defined belief systems and strict moral codes can provide certainty in a time of uncertainty and anomie. They often contain a promise that life will improve if members follow the guidelines they provide. This can give direction and hope. And the close-knit ties of sect life can provide a community where none exists on the outside.

Circumstances that lead to anomie Research suggests that the normative breakdown and insecurity which encourages the development of sects can result from a variety of factors.

First, the experience of disasters, whether natural or man-made. As Norman Cohn's studies of medieval Europe illustrate, sects may be preceded by outbreaks of plague, devastating fires, long droughts, serious economic slumps or calamitous wars, any of which may lead to a deep sense of doom and a fervent desire for salvation (Cohn, 1957).

Sects may be a response to unsettling contact with a powerful alien culture, especially if accompanied by the experience of being occupied and colonised. For example, the colonisation of Palestine by the Romans saw the birth of a sect which later became known as Christianity. In such contact between cultures, traditional norms, values and institutions may be shaken and undermined. And the contact often demoralises those who find themselves confronted by a more powerful society.

People who feel that their way of life is threatened or has collapsed experience a sense of disorientation, frustration,

deep anxiety and even rage. They will be predisposed to follow a messianic leader, such as Jesus Christ, who promises the coming of a new age.

A number of sociologists have argued that the social changes involved in the process of industrialisation and modernisation encouraged the emergence of sects. These changes can lead to social dislocation and a crisis of meaning and identity. People are less able to make sense of the world, they are increasingly unsure about who they are.

Sects can help some people to adjust to and make sense of a new situation. Bryan Wilson (1970) gives the example of Methodism which began as a sect. He sees the emergence of Methodism as a response by the new urban working class to the 'chaos and uncertainty of life in newly settled industrial areas'. Sects can provide a sense of community, clearly defined guidelines for living and a feeling of certainty.

Evaluation

The examples outlined in this section appear to support the view that sects are a response to social marginality, relative deprivation, rapid social change and social dislocation. However, there is evidence to question these explanations.

Beckford's (1975) study of Jehovah's Witnesses in Britain questions the significance of social marginality and relative deprivation. He found that most were upper working class and lower middle class. They showed no obvious signs of deprivation either financially or in terms of social status. Most had a religious upbringing and became disillusioned with mainstream religion. Sect membership offered an alternative religious direction which made sense and provided fulfilment.

Stark and Bainbridge (1985) examined the percentages of sects formed in the USA in different time periods during the first three-quarters of the 20th century. Sixteen per cent were formed in the 1950s, a period of social stability, 14% in the 1960s and only 3% from 1970 to 1977. The 1960s and early 1970s were a time of social unrest with student demonstrations, the hippie movement, Black riots and the Vietnam War. These findings cast doubt on the view that sects are most likely to emerge during periods of social change and social dislocation. However, it is important to note that Stark and Bainbridge use a fairly limited definition of a sect – a breakaway movement from an established religion. A broader definition may result in different figures and a different conclusion.

key terms

Theodicy of disprivilege A religious explanation for 'disprivilege' and a promise that things will get better in this life or the next.
Relative deprivation Deprivation which is relative to what people expect and feel they deserve.
Social dislocation A feeling of being uprooted, which can lead to a sense of anomie.

6.2 Cults and New Religious Movements

As outlined in the previous unit, cults are small religious groups which, unlike sects, believe that their teachings are just one of many paths to the truth. Compared to sects, cults are more tolerant of and open to the outside world. Many cults aim to develop the inner self and help people to experience their inner power.

Sociological explanations of cults are usually included within explanations of world-affirming New Religious Movements (NRMs), most of which can be classified as cults. They are also included within explanations of the New Age movement which contains many cult-like features. These explanations tend to focus on movements which developed in the West from the 1960s onwards.

The origins of NRMs

Rationalisation Roy Wallis (1984, 1985) draws on Max Weber's idea of *rationalisation* to explain the origins of NRMs. According to Weber, the meanings and motives which direct action in modern industrial society are rational. They are based on cold and deliberate reasoning, on precise calculations of the most effective ways of attaining goals such as making money and producing

activity24 *the origins of sects*

Item A *The Ghost Dance*

By 1890, the traditional way of life of the Native American Sioux had ended. They had been defeated by the US army, rounded up, and confined to reservations. The buffalo, their main source of food, had all but disappeared, slaughtered by professional White hunters such as Buffalo Bill.

The US government was determined to stamp out the Sioux way of life. Traditional customs such as the Sun Dance, an important religious ceremony, were banned. The reservation authorities tried to force the Sioux to become farmers – an occupation despised by Sioux warriors.

Farming was doomed to failure. The land was unsuitable, there was a drought and the cattle became diseased. Undernourished, the Sioux had little

The frozen body of Chief Big Foot, leader of the ghost dancers at Wounded Knee

resistance to the measles and whooping cough which swept through the reservations in 1890. On one reservation, the death rate rose to 45 a month in a population of 5,550.

In 1890, the Sioux received news of a messiah, a Paiute called Wovoka. He had been visited by Christ and founded a new religion – the Ghost Dance. This was his message.

In the beginning, God made the earth and then sent the Christ to earth to teach the people. But White men treated him badly, leaving scars on his body, and so he went back to heaven. Now he has returned to earth as a Native American. He will renew everything as it used to be and make it better.

In the next springtime, when the grass is knee-high, the earth will be covered with new soil which will bury all the White men. The new land will be covered with sweet grass and running water and trees. Great herds of buffalo and wild horses will come back. The Native Americans who dance the Ghost Dance will be taken up in the air and suspended there while a wave of new earth is passing, and then they will be set down among the ghosts of their ancestors on the new earth. There they will follow their traditional way of life, forever free from death, disease and misery. Only Native Americans will live on this regenerated earth – the White race will disappear.

About half the Sioux nation believed in the new religion. They danced the ghost dance and wore 'ghost shirts' which they believed made them invulnerable to White men's bullets. Fearing trouble, the authorities called in the army. Troops surrounded a group of ghost dancers at Wounded Knee Creek. Fighting broke out and 150 Sioux, including 60 women and children, were massacred. The Ghost Dance was over.

Source: Utley, 1963 and Brown, 1975

Item B *The Rastafarian movement*

The Rastafarian religion originated in the West Indies and was based on the ideas of Marcus Garvey, who preached that the only way for Black people to escape their poverty and oppression was to return to Africa. When Haile Selassie was crowned emperor of Ethiopia in 1930, and took the title 'Lion of Judah' (Ras Tafari), this was seen as a fulfilment of prophecy and followers claimed him as the Messiah, the incarnation of God. Rastafarians see themselves as the ancient lost tribe of Israel, enslaved and transported from Africa by Whites. They will remain forever oppressed and suffering, even in Jamaica, until they return to Africa. In Jamaica, its appeal has been greatest among the most disadvantaged sections of the Jamaican populace – the urban underclass. Some key beliefs are included in the 'Charter of the Rastafarians' below.

Rastafarian priests, Kingston, Jamaica

From the Rastafarian Charter

3 The Rastafarian Movement consists of the most advanced, determined and uncompromising fighters against discrimination, ostracism and oppression of the Black people of Jamaica.

4 The Rastafarian Movement stands for freedom in its fullest sense and for the recovery, dignity, self-respect and sovereignty of the Black people of Jamaica.

11 The Rastafarian Movement has as its chief aim the complete destruction of all vestiges of White supremacy in Jamaica, thereby putting an end to economic exploitation and the social degradation of the Black people.

Source: 'Charter of the Rastafarians' quoted in Williams, 1981

question

Give a sociological explanation for a) the Ghost Dance and b) Rastafarianism.

---

goods and services.

As a result of this process of rationalisation, mystery and magic, prophecy and the sacred have been pushed into the background. This has led, in Weber's words, to the 'disenchantment of the world', to *desacralisation* – the removal of the sacred, of religious meanings, guidelines and explanations. According to Wallis, many NRMs developed in response to this loss of the sacred.

Wallis is primarily concerned with explaining world-rejecting NRMs (many of which are similar to sects) and world-affirming NRMs (many of which are similar to cults).

World-rejecting NRMs

Wallis argues that the loss of the sacred was most acutely felt by young people in America and Europe during the 1960s and early 1970s. These were the years of political protest, counter-cultures and alternative lifestyles, when many young people sought to transform society. Their efforts largely failed. As a result, some young people believed that their lives and the wider society could not be transformed by human effort alone. They were therefore open to movements which claimed they could change the world by supernatural means, which claimed that a divine power would intervene to transform society.

Some disillusioned and disenchanted young people joined world-rejecting NRMs – sect-like organisations, often founded by a charismatic leader. Such movements were critical or even hostile to the outside world, seeing it as corrupt and lacking in spirituality. Examples of these movements are Krishna Consciousness (ISKCON) and the Children of God. Their members were usually middle-class young adults. For example, one survey found that 85% of Krishna Consciousness members in the USA were under 26 (Judah, 1974). And a number of studies found that many members of world-rejecting NRMs had previously been involved in hippie counter-cultural movements (Downton, 1979).

World-affirming NRMs

Many world-affirming NRMs can be classified as cults. They are concerned with self-realisation, self-improvement and the development of the inner self. As their name suggests, world-affirming NRMs generally accept the wider society.

According to Wallis, world-affirming NRMs have their origins in the values and concerns of advanced capitalist societies. These societies place a high value on status, achievement, self-confidence, personal attractiveness, happiness and self-fulfilment. For many people, these values are difficult to translate into reality. Some find an answer in world-affirming NRMs which offer them recipes, techniques and knowledge to find what they're looking for.

Movements such as Transcendental Meditation and Scientology promise success in personal relationships and in employment, a higher IQ and a route to personal fulfilment. The Human Potential Movement and Est offer personal and spiritual growth, self-realisation and happiness.

Members of world-affirming NRMs are usually older, more affluent and even more middle class than members of world-rejecting NRMs. One study found that the average age of participants in Human Potential groups was 35 (Stone, 1976). According to Wallis, they have paid a high price for their successful careers and lifestyles – a single-minded focus on work, a high level of self-control, and a repression of their inner selves. In Wallis' words, world-affirming NRMs can provide 'a context and method of liberating spontaneity, of contacting the "real" self behind the masks and performances, of feeling and sharing intimacy and love (if only for a weekend before a return to the harsh reality of urban industrial life)' (Wallis, 1985).

Evaluation

Much of the research on NRMs has focused on movements in the West from the 1960s onwards. It has looked at NRMs which were formed or developed during these years and tended to explain them in terms of the context of Western society at the time. There is a major problem with this approach.

NRMs are not just recent developments confined to the West. Both sects and cults are examples of NRMs and both have a long history and a global spread. It is therefore inappropriate to simply explain them as a response to specific developments in Western society during the second half of the 20th century (Hunt, 1992).

key term

Desacralisation The removal of the sacred – of religious meanings, explanations and guides to action.

6.3 The New Age movement

A number of sociologists have looked for an explanation of the New Age movement in the social context of the late 20th and early 21st centuries. Some have seen it as a reflection of *late modernity*. This is defined as a phase rather than a new era, the development of an existing type of society – modernity – rather than a new type of society. Others have seen it as an expression of *postmodernity*, a new era which is distinct from and follows modernity.

Who participates?

Survey data indicates that New Agers are mainly female, predominantly middle class and well-educated. There is a fairly even spread across the age groups with the highest percentage – 42% according to one survey – in the 35-49 age group (York, 1995).

According to Steve Bruce (2001), the New Age movement appeals to those who work in 'expressive professions' – teachers, social workers, nurses, counsellors, artists, writers and actors. People in these professions tend to be individualistic, and concerned with 'personal development' and 'human potential'. These concerns are reflected in many aspects of the New Age movement.

Late modernity and postmodernity

Individualism and the self *Individualism* and *reflexity* have been identified as characteristics of late modernity. Increasingly, the individual selects their own identity and designs their own lifestyle. They are more likely to be reflexive – to reflect on the self and what they are doing (Giddens, 1991, 2001).

Similarly, a concern with self has been identified as a feature of postmodernity. In the postmodern age, the individual has greater freedom to construct their own identity.

The New Age movement reflects these concerns. According to Paul Heelas (1996), it is a 'self-religion'. According to Steve Bruce (2002), it is concerned with self-discovery, personal choice, and the development of individual potential, freedom and autonomy.

Relativism Late modernity has been described as a time of uncertainty when traditional norms and values are breaking down at an increasingly rapid rate.

Postmodernity has been characterised as an era of *relativism* – as an era in which there are no absolute truths, in which no one belief system has a monopoly of the truth. *Metanarratives* – grand explanations – such as those of science and established religions have been undermined (Lyotard, 1984).

New Age spirituality is seen to thrive in this social context. Paul Heelas (1998) argues that the disintegration of the certainties of modernity has left a vacuum of meaning within which 'self-religions' emerge as individuals struggle to make sense of the situation.

Postmodernists argue that an age of relativism means that there is no longer a single truth – instead, there are many truths. This allows people to combine ideas, symbols and beliefs from the past and present, from a variety of cultures and from many parts of the world. This is exactly what New Age spirituality does. The relativism of postmodern society opens the door for the New Age movement and the individual construction of religion.

According to Bauman (1992), postmodernity has produced a 'crisis of meaning'. For some, the New Age movement provides answers.

Choice and consumption Both late modernity and postmodernity have been seen as times which emphasise individual choice and consumption. In particular, postmodernity has been characterised as an era in which people are preoccupied with choosing and consuming symbols, images, brands and goods in order to construct their own identities and lifestyles.

The New Age movement has been seen as a reflection of this concern. New Agers pick and mix from a vast range of ideas and beliefs – they select, match and construct to fit their image of self and their chosen lifestyle. According to Steve Bruce (2002), the individual consumer 'will decide what to believe' and 'the crucial test is personal experience'. If it works, if it provides meaning, satisfaction and fulfilment, the individual will 'buy into' New Age spirituality. If it doesn't work, they won't.

Life-as to subjective-life

According to Paul Heelas and Linda Woodhead (2004), there has been a 'massive turn' in Western culture from *life-as* to *subjective-life*. Life-as is life lived in terms of external roles, duties and obligations – for example, roles such as employer and employee, husband and wife, which are accompanied by a range of duties and obligations. These external roles, duties and obligations are 'higher authorities' which direct people's lives and give meaning to their existence. They are often supported by religion, by tradition and by the law.

Increasingly, people are moving from a focus on life-as to subjective-life which sees the inner feelings of each unique individual as primary. In Heelas and Woodhead's (2004) words, 'The goal is not to defer to higher authority, but to have the courage to become one's own authority. Not to follow established paths, but to forge one's own inner-directed … life'.

Assuming that Heelas and Woodhead are correct in their identification and description of recent changes in Western culture, then this 'cultural turn' helps to explain the growing attraction of New Age spirituality. With its focus on the inner-self, on subjective-life, on the unique individual, New Age spirituality can be seen as a reflection of broader cultural changes.

Evaluation

Relativism For Steve Bruce (2001), postmodernists take the argument too far. While he agrees that traditional authorities and established religions have been undermined, Bruce rejects the claim that the scientific 'metanarrative' has been abandoned. Scientific knowledge is still valued, and the idea that most people in Western societies now regard science as on a par with, for instance, the findings of palmistry or the reading of tea leaves, is nonsense.

Romanticism How new is the New Age movement? For Bruce (2001), New Age seekers' preferences for the more culturally alien and exotic religions and therapies is part of a romantic Western tradition 'as old as industrialisation itself'. There is a long tradition of 'romanticising the underdeveloped and finding true humanity and spirituality in the rural peripheries of the urbanising world'.

Tautology Explanations which see the New Age movement as shaped by late modernity and postmodernity are somewhat tautological. A tautology is a circular argument. For example, postmodern society is characterised by a concern with individualism and the self, choice and consumption and the relativity of beliefs and ideas. To argue that postmodern society shapes the New Age movement is a tautology because the New Age movement is part of postmodern society. What we need to know is what caused postmodernity *and* the New Age movement.

A similar criticism can be made of Heelas and Woodhead's explanation of New Age spirituality as a reflection of a more general cultural change. Again, what we need to know is what caused these more general changes *and* New Age spirituality.

key terms

Individualism An emphasis on the individual rather than the social group.
Reflexivity Reflecting and looking back on the self.
Life-as Life lived in terms of external roles, duties and obligations.
Subjective-life An approach to life which sees the inner feelings of each unique individual as primary.

6.4 The development of religious movements

So far, this unit has focused on the origins of religious movements. This section looks at their development.

Sects and denominations

From sect to denomination H. Richard Niebuhr (1929) argued that sects are short-lived – they must either evolve into a denomination or die. He gave the following reasons for this claim.

Members of sects tend to come from the margins of society. On joining the sect, they usually lead frugal and ascetic (strict, self-denying) lives. As a result, their social status is likely to rise and their wealth increase. Their new situation no longer fits with their rejection of the wider society – and it brings greater public acceptance. As their contact with mainstream society grows, they modify their more unconventional beliefs.

This process is accelerated by the next generation. They were not converted into the sect, they were merely born into it. As a result, they are unlikely to show the same enthusiasm and commitment as their parents. They are more likely to make compromises with, and be less critical of, the wider society.

The very success of a sect can lead to its downfall.

The more its membership grows, the greater the need for full-time officials to manage the organisation. This, coupled with the toning down of its more 'extreme' views and the rise in its members' status, leads the sect down the road to a denomination. The once radical sect now becomes a respectable denomination, sitting comfortably within mainstream society.

There is evidence that some sects follow the route outlined by Niebuhr. For example, the Quakers began as a sect in the 17th century. Within a few generations they had moderated their beliefs and entered mainstream society. So much so that several Quaker families played a major part in the development of the British banking system – Barclays Bank still bears the name of one of these families. Similarly, the Methodists began as a sect, moderated their strict beliefs and their criticisms of the wider society, and developed into a denomination.

Evaluation Death or denomination are not the only alternatives open to sects. Some survive as sects – they become *established sects* (Yinger, 1970). They often do so by isolating themselves from the outside world – for example, the Amish in Pennsylvania, isolate themselves from the rest of American society. And the Exclusive Brethren keep outside influences at bay by banning their members from watching television and using computers (Hunt, 1992).

The path to salvation According to Bryan Wilson (1970), the crucial factor which determines whether a sect develops into a denomination or remains a sect is the way it answers the question, 'What shall we do to be saved?'

The answer from some sects is to convert as many people as possible. These *conversionist sects* are likely to develop into denominations. They are typically found in the USA where they use large-scale revivalist meetings to generate conversions. They can become a denomination without compromising their primary aim – they can still save souls.

Other types of sect cannot maintain their basic position in a denominational form. The primary aim of *adventist sects*, such as Jehovah's Witnesses, Seventh Day Adventists and Christadelphians is to prepare themselves for the Day of Judgement. To do this, they must separate themselves from today's sinful and corrupt society and await the second coming of Christ. Only membership of the sect will guarantee them a place in the new world order. Becoming a denomination would compromise their position which demands separation from, rather than integration with, the wider society.

Wilson concludes that whether or not a sect becomes a denomination is largely determined by its prescription for salvation.

Cults and New Religious Movements

World-rejecting NRMs As noted earlier, most world-rejecting NRMs are similar to sects. Researchers who don't use the term NRM would classify many of them as sects.

Wallis (1984, 1985) sees two main routes for world-rejecting NRMs. The first is similar to the route described by Niebuhr. This involves a relaxation of the strict demands on members, a less critical view of the wider society, and a more conventional organisational structure. They move from world-rejecting to world-accommodating or world-affirming NRMs (see Activity 25, Item B).

Some world-rejecting NRMs take the opposite route, moving further inwards rather than outwards. According to Wallis, this is due to the intensity of their rejection of the wider society and the hostile reaction of the wider society to this rejection. In rare cases, this can lead to self-destruction where members of the movement commit suicide – the ultimate act of world-rejection (see Activity 25, Item A). In other cases, the movement goes underground – as in the case of the Children of God (Wallis, 1985).

World-affirming NRMs As noted earlier, world-affirming NRMs are similar to cults. Many support the norms and values of the mainstream culture and offer recipes for self-fulfilment and success in the wider society. They can be seen as serving clients or customers in a religious marketplace. From this point of view, their survival and development depend on the demand for the services they offer. To flourish, they must be sufficiently flexible to adapt their services to new demands and to compete with new brand names entering the market (Wallis, 1985).

Some do well when the economy is buoyant, but go to the wall during a recession – as did the Human Potential Movement. Others, such as Scientology and Est, vary their product to meet changing demands and attract a new clientele (Wallis, 1985).

key terms

Established sects Sects which survive over a relatively long period of time.
Conversionist sects Sects whose primary aim is to convert people.
Adventist sects Sects whose primary aim is to prepare themselves for the Day of Judgement, for the transformation of the world.

summary

1. The following explanations have been put forward for the origin of sects.

   ● Social marginality – Sects tend to recruit those on the margins of society. Their new status as the 'chosen few' provided by a theodicy of disprivilege can bring self-respect and hope for the future.

   ● Relative deprivation – Sects can provide a sense of community, mutual support and self-respect. The self-discipline and self-denial demanded by many sects can improve people's material situation.

   ● Social dislocation – This can result in anomie (a sense of normlessness). Sects, with their clearly defined belief systems and strict moral codes, can provide certainty and direction.

2. Circumstances which can lead to anomie include:

   ● Natural or man-made disasters

   ● Contact with, or colonisation by, a powerful alien culture

   ● The process of industrialisation and modernisation.

3. Wallis sees NRMs resulting from the processes of rationalisation and desacralisation. He sees world-rejecting NRMs during the 1960s and 70s as a response to the failure of young people to change society by protest and alternative lifestyles. He sees world-affirming NRMs as a response to the values of capitalist society – as a means of realising them or as compensation for the price paid for living up to them.

4. Some sociologists have seen the New Age movement with its emphasis on individualism, relativism, choice and consumption as a reflection of late modernity, while others have seen it as a reflection of postmodernity.

5. According to Heelas and Woodhead, the increasing emphasis on subjective-life, as opposed to life-as, accounts for the growth of New Age spirituality.

6. Niebuhr argued that sects are short-lived – they must develop into denominations or die.

7. But some sects survive – as established sects. They often do so by isolating themselves from the outside world.

8. According to Bryan Wilson, conversionist sects are likely to develop into denominations because they can still save souls in this form. Adventist sects cannot become denominations, because only membership of the sect will guarantee them a place in the new world order.

9. Wallis sees two main routes for world-rejecting NRMs. First, they can develop into either world-accommodating or world-affirming NRMs. Or second, they can turn further inwards and increase their isolation from the wider society.

10. Wallis argues that the survival and development of world-affirming NRMs depends on the demand for the services they offer. To flourish, they must respond to new demands.

activity25 the development of NRMs

Item A *The People's Temple*

The People's Temple was founded in the USA by the Reverend Jim Jones. He promised to create a utopia – a perfect society in which everybody worked for the common good. Most members were recruited from the poor.

As his following grew, Jones demanded more and more discipline and dedication, along with absolute loyalty to himself. He became a messiah-like figure, claiming at various times to be God, Buddha and Lenin. He forecast the destruction of the world and claimed that only members of the Temple would survive.

Jones and his followers grew increasingly hostile to the outside world. He vehemently criticised the 'enemies' of the People's Temple. Rumours of human rights abuses led to an investigation of the movement. Jones responded by leading around 1000 of his followers to Guyana in South America,

Jonestown after the mass suicide

where they hacked a settlement, known as Jonestown, out of the jungle.

Concerned relatives of the movement's members demanded an investigation which was led by Congressman Leo J. Ryan. Jones sent gunmen to ambush Ryan as he returned to his plane. The Congressman and several of his party were killed.

Next day, November 18, 1978, Jones announced that the community would soon be attacked. He ordered his followers to commit suicide as a sign of their dedication. They had rehearsed this many times. They drank a mixture of Kool-Aid (a soft drink) and cyanide. According to the few survivors, most people took their lives willingly, with mothers giving the cyanide to their children, then drinking it themselves. Over 900 people died.

Source: *Chronicle of America*, 1989 and www.apologeticsindex.org

Item B 3HO and Shambhala

3HO

According to their website, the 'Healthy, Happy, Holy Organisation (3HO) is a worldwide association of people dedicated to the excellence of the individual. The basic philosophy of 3HO affirms that you, as a human being, are so perfectly created that by using exercise, breathing and meditation, you can balance and revitalise the physical body, nervous and glandular systems and bring balance and peace to your life.

'3HO brings to the public the ancient science of Kundalini Yoga. It offers complete lifestyle guidelines on nutrition and health, interpersonal relations, child rearing and human behaviour. You may choose from a wealth of knowledge to find the exact techniques you are looking for to become healthy, happy and holy.'

Shambhala

Shambhala is based on the teachings of Buddha. According to their website, 'Buddhism is taking an increasingly prominent role in contemporary Western society as interest increases in this approach to life. A unique quality of the Buddhist teachings is that they can be expressed through existing cultural norms, making use of them rather than destroying or replacing them. This allows many Westerners to practise Buddhism today without renouncing their cultural heritage or radically changing their lifestyles. A careful sequence of group practice programmes ensures that students can develop according to their 'own interests and commitments.'

Sociological comment

New Religious Movements such as 3HO and Shambhala – whose members are mainly well-educated, middle-class, White Americans – have become increasingly world-affirming. This was a response to changing social and economic conditions. It provided a strong foundation on which the movements can grow. As Khasala (1986) states, 'What better way to become an accepted part of American society than by embracing some of the values that this country holds most dear: utilitarian individualism, capitalistic enterprise, and most definitely, financial success.'

Source: Hunt, 1992; Khasala, 1986; www.3HO.org; www.shambhala.org

questions

1 Discuss Item A in terms of Wallis' view of the development of world-rejecting NRMs.

2 Discuss Item B in terms of Wallis' view of the development of world-affirming NRMs.

3 The movements in Item B appear to be taking the route to denominationalism. What evidence is there for this statement?

Unit 7 Secularisation

keyissues

1 What is secularisation?

2 What is the secularisation thesis?

3 What are the arguments for and against secularisation?

Has the importance of religion changed over time? In some countries, such as Britain, religion is often seen as less important than in the past. The question of the changing significance of religion in modern societies has been central to sociology. Marx, Durkheim, Weber and many other sociologists have regarded it as an issue of major importance.

This unit looks at the argument that religion is declining in modern society – a process known as *secularisation*.

7.1 Defining secularisation

The word secular means not sacred, not spiritual, not religious. So, secularisation refers to the process of becoming less religious. And the claim that religion is declining in importance is known as the *secularisation thesis*.

However, defining secularisation is not as simple as this. Sociologists cannot agree on a definition of religion. As a result, they cannot agree on how to define – and measure – secularisation.

Two views of secularisation

Woodhead and Heelas (2000) identify two versions of the secularisation thesis – the *disappearance thesis* and the *differentiation thesis*.

The disappearance thesis This thesis states that modernity is bringing about the death of religion. The significance of religion both for society *and* for individuals is steadily declining. This process will continue until religion disappears.

The differentiation thesis This thesis states that religion is declining in *social* significance. It no longer plays an important part in society – for example, it no longer influences major social institutions such as the family and the educational, legal and political systems. It has become separated or differentiated from the wider social structure. However, it is likely to retain some significance in people's private lives.

Evaluation The distinction between the disappearance thesis and the differentiation thesis is important. Early sociological theorists such as Marx and Weber believed that religion would disappear. However, more recent British sociologists, such as Bryan Wilson, Roy Wallis and Steve Bruce state that their version of the secularisation thesis does *not* suggest that religion will disappear and everyone will eventually become an atheist. Instead, it means that the social significance of religion is declining (Bruce, 2002). In Bryan Wilson's (1982) words, 'It does not even require that most individuals have relinquished all their interest in religion. It maintains no more than that religion ceases to be significant in the working of the social system.'

The Broad and Narrow Approach

Sharon Hanson (1997) makes a distinction between religion on a social and individual level. She states there are two levels to the secularisation debate, and that these levels are often confused.

- The Broad Approach asks whether religion has lost significance on the level of the social system.
- The Narrow Approach focuses on religion at the level of individual consciousness.

Making this distinction is important. As noted earlier, secularisation may be occurring on the societal level, but not on the individual level.

Secularisation and the West

Most supporters of the secularisation thesis focus on the West – they do not see it as a global process. One of its main supporters, Steve Bruce (2002), limits the secularisation thesis to Europe, North America and Australasia. He sees the secular West as an exception in the sweep of human history.

7.2 Evidence for secularisation

The evidence in support of the secularisation thesis can be organised in terms of Bryan Wilson's (1966) definition of secularisation as 'the process whereby religious thinking, practice and institutions lose social significance'. So, compared to past ages:

1 What power, prestige and influence do religious institutions have?

2 What influence does religion have on people's beliefs, thinking, attitudes and consciousness?

3 How widespread are religious practices?

The power and influence of the church There can be little doubt that the power and influence of the church in Western Europe has declined over the last 1000 years. As a social institution, the Roman Catholic Church in medieval Christendom had power to rival that of kings. At its peak in the 12th and 13th centuries, the Roman Catholic Church was central to the political life of Western societies. It was the major employer, with its own courts and its own judges and lawyers, and its own physicians. In its heyday, it has been estimated that throughout Western Europe one out of every 30 adult males was in the service of the Church.

And it could shape and dominate the imagination. It provided one of the very few opportunities for literacy. And 'at a time when not one man in a thousand could read, the Church taught its story in stone, painting, glass and embroidery, in buildings which – in an age when most people lived in huts little bigger or cleaner than pigsties – towered above the landscape and blazed within with colour and wealth' (Bryant, 1953).

Today, in Western Europe, the power and prestige of religious institutions have long since shrunk. Church buildings can be seen in ruins or put to secular use. During the 20th century when the country's population almost doubled, the number of full-time clergy halved (Bruce, 2002). And, where once the churches played a major role as providers of information and guidance, this function has largely passed on to the media and to the medical profession.

Religious beliefs Supporters of the secularisation thesis claim that people's thinking and attitudes are no longer based on religious beliefs. To accept that secularisation has occurred, Wilson argues, 'All that needs to be assumed is that society was much more preoccupied with supernatural beliefs and practices, and accorded them more significance, than it does now' (quoted in Wallis & Bruce, 1989). Wilson accepts that superstitious and magical beliefs, indifference and unbelief were common in the Middle Ages. Nevertheless, he argues that those concerned were 'believers'. All shared a belief in the reality of the supernatural, even if they did draw on beliefs defined as deviant by the established church. Their beliefs were not secular in any modern sense.

The historian Peter Laslett came to similar conclusions. He studied evidence of the villagers living in Clayworth, Nottinghamshire in 1676 and concluded that they were 'literal believers, all of the time', though they might combine their Christian beliefs with others such as witchcraft (Hanson, 1997).

Surveys from the second half of the 20th century suggest a decline in religious belief. In 1947, 45% of British respondents said they believed in a 'personal God'. By 1981 this figure had dropped to 41%, by 1990 to 32% and by 2000 to 26% (Bruce, 2002).

Religious practices With regard to the mainstream churches and denominations in Western Europe, there is general agreement that religious practices have declined. The evangelical revivals of 18th and 19th century Britain (Methodism, Salvation Army, and others), led to gains in membership until perhaps the 1930s. Thereafter, most Protestant organisations declined. Church membership, church attendance, church marriage, church funerals, christenings, Sunday School and Bible reading are all down. According to Steve Bruce (1992), 'The high point for the British churches was between 1860 and 1910 when around 28% of the adult population were active members'. By 2002, only 17% claimed to be members and only about 8% attended church (Bruce, 2002). Even Roman Catholics – whose numbers grew until the early 1960s through immigration from Ireland and a high birth rate – appear to be part of this general decline in religious practice.

The decline might be greater than the figures suggest. A survey by Leslie Francis indicated that clergy in rural areas were overestimating Sunday attendances by an average of 40% (Morgan, 1997).

For most people, it appears that churches and denominations offer little more than ceremonial for the rites of passage of birth, marriage and death.

Privatised religion There is evidence of a decline in religious beliefs, particularly traditional Christian beliefs – for example, the belief in a personal God. And there is evidence of a decline in collective religious practices.

Some researchers argue that religion is becoming a 'private affair'. And this means a range of different beliefs rather than overarching, society-wide beliefs. Thomas Luckmann (1970) states, 'Once religion is defined as a "private affair", the individual may choose from the assortment of "ultimate" meanings as he sees fit'. And privatised religion does not encourage public, collective religious practice.

Grace Davie (1994) argues that there has been a separation of 'belief and belonging'. She claims that religious belief remains widespread but is less likely to be expressed in an institutional setting. People no longer feel they belong to a religious organisation.

If privatised religion is widespread, then, in terms of Hanson's Narrow Approach – religion at the level of individual consciousness – secularisation may not be occurring. However, in terms of the Broad Approach, secularisation may well be occurring. Religion appears to be losing its significance on the level of the social system. It no longer forms part of the mainstream culture. The major institutions of religion – churches and denominations – are declining in importance as their membership dwindles. This also provides support for the differentiation thesis which is an example of the Broad Approach. It states that secularisation is occurring if the *social* significance of religion is declining.

Beyond church and denomination Some religious groups outside the Christian mainstream have grown in Britain. Non-Trinitarian groups, such as the Christadelphians, Christian Scientists, Mormons and Jehovah's Witnesses have grown from 71,000 in 1900 to 533,000 in 2000. However, the 2000 figure is just one-sixth of the numbers lost to the main Christian Trinitarian churches over the same period (Brierley, 2000). (Trinitarian refers to a belief in the Trinity – God as Father, Son and Holy Spirit. Non-Trinitarian refers to a number of alternative views of God.)

As discussed in Unit 5, the last 40 years of the 20th century saw the emergence of a large number of New Religious Movements (NRMs) and the New Age movement. Eileen Barker (1983) estimated that the numbers involved in many of these NRMs in Britain were only in the hundreds. And, at any point in time during a 25 year period, the total involved in all NRMs was no more than 100,000. Socially as well as numerically, Steve Bruce (2002) regards NRMs as insignificant. Unlike earlier NRMs such as Methodism, they only affect the lives of their followers and make little or no difference to the wider society.

Bruce is equally dismissive about the New Age movement. He sees it as having minimal effect on society as a whole. And the commitment of New Age 'seekers' is slight as they flit from one spiritual novelty to the next. With the most popular aspects of New Age being relaxation techniques, meditation, yoga and massage, Bruce (2002) regards it not so much as an alternative to traditional religion as 'an extension of the doctor's surgery, the beauty parlour and the gym'.

Ethnic religions and secularisation In the UK, there has been a steady growth in the membership of ethnic minority group religions – for example, membership of the Muslim faith rose from 130,000 in 1970 to 675,000 in 2000 (Brierley, 2000). This reverses the trend shown by the majority population. Does this indicate a resurgence of religion amongst ethnic minorities – an opposite trend to secularisation?

At least part of this increase is due to continued immigration – for example, there are growing numbers of migrants from a Muslim background. Even this, however, does not fully account for the higher levels of religious participation amongst ethnic minorities. Steve Bruce (2002) suggests the following explanations.

Religion can remain a powerful social force when it provides resources for *cultural defence*. For example, in cases of ethnic conflict, it can be a positive source of ethnic identity and solidarity. Similarly, religion can provide a vehicle for *cultural transition* when an immigrant population settles in a new, and often unwelcoming, world. Religion can offer a sense of community and a sense of self-worth and support.

In the case of ethnic minority groups, religion may provide resources for cultural defence and cultural transition. However, it appears that this is only a short-lived adaptation. As Bruce (2002) notes, the third generation of Muslims is approaching 'the English level of religious indifference'. If this is so, ethnic religious enthusiasm is simply a blip in the overall trend to secularisation.

key terms

Cultural defence The strategies used by a group to defend its culture and group identity.
Cultural transition The change in culture when people – for example, immigrants – move from one social setting to another.

Evidence for secularisation – evaluation

Problems of measurement Does the data used to support secularisation provide a valid – a true and accurate – measure of the process? Different religious organisations measure membership in different ways. Many don't record attendance figures and those that do, don't always record them all year round and for all services. As noted earlier, some exaggerate attendance levels, as do many members of their congregations when asked how often they attend services.

Similarly, when people say they believe in God in response to a questionnaire-based survey, what does this mean? Is this belief of major significance to their lives? Or, is it something they rarely think about, something they regard as unimportant?

Religious beliefs are extremely difficult to measure. For example, over 37 million people in England and Wales described themselves as Christian in the 2001 census. They were asked to respond to the question 'What is your religion?' by ticking one of a number of options (*Social Trends*, 2004). For many, this statement of religion may mean little or nothing. It may simply be seen as a follow-on from being English.

David Martin (1969) argues that church attendance in Victorian Britain, particularly for the middle classes, was as much a sign of respectability as of religious conviction.

Belief and belonging As noted earlier, Grace Davie (1994) makes the distinction between belief and belonging. Some forms of religious belief still appear widespread. For example, European Values surveys from the 1980s to 2000 show that nearly 60% of Europeans describe themselves as 'a religious person' and around 50% claim that God plays a significant part in their life (Cook, 2000).

While belief may be fairly high, belonging – membership of and attendance at religious institutions – is low and getting lower. As discussed earlier, a decline in institutional religion does not necessarily indicate secularisation. Private or personal religion may remain relatively strong. Whether secularisation is occurring depends, in part, on how the process is defined – in terms of the Broad Approach or the Narrow Approach.

Historical comparisons Going to church is often assumed to be a valid indicator of religiosity. However, it may have different meanings at different times. For example, in the past it may have been an expression of community – a normal part of community life which had little to do with religion as such. Today, with the breakup of close-knit communities, collective worship may well be an expression of religious faith rather than a normal part of social life.

A 'golden age' of religion There is a tendency for some researchers to look back to a supposedly 'golden age' of religion in the Middle Ages as a point of comparison for today. There are a number of problems with this view.

- First, the religious practices of the land-owning nobility are much better documented than those of the peasantry.

- Second, there is some evidence that the peasantry were largely indifferent or even hostile to the Catholic Church.

- Third, although some supporters of the secularisation thesis accept that there was some apathy or indifference to religion in the Middle Ages, their critics argue that they have underestimated the extent of these views (Hamilton, 2001; Hunt, 1992).

Beyond major religious institutions Secularisation theorists have tended to focus on mainstream, institutional religion – on churches and denominations. They have dismissed NRMs as numerically and socially insignificant. And their tone is often scornful when it comes to the New Age movement. Yet the significance and potential of such movements may be much greater than they suggest (Heelas & Woodhead, 2003; 2004 – see pages 69-70).

The USA Compared to Europe, both belief and belonging in the USA are high. For example, surveys indicate that 90% of people believe in God and over 40% regularly attend a religious institution (Hunt, 1992). Does this evidence go against the secularisation thesis? This question will be discussed in Section 7.5, pages 70-72.

Further evaluation of the evidence used by secularisation theorists is contained in later sections.

activity26 evidence for secularisation

Item A **Medieval religion**

The God in whom medieval people believed was an intensely personal God, forever appearing in acts of nature, visions and apparitions, plagues and cures, storms, fires and miracles. And not only God, but the whole hierarchy of Heaven, angels and saints, apostles and martyrs, lay on the frontiers of the visible, tangible world, ready at any moment to reveal themselves.

So too did the Devil and the fiends, witches and ministers of evil. A flight of crows seemed a swarm of demons, the howling of the wind was the cry of some wicked lord, borne through the middle air to Hell. At a time when people knew little of the laws of nature or the world outside their village homes, they accepted such ideas with no more question than their 20th century descendants did of the latest scientific marvels.

Beyond all this lay a conception shared by rich and poor alike, educated and ignorant. It was that divine law governed the universe, from its greatest to its minutest part. Everything that happened in the world – everything that had happened, was happening and was going to happen – was a part of God's plan, only partly intelligible to people's puny intellect. The Church existed to help explain the plan, to help people obey it and, through Christ's love and sacrifice, to obtain forgiveness for them when they broke God's law.

Source: Bryant, 1953

Part of a medieval painting called the Great Doom. It shows some of the horrors of hell – a miser is being roasted and cheating traders are suspended over the fire on a bridge of spikes.

Item B **From sacred to secular**

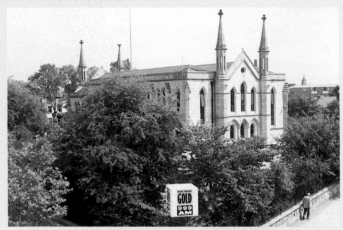

Former churches in Preston, Lancashire, converted into a radio station, an antique centre and a printing company.

Item C *Membership of religious groups (UK, thousands)*

Group	1970	1980	1990	2000
Christian: Trinitarian of whom:	9,272	7,529	6,624	5,917
Anglican (C of E)	2,987	2,180	1,728	1,654
Catholic	2,746	2,455	2,198	1,768
Free Churches	1,629	1,285	1,299	1,278
Presbyterian	1,751	1,437	1,214	989
Orthodox	159	172	185	235
Christian: Non-Trinitarian	276	349	455	533
Buddhist	10	15	30	50
Hindu	80	120	140	165
Jewish	375	321	356	383
Muslim	130	305	495	675
Sikh	100	150	250	400
Others	20	40	55	85

Source: Brierley, 2000

Item D *Religious beliefs*

Beliefs	1947	1981	1990	2000
There is a personal God	45	41	32	26
There is some sort of higher power, spirit or life force	39	37	41	21
There is something there	n.a.	n.a.	n.a.	23
I don't really know what to think	16	16	15	12
I don't really think there is any sort of God, spirit or life force	n.a.	6	10	15
None of these	n.a.	n.a.	1	3

Note: n.a. = not asked.

Source: Bruce, 2002

Item E *The social significance of New Age spirituality*

Although New Agers often use words like 'radical' and 'alternative', the effect is anything but. The anxious, repressed merchant banker who learns to meditate and gets his regular shiatsu massage, does not throw up banking and become a youth worker or an eco-warrior. He just becomes a happier and more relaxed merchant banker.

But even if the merchant banker does decide to throw it all in, buy a farmhouse in Wales and start a pottery with a side-line in horoscopes, the impact on the rest of the world is minimal. In the 18th and 19th centuries, the Methodists were responsible for a vast amount of social reform. They put a stop to child labour in factories and mines. They stopped young boy sweeps being forced to climb up the chimneys of Georgian houses. They restricted the length of the working day. They put an end to a system by which men were paid their wages in pubs. They ended slavery. They also founded schools, penny savings banks and public libraries.

Source: Bruce, 2002

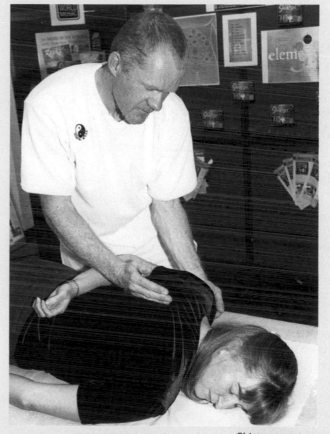

Shiatsu massage

questions

1 In what ways do Items A and B support the secularisation thesis?

2 a) Briefly describe the trends shown in Items C and D.

  b) What support do they provide for the secularisation thesis?

3 Using Hanson's concepts of the Broad Approach and the Narrow Approach, explain why Bruce (Item E) argues that the rise of New Age spirituality does not contradict the secularisation thesis.

7.3 Sociological theories and secularisation

This section looks at secularisation in terms of broader sociological theories of social change. Most of the sociologists examined here assume that secularisation is occurring in one form or another. Their aim is to explain the process. Others are less sure about the secularisation thesis. Some see a transformation of religious expression rather than a decline in religion as such.

Karl Marx

Marx believed that capitalism was the penultimate era of human society. The final era, communism, would follow the overthrow of capitalism.

As outlined earlier (see pages 23-24), Marx saw religion as a reflection of class society – it justified the position of the ruling class and provided compensation for the oppression of the subject class. Social classes and oppression would disappear in communist society. Since these are the social forces which generate religion, religion too would disappear.

Marx believed that capitalism itself contained the seeds of secularisation. It presented a materialist view of the world – its aim was to produce goods and make profits. And the social order was seen to be based on contracts rather than being ordained by God – for example, the wage contract between employer and employee.

Marx saw the death of religion as inevitable. His theory is an example of the disappearance thesis of secularisation.

Max Weber

As outlined in Unit 3, Weber saw rationalisation as the key process in the development of modern society (see pages 30-31). Reason steadily replaces faith. The world becomes demystified – its magic and mystery are taken away. The meanings which direct action are increasingly rational rather than religious.

Ironically, it was religion, in Weber's view, which spearheaded this process of rationalisation. Weber claimed that the spirit of capitalism had its origins in early forms of Protestantism, particularly Calvinism. And the spirit of capitalism was one of the main factors in the development of rational capitalism. Once on its way, modern society no longer needed religion to guide action – reason was now a sufficient guide.

Malcolm Hamilton (2001) summarises Weber's views. 'Calvinistic Protestantism was its own gravedigger. In many ways, it could not help but sow the seeds of secularisation in modern society by its own promotion of worldly activity and consequent expansion of wealth and material wellbeing.'

Peter Berger

Like Weber, Peter Berger (1973) sees the origins of secularisation in religion itself. He notes that it is the Christian world, and particularly the Protestant world,

which has experienced the greatest degree of secularisation. And it is Protestantism, more than any other branch of Christianity, which has cut out or cut down the sacramental, the sacred and the ritual elements of Catholicism, and the mystery, miracle and magic found in many other religions. In Berger's view, one of the main factors leading to secularisation is the rationality of Protestantism (see pages 31-33).

Berger argues that the process of secularisation has been accelerated by more recent changes in modern society. The growth of the media and increasing social and geographical mobility have exposed people to a range of different religions. Faced with this marketplace of religions with their competing sets of beliefs and practices, it has become increasingly difficult to accept the teachings of any one as the truth. This weakens the authority of all religions. And this accelerates the process of secularisation (see pages 31-33).

Bryan Wilson

The British sociologist Bryan Wilson (1966, 1976), argues for the differentiation thesis – that religion is declining in social significance. In Hanson's (1997) terminology, he takes the Broad Approach. Wilson gives the following explanations for secularisation.

Social differentiation As modern society developed, its various institutions became increasingly separate as they specialised in particular functions. This process is known as *social differentiation*. Religious institutions were once directly involved in politics, social control, social welfare, health and education. Now there are specialist institutions for each of these areas. As a result, religion is relegated to the margins of society where it 'ceases to be significant in the working of the social system' (Wilson, 1982).

Rational thinking and science Like Weber and Berger, Wilson argues that rational thinking has largely replaced religious views of the world. Like Weber, he sees early Protestantism contributing to rational thought. However, he places more emphasis on the development of science and the scientific method, which he sees as displacing religious explanations. In Wilson's (1966) words, 'Science not only explained many facets of life and the material environment in a way more satisfactory, but it also provided confirmation of its explanation in practical results'.

The decline of community Traditionally, religion has drawn its strength from close-knit communities. Communal values were expressed and reinforced in religious rituals. Events of significance to the community – from the harvest to births, marriages and deaths – were celebrated in the local church.

Industrialisation and urbanisation have led to the break-up of this type of community life. As a result, religion has lost much of its reason for being.

Emile Durkheim

The remaining views examined in this section are less sure about the secularisation thesis. Rather then seeing religion declining or disappearing, they are more likely to see a transformation of traditional religion into a new form of religion.

Looking back over the 19th century and the early years of the 20th century, Durkheim saw the rapid social changes brought about by industrialisation and urbanisation as a threat to religion. These changes led to the break-up of community and to anomie – a disruption of the norms which govern behaviour. The result was a weakening of social solidarity and collective consciousness. Since the close-knit community with its shared norms and values was the lifeblood of religion, religion itself was threatened.

Durkheim feared that religion would be relegated to a corner of life – a private matter, no longer capable of overarching society and unifying its members. However, he did not see the decline of religion as an irreversible trend, believing that all societies must have sacred symbols and communal ritual if they are to survive. So, in Durkheim's view, religion will not die, though it is likely to change its form. A possible example of this transformation of religion is the civil religion identified by Robert Bellah in the USA (see pages 20-22). If Bellah is correct, civil religion performs Durkheim's essential functions of religion – reinforcing collective consciousness and strengthening social solidarity.

Postmodernist views

According to Lyotard (1984), postmodern society is characterised by a loss of confidence in metanarratives the big stories or grand explanations provided by science, religion and politics. Their authority and certainty have been undermined, their claim to the truth has been questioned. As a result, traditional institutional religion with its claim to universal truth has been undermined (see page 34).

According to Zygmunt Bauman (1992), this produces a 'crisis of meaning'. Traditional religious metanarratives, such as Christianity, cannot deal with this crisis, which explains their decline. However, new religions or new expressions of religiosity can restore meaning. But these new expressions are very different from the old religions. They are tailored by individuals to fit their particular identities, rather than being imposed by institutions which claim an exclusive truth which everybody should believe. This can be seen in the decline of religious monopolies, such as Christianity, and the rise of the New Age movement.

key term

Social differentiation The process by which social institutions become increasingly specialised and separate.

7.4 The spiritual revolution thesis

In an important study known as the Kendal Project, a team of researchers led by Paul Heelas set out to test the *spiritual revolution thesis*. This thesis states that a spiritual revolution is underway, or may have already taken place (Heelas & Woodhead, 2003; 2005).

The researchers identified two possible trends. First, a decline in traditional Christianity with its emphasis on a God-on-high, who tells people how to live their lives. This is the argument put forward by secularisation theorists. Alongside this decline in the sacred is an alternative growth in the sacred in the form of New Age spirituality. Here the emphasis is on the spirituality of the inner self rather than conforming to some externally imposed morality. This is the argument put forward by *sacralisation theorists*.

Methodology The researchers chose Kendal as the setting in which to test the spiritual revolution thesis. Kendal is a town of some 28,000 people in the Lake District in northwest England. It was small enough to investigate systematically, but large enough to have a range of traditional religious activity and New Age spiritualities.

The focus of the research was a comparison between the 'congregational domain' and the 'holistic milieu'. The congregational domain was represented by 25 Christian churches and chapels in Kendal. A headcount was taken of those who attended on Sunday, 26 November, 2000. This avoided the problem of self-reporting where people tend to exaggerate their attendance rate.

The holistic milieu refers to those who practise activities which they see as involving the whole person – as combining the mind, body and spirit. The inclusion of 'spirit' is critical. If an activity such as yoga or tai chi is not seen as spiritual, then that person is not included in the holistic milieu. A questionnaire was used to count those involved in New Age spiritualities and in-depth interviewing explored the attractions of New Age.

The findings The headcount for attendance at churches and chapels was 2207, 7.9% of the population of Kendal – exactly the same as the percentage for Britain as a whole. Attendance figures for Kendal from the 1950s onwards show a significant decline. By comparison, the holistic milieu shows strong growth. There were 95 practitioners (providers) of spiritual activities in 2000. In the 1970s, there were only three such practitioners in the *Yellow Pages*, by 1999 this had grown to almost 40. Those taking part in 2000 numbered 600, 1.6% of the population of Kendal. However, only 55% considered these activities to be of spiritual significance, 0.9% of the population of Kendal.

Conclusion In Heelas and Woodhead's (2005) words, 'the spiritual revolution clearly has not taken place in Kendal'. At first sight, the 0.9% involved in holistic spiritual practices seems a long way from the 7.9% involved in the congregational domain. However, the trends suggest a different picture. If present trends continue, then the revolution will take place in 20 or 30 years, when numbers involved in the holistic milieu will overtake those in the congregational domain – see Activity 27, Item A.

Evaluation The Kendal Project is an important piece of research. First, it provides a measurement of New Age spirituality. Second, it looks at trends over time.

How do its findings fit into the secularisation debate? The trends identified in Kendal suggest that New Age spirituality cannot be dismissed as easily as some secularisation theorists argue. However, the numbers involved are still fairly small.

Can New Age spirituality be directly compared to religion? Although many people believe that holistic practices have a spiritual aspect, this is very different from believing in and praying to a supernatural being.

7.5 Religion in the USA

Is America an exception to secularisation in the West? This question has often been asked because of the apparently high levels of attendance at religious institutions in the

USA and the high proportion of Americans who say they believe in God.

Statistical evidence

Various surveys over the past 50 years indicate that between 90 and 95% of Americans claim to believe in God. And, over the same period of time, around 40% of Protestants and 50% of Catholics say they attended church in the past week.

These figures are based on self-reports – that is, people reporting their religious beliefs and practices to interviewers or on self-completion questionnaires. There is evidence that they overstate their commitment to religion in order to present themselves in the best possible light.

activity27 the spiritual revolution thesis

Item A *The timing of the revolution*

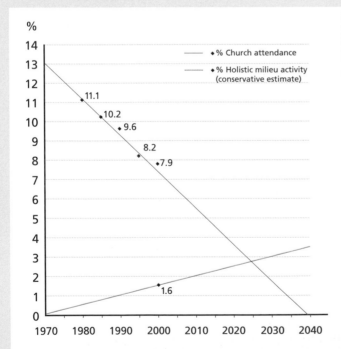

Source: Heelas & Woodhead, 2003; 2004

Item B *The scale of the revolution*

Findings from the Kendal Project show that 80% of those involved in holistic milieu activities are women, and 83% are aged over 40. Over half have attended university or college and many work in people-centred, caring jobs, such as nursing, where personal wellbeing is a major concern. Given the relatively small number of people with these characteristics, there is not much scope for expansion in the future. This means, of course, that the rate of growth of the holistic milieu is likely to slow down.

Source: Heelas & Woodhead, 2004

questions

1 Briefly summarise the trends shown in Item A.

2 New Age spirituality is very unlikely to become a majority concern. Discuss with reference to Items A and B.

For example, Hadaway and Marler (1999) conducted a head-count of people who attended church. They found actual attendance was about half the level of self-reported attendance – 'Instead of 40% of Protestants attending church, we found 20%. Instead of 50% of Catholics attending church, we found 28%'. However, even these levels are considerably higher than those in Britain.

The secularisation of religious institutions

When it comes to secularisation, America should be in the lead. As Bryan Wilson (1966) observed, it is 'a country in which instrumental values, rational procedures and technical methods have gone furthest, and the country in which the sense of the sacred, the sense of the sanctity of life, and deep religiosity are most conspicuously absent'. So how come there is high church attendance and widespread religious beliefs in a markedly secular society?

To Will Herberg (1960), the answer is simple. The religious content of churches, denominations and synagogues has been watered down. Religious institutions have compromised their beliefs and practices to fit in with the wider society. They have undergone a process of internal secularisation.

Herberg argues that the high level of attendance at religious institutions is directed by secular rather than religious concerns. He claims that to be an American – to demonstrate an American identity – requires a public commitment to religious beliefs within a religious organisation. Which religious organisation doesn't really matter. Either Protestant, Catholic or Jewish faiths are regarded as acceptable evidence of an American identity. Over time, these three religious traditions have become more and more alike in their teachings and in their function of supporting the nation. The central themes of American religion increasingly reflect the American Way of Life – the core values of American society such as freedom, democracy and achievement.

Herberg explains America's religious enthusiasm in terms of the unique experience of a nation which had to weld together a mix of people from across the world. In doing this, American religion has itself become secular. To a large extent 'religion' has gone out of religion. Despite its

summary

1. There are two main versions of the secularisation thesis – the disappearance thesis and the differentiation thesis.

2. Sharon Hanson makes a distinction between secularisation on the level of the social system (the Broad Approach) and on the level of the individual (the Narrow Approach).

3. Secularisation theorists claim that the power and influence of religious institutions, religious beliefs and religious practices have all declined.

4. They accept that religion may continue on an individual level – as privatised religion. However, they take the Broad Approach, arguing that religion is losing its significance on the level of the social system.

5. The evidence for secularisation has been questioned in the following ways.
   - Are the measurements of religious beliefs and practices valid – true and accurate?
   - If privatised religion remains widespread, is it reasonable to claim that secularisation is occurring?
   - Is the comparison of a 'golden age' of religion in the past with a secular present justified?
   - Does the rise of the New Age movement and high levels of religious belief and church attendance in the USA provide evidence against the secularisation thesis?

6. Sociological theories offer the following views of secularisation.
   - Karl Marx believed that religion will disappear with the overthrow of the capitalist system.
   - Max Weber argued that rationalisation is steadily eroding religion on both an individual and societal level.
   - Peter Berger claimed that the authority of all religions is weakened as they compete for clients in the religious marketplace. How can their competing and contradictory beliefs all be seen as true?
   - Bryan Wilson gave the following reasons for the decline of religion on a societal level – social differentiation, rational thinking and science, and the decline of community.
   - Emile Durkheim argued that the rapid social changes brought about by industrialisation and urbanisation and the resulting anomie led to a decline in religion. He did not see this as an irreversible trend – societies must have sacred symbols and communal rituals if they are to survive.
   - Some postmodernists argue that the loss of confidence in metanarratives has led to a decline in traditional religion. This produces a 'crisis of meaning'. However, they see new types of religion offering to restore meaning.

7. The Kendal Project indicated that the New Age spiritual revolution had not taken place. However, it suggested that if present trends continue, then the revolution will take place in 20 to 30 years.

8. Evidence on religious belief and attendance at religious institutions in the USA has been used to question the secularisation thesis. Even allowing for problems of measurement, attendance levels are high compared to Europe.

9. Will Herberg argues that religious institutions in the USA have retained support by becoming more secular.

10. In view of the different definitions of religion and secularisation and the problems of measurement, it is difficult to reach firm conclusions about the secularisation thesis.

apparent vigour, American religion has been secularised.

Evaluation Herberg's views have received some support. For example, Peter Berger (1970) argues that American religious institutions have maintained relatively high attendance levels by downplaying the supernatural and 'modifying their product in accordance with consumer demands' – that is, the demands of a secular society.

Whether American religion is becoming more secular depends on the researcher's view of religion. To Herberg, 'authentic religion' involves a strong belief in a supernatural power, a strong commitment to religious teachings and a refusal to compromise those teachings to fit in with the wider society. Other researchers might take a different view of religion and, as a result, reach different conclusions.

Herberg has been criticised for ignoring Christian fundamentalism in the USA. With their commitment to a literal interpretation of the Bible and to strict moral codes based on the 'word of God', the beliefs of Christian fundamentalists in many ways reflect Herberg's 'authentic religion'.

Conclusion

It is difficult to reach firm conclusions about the secularisation thesis. The term is used by different researchers in different ways. For some, it means the decline of religion on a societal level. For others, it means the decline of religion on an individual level.

Sociologists are unable to agree on a definition of religion. As a result, they will have different views of the secularisation process and how to measure it. In addition, they have their own views on 'authentic' religion. Is religion in the USA only a watered-down version of the real thing as Herberg and Berger claim? And what about New Age spirituality? Is it as real and significant as religious beliefs and practices? Or is it, as Steve Bruce (2002) claims, little more than 'an extension of the doctor's surgery, the beauty parlour and the gym'?

Even when sociologists agree on definitions of religion and secularisation, problems remain – in particular, the problem of measurement. How do you measure religious beliefs and practices? What do these measurements mean? Does a belief in God and regular church attendance reflect strong religious convictions? As this unit has indicated, we can't be sure.

In view of the different definitions of religion and secularisation and the problems of measurement, it is difficult to prove or disprove the secularisation thesis.

Unit 8 *Contemporary religion – a global perspective*

keyissues

1 Is there a global resurgence of religion?

2 If so, what are the reasons for this?

This unit returns to some of the issues raised earlier in the chapter and looks at them in a global context. Is secularisation occurring worldwide? Or is it confined to Europe as the title of Grace Davie's (2002) book, *Europe: The Exceptional Case*, suggests?

There is evidence of a recent rise in religious behaviour in many parts of the world. Is this a defensive reaction to the rapid social change brought about by modernisation and globalisation? Or is it a proactive movement to deal with this situation?

8.1 The resurgence of religion

Some sociologists who saw secularisation occurring in Europe believed it was only a matter of time before the rest of the world followed suit. This has not happened, nor is there any evidence that it is likely to happen. In fact, available evidence suggests just the opposite – that over the past 30 or 40 years there has been a resurgence of religion in the world outside Europe.

Islam

A number of researchers claim that Islam is the fastest growing of the world's major religions (Sutton & Vertigans, 2005). Although it is difficult to measure, this view is supported by estimates from the United Nations and the Vatican. Islam is now the world's second largest religion after Christianity. If present trends continue, it will become the world's largest religion by mid-21st century (www.religioustolerance.org, 2008).

There are other indicators of the rapid growth of Islam. According to the Saudi Arabian Press Agency, there has been a significant rise in the number of Muslims undertaking the hajj – the annual pilgrimage to the holy city of Mecca. The number in 1950 was less than 100,000; by 2008 it was over 2.5 million (www.about.com, 2008).

Pentecostalism

In terms of numbers, Pentecostalism is a success story – it is the fastest growing Christian religion. In Asia, its followers accounted for 0.5% of the population in 1970 rising to 4.2% in 2005; in Africa, 4.8% of the population in 1970 rising to 16.6% in 2005; in Central and South America, 4.4% of the population in 1970 rising to 28.1% in 2005 (World Christian Database, 2006). Often this growth has been very rapid. For example, in Rio de Janeiro in Brazil between 1990 and 1992 a new Pentecostal church was registered every weekday (Davie, 2007).

Religious conservatism

The main growth has been in the more conservative branches of religions. Phrases like Islamic fundamentalism and the Christian Right have been used to describe this development. The upsurge of conservatism can also be seen in the revival of the Russian Orthodox Church and in religions such as Hinduism, Buddhism and Judaism.

Western researchers sometimes use the term fundamentalism to describe conservative religious groups. Such groups tend to look to the past, to traditional faiths and to 'essential truths'. Recently, there has been a reaction against the term. For example, Peter Berger (1999) argues that fundamentalism implies 'superstitious', 'over-emotional', 'reactionary' and 'backward'. However, as the next section argues, so-called conservative religious movements don't only look backwards.

8.2 Theories of religious resurgence

Modernisation and globalisation

Religious resurgence, particularly in the developing world, has been seen as a response to modernisation and globalisation. Explanations are fairly general because they attempt to cover different religious groups – for example, Islam and Pentecostalism. And also because they attempt to cover differences within religious groups – for example, Muslims are divided by different types of Islam (such as Shiite and Sunni), nationality (such as Egypt, Iran, Pakistan, Malaysia, Indonesia), language and ethnicity.

Modernisation and globalisation have resulted in rapid social change. There has been large-scale migration within and between countries as 'economic migrants' seek to improve their living standards. This has resulted in social disruption, disorientation and threats to identity. Many migrants move from relatively stable, traditional rural communities to towns and cities. There they are often faced with high levels of unemployment and widespread poverty. The hope of a better life is sometimes dashed. The certainties of their old way of life are replaced by the uncertainties of their new environment. They are increasingly part of a global economy which shapes their lives, but over which they have little or no control (Davie, 2007; Furseth & Repsted, 2006; Sutton & Vertigans, 2005).

The resurgence of religion is seen as a response to the situation described above. It is seen primarily as a response of the poor. However, to some extent, members of the Western educated middle classes are becoming increasingly involved in the religious revival.

There are two main theories which attempt to explain religious resurgence. The first sees religion as a defensive reaction to modernisation and globalisation. The second sees religion as a proactive response, as a means of improving people's lives. Some researchers combine these theories.

Defensive reaction

A number of sociologists have seen the resurgence of conservative religious movements as a defensive reaction to modernisation and globalisation. Such movements provide a retreat into a religious haven. They provide certainty in an uncertain world by selectively retrieving traditional religious truths.

As globalisation undermines people's traditional sense of self, religion helps to build 'resistance identities', based in part on traditional doctrines (Castells, 1996). Globalisation often involves Westernisation – the spread of Western norms and values. Conservative religions can provide 'cultural defence' for local societies. This can be seen in Iran since the 1979 revolution when the religious leaders saw a return to traditional Islam as a cure for the 'disease' of 'westoxifaction' (Taheri, 1987). Activity 28 on page 74 provides evidence to support this view.

Proactive response

The resurgence of conservative religion has been seen as a practical response to the problems resulting from modernisation and globalisation. The rapid growth of Pentecostalism in Central and South America illustrates this view. Pentecostal churches impose a strict regime – services several times a week, Bible studies and committee meetings – plus a strict morality – no drinking, smoking or extramarital relations. There is an emphasis on self-improvement – a message sometime known as 'prosperity theology' and 'health and welfare gospel'. The churches offer business classes and teach congregations how to save. People are encouraged to better themselves, start their own businesses and pull themselves out of poverty.

Machismo – male virility and bravado – is widespread in Central and South America, particularly in the poorer urban areas. Machismo is expressed in drinking, gambling, womanising and partying. The strict morality of Pentecostalism works against this. The roles of husband and father become central, money spent on wine, women and song increasingly goes into the family, resulting in a better diet and education for the children (Brusco, 1995).

Developing societies are often former colonies. For many, the promise of independence has not led to prosperity. Neither colonial rule nor independence have encouraged a positive identity. Attempts at modernisation have been based on Western models and globalisation has been largely directed by Western corporations.

People in developing countries tend to feel marginalised as second-class class citizens in an increasingly global society. For many, Westernisation does not appear to be the answer.

Religion offers an alternative. It can help to build a secure and positive identity. For example, the resurgence of Islam can provide a positive, non-Western identity which draws on traditional culture (Martin, 2002). It can create an Islamic identity which crosses national boundaries and can mobilise Muslims to take political action in a global context (An-Na'im, 1999).

summary

1. While secularisation might be occurring in Europe, a religious resurgence appears to be occurring in the rest of the world.

2. Islam is growing rapidly. If present trends continue, it will be the world's largest religion by the mid-21st century.

3. Pentecostalism is the fastest growing Christian religion. It has grown dramatically in many developing countries.

4. The main growth has been in the more conservative branches of religions.

5. Religious resurgence has been seen as a response to the rapid social change and disruption resulting from modernisation and globalisation.

6. There are two main theories of religious resurgence: a) as a defensive reaction and b) as a proactive response.

7. As a defensive reaction, religious resurgence may provide:
   - A retreat into a religious haven
   - Certainty based on essential truths
   - Resistance identities
   - Cultural defence.

8. As a proactive response, religious resurgence may provide:
   - A strict morality
   - A guide to self-improvement
   - A recipe for upward mobility
   - Support for the family
   - A positive non-Western identity.

activity28 the resurgence of religion

Item A Islamic revival in Egypt

Estimates of how many new mosques have been built in Egypt over the past few decades vary a lot, from tens to hundreds of thousands, depending on whom you ask.

Islam is increasingly entering daily life. Even the usual Egyptian 'hello' and 'goodbye' (ahlan, ma'a al-salama) appear to be giving way to 'There is No God but Allah', a phrase used only in religious contexts before.

By the 1960s the veil was a thing of the past in Egypt. Now more and more professional and well educated women – doctors, broadcasters, engineers, lawyers – say they have donned the veil voluntarily.

However, this is not the severe black veil of their grandmothers. Wherever you go, most of the women you are most likely to see in public places are wearing a colourful headscarf with a Western-style dress that covers the whole body.

Source: Abdelhadi, 2003

Student at Cairo University, Egypt

Item B Pentecostalism in Guatemala

In churches like Showers of Grace, Pentecostals are told they can escape from poverty with the help of God and by their own efforts.

'Our purpose is to bring people with few resources to different levels,' says Nestor Mendez, a pastor of Showers of Grace, whose desk is cluttered with books such as *First Time Manager* and *Let Your Dreams Soar*. 'I believe we can change not only their lives but the country.'

Edmundo Guillen, the head pastor of Showers of Grace, explains their mission: 'Our greatest dream is that they all become entrepreneurs'.

Source: Llana, 2007

Pentecostal worshippers in South America

questions

1 What effect might the Islamic revival in Egypt have on people's identities?

2 How can Item B be seen as a positive and practical response?

Introduction

Can you imagine a day going by without watching a television programme or a DVD; listening to music on the radio, or an MP3 player; logging onto a website or reading a newspaper, magazine or book? If your answer is yes then you're a pretty unusual person! We live in a world where we are surrounded by print and electronic media and depend upon them for information and entertainment.

Media products are often produced by organisations. Does it matter who owns and controls these organisations?

We rely upon the media for much of our information and entertainment. Are the media giving us an accurate picture of the world?

BT satellite dish

We watch, listen to and read media messages. How do we respond to these messages?

What effect are the new media, such as the internet and satellite broadcasting, having on our lives?

These are some of the questions examined in this chapter.

chaptersummary

▶ **Unit 1** examines the main types of media institutions.

▶ **Unit 2** looks at the ownership and control of media institutions.

▶ **Unit 3** focuses on the media in global society.

▶ **Unit 4** examines the selection and presentation of news.

▶ **Unit 5** looks at the media representations of gender, ethnicity, class, age, sexuality and disability.

▶ **Unit 6** considers the effects of the media on audiences.

▶ **Unit 7** assesses the impact of the new media.

▶ **Unit 8** looks at the media in postmodern society.

Unit 1 Media institutions

keyissues

1 What are the key characteristics of the media?

2 Who owns and controls media institutions?

1.1 Defining the media

What are the mass media? The term *media* describes different means of communication. Some media – such as the telephone – enable communication between two people. However, others allow communication with a *mass* audience. These include newspapers, television, radio, and the internet.

For much of human history, social relations have been face to face. People communicated by talking and through body language. Now technological developments have made it possible to communicate with large numbers of people at one time. It is these forms of communication that have come to be known as the *mass media*.

'The mass media are simply the means through which content, whether fact or fiction, is produced by organisations and transmitted to and received by an audience' (McCullagh, 2002).

This definition identifies three key aspects of the mass media.

● The production of messages by media institutions

● The content of media messages

● The reception of messages by audiences.

While these three dimensions are interrelated, it is

important that each is examined separately. We cannot understand what factors shape media content without looking at the production process. We cannot understand the meanings of media messages without analysing their content. And we cannot reach an informed judgement about media effects without examining how audiences interpret media messages.

We shall examine each of these processes in turn, beginning with media organisations.

1.2 Media organisations

Types of media organisation There are three forms of media organisation.

- Community based media organisations, eg a radio station in a local hospital
- Public/state owned media organisations, eg the BBC
- Privately owned media organisations, eg News Corporation (Devereux, 2003).

While all three forms still survive, privately owned media organisations are by far the most significant. Community based media continue to play a minor role, usually appealing to limited local audiences. Public/state owned media organisations, although in an earlier media age often enjoying a national monopoly, have steadily lost their dominance. They have either been privatised or face significant competition from a limited number of privately owned global media institutions.

activity1 defining the mass media

question

Why is each picture an example of the mass media?

Trends in media ownership

Increasing media choice? In the last 15 years there has been a rapid increase in the range of media outlets. 'In 1988 there were four TV channels in the UK; today over 250; there were 60 commercial radio stations, today over 350; 14 cinema multiplexes, today nearly 2000; zero web pages, today billions' (Peake, 2002, updated 2009). These changes suggest a much wider range of choice. However, the source of these 'choices' is a smaller and smaller number of extremely large and powerful media institutions. And, as the next unit indicates, some researchers see this development as reducing choice.

Increasing concentration of media organisations 'Fewer and fewer large companies increasingly own what we see, hear and read' (Williams, 2003). This process is known as the *concentration of media organisations*.

The increasing concentration of media organisations is the result of three major developments:

- *Vertical integration*
- *Horizontal integration* and multi-media ownership
- The expansion of *transnational ownership*.

Let's take each in turn.

Vertical integration This refers to 'the process by which one owner acquires all aspects of production and distribution of a single type of media product' (Croteau & Hoynes, 1997). Vertical integration is not new. Production and distribution of movies were concentrated in the hands of the big five Hollywood companies in the early part of the twentieth century. This enabled them to build a dominant position in world film production. Although film industries subsequently developed elsewhere, Hollywood still retains its dominance. 'The most comprehensive survey of cinema-going in Britain by the Film Council reveals that although younger people are flocking to the cinema in ever increasing numbers, they are overwhelmingly watching films made by the big US studios' (Kennedy, 2003).

Horizontal integration This refers to 'the process by which one company buys different kinds of media, concentrating ownership across different kinds of media' (Croteau & Hoynes, 1997). Horizontal integration has developed rapidly in recent years. The largest media groups own a range of media. Take News Corporation owned by Rupert Murdoch. Although this company initially produced newspapers, it now has interests in a range of other media, including book publishing (eg, Harper Collins), television (eg, BSkyB), radio (eg, Sky), film (eg, 20th Century Fox), and the internet (eg MySpace).

Transnational ownership The major media organisations operate across national boundaries. Take News Corporation again. Although the company originated in Australia, it now operates on a global scale. It produces over 175 newspapers in Australia, Britain and the USA; it owns 37 television stations; and it is able to beam programmes into homes through its ownership and control of cable programming and satellite operations across Europe, Asia, Australia, Latin America and the USA.

Explaining increasing concentration

Media products such as newspapers and films are costly to produce. They require a large upfront investment. But while producing the first newspaper or film is expensive, the cost of reproducing copies is cheap. This encourages media organisations to maximise their audiences. Hence the three developments outlined above – all of which have led to increasing concentration.

Vertical integration has enabled Hollywood companies to sell their films more easily. Horizontal integration has allowed organisations to promote their products across a range of media. '*Batman* was developed into a film by Time Warner, publicised through its magazines and promoted via its cable and television networks, the soundtrack of which was released on its record labels and whose merchandising included children's toys produced through its manufacturing interests' (Williams, 2003).

What is more, the development of multi-media organisations operating across the world enables them to search for markets on a global scale. 'The marketing of *The Lion King, Pocahontas*, and many other animated characters, by Disney (the film, the dolls, the books, the jigsaw puzzles, lunchboxes and so on) is but one of many examples of this (worldwide) exploitation of one product in as many markets as possible' (Newbold et al., 2002).

key terms

Mass media Means of communication through which content – news, sport, music, drama, writing, advertising – are transmitted to large audiences.

Media concentration The concentration of mass media ownership into fewer and fewer organisations.

Vertical integration One company acquiring all aspects of the production and distribution of a single type of media product.

Horizontal integration One organisation buying up companies from different media, concentrating ownership across different kinds of media.

Transnational ownership The ownership by a single company of media organisations which operate in two or more countries.

summary

1. The mass media are the means of communication through which messages are produced by organisations and received by audiences.

2. Most people use the mass media extensively for information and entertainment.

3. Ownership and control of the mass media has become increasingly concentrated in recent years due to vertical integration, horizontal integration and transnational ownership.

activity2 media integration and concentration

Item A Time Warner

Time Warner, the world's largest media company, has grown through mergers and acquisitions.

- In 1990, Time merged with Warner Communications and became Time Warner.
- In 1996, Time Warner acquired Turner Broadcasting System.
- In 1996, Time Warner merged with AOL (America Online).

Time Inc. is the largest magazine publisher in the USA and a leading publisher in the UK and Mexico. Its magazines include *Time, Fortune, Ideal Home* and *Nuts*.

Warner Bros. Entertainment produces feature films and TV series and distributes DVDs worldwide.

Turner Broadcasting System owns a number of television networks. It produces CNN, a 24-hour cable TV news service and CNN Internation which reaches more than 200 countries.

AOL is a leading global web services company with a worldwide audience.

HBO (Home Box Office) delivers two 24-hour pay television services offering movies on demand with over 40 million US subscribers. It has joint ventures in various countries, for example HBO Brasil, HBO Poland and HBO India.

Time Warner Cable is the second largest cable operator in the USA.

Joint operations There are joint operations between the divisions within Time Warner – for example, between In2TV and TMZ.com and AOL and Warner Bros.

Source: timewarner.com, 2009

Time Warner Center, New York

Item B Media concentration in the USA

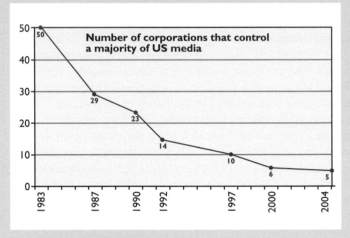

Number of corporations that control a majority of US media

The five corporations which controlled most of the mass media in the USA in 2004 were Time Warner, Disney, Viacom, News Corporation and Bertelsmann.

Source: Bagdikian, 2004

questions

1 How does Item A illustrate both vertical and horizontal integration?

2 How do Items A and B indicate media concentration?

Unit 2 Ownership and control of the media

keyissues

1 Does it matter who owns and controls the media?

2 Do the media provide the information required for an informed citizenship?

What is the relationship between ownership and control of the mass media? To what extent do the owners of media corporations control the content of the media they produce? Does media concentration matter? Are we well served by the mass media on offer? These are some of the questions addressed in this unit. These questions are examined in terms of two sociological theories – pluralism and Marxism.

2.1 Pluralism

Pluralism – the theory

Pluralism is a sociological theory which presents the following picture of Western societies. These societies are seen as *representative democracies* – societies in which the concerns and interests of the population as a whole and of particular groups within the population are represented. The electorate – those entitled to vote – elect politicians whose job is to represent the nation as a whole. The electorate has the freedom to choose between competing political parties.

Pressure groups or interest groups represent sections of the population. For example, there are a range of interest groups representing various occupations – for instance, professional associations such as the British Medical Association representing doctors and trade unions such as the National Union of Teachers representing teachers. Pressure groups, as their name suggests, put pressure on the government to further the interests of their members. Some pressure groups represent more vulnerable groups in society – for example, the Child Poverty Action Group represents the interests of the poor. And, at the other end of the scale, the Confederation of British Industry represents the interests of the owners, managers and shareholders of private industry.

From a pluralist point of view, no one group is dominant in society – to some extent all groups have a say in the running of society, and all adults have the freedom to choose who governs society.

Pluralism and the media

Reflecting public demand The pluralist picture of a representative democracy is reflected in pluralist views of the media. It states that the content of the mass media mirrors what the public, or a section of the public, wants. The media cater to the public as a whole or to particular groups in society. Put another way, the media simply respond to the demands of the market.

Those who own and control the media usually take a pluralist view, arguing that they must satisfy public demand to stay in business. If they failed to do this, nobody would buy their newspapers or watch their TV programmes.

Diverse society, diverse media The media present a range of views which reflect the diversity of opinions in society. The pluralist theory of power states that no one group dominates the whole of society – power is shared among a range of groups. The mass media mirror this diversity. They present a wide range of views, which allows the audience freedom to choose between them. Minority views and tastes are catered for because of the choice of newspapers, magazines, films, radio and TV channels available in a free market.

The media may be biased in certain ways but this is simply because the views they broadcast are those that most people sympathise with and want to hear. If asylum seekers are represented as a 'problem', it is because this reflects the majority view; if women are portrayed in domestic roles, this reflects the reality of most women's lives.

Digital technology All forms of communication, from statistical data to the human voice, can be coded, stored and relayed in a digital form. Increasingly, consumers can access this material – for example, they can select films and music from huge digital libraries. From a pluralist view, this can be seen as a transfer of power from owners to audiences. It puts audiences in the driving seat – they choose what and when to access (Murdock & Golding, 2005). According to Rupert Murdoch, owner and chief executive of News Corporation, 'This technology has liberated people from the once powerful media barons' (quoted in Greenslade, 1993).

Media concentration Does media concentration matter? Are we, the audience, well served by the concentration of ownership and control in the hands of a few, extremely powerful, media magnates?

Many pluralists argue that concentration of ownership is essential for survival in an increasingly global market. Only global companies such as Time Warner, Viacom and News International have the resources to provide audiences with a wider choice and a greater range of media products at affordable prices. Increasing media concentration should therefore be welcomed (Curran & Seaton, 1997).

Media deregulation In many countries there are laws which regulate the ownership and content of the media. For example, in the UK, television broadcasts were formerly limited to the BBC, a state-owned organisation controlled by a board of governors appointed by the Home Secretary. The content of broadcasts was regulated by the rules of public service broadcasting which stated that the BBC should 'inform, educate and entertain'. In practice, this meant a balance between entertainment on the one hand and news and documentaries on the other hand.

From 1954, with the introduction of commercial television, there has been steady reduction of the regulations governing the media. This process is known as *media deregulation*. In terms of television, this has resulted in a rapid expansion in the number of channels and increased competition between terrestrial, satellite and cable companies. The rules governing programme content have been reduced – for example, MTV is clearly not bound by the requirements of public service broadcasting.

In most countries, there are laws which limit the concentration of media ownership. They are designed to prevent organisations from dominating large sections of the media. In recent years, these laws have been relaxed. This is a further example of media deregulation.

In general, pluralists welcome media deregulation. They

key terms

Pluralism A theory which sees power widely dispersed in democratic societies.

Representative democracy A system of government in which the people are represented by elected officials.

Media deregulation The reduction or abolition of laws limiting media ownership and regulating media output.

argue that private ownership of the media is the most effective way to provide a wide range of choice. Privately owned media organisations compete with each other to give audiences what they want. If audiences reject their products, they would go out of business. By contrast, publicly owned media and state regulation can be seen as dangerous since they concentrate too much power in the hands of government, offer limited choice and are unresponsive to their audience.

activity3 catering for all tastes

question

What support do these items provide for the pluralist view that the media cater for a range of groups in society?

2.2 Pluralism – an evaluation

The previous section outlined pluralist views of the relationship between ownership and control of the media and presented evidence to support those views. This section looks at criticisms of pluralist views.

Media concentration and democracy

In *The New Media Monopoly*, Ben Bagdikian (2004) makes the following criticisms of pluralist views. His evidence is drawn mainly from America.

In 1983, most of the mass media in the USA was owned and controlled by 50 corporations. By 2004, the media were dominated by five giant corporations – Time Warner, Disney, News Corporation, Bertelsmann and Viacom. According to Bagdikian, this increasing media concentration has very serious consequences. It has moved politics in the USA towards the far right – the views broadcast are increasingly conservative and there is little room for liberal or radical voices. These views reflect those of the media owners – and the advertisers on whom the owners depend for their profits.

Media concentration has also resulted in less and less local news and local voices. For example, the largest radio chain has over 1,200 local radio stations but only 200 employees. The programmes are pre-recorded and the same programmes are broadcast by local stations throughout the USA.

Bagdikian argues that both local and national democracy are under threat. Despite more and more TV channels and radio stations, choice has been narrowed since they're all broadcasting more and more of the same thing – more 'reality' shows, more sitcoms and soaps, more movies. There is little diversity of opinion in the news and little access to local TV and radio.

In a democracy, citizens need to be informed – they need a range of views, a variety of opinions and information from which to make informed choices. Broadcast media are required by law to operate 'in the public interest'. According to Bagdikian, they are failing to do this and, in the process, failing to produce the informed voters essential for a democracy.

The drive for profits

In the UK, the BBC is funded by a licence fee. All other broadcasting media – commercial TV and radio – are funded by advertising (eg, ITV) or subscription (eg, BSkyB). As a public service broadcaster, the BBC is required to 'inform, educate and entertain'. The information it broadcasts should be 'accurate and impartial' and it should produce a variety of programmes to cater for all groups in society. Ofcom – the Office for Communications – regulates the output of both the BBC and commercial broadcasters. As with ownership, the rules governing the content of broadcasting have been relaxed. For example, TV channels can now specialise in popular music (eg, MTV), sport (eg, Sky Sports 1 and 2) or shopping (eg, the Shopping Channel).

Privately owned commercial broadcasters are in business to make money. Their primary aim is profit rather than public service. And this is the main influence on media content. Evidence to support this view is given in the following examples.

Infotainment The need to make more money by increasing readership of newspapers has led to the growth of the 'human interest' story. This has largely replaced political coverage in the tabloid press (McCullagh, 2002). Now news has become 'infotainment' – part of the entertainment industry. Gossip about the 'instant stars' created by reality TV programmes such as *Big Brother* is regularly reported in tabloid newspapers. Investigative journalists have been replaced by celebrity columnists and presenters (Franklin, 1997).

Advertising revenue The importance of advertising as a major source of revenue has encouraged media organisations to focus on audiences with significant purchasing power. This means mass audiences – in general, the larger the audience the higher the advertising fees – or smaller audiences with spending power such as the young people who watch MTV and the readership of 'quality' newspapers such as the *Times* and *Telegraph*. This has led to a decline in the number of newspapers and minority interest programmes whose audiences are relatively poor (Curran & Seaton, 1997).

At the same time, the boundary between media content and advertising is being broken down (Murdock, 1992). For example, companies pay for products to be 'placed' in films.

Digital technology

Does digital technology increase audience choice and control as some pluralists argue? The first criticism of this view is that audiences often have to pay to access the vast libraries of digital products. This excludes some who cannot afford to pay.

Secondly, power lies with those who own and control cultural products such as films, books, newspapers, recorded music and images. Media corporations can decide what is made available and at what price (Murdock & Golding, 2005).

The influence of proprietors

The pluralist view argues that the power of media proprietors (owners) to influence media content is limited by their need to make profits. If proprietors printed or broadcast views which did not reflect those of their audience, then they may well go out of business.

How much do proprietors influence the content of the media they produce? Answers to this question fall into two main approaches – the *instrumental* and the *structural*.

The instrumental approach This approach argues that the proprietors of media organisations directly influence the content of the media they own. Between the two world wars, press barons such as Lord Rothermere and Lord Beaverbrook used their newspapers to put across conservative political views. Some researchers argue that the growing concentration of the media has increased the power of proprietors who frequently mount propaganda campaigns 'to defend the economic, social and political agenda of privileged groups' (Herman & Chomsky, 1988).

For example, Rupert Murdoch, owner and chief executive of News Corporation admits that he exercises editorial control on major issues in many of the newspapers in his global empire. In newspapers like *The Sun* and *News of the World,* he decides policy on the European Union and which political party to support in a general election (House of Lords, 2008).

The structural approach This approach also recognises that top media executives exercise considerable power.

activity4 the influence of proprietors

Item A Rupert Murdoch

Rupert Murdoch is the owner and chief executive of News Corporation, a global media company. Murdoch owns 175 newspapers on three continents. They publish 40 million papers a week and dominate the newspaper markets in Britain, Australia and New Zealand. In an interview in his own *Sydney Daily Telegraph*, Murdoch backed President Bush's stance against Saddam Hussein and called for war against Iraq. And the editors of his 175 newspapers around the world mirrored his views, supporting military action against Saddam.

Source: *The Guardian*, 17.2.2003 and *The Independent*, 18.10.2004

Item B Conducting his campaign

This graphic by Steve Caplin gives one view of Murdoch's campaign for war against Iraq.

Item C What his papers say

The tyranny of Saddam and the danger to innocent lives demand the world responds.

Sydney Daily Telegraph

There comes a time when evil must be stopped, and it is better to do that sooner rather than later.

Brisbane Courier-Mail

The doubters must say how much more time they would give Saddam to play his delaying games.

Wellington Dominion-Post

Stick with the friend you can trust through and through – America.

The Sun

Item D Murdoch's leadership style

Richard Searby, one-time chairman of News Corporation, describes Rupert Murdoch's leadership style.

'Most company boards meet to take decisions. Ours meets to ratify – confirm and rubber stamp – Rupert's decisions. For much of the time, you don't hear from Rupert. Then, all of a sudden, he descends like a thunderbolt from hell to slash and burn all before him. Since nobody is ever sure when the next autocratic intervention will take place (or on what subject), they live in fear of it and try to second guess what he would want, even in the most unimportant of matters.'

Quoted in Neil, 1996

The Sun and the *News of the World*, owned by Rupert Murdoch's News Corporation, used to support the Conservative Party. In the 1997 election, both papers changed their support to Tony Blair's Labour party. According to Andrew Neil who worked for Murdoch as a newspaper editor for 11 years, the decision to back Labour 'was entirely Rupert's. Their editors played almost no part in the decision and many of the staff, especially on *The Sun*, were very unhappy about it. But they had no say in the matter and were never consulted.'

Source: House of Lords, 2008

question

How do Items A, B, C and D support the claim that proprietors sometimes influence the content of the news media?

However, those who favour this approach argue that it is impossible for one individual to control the day-to-day output of huge media organisations such as Rupert Murdoch's News Corporation. They see Murdoch's power as *allocative control* – the power to set the goals of the organisation, to make key financial decisions and to set the tone and politics of his products (Williams, 2003). In Murdoch's case, key decisions relating to the press have involved:

- Relocating the production of his British newspapers in 1986 from Fleet Street to Wapping, where new technology could be employed to destroy the power of the print unions

- Appointing editors who share his views and firing those who do not toe the line

- Reducing the price of his newspapers to drive out competitors (Eldridge et al., 1997).

Despite the limitations of allocative control, it is still possible for proprietors to express their own views in the media they own. Evidence to support this claim is given in Activity 4.

2.3 Marxism

The theory

Karl Marx (1818-1883) argued that human society was made up of two parts – the *infrastructure* or economic base and the *superstructure* which, in capitalist industrial society, includes the political, legal and educational systems, the mass media and beliefs and values. The superstructure is largely shaped by the infrastructure – in other words, the economic base largely shapes the rest of society.

Social classes According to Marx, every society has two main social groups, a *ruling class* and a *subject class*. The power of the ruling class comes from its ownership of what Marx called the *means of production*. This includes the land, raw materials, machinery, tools and buildings used to produce goods. Thus in Western industrial society, *capitalists* – those who own private industry – form the ruling class. The subject class – the *proletariat* – is made up of workers who sell their labour in return for wages.

There is a basic conflict of interest between capitalists and workers. The workers produce wealth in the form of goods yet a large part of that wealth is taken in the form of profits by the capitalist class. Thus one group gains at the expense of the other.

Marx believed that this conflict could not be resolved within the framework of capitalist society. It would eventually result in the overthrow of the capitalist class. A workers' revolution would lead to a communist society in which the means of production would be owned by everyone, classes would disappear, and exploitation and oppression would end.

Ruling class ideology This, however, would only happen when workers became fully aware of their exploitation. But this awareness will not occur overnight because of the way society is structured. Since the infrastructure largely shapes the superstructure, the relationship of dominance and

activity5 the drive for profits

Item A Infotainment

AND TONIGHT, AS IRAN DECLARES WAR ON CHINA AND UNEMPLOYMENT REACHES SEVEN MILLION, WE ASK, WHAT ABOUT THAT ROYAL DIVORCE?

NEWS 24-7

Based on an idea from Glasgow Media Group, 1982

question

Use Items A, B and C to show how the drive for profits may affect media content.

Item B Concentration – local interests

In the 1990s, the USA relaxed radio ownership rules. As a result, large transnational companies started buying up local radio stations. Clearchannel bought large numbers and ended up with three times more stations than its nearest rival. It was accused of ignoring local interests. For example, there was a train derailment of toxic chemicals in Minot, North Dakota in 2002. The *New York Times* claimed that the local Clearchannel station failed to report the incident. This was seen as a result of national programming and the centralisation of news production.

Source: House of Lords, 2008

Item C Concentration – cross promotion

A US study published in 2001 found that media outlets covered their parent company's products much more than those of their rivals. For example, CBS was then owned by Viacom (they are now a separate company) whose holdings included MTV, Simon & Schuster book publishers and Paramount film studios. CBS's morning magazine news programmes were nearly twice as likely to cover Viacom products as those of ABC and NBC combined. The coverage ranged from interviews with contestants on other CBS shows to interviews with the stars of Paramount movies.

Source: House of Lords, 2008

---

subordination between the ruling class and subject class will be reflected in the superstructure. Thus, the political and legal systems will support ruling class power – for example, laws will protect the rights of capitalists to own industry and take profits. In the same way, the beliefs and values of society will support ruling class domination. Thus, capitalism will be seen as reasonable and just, rather than exploitative and oppressive. In this way, beliefs and values will disguise and distort the true nature of society.

In Marxist terms, beliefs and values form a *ruling class ideology*. This produces a *false consciousness* which prevents people from seeing the reality of their situation.

Marxism and the media

In Marx's words, 'the ruling ideas are the ideas of the ruling class'. As part of the superstructure, the mass media will reflect the economic base and present capitalism as normal, reasonable and acceptable. And, as part of the ruling class, those who own and control the media will have a vested interest in portraying capitalist society in a positive light. As a result, the media transmit a conservative, conformist view, promote established attitudes and values, and reinforce the position of the powerful.

Ideology Ralph Miliband's study *The State in Capitalist Society* (1973) provides an example of a Marxist approach to the media. The ruling class have to convince the rest of the population to accept the widespread inequalities which are inevitable in capitalist societies. Miliband points to the power of the dominant classes to control the way people think through *ideology* – a false view of reality. This control

is exercised in part through the mass media.

Miliband rejects the idea of pluralist diversity. He sees the choice of alternative options and ideas presented by the media as very limited. The content of the media reflects the viewpoint of the dominant group in society – the White, male, ruling class. It is not just political reporting that supports the system, the content of entertainment programmes is also seen as supporting the way things are by portraying the capitalist system in a favourable light.

The new 'opium of the people' Miliband describes the media as the new 'opium of the people', adapting Marx's famous phrase, 'religion is the opium of the people'. He sees the media acting like opium, a hallucinatory drug which creates illusions and produces a feeling of wellbeing. This keeps the working class quiet and encourages them to accept a system which, in reality, exploits them.

In a similar vein, Herbert Marcuse (1964) suggests that programmes which simply entertain, plus the promise of consumer satisfaction that advertisements and game shows provide, help to remove any doubts people may have about the organisation of society. Programmes such as *EastEnders* and *Coronation Street* divert attention from the unfair nature of society, give the impression that nothing is radically wrong with the world we live in, and provide enjoyment and a sense of well-being for millions.

Neo-Marxism and cultural hegemony

The picture presented so far is of a society brainwashed by a pervasive ruling class ideology. There appears to be little or no challenge to this ideology. In particular, the media fail to provide alternative views and critical voices.

activity6 entertainment

Item A EastEnders

Item B The National Lottery

question

How might a Marxist interpret Items A and B?

Neo-Marxists ('new' Marxists) present a somewhat different picture. They draw in part on the work of the Italian Marxist, Antonio Gramsci (1891-1937). Gramsci argues that beliefs and ideas are not simply shaped by the economic base. To some extent they have a life of their own.

Cultural hegemony Gramsci refers to the power of ruling class ideology as *cultural hegemony* – the dominance of one set of ideas and beliefs over others. He argues that there are always ideas and beliefs which challenge the dominant ideology and which threaten cultural hegemony. For example, as a result of their experience in capitalist society, workers will, at least partially, see through the dominant ideology and may develop views in opposition to it.

The British sociologist Stuart Hall (1995), has developed Gramsci's argument. He claims that the economic base places real limits on the development of alternative views but it cannot always prevent them. As a result, cultural hegemony is never complete, never totally dominant. To some extent, there are always competing viewpoints, there are always people who challenge dominant beliefs. And these challenges to cultural hegemony can change society.

The media and cultural hegemony To what extent does the media challenge cultural hegemony? Very little, according to researchers such as Ben Bagdikian – see page 81. However, as Activity 7 shows, it is possible to find examples which challenge dominant beliefs.

Marxism – an evaluation

From a Marxist viewpoint, it doesn't particularly matter who owns and controls the mass media – whether it is state owned like the BBC or privately owned like commercial TV. Because of the structure of capitalist society, the media will reflect the views of the capitalist class and broadcast the dominant ideology. Critics have argued that this is not always the case. To some extent, their criticisms have been taken on board by neo-Marxists who accept that there are challenges to cultural hegemony.

Marxists make a judgement about what they see as the dominant ideology. They judge it to be a distorted view of reality which serves to disguise the oppression and exploitation of the capitalist system. As purveyors of the dominant ideology, the mass media are seen as instruments of oppression. Clearly, pluralists would reject this view and see it simply as a value judgement, with little or no basis in reality. From a pluralist viewpoint, the media reflect the concerns and interests of all the major groups in society.

key terms

Allocative control The power to set the goals of an organisation and make key financial decisions rather than day-to-day control.

Infrastructure The economic base of society.

Superstructure The rest of society, including the mass media.

Means of production The things used to produce goods – for example, machinery and raw materials.

Ruling class Those who own the means of production.

Subject class Those who actually produce the goods.

Ruling class ideology A false and distorted picture of society which supports the position of the ruling class.

False class consciousness A false picture of the class system which prevents people from seeing the reality of their situation.

Cultural hegemony The dominant ideas and beliefs in society. There are always alternative ideas and beliefs which threaten cultural hegemony.

activity7 challenging cultural hegemony

Item A Michael Moore

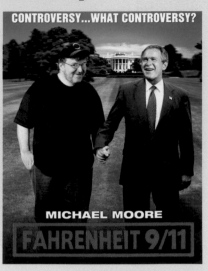

Produced, directed and written by Michael Moore, (holding Bush's hand on the DVD cover), *Fahrenheit 9/11* was a box office success in cinemas across the USA. It was a scathing attack on the Bush administration. In a nutshell, Bush and those surrounding him were portrayed as liars, cheats and frauds, representing the interests of big business rather than those of the people.

A flavour of the film can be seen from the following example. In 2001, the Bush administration said that Iraq did not present a threat to America or the rest of the world. By 2003, all this changed. Iraq had weapons of mass destruction which threatened world peace and there was a close link between Iraq and al Qaeda. We now know that neither of these claims was true. Despite this, President Bush stated that the invasion of Iraq in 2003 was 'to save the world from great danger' and to bring democracy and freedom to the Iraqi people. However, *Fahrenheit 9/11* suggests another reason. In the words of one of the participants, 'If it wasn't for the oil, nobody would be there'.

Item B Reporting Hurricane Katrina

Thousands of desperate people outside the Superdome in New Orleans waiting to be rescued

On August 29, 2005, Hurricane Katrina smashed into the Gulf Coast of the USA. Over 1,000 people were killed and over a million made homeless. New Orleans was flooded when the hurricane broke through its sea defences. Over 60 fires blazed in the city and hundreds of people were trapped in bedrooms and on rooftops. The scenes were horrific. One woman tells how she couldn't get the images of dead babies, women and men floating along the streets out of her head.

Ray Nagin, the mayor of New Orleans, described the rescue operation as a 'national disgrace'. Over 50,000 people were trapped in the city for nearly a week with no electricity, sanitation or medical care and very little food and water. People shouted to the TV cameras: 'We're dying.' 'We haven't eaten for days.' 'Doesn't anybody care?' Many of those who got out were stranded for days on a motorway just outside New Orleans. Buses sent to rescue them did not arrive because there were no plans for housing them. The United States government was totally unprepared for a disaster on this scale, despite being warned for years that it was going to happen.

The American media, not known for their critical stance, became increasingly angry and hostile towards the government. The *New York Times* asked 'Who are we if we can't take care of our own?' The same newspaper stated, 'Thousands of Americans are dead or dying, not because they refused to evacuate New Orleans, but because they were too poor or too sick to get out without help – and help wasn't provided.' Jack Cafferty, a veteran newscaster on CNN TV News angrily stated, 'I have never seen anything as bungled and as poorly managed. Where the hell is the drinking water for these people? Why can't sandwiches be dropped? This is a disgrace.'

Media coverage shocked America. Those who suffered most were poor and Black. Nearly a third of the population of New Orleans lived below the poverty line and around 85% of them were Black. The comments of Jesse Jackson, a civil rights leader, were broadcast across America: 'Today, I saw 5,000 African Americans on Highway 10, desperate, perishing, dehydrated, babies crying – it looked like the hold of a slave ship.'

The results of years of racial discrimination and government indifference to the poor were clear for all to see. Questions were increasingly asked about the Bush administration's policy of cutting taxes for the rich and cutting welfare for the poor. George W. Bush, forced to cut short one of his many holidays to make a personal appearance in New Orleans, denied that race was an issue. Yet, even he, faced with TV pictures which said the opposite, was forced to admit that 'poverty has roots in a history of racial discrimination which cut off generations from the opportunity of America.' What was out of sight, out of mind, ignored and brushed under the carpet, now stared mainstream America in the face.

Source: Various issues of *The Observer* and *The Guardian*, September, 2005

question

How can Items A and B be seen as challenges to cultural hegemony in the USA?

Unit 3 *Globalisation, the media and culture*

keyissues

1 What is globalisation?
2 What part does the media play in the process of globalisation?

3.1 What is globalisation?

Globalisation is the process by which societies become increasingly interconnected. Many researchers believe that the pace of globalisation has speeded up over recent decades. Events in one part of the world increasingly affect other parts, activities in one nation have a growing impact on other nations. Global interactions become more and more frequent as goods, capital, people, knowledge, culture, fashions and beliefs flow across national boundaries. Here are some examples of globalisation.

Economic globalisation Financial transactions are increasingly global. The existence of stock exchanges in various countries means that the buying and selling of shares can continue round the clock. The financial market is now global. For example, the 'credit crunch' in 2008/09 began in the USA and rapidly spread to financial markets across the world.

The economies of nation-states are increasingly part of a global economic system. There has been a rapid growth in the size of transnational corporations (TNCs) – companies which operate in a number of countries, for example Ford, Sony, Nestlé and Nike. They can move production from one country to another, wherever economic conditions are most favourable. And they sell their products to world markets.

activity8 globalisation

Item A *9-11*

Attack on the World Trade Center, New York, September 11, 2001

Item B *Coca-Cola*

Playing dominoes in Egypt beneath a Coca-Cola advert

question

How do Items A and B illustrate globalisation?

Political globalisation More and more nation-states are becoming members of international organisations. These organisations include the UN (United Nations), NATO (North Atlantic Treaty Organisation) and the EU (European Union). International financial institutions such as the World Bank and the IMF (International Monetary Fund) have steadily grown. For example, the IMF, which among other things provides loans for its members, has grown from 25 members in 1945 to 185 in 2008 (imf.com, December 2008).

Cultural globalisation The world is increasingly exposed to Western tastes, styles and fashions, music and films, transmitted by international marketing corporations and transnational media corporations. According to some researchers, this is leading to the emergence of a global consumerist culture (Sklair, 2003).

Globalisation and risk According to the German sociologist Ulrick Beck (1992), we live in a *global risk society*. Global risks cross national boundaries. For example, the explosion at the nuclear power station at Chernobyl in the former Soviet Union in 1986 resulted in radioactive material blown westward across Europe reaching 20 countries (see page 10). Global risks include global warming, pollution, deforestation, depletion of fish stocks in the world's oceans, devastating accidents such as major oil spills, diseases such as AIDS, and international terrorism.

3.2 Media imperialism and cultural imperialism

Media imperialism From the 1960s to the mid-1980s, the media's role in globalisation was often seen in a negative light. Many researchers saw the developing world as subordinate to Western interests – transnational corporations were seen to exploit developing countries.

The part played by global media organisations in this process was known as media imperialism. The power and influence of transnational media corporations was seen as a new form of imperialism – similar, in certain respects, to the colonial rule of European powers in the 19th and first half of the 20th century.

Cultural imperialism Media imperialism was seen to result in cultural imperialism – the imposition of Western culture on developing countries. Transnational media organisations were said to transmit Western values and attributes across the developing world. Here is an example of this view. 'The global television music of MTV, the global news of

activity9 cultural imperialism

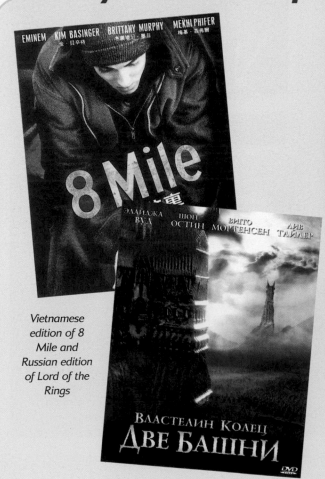

Vietnamese edition of 8 Mile and Russian edition of Lord of the Rings

Buying pirated videos and DVDs in Shanghai, China. Titles include Gone With The Wind and Disney's Sleeping Beauty.

question

How can these items be used to support the idea of cultural imperialism?

CNN, the global box office hits of Hollywood films and the global soap operas shape the cultures of the developing world, ensuring their Westernisation' (Williams, 2003).

From this point of view, Western media corporations such as Time Warner, Disney and News Corporation dominate mass media news and entertainment in the developing world. As a result, local cultures will be battered into submission, swamped with Western media output and will eventually disintegrate.

Evaluation

Many researchers now argue that theories of media and cultural imperialism either go too far or are no longer applicable. Here are some of their criticisms.

Cultural response Research indicates that different cultures interpret media output in different ways. Even when the same TV programmes are shown around the world, people don't necessarily respond to them in the same way. For example, Dutch viewers enjoyed the glossy US soap opera *Dallas* but rejected the programme's celebration of American capitalism (Ang, 1985). And when the rights to programmes such as *Who wants to be a millionaire?* and *Big Brother* are sold to TV companies across the globe, local versions reflecting local cultures are produced. Examples such as these can be used to question cultural imperialism.

National and regional broadcasting There has been a steady increase in local broadcasting specifically aimed at national or regional populations. For example, Aljazeera, a 24-hour satellite news station, was set up in 1996 by the Emir of Qatar. Its main audience is in the Middle East (see Activity 10). There are a growing number of independent media production centres outside the USA and Europe. For example, TV Globo in Brazil produces many of its own programmes and is the dominant force in Brazilian television (Sparks, 2007).

In many countries home produced programmes are steadily replacing imports. They are more attractive to local audiences because they gel with local cultures. Research in Asia showed that in seven of nine countries studied more hours of locally produced television were broadcast than imported programmes (Gorman & McLean, 2003). This suggests that local cultures are not being overwhelmed by Western media products.

Minority ethnic media In some cases, the flow of programmes may be reversed so that local programmes from developing countries are exported to Western societies. For example, British Asians 'maintain strong ties with their countries of origin through the consumption of popular film and television exported from the Indian sub-continent' (Gillespie, 1995). And, in many cases, minority ethnic groups produce their own media products reflecting the culture of their countries of origin. For example, in the USA, Spanish speaking Latinos produce large quantities of recorded music, listen to their own radio stations and watch cable TV programmes specifically designed for their cultural requirements.

3.3 Globalisation and the media

By the 1990s, theories of media and cultural imperialism were partly replaced and partly re-labelled by the more fashionable term globalisation (Sparks, 2007). Here are some of the main views of globalisation theory and the media.

Changing reality Globalisation changes people's perception of reality. It compresses the world – the world seems to be shrinking. Time is also compressed – it appears to be speeding up as events in one part of the world can sometimes be seen thousands of miles away as they occur.

This new reality is known as *time-space compression*. The mass media play an important part in this process. Communication satellites can broadcast events across the globe as they happen. For example, people all over the world watched live transmissions of the destruction to the World Trade Center in New York.

Cultural products As noted earlier, global media corporations have not destroyed local cultures. The situation is complex and multi-layered with a) global, b) regional, c) national and d) local markets and products. From this point of view, Western media corporations do not dominate global markets. Nor are the products they broadcast necessarily Western in content. Often they are hybrid cultural products, combining aspects of several cultures (Sparks, 2007).

TNCs and state power Some globalisation theorists argue that the globalisation of the media has reduced the power of nation-states to control what their populations see and hear. Transnational media corporations transcend nation-states; satellite broadcasting systems and the internet bypass national boundaries.

Evaluation

Some researchers reject the view that the power of nation-states to control media output has been reduced. There is evidence to show that nation-states are not helpless in the face of global media corporations. For example, attempts to establish hard-core pornographic satellite TV subscription

key terms

Globalisation The process by which societies become increasingly connected.

Transnational corporations Companies which operate in a number of countries.

Global risk society A global society in which human-made risks cross national boundaries.

Media imperialism A new form of imperialism in which Western media corporations dominate global media output.

Cultural imperialism The imposition of Western culture on developing countries.

Time-space compression The process by which time seems to be speeding up and space appears to be getting smaller.

services for the UK have been prevented by domestic British law.

The power of the state to regulate satellite broadcasting can be seen from negotiations between China and Rupert Murdoch's News Corporation. Murdoch's Star TV satellite service was designed to broadcast to China. In order to do so, it had to abide by Chinese law and adapt its programmes to fit government requirements. For example,

activity10 questioning cultural imperialism

Item A Aljazeera

Aljazeera newsroom, Qatar

Aljazeera provides an alternative to Western produced global news channels such as CNN. It was set up in 1996 by Sheik Hamad, the Emir of Qatar, a small state in the Middle East. Its income comes from an annual grant from the Emir, from adverts, and from syndicating its programmes to other TV channels. It has 30 news-gathering offices around the world and an estimated 50 million viewers, mainly in the Arab Middle East.

Source: Haralambos & Jones, 2006

Poster, Brick Lane, London

Item B Minority ethnic media

Red Records, Brixton, South London, specialising in African-Caribbean music

Reading The Voice, an African-Caribbean newspaper

Radio presenter at Sunrise Radio, an Asian radio station

question

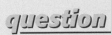

How can these items be used to question the idea of cultural imperialism?

the BBC world news was removed from Star TV because the authorities considered it too critical of China (Sparks, 2007).

The above examples show that nation-states have the power to regulate the output of transnational media corporations.

summary

1. There are a number of aspects to globalisation. They include:
   - Economic globalisation
   - Political globalisation
   - Cultural globalisation.
2. According to Beck, we live in a global risk society.
3. Some researchers accuse Western transnational media corporations of media imperialism and cultural imperialism.
4. Critics of media and cultural imperialism make the following points.
   - Different cultures interpret the same media output in different ways.
   - Local versions of Western programmes reflect local cultures.
   - There has been a steady increase in local media products specifically aimed at national or regional populations.

- Minority ethnic groups often consume media products imported from their countries of origin.
- Minority ethnic groups often produce their own media products which reflect the culture of their countries of origin.

5. To some extent media and cultural imperialism theory was replaced in the 1990's by globalisation theory.
6. According to globalisation theory:
   - Global media output plays an important part in time-space compression.
   - Western media corporations do not dominate global markets.
   - The increasing globalisation of the media has reduced the power of nation-states to regulate media output.
7. Critics argue that nation-states have the power to regulate the output of transnational media corporations.

activity11 state regulation

Liu Chang Lee, Chairman of Phoenix TV, a Chinese television company, gives the following advice to foreign media companies seeking to broadcast to China.

'Foreign media companies need to develop a dialogue with bureaucratic agencies that regulate the media and entertainment market. The purpose of this dialogue is on the one hand to enable the foreign company to understand the Chinese environment more clearly, and at the same time convince the Chinese side that foreign media organisations are not seeking to destabilise China, sow the seeds of social or political trouble, or weaken China's sense of cultural identity.'

Source: quoted in Sparks, 2007

James Murdoch (Rupert's son) chairman and CEO of Star TV after signing an agreement in 2001 to broadcast a 24-hour Mandarin language entertainment channel in southern China.

question

Why does the Chinese government want to regulate the output of foreign media companies?

Unit 4 Selection and presentation of news

keyissues

1 How is news constructed?

2 What are moral panics and how do they arise?

4.1 The construction of news

This unit looks at the selection and presentation of news. Williams (2003) identifies three important influences on media content.

- The power of those who actually work in the media – people like journalists

- The day-to-day organisation and routine of media companies

- The culture of society – its wider norms and values.

We shall examine each of these factors in terms of the production of news.

The influence of media workers

An influential study conducted by White in 1950 argued that particular individuals play a significant role in determining which items make news. This study was based on the decisions made by one news editor on what should appear as national and international news in a small American newspaper. White's study suggested that the editor's individual prejudices played a significant role in the selection process. He acted as a *gatekeeper,* only allowing his preferred stories to pass through the 'gate' into the news.

Later research has challenged this view. An investigation of the selections made by a number of news editors did not find any significant variation in the news items they chose (Williams, 2003). This suggests that individual media workers are influenced in their decision-making by the organisations in which they work rather than their own preferences. Such a suggestion is reinforced when we realise that the selection of news involves many people – no one individual can be held responsible for the final product.

The influence of organisational structures

Watch the 10 o'clock news on ITV and BBC. While there is some variation in the events reported, there is also a noticeable similarity between the two news broadcasts on any day. This agreement over what counts as 'news' is the starting point for sociologists who highlight the importance of organisational structures in shaping the news. They believe that the routines of news organisations and the occupational socialisation of journalists are vital in explaining the content of the news.

Routines A daily newspaper works on a 24-hour cycle. To ensure that the news is fresh, one routine adopted is to focus on events that occur within that cycle. A train crash occurring since the previous day's newspaper is more likely to be reported as news than a famine that unfolds over time.

To make the reporting of events manageable, newspapers are divided up into sections (foreign news, crime news, sports news etc) and specialist correspondents are allocated to report on different kinds of news. Events happening in the real world are squeezed into these sections, with those occurring in locations where journalists are placed the most likely to be reported. So we know more about what is happening in North America and Europe than in South America and Africa.

News values Journalists learn the kind of events seen as newsworthy in the course of their professional socialisation. They pick up a set of informal rules or *news values* which enable them to identify what is newsworthy. A former editor of *The Guardian* identifies these news values as follows:

Significance: social, economic, political, human.

Drama: the excitement, action and entertainment in the event.

Surprise: the freshness, newness, unpredictability.

Personalities: royal, political, 'showbiz', others.

Sex, scandal, crime: popular ingredients.

Numbers: the scale of the event, numbers of people affected.

Proximity: on our doorsteps, or 10,000 miles away?

(Hetherington, 1985).

Events that correspond to these values are more likely to be identified as newsworthy than others. What's more, in reporting these events, journalists tend to present them in dramatic and personalised terms. 'Surprises' become 'shocks'; 'disagreements' become 'open conflicts'; and political debates are translated into choices between rival personalities (McCullagh, 2002).

News values have to be interpreted on a daily basis, with newspapers differing in the priority they give to some news values over others. However, there is often a remarkable similarity across the British news media when it comes to the main story of the day (Allan, 1999).

Objectivity Journalists often claim to be objective – to provide balanced and neutral accounts of events. Tuchman (1978) argues that the desire for objectivity means that the news media adopt a number of conventions in reporting the news. Facts are distinguished from opinions, with hard news, for example, being separated from editorial comment. The most important elements of the story are presented first, with the background outlined later. Different sides of the story are given; supporting evidence is produced for the claims made; and reliable sources are quoted.

However, in practice, these conventions mean that the voices of powerful organisations such as the government are often given prominence as they tend to be seen by the media as credible and authoritative.

Frameworks To enable newsworthy events to be understood by audiences, the news media place them within familiar frameworks. Take the coverage of two seemingly similar tragedies, the shooting down of a Korean civilian airliner by the Soviet Union in 1983 and the shooting down of an Iranian airbus by the USA in 1986. Both events took place during the 'cold war' when communism was seen as a threat to Western societies. In this context, a common way of interpreting events involved a contrast between the civilised West and the uncivilised East. In both the American and British news media, this familiar framework was employed to interpret what happened in 1983 and 1986. The first event was presented as 'a barbaric, terrorist, heinous act', while the second was presented as 'an understandable accident' (McNair, 1996).

This framework was of course not the only one that could have been used. The Soviet (Russian communist) news media reversed the Western view and interpreted the first event as an unfortunate accident and the second as a terrorist act.

In Britain and America the same framework was used across the news media and reflected how both governments saw these incidents. Hall et al., (1978) argue that this is not uncommon and that powerful groups are able to act as *primary definers*. Less powerful voices may be heard, but these voices are often drowned out. And when they are not drowned out, they are often ridiculed.

Evaluation Sociologists agree that we need to take account of the influence of both media owners and organisational factors in order to understand the production of media messages. In many cases, these influences mean that media coverage reflects the interests of powerful groups. However, this is not always the case.

Powerful groups do not always speak with one voice. This means that there can be conflict over how events are to be interpreted. Powerful groups disagreed about war with Iraq in 2003. And they are bitterly divided over Britain's adoption of the euro as its currency. In these instances, it is not possible to identify one primary definition of the issues.

The media sometimes challenge powerful groups. Some investigative journalists can become the primary definers, with powerful groups being obliged to respond to the way the media define the issues. Two journalists on the

activity12 *news values*

Item A Islanders consider exodus as sea levels rise

Tuvaluan children playing in the sea which threatens to swamp their island

Faced with the prospect of being swamped by rising sea levels, the Pacific island nation of Tuvalu is considering evacuating its 9,300 residents.

With sea levels predicted to rise by more than 80 cm over the next century due to global warming, Tuvaluans are living on borrowed time. The most recent figures suggest that Tuvalu's sea levels have risen nearly three times as fast as the world average over the past decade, and are now 5 cm higher than in 1993.

Source: *The Guardian*, 19.7.2003

Item B Harry is 'out of control'

Prince Harry's late-night drinking and wild behaviour have forced one of his royal protection officers to quit. Sergeant Ieuan Jones was transferred to other duties after telling colleagues he could not cope with the tearaway Prince.

One Buckingham Palace worker said: 'He won't do what he is told and when you are dealing with the safety of someone like him that is a dangerous situation. They get totally fed up sitting around in pub after pub while Harry knocks back drink after drink. They can only have tonic water or coke and it gets very boring indeed for them.'

Source: *Sunday Express*, 20.7.2003

Item C A balanced discussion

"AND TO ENSURE A BALANCED AND IMPARTIAL DISCUSSION OF THE LATEST GOVERNMENT MEASURES, I HAVE WITH ME A GOVERNMENT SPOKESMAN AND A WILD-EYED MILITANT FROM THE LUNATIC FRINGE."

Source: Developed from an idea in *Glasgow Media Group*, 1982

Item D Reporting the intifada

The Glasgow Media Group analysed coverage of the Palestinian intifada (uprising) in 89 TV news bulletins broadcast by BBC1 and ITV in 2000. They found important differences in the language used to describe Israeli and Palestinian deaths. When Israelis were killed, words such as 'murder', 'atrocity', 'lynching' and 'savage cold-blooded killing' were used. But when Palestinians died at Israeli hands, the language used was considerably more moderate.

Source: Philo & Miller, 2002

questions

1 Assess the 'newsworthiness' of the news stories in Items A and B using the list of news values.

2 What point is being made by the cartoon in Item C? What does it suggest about the influence of the powerful?

3 What does Item D suggest about the claim that TV news is objective?

Washington Post, for example, uncovered a range of illegal activities by the US government that culminated in the resignation of the President in 1974 (Schlesinger,1991). And in 2005, the *Washington Post* revealed the existence of a network of detention centres in eastern Europe set up by the USA to interrogate suspected terrorists.

The influence of wider culture

What counts as news and the way it is reported will, to some extent, reflect the wider culture – the shared norms, values, concerns and beliefs of society. To take an obvious example, baseball, ice hockey, basketball and American football dominate sports reporting in newspapers in the USA. They are rarely found in British newspapers.

News often reflects strongly held values. For example, murder is regularly reported and condemned. This reflects the high value placed on human life.

News reporting often draws on widely held cultural stereotypes. For example, Schudson (2000) argues that news reports which represent young Black people as a problem and women as sex objects reflect shared cultural stereotypes.

We live in an age where organisations attempt to manage the news, to 'spin' information in order to present themselves in the best possible light. They try to ensure that their actions are seen to be in line with society's norms and values. For example, Tony Blair's Labour government was accused of exaggerating the threat of weapons of mass destruction in order to justify the war against Iraq and the deaths of British soldiers and Iraqi civilians.

However, governments and powerful organisations are not always able to portray their actions as fitting the norms and values of society. For example, it is difficult for governments and business organisations to control media coverage when accidents such as oil spills and explosions at nuclear plants occur (McCullagh, 2002).

Conclusion

Most researchers see the construction of news in the following way. Here's how Graeme Burton (2005) summarises the process of news creation.

- News is socially constructed – it is created within a framework of social relationships and cultural beliefs.

- There is no 'truth out there' which is reported in the news.

- News consists of information that is selected and interpreted on the basis of national norms, values and concerns.

- Those who actually construct the news – editors and journalists – do so within organisational structures and in terms of news values. These structures and values define what counts as news.

key terms

Gatekeeping Making decisions about what will and will not become 'news'.

News values A set of informal rules used by journalists to identify what is newsworthy.

Primary definers Individuals and groups who are able to influence what events become news and how they are reported.

activity 13 news frameworks

The Gulf War (1990-91) was fought between Iraq, led by Saddam Hussein, and the Allies (USA, Britain and a number of other countries) led by the American President George Bush Sr. The table below shows some of the words and phrases used by the British media to describe each side.

Mad dogs and Englishmen

We have	They have
Army, Navy and Air Force	A war machine
Reporting guidelines	Censorship
Press briefings	Propaganda

We	They
Take out	Destroy
Suppress	Destroy
Eliminate	Kill
Neutralise	Kill
Dig in	Cower in their foxholes

We Launch	They Launch
First strikes	Sneak missile attacks
Pre-emptively	Without provocation

Our boys are...	Theirs are...
Professional	Brainwashed
Lion-hearts	Paper tigers
Cautious	Cowardly
Confident	Desperate
Heroes	Cornered
Dare-devils	Cannon fodder
Young knights of the skies	Bastards of Baghdad
Loyal	Blindly obedient
Desert rats	Mad dogs
Resolute	Ruthless
Brave	Fanatical

Source: *The Guardian*, 23.1.1991

questions

1 What framework is the British news media using?
2 The Iraqi news media was tightly controlled by Saddam Hussein's regime.
   a) What framework might they use?
   b) Suggest two phrases they might use to describe the Allies.

4.2 The news and moral panics

Journalists often claim that the news represents a 'mirror on the world' (Allan, 1999). They believe that the news gives an accurate and impartial reflection of events. Research evidence gives a somewhat different picture. Section 4.1 showed that the news media not only select certain events as newsworthy, but also place a particular interpretation on those events. From this point of view, the media construct news rather than mirror the world.

Mods and rockers It is not unusual for the news media – especially the tabloid press – to sensationalise the events they report. This can be seen from the following research. In a groundbreaking study conducted in the 1960s, Stanley Cohen looked at media coverage of the activities of two youth subcultures – mods and rockers. On Easter bank holiday in 1964, large numbers of young people, including mods on their scooters and rockers on their motor cycles, went to Clacton for a day out at the seaside. Cohen was interested in how the media reported their behaviour and the consequences of that reporting.

The media presented a picture of two rival gangs 'hell bent on destruction'. Fighting, vandalism and anti-social behaviour were reported as widespread and those responsible were identified as mods and rockers.

On closer inspection, Cohen found little evidence of serious violence and vandalism. True, there were large crowds of often noisy young people. And there were mods and rockers baiting each other and sometimes getting into scuffles. But most young people did not identify with either group, and were not involved in any disturbances.

The mass media had presented a distorted and sensationalised picture of events. And this media picture created public fears and concerns about mods and rockers. The police responded to these concerns by increasing their presence at seaside resorts on future bank holidays and by making more and more arrests. Young people resented what they saw as heavy-handed and unjustified police behaviour and were more likely to identify with mods and rockers. There were further disturbances followed by yet more sensationalised reporting, and increased police activity in response to public demands to deal with the 'problem'.

Moral panics Cohen argued that the reaction of the media created what he called a *moral panic*. A moral panic exists when 'a condition, episode, person or group of persons emerges to become defined as a threat to societal values and interests' (Cohen, 1987). In this particular case, mods and rockers were singled out as *folk devils* whose behaviour was seen as a threat to social order.

Creating a moral panic Moral panics occur on a regular basis. Newspapers (especially tabloid newspapers) often play a key role in their creation. They sensationalise issues by using emotive headlines, language and pictures. They present groups as stereotypes. They associate those groups with stereotypical behaviour – for example, New Age Travellers with drugs; Black youth with street crime; English football supporters abroad with violence. Contrasts are drawn between a rosy image of the past and a decline in modern-day morals. Finally, the media clamour for a clampdown on the group, and/or the behaviour identified as a threat.

Young people and moral panics Young people continue to be the focus of moral panics. Their behaviour has frequently been identified as a problem. Examples include youth subcultures such as hippies, skinheads and punks, and behaviour associated with young people such as street crime, football hooliganism and drug taking.

Young people are sometimes seen as the victims in moral panics. Critcher (2003) argues that moral panics increasingly focus on threats to children. Concern over child abuse, paedophilia and the influence of violent films on young viewers are examples of these kinds of moral panics.

Features of a moral panic The term moral panic has been taken up widely and is now regularly used by politicians and journalists. Often the term is used quite loosely. Goode and Ben-Yehuda (1994) try to define moral panic precisely. They argue that moral panics have five distinguishing features.

- Increased public concern over the behaviour of a certain group
- Increased hostility towards the group
- A certain level of public agreement that there is a real threat and that it is caused by the group
- Public concern is out of proportion to the real harm caused by the group
- Moral panics appear and disappear very quickly. (Goode & Ben-Yehuda, 1994)

activity14 paedophilia: a moral panic?

Item A Tabloid headline

WE TRAP INTERNET CHILD SEX SICKO

Shocking Internet peril that all concerned parents should be aware of

Source: *The People*, 20.7.2003

Mothers of four murdered children lead a march through central London demanding more action to protect youngsters from paedophiles.

question

With reference to the items, explain how media concern over paedophilia can be described as a moral panic.

Item B Public reaction

Eight-year-old Sarah Payne was abducted while playing near her grandparents' house in West Sussex on July 1st 2000. Her half-buried body was found by a farm labourer on July 17th. On December 12th 2001, a 42-year-old local man and convicted sex offender, Roy Whiting, was found guilty of her 'sexually-motivated' murder and sentenced to life imprisonment.

When Sarah Payne's body was discovered, the *News of the World* launched a campaign: How do you know if there's a paedophile in your midst? The paper published the names and photographs of 50 people it claimed had committed child sex offences, and promised: 'We pledge we will pursue our campaign until we have publicly named and shamed every paedophile in Britain'.

The paper produced figures suggesting 88% of Britons believed parents should be told if a child sex offender was living in their area. It provided a website on which parents could use an interactive map to find their local paedophiles. It asked readers to report any convicted child abusers living in their area. And it published an endorsement of the campaign from Sarah's parents, Sarah and Michael Payne, who later spoke of their unease at being press-ganged into giving the campaign their support.

From Plymouth to Portsmouth, Manchester to London, wrongly identified men and known paedophiles found themselves being hounded by mobs up to 300 strong. The vigilante action was most severe on the Paulsgrove estate in Portsmouth, where protesters circulated a list of 20 alleged sex offenders in the community and proceeded to target them.

The crowds – 40 of whom were later charged with offences – smashed windows, torched cars and forced five families, wrongly identified as harbouring sex offenders, out of their homes. A suspected paedophile in nearby Southampton shot himself dead and a female registrar was hounded from her South Wales home because neighbours confused 'paediatrician' with 'paedophile'.

Source: *The Guardian*, 13.12.2001

Evaluation Critcher (2003) examined five case studies – AIDS, ecstasy and raves, video 'nasties', child abuse in families, and paedophilia. In his view, only two of these cases were full moral panics – video 'nasties' and paedophilia. In these cases an issue was seen as a threat; the media defined the 'problem' in the same way; organised groups generally supported the panic; and the state eventually responded by bringing in new legislation to combat the apparent threat.

Critcher challenges the view that moral panics are always triggered by a concern over identifiable folk devils. What triggered concern in the cases he examined was the death of children or young people. These events were seen to reflect major social problems. In only one of the cases was there an indisputable folk devil – the paedophile.

Critcher argues that a consensus (agreement) is necessary for a moral panic to develop. Some newspapers

*activity*15 *video 'nasties'*

Item A **The Video Recording Bill**

The Video Recording Bill was passed by the Conservative government in 1984. Its aim was to place strict controls on video 'nasties' – videos with high levels of violence and sex which were seen as harmful to children.

Source: Harris, 1984

Item B **Child's Play**

In November 1993, two 11-year-old boys from Merseyside were found guilty of murdering a two-year-old child. The 'horror' video *Child's Play 3* had been rented by the father of one of the boys shortly before the murder. There were certain similarities between scenes in the video and the killing of the child. But there was no evidence that either boy had seen the video. Despite this, the judge at the trial stated, 'I suspect that exposure to violent films may in part be an explanation'.

Source: *The Guardian*, 26.11.1993

Item C **The police view**

Merseyside police detectives who had interviewed the boys for several weeks before the trial rejected any suggestions that 'horror' videos had influenced the boys' behaviour. One detective said, 'I don't know where the judge got that idea from. I couldn't believe it when I heard him. We went through something like 200 titles rented by the family. There were some you or I wouldn't want to see, but nothing – no scene, or plot, or dialogue – where you could put your finger on the freeze button and say that influenced a boy to go out and commit murder.'

Source: *The Independent*, 26.11.1993

Item D **Reaction in Parliament**

In the Commons, the Conservative MP Sir Ivan Lawrence QC called for action to curb 'the constant diet of violence and depravity' fed to youngsters through television, videos and computer pornography. Sir Ivan, chairman of the Home Affairs Select Committee, said it was becoming 'daily more obvious' that this was a major reason for the rise in juvenile crime.

Source: *The Independent*, 26.11.1993

Item E **Burning videos**

Azad Video, Scotland's largest video renting chain, burned its *Child's Play* videos including 300 copies of *Child's Play 3*. Xtra-Vision, the Irish Republic's biggest video chain, withdrew *Child's Play* from its shelves.

Source: *The Sun*, 26.11.93

Item F **The Sun's reaction**

The Sun, 26.11.1993

Item G **Moral panics**

At the turn of the century, there was great concern about violent images in Penny Dreadful comics. In the 1950s, panic that horror comics would lead to children copying the things they saw, led to the Children and Young Persons (Harmful Publications) Act 1955. In the 1980s, there was the huge panic about films such as *Drillerkiller*, which also led to a new law. There's been a recurrent moral panic about violent images which looks to a mythical golden age of tranquil behaviour.

Source: T. Newburn, Policy Studies Institute, quoted in *The Guardian*, 26.11.1993

Item H Press editorials, 26.11.1993

The uncanny resemblance between the film *Child's Play 3* and the murder must be of concern. A link between the film and the crime would not prove that the former caused the latter. Yet it seems quite possible that exposure to images of brutality could turn an already disturbed child towards violence.

Source: *The Independent*

More and more children are growing up in a moral vacuum, which for so many is being filled with fetid (stinking) junk from the lower depths of our popular culture – video nasties, crude comics and violent television.

Source: *Daily Express*

Instead of urging legislation to ban violent films, it would surely be more to the point if we took it upon ourselves as adults to ensure their prohibition in our own homes.

Source: *Daily Telegraph*

questions

1 Read Items A, B, C and D. What justification is there for the views of the judge and Sir Ivan Lawrence? Why do you think they reacted in this way?

2 Do you think the reactions in Items B, D, E, F and H can be described as a moral panic? With some reference to Item G, give reasons for your answer.

Chucky, the evil doll in Child's Play

tried to create a moral panic over AIDS by identifying it as 'a gay plague'. They were unsuccessful because experts challenged this view and AIDS was eventually seen as a health risk to the population as a whole.

Critcher disagrees with the last feature of moral panics identified by Goode and Ben-Yehuda – that they appear and disappear very quickly. He gives examples of moral panics that last for years.

For instance, a moral panic over drugs has continued over the past 40 years. And even when a moral panic ends, it often comes back. For example, there was a moral panic over video nasties from 1982-84. It re-appeared in 1993, as Activity 15 shows.

key terms

Moral panic Widespread public concern, usually fuelled by sensational media coverage, that an event or group is threatening society.

Folk devils Groups whose behaviour is seen as a threat to social order.

summary

1. The production of media content is influenced by professionals such as editors and journalists.

2. The work of professionals in the news media is influenced by organisational factors such as the routines of news reporting and by ideas about what is newsworthy (news values).

3. The wider cultural environment also influences media content. Powerful organisations usually have the ability to become primary definers of the news. And journalists are influenced by dominant cultural values and assumptions.

4. The mass media select certain events as newsworthy and place

a particular interpretation on those events. In this way, the media construct news rather than mirror the world.

5. At times, the media sensationalise the events they report. This can lead to moral panics.

6. Certain groups of young people are seen as a threat to social order and a cause for public concern. Sensationalised reporting of their activities can result in a moral panic.

7. Moral panics sometimes view young people as victims – for example, as victims of paedophiles.

Unit 5 Media representations

keyissues

1 What are representations?

2 How do the media represent different social groups?

5.1 Representations and stereotypes

Representations We experience many events first-hand. We meet other people, go to school or college, visit different areas and so on. The judgements we make about these people, events and places are based on our own direct impressions.

However, we directly experience only a tiny proportion of the world. We rely on the media for knowledge about unfamiliar places, people and events. The sort of information we gain from the media is indirect – the media actually re-present the world to us. In providing these *representations* of the world, the media will highlight some aspects and neglect others. The language they use and the pictures they choose will give particular impressions.

In general, the media do not have very long to provide background detail. For example, news broadcasts are made up of a number of short items. This means that 'shorthand' methods are often used to describe people and events. The media tend to rely on the images of particular groups that are already in the heads of their audience. In other words, they rely on *stereotypes*.

Stereotypes The term stereotype was introduced by the journalist Walter Lippman in his book *Public Opinion*, published in 1922. He described stereotypes as 'the little pictures we carry around in our heads'. Stereotypes are widely-held beliefs about the characteristics of members of social groups. Simply because they belong to a particular group, people are seen to have certain attitudes and behaviour.

Stereotypes are generalisations – they are applied to all members of a group. For example, Germans may be seen as efficient, Black people as good athletes and students as layabouts. Stereotypes can be positive or negative, they can offer a favourable or unfavourable image of a group. Nurses are usually pictured as kind and caring, whereas dealers in stocks and shares are often portrayed as money-grabbing and selfish.

Representations of social groups Representations are important because we depend on the media for much of our information about society. Even when we have direct experience of different social groups, media representations will still be in our heads. This will affect the way we think about and interact with others.

This unit looks at representations of gender, ethnicity, social class, age, sexuality and disability.

activity16 stereotyping

Item A Racial stereotypes

A number of experiments were conducted in the USA using the following procedure. After being shown this picture, one participant described it to a second participant, who then described it to a third, and so on. After six descriptions, over half the final participants reported that the Black person, not the White person, was holding the razor. Some even had the Black person waving the razor in a threatening manner.

Source: Allport & Postman, 1947

Item B American stereotypes of Japanese

1932	1950	1967
intelligent	treacherous	industrious
industrious	sly	ambitious
progressive	extremely nationalistic	efficient

Source: Katz & Braly, 1933; Gilbert, 1951; Karlins, Coffman & Walters, 1969

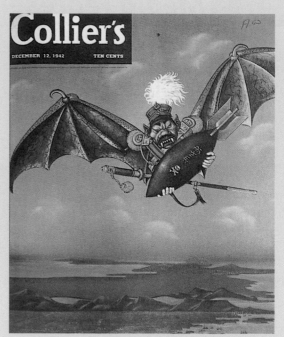

The cover of an American magazine published after the Japanese bombed the American fleet at Pearl Harbor in 1941.

A response by an American cartoonist to the torture and execution of American airmen who had bailed out from damaged planes during a bombing raid over Japan. (Tojo was the Japanese Prime Minister during the Second World War.)

questions

1 Explain the results of the experiment in Item A, using the idea of stereotypes.

2 Look at Item B.
   a) Describe the changes in American stereotypes of Japanese.
   b) Suggest reasons for these changes.

5.2 Representations of gender

Gender stereotypes: the 1950s to 1970s What is a woman? Judging from media representations of women from the 1950s to the 1970s, a woman is a:

- housewife and mother
- domestic servant
- domestic consumer
- sex object.

This stereotypical view of women was particularly apparent in advertising where the roles of housewife, domestic servant and domestic consumer were often combined. For example, women were regularly presented as cleaners, consuming particular brands of washing powder, washing-up liquid, furniture polish, toilet cleansers, air fresheners, disinfectants and the like. At other times, they were presented as sex objects selling products to women to make them appear more attractive to men, or using their sex appeal to sell products to men.

When the media portrayed women outside this narrow stereotype, it was often in negative terms. A study of gender representations in the American media from the 1950s to the 1970s found that women shown in paid employment on TV programmes often had unstable or unsatisfactory relationships with male partners. Married women with jobs, particularly more demanding, higher-status jobs, were much more likely than full-time housewives to be portrayed as unhappily married in television drama and comedy (Tuchman, 1981).

The following quotation by Tunstall (1983) provides a summary of the main findings of research into gender representation in the media from the 1960s and 70s.

'The presentation of women in the media is biased because it emphasises women's domestic, sexual, consumer and marital activities to the exclusion of all else. Women are depicted as busy housewives, as contented mothers, as eager consumers and as sex objects. This does indeed indicate bias because, although similar numbers of men are fathers and husbands, the media has much less to say about these male roles. Just as men's domestic and marital roles are ignored, the media also ignore that well over half of British adult women go out to paid employment, and that many of both their interests and problems are employment-related'.

Patriarchy From a feminist perspective, the gender representations outlined above are an aspect of patriarchy – a social system based on male domination. Women are portrayed either as domestic servants providing comfort and support for men, or as sex objects to service men's sexual needs. In both cases, women play subordinate and subservient roles.

Such media representations suggest that these roles are natural and normal. Feminists see this as an example of patriarchal ideology – a set of beliefs which distorts reality and supports male dominance.

Changes in media representations of gender

There is some evidence that the representation of gender roles has become more equal and less stereotyped. Drawing upon two content analysis studies of gender representations on prime-time TV shows, Gauntlett (2002) identifies the following changes.

- A significant increase in the proportion of main female characters, from 18% in 1992-93, to 43% in 1995-96.
- A massive decrease since the 1970s in the proportion of women whose main occupation was represented as housewife – now only 3%.
- A marked shift towards equality within the last two decades. 'Female and male characters are likely to be as intelligent, talented and resourceful – or stupid – as each other' (Gauntlett, 2002).

Films, soaps and sit-coms

Further evidence that gender representations are changing comes from analysis of films, soap operas and situation comedies. Gauntlett (2002) argues that women and men tend to have similar skills and abilities in films today. While a film like *Charlie's Angels* does focus on women as physically attractive, they are also presented as 'amazingly multi-skilled'.

Strong female characters are central to British soap operas and many actually drive the stories, for example Peggy Mitchell of *EastEnders* (Abercrombie, 1996).

In situation comedies, women are no longer portrayed in traditional 'feminine' roles. For example, both *Roseanne*

activity 17 gender stereotypes

questions

1 What stereotypes are illustrated in these representations of women?
2 How can they be seen as examples of patriarchal ideology?

and *Absolutely Fabulous* show 'unruly women who refuse the straightjacket of femininity' (Newbold et al., 2002).

Women's magazines Evidence of changes in gender representations are also evident in magazines targeted at young women. Ferguson (1983) conducted a study of young women's magazines from 1949 to 1980 and found that they promoted a traditional idea of femininity. The dominant assumption was that girls should aspire to be beautiful in order to get a husband and once married should become home makers and carers.

By contrast, the focus of magazines since the 1980s is on young women seeking to control their own lives rather than being dependent on men. There is now more emphasis on sexuality and less on romance. Articles such as 'The hottest sex you'll ever have' (*MORE!* May, 2003) illustrate this shift. The traditional idea of femininity is challenged, with women no longer portrayed as the weaker sex. Instead, young women are encouraged 'to be assertive,

confident, and supportive of each other' (McRobbie, 1999). In some ways, these magazines turn the tables on men by encouraging women to be sexual aggressors rather than sexual objects (Gauntlett, 2002).

Evaluation Are the changes in media representations of women as significant as the above studies suggest? Think about the following evidence. A study of gender representations on American TV in 1995-96 found that men took 63% of the speaking roles compared to women's 37% (Gauntlett, 2002). Research on television sports coverage reveals that sportswomen continue to be under-represented. What little coverage there is 'tends to sexualise, trivialise and devalue women's sporting accomplishments' (Newbold et al., 2002).

While accepting the above points, available evidence indicates that media representations of women are now less likely to rely on traditional stereotypes and less likely to portray women in a narrow range of subordinate roles.

activity 18 *changing representations of women*

Angelina Jolie as Lara Croft in Tomb Raider

questions

1 How do the items illustrate changes in media representations of women?

2 To what extent do you think the items accurately represent media representation of women today?

5.3 Representations of ethnicity

Research into the media treatment of ethnicity has emphasised the way in which minority ethnic groups are almost always represented as a 'problem'. They tend to be reported as the cause of social disorder (eg, riots) and crime (eg, 'mugging'). While Black youths *are* involved in these actions, so are large numbers of White youths. The negative representation of minority ethnic groups was particularly noticeable in earlier decades, as the following example from the 1980s illustrates.

Racism and the press In a detailed examination of racism and the press, Van Dijk (1991) focused on the reporting of ethnic relations in the 1980s. He studied a sample of British newspapers from 1985 and 1989. His main finding was a positive presentation of White British citizens and a negative presentation of non-White British citizens. Minority group members were quoted less often and less fully than majority group members – even when minority 'experts' were available for comment. White authorities – especially the police and politicians – were the major speakers.

Van Dijk showed that the voice of the British press was predominantly 'white' in both 1985 and 1989, although some improvement was noticeable in the later sample.

Racial stereotypes Most recent studies argue that minority ethnic groups continue to be represented in a stereotypical way. The research, almost without exception, has emphasised the large proportion of negative images in the portrayal of Black and Asian people (Cottle, 2000). Complex differences – for example, those between different minority ethnic groups – are ignored. The point of view is virtually always a White one: that 'of the dominant looking at the subordinate: how *they* are different from us rather than how *we* are different from them' (Ross, 1996)

Overt and inferential racism Both press and television news are often seen by these studies as racist. However, there is a difference between what Hall (1995) calls 'overt' and 'inferential' racism. Overt racism is apparent when racist arguments are presented favourably. Sometimes overt racism does occur but more often what is at issue is inferential racism.

Inferential racism occurs when coverage seems balanced but is based on racist assumptions. Television news and current affairs programmes make an effort to be balanced yet debates are often based on the assumption that Black people are the 'source of the problem' (Hall, 1995).

Changes in media representations of ethnicity

Much of the research on racism and the media relates to the 1970s and early 1980s. In recent years there has been a growth in both the number and range of representations of minority ethnic groups.

Film and television drama and comedy In Britain the ideal of public service broadcasting has allowed Black programming to develop on Channel 4 and BBC2 (Daniels, 1996). This has led to the emergence of Black British cinema through films such as *My Beautiful Launderette* (Higson, 1998).

In recent years, programmes and films developed primarily for minority audiences have become popular with White audiences, for example, the Black sit-com, *Desmond's* and the Asian comedy, *Goodness Gracious Me*. Although integrated casting is still exceptional, Black and Asian actors 'are now playing "ordinary" characters and the new way of presenting Black (and Asian) people effectively says to the audience that Black [and Asian] people are just like White people' (Abercrombie, 1996). This is apparent in popular programmes such as *The Bill* and *EastEnders* in Britain and *The Cosby Show* in America.

It is still rare for Black or Asian actors to receive star billing but even this has become more common. In some cases this has resulted in the production of positive images of minority communities as in the representation of the Black middle-class family the Huxtables in *The Cosby Show*. The overall result has been an expansion in 'the *range* of racial representations and the *complexity* of what it means to be Black [or Asian]' (Hall, 1997).

Advertising Changing representations are also evident in advertising. 'Colonial images and crudely nationalistic emblems are relatively rare in the current period' (Solomos & Back, 1996) and the under-representation of non-Whites in advertising is no longer evident (Glasgow Media Group, 1997). Instead, some multinational corporations now acknowledge and celebrate difference. A classic example is the 'United Colours of Benetton' advertising series in which the message of human unity is based on an acceptance of ethnic and cultural differences (see Activity 19, Item A). While this campaign and others have been criticised for reinforcing ethnic stereotypes, shifts towards a positive valuation of difference can challenge racism (Solomos & Back, 1996).

Even more unsettling to racist beliefs are the attempts by some artists to challenge our traditional ways of looking through the development of new forms of representation. An example is the presentation by Toscani, the photographer responsible for the Benetton campaign, of a series of well known people with transformed racial characteristics. The picture of the 'Black Queen', for example, reveals and challenges our taken-for-granted assumptions about the necessary whiteness of British identity (see Activity 19, Item C).

The news A study from the 1990s of news reporting on TV, radio and in newspapers presents an optimistic picture. The content analysis, conducted over a six-month period from November 1996 to May 1997, revealed that most news items that dealt with racial issues put across an anti-racist message.

No explicit racist messages in cartoons could be found. Extensive coverage was given to instances of racism.

Immigration was treated in a sympathetic way and press silence on racist attacks was no longer evident. Multiculturalism and Islam were more likely to be valued than attacked. And minority voices were more likely to be heard.

However, the extent of progress should not be exaggerated. While deliberate bias against minorities was found to be rare, about a quarter of news items still conveyed a negative message about minority groups. And the old framework depicting minority ethnic groups as a social problem was at times all too evident, especially in the tabloid newspapers (Law, 1997).

Evaluation Research indicates that media representations of ethnicity do change. They are not simply based on the same old negative stereotypes. While old stereotypes do persist, for example in coverage of Islam after September 11th,

media representations of ethnicity are becoming more diverse and more positive.

key terms

Representations The way the mass media portray particular social groups, individuals or events.

Stereotypes Widely-held beliefs about the characteristics of members of social groups.

Content analysis A method of analysing the content of the mass media by counting the number of occurrences of particular words, phrases or images.

Patriarchal ideology The idea that traditional gender roles are natural and inevitable.

activity19 changing representations of ethnicity

Item A   Benetton advertisements

Item B   Obama/McCain colour switch

Item C Queen Elizabeth II

Item D Goodness, Gracious Me

The following dialogue is from the comedy programme *Goodness, Gracious Me*.

The setting is late on a Friday night at an English restaurant in downtown Bombay. Several drunken Indians stagger in. A White waiter helps them into their seats.

'I'm totally off my face. How come every Friday night we end up in a Berni Inn?'

'Cos that's what you do innit? You go out, you get tanked up and you go for an English.'

They peer bleary-eyed at the menu.

'Could I just have a chicken curry?'

'Oh no, Nina, it's an English restaurant, you've got to have something English – no spices.'

'But I don't like it, it's too bland.'

'Jam-mess (*mispronouncing James – the waiter*) What've you got that's not totally tasteless?'

'Steak and kidney pie sir?'

'There you are, steak and kidney pee.'

'No, no. It blocks me up. I won't go to the toilet for a week.'

'That's the whole point of having an English.'

Source: Gillespie, 2002

question

How does each of the items demonstrate that media representations of ethnicity are changing?

5.4 Representations of social class

Media representations of social class have received less attention recently than those of gender and ethnicity. Research has focused primarily on representations of the working class.

Under-representation of the working class Many researchers note how rarely the average working person is represented in the media. 'Studies of 50 years of comic strips, radio serials, television dramas, movies and popular fiction reveal a very persistent pattern, an under-representation of working-class occupations and an over-representation of professional and managerial occupations among characters' (Butsch, 1995). And when it comes to the news, 'working-class people are likely to cross the screen only as witnesses to crimes or sports events, never as commentators or – even when their own lives are under discussion – as "experts"' (Ehrenreich, 1995).

The few representations there have been of the working class have consistently tended to be negative, as the following examples from situation comedies and the news illustrate.

Situation comedies and social class An American study of situation comedies over four decades from 1946 to 1990 showed that working class males were typically represented as buffoons. 'They are dumb, immature, irresponsible or lacking in common sense. This is the character of the husbands in almost every sitcom depicting a blue-collar (White) male head of house, *The Honeymooners*, *The Flintstones*, *All in the Family* and *The Simpsons* being the most famous examples. He is typically well-intentioned, even loveable, but no one to respect or emulate. These men are placed against more mature, sensible wives'. In contrast, situation comedies featuring the middle class typically do not represent either parent as a buffoon but, where they do, it is the 'dizzy wife' as in *I Love Lucy*, with the husband here being portrayed as sensible and mature (Butsch, 1995).

The news and social class In Britain, the Glasgow Media Group have carried out a series of detailed studies of television news (Eldridge, 1995). They argue that the news is not impartial but reflects the interests of powerful groups. The coverage of industrial disputes – involving, for example, strikes of the Glasgow refuse collectors in the 1970s and miners in the 1980s – illustrates this.

- In terms of access to the media, management and the 'experts' receive far more coverage than trade unionists – in the Glasgow refuse strike for example, not one of the 21 interviews broadcast nationally was with a striker.

- Management and trade unionists are treated very differently. The former were usually allowed to make their points quietly and at length; the latter often had to shout over the noises around them or were interrupted by reporters.

The Glasgow Media Group conclude that the overall impression given by the media was that workers caused strikes and that 'excessive' wage demands caused inflation. What is in fact just one interpretation of the cause and effects of industrial disputes is presented as the dominant and authoritative one. This dominant view represents the working class in a negative way.

Even more negative is the depiction of the poor, many of whom are pictured as an underclass. One study showed that welfare issues only become newsworthy when associated with crime and fraud. By focusing on cases of welfare abuse, the media have portrayed the underclass as the undeserving poor, sponging off the welfare state (Golding & Middleton, 1982).

Soap operas and social class So far research has indicated that:

- the working class has typically been under-represented in the media:

- when it has appeared, it has often been depicted in a negative manner.

British soap operas are something of an exception. Series such as *Coronation Street* and *EastEnders* feature the working class which continues to be represented as a close-knit community. While this community is portrayed as resilient, it is also increasingly depicted as multi-ethnic and threatened by outside criminal and racist forces (Dodd & Dodd, 1992).

Framing class

A recent American study based on a systematic content analysis of media representations of social class analysed the archives of major newspapers as well as 50 years of television entertainment programming (Kendall, 2005). It argues that the media selectively frame the world. 'A frame constitutes a storyline about an issue' and this directs people's attention to some ideas rather than others. Surveying news stories and television entertainment across a range of media reveals a remarkable similarity in how events are framed. An example is the common coverage at Christmas of stories which feature charity towards the poor. 'These media representations suggest that Americans are benevolent people who do not forget the less fortunate' (Kendall, 2005).

Framing the rich and upper class In contemporary America, the upper class continues to be depicted generally in flattering terms. Kendall identifies four positive media frames.

- The consensus frame: the wealthy are like everyone else.

- The admiration frame: the wealthy are generous and caring people.

- The emulation frame: the wealthy personify the American Dream (anyone, whatever their origins, can be successful).

- The price-tag frame: the wealthy believe in the gospel of materialism.

While the above positive frames are dominant, two negative frames can also be distinguished.

- The sour grapes frame: the wealthy are unhappy and not well-adjusted.

- The bad apple frame: some wealthy people are scoundrels.

Framing the poor and the working class In contrast to the generally sympathetic framing of the wealthy, 'much media coverage offers negative images of the poor, showing them as dependent on others (welfare issues) or as deviant in their behaviour and lifestyle' (Kendall, 2005). Two common frames can be detected.

- The exceptionalism frame: if this person escaped poverty, why can't you?

- The charitable frame: the poor need a helping hand on special occasions like Christmas.

While the charitable frame exhibits some sympathy for the poor, it is very unusual to find any coverage that suggests the need to address the structural causes of poverty.

The working class is typically distinguished from the poor in America. This class also, is usually represented in a negative way.

- The shady frame: greedy workers, union disputes and organised crime.

- The caricature frame: rednecks, buffoons, bigots and slobs.

- The fading blue-collar frame: out of work or unhappy at work.

Occasionally a more positive frame can be detected.

- The heroic frame: working-class heroes and victims.

Framing the middle class Three key frames are evident.

- The middle-class values frame: middle-class values are the core values of American society to which people should aspire.

- The squeeze frame: the middle class is finding it difficult to maintain its (costly) life style.

- The victimisation frame: middle-class problems are caused by the actions of people from other classes.

All tend to represent the middle class in a positive way, enabling most readers/viewers to identify with this class.

Conclusion Media representations of social classes typically mean that the upper and middle classes are depicted in a positive way and the working class and poor are depicted in a negative way. The result is that the media put forward an ideology which justifies class inequality and 'the ever widening chasm between the haves and have-nots' (Kendall, 2005).

5.5 Representations of age

Nature and nurture

Over the course of the life cycle, children become teenagers; youths become adults; and middle-aged adults become old. This is normally thought of as a natural process since ageing entails inevitable biological changes. And these biological changes are often accompanied by changes in our attitudes and behaviour. Sociologists, however, argue that these social changes are not just a result of the biological clock ticking away. Indeed the stages themselves – childhood, youth, maturity, old age – have not always been distinguished in the ways we do now (Richardson, 2005).

Childhood Some historians argue that for most of human history children (at least after the age of six or seven) were seen as miniature adults. The idea of childhood as a period of innocence and dependence only began to emerge around the 15th century. And even then, the expectation that children should be engaged in education rather than employment took a long while to become the norm. Childhood is now seen as an extended stage of the life cycle and sharply distinguished from adulthood.

Youth For many historians, youth only became recognised as a separate stage of the life cycle after the discovery of childhood. Indeed, it was only in the post-war period that teenagers were affluent enough to become significant consumers of mass media products such as rock and roll, and develop youth cultures. Youth is now recognised to be a stage somewhere between childhood and adulthood.

Adulthood and old age For much of human history, adults were obliged to work for a living until they died. Old age, however, is now seen as a distinct stage in the life cycle when people are entitled to a pension and not expected to be employed.

Representations of age groups

The status of different age groups in Western societies is linked to their economic circumstances. Those in the middle – adults in work – have the most status. By contrast, those at either extremes – the young and the old – whom it is assumed (often incorrectly) do not work, have less status. The different status of age groups results in corresponding variations in mainstream representations. According to McQueen (1998), 'These, broadly, are that: children are helpless and innocent; teenagers irresponsible and rebellious; middle-aged people responsible and conformist; and old people vulnerable and a "burden" on society'. We shall now look at the portrayal of the groups with less status.

Children A study of children's television has identified three main strands (McQueen, 1998). The first is a commercial strand and targets children as consumers of cartoons (eg *Tom and Jerry*) and action programmes. The second is a public service strand and seeks to be distinctly educational (eg *Blue Peter*). The third, and most recent, is an adult strand which recognises that children often prefer 'adult' programmes (eg *Neighbours*). In Britain, the second strand – though once dominant – has declined and the third strand has grown. While the former represents children as totally dependent and in need of protection and guidance from adults, the latter recognises diversity among children and their capacity to deal with complex issues.

Youth The most common depiction of young people in the news is the representation of youth as trouble. Hence a series of moral panics in the post-war period about 'depraved youth' who have no respect for authority (Muncie, 1999). Teddy boys were the first 'folk devils' to be identified in the post-war period but they were followed in successive decades by, among others, mods and rockers (see Section 4.2), muggers, punks and joy-riders. In each of these cases, a group of young people was identified as trouble. The behaviour of this group in turn served to symbolise what was wrong with youth and, by extension, society generally.

Representing youth in this way – youth as trouble – is not new. An analysis of newspapers over a number of centuries reveals that, in every age, it is common to portray youth as a problem and to contrast contemporary youth with the situation of 20 years ago when young people respected authority and society was in a better state (Pearson, 1983).

Old age Older people are much less likely to be represented on television or in the mass media than younger people, 'with 11 per cent of the population who are aged over 65 years, reduced to only 2.3 per cent of the television population' (McQueen, 1998). When older people are represented, White middle-class men are much more commonly found than women, ethnic minorities or the poor. As for the nature of the images, these are according to one recent account 'overwhelmingly negative, comic or grotesque' (McQueen, 1998).

5.6 Representations of sexuality

The term sexual orientation refers to an individual's sexual preferences – for people of the same sex (homosexuality), persons of the opposite sex (heterosexuality) or persons of either sex (bisexuality). In all societies, there are rules governing what are deemed acceptable sexual relations. While these vary from society to society, in many societies heterosexuality is considered the norm and homosexuality/bisexuality as deviant. Indeed, as late as the 1960s, gay male sexual relations were completely illegal in Britain. And it is only since 2003, with the incorporation into law of the Employment Equality (Sexual Orientation) Regulations, that it has been illegal to discriminate against people because of their sexual orientation. And it was not until 2005 that same-sex couples (lesbians and gays) have

activity20 hooligans and yobs

Item A Hooligans

At twelve—his literary
education

At seventeen—a full-fledged Hooligan

Source: *The Daily Graphic*, 5.12.1900

Item B Yobs

ONE MORE VICTIM OF OUR YOB CULTURE
A father of four was kicked to death by yobs after being asked for a light.

LOUTS DESTROY ANOTHER FAMILY
Britain's yob culture has claimed the life of yet another family man.

ATTACKED BY A TEEN GANG
A barrister was in a coma last night after becoming the latest victim of a teenage street gang. Yobs are intimidating entire neighbourhoods.

Source: *Daily Mail*, June and July, 2005

question

What impression of youth is provided by Items A and B?

---

been given, through civil partnerships, similar rights as married heterosexual couples.

Representations of lesbians and gay men Analysis of media content has repeatedly produced the following findings.

- Sexual minorities 'mostly are ignored or denied'.
- When they do appear they do so in order to play a supportive role for the natural order and are thus narrowly and negatively stereotyped' (Gross, 1995).
- Common stereotypes include those of 'homosexual men' being 'identified by a mincing walk and camp voices' and 'lesbians as butch dungaree-wearing feminists' (McQueen, 1998).

Changing representations of sexuality With more societal acceptance of diversity, including diverse sexual orientations, lesbians and gay men have become both more visible and less narrowly and negatively stereotyped. This is evident in a number of ways.

- The greater visibility of gays is evident in advertising, the news and fictional television programmes. Advertisers for example are now more likely to engage in gay-positive marketing campaigns. This is partly in order to attract a previously untapped market – gay consumers – and partly to draw on the perceived hipness of the gay lifestyle in order to sell products to a mass market (Media Awareness Network, 2005).
- In the period from 1981, when AIDS was first identified, to 1985 when a potential AIDS epidemic was recognised, some sections of the press identified gay

men as folk devils responsible for what was presented as 'a gay plague'. Gay activists and medical authorities, however, successfully challenged this interpretation of AIDS and indeed persuaded governments after 1986 to develop campaigns in order to promote safe sex (Critcher, 2003).

- While gay men are often represented as camp in situation comedies, less stereotypical representations are evident in soap operas. In contrast to situation comedies and one-off dramas, it is not necessary in soap operas, which comprise an ongoing drama, to identify immediately whether a character is gay. There is room for some character development and it is possible therefore that it may emerge that certain individuals happen to be gay. Despite this, one analysis indicates that plots featuring gays typically 'dealt with the issue of heterosexuals coming to terms with gayness'. In other words, 'media representations are not representing in most cases a gay/lesbian perspective – they are constructed from a heterosexual point of view and aimed at a heterosexual audience' (Bernstein, 2002).
- Although the mainstream media often continue to represent gays and lesbians as the Other, they do present a wider range of images of gay people than was the case. Talk shows provide an opportunity for people outside the sexual mainstream to voice their concerns. And cutting-edge drama series have emerged, such as Channel 4's *Queer as Folk,* which focused on the lives of three gay men living in Manchester.

*activity*21 *double standards*

Item A *Censorship?*

Tesco has so far been unwilling to sell a new women's magazine, *Scarlet* because its raunchiness is thought to be tasteless and might offend customers. In contrast, equally raunchy lads' weeklies such as *Nuts* and *Zoo* are widely available. Referring to Tesco's decision and to the refusal of many outlets to stock gay and lesbian magazines, the chairperson of Object, an organisation against sexual stereotyping says, 'This is social control of women's and gay men's sexual rights by the distributors. Why are male bodies being censored and protected but not women's bodies? Is it because they are afraid of female erotica and homosexuality?'

Source: *The Guardian*, 28.11.2005

Item B *Steering clear*

When the American version of *Queer as Folk* was in production, fashion houses such as Versace, Pravda, Polo, Ralph Lauren and Abercrombie & Fitch refused to allow their brands to appear in the series. And although the show is set in Pittsburgh, the marketing director of Pittsburgh Steelers wrote a letter to the producers demanding that all references to the team be removed.

Source: *Media Awareness Network*, 2005

questions

1   Look at Item A. What evidence is there of double standards in the treatment of *Scarlet* and *Zoo*?
2   Look at Item B. Why are some companies unwilling to be associated with the drama *Queer as Folk*?

5.7 Representations of disability

There are two main ways of understanding and representing disability:

- The medical model
- The social model.

The medical model This 'views disability as a product of impairment' (Bulsara, 2005). Here the focus is on physical difference such as blindness and being wheelchair bound. The disabled are defined as a group whose bodies do not function normally and who, as a result, are not capable of enjoying an ordinary lifestyle.

The social model By contrast, this model views disability as the outcome of social barriers. Here the focus is on the obstacles and discriminatory practices that people with disabilities face. It is recognised that some people experience impairments, but what is highlighted are the social barriers that prevent these people from enjoying an ordinary lifestyle.

Under-representation of disability

Content analysis of representations of disability on television conducted between 1993 and 2002 indicates that people with disabilities appear infrequently and that there has been little change over the years. In 2002, they made an appearance in 11% of the programmes surveyed but accounted for only 0.8% of all the people who spoke. What is more, the range of disabilities portrayed was very limited, being those highlighted in the medical model, notably blindness and being wheelchair bound (Agyeman, 2003).

Images of the disabled

According to Barnes (1992), there are a range of images of the disabled. Content analysis of both electronic and print media identified the following.

- The disabled person as pitiable and pathetic. Such an image was common on programmes such as *Children in Need* and telethons where the disabled were presented as objects of pity in order for the able-bodied to feel compassion and give money.

- The disabled person as an object of violence, a common scenario in television programmes where disabled people appeared.

- The disabled person as sinister and evil – for example, Shakespeare's *Richard III* or *Treasure Island's* Blind Pew.

- The disabled person as atmosphere or curio – for example, a character with a humped back, such as Igor in the film *Frankenstein,* being used as a metaphor for evil.

- The disabled person as 'super cripple'. This image of an individual heroically overcoming obstacles is evident in films such as *My Left Foot*, where the central character, Christy Brown is played in fact by an able-bodied actor, a common occurrence in Hollywood films.

- The disabled person as an object of ridicule – for example, Mr Magoo, a partially-sighted cartoon character.

- The disabled person as their own worst enemy able to overcome obstacles if he (or occasionally, she), put their minds to it and ceases to be self pitying.

- The disabled person as a burden who is dependent and needs to be looked after.

- The disabled person as sexually abnormal.

- The disabled person as incapable of participating in community life.

- The disabled person as normal.

While a range of media representations of the disabled can still be identified, the most prevalent ones 'commonly perpetuate negative stereotypes' (Roper, 2003). 'Three potent images are conjured up: pity, dependent and flawed' (Bulsara, 2005). For the most part, media representations thus 'represent disabled people as deviant outsiders in clear juxtaposition to the normal and "able bodied" majority' (Hughes, 1998). While most images of disabled people illustrate that the medical model of disability continues to be dominant, there is little doubt that – as disabled people have become more vocal in their demand for civil rights – more media representations draw upon the social model of disability. In 42% of those cases where people with disabilities appeared on television, for example, issues of prejudice, stereotyping or discrimination were highlighted. It still remains rare, however, for disability to be 'portrayed as an everyday, incidental phenomenon' (Agyeman, 2003) with 'disabled people nipping into the Queen Vic for a drink, and then leaving again' (Furner, 2005).

How important are representations?

The previous sections have demonstrated continuity and change in media representations of different social groups. But how important are these representations? Do they actually influence viewers, listeners and readers?

Their impact cannot be assessed without looking carefully at how audiences respond to the media. The problem here is that people do not respond in a simple and straightforward way to what they see, hear or read. The effects of the mass media on audiences are discussed at length in Unit 6.

summary

1. The mass media represent various social groups. These representations are often based on stereotypes.

2. Studies of gender representations from the 1950s to the 1970s showed that the media presented a stereotype of women as domestic servants and sex objects.

3. More recent evidence indicates that media representations of women are less likely to be based on traditional stereotypes.

4. Media representations of ethnicity have tended to rely on negative stereotypes. Black people were routinely presented as a 'threat' and a 'problem'. Ethnic issues were seen from a White point of view.

5. Recent research indicates more positive representations of minority ethnic groups and a growth in the number and range of representations. However, old stereotypes persist.

6. The working class are under-represented in the media and tend to be pictured in a negative way. The middle class are represented in a more positive light.

7. There has been a move from representing children as dependent and in need of protection to recognising their capacity to deal with complex issues.

8. The most common representation of youth in the news is 'youth as trouble'.

9. Older people are under-represented in the media and tend to be pictured in negative or comic ways.

10. Sexual minorities have tended to be ignored or represented in terms of negative stereotypes. There is some recent evidence of more diverse and positive representations.

11. The disabled are under-represented in the media. Although a range of media images can be identified, the most common continue to reflect negative stereotypes.

12. People do not respond in a straightforward way to what they see, hear and read. As a result, it is difficult to assess the effect of media representations.

Unit 6 Media effects

keyissues

1 What effects do the media have on audiences?

2 Do the media make us more violent?

6.1 Two views of media effects

How do the mass media affect their audiences? There are two main views. The first view sees the media as powerful and their audience as passive. The media are seen to shape the beliefs and behaviour of the audience who passively accept what they see, hear and read and act accordingly. In terms of this view, the audience is pictured as a mass of isolated individuals who are vulnerable to media manipulation and control.

The second view sees an active audience. They use the media to meet their own needs, selecting what they see, hear and read. Rather than simply accepting, they interpret media output, actively constructing their own meanings. And different individuals and groups interpret the media in different ways depending on their individual experiences and group membership.

Research on media effects has tended to swing between these two contrasting views of the audience. However, more recent research has shown a preference for the active audience view.

Hypodermic syringe theory

Early theories of media effects claimed that the mass media have a direct and immediate effect on behaviour. Hypodermic syringe theory likened the effect of the media to the injection of a drug into a vein. The media were seen to have an immediate effect on people's moods and actions. For example, violence in a movie produces feelings of aggression which can lead to violent behaviour.

Evaluation This view pictured a powerful media which could manipulate and control audiences. Much of the evidence used to support hypodermic syringe theory came from laboratory experiments. But the way people behave in laboratories is often very different from their behaviour in real life situations.

activity22 the Martians are coming

Orson Welles broadcasting War of the Worlds

'The girls huddled around their radios trembling and weeping in each other's arms. They separated themselves from their friends only to take their turn at the telephone to make long distance calls to their parents, saying goodbye for what they thought might be the last time. Terror-stricken girls, hoping to escape from the Mars invaders, rushed to the basement of the dormitory.'

With these words, an American college student recalls the reaction of herself and her friends to a radio broadcast in 1938. The broadcast was a radio play by Orson Welles based on H.G. Wells' *The War of the Worlds*, a novel about an invasion from Mars. It was so realistic that hundreds of thousands of people, who missed the announcement that it was only a play, were convinced the Martians had invaded. There was widespread panic at the news that millions had been killed by Martian death rays.

Many people just didn't know how to respond. They turned to family and friends to see whether they should believe what they'd heard. They interpreted what they saw in terms of the radio programme. One person looked out of his window and saw that Wyoming Avenue was 'black with cars. People were rushing away, I figured.' Another recounted, 'No cars came down my street. Traffic is jammed on account of the roads being destroyed, I thought.'

Thousands fled towns and cities and took to the hills.

Source: Cantril, 1940

New York Times

Radio Listeners in Panic, Taking War Drama as Fact

Many Flee Homes to Escape 'Gas Raid From Mars'—Phone Calls Swamp Police at Broadcast of Wells Fantasy

A wave of mass hysteria seized thousands of radio listeners throughout the nation between 8:15 and 9:30 o'clock last night when a broadcast of a dramatization of H. G. Wells's fantasy, 'The War of the Worlds,' led thousands to believe that an interplanetary conflict had started with invading Martians spreading wide death and destruction in New Jersey and New York.

The "radio war," as it were, took place at various points and radio stations here and in other cities of the United States and Canada seeking advice on protective measures against the raids.

The program was produced by Mr. Welles and the Mercury Theatre on the Air over station WABC and the Columbia Broadcasting System's coast-to-coast network, from 8 to 9 o'clock.

question

To what extent does the behaviour of the radio audience support the hypodermic syringe theory?

Two-step flow theory

Hypodermic syringe theory largely ignores the fact that people are social beings, that they have families, friends and work colleagues. Katz and Lazarsfeld's influential *two-step flow theory* (1955) emphasised the importance of social relationships in shaping people's response to the media. They argued that opinions are formed in a social context.

Within this context certain people – *opinion leaders* – are influential in shaping the views of others. These individuals are more likely to be exposed to the media, for example to read more newspapers and magazines. As a result, they are more likely to be influenced by the media and, as opinion leaders, to transmit media messages to others. Hence the idea of a two-step flow – attitudes and ideas 'flow *from* radio and print to opinion leaders and *from them* to the less active sections of the population' (Katz and Lazarsfeld, 1955).

Evaluation Two-step flow theory was largely based on research into short-term changes in attitudes and opinions. For example, media presentations of election campaigns were examined in order to discover to what extent they changed people's voting intentions. Often, such studies showed that the media had little effect on people's opinions.

Uses and gratifications theory

The uses and gratifications approach directly challenged the hypodermic syringe theory. Rather than asking what the media do to audiences, it asked what do audiences do with the media. It argued that people use the media to gratify certain needs. To find out what those needs are, you ask people what they get from watching particular programmes. Using this method, McQuail et al. (1972) identified four needs that are met by watching television. The first was escapism, the need for people to forget about everyday problems. The second was companionship, the need to feel in contact with others, for example with characters in a TV soap. The third was personal identity, for example the need to confirm how clever you are by taking part in TV quizzes from your armchair. The fourth was information, the need to know what is going on in the world.

The uses and gratifications approach puts the audience in the driving seat – they choose from what the media has to offer in order to gratify their needs.

Evaluation There are two main criticisms of this view. First, how do we identify audience needs? When people say that television provides escapism, are they saying that is what they want from television or that's what they get from television? Second, are audiences as active in their choice of programmes as the uses and gratifications approach suggests? Here research 'indicates that, for the most part, they are not selective in their choice of viewing' – more often than not, they watch what they're given (McCullagh, 2002).

Cultural effects theory

This theory assumes that the media does have important effects on its audience. These effects are not as immediate and dramatic as those indicated by the hypodermic syringe theory. Nor are they relatively insignificant as suggested by the two-step flow theory. Rather, they can be seen as a slow, steady, long term build-up of ideas and attitudes.

Cultural effects theory assumes that if similar images, ideas and interpretations are broadcast over periods of time, then they may well affect the way we see and understand the world. Thus, if television and radio broadcasts, newspapers and magazines all present, for example, a certain image of women, then slowly but surely this will filter into the public consciousness.

Like the two-step flow theory, cultural effects theory recognises the importance of social relationships. It argues that media effects will depend on the social position of members of the audience, for example, their age, gender, class and ethnicity (Glover, 1985).

Evaluation Cultural effects theory is difficult to evaluate. Because the effects it claims take place over long periods of time, it is difficult to show they are a result of media output. They may be due to other factors in the wider society.

Media as texts

This approach states that the media output – TV programmes, films, books, advertisements – can be seen as 'texts' which are 'read' by the audience. The way that these texts are 'written' determines how audiences understand

activity23 madonna

question

How would you interpret this image of Madonna?

them. For example, Mulvey (1975) argues that many Hollywood movies encourage us to adopt a 'male gaze' – to identify with male characters and see women as sex objects. This suggests a powerful media which directs audiences to interpret media output in a particular way.

Evaluation This approach pictures a passive audience who simply read 'texts' as they have been 'written'. However, research on audiences suggests that media texts can be read in a variety of ways. As the case studies in the following section indicate, people interpret media output in terms of their personal experience and membership of social groups. For example, their age, gender, ethnicity, sexual orientation, social class and nationality will all influence their interpretation and understanding of the media. John Fiske (1987) uses the example of Madonna's videos to make this point. Researchers might see these videos as reflecting the 'male gaze' with Madonna flaunting her sexuality for the benefit of men and 'teaching young women to see themselves as men would see them'. However, judging

from letters in a teenage magazine, many young girls saw Madonna as a strong, liberated woman who challenged the mainstream model of femininity.

6.2 Case studies of media effects

So far this unit has looked at general theories of media effects. This section looks at case studies which examine how particular audiences respond to particular aspects of media output.

The 1984/5 miners' strike

The 1984/5 miners' strike was regularly reported by the news media. Activity 24 is based on a study by the Glasgow Media Group of television news coverage of the strike (Philo, 1993). The study examines how people interpreted TV news' version of events. It shows that media effects are not simple and direct. Instead, media output is interpreted in various ways in terms of people's beliefs and experiences.

activity24 audience interpretation

Item A The strike

Item B The research

One hundred and sixty-nine people were interviewed a year after the miners strike of 1984/5. Television news programmes had focused on violent incidents during the strike – clashes between picketing miners and police. Those selected for interview included miners and police who had been involved in the strike, plus a range of people from different parts of the country and with different social backgrounds.

The researchers found that people interpreted the media's version of the strike in terms of their experiences and previously held attitudes and beliefs. Of those interviewed, 54% believed that the picketing was mostly violent. This reflected media coverage of the strike. However, none of those who had direct knowledge of the strike – the miners and police – believed that picketing was mostly violent. They rejected the impression given by the media. According to them, strikers and police spent most of their time standing round doing nothing.

Source: Philo, 1993

questions

1 a) Which picture is typical of the strike?

   b) Why do you think TV news focused on violent confrontations?

2 Why did people interpret the news in different ways?

Neighbours – a Punjabi perspective

The Australian soap *Neighbours* was popular with many young people in the Punjabi community in Southall. Research by Marie Gillespie (1995) shows why. *Neighbours* offered the Southall teenagers a picture of family and community life with which to compare their own. Many of them experienced a tension between British and Indian norms and values as they grew up. 'Soap talk' based on *Neighbours* allowed them to contrast, evaluate and criticise their own family life. Many identified with characters in *Neighbours* and appreciated the freedom that young people appeared to have. By comparison, some felt the restrictions of their family were unfair. One girl talks about the emphasis on respect and obedience to elders: 'It drowns your own sense of identity, you can't do what you want, you always have to think of your family honour.' Another girls comments: 'You can see that families in *Neighbours* are more flexible, they do things together as a family, they don't expect that girls should stay at home and do housework and cooking, boys and girls are allowed to mix more freely.'

The young Punjabis interpreted *Neighbours* in terms of their own experiences, concerns and values. This is an important study because it suggests that there are many different audiences 'out there' and that each will interpret media output in a somewhat different way.

Tyneside rappers

Hip-hop/rap is a global music. Yet young people around the world interpret it in terms of their particular meanings and experiences. This can be seen from Andy Bennett's (2001) study of White rappers in Newcastle upon Tyne. They saw hip-hop as a street thing rather than a Black thing. They dropped the 'Americanisms', rapping with local accents, giving accounts of their own lives and

dealing with local problems – for example, crack was replaced by Newcastle Brown Ale, problems of excessive drinking and alcohol related violence. In their eyes, they created 'pure Geordie rap'.

Again, we see media output being interpreted in terms of the experiences and concerns of a particular audience.

Media effects – conclusion

This unit began with two views of media effects. The first saw the media as powerful and their audience as passive. The media largely shape the beliefs and values of the audience who tend to accept what they see, hear and read. The second view sees the audience as active – selecting and interpreting media output and constructing their own meanings based on individual experience and group membership.

There is evidence to support both views of audience response to media output. For example, the Glasgow Media Group's study of TV news' coverage of the 1984/5 miners' strike found that over half the people interviewed accepted the TV version of events as 'mostly violent'. Summarising the findings of this and other studies, some members of the Glasgow Media Group concluded that in terms of news: 'Most of us, most of the time go along with what the media tell us to be the case' (Eldridge et al., 1997). On the other hand, those who had direct knowledge of the strike rejected the version given by the media.

The case studies examined in this section indicate that audiences are not passive, that their interpretations and meanings are not simply shaped by the media. They bring with them a lifetime of experiences, concerns, expectations and values in terms of which they interpret and give meaning to media output.

summary

1. There are two main views of media effects. The first sees the media as powerful and the audience as passive. The media are seen to shape the beliefs and behaviour of the audience. The second view sees the audience as active – they interpret media output and construct their own meanings.

2. The hypodermic syringe theory sees the media having an immediate and direct effect on people's moods and actions.

3. Two-step flow theory argues that attitudes and ideas flow from the media to opinion leaders to the rest of the population.

4. Uses and gratifications theory argues that people use the media to gratify certain needs – the needs for escapism, companionship, identity and information.

5. Cultural effects theory sees media effects as a slow, steady, long-term build-up of beliefs and attitudes in response to the frequent transmission of similar images and ideas over fairly long periods of time.

6. The media as texts approach sees media output as 'texts' which are 'read' by the audience. It argues that the way these texts are 'written' determines how the audience understands them.

7. Case study research shows how particular audiences draw on their beliefs, values, knowledge and experience in order to interpret media output.

activity25 interpreting hip-hop

Item A Dizzy Rascal

London rapper, Dizzy Rascal. American rapper Jay-Z said, 'I like his beats but I can't understand a word he says'.

Item B 50 Cent

American rapper 50 Cent performing in Venice, Italy

Item C Chinese hip-hop fans

Dancing to hip-hop music at the Beijing Pop Music Festival, 2007

Item D Skinnyman

London rapper, Skinnyman

question

Use these pictures to support the view that hip-hop/rap is interpreted differently by different performers and audiences.

Unit 7 *The new media*

key issues

1 What are the new media?

2 How does the internet affect news output?

3 How might the new media affect the democratic process?

4 What is the significance of social networking sites?

This unit looks at recent developments in the media such as the internet and satellite broadcasting. It examines some of the key questions addressed in this chapter in terms of the new media. For example, is the internet an instrument for revitalising and expanding democracy? Or does the internet simply extend the dominance and further the interests of the powerful?

Many sociologists believe that we are in the middle of a communications revolution which is transforming the way images, text and sounds are communicated. Three technological developments are seen as particularly important in bringing about this revolution.

- The development of relatively cheap personal computers allowing access to the internet for millions of people at home and at work

- The emergence of new ways of sending audio-visual signals to individual households

- The growth of digital technology causing changes in the way information (images, texts and sounds) is stored and transmitted.

7.1 New media

The internet, along with cable television and satellite broadcasting, are examples of *new media*. The new media share three characteristics:

- 'They are screen based', with information being displayed on a television screen, PC monitor or a mobile telephone.

- 'They can offer images, text and sounds.'

- 'They allow some form of interaction.'
  (Collins & Murroni, 1996)

The internet The internet is a global system of interconnected computers. It is not owned by any individual or company, but comprises a network that stretches across the world. The best known part of the internet is the World Wide Web (www), effectively a global multi-media library.

The internet was created in 1969 by the American military to enable scientists working on military contracts across the USA to share resources and information. It developed further in the 1980s within universities, but it

was not until the second half of that decade, with the increased availability of PCs in the home, that the internet really took off (Gorman & McLean, 2003). The growth in internet access has been dramatic. In 2008, 16 million households in Britain (65%) had internet access, an increase of 5 million since 2002 (National Statistics Online, 2009).

Cable television and satellite broadcasting Terrestrial broadcasting by the BBC and ITV operates by sending audio-visual signals through the air which are picked up by ordinary television aerials. By contrast, cable television relies on a physical cable link and satellite broadcasting on dishes to pick up signals.

In contrast to the USA and the rest of Europe, cable television in the UK is less popular than satellite broadcasting. In 2002, only 14.7 per cent of homes in the UK where cable is available had taken out a television subscription, compared to 25% with satellite dishes (Peake, 2002). Subscribers to BSkyB have risen steadily from over 6 million in July 2002 to nearly 9.1 million in September 2008 (Ofcom.org.uk, 2008). The development of cable television and satellite broadcasting enables people to choose from a much larger number of television channels.

Digitalisation Of central importance to recent technological developments in the media is *digitalisation* – the shift from analogue to digital coding of information. Digital systems translate all information – images, texts, sounds – into a universal computer language. The use of this common language reduces the boundaries between different media sectors. 'Digital transmission technology has a broadcasting capacity many times bigger than analogue, opening the door on a new era: many more TV channels and radio stations; higher quality pictures and sound; multimedia facilities; and interactivity (home shopping, games, video on demand)' (Peake, 2002).

Diversity and choice In one respect, the new media have led to more consumer choice. For example, cable television and satellite broadcasting have increased the number of television channels. While many of these are entertainment channels, the number of news channels has also increased. Sometimes these provide views of world affairs that are very different from British and American sources. For example, the 24-hour Arab satellite news station Aljazeera often provides alternative content and perspectives to Western news programmes.

Quality The government exercises some control over the quality and range of programmes on the BBC and ITV. However, the main providers of cable and satellite broadcasting – NTL, Telewest and BSkyB – face 'no regulatory directives on either the range or the sources of programme material' (Negrine, 1994). Anxious to make as much profit as possible on their massive investments, cable and satellite broadcasters fill their channels with cheap imported material, films, or sport.

Other broadcasting organisations are tempted to follow suit as they too search for large audiences to generate advertising revenue or, in the case of the BBC, to justify the license fee. According to many commentators, 'there is a consequent loss in both the quality, and the range, of programmes produced' (Negrine, 1994). Increased choice does not therefore mean increased diversity.

Inequality There is also inequality of access to the new media. As subscription channels and pay-per-view become more popular, poorer people become excluded from key world events, especially in entertainment and sport.

7.2 News online

This section looks at news on the internet and its effect on the other news media.

Sources of news

In the USA, the Pew Research Center for People and the Press conducts regular surveys of media use. The December 2008 survey showed that the internet had overtaken newspapers as a news outlet. Its growth as a source of news has been rapid. In September 2007, 24% of Americans reported that the internet was one of their main sources of national and international news. By December, 2008, this figure was 40% (see Activity 26, Item A). Television was still a main source of news for 70% of the population. For young people (aged 18 to 29), television and the internet were neck and neck at 59%. (Figures add up to more than 100% because multiple responses were allowed.) (people-press.org, 2009).

The trend in the UK is similar but slower moving. According to the Office of Communications (Ofcom), the internet is 'the fastest growing platform for news'. However, the actual number of people who use the internet as their main source of news remains small – only 6% of UK adults in 2006, up from 2% in 2002 (Ofcom, 2007). In 1994, adults watched an average of 108.5 hours of television, in 2006 this was down to 90.8 hours. Television remains the main source of news though viewing of TV national news has declined. Newspaper readership has declined rapidly from 26.7 million adults reading a daily newspaper to 21.7 million in 2006 (House of Lords, 2008).

Types of online news

Repackaging Many of the online news outlets are operated by traditional news providers. The major newspapers have their own site as do television news providers. Much of the news they provide online is repackaged from their existing sources. For example, a survey conducted in 2003 in 16 countries compared the front pages of major national print and online newspapers. The results showed that 70% of the main stories in both media were identical (Van der Wurff & Lauf, 2005). One of the main differences is that the internet enables providers to present breaking news immediately, an advantage shared by 24-hour television news channels.

Repackaging means that ways of accessing the news have increased rapidly but this has not been matched by an increase in news content.

News aggregator sites Sites such as Google News and Yahoo! News present stories on particular topics from a wide range of sources. They 'aggregate' – bring together – news stories, hence the term *news aggregator* site. While this allows users to compare the coverage of a particular story, it adds nothing new to existing coverage. News aggregation sites do not invest money in journalism.

User generated content This phrase refers to news content provided by users – by the public rather than the owners of news websites. Some online news sites invite comment from users, giving them the opportunity to broadcast their views. Increasingly the public provides content, often recorded on video cameras and mobile phones.

Blogs *Blog* is short for *weblog*. A blog is an online journal, newsletter or diary which is regularly updated. Usually created by individuals, blogs deal with a vast range of topics from politics and social issues to music and celebrities. Estimates of the number of blogs worldwide vary considerably – one estimate for 2008 gave 184 million (technorati.com/blogging).

Many blogs comment on the news, sometimes they generate news and occasionally they break a big story. Some bloggers such as Salam Pax, 'the Baghdad Blogger' become very influential – see Activity 26, Item C.

News online – conclusion

Although the internet has provided many more ways to access the news, this has not been matched by a corresponding expansion of news content and news gathering services. Much online news consists of repackaging material generated by more traditional media. However, there have been some important changes. User generated content is a feature of many online news sites. And blogging is a growing aspect of online news.

Online news is becoming increasingly important, particularly for young people. It may well compensate for the decline in other news outlets, particularly the fall in newspaper readership. And some commentators argue that it may well reduce the threat of media concentration (House of Lords, 2008).

key terms

News aggregator sites Websites which present news stories on particular topics from a wide range of sources.

Blog An online journal, newsletter or diary which is regularly updated.

activity26 online news

Item A Sources of news in the USA

Where do you get most of your national and international news?

(percentages)

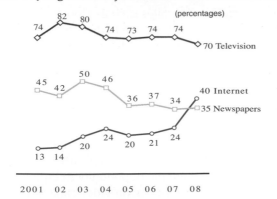

74 82 80 74 73 74 74 70 Television

45 42 50 46 36 37 34 40 Internet / 35 Newspapers

13 14 20 24 20 21 24

2001 02 03 04 05 06 07 08

Source: people-press.org, 2009

Item B Young people and online news in the USA

Internet rivals TV as main news source for young people*

Main source of news	Aug 2006 %	Sept 2007 %	Dec 2008 %	07-08 Change
Television	62	68	59	-11
Internet	32	34	59	+25
Newspapers	29	23	28	+5
Radio	16	13	18	+5
Magazines	1	*	4	+4
Other	3	5	6	+1

*Ages 18 to 29.
Figures add to more than 100% because multiple responses were allowed.

Source: people-press.org, 2009

Item C The Baghdad Blogger

In early 2003, a special voice emerged in Iraq to tell the world what it was like to be an ordinary person in Baghdad. Salam Pax, 'the Baghdad Blogger' began his online reports of life after the American invasion. 'Closely observed, intelligent, sometimes passionate, frequently funny, he spared neither regime nor invader.' Salam captured a worldwide audience.

Source: Plommer, 2009

Item D Views on blogging

'It's like all the stuff on the web,' Mike Smartt of BBC News Online states, 'dissemination of information is great, but how much of it is trustworthy?'

Robert L Belichick, a health care worker from Chicago, is a regular reader of blogs. 'The main reason for going to the blogs is for information that will never see the light of day in print or TV media. For example, not one major media outlook in the USA reported that the USA excised (removed) over 8,000 pages from the Iraq declaration since they contained information about the US companies that supplied all the biological and chemical weapons to Saddam.'

Source: Raynsford, 2003

questions

1 Outline the trends indicated in Items A and B.
2 Assess the importance of blogs.

7.3 Politics online – a case study

This section looks at the role played by the internet in Barack Obama's campaign for the presidency in 2008. It shows the potential of the internet in politics as indicated by phrases such as 'the internet election' and 'the first internet presidency'.

Social networking sites Obama's team made extensive use of social networking sites. One count during the campaign showed that Obama had:

- 98,623 followers on Twitter
- 709,606 friends on MySpace

- 2.14 million Facebook supporters (von Leyden, 2008)

myBo Obama had his own social networking site, my.BarackObama.com nicknamed myBo by his supporters. The site has a database which enables volunteers to identify and contact Obama supporters to urge them to vote. It includes a Neighbour-to-Neighbour tool which allows volunteers to find and canvass registered voters in their area. Volunteers are encouraged to feed back local information which is used to direct the campaign. Regular bulletins update volunteers on events and strategy. And myBo and email blasts were used to raise millions of dollars to pay for the election campaign (Wagner, 2008).

YouTube Specially created campaign videos, often fronted by celebrities such as Justin Timberlake and Jessica Biel, were placed on YouTube. The videos were watched for 14.5 million hours. To buy that amount of time on television would cost $47 million (Miller, 2008).

The internet as a news source Surveys by the Pew Research Center for People and the Press show that the internet was a major source of news about the presidential campaign. In 2008, 24% of Americans said they regularly learned something about the campaign from the internet, almost double the percentage in the 2004 campaign.

The internet was particularly important for young people. Forty-two per cent of people aged 18 to 29 said they regularly learned about the candidates and the campaign from the internet, the highest percentage for any news source for this group. (people-press.org, 2008).

Conclusion The Obama team's use of the internet changed the way politicians communicate and organise their supporters. And it engaged their supporters, making them feel a part of the whole campaign process.

7.4 Digital citizenship and democracy

Democracy is a political system in which citizens have a say in the way they are governed. Western societies are representative democracies in which the interests of the people are represented by elected officials. Political participation is essential if a democracy is to operate effectively. At a minimum, citizens must vote in elections in order to choose those who will represent them in government.

Researchers who accept this view of democracy argue that the internet is playing a steadily growing part in the democratic process. The previous section, which outlined the role of the internet in Barack Obama's presidential campaign, provides evidence to support this view.

Digital citizenship Many researchers now argue that the ability to participate online is essential for a fully democratic society. The term *digital citizenship* has been coined to describe 'the ability to participate in society online'. '*Digital citizens* are those who use the internet regularly and effectively' (Mossberger et al., 2008)

In *Digital Citizenship: The internet, society and participation*, Karen Mossberger, Caroline Tolbert and Ramona McNeal make the following points. Their analysis is based largely on survey data from the USA.

The internet is now so important that participation is essential if people are to play a full part in mainstream society. In particular, to become full citizens in a democracy, people must have access to the internet and the skills to use it. Survey evidence shows that internet use increases the likelihood of voting and participating in the political process. Politics online is now a vital part of politics 'on the ground' (Mossberger et al., 2008).

The digital divide Access to the internet is not spread evenly across the population. Social inequalities are reflected in internet use. The higher a person's social class, income and educational attainment, the more likely they are to use the internet. Those who might benefit most from internet use – the poor and the disadvantaged – are least likely to be online. The *digital divide* means that those who are excluded from terrestrial society are most likely to be excluded from online society (Mossberger et al., 2008).

Repressing the internet The internet allows people 'to participate in a free flow of information and ideas with others across the world' (Amnesty International, 2006). A number of governments have attempted to suppress this freedom of expression by censoring material on the internet and persecuting citizens who criticise them online. Countries accused of internet repression include China, Vietnam, Tunisia, Iran, Israel, Saudi Arabia and Syria.

Western IT companies such as Microsoft, Google and Yahoo! have been criticised for 'helping to build the systems that enable surveillance and censorship to take place' and for participating in the suppression of information and the identification of bloggers who speak out against their governments (Amnesty International, 2006).

key terms

Digital citizenship The ability to participate in online society.

Digital citizens Those who use the internet regularly and effectively.

Digital divide The divisions between those with access to the internet and the skills to use it and those who lack access and the appropriate skills.

7.5 The public sphere

The media as a public sphere The idea of a *public sphere* refers to a space where people can freely debate issues that are of importance to them as citizens. Habermas (1992) argues that the public sphere emerged in 18th century coffee houses where individuals could meet to discuss the issues of the day. This sphere was independent of both commerce and the government. The mass media in Habermas' view threaten this space because they are primarily concerned to make profits. This means they seek to manipulate our thoughts and behaviour in order to make money.

This picture of the mass media has been criticised because it ignores the pressures on the news media to be 'objective' and does not take account of public service broadcasting. In Britain, for example, the BBC was established as a public service organisation funded by the license fee and obliged to present news and current affairs in an impartial way. While increased competition for readers and viewers has, in the view of many sociologists, led to more 'infotainment', public service broadcasting survives.

The internet as a public sphere The spectacular growth of the internet has suggested to some people that the public sphere is being given a new lease of life. There are two main reasons for this.

- In contrast to conventional news media, where editors and journalists define what counts as news, the internet provides individuals with the opportunity to access a wider range of information and interpretations. Any

activity27 democracy and the internet

Item A **Blogs in Iran**

An Iranian blog in English

In the last five years, the Iranian judiciary have closed down around 100 publications, including 41 daily newspapers. The mullahs – religious leaders – impose strict rules on dress and behaviour and censor media output in line with their views on religious correctness. In the absence of freedom of speech, an estimated 75,000 Iranians have turned to weblogs. Farsi, the main language of Iran, is now the fourth most popular language for online journals. Blogs provide people with anonymity and freedom of expression. They allow them to criticise the government and to indulge their tastes for things banned by the regime – from Harry Potter to Marilyn Manson.

Source: guardian.co.uk, 2005

Item B Riots in France

Both the government and the rioters used the internet during the riots in French towns and cities in November, 2005. Three young bloggers were arrested for urging people to burn down their nearest police station. The interior minister, Nicolas Sarkozy took out ads on Google to broadcast the government's point of view. A few years ago, he would have held a press conference – now he speaks through a search engine.

Source: Jarvis, 2005

Item C The Zapatistas

The Zapatistas are a revolutionary movement in Chiapas, a state in southern Mexico. They have formed a grass-roots movement for self-government – in their words, for 'autonomy, justice and freedom'. They have an extensive website and make widespread use of the internet to organise their movement and gain international support. They invite visitors to their website to express their own views and participate in the movement. They see their struggle in part as a 'cyberwar' – a battle for hearts and minds in cyberspace. In their words, 'The revolution will be digitised'.

Source: Zapatista Net of Autonomy & Liberation, 2005

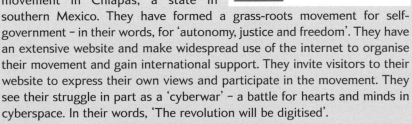

Riots in Toulouse, France

Zapatista leader, Subcommander Marcos

Item D A presidential election

From Barack Obama's website

From YouTube

Item E Repression of the internet

George Brock, president of the World Editor Forum, reads the Golden Pen for Freedom award motivation for Shi Tao in 2007

Shi Tao is a Chinese journalist serving a 10-year prison sentence for 'illegally providing state secrets to foreign entities'. His crime was to use the internet to email a US pro-democracy site about warnings from the Beijing authorities to news outlets against covering demonstrations to mark the anniversary of the 1989 Tiananmen Square democracy protests where hundreds of protesters were killed.

Shi Tao sent that email from his Yahoo account. One year later he was in court, where account-holder information provided by Yahoo's Chinese partner company was used as evidence to convict him. While Yahoo was quick to condemn the punishment of people for free expression, it has supplied information to the Chinese government that has led to prosecutions in such cases.

Source: Amnesty International, 2006

questions

1 What support do Items A, B, C and D provide for the view that the internet has an important part to play in the democratic process?

2 Amnesty International and *The Observer* launched a campaign against internet repression in 2006. Do you support this campaign? Refer to Item E in your answer.

point of view, no matter how extreme, can be found on the internet.

- The internet provides individuals with the opportunity to engage in online discussions and debates across the globe. In contrast to conventional news media, where communication is predominantly one way, the internet provides a means through which people can interact with others.

The internet and democracy Can the internet really revitalise democracy? Can people directly participate in the democratic process via the internet? And can their participation in cyberspace actually change things on the ground?

It's early days yet, but some believe that the answer to these questions is 'eventually, yes'. They argue that the internet gives voice to those who might otherwise go unheard; it allows like-minded people to join together and take action which may lead to social change; it allows the powers that be to be challenged; it provides a means for citizens to direct communication, send and receive messages, discuss and debate. In other words, it may develop into the public sphere which Habermas believes is lost (Livingstone, 2004).

Others are not so sure about the promise of the internet. While recognising that there is a lot of political activity online, they believe it will have little effect 'on the ground'

– politics will continue as usual (Graber et al., 2004). Some believe that the digital divide will widen social inequality and that this may discourage low income groups from participating in the democratic process.

> ## key term
>
> **Public sphere** A space where people can freely debate issues which are important to them as citizens.

7.6 The internet and e-commerce

E-commerce – commercial activities conducted on the internet – is here to stay. For example, Amazon, which began as an online bookseller and moved into DVDs, CDs, electrical goods and white goods (washing machines, fridges), goes from strength to strength. And every major company has its own website from which it advertises and often sells its goods and services. In the UK, internet sales rose by 30% in 2007 to £163 billion. This represents 7.7% of the total value of all sales by non-financial sector businesses in 2007 (Office of National Statistics, 2008).

Some see e-commerce as a positive development. It offers more choice to consumers, it increases competition, it often leads to lower prices and it puts consumers in control – they can compare prices and pick and choose from a vast range of products. Others see the development of e-commerce in a negative light. It encourages materialism and consumerism and furthers capitalist domination and control.

7.7 Social networking

Social networking sites are internet websites which allow people to communicate with each other online. Examples include MySpace, Facebook and Bebo. Social networking sites are usually free to join, with members having their own homepage with a photograph and some biographical information. Members can register with each other as friends which provides them with access to more private content, for example photographs and videos.

Numbers Social networking sites have grown dramatically in the last few years. MySpace, set up in 2003 and bought by Rupert Murdoch's News Corporation in 2005, is the largest with 253 million registered users in 2008. Facebook had 140 million and Bebo 40 million registered users in 2008. This is only one of many measures. An alternative is 'monthly unique visitors' – the number of different people who log on each month. For example, in January 2008, MySpace had 76 million unique visitors in the USA and Facebook had 55 million (comscore.com, 2009; techcrunch.com, 2009).

Users Who uses social networking sites? Research conducted in the UK in 2007 by Ofcom (Office of Communications) shows that 22% of adult internet users aged 16+ and 49% of children aged 8-17 who use the internet have joined a social networking site. For adults, the likelihood of joining is highest among 16-24 year olds (54%) and decreases with age (Ofcom, 2008). Research in the USA provides a similar age breakdown, with a higher proportion of each age group using social networking sites (pewinternet.org, 2009).

Friendship Most people use social networking sites to keep in touch with their close friends. However, all their contacts on these sites are usually referred to as 'friends'. A UK questionnaire survey by Will Hallam found that 90% of the 'close friends' that people contacted on the networking sites, they had already met face to face. Most people have about five close friends, whether or not they use a social networking site. The difference occurs with acquaintances – those using networking sites often have many more casual acquaintances (Randerson, 2007)

The Ofcom research

The largest research project on social networking in the UK was conducted in 2007 by Ofcom. It was based on in-depth and structured interviews with over 6,000 children and adults.

Distinct groups The research indicated that social networkers fell into five distinct groups. They are:

- Alpha Socialisers – (a minority) people who use sites in intense short bursts to flirt, meet new people, and be entertained.
- Attention Seekers – (some) people who craved attention and comments from others, often by posting photos and customising their profiles.
- Followers – (many) people who joined sites to keep up with what their peers were doing.
- Faithfuls – (many) people who typically used social networking sites to rekindle old friendships, often from school or university.
- Functionals – (a minority) people who tended to be single-minded in using sites for a particular purpose.

(Ofcom, 2008)

Communication Users communicated mainly with people who they had first met offline. For example, 69% of adults used social networking sites to talk to friends and family they already saw regularly. For many, the sites were a means of managing their social relationships (Ofcom, 2008).

User generated content The content of social networking sites is created and shared by users. Profiles often contain detailed information about the user in words, photographs and video. Profile information ranges from 'date of birth, gender, religion, politics and home town, to their favourite films, books, quotes and what they like doing in their spare time' (Ofcom, 2008).

> ## key term
>
> **E-commerce** Commercial activities conducted on the internet, eg advertising and selling goods and services.

summary

1. Digital technology forms the basis for the new media.
2. Online news has a rapidly growing audience – particularly among young people.
3. Online news is often repackaged from other sources.
4. There is an increasing amount of user generated content in online news.
5. Many blogs comment on the news. They sometimes generate news and occasionally break a news story.
6. Obama's election as president of the USA shows the potential of the internet to the political process.
7. A number of researchers argue that digital citizenship is essential for full participation in the political process.
8. The internet has been seen as a public sphere which can provide a space for people to debate freely.
9. The digital divide means that those who are excluded from terrestrial society are most likely to be excluded from online society.
10. A number of governments have attempted to suppress freedom of expression on the internet.
11. E-commerce is growing rapidly.
12. Social networking sites have grown dramatically in recent years.
13. Children and young adults are the main users.
14. Most people use social networking sites to keep in touch with close friends and family – relationships which were formed outside the sites.

Unit 8 Postmodernism

keyissues

1 How do postmodernists see today's society?

2 What is the role of the media in postmodern society?

8.1 Postmodern society and the media

Some researchers believe we are living in a *postmodern society*, a society that comes after and is different from modern society. This new age is known as *postmodernity*. Those who take this view are known as *postmodernists*. This section looks at some of the key features of postmodern society and their relationship to the media.

Media realities

Multiple realities We live in a media-saturated society. The media bombard us with images which increasingly dominate the way we see ourselves and the world around us. Media images, it is argued, do not reflect or even distort social reality. They are themselves realities. Our consciousness is invaded by the *multiple realities* provided by news, documentaries, pop music, advertisements, soaps and movies set in the past, present and future, on this world and other worlds.

The media not only provide multiple views of reality – these views are also open to a multitude of different interpretations. Media audiences are active – individuals place their own interpretations on what they see, hear and read.

Simulation Increasing exposure to the media blurs the division between our everyday reality and media images. The media provide us with much of our knowledge about the world. But this knowledge is not drawn from our direct experience. Instead it is reproduced knowledge, it is a *simulation* – it represents the real thing but it is not a true or genuine representation. In this sense, it has similarities to a *PlayStation* game.

To some extent, postmodernists apply this view to every aspect of the media – from the news, to soaps, to advertisements. From this perspective media simulations remove the distinction between image and reality – images become part of our reality.

Multiple truths As a result of the multiple realities and the variety of simulations presented by the media, the idea of an absolute truth has gone. There is no longer a single dominant meaning. Instead there are a multitude of meanings. A single truth has been replaced by many truths as the media broadcast different perspectives and different views from across the world and from the past and the present.

Living the image Images we experience from the media become as, if not more, real and significant than things we directly experience in everyday life. For example, the death of Princess Diana resulted in an outpouring of grief across the world – but for the vast majority she existed only through the media. And the same applies to the footballer George Best. His image was kept alive by the media and his death was headlined by TV news and national newspapers.

Even fiction can become 'real'. A death, a divorce or a marriage in a soap opera glues millions to the screen and is talked about next day as if it actually happened. As its name suggests, reality TV brings 'real' people into our homes and conversations. And it sometimes draws audiences further into this reality as they vote for which participants are to stay or go in shows like *Big Brother* and *I'm A Celebrity, Get Me Out Of Here*.

Postmodern identities

Identity and choice In modern societies, people's identities were usually drawn from their class, gender, occupation and ethnic group. In postmodern society, people have more opportunity to construct their own identities and more options to choose from. For example, a woman can be heterosexual, bisexual or lesbian, a business executive and a mother, she can be British, a Sikh and a member of Greenpeace. And her lifestyle and consumption patterns can reflect her chosen identity. Brand-name goods such as Gucci and Dolce & Gabbana can be used as statements of her identity.

With all the choices on offer, it is fairly easy for people to change their identities, or to have several identities which they put on and take off depending on their social situation. As a result, postmodern identities are more unstable and fragile. They offer choice, but they don't always provide a firm and lasting foundation.

Identity and the media The media offer a wide range of identities and lifestyles from which we can pick and choose and act out. Adverts sell images and style rather than content and substance. Jeans are not marketed as hard wearing and value for money but rather as style in the context of rock, R&B or hip-hop music. Drinks like Tango, Bacardi and Smirnoff Ice are sold on style and image rather than taste or quality. Coca-Cola is the 'real thing' despite the fact that it mainly consists of coloured sweetened water.

According to postmodernists, people are increasingly constructing their own identities from images and lifestyles presented by the media.

Time, space and change

Time and space The media allow us to criss-cross time and space. *Romeo and Juliet* was written by Shakespeare in the 16th century but the film starring Leonardo di Caprio takes place in the present day. Watching TV news we can go round the world in 30 minutes from Iraq to the USA, from Afghanistan to Northern Ireland. Adverts use music from the 1950s, 60s and 70s to sell beer, washing powder and jeans. And fashions in clothes, such as Miss Sixty, recreate styles from the past. As a result, 'time and space become less

stable and comprehensible, more confused, more incoherent, more disunified' (Strinati, 1992)

Change Images and styles are constantly changing. The media regularly present new styles of music and fashion, new types of food and drink, new and improved household products, many of which are linked to new lifestyles. Often these products are associated with media personalities – for example, Glow by JLO, advertised as 'the new fragrance by Jennifer Lopez'.

As a result of this constant change and emphasis on the new, things appear fluid – nothing seems permanent and solid. The mainstream culture of modern society is replaced by the fleeting, unstable, fragmented culture of postmodern society.

8.2 Postmodernism and the media – evaluation

Many sociologists are critical of the picture of the media and society presented by postmodernists. Greg Philo and David Miller (2001) make the following points.

- There is no way of saying that reality is distorted by media images because, according to postmodernists, those images and the way that people interpret them are the reality. This is carrying the idea of an active audience to a ridiculous extreme.

- People are well aware that there is a reality beyond the images broadcast by the media. They recognise that media messages are often one-sided, partial and distorted.

- Many people are not free to construct their own identities and select their own lifestyles. For example, people living in poverty simply don't have the money to buy Gucci sunglasses or Jean Paul Gaultier fragrance.

Despite these criticisms, many sociologists accept that the media are increasingly influential in today's society. And they accept that there is something to many of the points made by postmodernists, but see their argument as going too far.

activity28 postmodernism and the media

Item A *Identity cards*

SUPERMODEL

POP STAR

Dream Identity Card

SPORTS STAR

FILM STAR

Will it ever come to this? The Government is planning to sell Identity Scratch Cards. Scratch off the special square and you may win a year's worth of free identity. The winner gets to choose a dream identity, for example, a pop star or a major sports personality.

Source: Iannucci, 1995

Item B *The Truman Show*

In the film *The Truman Show* a man discovers that his life has been constructed as a soap opera. His family, friends and neighbours are all actors and he is the central character. Everything around him is an illusion, created by the media.

question

How do these items illustrate the postmodernist view of the media and society?

key terms

Postmodern society A society that comes after and is different from modern society.

Postmodernists Researchers who argue that we now live in a postmodern age.

Multiple realities The idea that the media present a number of different realities.

Simulation Images projected by the media rather than drawn from our direct experience. Despite this, these images become part of our reality.

summary

1. According to postmodernists, we live in a media-saturated society.
2. The media bombard us with multiple realities. These realities are simulations. Despite this, they become part of our reality. As a result, the division between everyday reality and media images disappears.
3. A single truth becomes multiple truths as the media present different views from across the world.
4. The media offer a wide range of identities and lifestyles from which we can pick and choose.
5. The media constantly present new images and styles. As a result, nothing seems permanent and solid.
6. Many critics argue that postmodernists have overstated their case, but accept there is something in what they say.

3 Crime and deviance

Introduction

We are fascinated by crime and deviance. This is evident from the mass media – from crime series on TV and crime reports in newspapers, from detective novels which are concerned with finding the criminal and explaining the crime, and from movies which often portray the more colourful, lurid and violent aspects of crime.

Why this fascination? Criminal behaviour appears unusual and different. It involves risks which endanger those who commit crimes and their victims. For many people, out-of-the-ordinary behaviour seems much more interesting than their own humdrum activities. And to those of us looking on, the risks and dangers involved are often experienced as exciting and entertaining – from a safe distance!

Crime and deviance break social norms – they deviate or diverge from conventional behaviour. This can be disturbing. We often fear crime and feel worried and anxious when taken-for-granted norms are broken. Why? Because such activities disrupt our sense of social order and threaten our view of the way things should be.

And this adds to our fascination with crime. It should therefore come as no surprise that crime and deviance is one of the most popular topics in sociology.

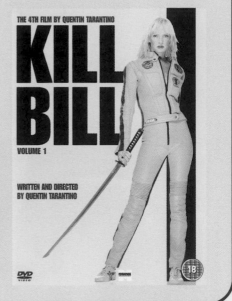

chaptersummary

▶ **Unit 1** looks at the meanings of deviance, crime and social control.

▶ **Unit 2** investigates evidence on the extent of crime, trends in the crime rate, and the identity of offenders.

▶ **Unit 3** examines media representations of crime and deviance.

▶ **Units 4, 5 and 6** outline and evaluate various sociological theories of crime and deviance, including functionalist, interactionist and Marxist approaches.

▶ **Units 7 and 8** examine two opposing theories of crime, social order and social control – right realism and left realism.

▶ **Unit 9** looks at the relationship between globalisation and crime, focusing on green crime and state crime.

▶ **Units 10, 11 and 12** look at the relationship between ethnicity and crime, gender and crime, and age and crime.

▶ **Unit 13** examines the spatial distribution of crime.

▶ **Unit 14** looks at social control, crime reduction and social policy.

▶ **Unit 15** examines sociological studies of suicide, focusing on the methodologies they use.

Unit 1 The nature of crime, deviance and social control

keyissues

1 What are crime, deviance and social control?

2 What is distinctive about the sociological approach to crime, deviance and social control?

1.1 Defining crime and deviance

Human social life is governed by norms and values – by norms which define appropriate and acceptable behaviour, and by values which define behaviour as right or wrong.

Sociologists have long been concerned with how society's norms and values are maintained.

However, there is another side to the story – how and why are norms broken and values rejected? In other words, how and why does *deviance* occur?

Deviance

Deviance is usually defined as behaviour which goes against conventional norms and generally accepted values. In terms of this definition, deviance is behaviour which most people would regard as inappropriate, or more strongly, as unacceptable and wrong. As a result, deviance is usually subject to a variety of social controls ranging from mild disapproval to severe punishment.

This view of deviance is reflected in the following definition by Downes and Rock (2003). 'Deviance may be considered as banned or controlled behaviour which is likely to attract punishment or disapproval.' This definition covers acts such as murder and rape which are explicitly banned in most cultures and subject to severe punishment. It also covers relatively trivial acts such as burping and farting in public which usually attract little more than a disapproving glance or a negative comment.

Crime

At first sight, *crime* is a much more specific category than the wide and varied range of activities covered by deviance. Often, crime is simply defined as an infraction of the criminal law – as lawbreaking. Crimes are usually seen as particularly serious and negative forms of deviance – hence laws which ban them and agents of social control such as the police and judges who deal with them. This view of crime is reflected in the following definition. 'Crimes are those actions deemed so disturbing to citizens or disruptive to society as to justify state intervention' (Pease, 2002).

This type of definition has its limitations. We cannot assume that crimes are always more disturbing to citizens or more disruptive to society than non-criminal behaviour. Think of all the non-criminal behaviour that contributes to global warming, global pollution and the destruction of the world's wildlife. In Muncie's (2001) words, 'Any number of damaging events are far more serious than those that make up the "crime problem".'

What is more, breaking the criminal law covers a vast array of actions from the trivial to the serious. Crime, like deviance, covers a highly varied range of behaviour. This leads some sociologists to talk about crimes in the plural rather than crime in the singular. In other words, there's 'crime and crime'.

There are many different definitions of deviance and crime. None are without their problems as Activity 1 illustrates. It looks at vandalism which the *Concise Oxford Dictionary* defines as the wilful or malicious destruction or damage of property. This destruction or damage may or may not be seen as deviant. It may or may not be defined as criminal damage.

key terms

Deviance Actions which deviate from the norms and values of society.
Crime A form of deviance which breaks the law.

activity1 vandalism

Item A

Item B

Item C

Item D

Item E

Item F

questions

1 Look at the pictures. Which (if any) would you see as examples of vandalism? Give reasons for your answer.
2 Using examples from this activity, briefly discuss the problems of defining crime and deviance.

1.2 The contexts and diversity of deviance

Deviance takes varied forms in society. For example, we can distinguish between *secret and private deviance* as against *open and public deviance*, and between *individual deviance* as against *collective deviance*.

Secret and private deviance This form of deviance is often concealed – not least due to the heavy personal costs of exposure to the public gaze. It is often undercover and may be hidden in normal settings such as the home or the workplace. Secret deviance may be legal – for example, a group with unusual sexual practices who meet in each other's homes. Or it may be illegal, as in the case of the Gloucester serial killer, Frederick West.

West appeared to be a fairly average family man with a normal occupation as a self-employed builder. Yet, in the privacy of his home, he murdered two members of his family and a number of vulnerable young women. Furthermore, he was able to use his 'normal' skills as a builder to hide the dead bodies in his house and garden.

Open and public deviance This form of deviance often involves conforming to the norms and values of a clearly defined outsider group – norms and values which differ from those of the wider society. Take the example of the so-called New Age Travellers in Britain today. Their lifestyle is very different from that of the mainstream population. They tend to be seen as a deviant group and are viewed with distaste and hostility by some members of society. They are an example of public and collective deviance.

1.3 The relativity of crime and deviance

Crime and deviance are relative to time, place and culture. In other words, what counts as crime and deviance varies from time to time, place to place and culture to culture.

Societal and situational deviance Ken Plummer (1979) captures this point in his distinction between societal and situational deviance. *Societal deviance* refers to behaviour which breaks the law or which is seen as deviant by most members of society. It is judged to be deviant on the basis of their shared values and beliefs and what 'common sense' tells them. There is general agreement about the identification of societal deviance – for example, most people regard armed robbery as wrong, as deviant and as criminal.

Situational deviance refers to the effect of the context or situation on the classification of deviance. In one situation an act may be seen as deviant, in another situation it may not. People interpret what counts as deviance in their personal worlds of friends, colleagues and acquaintances. Plummer accepts that the beliefs and values of the wider society affect views of situational deviance. However, he argues that in certain contexts people either neutralise or reject the societal version of deviance.

Plummer uses the example of homosexuality to illustrate this point. Homosexuality is societally deviant but not always situationally deviant. In certain contexts, such as gay bars and clubs, homosexuality is no longer deviant – it becomes the norm.

Culture and deviance Crime and deviance are relative to culture. Different cultures have different norms and values. As a result, what is considered normal and deviant will vary from one culture to another. For example, in many non-Western societies marriage is polygynous – a man may have two or more wives. In the West, this is not only deviant, but criminal.

As cultures change, so do definitions of deviance and crime. At certain times in Western societies it was considered deviant for women to use make-up and consume alcoholic drinks in public. Today, this is no longer the case. In the same way, definitions of crime change over time. Sexual relations between men were once a criminal offence in Britain. Since 1969, homosexual acts between consenting adults in private have no longer been illegal.

activity2 deviance is relative

Item A Smoking banned

On Saturday, 29 March 2003, Robert de Niro and Danny de Vito joined 280 guests in the ballroom of the Regent Wall Street Hotel in New York for a $95-a-head Last Smoke dinner. The prime rib steak smoked in tobacco leaves went down well. De Niro and De Vito lit up their Cuban Montecristo cigars.

When the clock struck midnight, the Last Smoke was over. Smoking was banned in 13,000 New York bars and restaurants which were not covered by an earlier smoking ban.

The city hired an army of inspectors to tour bars and restaurants, confiscating ashtrays and issuing warnings in a 30-day grace period before fines of up to $3000 start being slapped on owners.

Source: *The Observer*, 30.3.2003

After the ban

Item B Endorsing Camels

The late American film star John Wayne advertising Camel cigarettes

questions

1 Use information from Items A and B to illustrate the point that deviance is relative to time and place.

2 Look at Item B. Why would it be unlikely for a film star today to endorse cigarettes?

1.4 Social control

Every society has methods of making its members toe the line, of making sure that they stick to the straight and narrow. These methods are known as mechanisms or methods of *social control*. They ensure that most of the people, most of the time, conform to society's norms and values. For social order to exist, shared norms and values are necessary and conformity to them must be enforced. Enforcing conformity means discouraging deviant and criminal behaviour – behaviour which breaks social norms and goes against shared values.

Social control takes many forms. Some researchers have distinguished between *formal* and *informal* methods of social control.

Formal methods of social control Formal methods refer to institutions specifically set up to enforce social control. In modern industrial societies, this mainly involves institutions which create and enforce the law – for example, parliament which enacts the law and the police, judiciary and prison service which enforce the law.

The ultimate and most obvious form of social control is physical force. Under certain circumstances, some have the right to use physical force against others in an attempt to control their behaviour. In modern industrial societies, the police are an obvious example. Other formal methods of social control include judicial punishments such as fines and imprisonment.

Informal methods of social control Informal methods of social control involve institutions and social groups which are not directly concerned with enforcing social control and upholding the law. These groups and institutions include the family, schools, religious organisations and significant others.

The family and the school socialise young people, teaching them the norms and values of the wider society. Conformity to these norms and values is usually rewarded, deviance from them is usually punished.

Religious teachings often reinforce the values of society. For example, the Christian Commandments 'you shall not kill' and 'you shall not steal' reinforce the values placed on human life and private property. And, in turn, they back up secular laws protecting life and property. Religions offer rewards to those who follow their teachings and punishments to those who deviate from them. In this way, religion acts as a mechanism of social control.

Significant others are people who matter to an individual. They usually include his or her immediate family, friends, neighbours and workmates. People are concerned about what significant others think about them. Their approval makes them feel good, their disapproval upsets them. Because the opinion of significant others is held so highly, they can play an important part in controlling the behaviour of an individual. People often conform to social norms in order to gain the approval and acceptance of significant others and to avoid their disapproval and rejection.

Many sociologists see informal social controls as more important and effective than the more obvious formal controls.

key terms

Social control Methods of controlling people's behaviour – encouraging them to conform to society's norms and values and discouraging deviant and criminal behaviour.
Formal methods of social control Institutions specifically set up to enforce social control – in particular, institutions which create and enforce the law.
Informal methods of social control Institutions and groups which are not directly concerned with enforcing social control yet still play an important part in controlling the behaviour of others.

summary

1. The term deviance covers a wide range of behaviour which deviates from the norms and values of society.

2. The term crime also covers a variety of activities – from the trivial to the serious.

3. Crime and deviance may be secret and private or open and public; individual, involving one person, or collective, involving a group of people.

4. Crime and deviance are relative to time, place and culture. What counts as crime and deviance varies from time to time, place to place and culture to culture.

5. Every society has mechanisms of social control which discourage crime and deviance.

6. Formal mechanisms of social control include institutions which create and enforce the law – for example, parliament, the police and the judiciary.

7. Informal mechanisms of social control include the family, schools, religious organisations and significant others. Although not directly concerned with social control, sociologists see them as powerful control mechanisms.

activity3 social control

Item A Police

Item B Family

Item C Friends

Item D Prison

questions

1 Which of the items are examples of a) formal social control and b) informal social control?

2 Briefly suggest how each item may help to enforce social control.

Unit 2 Crime statistics

key issues

1 How are the volume and trends in crime measured?
2 How are offenders identified?
3 How valid and reliable are data on crime and offenders?

2.1 Measuring crime

The two main measures There are two main measures of crime in Britain. The first, *police recorded crime*, is based on police records – records kept by the police of crimes which they have recorded. The second, the British Crime Survey (BCS), is based on interviews with a representative sample of adults. It asks whether they have been victims of particular crimes during the previous year.

Sections 2.2 and 2.3 look at the 'official' picture of crime presented by police recorded crime. Section 2.4 looks at the picture presented by the British Crime Survey.

The official picture Each year, statistics produced from police records provide an official account of the volume of crime and trends in crime. In addition, statistics compiled from court records and police cautioning records give an official picture of those responsible for criminal offences – that is the 'criminals'. Together, these statistics present a picture of the 'crime problem' – a picture interpreted for us by politicians and transmitted to us by the mass media.

But are official statistics a valid measure of crime? Do they provide an accurate measure of the extent of crime and of trends in crime? Do they present a true picture of those who commit crimes? The short answer to all these questions is probably not.

2.2 The volume of crime

According to official statistics based on police records, there were around six million cases of recorded crime in the United Kingdom in 2006/07 (*Social Trends*, 2008). Nearly three quarters (73%) of these were offences against property – theft, handling stolen goods, criminal damage, burglary, fraud and forgery.

These statistics do not represent the total volume of crime. There is a so-called 'dark figure' or 'hidden figure' of unrecorded crime. There are various reasons why the official picture is incomplete. And there are reasons why this picture may be systematically biased – for example, it may repeatedly underestimate certain kinds of crime.

Recorded versus known offences Official statistics do not even give a complete record of criminal offences known to the authorities. For example, until 1998 they didn't cover *summary offences* – those tried in Magistrates' Courts as opposed to Crown Courts. Such offences include driving after consuming alcohol over the legal limit. Nor do statistics on recorded crime cover offences dealt with *administratively* by organisations such as the Inland Revenue. Generally speaking, the Inland Revenue negotiate a monetary settlement with people who commit a tax offence – for example, with a business which does not record all its takings and so pays less tax than it should.

There may be some justification for omitting the above offences if they were trivial. But consider this. Over half of crime statistics are made up of criminal damage and theft from a vehicle or from shops. Often such crimes involve small amounts of damage or loss. It is questionable whether they can be seen as more serious than summary offences or offences dealt with administratively.

Police recording practices A further example of known offences not appearing in official statistics is provided by police recording practices. Over 30% of offences reported to the police in 2002/03 were not recorded (Simmons & Dodd, 2003). While the police have a statutory obligation to record crimes, they also have some discretion over whether a crime is serious enough to warrant their attention.

This discretion can be used in different ways by different police forces. For example, in 1981, Nottinghamshire appeared to be the most criminal area in the country. This was largely due to many more crimes involving £10 or less being recorded in Nottinghamshire than in comparable counties such as Leicestershire and Staffordshire (Holdaway, 1988).

The Home Office provides police forces with 'counting rules' to calculate the extent of crime. The basic rule is that the statistics should indicate the number of victims rather than the number of criminal acts. For example, if a single victim has been assaulted by the same person on several occasions, only the most serious offence is counted (Maguire, 2002). This can make some crimes appear less serious than they are. For example, it can understate the extent of domestic violence which often involves numerous assaults over a prolonged period.

Police priorities The number and type of offences discovered by the police in the course of their operations will vary according to their priorities. And this, in turn, will affect crime statistics.

Police priorities are influenced by the concerns of local and national government, pressure groups, public opinion and the media. For example, in recent years, the police have directed more resources to combat paedophilia, due, in part, to increased media concern with this offence.

An ongoing police priority is to improve their clear-up rate – solve more crimes and catch more offenders. With this in mind, resources tend to be targeted at certain crimes. In the words of a retired police officer, 'If you don't catch a burglar, he will go out and he will commit a lot of crime which will then be reported and it will damage your detection rate' (Davies, 1994).

Reporting and non-reporting Over 80% of all recorded crime results from reports by the public (Bottomley & Coleman, 1981). Some types of crime are more likely to be reported than others. For example, 93% of thefts of vehicles were reported to the police in 2007/08, as an official record of the incident is needed for insurance purposes. This compares with estimates which suggest that only around a third of incidents of vandalism and theft from the person are reported (Kershaw et al., 2008).

There are many reasons why crimes are not reported to the police.

- There may be a lack of awareness that a crime has taken place – eg, fraud.
- The victim may be relatively powerless and frightened of the consequences of reporting – eg, child abuse and domestic violence.
- The offence may seem too trivial – eg, vandalism.
- There is no apparent victim – eg, prostitution.
- A view that the police can't do anything about the incident.
- The matter was dealt with privately.

Crime statistics rely heavily on the public reporting incidents to the police. Since some types of crime are more likely to be reported than others, official statistics will not reflect the overall pattern of crime.

The significance of crime statistics Numbers aren't everything. For example, violence against the person, sexual offences and fraud may form a relatively small proportion of recorded crime, but there are other ways of measuring their significance.

Violent and sexual offences often have a traumatic effect upon victims and their seriousness is evident from the number and length of prison sentences they bring – around a third of prisoners are serving sentences for violent or sexual offences.

Fraud may only account for 6% of recorded crime but its monetary value is far greater than this suggests. In Mike Maguire's (2002) words, 'If one measures the importance of property offences in terms of the value stolen, rather than the quantity of incidents, fraud comes out as of enormously greater significance than other categories'. If we take any one of the major cases of alleged fraud investigated by the Serious Fraud Office in the early 1990s – Barlow Clowes, Guinness, Maxwell, BCCI, Polly Peck – we find that, by itself, it exceeded the total amount stolen in thefts and burglaries recorded by the police (Levi, 1993).

Conclusion Official statistics on recorded crime are drawn from police records – they are based on data collected by the police. The evidence presented in this section indicates that these statistics fail to provide a reliable and valid measurement of crime. And they may be systematically biased in underestimating the extent of certain crimes.

Official statistics on recorded crime are *not* simple, straightforward facts. Instead, they are a *social construction* – they are constructed during the process of social interaction, they are based on a series of interpretations, definitions and decisions which are influenced by a variety of factors, and vary from situation to situation. In the words of Simon Holdaway (1988), 'Official statistics of crime are not so much the facts about crime, as the end product of a complex series of decisions. An incident occurs and someone decides that it is a crime. A decision is made to telephone a police officer and the police officer receiving the call decides to regard the incident as a crime. Another officer attends the scene and, hearing the various accounts of the incident, makes a further decision about its being a crime, and so on. The official statistics are socially constructed; they are the end product of a range of decisions.'

key terms

Police recorded crime Crimes recorded by the police from which official statistics on crime are drawn.
Summary offences Crimes dealt with by Magistrates' Courts as opposed to Crown Courts. They were not included in official statistics until 1998.
Crime dealt with administratively Crimes which are not prosecuted – not taken to court. They are dealt with by organisations such as the Inland Revenue and do not appear in police recorded crime.
Social construction Definitions and meanings constructed in the course of social interaction.

activity4 domestic violence and fraud

Item A Domestic violence

Domestic violence includes violent incidents which involve partners, ex-partners, household members or other relatives. According to the British Crime Survey, only one in three victims of domestic violence report the incident to the police. Reasons for non-reporting include a desire for privacy, fear of reprisals and of family break-up.

Domestic violence often involves a series of incidents over a period of time – for example, a woman may be assaulted many times by her partner. However, the police only record the most serious incident.

A study conducted jointly by the police and the Crown Prosecution Service investigated 465 incidents of domestic violence to which the police were called. There should have been 260 crime reports, but only 118 incidents were recorded. Only 21% of these resulted in charges and there was a conviction in just 11%. In nearly half the cases received by the Crown Prosecution Service, the victim withdrew the complaint.

Source: Cowan, 2004

A Women's Aid poster – the organisation helps women who have been victims of domestic violence

Childbirth isn't the only strain associated with pregnancy...

Domestic violence often starts or increases during pregnancy.*

From bruises and broken bones to forced sex or the psychological damage of living in fear... domestic violence is no accident.

Contact the Freephone 24 Hour National Domestic Violence Helpline for information and support:

0808 2000 247 (Run in partnership between Women's Aid and Refuge)

WARNING: DOMESTIC VIOLENCE DAMAGES YOUR HEALTH
You can contact your local Women's Aid group or other local help services on:

Item B Fraud

In June 2002, WorldCom, the second largest long-distance telephone company in the USA, was forced to admit a $4 billion hole in its accounts. In other words, the company had fraudulently claimed to have $4 billion more than it actually had. WorldCom shares dropped from a peak of $64 to a mere 20 cents. Investors lost a fortune because of this accounting fraud.

Fraud is a difficult crime to define. It ranges from avoiding VAT and alcohol and tobacco smuggling – estimated by the Home Office to be worth around £7 billion a year – to credit card fraud which rose in value by 30% between 2000 and 2001 to an estimated £411 million. The value of cases of fraud in the City investigated by the Serious Fraud Office – for example, illegal share dealing – totalled £1.75 billion in 2001/02. Social security fraud is estimated at £2 billion a year. But the above examples are dwarfed by tax fraud. One estimate, by the accountancy firm Deloitte and Touche, puts the cost of 'tax dodging' between 1976 and 1996 at £2000 billion – the equivalent of six years of government expenditure.

Fraud is difficult to detect – the cases uncovered are probably only the tip of the iceberg. Often they involve a large number of fraudulent acts. But, when they are detected, only one or two 'sample' offences are recorded by the police. And many cases of detected fraud never enter police records. Tax, social security and VAT fraud are usually dealt with administratively. The Inland Revenue rarely prosecutes detected offenders, despite the enormous sums involved.

Source: Croall, 2001; Maguire, 2002; *The Guardian*, 12.7.2002

Bernard Ebbers, former WorldCom chief executive officer (centre), escorted by US federal agents after turning himself in to face fraud charges

question

Police recorded crime statistics present an incomplete picture of crime. They seriously underestimate certain types of crime. They fail to indicate the significance of certain types of crime.

What support do Items A and B provide for these views?

2.3 Trends in crime

Police recorded crime

Each year, when the government publishes statistics on recorded crime, newspapers respond with headlines such as: Violent crime up 20%; Burglary up 10%. These headlines are usually based on a comparison of the present year's figures with those of the previous year. This section looks at trends in crime over longer periods of time.

Official statistics since 1876 show little change in annual crime figures until the 1930s. Then, there is a gradual rise to the early 1950s, followed by a sharp increase until the early 1990s. Since then, the figures have gone up and down, but remained at a high level compared to earlier years – see Activity 5, Item B.

If there are problems with official crime statistics in any one year, these are magnified when we examine trends over time. First, more crimes may be reported as time goes on. Second, new types of crime may be emerging and new opportunities opening up for existing crimes. Third, changes in legislation and law enforcement may result in more crimes being recorded. These are some of the factors which must be considered before drawing any conclusions from trends in crime statistics.

More crimes may be reported Since the mid-1990s, the proportion of crime reported to the police has remained more or less the same – around 44% of all crime. This is significantly higher than in the early 1980s (Simmons & Dodd, 2003). A number of reasons have been suggested for the increase in reporting rate.

- Increased telephone ownership, especially of mobiles, which makes reporting easier.
- The growth of reported burglary between 1981 and 1993 may be related to an increase in valuable goods in the home – for example, TVs and videos – to wider car ownership, and more insurance policies covering house contents and cars. Insurance companies require a police report when a crime has been committed (Mayhew et al., 1994).
- People may be less willing to tolerate certain types of crime. For example, the increase in reported violent crime may, at least in part, be due to less tolerance of violence. Recorded incidents of robbery, rape and theft from the person more than doubled between 1991 and 2000/01 (Maguire, 2002).
- The break-up of traditional, close-knit communities may result in people being more inclined to bring in the police to deal with incidents rather than sorting things out for themselves (Maguire, 2002).

New crimes and new opportunities Trends in crime change. New crimes emerge as do new opportunities to commit existing crimes. The invention of credit and debit cards and computers provides opportunities for theft and fraud which did not exist 50 years ago. Today, thefts of, or from, motor vehicles make up around one fifth of recorded crime. In the 1950s, these offences were relatively rare as there were far fewer cars on the road (Maguire, 2002).

Changes in legislation and law enforcement These changes may result in more crimes being recorded. This can be seen from the following examples.

The decision in 1977 to include offences of criminal damage of £20 or less in police crime statistics raised the annual total by around 7% (Maguire, 2002). And the decision in 1998 to include summary offences, such as common assault, again boosted the total of recorded crime, as well as giving the impression of a major increase in violent crime. It is estimated that this change, plus new counting rules, increased the total number of recorded offences by up to 14% (Maguire, 2002). In 2002, the introduction of a new National Crime Recording Standard, designed to reduce police discretion in recording reports of offences from the public, resulted in the highest proportion of reported crime ever recorded by the police (Simmons & Dodd, 2003).

In the 1970s, the increased use of formal cautions for young people added substantially to the volume of recorded crime. According to one estimate, this change accounted for the whole increase in recorded crime for boys under 14 during the 1970s (Pearson, 1983).

Finally, the increase in the numbers of police officers – an increase of over 50% since the 1980s – coupled with more sophisticated technology, is likely to have resulted in more crimes being recorded.

Conclusion Does the rise in recorded crime mean that more crimes are being committed? The evidence presented in this section suggests that this may not be the case. It shows that at least part of the increase in recorded crime may have nothing to do with changes in the actual volume of crime.

2.4 The British Crime Survey (BCS)

Methodology

The British Crime Survey (BCS) is a *victim study* – it asks people if they have been a victim of particular crimes. The survey was conducted every two years from 1982 to 2000, and since then every year.

The BCS is based on a representative sample of adults (aged 16 and over) living in private households in England and Wales. The response rate – those who agreed to be interviewed – in the 2007/08 survey was 76%. Nearly 47,000 interviews were conducted. Respondents were asked to recall crimes against themselves or any other member of the household over a 12 month period preceding the interview (Kershaw et al., 2008).

Various crimes are excluded from the BCS – crimes such as murder, where the victim is no longer available for interview, so-called victimless crimes (eg, drug possession or dealing), fraud, and offences against non-domestic targets such as businesses. BCS estimates exclude sexual offences due to the small number reported to the survey and concerns about people's willingness to disclose such offences (Simmons & Dodd, 2003).

BCS findings

The 2006/07 British Crime Survey provides the following picture of crime in England and Wales.

The volume of crime On the basis of interviews conducted in 2006/07, the BCS estimates that 11.3 million crimes were committed against adults living in private households. Police recorded crime for England and Wales for the same period was just under 5.5 million. The BCS estimate is, therefore, more than double police recorded crime.

Unreported and unrecorded crime Not all BCS crimes can be directly compared with police figures – for example, thefts involving household and personal property are placed by the police in the same category as thefts of business property and shoplifting, crimes which are not included in the BCS. However, just over 9.5 million BCS crimes are comparable with those in police statistics. Of these, 43% were reported to the police, and of those reported, 68% were recorded by the police. This means that only 29% of all BCS crimes were actually recorded by the police and entered the official statistics of police recorded crime (Simmons & Dodd, 2003).

Since the BCS includes both unreported and unrecorded crime, it gives a more complete estimate of many crimes than police records.

Trends in crime From 1981 to 1995, British Crime Survey estimates show a steady rise in crime. Since then, there has been a steady fall, apart from a slight rise in 2006/07 – see Activity 5, Item C.

In general, the BCS trends in the volume of crime are reflected in the trends in police recorded crime. However, they diverged when a new counting rule for recorded crime was introduced in 1998 and the National Crime Recording Standard came into operation in 2002.

key term

Victim study/survey A study of the victims of crime. Such studies usually ask people to report the crimes that have been committed against them, or any other member of the household, during the previous year.

activity5 the British Crime Survey

Item A The BCS and police recorded crime

	% of BCS crimes reported to the police	% of reported BCS crimes recorded by the police	% of all BCS crimes recorded by the police
Vandalism	31	70	22
PROPERTY CRIME	50	75	38
Burglary	65	71	46
Burglary attempts and no loss	49	42	21
Burglary with loss	87	94	81
All vehicle thefts	50	84	42
Thefts from vehicles	47	75	35
Thefts of vehicles	97	84	81
Attempted vehicle theft	36	100	38
Bicycle theft	50	56	28
Thefts from the person	33	59	19
VIOLENCE	41	52	21
Common assault	34	46	16
Wounding	46	57	26
Robbery	53	54	28
ALL COMPARABLE CRIME	43	68	29

Source: Simmons & Dodd, 2003

Item B *Police recorded crime trends*

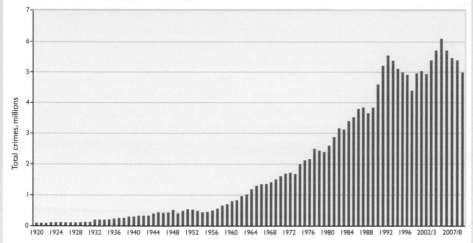

Crimes recorded by the police, England and Wales, 1920–2007/08

New counting rules were introduced in 2002/03

Note: From 1997, the figures are based on the financial year (ie, April to March).

Source: Maguire, 2002 and Kershaw et al., 2008

Item C *BCS trends*

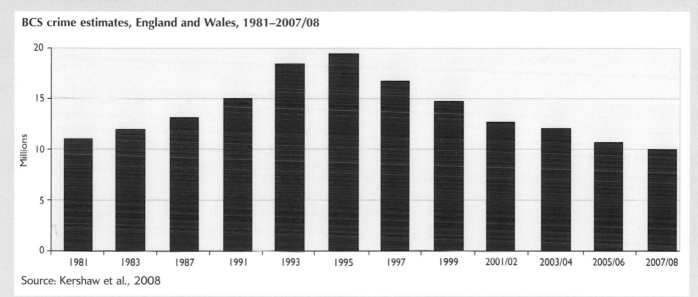

BCS crime estimates, England and Wales, 1981–2007/08

Source: Kershaw et al., 2008

questions

1 a) Briefly summarise the differences between the police and BCS figures in Item A.

  b) Why are some crimes more likely to be reported to the police than others?

  c) Why are some crimes reported to the police more likely to be recorded than others?

2 a) Briefly summarise the trends shown in Items B and C.

  b) Suggest reasons for any differences in recent trends between police recorded crime and BCS estimates.

These new measures increased the volume of police recorded crime. For example, the National Crime Recording Standard raised the volume of police recorded crime by 10% in 2002/03. This 10% 'increase' was simply due to a change in recording practice, it does not reflect a real increase in crime.

Without these changes in recording practices, the trends in police recorded crime would be similar to the BCS trends – they would show a steady decline in the volume of crime from the mid-1990s (Simmons & Dodd, 2003).

Evaluation of the BCS

Advantages For the crimes it covers, the British Crime Survey provides a more accurate picture of the extent of crime and of trends in crime than police recorded crime. There are two main reasons for this.

- First, BCS estimates include unreported and unrecorded crime.
- Second, the trends identified by the BCS are not affected by changes in recording practices, unlike the trends identified from police records.

Disadvantages There are a number of disadvantages of the BCS. They include the following.

- Only three-quarters of BCS crimes can be directly compared to police recorded crime.

- Because it is a household survey, the BCS does not cover a range of crimes which appear in police statistics. These include crimes against corporate and commercial organisations – such as fraud and shoplifting – motoring offences and so-called victimless crimes – such as possession or dealing in drugs (Maguire, 2002).
- Locally-based surveys of women indicate that the BCS underestimates assaults committed by people known to the victims – for example, partners.
- The BCS is a national survey. However, crime is not spread evenly across the country. In certain inner-city areas, the risks of serious crime are high. A local victim survey in Islington revealed that one-third of all households reported being a victim of burglary, robbery or sexual assault within the previous year (Jones et al., 1986). This is considerably higher than the national figure.

2.5 The social characteristics of offenders

Sociologists often explain behaviour in terms of people's social characteristics – for example, their social class, ethnicity, gender and age. Sociologists are therefore interested in the social characteristics of offenders. For instance, if offenders are primarily young, male and working class, then these factors may help to explain their criminal behaviour.

There are two main sources for identifying the social characteristics of offenders – official sources and self-report studies.

The official picture

Known offenders Statistics compiled from court records and police cautioning records provide an official picture of offenders. It is important to note that the number of 'known offenders' is small compared to the number of recorded offences. For example, in 2000, some 325,000 people were sentenced in court in England and Wales and 151,000 were cautioned by the police. This compares with over 5 million recorded crimes. The proportion of known offenders becomes even smaller when a comparison is made with BCS data. According to one estimate, only 3 in 100 BCS crimes resulted in an offender being convicted or cautioned (Barclay & Tavares, 1999).

We cannot assume that all offenders are similar to this small proportion of known offenders. In other words, we cannot generalise from such a small, and probably unrepresentative, sample.

Social characteristics Of the 476,000 offenders convicted or cautioned in 2000, 80% were male and 41% under the age of 21. Often gender and age are the only characteristics of offenders available from court and police cautioning records.

A fuller picture is provided by the National Prison Survey which was conducted in England and Wales in 1991

(Walmsley et al., 1992). The main findings were as follows.

- 62% of inmates were under 30 compared with 25% in the population as a whole.
- A disproportionate number were from the lower levels of the class system – 41% of males formerly had unskilled or partly-skilled manual jobs compared with 18% of the population as a whole.
- Given their numbers in the general population, a disproportionate number of prisoners came from ethnic minorities – particularly African Caribbean.

Overall, the findings of the National Prison Survey reveal a very different pattern than that found in the wider population.

Mike Maguire (2002) describes the picture presented by official sources of the social characteristics of offenders. 'There are many more males, young people, Black people, poor people, poorly-educated people, and people with disturbed childhoods than one would find in a random sample.'

Self-report studies

Only some 3% of crimes result in a conviction or caution. What about the other 97%? Do those who committed these offences share the same characteristics as the 3%? *Self-report studies* may help to provide an answer to this question.

Self-report studies of crime ask people whether they have committed a series of offences. They are usually based on a self-completed questionnaire or an interview. Respondents are presented with a list of offences and asked which they have committed over a period of time – for example, during the past 12 months or during their lifetime.

Crime is normal Self-report studies suggest that most of us have committed at least one crime at some stage in our lives. This questions the view that a clear distinction can be made between law-abiding people and offenders. Gabor (1994) argues that many of us have done one or more of the following: 'taken home linens, silverware, art and other "souvenirs" from hotels in which we have stayed; made inflated insurance claims following a fire or theft; illegally copied computer software or videos; used prohibited drugs or abused prescription drugs; exhibited disorderly conduct in public; physically struck another person intentionally'.

It is possible to argue that crime is 'normal'. If this is the case, then there is nothing particularly distinctive about the social characteristics of those who break the law. However, there are problems with this view. What kinds of crime are we talking about? Many of the crimes committed by most people can be seen as fairly trivial. And how many crimes do most people commit? Self-report studies indicate that committing one or two criminal acts is a 'normal' part of growing up for most boys. However, frequent lawbreaking is relatively rare (Hood & Sparks, 1970).

Gender Self-report studies indicate that far more males than females commit crimes. This reflects the picture given by official statistics. In a self-report study conducted by the

Home Office, over 30% of 22-25 year-old males admitted a criminal offence within the previous year, compared with only 4% of females in the same age group (Graham & Bowling, 1995).

Social class Most self-report studies suggest a link between social class and criminal behaviour. They indicate that the lower a person's position in the class system, the more likely they are to commit a crime. Again, this reflects the picture given by official statistics (Coleman & Moynihan, 1996).

This link appears strongest in terms of 'street crime' – burglary, robbery, theft of or from a vehicle – and the so-called *underclass* – those at the base of the class system, the long-term unemployed and those dependent on welfare benefits (Farnworth et al., 1994).

However, there are problems with this apparent link between class and crime. Street crimes are the typical crimes of the poor. They are a police priority and are the types of crime which the police are most likely to deal with. And they are the types of crime which tend to be listed by researchers in self-report questionnaires and structured interviews. Other types of crime, such as fraud, domestic violence and child abuse, are less visible and less likely to appear on a list in self-report studies. In view of this, it is not surprising that the poor appear to commit more crimes than their better-off counterparts (Maguire, 2002).

Age Self-report studies, like official statistics, suggest that crime is a 'young person's game'. However, it is important to note that young people tend to offend in groups and in public – they are more visible and more likely to be apprehended. Also the crimes young people commit are more likely to be listed in self-report studies (Coleman & Moynihan, 1996). And they are more likely to be reported to the police – for example, vehicle theft.

Ethnicity There is little difference between Blacks and Whites in self-reported crime. This is at odds with the picture presented by official statistics which shows a relatively high proportion of Black offenders.

Evaluation and conclusion

Official statistics reveal the social characteristics of those who have been processed by the criminal justice system – that is, those who have been cautioned, those found guilty by the courts, and those imprisoned. They reflect the priority given by the police to certain kinds of crime and certain types of lawbreakers. As such, they are useful.

However, official statistics are unlikely to present a picture of the social characteristics of lawbreakers in general. They indicate that young, working-class males are a major crime problem. But this may simply reflect the fact that 'most police resources are devoted to uniformed patrol of public space' where most young working-class males are likely to spend their social lives (Reiner, 1994). And police priorities and perceptions might well be the main reason for the apparent class/crime link. According to William Chambliss (1969) 'The lower class person is (i) more likely to be scrutinised and therefore to be observed in any violation of the law, (ii) more likely to be arrested if discovered under suspicious circumstances, (iii) more likely to spend the time between arrest and trial in jail, (iv) more likely to come to trial, (v) more likely to be found guilty, and (vi) if found guilty, more likely to receive harsh punishment than his middle or upper-class counterpart.'

Self-report studies The results of self-report studies must be approached with caution. Traditionally, they have focused on male juvenile delinquency – the criminal behaviour of young men. And the lists of crimes presented in self-report studies tend to reflect those typically committed by young working-class males – in particular 'street crime'. They tend to omit 'hidden crimes' and adult crimes, such as domestic violence and child abuse, crimes which are likely to be spread more evenly across age and class groups. And they are unlikely to include fraud, often committed by middle-class, middle-aged men. As a result, self-report studies provide only a partial view of crime. And this leads to a one-sided picture of the social characteristics of offenders.

key terms

Self-report study A survey in which respondents report on aspects of their behaviour – in the case of crime, the offences they have committed over a period of time.
Underclass Some sociologists claim that an underclass, a class below the working class, has developed in modern societies. Characteristics of the underclass include dependency on welfare benefits and long-term unemployment.

summary

1. There are two main measure of crime in Britain – police recorded crime based on police records, and the British Crime Survey (BCS), a victim study based on a representative sample of adults.

2. Police recorded crime statistics do not represent the total volume of crime. There is a 'dark figure' or 'hidden figure' of unrecorded crime.

3. Certain offences, for example many tax offences, do not enter police records because they are dealt with administratively by organisations such as the Inland Revenue.

4. Many of the offences reported to the police are not recorded – over 30% in 2002/03. Often this is because the offences are seen as too trivial to record.

5. Police priorities affect the crimes they target, the number and

type of offences they discover, and the crime statistics they produce.

6. Some crimes are more likely to be reported to the police than others. For example, vehicle theft is much more likely to be reported than domestic violence.

7. Police recorded crime provides statistics. It has nothing to say about the significance of crime. For example, in monetary terms fraud is much more significant than other property offences.

8. Police recorded crime fails to provide a reliable and valid measure of crime. It may be significantly biased in underestimating certain types of crime – for example, fraud and domestic violence.

9. Police crime statistics are a social construction. They are constructed during the process of social interaction and based on a series of interpretations, definitions and decisions.

10. Police recorded crime provides the following picture of trends in crime. There is little change in the annual crime figures from 1876 until the 1930s. Then, there is a gradual rise to the 1950s, followed by a sharp increase until the early 1990s. Since then, the figures have gone up and down, but remained high compared to earlier years.

11. The following reasons have been given for the increase in police recorded crime.
    ● The proportion of crime reported to the police rose significantly between the early 1980s and mid-1990s.
    ● New crimes and new opportunities for crime have developed – for example, credit card fraud.
    ● Changes in police recording practices have increased the total of recorded crime.

12. The rise in police recorded crime does not necessarily mean that more crimes are being committed. However, evidence from the British Crime Survey indicates an actual rise in crime from the early 1980s until 1995.

13. The British Crime Survey (BCS) is a victim study based on a representative sample of adults in England and Wales.

14. It estimates that the total volume of crime is more than double the total given by police recorded crime.

15. The BCS indicates a steady rise in crime from 1981 to 1995, followed by a steady fall.

16. Differences between BCS and police recorded crime trends since 1995 are probably due to changes in police recording practices. These changes increased the level of recorded crime.

17. Compared to police recorded crime, the BCS has the advantage of including both unreported and unrecorded crime. Also, it is not affected by changes in recording practices.

18. The BCS has a number of disadvantages. They include:
    ● The BCS does not cover certain crimes which appear in police statistics – for example, fraud.
    ● It underestimates certain crimes – for example, domestic violence.

19. There are two main sources for identifying the social characteristics of offenders – official sources and self-report studies.

20. Statistics from court records and police cautioning records provide an official picture of offenders. However, the number of 'known offenders' is small compared with the number of recorded offences.

21. This number becomes even smaller when BCS crimes are taken into account. Only around 3 in 100 BCS crimes result in an offender being convicted or cautioned. We cannot generalise from such a small and probably unrepresentative sample.

22. According to official sources, the typical offender is young, male and working class.

23. Self-report studies indicate that most people have committed at least one crime. In this respect, there is nothing distinctive about people who break the law.

24. Self-report studies give the following picture of the social characteristics of offenders. It reflects the picture provided by official statistics.
    ● Significantly more males than females commit crimes.
    ● The lower a person's position in the class system, the more likely they are to commit crimes.
    ● Younger people are more likely to commit crimes than older people.

25. The social characteristics of offenders provided by official statistics reflect the priorities given by the police to certain kinds of crime and certain types of lawbreakers.

26. Self-report studies tend to focus on the types of crime committed by young working-class males. They tend to omit adult crimes, such as domestic violence and fraud, which are likely to be spread more evenly across age and social class groups.

27. Both official sources and self-report studies give only a partial view of crime. This leads to a one-sided picture of the social characteristics of offenders.

activity6 your self-report

Incident	Offence	Maximum Penalty
1. Have you ever bought goods knowing or believing they may have been stolen?	Handling stolen property	£5,000 and/or 6 months imprisonment
2. Have you taken stationery or anything else from your office/work?	Theft	£5,000 and/or 6 months imprisonment
3. Have you ever used the firm's telephone for personal calls?	Dishonestly abstracting electricity	£5,000 and/or 6 months imprisonment
4. Have you ever kept money if you received too much change?	Theft	£5,000 and/or 6 months imprisonment
5. Have you kept money found in the street?	Theft	£5,000 and/or 6 months imprisonment
6. Have you taken 'souvenirs' from a pub/hotel?	Theft	£5,000 and/or 6 months imprisonment
7. Have you tried to evade customs duty on a small item bought on holiday?	Intending to defraud	Three times value of goods or £5,000 fine, whichever is greater and/or 3 years imprisonment
8. Have you used a TV without buying a licence?	Using a TV without a licence	£400 fine
9. Have you ever fiddled your expenses?	Theft	£5,000 and/or 6 months imprisonment
10. Have you ever driven a car knowing you are 'over the limit'?	Driving with excess alcohol	£5,000 and/or 6 months imprisonment

Source: Muncie, 1996

questions

1 a) How many of these offences have you committed?

   b) Add up the maximum penalties which you could have received.

   c) Compare your answers to a) and b) with those of other students.

2 What do your answers to Question 1 suggest about a) the accuracy of official statistics and b) the picture of the 'typical criminal' drawn from official statistics?

Unit 3 Media representations of crime

keyissues

1 What pictures of crime do the media present?

2 What factors influence media representations of crime?

3 To what extent do the media shape popular perceptions of crime?

3.1 Media images of crime

The previous unit looked at the pictures of crime and the criminal presented by official statistics, victim studies and self-report studies. This unit looks at the pictures presented by the mass media.

Judging by the output of the media, the public have an enormous appetite for crime. A significant proportion of newspaper articles, broadcast news (TV and radio), films, novels, comics, drama, documentaries and reality TV focuses on crime. And the pictures of crime and the criminal presented by the media are often different from those provided by official statistics, victim studies and self-report studies.

Methodology

Most of the studies of media representations of crime are based on content analysis.

Formal content analysis This method aims to classify and quantify media content in an objective manner. For example, it is used to measure the amount of space devoted to crime and the types of crime covered in newspapers. Researchers usually have a checklist of crimes which they use to classify and quantify newspaper coverage. Formal content analysis can often effectively measure simple, straightforward aspects of content. However, it says little about the meaning of content to the audience.

Thematic analysis This form of content analysis looks for themes which underlie the content. For example, the police may be regularly presented in a positive light – as sympathetic, honest, just and efficient. This theme may underlie many news reports on crime. However, the themes interpreted by sociologists may have little to do with the interpretations of the audience.

Textual analysis This form of content analysis involves a close examination of the 'text' in order to see how it encourages a particular reading and creates a particular impression. Ray Pawson (1995) gives the following example from a newspaper headline, GIRL GUIDE, 14, RAPED AT HELLS ANGELS CONVENTION. This is an example of the 'innocent victim'/'wicked perpetrator' pair which creates the impression of two extremes, one good, the other evil. It is one of the many tricks of the trade used to convey particular messages.

As with thematic analysis, the problem with textual analysis is reading things into the text which may have little or nothing to do with interpretations of the audience.

The extent of crime in the news

Most analyses of crime in the media have focused on the news. The results show that crime forms a significant part of news' content. For example, a study comparing the coverage of ten national daily newspapers for four weeks in 1989 found that 12.7% of the events reported were about crime. The proportion of space given to crime was greater the more down-market the paper – *The Guardian* containing only 5.1%, *The Sun* 30.4% (Williams & Dickinson, 1993).

Another study found that broadcast news devoted even more attention to crime than the press, with commercial stations containing a higher proportion of crime features than the BBC (Cumberbatch et al., 1995).

Studies indicate that the proportion of news devoted to crime has increased over the past 50 years. For example, one study found that the proportion of space given to crime reports in the *Daily Mirror* and *The Times* from 1945 to 1991 rose from 8% to 21% (Reiner et al., 2000).

The pattern of crime news

Content analysis conducted at different times and places reveals the following patterns in crime news.

Types of crime The coverage of violent and sexual crimes is significantly greater than their incidence as measured by official statistics, victim studies and self-report studies. Homicide accounts for one-third of all crime news. Williams and Dickinson's (1993) study of ten national newspapers in 1989 found that 64.5% of crime stories dealt with violence against the person. According to British Crime Survey, only 6% of crimes reported by victims in 1989 were violent.

The proportion of violent and sexual crimes tended to be greater the more down-market the newspaper. Television news coverage is closer to the tabloids (eg, the *Sun*) than the broadsheets (eg, *The Guardian*) (Reiner, 2002).

Social characteristics of offenders Like official statistics and self-report studies, crime news portrays offenders as overwhelmingly male. But here the similarity ends. Offenders in crime news are older and higher status – they are more likely to be middle class. In this respect, the media may present a more accurate picture, since official statistics tend to underestimate the proportion of older, higher status offenders (Reiner, 2002).

Incidents rather than causes Crime news focuses on actual incidents of crime. It tends to describe events and pays little attention to the causes of crime. There are exceptions – broadsheets, such as *The Guardian*, are more likely to contain some analysis of the causes of crime (Carrabine et al., 2002).

The criminal justice system The news media usually present a positive picture of the criminal justice system. For example, the success of the police in detecting crime is often exaggerated. There are stories exposing police corruption and malpractice. However, such wrongdoing tends to be portrayed as the failings of individuals rather than the criminal justice system as a whole (Chibnall, 1977). When the system is clearly to blame, the media usually report that reforms have been made and all is now well. Again, the legitimacy of the criminal justice system is safeguarded.

Crime and reality TV

The emergence of reality TV has blurred the boundaries between news and fiction. *Crimewatch UK* is one of the earliest reality TV programmes – it presents dramatised reconstructions of crime. It aims to both entertain and to help the police solve crimes. And it still continues to attract a far larger audience than the news.

In its portrayal of crime, *Crimewatch UK* is similar to the news – it focuses on murder, armed robbery with violence, and sexual crimes (Dobash et al., 1998). This focus is very different from the picture presented by official statistics, victim studies and self-report studies. In some ways this is nothing new. In Victorian times, today's reconstructions of crime were matched by the popular *Penny Dreadful* – cheap sensational accounts of recent murders which whetted the Victorian appetite for both blood and indignation in a tantalising cocktail.

More recent reality TV programmes such as *Crime Beat*, *Police Camera Action* and *Car Wars* are different. They use CCTV footage as opposed to dramatised reconstructions and highlight 'the "everydayness" of the crimes portrayed and the frequency of their occurrence in "everyday life" ' (Brunsdon et al., 2001). In other words, they portray crime as a routine and regular event and address the viewer 'as a threatened consumer' who must take responsibility for crime prevention (Carrabine et al., 2002).

Crime fiction

The extent of crime fiction Crime has always been a staple ingredient of media fiction. One estimate suggests that between a quarter and a third of paperback novels could be categorised as crime stories (Mandel, 1984). Since 1945, around 20% of all films are crime movies and around 50% have a significant crime content (Allen et al., 1997). And, since 1955, some 25% of the most popular British TV programmes have been crime or police series (Reiner et al., 2000).

Crime in fiction In many respects, the picture of crime in media fiction is similar to that presented by crime news. As such, it is very different from the picture given by official statistics, victim studies and self-report studies.

- Media fiction focuses on murder and other violent crimes. Murder was the most frequent offence in crime movies since 1945 (Reiner, 2002).

- Offenders in crime fiction are mainly middle-aged, middle-class males as opposed to the young, working-class males in official statistics and self-report studies (Reiner, 2002).

- The police clear-up rate is very different from the picture given by official statistics. In crime fiction, the police usually 'get their man'. According to official statistics, they usually don't.

The police tend to be presented in a positive light in crime fiction – as protecting citizens from harm. However, in recent years, there has been increasing criticism of the criminal justice system – in terms of both its effectiveness and its honesty (Reiner, 2002).

activity7 media pictures of crime

Item A *Newspaper reports*

Murdered by a savage out on bail

A drug addict murdered a widow of 82 for her pension money while on bail for another violent crime.

Wayne Franks, 29, was jailed for life yesterday for a savage attack in which he hit Mabel Whitelam over the head with a hammer, strangled her and stabbed her 22 times.

Financial adviser accused of murdering his client

A financial advisor seduced a lonely and vulnerable elderly woman before stealing £280,000 and murdering her in her bed, a court heard yesterday.

Aged 64, married and a father of three, he allegedly began an affair with his client after she contacted him for advice on investing her £500,000 savings. He stole her money to help clear his debts and pay for his affluent lifestyle, Chester Crown Court was told.

Terror of 'SAS' rapist

A builder who terrorised a family after convincing them he was a member of the SAS was jailed for 20 years yesterday.

Over 16 months, Nigel Da Costa carried out a series of indecent assaults and rapes and held members of the family prisoner.

The 33-year-old shaven-headed thug subjected them to the degrading attacks, often at gunpoint, telling them they had threatened national security by searching for his name on the internet.

He maintained his grip on their lives by threatening to have them killed.

His wife Helen, 29, a former primary school teacher, was jailed for five years for going along with her husband's fantasies. She was present at many of the attacks.

Source: All reports from the *Daily Mail*, May 2004

Item B *Images of violence*

CCTV still from the attack on Securitas in Tonbridge, Kent

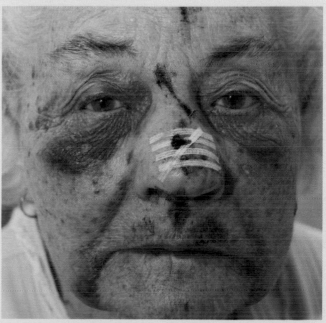

Lillian Young, age 81, after being mugged and beaten up near her South Shields home.

Item C Crime fiction

questions

1 In what ways are the crime reports in Item A and the images in Item B typical of newspaper representations of crime?

2 Judging by Item C, how does crime fiction picture crime?

3 How do the representations of crime in Items A, B and C differ from those presented by official statistics, victim studies and self-report studies?

3.2 Explaining media representations of crime

Little is known about the production of representations of crime in media fiction. However, there have been a number of studies of the production of crime news.

News values What makes 'news'? In the course of their professional socialisation, journalists are taught what makes a good news story and what events are newsworthy. In other words, they learn *news values*.

In terms of these values, a good news story should include the following:

- Novelty, freshness and surprise
- Drama and excitement
- Titillation
- A focus on personalities (Chibnall, 1977).

Given these news values, it is not surprising that violent and sexual crimes predominate in the news, that the focus is on criminal incidents rather than an analysis of causes, and that the offenders and victims portrayed tend to be well-known personalities, often celebrities.

Sources of crime news The police and the courts are the main sources of crime news. As a result, journalists are largely dependent on official sources for their information. These sources have become *primary definers* – they define

what counts as crime, what counts as justice, and what crimes are significant. And, in doing so, they reflect the concerns of the powerful – the agents of social control and the state (Hall et al., 1978).

What about alternative ways of defining crime and its significance? Human rights organisations such as Amnesty International identify a variety of 'state crimes', for example the treatment of so-called asylum seekers and suspected terrorists in Britain. Occasionally, their views are reported. But, for the most part, their voices are drowned out by the primary definers. In view of this, it is not surprising that the criminal justice system tends to be presented in a positive light.

key terms

News values Values which define what is newsworthy.
Primary definers Those who have the power to define the way things are – in this context, what counts as crime and justice.

3.3 The media and perceptions of crime

Do media representations of crime influence people's views of crime? Do they amplify people's fear of crime?

The British Crime Survey includes questions about

perceptions of and concerns about crime. It also asks questions about newspaper readership. Findings from the three surveys from 2001 to 2003 indicate the following.

The crime rate Over the three years in question, an increasing proportion of respondents believed that the national crime rate had risen 'a lot' (25% in 2001, 30% in 2001/02 and 38% in 2002/03). However, the BCS indicated a steady fall in crime over these years.

According to the 2002/03 survey, 43% of those who read a national tabloid newspaper thought that the crime rate had risen 'a lot', compared to 26% of broadsheet readers (Simmons & Dodd, 2003).

Concerns about crime The BCS found that concern about particular types of crime was associated with newspaper readership. Compared to broadsheet readers, readers of tabloids were twice as likely to be 'very worried' about burglary, mugging, physical attack and rape (Simmons & Dodd, 2003).

Newspaper readership and perceptions of crime Is there a causal link between newspaper readership and perceptions of crime? As noted earlier, tabloids are more likely to report violent and sexual crimes than broadsheets. And they are more likely to headline the more dramatic and negative aspects of official crime statistics – for example, CRIME SOARS – Muggings up by 28% (*Daily Mail*, 12.7.2002). Since tabloid readers are more likely to be concerned about violent crime, and more likely to believe that the crime rate is rising, it is tempting to argue that their perceptions are influenced by the papers they read.

However, there is another view. Tabloid readers tend to be working class and broadsheet readers middle class. The BCS found that people living in inner-city areas and council estates are particularly concerned about crime, especially violent crime. These are the areas where working-class people are likely to live and the areas where violent crime is probably highest. Rather than causing this fear of crime, tabloid newspapers may simply be reflecting it. As Crawford et al., (1990) put it, 'in inner-city areas, mass media coverage of crime tends to reinforce what people already know'.

summary

1. Most of the studies of media representations of crime are based on content analysis.
2. There are three main types of content analysis, each with its strengths and weaknesses.
   - Formal content analysis
   - Thematic analysis
   - Textual analysis.
3. A significant proportion of space in newspapers is devoted to crime news. The more down-market the paper, the greater the proportion of crime news.
4. Broadcast news tends to devote more attention to crime than the press.
5. News coverage of violent and sexual crimes is significantly greater than their incidence as measured by official statistics, victim studies and self-report studies.
6. Offenders in crime news are more likely to be older and middle class than those who appear in official statistics and self-report studies.
7. Reality TV programmes, such as *Crimewatch UK*, focus on murder, armed robbery with violence, and sexual crimes. More recent reality TV programmes tend to focus on routine, 'everyday' crimes.
8. Media fiction concentrates on murder and other violent crimes. Offenders tend to be middle-aged, middle-class males as opposed to the young, working-class males who predominate in official statistics and self-report studies.
9. In both crime news and crime fiction, the police are usually portrayed in a positive light.
10. Media representations of crime are largely shaped by news values and official sources – the police and the courts.
11. Despite a recent decrease in the crime rate, a growing number of BCS respondents believe the rate is increasing. Those who read tabloid newspapers are more likely to take this view.
12. Tabloid readers are twice as likely as broadsheet readers to be very concerned about violent crime.
13. Tabloids are more likely to report violent crime and to headline negative trends in official crime statistics than broadsheet newspapers. This may influence tabloid readers' perceptions of crime.
14. There is an alternative argument. Tabloid readers tend to be working class and to live in areas with a high rate of violent crime. The tabloids may simply reflect their concern with crime rather than shaping it.

activity8 definitions and perceptions of crime

Item A News values

Cilla Black returning home after the burglary

Thugs target the famous

The vicious gang who struck at Cilla Black's home had earlier robbed Tony Blair's friend Lord Levy it emerged last night. Detectives revealed several chilling similarities, including the degree of violence used.

The armed gang held a hunting knife to the throat of Miss Black's youngest son as they stole jewels, cash and gold worth more than £1 million.

Five months earlier, Lord Levy, the Prime Minister's special envoy to the Middle East, and his wife were handcuffed to chairs and beaten after three masked men broke into their £5 million North London mansion. The gang made off with £80,000 in cash and jewellery.

Source: *Daily Mail*, 24.5.2004

Item B Violent crime

Figures show how promise to crack down on thugs is failing

Heat on ministers as violent crimes go up by 20pc

VIOLENT crime has soared by 20 per cent in a year, official figures are expected to show.

Despite the Government's pledge to crack down on crime,

By Jo Butler
Home Affairs Correspondent

increase in violent crime and an overall rise of 8 per cent.

But the latest figures still make

Looking down the barrel of a gun: Violent crime is on the increase

Source: *Daily Mail*, 26.5.2003

Item C Concern about crime

Worry about crime and newspaper readership

Percentages

% very worried about:	National tabloids	National broadsheets
Burglary	17	9
Mugging	16	7
Physical attack	17	6
Rape	18	7
Being insulted or pestered in a public place	9	5

Source: Simmons & Dodd, 2003

questions

1 What news values are reflected in Item A?

2 What impression might readers form from the newspaper report in Item B?

3 a) Briefly summarise the table in Item C.

   b) Suggest explanations for the apparent link between newspaper readership and concern with crime.

Unit 4 *Explaining crime and deviance: functionalism, strain theory and subcultural theory*

key issues

1 What is distinctive about the sociological approach to crime and deviance?

2 What are the main sociological explanations of crime and deviance that flow from a functionalist perspective?

3 What are the strengths and weaknesses of these explanations?

4.1 Normalising the criminal

Sociology is not the only subject concerned with crime and deviance. Cesare Lombroso, the first writer who tried to explain crime scientifically, drew on biology. Writing in the 19th century, he claimed that criminals were biologically distinct from non-criminals and that this difference explained their criminal behaviour. Other researchers have drawn on psychology, arguing that there is a psychological basis for criminal behaviour. What these approaches have in common is a picture of the criminal as somehow different from the rest of us.

For some researchers, this difference is mainly due to heredity – to the inheritance of particular genes which predispose individuals to criminal behaviour. For others, the difference arises from people's experiences, particularly childhood experiences, which again are seen to predispose them to crime. In both cases, the criminal is seen as abnormal in a normal population.

Sociologists tend to be sceptical of these views. They insist that a satisfactory explanation of crime and deviance must take the social context into account. As noted earlier, crime and deviance are socially constructed. What counts as crime and deviance is based on meanings, definitions and interpretations of behaviour which develop in the context of social interaction. Even crime statistics are socially constructed – based on countless decisions which, in turn, are based on definitions and interpretations which change from time to time and context to context.

Sociologists look to the social situation for explanations of why people commit criminal acts or are defined as criminal. For example, they look at people's position in the class structure, their power and influence in society, their age, gender and ethnic groups, their culture and subculture for these explanations. There is no suggestion of abnormal genes or abnormal personalities. From a sociological viewpoint, the 'criminal' is as normal as the rest of us.

activity 9 *criminals are different*

Item A *Throwbacks*

Cesare Lombroso is credited with being the founding father of criminology, a new discipline which sought to explain crime scientifically. From his studies of convicted criminals he claimed to have discovered biological characteristics which were the outward signs of an inborn criminal nature. These included 'enormous jaws, high cheek bones, prominent superciliary arches (eyebrow ridges), solitary lines on the palms, extreme size of the orbits, handle-shaped or sessile ears found in criminals, savages and apes, insensibility to pain, extremely acute sight, tattooing, excessive idleness, love of orgies and the irresistible craving for evil for its own sake'. Lombroso believed that criminals were a throwback to an earlier and more primitive form of human being.

Source: C. Lombroso, *L'Uomo Delinquente*, first published in 1876

Item B *Cartoon from Punch, 1881*

CIVILISATION OF THE ROUGH
Professors of Dancing and Deportment giving Lessons to the Convicts.

Item C Criminal types

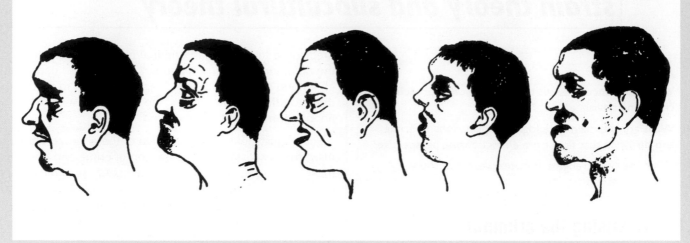

Typical 'criminal types' identified by the Victorian criminologist Havelock Ellis

Item D Personality and crime

Hans Eysenck argues that personality is largely inherited – that is, genetically based. Certain types of personality are more prone to react to particular environmental factors with criminal behaviour. Personality and environment are equally important. It is the interaction between the two which is probably the most important factor.

Eysenck identified a number of dimensions of personality. One dimension ranged from introversion at one end of the scale to extraversion at the other. Introverts learn the norms and values of society more quickly and effectively than extraverts. They are therefore more likely to respond to mechanisms of social control. Introverts are quiet and reserved, they tend to avoid high levels of stimulation. Extraverts, on the other hand, seek stimulation and excitement, they are impulsive and enjoy taking risks.

Eysenck devised a questionnaire to measure extraversion. He claims that those with a high extraversion score are more likely to commit criminal acts. For example, in one study he found that young men who repeatedly offended had high extraversion scores.

Source: Eysenck, 1987

questions

1 The criminal types identified by Victorian criminologists were little different from popular stereotypes of the day. Discuss with reference to Items A, B and C.

2 What similarities and differences are evident in Lombroso's and Eysenck's explanations of criminal behaviour? (Items A and D)

4.2 Functionalism and crime

Sociological theories of crime and deviance are diverse and often competing. But they share one thing in common – they offer social rather than biological or psychological explanations.

In this and the next two units, these theories are grouped under three major perspectives within sociology – functionalism, interactionism and Marxism. It is important to recognise that these perspectives are broad schools of thought which contain many variations, and that a number of sociological theories of crime and deviance straddle different perspectives. Nonetheless, this approach provides a chronological overview which shows how new theories developed from a critique of earlier work.

Functions of crime and deviance

Crime and deviance as 'normal' Functionalists see shared norms and values as the basis of social order and social solidarity. It is not surprising that they consider crime and deviance, beyond a certain level, to be *dysfunctional* or harmful to society – a threat to social order and to the survival of the social system. What *is* perhaps surprising is the view that a certain amount of crime and deviance is not only 'normal' but also 'an integral part of all healthy societies' (Durkheim, 1964).

A crime-free or a deviance-free society is seen as a contradiction in terms. Writing in 1895, the French sociologist Emile Durkheim asked us to 'Imagine a society of saints, a perfect cloister of exemplary individuals. Crimes, properly so called, will there be unknown; but faults which appear venial (trivial) to the layman will create there the same scandal that the ordinary offence does in ordinary consciousness.'

While too much crime or deviance constitutes a threat to social order, too little crime or deviance is unhealthy. It indicates that the norms and values are so strong and constricting that they prevent the innovation and change necessary for a healthy society.

Crime and deviance as functional How then is a certain amount of crime and deviance functional? For Durkheim, it is functional because of the response such activities draw forth from society. Through *degradation ceremonies* such as criminal trials and public punishment, we are reminded of our shared norms and values. By publicly condemning those who have broken significant rules, not only are norms and values reaffirmed but also we learn the limits of toleration and unite against the condemned. Crime and deviance, or at least the public response to them, are functional because they serve to reinforce social solidarity and integrate society.

Do crime and deviance serve any other functions? Some functionalists believe they do. For example, Kingsley Davis (1961) argued that crime and deviance can act as a 'safety valve'. He claimed that there is a conflict between man's instinctual need for sexual satisfaction and society's need to restrict the legitimate expression of sex to within the family. Prostitution, in this context, is functional because it provides sexual satisfaction without threatening the family as an institution. Another writer has identified a 'warning function' of crime and deviance. They 'may serve as a signal or warning that there is some defect in the social organisation' which may 'lead to changes that enhance efficiency and morale' (Clinard, 1974). For example, truancy from school may indicate unsuspected causes of discontent and the need for changes in the education system.

Evaluation Suggesting functions for crime and deviance, however, is not the same as finding an explanation for them. To argue that crime and deviance have certain social consequences does not explain their presence in the first place. 'It is one thing to assert that crime can be made to serve some social end or other once it has occurred – for example, to heighten solidarity by uniting against the offender. It is another step altogether to explain crime as promoted in advance by society to bring about that end' (Downes & Rock, 2003).

key terms

Dysfunctional Activities which are harmful to society – for example, they weaken social solidarity and disrupt social order.
Degradation ceremonies Ceremonies which degrade and condemn wrongdoers – for example, public punishment.

activity10 *functions of crime and punishment*

Item A Public execution

Hogarth's engraving of a public execution at Tyburn

Item B Prostitution

A prostitute

Item C Riots

Bradford, 2001

question

Suggest how the activities in Items A, B and C can be seen as functional for society.

4.3 Strain theory

In the 1930s, the American sociologist Robert K. Merton wrote an article entitled *Social Structure and Anomie*. It became one of the most influential explanations of crime and deviance. Merton's theory was sociological – he offered a social rather than a psychological or biological explanation. In particular, it was a *structuralist theory* as it saw the structure of society shaping people's behaviour.

Culture and norms According to Merton, American culture attaches great importance to success – and success is measured in terms of money and material possessions. There are norms which define legitimate means for achieving success. These legitimate means include gaining skills and qualifications and career advancement. The American Dream states that anybody can make it to the top if they try hard enough.

Anomie So much emphasis is placed on material success that many people experience pressure to deviate from accepted norms and values. Deviance occurs when they reject the goal of success and/or the legitimate means of reaching that goal. For example, some people are tempted to use any available means of getting to the top – even if this involves criminal behaviour.

   Merton refers to this pressure to deviate as a 'strain to anomie'. *Anomie* means normlessness – it refers to a situation where norms no longer guide behaviour, where 'anything goes'.

Social structure Despite what the American Dream says, not everybody has an equal chance of success. The social structure prevents equal opportunity. In particular, the strain to anomie is most strongly felt by those at the bottom of the

class structure. They are less likely to acquire the skills and qualifications needed to reach the top. As a result, they are more likely to seek alternative routes to success.

Adaptations Merton identifies five possible adaptations or responses to the strain of anomie in American society – see Table 1. The first is conformity – aiming for success and sticking to the rules. The other four are deviant adaptations – they reject the goal of success and/or the norms for achieving it.

Table 1 Goals and means

	Cultural goal	Normative means
Conformity	acceptance	acceptance
Deviant adaptations		
Innovation	acceptance	rejection
Ritualism	rejection	acceptance
Retreatism	rejection	rejection
Rebellion	replacement	replacement

Conformity According to Merton, most people conform despite the strain to anomie. Even if they don't make it, they continue to strive for success and follow the normative means of getting there.

Innovation People who adopt this deviant adaptation accept the goal of success but, in Merton's words, they have 'little access to conventional and legitimate means for becoming successful'. As a result, some innovate – they turn to illegitimate means, to crime. The pressure to select this adaptation is greatest for those in the lower levels of the class system.

Ritualism People who follow this deviant route abandon the goal of success, but stick rigidly to the rules – for example, people in dead-end, white-collar occupations who follow their job descriptions to the letter.

Retreatism This deviant adaptation involves a rejection of both the goal of success and the normative means of achieving it. It applies to people who 'drop out' – tramps, drug addicts and habitual drunkards.

Rebellion This involves a rejection of conventional goals and means and their replacement with alternatives. The revolutionary who seeks to change society illustrates this type of deviant adaptation.

Evaluation of strain theory

Advantages Merton's strain theory was an early attempt to explain crime and deviance in terms of the culture and structure of society. It provided a sociological alternative to biological and psychological theories. In particular, it offered an explanation for working-class crime. Whatever its weaknesses, Merton's work provided a spur for the development of further sociological theories of crime and deviance.

Disadvantages Merton's theory raises a number of unanswered questions.

- First, why do some people but not others adopt deviant adaptations? For example, why do some people in the lower levels of the class system turn to crime but others do not?
- Second, Merton's theory focuses on individuals rather than groups. Crime and deviance are often collective activities. How can this be explained in terms of strain theory?
- Third, crime and deviance are not always motivated by a desire for monetary gain. How can activities such as vandalism and fighting between rival gangs be explained in terms of Merton's theory?

In search for answers to these questions, subcultural theory was born.

4.4 Subcultural theory

Albert Cohen – status frustration

Albert Cohen (1955) was the first sociologist to develop a subcultural theory of working-class crime and deviance. He examined delinquent gangs in low-income, inner-city areas. *Delinquency* refers to the criminal and anti-social acts of young people.

Cohen agreed with Merton that the mainstream value of success creates problems for young working-class males. Many do badly at school and fail to acquire the skills and qualifications needed for success.

Status frustration Defined as failures by the wider society, many working-class adolescents experience *status frustration*. They are frustrated with their low status as 'losers' and are given little or no respect.

A subcultural solution Faced by a common 'problem of adjustment' – a problem they share – some working-class adolescents develop a deviant solution. They create their own *subculture* – their own norms and values which differ from those of mainstream society. In Cohen's words, 'the delinquent subculture takes its norms from the larger culture but turns them upside down'.

Anti-social and criminal behaviour, which are condemned by the wider society, are valued by the delinquent subculture. And, most importantly, they provide a means by which 'failed' working-class young people can solve the problem of status frustration. By succeeding in terms of the values of the delinquent subculture, they gain respect and admiration from their peers – those in a similar situation.

This is where collective deviant activities come in. Gang members require an audience to gain respect. The 'successful' delinquent gains status in the eyes of his peers.

Non-utilitarian crime If status frustration is the main problem, then criminal activities to achieve monetary success – Merton's 'solution' – may not be necessary. Vandalism, joy-riding, fighting, anti-social behaviour such as giving cheek to teachers and disrupting the classroom, can bring respect. These are examples of *non-utilitarian crime* and deviance – not 'useful', not directed to monetary gain.

Acting in terms of the deviant subculture, young men not only gain status in each other's eyes, they also hit back at a society which has denied them the opportunity to succeed and branded them as failures.

Evaluation Cohen's subcultural theory offered explanations for non-utilitarian crime and collective deviance – explanations which Merton's strain theory failed to provide. However, there are other explanations for working-class delinquency, as the following sections illustrate.

Cloward and Ohlin – opportunity structures

The American sociologists Richard Cloward and Lloyd Ohlin (1961) provide an explanation for different types of working-class delinquency. They argue that both Merton and Cohen fail to explain why delinquent subcultures take different forms. Why, for example, are some gangs mainly concerned with theft while others focus on violence?

Cloward and Ohlin agree with Merton that delinquency results from legitimate opportunity structures being largely closed to many young, working-class males. However, their response to this situation varies depending on the social environment in which they grow up. Different social environments provide different opportunities for crime and deviance which, in turn, encourage the development of different delinquent subcultures. Cloward and Ohlin identify three types of delinquent subculture.

The criminal subculture This type of subculture tends to develop in areas where there is a well-established pattern of adult crime. This provides an illegitimate opportunity structure. Young men are presented with role models from whom they can learn the tricks of the trade. They are given the opportunity to climb the professional criminal hierarchy and to become 'successful' by participating in crime which brings monetary gain.

The conflict subculture This type of subculture tends to develop in areas where an *illegitimate opportunity structure* is absent. These areas usually have a high turnover of population and a low level of social cohesion – this prevents established patterns of adult crime from developing.

With little opportunity to succeed by either legitimate or illegitimate means, young men become frustrated and angry. They often respond to this situation with gang violence which gives them the opportunity to gain status and respect from their fellow gang members.

The retreatist subculture This type of subculture tends to emerge among those who have failed to succeed either by legitimate means or as members of either criminal or conflict subcultures. These 'double failures' sometimes form retreatist subcultures based on illegal drug use.

Evaluation Cloward and Ohlin develop both Merton's strain theory and Cohen's subcultural theory. They show that working-class delinquency is not simply concerned with material gain. And they identify, and provide explanations for, a number of delinquent subcultures.

However, Cloward and Ohlin tend to box off the subcultures they identify and ignore the overlaps between them. For example, gangs involved in the conflict subculture often deal in drugs and make large sums of money in the process. The same applies to members of the retreatist subculture – some addicts also 'successfully' deal in drugs (Winlow, 2001).

key terms

Structuralist theory A theory which sees the structure of society shaping people's behaviour.

Anomie A state of normlessness – where norms no longer direct behaviour.

Delinquency The criminal behaviour of young people.

Status frustration Dissatisfaction and frustration with the status and respect given by others.

Subculture Distinctive norms and values shared by a group within society. These norms and values differ from those of the mainstream culture.

Non-utilitarian crime Crime which is not directed to monetary gain – for example, vandalism.

Illegitimate opportunity structure A structure which provides illegal opportunities for monetary gain.

Lower-class subculture

The theories we've looked at so far present a similar picture of society. They assume that there is a consensus or agreement about values. Members of society are socialised into a common value system and become committed, at least in the USA, to the ideal of success in monetary terms. Criminal and deviant subcultures are seen as reactions by young working-class males to their inability to obtain this goal by legitimate means.

The American sociologist Walter B. Miller (1958) takes a different view. He sees society as consisting of different social classes, each with a distinct set of values. Miller argues that there is a distinctive lower-class subculture which is passed on from generation to generation. It arose partly from the experience of low-skilled labour which involved boring, repetitive, dead-end jobs, interspersed with periods of unemployment. Lower-class subculture provides ways of living with this situation and of finding satisfaction outside of work.

activity11 Hispanic gangs

Item A Hispanic gangs in LA

East Los Angeles is a mainly Hispanic area. Hispanics or Latinos have their origins in Spanish speaking countries in Central and South America. Hispanics in the USA are twice as likely to live in poverty as White Americans.

East LA has at least 800 Hispanic gangs with more than 100,000 members. The level of gang violence is extremely high. LA is known as the murder capital of the USA. Most of these murders are gang-related.

The Hispanic gangs are split into two groups. The *chicanos* are Mexican-Americans born in the USA who often don't speak any Spanish. Their rivals are gangs whose members are recent immigrants from Mexico and other Spanish speaking countries who have evolved a language of their own called *calo*. Older members *(veteranos)* are held in great respect by their 'home boys', having defended the honour of their neighbourhood with fierce urban warfare.

Each gang has its own initiation ceremony. For example, to become a Playboy, a new member has to get 'jumped in' – beaten up – by a minimum of three gang members. While the beating takes place, others look on and count up to 13 slowly. Once initiated, members take on nicknames and adopt the dress codes of their comrades.

Many gang members deal in drugs. At the age of 15, former gang member Luis Rivera was earning $1000 a day selling crack cocaine. 'I had my first car at the age of 16. I had no shortage of money.'

Source: *The Observer*, 6.2.1994, 7.7.2002; Winant, 1994

Item B **Hand signals and tattoos**

Hand signals representing the Playboys

Hand signals and tattoos are important signifiers of gang loyalties. Tattoos are usually done by *carnals* (fellow gang members), often using home-made instruments. They are a symbol of identity and defiance.

Young men who want to escape from gang life sometimes get their tattoos removed with a laser gun. Jose, a former gang member, states, 'The quicker I get 'em off, the quicker I get out of the gang. If I get them removed, then I'll no longer be a gang member.'

Source: *The Observer*, 6.2.1994, 7.7.2002

A member of the Playboys

question

Read Items A and B and look at the pictures.

Explain the behaviour of Hispanic gangs in terms of

a) Merton's strain theory, b) Cohen's subcultural theory, and c) Cloward and Ohlin's opportunity structure theory.

Focal concerns According to Miller, lower class subculture has a number of *focal concerns* – major interests and involvements. They include a desire for excitement and thrills, an emphasis on toughness – on a macho form of masculinity – and a concern with 'smartness' – with conning and outwitting others. These concerns are exaggerated by lower-class young men because of their desire for status in the eyes of their peer group.

Lower-class delinquency results from young men acting out the concerns of lower-class subculture. In doing this, they often break the law. The concern with toughness can lead to fights, the concern with excitement can result in a range of criminal activities from joy-riding to robbery, and the concern with smartness can be seen in the repertoires of the hustler and the con man.

Evaluation Miller pictures lower-class subculture as a 'distinctive tradition, many centuries old'. Lower-class young men are seen to act out this subculture with little reference to mainstream society. They appear to live in a world of their own. While accepting that a lower-class subculture may well exist, it is unlikely that lower-class young men are as insulated from the wider society and its values as Miller suggests (Bordua, 1962).

key term

Focal concerns Main interests, concerns, involvements.

4.5 Delinquency and drift – David Matza

The theories examined so far tend to see criminal and deviant behaviour resulting from forces beyond the individual's control. For example, in terms of Merton's strain theory, those at the bottom of the class structure are under considerable pressure to turn to crime. And Cohen's subcultural theory suggests that the deviant behaviour of many young working-class males is directed by a delinquent subculture. To an extent, these theories picture people as prisoners of the social structure, acting out predetermined roles with little or no say in the matter.

David Matza (1964) sees three main problems with this approach.

● First, it tends to make deviants more distinctive than they really are. For example, the idea of deviant subcultures suggests that those involved are very different from members of mainstream society.

- Second, it 'over-predicts' delinquency – it accounts for more delinquency than there actually is. Why doesn't everybody in a particular position in society become a delinquent?
- Third, it suggests that the deviant has little or no freedom of choice – that their behaviour is determined by social forces beyond their control.

How different are delinquents?

Matza rejects Cohen's view that delinquents are different, that they have a distinctive subculture in opposition to mainstream society.

Subterranean values Matza argues that delinquent behaviour is often directed by *subterranean values* which are found throughout society. These 'underground values' are only expressed in particular situations. They include an emphasis on excitement and toughness. In mainstream society they are expressed in competitive sports – for example, on the football field. If, as Matza claims, they often direct delinquent behaviour, then in this respect, delinquents are little different from other young people (Matza & Sykes, 1961).

Techniques of neutralisation How do young people view their delinquent behaviour? According to Matza, many express guilt and shame for their delinquent acts. This suggests at least some commitment to mainstream norms and values. If this is so, why does delinquent behaviour occur? Part of the answer is *techniques of neutralisation* which open the door to delinquency and provide a justification for it. Matza identifies five techniques which neutralise the blame for delinquent acts and make them acceptable (Sykes & Matza, 1962).

- **Denial of responsibility** This technique states the delinquent was not responsible for his own actions. He got in with a bad crowd and came from a poor neighbourhood. As a result, 'It wasn't my fault'.
- **Denial of injury** Nobody was really hurt. For example, stealing from those who could afford it, 'borrowing' a car for joyriding.
- **Denial of the victim** They had it coming to them – the person concerned was not a victim but someone who deserved to be punished.
- **Condemning the condemners** Those who condemn the delinquent are themselves wrongdoers – for example, the police are corrupt and brutal.
- **Appeal to higher loyalties** Criminal behaviour is justified in terms of mainstream values such as duties and obligations to families and friends – stealing to provide food for their family, fighting to defend their friend.

According to Matza, techniques of neutralisation suggest that delinquents largely accept the values of the wider society. They justify their criminal acts in terms of mainstream values. And there is little evidence for a distinctive delinquent subculture. Delinquents are therefore similar to young people in general.

Drifting into delinquency Subcultural theory suggests that many young males are committed to a distinctive subculture and a deviant lifestyle. In *Delinquency and Drift*, David Matza (1964) rejects this view. He argues that many young men drift in and out of delinquency. Their delinquent acts are casual and intermittent rather than a way of life. This fits with evidence indicating that most young people have little difficulty giving up delinquent activities as they grow older.

Again, the delinquent is pictured as little different from young people in general.

Evaluation of Matza

Advantages Matza provided a view of delinquency which answers the criticisms of strain theory and subcultural theory. Delinquents are no longer seen as prisoners of the social system directed by their position in the social structure and/or their distinctive subcultures.

According to Downes and Rock (2003), Matza's view describes the criminal behaviour of many young men in Britain. The most frequent reason they give for their delinquency is boredom. And delinquency offers plenty of opportunity for risk, daring and excitement to relieve boredom.

Disadvantages

- In seeking to remedy theories which over-predict delinquency, Matza may have gone too far in the opposite direction – and under-predicted. For example, one in three British men born in a single month in 1953 had a criminal record by the time they reached 30 (Carrabine et al., 2002).
- Matza's picture of young men drifting in and out of delinquency with little commitment to a deviant lifestyle does not fit the highly organised gangs in the USA. The life of the young men in the Hispanic gangs described in Activity 11 shows a real commitment to a deviant subculture. If there are over 100,000 Hispanic gang members in Los Angeles, this is hardly casual and intermittent behaviour.
- According to Stanley Cohen (2003), techniques of neutralisation don't necessarily indicate a commitment to conventional norms and values. They may simply be a public justification and excuse for criminal behaviour. For example, at the Nuremburg trials after the Second World War, neutralisation techniques were used by Nazis in their defence for the murder of millions of Jews.

key terms

Subterranean values Values which are only expressed in particular situations.
Techniques of neutralisation Techniques which neutralise the blame for actions which are defined as unacceptable or wrong by society's norms and values.

4.6 White-collar crime

The starting point for the theories of crime and deviance examined so far is the social pattern reflected in official statistics – that most offences are committed by young working-class males. As a result, these theories have little to say about *white-collar crime.*

Defining white-collar crime

The American criminologist Edwin Sutherland (1949) defined white-collar crime as 'a crime committed by a person of respectability and high social status in the course of his occupation'. He challenged the view that crime was mainly a 'working-class problem', claiming that the financial cost of white-collar crime was probably several times greater than the cost of working-class crime.

Today, many researchers identify two types of white-collar crime – *occupational crime* and *corporate crime.* Occupational crime refers to crimes committed at the expense of the organisation, for example employees stealing money or goods from their employer. Corporate crime refers to crimes committed on behalf of the organisation, such as non-payment of VAT.

Some researchers identify a third type of white-collar crime – *state crime.* This involves crimes committed by the state or agencies of the state such as the police or the military. Such crimes are committed on behalf of the state. For example, many people regard the treatment of suspected terrorists held by the USA government at Guantanamo Bay in Cuba as a criminal offence. State crime will be examined in more detail in Unit 9.4.

Corporate crime

There are many types of corporate crime. They include the following.

Crimes against consumers These include manufacturing or selling food which is unfit for human consumption, manufacturing or selling dangerous goods, and falsely describing the content of goods – for example, of food.

These crimes can have disastrous consequences. In the 1970s, mechanical defects in the Ford Pinto may have led to between 500 and 900 deaths in the USA. The company was fully aware of these defects (Box, 1983). And from the 1950s and 60s, the deliberate fabrication of test data on the fertility drug thalidomide resulted in the births of thousands of deformed babies.

Many instances of companies harming consumers are not dealt with as a criminal offence. Accidents and 'disasters' for which companies are held to be responsible provide an example. In 1987, the capsizing of the cross-Channel ferry *Herald of Free Enterprise* led to the deaths of 154 passengers and 38 crew members. An official inquiry blamed the owners, P&O Ferries, for failing to provide a safe operating system. However, attempts to prosecute the company for 'corporate manslaughter' failed (Croall, 2001).

Crimes against employees These include failing to meet health and safety regulations which can lead to the injury or death of employees. Between 1965 and the mid-1990s in the UK, around 25,000 people were killed at work. According to the Health and Safety Executive, 70% of these deaths were due to the failure of management to meet safety regulations (Hughes & Langan, 2001).

Environmental offences These include polluting the environment with toxic waste. For example, ICI was fined £300,000 by the Environment Agency in 1999 for polluting groundwater in Runcorn. However, most fines are much lower, averaging £4300 in 1998 (Croall, 2001). Green crime will be examined in more details in Unit 9.3.

Financial frauds These include false accounting, insurance frauds and the making of false claims by sellers about the benefits of pension schemes and savings plans. Fraud can involve vast sums – over $4 billion in the case of WorldCom's false accounting (see Activity 4, Item B). And the consequences can be extremely serious – in WorldCom's case, 17,000 workers were made redundant and many investors lost their life savings.

Views of white-collar crime

Compared to more visible and obvious types of crime such as burglary and murder, white-collar crime is often seen and treated differently by the public, police, courts and regulatory bodies. According to Gordon Hughes and Mary Langan (2001), this is due to four main factors.

Low visibility Street crimes and their consequences are highly visible. White-collar crimes are largely hidden from the public gaze. And when they are detected, it is often difficult to pinpoint blame – for example, which individuals were responsible for neglecting health and safety regulations?

Complexity Large-scale frauds are highly complex operations. They are difficult to unravel and it is hard to allocate blame. They involve different companies, various bank accounts, a multitude of transactions, and a variety of individuals who are more, or less, aware of what's going on. Teams of expert investigators spend years attempting to get to the bottom of large-scale frauds.

Diffusion of responsibility Responsibility for corporate crime is often diffused – widely spread. It is difficult to allocate blame to particular individuals. In the case of the *Herald of Free Enterprise* disaster, a variety of people and organisations were blamed – crew members, their commanding officers, the company and the regulatory authorities.

Diffusion of victimisation Many white-collar crimes are described as 'crimes without victims'. In many cases, there is no obvious victim as in cases of murder or robbery. However, there are victims but they are spread out or diffused. For example, environmental pollution can affect thousands of people. And we all have to pay for white-collar crime – in higher prices, insurance premiums and taxes (Hughes & Langan, 2001).

Regulating corporate crime

Compared to many other forms of crime, corporate crime has a lower rate of detection and prosecution, and more lenient punishments (Croall, 2001).

Regulatory offences Many corporate offences are dealt with by regulatory bodies rather than the criminal justice system. Bodies such as the Health and Safety Executive, the Environment Agency and the Trading Standards Agency deal with violations of health and safety, environmental health and trading standards regulations. They are more likely to issue 'official warnings' to put matters right rather than pursue prosecutions.

In the case of professionals, such as doctors and lawyers, 'misconduct' is usually dealt with by professional associations such as the British Medical Association. Only the most serious cases result in prosecution.

Many private companies operate a system of self-regulation. For example, the London Stock Exchange and Lloyds attempt to regulate their own affairs, even if this means a certain amount of loss through fraud.

Risk of prosecution Regulatory bodies are primarily concerned with securing compliance with regulations rather than identifying offenders. They advise and warn rather than punish.

Organisations such as the Inland Revenue and Customs and Excise tend to deal with offences administratively rather than prosecute. Their main aim is to recover the money lost from tax evasion and VAT fraud rather than charge the offender with a criminal offence.

Lenient punishment When white-collar offenders are prosecuted and found guilty of a criminal offence, their punishment tends to be lenient. Compared to 'ordinary criminals' such as burglars, they are more likely to be 'punished' with community service, a fine, or a short sentence in an open prison.

Explaining white-collar crime

White-collar crime covers a vast array of offences from petty occupational crime, such as fiddling expenses and stealing small items from employers, to corporate crime such as large-scale frauds. It is difficult to find an explanation for this variety of offences.

Strain theory revisited Merton's strain theory has been developed in an attempt to explain white-collar crime. A typical explanation goes as follows. All members of society face the same success goals – there is pressure on all social

summary

1. Sociologists look to society for an explanation of crime and deviance rather than the biological or psychological make-up of the individual.

2. According to Durkheim, a certain amount of crime is not only 'normal' but also an 'integral part of all healthy societies'. Society's values and norms must not be too strong – this would prevent the innovation and change necessary for a healthy society. Crime can be seen as a byproduct of this necessity.

3. Some crimes can be functional for society – for example, they may indicate that something is wrong with the way society is organised.

4. Merton's strain theory argues there is a 'strain to anomie' when the normative means for attaining cultural goals are blocked. This strain is most strongly felt by those at the bottom of the class structure. Some 'innovate' and turn to crime to attain monetary success.

5. Cohen's subcultural theory argues that many young working-class males experience status frustration. Some respond by developing a delinquent subculture in terms of which they can gain status and respect.

6. Cloward and Ohlin provide an explanation for different types of working-class delinquency. They argue that different social environments provide different opportunities for crime and deviance. This encourages the development of different delinquent subcultures.

7. David Matza argues that many sociological theories picture delinquents as more distinctive than they really are. He sees delinquents responding to subterranean values which are found throughout society. They use techniques of neutralisation which indicates that they largely share the values of the wider society. And they drift in and out of delinquency rather than being committed to a delinquent subculture.

8. Many sociological theories of crime and deviance tend to ignore white-collar crime.

9. There are two main types of white-collar crime – occupational crime and corporate crime.

10. Corporate crime includes crimes against consumers, crimes against employees, environmental offences and fraud.

11. Corporate crime is seen and treated differently from crimes such as burglary and murder. Reasons for this include:
    - Its low visibility
    - Complexity
    - The diffusion of responsibility
    - The diffusion of victimisation.

12. Compared to many other forms of crime, corporate crime has a lower rate of detection and prosecution, and more lenient punishments.

13. Merton's strain theory has been adapted to explain white-collar crime. This version states that some middle-class people experience relative deprivation when they make comparisons with those better off than themselves. In the absence of legal means to reach this level of success, some turn to crime.

14. Subcultural theory has been developed to explain middle-class crime. Many corporations have a subculture which emphasises the pursuit of wealth and profit. For some, the pressure to succeed in terms of this subculture leads to criminal acts.

classes to succeed. When people in white-collar occupations find the routes to pay increases and promotion blocked, they sometimes 'innovate', just like members of the working class. In other words, they turn to illegal means to become successful and attain monetary goals. They experience the same strain to anomie, to normlessness. This weakens the mechanisms of social control – the norms which would otherwise restrain criminal behaviour.

But why should middle-class people experience a strain to anomie when they are better off than those at the bottom of the class structure? One suggestion is that deprivation is relative. Middle-class people may feel deprived relative to, that is in comparison to, others who are considerably better off than themselves. And, given the pressure to succeed, they experience a strain to anomie. As a result, they innovate, just like their working-class counterparts.

In much the same way, corporations may find that legal ways of maintaining or increasing their profits are ineffective. As a result, there is a strain to anomie and pressure to turn to illegal means. The desired result may be obtained by fraud or by ignoring health and safety and environmental regulations (Box, 1983).

key terms

White-collar crime The crimes of people in white-collar occupations. It includes occupational crime and corporate crime.

Occupational crime Crimes committed by employees at the expense of the organisation.

Corporate crime Crimes committed on behalf of and for the benefit of the organisation.

State crime Crimes committed by the state or by agencies of the state on behalf of the state.

Subcultural theory revisited The hero of the film *Wall Street* – the street where the big New York stockbroking firms are located – stated that 'greed is good'. Some sociologists have argued that many corporations, especially financial institutions, have a subculture which emphasises the pursuit of wealth and profit. This so-called enterprise culture places a high value on risk-taking and monetary success. For some, it is a short step to 'success at all costs', even if this means fraud, bribery and corruption.

Further explanations of white-collar crime are examined in Unit 6 which looks at Marxist theories of crime.

activity 12 corporate crime

Item A Enron

Under its president Kenneth Lay, the US company Enron became the world's largest energy trading company. It specialised in contracts to deliver natural gas and electricity to customers at a future date. In December 2001, Enron filed for bankruptcy, billions of dollars in debt.

Investors lost a fortune with Enron shares practically worthless. Enron's 19,000 employees lost both their jobs and their savings because they belonged to a retirement plan based on Enron shares. 20,000 creditors were owed an estimated $67 billion. Most received less than 20 cents for every dollar they were owed.

Investigations revealed fraud on a vast scale. Top executives lined their pockets while concealing massive debts. False accounting practices boosted reported income and lowered reported debt. As a result, share prices remained high, bearing no relationship to the true value of the company.

Shortly before bankruptcy was declared, the company president Kenneth Lay borrowed $74 million and repaid it with company shares. And a number of senior executives were given payments totalling $55 million.

Source: Various issues of *The Guardian*, 2001, 2002, 2003

An effigy of Enron president Kenneth Lay (right) at an anti-capitalist demonstration in New York

Item B The Piper Alpha disaster

On July 6, 1988, there was an explosion on the oil rig Piper Alpha, 100 miles off the east coast of Scotland. It was caused by an escape of flammable gas and resulted in the deaths of 167 workers. The rig was owned by the Occidental Group.

A public enquiry led by Lord Cullen looked into the causes of the disaster. They included:

- An inadequate assessment by the company of the risks involved
- A failure to put right known deficiencies in the system
- Management neglect of safety standards and regulations.

Source: Cullen, 1990

Piper Alpha two days after the explosion

Dear G E Rald,

We should like to take this opportunity to inform you that on 12th of March this year you were seen entering empty handed into the private premises of Ms P C Edwards of Convent St, Folkestone, and leaving shortly afterwards with your hands full.

In our opinion, this constitutes a violation of the Theft Act 1968 subsection 32(c) and we would be grateful if you would consider the following advice: please stop going down Convent St and entering houses without the owners' permission.

We should warn you that next March 12th another police constable will be on foot duty in Convent St, and should he notice a repetition of your behaviour, we shall have to consider the possibility of taking even more stringent action than we have on this occasion.

Item C A warning

Many regulatory bodies inspect companies to check that regulations, for example on health and safety, have been followed. Warnings are issued if any regulations have not been met and companies are revisited to check that matters have been put right. On the left is a spoof letter, using similar procedures, written to a young burglar.

Source: Box, 1983

questions

1. The consequences of corporate crime can be extremely serious. Discuss with reference to Item A.
2. Would you describe the Piper Alpha disaster (Item B) as a crime? Give reasons for your answer.
3. How does Item C illustrate the difference between the way many corporate offences and 'ordinary crimes' are seen?

Unit 5 Interactionism and labelling theory

keyissues

1. What is distinctive about the interactionist approach to crime and deviance?
2. What are the strengths and weaknesses of labelling theory?

5.1 The interactionist approach

To move from functionalism to interactionism is to move to a very different theoretical perspective. Gone are the social systems and social structures which direct behaviour. In their place are small-scale interaction situations in which people act in terms of meanings and definitions of the situation. The interactionist approach to crime and deviance became popular in the 1960s.

The interactionist perspective According to Herbert Blumer (1969) interactionism, or more specifically symbolic interactionism, is based on three central views.

- First, 'human beings act towards things on the basis of the meanings that things have for them'. Human behaviour is not determined by social forces. Rather, people are self-conscious beings who choose what to do on the basis of their subjective perceptions – how they see things.

- Second, 'the meaning of things is derived from, or arises out of, the social interaction that one has with one's fellows'. Meanings are not fixed but are continually modified as people negotiate with each other.

- Third, 'group action takes the form of a fitting together of individual lines of action'. Society is not so much a determinant of human action as a product of human activity. People make society, rather than society making people.

The challenge to functionalism In terms of its approach to crime and deviance, functionalism was challenged on three grounds.

- First, the assumption that there is agreement about what forms of behaviour constitute crime and deviance. What intrigued interactionists was why the same behaviour is defined as criminal or deviant in some contexts but not others.

- Second, the claim that deviants are somehow distinctive, comprising a specific group of the population. We are asked instead to look at the process of interaction and question why certain individuals or groups are more likely to be defined as deviant.

- Third, the search for the causes of deviance is seen to be fruitless. We all commit acts which break rules. What is more interesting is the way that agencies of social control respond to different individuals and the effects of that response on their future actions.

5.2 Labelling theory

From an interactionist perspective, deviance is an act which is labelled as such. There is nothing essentially or intrinsically deviant about any act. It only becomes deviant when it is seen as such and labelled as such.

The classic statement of this view is given by Howard Becker (1963). In his words, 'social groups create deviance by making the rules whose infraction constitutes deviance and by applying those rules to particular people and labelling them as outsiders. From this point of view, deviance is not a quality of the act the person commits but rather a consequence of the application by others of rules and sanctions to an "offender". The deviant is one to whom that label has successfully been applied; deviant behaviour is behaviour that people so label.'

Becker's words are frequently quoted because they represent a new approach within the sociology of crime and deviance. The focus moves away from a concern with the deviant and the causes of deviance to a concern with the agencies of social control – with the process by which they label certain acts as deviant and the consequences of this labelling. How, then, is deviance created?

Defining deviance Society creates the rules. Deviant behaviour is not a distinctive form of behaviour but behaviour which is seen to contravene these rules. Becker (1963) illustrates this point well. 'The act of injecting heroin into a vein is not inherently deviant. If a nurse gives a patient drugs under a doctor's orders, it is perfectly proper. It is when it is done in a way that is not publicly defined as proper that it becomes deviant.' What applies to the use of drugs also applies to other forms of behaviour. Even the act of taking someone else's life is, in some contexts, considered appropriate. Indeed, in a war it is the refusal to kill which is often seen to be deviant.

Labelling Acts labelled as deviant tend to be committed by certain types of people. For example, the police tend to target specific groups. Studies of policing indicate that 'those who are stopped and searched or questioned in the street, arrested, detailed in the police station, charged, and prosecuted are disproportionately young men who are unemployed or casually employed, and from generally discriminated against ethnic minorities' (Reiner, 1994). For labelling theorists, this is due to the perceptions held by the police of the 'typical criminal'. They are more likely to see the activities of young men from the lower levels of the class structure and from certain ethnic minority groups as suspicious.

Aaron Cicourel's (1976) study of police and juvenile (probation) officers in California illustrates this point. Both groups held a similar picture of the 'typical delinquent' – as 'coming from broken homes, exhibiting "bad attitudes" towards authority, poor school performance, ethnic group membership, low-income families and the like'. As a result, young people who fitted this picture were more likely to be arrested and handed over to the juvenile officers. And, in turn, those who came closest to the picture of the 'typical delinquent' were more likely to be charged with a criminal offence by the juvenile officers. The middle-class minority who were arrested were usually 'counselled, cautioned and released' by the juvenile officers.

In the process, the police and probation officers not only created typical delinquents, they also created the social characteristics of the typical criminal shown in official statistics – young, working class and male.

Primary and secondary deviance

Edwin Lemert (1972) makes a distinction between *primary* and *secondary deviance*. Primary deviance refers to deviant acts which have not been publicly labelled. Most of us have engaged in such acts at one time or another, and for all sorts of reasons. Usually, this has little effect on our identity and status in society, or on our future lives.

Secondary deviance refers to acts which have been publicly labelled as deviant and to the deviance which is generated by this labelling.

Societal reaction The reaction of society – the way others react to someone labelled as deviant – may have a dramatic effect on that person's status and identity and may lead to further deviant acts.

Labelling people as deviant will tend to mark them out. The label may become a *master status* which overrides all other statuses. As a result, the individual is no longer seen as a parent, a friend or a worker but only as a criminal. Rejected by conventional society, they may embark on a deviant career – engage in further deviant acts and ultimately join an organised deviant group. Public labelling may result in a *self-fulfilling prophecy* whereby the person labelled deviant not only commits further deviant acts but also accepts the label.

Jock Young's (1971) study of hippie marihuana users in Notting Hill during the 1960s illustrates this process. The police targeting of a group, whose lifestyle included smoking marihuana, served to widen the differences between the hippies and conventional society. In the process, drug taking, which had been 'essentially a peripheral activity' became 'of greater value to the group as a symbol of their difference and of their defiance against perceived injustices' (Young, 1971). In this context, a deviant subculture developed. Individuals labelled outsiders began to see themselves as different from non-drug takers, all of which made it difficult for them to re-enter the wider society.

Evaluation of labelling theory

Advantages Labelling theory has a number of advantages.

- First, it has drawn attention to the importance of labelling and societal reaction. These processes can, in themselves, generate deviant and criminal behaviour.
- Second, it has shown that certain types of people are singled out for labelling.
- Third, it has shown that this results from the definitions and perceptions of the agents of social control – for example, their perceptions of the 'typical delinquent'.

Disadvantages Critics have pointed to the following weaknesses of labelling theory.

- **Origins of deviance** Labelling theorists see the search for the origin of deviant acts as largely fruitless. But deviance is not simply created by the label. People do not become burglars simply because they are labelled as such. They know that their actions are deviant, they are aware that they are breaking the law. Why do they become burglars? This example suggests that looking for the origins of deviance is an important sociological question.
- **Selection of deviants** Labelling theory fails to explain why certain types of people are selected as likely deviants rather than others. It is not sufficient to say that they fit definitions of likely deviants held by the agents of social control. Where do these definitions come from? They don't appear to be simply created in interaction situations. The picture of the 'typical

delinquent' is common to criminal justice systems in the UK, USA and elsewhere.

- **Who makes the rules?** According to Howard Becker (1963), 'social groups create deviance by making rules whose infraction constitutes deviance'. But who are these people who make the rules? And why do they make these particular rules? For example, are rules made by the powerful for their own benefit? This possibility is examined in the next unit which looks at Marxist approaches to crime and deviance.

---

key terms

Primary deviance Deviant acts which have not been publicly labelled.
Secondary deviance Acts which have been publicly labelled as deviant and the deviance which is generated by the label.
Societal reaction The reaction of others to an individual. In this case, the reaction of others to someone labelled as deviant.
Master status A status which overrides all other statuses. The status in terms of which a person is seen by others.
Self-fulfilling prophecy A prophecy which comes to pass simply because it has been made. The prophecy therefore fulfils itself.

5.3 Deviancy amplification

A number of sociologists who do not share the same theoretical perspective as the interactionists have also focused on societal reaction. The following study looks at societal reaction to mods and rockers in the mid-1960s.

Mods and rockers Mods and rockers are youth groups who differed from each other in terms of dress, musical tastes and modes of transport – mods rode scooters, rockers rode motor bikes. Stanley Cohen's (1987) study looked at societal reaction to disturbances involving mods and rockers which took place in Clacton over the Easter bank holiday in 1964.

The mass media represented these disturbances as a confrontation between rival gangs 'hell bent on destruction'. On inspection, however, Cohen discovered that the amount of serious violence and vandalism was not great and that most young people who'd gone to the seaside that weekend did not identify with either the mods or the rockers. The mass media had produced a distorted picture of what went on.

Deviancy amplification spiral Media coverage led to considerable public concern with mods and rockers. And this set in motion a *deviancy amplification spiral*. Sensitised to the 'problem', the police made more arrests, the media reported more deviance, and young people were more likely to identify with either mods or rockers. Further disturbances followed on subsequent bank holidays, attracting more police attention, more arrests, increased media interest and more young people reacting to what they saw as heavy-handed and unjustified treatment from the police.

activity 13 labelling theory

Item A *Defining deviance*

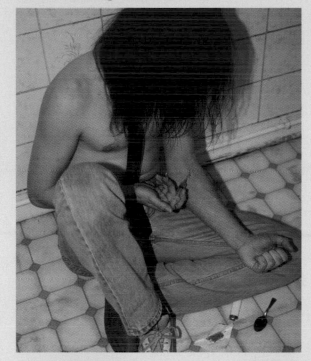

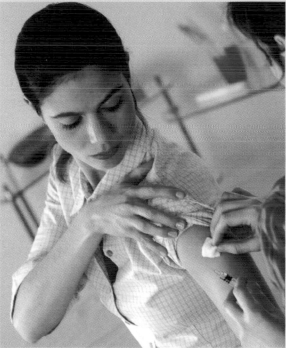

Item B *Labelling deviance*

Item C *Secondary deviance*

Stop and search

questions

1 Which act or acts in Item A might be defined as deviant? Give reasons for your answer.

2 If there was trouble at a soccer match, which of the people in Item B would the police be more likely to question and arrest? Give reasons for your answer.

3 How might the police activity in Item C lead to secondary deviance?

The reaction to the initial disturbances over the Easter bank holiday not only exaggerated the amount of deviance, it also generated more deviance.

Moral panics

Stanley Cohen claimed that the reaction of the media to events in Clacton generated a *moral panic*. A moral panic occurs when 'a condition, episode, person or group of persons emerges to become defined as a threat to societal values and interests' (Cohen, 1987). In the above case, mods and rockers were singled out as 'folk devils' whose behaviour constituted a threat to the social order. The 1960s were a decade of widespread social change, in which cherished norms were challenged. The mods and rockers served as symbols of what was wrong with society. In subsequent decades, young people continued to be the focus of moral panics. The 1970s saw the moral panic of mugging, and the 1980s the moral panic of football hooliganism (see Activity 14).

More recently, moral panics have focused on threats to children with concerns over child abuse, paedophilia and the influence of violent films on young viewers (Critcher, 2003).

The media's reaction to deviance may lead to a deviancy amplification spiral, a moral panic and more authoritarian forms of control. This process is illustrated in Figure 1.

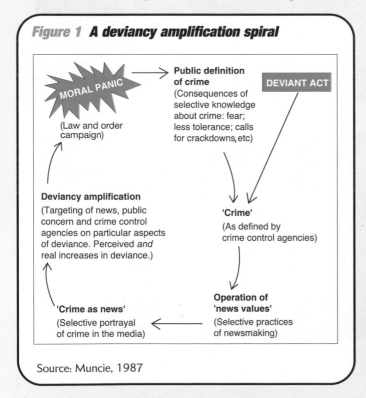

Figure 1 A deviancy amplification spiral

Source: Muncie, 1987

Evaluation

There is evidence that societal reaction can amplify deviance. And there is evidence that this reaction can reach the level of a moral panic. When it reaches this level, it is out of proportion to the situation – it is 'over the top'.

But who's to say that a so-called moral panic is unreasonable? Jock Young (1986) criticises the concept of a moral panic because it implies that crime is, in large part, constructed by the media. Young accepts that the media may exaggerate the 'crime problem', but it does not create it. He argues that the reality of crime, and the human suffering it produces, must be taken seriously and not reduced to a media construction.

key terms

Deviancy amplification spiral A process in which deviance is increased by societal reaction.
Moral panic According to Cohen (1987), a moral panic occurs when 'a condition, episode, person or group of persons emerges to become defined as a threat to societal values and interests'.

summary

1. From an interactionist perspective, people act in terms of meanings and definitions which arise in social interaction. The interactionist approach to crime and deviance became popular in the 1960s.

2. Interactionists challenge the view that deviants are essentially different from non-deviants.

3. In terms of labelling theory, deviance is behaviour which is labelled as such, a deviant is someone to whom a label has successfully been applied.

4. Labelling theory focuses on the agents of social control, on the way they define certain acts and certain kinds of people as deviant, and the consequences of this.

5. Societal reaction to someone labelled as deviant can lead to a self-fulfilling prophecy. Individuals so labelled may be encouraged to commit further deviant acts and may see themselves in terms of the label.

6. Although it has a number of advantages – for example, showing the importance of societal reaction – labelling theory has been criticised for failing to explain:
    ● The origins of deviance
    ● Why certain types of people are seen as likely deviants
    ● Who makes the rules.

7. Societal reaction can lead to a deviancy amplification spiral in which the response to the initial deviance generates further deviance.

8. Societal reaction can take the form of a moral panic.

9. The idea of a moral panic has been criticised because it implies that crime is largely constructed by the media. According to Jock Young, it tends to ignore the reality of crime.

*activity*14 *football hooliganism*

Item A *Moral panics and social control*

```
┌─────────────────────────────────────┐
│      IDENTIFICATION OF A PROBLEM     │
│         (eg football hooliganism)    │
└─────────────────────────────────────┘
                   ↓
    Identification of a subversive minority
(eg the 'few who spoil the enjoyment of millions': identification
            by styles - skinheads, etc)
                   ↓
            Simplification of cause
  (eg decline in moral standards, lack of discipline etc)
                   ↓
       Stigmatisation of those involved
 (Media use of emotive and disparaging significations eg
        'morons'; 'animals'; 'savages' etc)
                   ↓
         Stirring of public indignation
    (eg media campaigns calling for 'action': criticism of 'soft'
      sentences; evocation of the 'national image', etc)
                   ↓
            Stamping down hard
(eg government responds to 'public demand' as presented by
   the media. Stiffer sentences; more 'anti-hooligan' legislation;
              bans on spectators etc)
┌─────────────────────────────────────┐
│   MORE AUTHORITARIAN FORMS OF CONTROL│
└─────────────────────────────────────┘
```

Source: Muncie, 1987

Item E *The police response*

In the last 20 years increasing attempts by police to control football hooliganism have included separating rival groups at matches in pens surrounded by spiked fences; closed circuit television crowd surveillance techniques; the use of identity card schemes; soccer hooligan group infiltration through police undercover operations and the formation of a National Football Intelligence Unit with computerised data banks on known soccer hooligans.

Source: Kerr, 1994

Item F *A hooligan's view*

We just don't have the time we used to have. The moment a fight starts we're immediately surrounded by dogs and horses. That's why everyone has started using knives. I suppose it might sound stupid but, because the policing has got so good, we've got to the point where we have to inflict the greatest possible damage in the least amount of time, and the knife is the most efficient instrument for a quick injury. In fact the knifings – because there is so little time – have been quite symbolic. When someone gets knifed, it amounts to an important victory to the side that has done the knifing. If the policing was not so good, I'm sure the knifings would stop.

Source: Kerr, 1994

Item B *Newspaper headlines, 1988*

Before the European Championship
Sun: Euro hoolies league
Daily Mirror: Plague of the Euro yob: Dutch go top of the Thug's Table

During the European Championship
Sun: World War III
Star: Yobs Plot War

Item C *Margaret Thatcher's reaction*

'We must really eradicate this blot on our reputation We want those guilty of it caught and convicted, and given a severe sentence as an example to others.'

Then prime minister Margaret Thatcher, 1988, after rowdiness by some English fans at the European championships. Comments made at the Welsh Conservative Conference and reported in *The Times*.

Item D *Pictured in the media*

Liverpool vs Juventus, European Cup Final, Brussels, 1985

questions

1 To what extent does the societal reaction in Items B to E fit the process outlined in Item A?

2 How might societal reaction generate further and more serious deviance? Refer to Item F in your answer.

Unit 6 *Marxism and radical criminology*

keyissues

1 What is distinctive about the Marxist approach to crime, deviance and social control?

2 What are the strengths and weaknesses of this approach?

6.1 Traditional Marxist approaches

This unit examines two Marxist approaches to crime and deviance which emerged in the 1970s. The first is a fairly traditional development of Marxist ideas. The second – radical criminology – incorporates certain aspects of the interactionist approach.

From a Marxist perspective, crime and deviance in Western society can only be understood in terms of capitalism and the class struggle. Coercion and conflict are seen as the key features of capitalist society in contrast to functionalism's emphasis on consensus and integration. However, like functionalism, Marxism sees the structures and institutions of society as largely determining how people behave.

Causes of crime From a Marxist viewpoint, crime is systematically generated by the structure of capitalist society. Capitalism is an economic system based on the private ownership of the means of production and the maximisation of profit. As such, it emphasises individual gain rather than collective wellbeing. Capitalism is a competitive system which encourages aggression and emphasises the importance of winning. It is also an exploitative system in which some gain at the expense of others.

Given these priorities it is a short step to seeing the end as justifying the means – to be so obsessed with personal gain and coming out on top that breaking the law seems a minor barrier to success. Pressures to break the law will affect people across the social spectrum from wealthy business people to the poverty-stricken unemployed. In this respect, fiddling business expenses and fiddling the dole have similar causes.

From a Marxist perspective, capitalism encourages greed and self-interest, it generates frustration and aggression. Breaking the law can be seen as a rational step in order to satisfy these desires and express these feelings. Crimes motivated by financial gain can be seen as a logical outcome of the priorities of profit. Crimes with no apparent financial motive can be seen as an expression of the frustration, aggression and hostility which the system produces.

The law Laws in capitalist society are seen to reflect the interests of the dominant capitalist class. Thus the many laws protecting private property, which have appeared on the statute books over the past 200 years, reflect the growth of industry and the expansion of trade and commerce. In this respect, private property, the essence of capitalism, is protected.

Laws which appear to protect the interests of workers can be seen as concessions to the working class to maintain, if not its loyalty, then its acceptance of the system. For example, health and safety laws protecting workers can be seen in this light – and they have the additional benefit to capitalism of helping to provide a fit and healthy workforce.

Law enforcement 'There is one law for the rich and another for the poor.' This piece of folk wisdom summarises how many Marxists characterise law enforcement in capitalist society. The law is enforced selectively – there is a systematic bias in favour of those at the top. The crimes of the powerful such as corporate crime – for example, failing to pay business taxes and breaking trading laws – if discovered are rarely prosecuted. By comparison, those at the bottom of the class system who are caught breaking the law are regularly prosecuted. Yet in monetary terms their crimes are a drop in the ocean compared to the vast sums involved in the criminal activities of those at the top. Some of the evidence for this claim can be seen in Activity 15.

Evaluation Marxist approaches have the advantage of combining explanations of crime which cover members of all social classes, a wide variety of offences, the nature of law in capitalist society and the selective enforcement of the law. However, these explanations are very general and depend for their force on an acceptance of a Marxist view of capitalism. Many sociologists reject the view that there is a fundamental conflict of interest between the ruling and subject classes in capitalist society and the exploitation of one by the other.

6.2 Radical criminology

Radical criminology is the most influential attempt to apply a Marxist perspective to the study of crime and deviance. It emerged in Britain in the 1970s out of dissatisfaction with existing theories – including the more traditional Marxist approaches.

Radical criminology focuses on the process by which the state defines certain activities as criminal and thereby criminalises certain groups, particularly the oppressed and disadvantaged. This stress on the process of criminalisation is reminiscent of labelling theory. While accepting that interaction between lower-level agents of social control, such as the police, and deviants is important, radical

activity15 *scrounging*

Item A **Two views of capitalist society**

'I got the loot, Charlie, but after bank costs, services and handling charges, we owe them £6.25p.'

Item B **'The real scroungers'**

Cost of dole fraud	£500 million	Cost of tax fraud	£5,000 million
Number of prosecutions	14,000	Number of prosecutions	20

In the eyes of the law, all people may be equal but the government's treatment of tax and social security offenders suggests there is one law for the rich and another for the poor. For every individual who is pursued through the courts for tax fraud, about 700 are prosecuted for welfare offences. This disparity cannot be accounted for by arguing that benefit fiddling is a more serious social menace than tax fraud. Official estimates indicate that losses from benefit abuses are dwarfed by losses from tax evasion. The Inland Revenue sees prosecution as a last resort and seeks to secure 'a reasonable settlement by agreement'. As one tax accountant put it, 'You have to be very unlucky, very stupid and very crooked to be done by the Revenue'.

Source: *The Observer*, 23.10.1988

questions

1 Using a Marxist perspective, briefly comment on the cartoons in Item A.

2 Read Item B. Suggest reasons for the different treatment of tax fraud and welfare fraud.

---

criminology demands a wider focus. It looks at the process of criminalisation in relation to the state as it seeks to manage the capitalist system.

A 'fully social theory of deviance'

The ambition of radical criminology is evident in the final chapter of *The New Criminology* by Ian Taylor, Paul Walton and Jock Young (1973). There the authors outline a model which they term a 'fully social theory of deviance'. The model has seven dimensions:

1 'The wider origins of the deviant act'

The radical criminologist needs to locate the deviant act within the wider social system – capitalism and its class divisions.

2 'The immediate origins of the deviant act'
They then need to look at the immediate social context within which an individual chooses to commit an act of deviance.

3 'The actual act'
Attention needs to be given to what the deviant act means to the individual concerned.

4 'The immediate origins of social reaction'
They need to look at the immediate response of other people, such as members of the deviant's family and the police, to the discovery of deviance.

5 'Wider origins of deviant reaction'

The immediate reaction needs to be located within the wider social system, with particular attention given to the question of who has the power to define certain activities as deviant.

6 'The outcomes of social reaction on the deviant's further action'

While most deviants recognise that there will be a reaction against them, it is important to examine the effects of the labelling process on the deviant.

7 'The nature of the deviant process as a whole'

Finally the six aspects of the deviant process need to be connected together for there to be a 'fully social theory of deviance'.

The closest approximation to a 'fully social theory of deviance' is *Policing the Crisis* by Stuart Hall et al. (1978). It is a study of the moral panic which took place in the early 1970s over 'mugging'. In the following summary, particular attention is given to the way this study illustrates a 'fully social theory of deviance'.

Policing the crisis

The wider origins of mugging Mugging is a term imported from America. It refers to the street crime of robbery or theft involving the threat or actual use of violence. During the early 1970s in Britain, a moral panic developed about the dangers of street crime and, in particular, the threat of the young Black mugger. Stuart Hall et al. (1978) argue that this societal reaction to mugging must be seen in the wider context of capitalism and the class system.

Street crime has traditionally been one 'survival strategy' for those at the bottom of the class system, particularly during an economic crisis.

Partly as a result of racism, the first generation of African-Caribbean migrants were the most disadvantaged members of the working class. The majority found low-paid employment and made the best of their situation.

The immediate origins of mugging Acutely aware of the racism of British society, Black youth were less willing than their parents to accept the situation. This sometimes caused conflict between the generations, resulting in some young people leaving home, taking to the streets and drifting into petty crime. In this context, a small minority of Black youngsters adopted the 'mugging solution' as a survival strategy.

The immediate origins of the social reaction to mugging The media were central in 'orchestrating public opinion' against the Black mugger. Between August 1972 and August 1973, the national daily newspapers reported 60 incidents as 'muggings'. They pictured Black youth creating mindless havoc in the inner cities. Yet mugging was neither a new problem, nor was it growing at an alarming rate – in fact, the rate of growth was less than half the rate in the 1960s. Hall et al. see the societal reaction to mugging as a moral panic.

The wider origins of the social reaction to mugging Hall et al. argue that this moral panic must be seen in the context of the problems that British capitalism was experiencing in the early 1970s.

Since 1945, full employment, rising living standards and the growth of welfare services resulted in the working class accepting the authority of the state. However, an economic crisis in the early 1970s brought rising unemployment, a slowing down of the rise in people's living standards and a halt to the expansion of welfare services. As a result, the authority of the state came under challenge from various groups, especially trade unions. For example, in 1972, there were more workdays lost by strikes than in any year since 1919. (See Chapter 5, Activity 7, pages 276-277.)

The state reacted by presenting this challenge to its authority as a 'law and order' issue. The stability of society was threatened by lawlessness and the state must respond. The focus on the Black mugger served to symbolise this threat to social order. The result was to divide the working class on 'racial' grounds, so weakening any challenge to the state. And, the apparent need to stamp out mugging as quickly as possible justified the state increasing its powers.

The outcome of social reaction Responding to the perceived threat of mugging, the police targeted this crime and Black youth in particular. Increasing numbers of young Black men were randomly stopped, searched and questioned in the street. Many saw this as unjustified and some responded with verbal abuse or violence. This often led to their arrest and appeared to confirm that they were indeed prone to crimes of violence. The result was a process of deviancy amplification. The labelling of Black youth as deviant led to more arrests which, in turn, justified even stronger police measures against so-called Black muggers, all of which provided further headlines for the newspapers.

A fully social theory *Policing the Crisis* looks at the moral panic of mugging from a variety of viewpoints. It analyses the crisis faced by British capitalism in the early 1970s and the resulting threat to the authority of the state. It argues that the state responded to this crisis by mounting a law and order campaign which led to a moral panic over mugging. As a result, Black youths became increasingly criminalised and the state was able to justify its growing powers. This analysis looks at the 'problem of mugging' on various levels – from society as a whole right down to street level.

Evaluation of radical criminology

Advantages Radical criminology combines a number of different perspectives in an attempt to provide a fully social theory of deviance. Within a Marxist framework, *Policing the Crisis* includes labelling theory along with concepts such as societal reaction, moral panics and deviancy amplification. In doing so, it offers a more comprehensive picture than previous perspectives.

Disadvantages In adopting a Marxist framework, radical criminology ultimately explains crime and deviance in terms of the nature of capitalist society, the conflict of interest between social classes and the role of the state in representing the capitalist class. Can all crime and deviance be explained in terms of this framework? Critics argue that many laws and much police activity cannot simply be seen as an expression of the interests of the capitalist class – for example, traffic laws and their enforcement (Rock, 1979).

According to Lea and Young (1993), radical criminology tends to trivialise and underplay the reality of crime. While moral panics do occur and societal reaction can amplify deviance, crime has risen. And the consequences are serious. Both the victims and the perpetrators of street crime are usually working class and, in many inner-city areas, this is a major problem. Radical criminology has little to say about the victims of crime.

According to Downes and Rock (2003), *Policing the Crisis* was a brave but unsuccessful attempt to provide a fully social theory of deviance. In particular, the authors failed to demonstrate that the societal reaction to mugging was caused by a crisis of capitalism. At the very least, they needed to show a link between economic crises and moral panics at other times and places. And this was not done.

summary

1. Marxist theories of crime and deviance became popular in the 1970s.
2. Traditional Marxist approaches argued that:
   - Crime is systematically generated by the structure of capitalist society.
   - Laws reflect the interests of the dominant capitalist class.
   - Laws are enforced selectively - there is a systematic bias in favour of those at the top.
3. Radical criminology adopts a Marxist framework but includes other perspectives - for example, interactionism.
4. It focuses on the process by which the state defines certain activities as criminal and thereby criminalises certain groups, particularly the disadvantaged. It looks at the process of criminalisation in relation to the state's management of the capitalist system.
5. Radical criminology aims to provide a 'fully social theory of deviance' - to explain every aspect of deviance from the activity of the state to crime on the streets.
6. Policing the crisis argued that the state manufactures a crime problem in order to justify strengthening its control over the population.
7. Radical criminology has been criticised for:
   - Seeing the actions of the state and the agents of social control as solely serving the interests of the capitalist class.
   - Downplaying the significance of crime and largely ignoring the victims of crime.

Unit 7 Right realism, social order and social control

keyissues

1 What is distinctive about right realist approaches to crime?

2 What are the strengths and weaknesses of these approaches?

right realism and *left realism*. Both see crime as a major problem in society, especially for its victims, and both claim to take crime seriously and to put forward practical proposals to combat it. 'Realist' approaches can be seen as a reaction to both labelling theory and radical criminology. Neither of these perspectives appeared to show much concern for the victims of crime. Indeed, labelling theory implied that in many cases the 'victim' was the person who had been labelled as 'criminal'.

7.1 Recent developments in the sociology of crime

New approaches to crime and deviance are partly a reaction to the shortcomings of previous approaches, partly a reflection of changing academic and political priorities, partly a response to changing fashions.

In the 1980s and 90s there was increased concern about law and order in Britain and the USA. This was accompanied by a growing awareness of high levels of unreported victimisation, especially amongst the most vulnerable sections of the population. These concerns were reflected in two new approaches to the study of crime –

7.2 The right realist approach

Conservative theorists were the first to adopt a realist approach. James Q. Wilson (1975), an American New Right theorist and policy adviser to President Reagan, was one of the earliest authors to question the predominant liberal and left analyses of law and order which prevailed in sociology. What then are the central features of the right realist analysis of crime?

Poverty, unemployment and crime

First and foremost, right realists question the view that

economic factors such as poverty or unemployment are responsible for the rising crime rate. In the following passage, Wilson makes a telling critique of this view by arguing that affluence and prosperity may go hand in hand with rising crime.

'If in 1960 one had been asked what steps society might take to prevent a sharp increase in the crime rate, one might well have answered that crime could best be curtailed by reducing poverty, increasing educational attainment, eliminating dilapidated housing, encouraging community organisation, and providing troubled or delinquent youth with counselling services.

Early in the decade of the 1960s, this country (the USA) began the longest sustained period of prosperity since the Second World War. A great array of programmes aimed at the young, the poor and the deprived were mounted. Crime soared. It did not just increase a little; it rose at a faster rate and to higher levels than at any time since the 1930s, and, in some categories, to higher levels than any experienced in this century' (Wilson, 1975).

Explaining rising crime

According to James Q. Wilson and Richard Hernstein (1985), 'crime is an activity disproportionately committed by young men living in large cities'. They explain this in terms of both biological and social factors. In their words,

'It is likely that the effect of maleness and youthfulness on the tendency to commit crime has both constitutional [biological] and social origins: that is, it has something to do with the biological status of being a young male and with how that young man has been treated by family, friends and society.'

Wilson and Hernstein picture young men as 'temperamentally aggressive'. This aggression is partly biologically based and makes them prone to crime.

An increase in the proportion of young men in the population is therefore likely to increase the crime rate. In the USA and Britain in the 1970s, the proportion of young men in the population and the crime rate both increased. Since the early 1980s, the proportion of young men has decreased but the crime rate has continued to increase. Wilson and Hernstein offer a social explanation for this increase.

Culture and socialisation Wilson and Hernstein argue that the way young men are socialised in the family, school and wider community has an important effect on their behaviour. Consistent discipline inside and outside the home encourages individuals to learn and follow society's norms and values and develop self control.

Wilson and Hernstein see the growth of a culture which emphasises *immediate gratification* – the immediate satisfaction of wants and desires – *low impulse control* – less control over desires and emotions, fewer restraints and checks on behaviour – and *self-expression* – the outward expression of feelings. These aspects of culture have produced a less effective learning environment for many young men and reduced the restraints on their behaviour. As a result, they are less likely to conform to society's norms and values and more likely to commit crime.

Costs and benefits Wilson and Hernstein argue that the crime rate will change with changes in the costs and benefits of crime, particularly property crime. The more the benefits rise – for example, the more successful criminals are – and the more the costs fall – for example, the less likely they are to be caught – the more the crime rate will rise.

7.3 Social control

Control theory

Many right realists argue that individuals are more likely to commit crime when the social constraints on their behaviour are weakened. Control theory is mainly concerned with identifying the factors which prevent individuals from committing crimes.

According to the American sociologist Travis Hirschi (1969), none of us is immune from the temptations of crime. What stops most of us from committing crime are strong social bonds which link us together. Social bonds consist of four main elements: attachment, commitment, involvement and belief. The stronger our attachments to key social institutions such as the family and school, the more we develop commitments to those involved – parents and teachers. Such commitments in turn foster involvement in family life and learning, and encourage a belief in conforming to the rules. Effective social bonds mean that we have too much to lose by committing crime. To do so would risk losing the good opinion of significant others – those who matter to us.

In support of his theory, Hirschi reports the findings of a large-scale self-report study of over 4000 young people aged 12-17 in California. Variations in their reported bonds with parents and teachers were much more significant than economic factors in accounting for variations in reported delinquency. Drawing on a range of studies, Hirschi has put forward a general theory of crime. He argues that the primary distinguishing feature of offenders is a lack of self-control. This, in turn, stems from poor socialisation in families and schools (Gottfredson & Hirschi, 1990).

Social control and the underclass

The American New Right theorist Charles Murray (1990, 1996) claims that an underclass is emerging in modern Western societies. For Murray, an underclass does not simply consist of those with the lowest income at the base of the class system. Instead, it consists of those with low income who behave in a certain way. In Murray's words, 'When I use the term *underclass*, I am indeed focusing on a certain type of poor person defined *not* by his condition, eg long-term unemployed, but by his deplorable behaviour in response to that condition, eg unwilling to take the jobs that are available to him'.

Murray sees births outside marriage 'as the leading indicator of an underclass'. Such births often lead to lone-parent families, the majority of which are headed by women. When lone-parent families become widespread, they form the basis of and the 'breeding ground' for an underclass. And 'proof that an underclass has arrived is that large numbers of young, healthy, low-income males choose not to take jobs'.

Inadequate socialisation Many of these young men have grown up in a family without a father and male wage earner. As a result, they lack the male role models of mainstream society. Within a female-headed family dependent on welfare benefits, the disciplines and responsibilities of mainstream society tend to break down. Murray believes that work must become the 'centre of life' for young men. They must learn the disciplines of work and respect for work. And they must learn to become 'real fathers', accepting the responsibilities of parenthood. However, 'Little boys don't naturally grow up to be responsible fathers and husbands. They don't naturally grow up knowing how to get up every morning at the same time and go to work. They don't naturally grow up thinking that work is not just a way to make money, but a way to hold one's head high in the world.' Murray believes that the socialisation and role models required to develop these attitudes are often lacking in female-headed low-income families.

Crime and the underclass According to Murray (1990), crime is a characteristic of the underclass. He argues that 'men who do not support families find other ways to prove that they are men, which tend to take various destructive forms'. Many turn to crime – particularly violent street crime – and to drug abuse. The high crime rate and high levels of victimisation result in fragmented communities which reinforce already inadequate socialisation.

Welfare benefits and family Although Murray appears to blame members of the underclass for their situation, he places most of the blame on government policy. It is the availability of overgenerous welfare benefits which has allowed the underclass to develop. Members of the underclass have become dependent on the state which has funded their unproductive lifestyles. Murray's solution is a sharp reduction or withdrawal of welfare benefits in order to force people to take responsibility for their own lives. In addition, Murray (1996) recommends penalising births outside marriage and reaffirming 'the value of marriage and the nuclear family'.

Without these changes, Murray believes that the underclass will reproduce itself from generation to generation.

7.4 Social order and crime prevention

Right realists are concerned with practical measures to reduce crime and maintain social order. Some of those measures are based on rational choice theory.

Rational choice theory As noted earlier, Wilson and Hernstein (1985) argue that there is an important element of choice when deciding whether or not to commit a crime. They picture the individual weighing up the costs and benefits of criminal activity and coming to a rational decision. In terms of this view, crime reduction means increasing the costs of crime and raising the benefits of conformity.

Two measures which increase the costs of crime are *target hardening* and *surveillance*. Target hardening reduces the physical opportunities for offending. Examples include installing tougher coin boxes in phone kiosks, making it more difficult to break into buildings, and gated communities with security guards. Surveillance refers to systems like CCTV (closed circuit television) which can film criminal activities. These measures increase the costs of crime – the cost of failure and the cost of getting caught.

Informal social controls In James Q. Wilson's view, it is not practical to deal with the fundamental causes of crime – the biological and social factors outlined in Section 7.2. The central concern of the criminal justice system should be the maintenance of social order. Since informal controls are fundamental in preventing crime, the police should seek to prevent further deterioration of communities before it is too late.

In a highly influential article, Wilson and Kelling (2003) argue that crime and social disorder are closely connected. Leaving broken windows unmended and ignoring anti-social behaviour can result in a vicious cycle whereby graffiti proliferates, noise levels increase, vandalism grows and more windows get broken. The consequence of inaction is to tip a neighbourhood into decline – property values spiral downwards, respectable members of the community are afraid to go out, they eventually leave the neighbourhood, and crime and disorder become widespread.

The role of the police is to prevent an area from deteriorating by clamping down on the first signs of petty crime and disorderly behaviour. By working with local residents to deal with undesirable behaviour, the police can help to prevent the deterioration of neighbourhoods and reinvigorate informal social controls. Since the police have limited resources, prioritising areas where there is still a possibility of regenerating communities means that there is little point in wasting valuable resources on the worst inner-city areas. The most that can be done there is to contain the crime problem by adopting more punitive measures – for example, longer prison sentences – to deal with 'wicked people' (Wilson, 1975). The prison population in the USA has tripled since the late 1970s (from 500,000 to 1.8 million in 1998) and is now the highest per capita in the world (Carrabine et al., 2002).

7.5 Evaluation of right realism

What's 'real' about right realism? Right realists see the rising crime rate as a real indicator of a *real* social problem

– a problem which must be tackled with practical methods. However, as discussed in Unit 2, at least part of the rise in crime indicated by official statistics may result from changes in recording and reporting crime (Walklate, 2003).

Economic change and crime Right realists make an important point when they argue that economic growth and rising living standards have gone hand in hand with rising crime since the 1960s. However, this does *not* mean that social inequality ceases to be an important factor in generating crime. Despite rising living standards, the gap between top and bottom has widened over the past 25 years. This can result in a sense of relative deprivation which may lead to an increase in crime.

Disorder and community deterioration Do signs of disorder – 'broken windows' and anti-social behaviour – lead to a vicious cycle of community deterioration and rising crime? A study of 196 neighbourhoods in Chicago questions this view. It found that economic disadvantage underpinned *both* growing disorder and crime (Sampson & Raudenbush, 1999). Again, this points to the importance of relative deprivation in generating crime.

Young males Right realists focus on young males and street crime. They are the real problem, and the type of crimes they commit are the real threat to social order. This view is questionable. Other types of crime may be equally, if not more harmful – for example, corporate crime and domestic crime.

Right realists assume that young males in inner-city areas are responsible for most crimes. Again, this is questionable. It assumes that official statistics provide a valid picture of the typical offender.

key terms

Immediate gratification The immediate satisfaction of wants and desires.
Low impulse control Little control over emotions, few restraints on behaviour.
Self-expression The outward expression of feelings.
Target hardening Reducing the physical opportunities for offending by 'hardening' the targets of crime – for example, more secure buildings.
Surveillance Close observation, particularly of suspected persons.

Crime prevention According to Wilson (1975), 'wicked people exist' and the only thing that works is to 'set them apart from innocent people'. More imprisonment and longer sentences keep wicked people out of circulation and reduce the crime rate. Not only is this a very expensive measure, there is no sound evidence that it works (Walklate, 2003).

Civil liberties The major concern of right realists is to maintain order in society. For some, their prescription for producing order is based on a 'culture of control' – social control, situational control and self-control. This has alarmed some sociologists who see it as a threat to civil liberties – for example, the widespread use of surveillance techniques intruding on people's privacy (Hughes, 2000).

summary

1. Right realists accept the view that the crime rate rose dramatically in the second half of the 20th century.

2. They reject the view that economic factors and social inequality explain this rise.

3. Wilson and Hernstein argue that the rise in crime results from the growth of a culture which emphasises immediate gratification, low impulse control and self-expression. This results in a less effective learning environment for many young men. As a result, they are less likely to conform to society's norms and values.

4. Control theory states that strong social bonds result in high levels of social control. These are the main factors which prevent criminal behaviour.

5. Charles Murray argues that the underclass is a 'breeding ground' for crime. The 'deplorable behaviour' of young males results from inadequate socialisation in female-headed families and a lack of mainstream role models. Murray argues that overgenerous welfare benefits have allowed the underclass to develop.

6. Rational choice theory states that individuals weigh up the costs and benefits of criminal activity. Crime reduction therefore means increasing the costs of crime and the benefits of conformity.

7. Target hardening, surveillance, more imprisonment and longer sentences increase the costs of crime.

8. The primary role of the criminal justice system is to maintain public order. According to Wilson, strong informal social controls are the most effective method for maintaining order.

9. Disorder indicates a weakening of informal controls. The police should clamp down on the first signs of disorder to prevent community deterioration and rising crime.

10. Right realism has been criticised for:
    - Accepting the picture of crime presented by official statistics
    - Rejecting the view that economic factors and social inequality can generate crime
    - Focusing on young males and street crime and largely ignoring other types of offenders and crime.
    - Placing too much emphasis on control which some see as a threat to civil liberties.

activity 16 controlling crime and anti-social behaviour

Item A Maintaining order

How to sweep these beggars from our streets

by David Marsland

In all of our major cities and larger towns beggars have multiplied over recent years like fungus spreading in a damp cellar. Their aggressive hassling of men, women, and children is an intolerable blot on the complex but orderly copy-book of a modern civilised society.

Their arrogant contempt for the values of most decent, ordinary people - honesty, hard work, and civility foremost among them - is intolerable. Their possessive occupation - like locusts swarming on the harvest - of the most celebrated and attractive streets and squares they can find, is contemptible.

Analysis of historical and international evidence serves to disprove most fashionable explanations of begging. Neither 'capitalism' nor poverty is the cause. Begging on any scale is unheard of in some of the richest countries in the world - such as Switzerland - and some of the poorest - such as Malaysia.

Nor is it unemployment which causes begging. The current scale of begging was unheard of in the Britain of the 1930s, when unemployment was at much higher levels and much crueller in its impact.

Victorian experience provides the clue to the real explanation. Faced with a problem very like today's, politicians, businessmen and community leaders carefully analysed cause and effect, and rapidly set up a practical system which solved the problem in short order.

The Poor Laws and the work-houses were modernised and toughened up.

Help without a return of effort was out-lawed. The values of hard work, self reliance and respectability were reinforced and unapologetically defended by a powerful consensus of public opinion in the schools, the churches, the media and Parliament. Begging was shamed out of existence.

What is causing the escalation in modern begging is:

- The hand-out culture of the decaying welfare state.
- The cultivation of tolerance for 'doing nothing' and 'doing your own thing' by teachers, intellectuals and political leaders.
- The impact on established British values of the sloppy, alien thinking of the Sixties.

Source: *Daily Mail*, 1994

Item B Controlling crime

Closed circuit television

Gated community

Former Metropolitan Police Chief Sir Paul Condon (centre) promoting the Neighbourhood Watch Scheme

questions

1 In what ways does Item A reflect the right realist approach?

2 How do the pictures in Item B illustrate right realist views on crime control?

Unit 8 Left realism, social order and social control

keyissues

1 What is distinctive about the left realist approach?
2 What are its strengths and weaknesses?

8.1 The left realist approach

The emergence of left realism Left realism developed in the early 1980s. It was a reaction to both right realism and radical criminology. It was led by the British sociologist Jock Young.

Left realism accused the right of over-dramatising the crime problem with its picture of crime rates out of control. It rejected right realism's view of moral decay and sick societies. And it accused the right of failing to understand the real causes of crime.

Marxism and radical criminology were criticised for focusing on the crimes of the powerful and for failing to understand working-class crime. In particular, left realism argued that street crime could not simply be dismissed as a moral panic fuelled by a crisis of capitalism. Left realism accused radical criminology of failing to take working-class crime seriously.

Taking crime seriously Left realism, as its name suggests, claims to focus on the reality of crime. Its rallying cry to sociologists is to 'take crime seriously'. And this means starting from 'problems as people experience them' (Young, 1986). Although left realists do not discount the importance of white-collar and corporate crime, they see street crime as 'the most transparent of all injustices' (Lea & Young, 1993). Its effects can be traumatic, it can leave people living in fear, it can impoverish victims. Left realists see crime committed by working-class people against working-class people as a problem of the first order.

Explaining crime Left realists argue that earlier explanations of crime failed to see the whole picture. For example, they looked at offenders and ignored victims, or focused almost exclusively on the criminal justice system. Left realists argue that an understanding of the reality of crime requires an examination of four basic elements and how they interact (Young, 1997).

- The victims – how they see and experience crime
- The offenders – why they commit crime
- The reaction of the formal agencies of the state – for example, the police and the courts
- The response of the public and the nature of informal methods of social control.

8.2 The victims

Left realists see crime as a real problem and the public's fear of crime as largely rational and justified. And they see the social survey as the main research method for studying the victims of crime.

Victim studies According to Jock Young (1992), victim surveys 'allow us to give voice to the experience of people' and to take their needs seriously. They reveal the extent of victimisation, the concerns and priorities of the victims of crime, and they provide information on which to base policies of crime prevention.

Left realists accept that estimates from national surveys, such as the British Crime Survey, show that the average chance of being a victim of crime is small. However, national surveys underestimate the risks faced by low-income groups in inner-city areas. For example, the Islington Crime Survey found that 36% of local residents saw crime as a major problem, 56% were anxious about being burgled, 46% had been a victim of a street robbery and a third of women avoided going out after dark for fear of sexual harassment (Jones et al., 1986).

In contrast to some earlier approaches, such as labelling theory and radical criminology, left realists highlight the plight of victims. It is disadvantaged groups living in the inner cities who are most at risk from being harmed by street crime. And since these groups are on low incomes, they often suffer more – petty theft is a lot more serious when people are living in poverty.

8.3 The offenders

Left realists largely accept the picture presented by official statistics – that there has been a significant growth in crime, especially working-class crime. They see the increase in working-class crime as a particularly disturbing development – most of the victims are not the rich but the most vulnerable members of society. And most of the offenders come from the same social groups as their victims.

Why do people commit crime? The key concept used by left realists to answer this question is *relative deprivation*.

Relative deprivation Jock Young notes that the rise in crime between 1960 and 1975 occurred at a time of full employment and rising living standards. And since then 'as the West became wealthier, the crime rate rose' (Young, 1999). Deprivation, as such, clearly does not cause a rise in crime. What does, according to left realists, is how people see or perceive deprivation. In other words, what matters is *relative deprivation*.

People see themselves as deprived in comparison to, or relative to, other people. This comparison may be relative to people in the same social category as themselves – for example, in the same social class or ethnic group – or to people in other social categories – for example, in different social classes or ethnic groups to themselves.

Crime and deviance 173

In late modern society – from the 1970s onwards – there has been an increase in relative deprivation. And this increase has been particularly acute for those at the base of the class structure and for those in certain ethnic groups. Reasons for this will be examined shortly.

Relative deprivation does not necessarily lead to crime. It breeds discontent which can be expressed in many different ways – crime is only one of them. It is the combination of relative deprivation and *individualism* that provides a recipe for crime. In Jock Young's (1999) words, 'The lethal combination is relative deprivation and individualism'.

Individualism A number of sociologists see the rise of individualism as one of the main characteristics of late modern society. Individualism refers to a focus on and concern with the self, to a demand for individual freedom and autonomy. It is partly responsible for, and partly a result of, the breakdown of close-knit communities and the break-up of families. It undermines the relationships and values necessary for social order and weakens the informal mechanisms of social control in the community. And it often results in the pursuit of selfish interests.

According to Jock Young (1999), the combination of relative deprivation and individualism is the main cause of crime in late modern society. As a result of this combination, 'the working-class area implodes upon itself', anti-social behaviour is widespread, 'neighbours burglarise neighbours' and 'aggression is widespread'.

Late modern society and rising crime

What are the changes in late modern society that have led to the disintegration of community, the increase in relative deprivation and rising crime rates? Left realists provide the following picture with particular reference to the lower working class.

Changes in the economy There has been a rapid decline in manufacturing and manual jobs, particularly unskilled and semi-skilled occupations. Lower working-class males have been particularly hard hit, as have African Caribbeans in Britain and African Americans and Hispanics in the USA. And within these groups, the young are most likely to experience unemployment – many have never had full-time work. This has led to acute feelings of relative deprivation because of a lack of fit between their situation and what they see as reasonable expectations in terms of jobs and material rewards.

Changes in the economy have led to the disintegration of many lower working-class families and communities, and the informal social controls they provided.

Government policy has not helped. Most Western governments have adopted free-market policies which discourage state intervention in the economy to provide jobs. Alongside this, many governments have reduced welfare benefits.

Exclusion Those at the base of the class structure are increasingly excluded from mainstream society.

- They are largely excluded from the labour market.
- They face increasing social exclusion as the middle classes flee from the inner city to areas where the poor cannot afford to live and, in some cases, cannot enter as the rich increasingly live in gated communities with security guards at the entrance.
- And they are excluded from society, as prison populations increase dramatically. For example, in the USA, 1 in 9 Black males in their 20s are in prison compared to 1 in 135 of the total population (Mauer, 1997).

The mass media and inclusion There is one area where those at the base of the class structure are included – the mass media, especially television. Living in a world which excludes them, they remain 'glued to the television sets which alluringly portray the glittering prizes of a wealthy society' (Young, 1999). And, sharing the materialistic values of the mainstream culture, they are faced every day with comparisons which fuel relative deprivation.

Jock Young (2002) argues that the lower working class live in a *bulimic society* – a society constantly exposed to the material goods taken for granted by most of the population, but unable to consume them. In this sense, they are starving. In Young's words, 'The process is not that of a society of simple exclusion. Rather it is one where both inclusion and exclusion occur simultaneously – a bulimic society where massive cultural inclusion is accompanied by systematic structural exclusion.'

8.4 Dealing with crime

The public and informal control

Left realists agree with the right realists that the police and other criminal justice agencies can only play a limited role in preventing crime. Far more important are the forces of informal control. 'It is not the "Thin Blue Line" but the social bricks and mortar of civil society which are the major bulwarks against crime. Good jobs with a discernible future, housing estates that tenants can be proud of, community facilities which enhance a sense of cohesion and belonging, a reduction in unfair inequalities, all create a society that is more cohesive and less criminogenic' (Young, 1992).

On the local level, what's needed is a concerted effort by all the agencies which may have an impact on crime. Left realists refer to this as *multi-agency intervention*. Local authorities must coordinate their various departments – for example, housing, education, social services and planning – in order to rebuild disintegrating communities. On the national level, the state must reduce economic inequalities and create a more just society.

The police and formal control

Left realism accepts that good policing can play an important part in reducing crime. But, low clear-up rates and a decline in public confidence have made members of some communities reluctant to help the police. Where the

activity17 life at the bottom

Item A Watching TV

A study of a low-income Black ghetto in Philadelphia found that African Americans watch TV half as much again as whites – in the average Black household TV is on for 11 hours a day. By the age of five and six, children are familiar with adult luxury – from Gucci, Evan Piccone and Pierre Cardin, to Mercedes and BMW. By the age of ten they are thoroughly engrossed in Nike's and Reebok's cult of the sneaker.

Source: Nightingale, 1993

Item B Dealing in drugs

A study of Puerto Rican immigrants in East Harlem drew the following conclusion.

I want to place drug dealers and street level criminals into their rightful position within the mainstream of US society. They are not 'exotic others' operating in an irrational netherworld. On the contrary they are 'made in America'. Like most other people in the United States, drug dealers and street criminals are scrambling to obtain their piece of the pie as fast as possible. They are aggressively pursuing careers as private entrepreneurs: they take risks, work hard, and pray for good luck. They are the ultimate rugged individualists, braving an unpredictable frontier where fortune, fame, and destruction are all just around the corner, and where the enemy is ruthlessly hunted down and shot.

Source: Bourgois, 1995

Item C Riots

Two youths stole a police BMW motorbike in Hartcliffe, Bristol. In the police chase which followed, they crashed and were killed. Trouble ensued – crowds of young people, White and Black, set fire to the local library and community centre, and looted shops. The following night, there were more riots. It is a familiar pattern, repeating what has occurred in depressed estates from Teeside to Salford.

The affluent societies of the West have fostered new expectations. Advertising and the rules of an economy based on mass consumption teach us that if we are truly to belong to our society, we must possess its glittering prizes. Hunger no longer propels riots – in its place are the DVD player, the mobile phone and the BMW.

Source: Young, 1992

Looting during a riot in Miami, Florida 1990

Item D Exclusion

US population in prison, on parole or on probation, 1995		
	In prison	In prison, on parole or on probation
Total population	1 in 135	1 in 37
Black males	1 in 24	1 in 13
Black males in 20s	1 in 9	1 in 3

Source: Mauer, 1997

Inmates from a maximum security prison, Miami

questions

1 In what way does Item A illustrate Young's view of the bulimic society?

2 How does Item B indicate that those at the bottom share the values of mainstream society?

3 Use the concept of relative deprivation to explain the behaviour outlined in Items B and C.

4 How can Item D be seen as the ultimate form of exclusion?

flow of information from the public – which is crucial to the solution of many crimes – has ground to a halt, the police have responded with more direct methods such as stopping and searching large numbers of people.

This can lead to 'a drift towards military policing' which can make it well nigh impossible to police with the consent of the community (Lea & Young, 1982). In some Black low-income inner-city areas, the police are regarded by some as an army of occupation. And in Brixton in 1981, a police operation, which swamped an area with officers on a stop and search mission, triggered riots.

In line with its concern about what is to be done about law and order, left realism calls for greater democratic control of the police. A genuinely accountable police force will be more efficient since it will restore the flow of information from the public. And it will reflect the concerns and priorities of the community.

In addition, left realism urges the state to decriminalise minor offences such as the possession of cannabis, find more alternatives to imprisonment, and develop multi-agency and community-based forms of crime prevention.

8.5 Evaluation of left realism

Left realism is a genuine attempt to take crime seriously. And it is a comprehensive approach which looks at both victims and offenders, and informal and formal methods of social control. Despite these advantages, it has been criticised in various ways.

Focus on street crime While left realists accept that crime takes place across the class structure, their primary focus is on street crime and lower working-class offenders and victims. In their defence, such crimes loom large in victim surveys and are particularly harmful to victims. However, some sociologists criticise left realists for neglecting white-collar and corporate crime – which may be even more harmful (Walklate, 2003).

Over-predicting crime The view that relative deprivation plus individualism and economic inequality generate crime 'over-predicts the level of crime' (Jones, 1998). Since this explanation appears to fit most people, why isn't there more crime?

A trend towards inclusion Some sociologists question whether the trends identified by left realists are as serious and permanent as they suggest. According to the British Crime Survey, crime rates have been falling since the mid-1990s. And so have unemployment rates.

It is possible to detect trends towards inclusion as well as exclusion in late modern societies (Downes & Rock, 2003). For example, the Labour government in Britain has introduced the minimum wage, raised child benefits, set up the New Deal to help the unemployed return to work, and created the Social Exclusion Unit with the aim of bringing the excluded into mainstream society.

Victim surveys Left realists rely heavily on victim surveys to measure the type, extent and fear of crime in low-income inner-city areas. As outlined earlier, victim studies have their limitations (see pages 137-138). Certain types of crime are under reported or not reported – for example, domestic violence and child abuse. And victim studies do not capture how people define and experience criminal victimisation – for example, do women define domestic

summary

1. Left realism aims to 'take crime seriously'. It sees street crime as particularly damaging to victims.

2. Understanding crime requires an examination of four basic elements and how they interact – victims, offenders, the police and the criminal justice system, and the public and informal control.

3. Local victim studies reveal the type and extent of crime in low-income, inner-city areas. They present a disturbing picture.

4. Relative deprivation is the key concept used by left realists to explain crime. Relative deprivation is felt most acutely by those at the base of the class structure.

5. In late modern society, the combination of relative deprivation and individualism is the main driving-force generating crime.

6. Changes in late modern society have led to the disintegration of community and informal social controls, an increase in relative deprivation, and rising crime rates. These changes include:
   - Economic change and the loss of many unskilled and semi-skilled jobs
   - The growing exclusion of those at the base of the class structure from mainstream society.

7. One area where those at the bottom are included is the mass media. They are presented daily with expensive goods and lifestyles but are unable to consume them. In Jock Young's words, they live in a 'bulimic society'. The media fuels relative deprivation.

8. Left realists argue that the criminal justice system has only a limited role in preventing crime. Informal mechanisms of social control are far more important.

9. Left realists argue that multi-agency intervention on the local level can help to reduce crime rates.

10. The police have an important part to play but they need the support of the public. This requires an accountable police force under local democratic control.

11. Left realism has been criticised for:
    - Paying too much attention to street crime and largely ignoring white-collar and corporation crime
    - 'Over-predicting' the level of crime
    - Ignoring trends towards inclusion in late modern society
    - Relying too heavily on victim studies as a source for information.

violence by their partner as a crime and, if so, what level of violence? In-depth interviews rather than survey questionnaires are more likely to answer this and similar questions.

Unit 9 Globalisation and crime

keyissues

1 What impact does globalisation have on crime?

2 How significant is green crime?

3 Do states commit human rights crimes?

9.1 Globalisation and transnational crime

Globalisation refers to the process by which societies become increasingly interconnected. Many sociologists believe that in the last few decades we have entered a new phase of globalisation. This new phase has meant that globalisation has speeded up to such an extent that it is no longer possible for a society to remain insulated from significant events across the globe. In 2008, for example, the collapse of some financial institutions in the USA triggered a worldwide 'credit crunch' as banks grew increasingly reluctant to lend money. This in turn led to a recession, with societies across the world experiencing a contraction in their economies and a rise in unemployment.

A key factor in globalisation has been the development of information and communications technology. For example, the computerisation of financial markets enables vast amounts of capital to be transferred each day from one side of the world to the other, with sometimes devastating effects on national economies. And the advent of satellite communication makes it possible for there to be instantaneous communication across the globe and for national boundaries to be crossed with ease. The result is that events occurring thousands of miles away can now have an almost immediate impact on us.

Transnational crime Globalisation entails not only a considerable movement of money and information across national boundaries, but also facilitates increasing flows of people between countries. For many countries, tourism is now their most important source of revenue. While globalisation has had a significant impact on legitimate enterprises, it also has created new opportunities for transnational organised and corporate crime – 'opportunities that territorially bound state criminal justice agencies are poorly placed to stem'. *Transnational crime* – crime that crosses national boundaries – includes the following: 'cross-border smuggling of drugs, weapons, radioactive materials, information, art, cars, and other stolen goods; trafficking in illegal immigrants, women and children (often to work in the sex industry), and body parts; counterfeiting, international fraud and other financial crime, and espionage, terrorism, extortion, and kidnapping – modes of illicit action that depend crucially upon money laundering by the hundreds of billions of dollars' (Loader & Sparks, 2007).

Transnational organised crime Globalisation provides new opportunities for organised crime to engage in criminal activities across national boundaries. Such activities are often referred to as *transnational organised crime*.

When we think of organised crime, it is likely that images of American gangsters come to mind – the Corleone family, the subject matter of *The Godfather* film trilogy or Tony Soprano, the hero of *The Sopranos* television series. Here, organised crime conjures up images of a 'monolithic, hierarchically structured, ethnic Italian Mafia' (Rawlinson, 2005). Such images can be very misleading. While definitions of organised crime differ, criminologists usually use the term in contexts where people come together in a criminal enterprise to exploit opportunities, including illegitimate ones, for economic gain. This definition leaves open the question whether people come together as a hierarchically structured group or as a flexible network. It also leaves open the question whether people who come together do or do not share a particular ethnicity.

Organisational structure So far as the question of organisational structure is concerned, criminological research indicates that 'there is no Blofeld figure or SMERSH collective organising "crime" or "terrorism" worldwide. Rather there are layers of different forms enterprise criminal, some undertaking wholly illegal activities and others mixing the legal and illegal' (Levi, 2007). There is little doubt, however, that monolithic, hierarchically structured organisations, a description used to characterise the Mafia, are less likely to survive. They tend over time to be replaced by more flexible networks.

In an ethnographic study of organised crime in Britain, Hobbs and Dunningham (1998) argue that organised crime increasingly entails individuals coming together in loose-knit networks to exploit any entrepreneurial opportunities. In Downtown, a locality which had experienced deindustrialisation, the authors did not discover a large criminal organisation, like that of the Krays in London in the 1960s. Instead they discovered individuals with extensive criminal contacts who played key roles in putting together people with the appropriate skills for particular illegal activities.

Ethnicity In a similar vein, Levi challenges the notion that individuals involved in organised crime in America share a common ethnicity: 'Rather than being viewed as an alien group of outsiders coming in and perverting society, organised crime in America is best viewed as a set of shifting coalitions between groups of gangsters, business people, politicians, and union leaders' (Levi, 2007). The new opportunities for crime provided by globalisation not only involve a wide range of ethnic groups, but also help to break down ethnic boundaries. In the case of drug trafficking, for example, there has been increased communication between different traffickers and this has facilitated the formation of multi-ethnic teams (Dorn et al., 2005).

Glocal contexts While organised crime increasingly entails international collaboration and operations in different countries, we must remember that 'organised crime is local at all points' (Hobbs & Dunningham, 1998). While organised crime increasingly seeks to exploit the new opportunities generated by globalisation, and can thus be characterised as transnational, activities such as drugs and human trafficking 'and the actors involved are locally based and will be affected by local conditions' (Rawlinson, 2005). Hobbs and Dunningham demonstrate, for example, how criminal entrepreneurs initially rely on local networks of contacts. While some may become involved in wider networks and operate across national boundaries, they usually retain strong local links. Transnational organised crime in this view is not typically committed by large centrally organised, global organisations but instead operates as a *glocal system*. In other words, it 'is able to occupy both a local and global context'. It remains locally based but has global connections.

key terms

Transnational crime Criminal activity which crosses national boundaries.
Transnational organised crime Transnational crime that involves an organised group.
Glocal system A context in which a group operates at both local and global levels.

activity18 transnational organised crime

Item A Media images

Donald Pleasence as Blofeld in the Bond movie You Only Live Twice

Marlon Brando as The Godfather in the film of the same name

James Gandolfini as Tony Soprano in the TV series The Sopranos

Item B *The Mafia*

On 20 December 1946, Colonel Garland Williams of the Federal Bureau of Narcotics gave Americans a new way of understanding organised crime. He announced that the Mafia 'is a very dangerous criminal organisation that is being used to undermine the principles of American ideals of law enforcement'. He then elaborated: 'The organisation is national in scope. Its leaders meet annually, usually in Florida, and there agree upon policies for the control and correlation of their various criminal enterprises (Woodiwiss, 1993). This idea gained in momentum in subsequent decades, eventually dominating not just American but also international perceptions of organised crime. The basis of the idea was that of an alien, implanted conspiracy (of Sicilian origins) which was centrally organised and also dominated organised crime.

Source: Hughes & Langan, 2001

questions

1 What are the common features of organised crime suggested by Items A and B?

2 In what ways may these items provide a misleading image of transnational organised crime?

9.2 Critical criminology, globalisation and crime

Critical criminologists have sought to identify changes in the structure of advanced societies that have shaped criminal activity. In Britain, Taylor (1997) and in America, Currie (1997; 2003), for example, point to the effects that changes in the political economy have had on crime. In particular, they highlight the way changes in the global economy and the response of governments to these changes have generated increasing criminality.

The political economy of crime in a global age

Taylor (1997) identifies a number of significant changes in the political economy that he believes have increased criminal behaviour. These include:

- **The development of a global economy** The economies of different countries have been interdependent for a long time. Taylor argues that they have become more interdependent in the last three decades as a result of the growth of transnational corporations(TNCs) and, until 2008, the deregulation of financial markets. TNCs operate in different countries and increasingly move their businesses from country to country in search of profits. At the same time, 'financial institutions move enormous sums of money, sometimes in excess of one nation's gross national product, around the international stock exchange in the search for increasingly competitive advantage' (Taylor, 1997). These developments make it increasingly difficult for governments to control their own economies and have in turn entailed increased economic insecurity.

- **The decline of mass manufacturing** The shift from manufacturing to services in advanced societies has been accompanied by a decline in mass production. This in turn led to a significant rise in unemployment in the 1970s and 1980s.

- **Free market policies** Accompanying these changes in the 1980s and 1990s was a growing commitment of governments, especially in Britain and America, to free market economic policies and the reduction of public expenditure on welfare services. The destructive effects of economic insecurity and unemployment were 'magnified, rather than modified by such policies' (Taylor, 1997).

The above changes have entailed a significant extension in market forces and these in turn have resulted in increasing inequality. In a similar manner to the left realist perspective of Young, Taylor argues that the growth of such inequality at a time when the good life is increasingly portrayed in terms of the consumption of fashionable consumer goods generates increased crime among the disadvantaged. At the same time, Taylor emphasises the need to focus 'on the powerful corporate institutions and individuals at the core of the major crimes in the new international markets' (Taylor, 1997). Examples include the use of tax havens to launder 'hot' money gained through the international drugs trade and other criminal activities, and insider trading where people make profits by trading in stocks and shares on information gained from insiders in the company.

activity19 transnational corporate crime

Item A *A thin line*

The line between what is unethical and what is illegal in politics, and what is reckless and what is fraudulent in finance, has become increasingly blurred.

In 2008, the American financier Bernard Madoff was arrested after he confessed to defrauding investors of some $50 billion in an elaborate global fraud. Madoff was a highly respected pillar of the community. In Palm Beach, Florida, people joined the country club and the golf club just to meet him. They virtually begged him to invest their money.

In Illinois, the state governor Rod Blagojevich had the right to appoint a successor to the Senate seat left vacant by Barack Obama. He was arrested after wiretaps allegedly revealed that he was about to sell the seat to the highest bidder.

The actions of these two men reflect the blurring of right and wrong in finance and politics in American society. Power, politics and financial gain often go hand in hand. And a blind eye is often turned to fraudulent activity conducted by highly respected operators in the financial world. The opportunity for, and magnitude of, such frauds are multiplied in a global economic system.

Source: Younge, 2008

Bernard Madoff leaving the US District Court in Manhattan

Item B *Financial fraud*

In 1991, in one of the biggest scandals of recent banking history, BCCI (Bank of Credit and Commerce International), with a large branch outside the super-respectable Dorchester hotel in London's Park Lane went 'belly up'. Investigations by the US Senate found that it had engaged in 'illicit financial services for varied groups of clients, including Columbian narco-traffickers, Middle East terrorists and Latin American revolutionary groups, as well as tax evaders, corrupt politicians and several multinational companies' (Strange 1996: 118).

Source: Cohen & Kennedy, 2007

questions

1 How do Items A and B suggest that there is a thin line separating legitimate and illegitimate corporate practices?

2 How do they indicate that financial fraud is often transnational?

The political economy of the drugs trade in a global age

An analysis of the drugs trade helps to illustrate how the social changes identified by Taylor impact on crime. Drawing on a study of Los Angeles by Mike Davis (1990), Taylor argues that the 1980s saw a decline in manufacturing and the relocation of service industries to the suburbs. This resulted in high unemployment for many African Americans. Confronted by racism and frustrated by a lack of opportunity for gainful employment in the legitimate business sector, many young Blacks became entrepreneurs in the illegitimate business sector, notably the drugs trade.

The opportunity to enter this sector arose from the re-routing of the cocaine trail during this period from Florida to California. With the increasing popularity of crack cocaine, crack houses were set up for distilling and cutting crack cocaine. The development of this lucrative trade entailed significant competition as gangs fought for control of the trade. By 1988, it is estimated that the membership of gangs amounted to approximately 15,000, with 'gang-related killings running at one a day' (Taylor, 1997).

It is not possible to gain a full understanding of the drugs trade without taking account of changes in the global economy. The decline in manufacturing in Los Angeles was partly due to the fact that corporations found it more profitable to locate plants in low wage economies overseas. What is more, the production of the coca plant in particular countries such as Columbia and Bolivia is not an accident. The countries that continue to produce the plant are the ones 'that have been disadvantaged in the new international global political economy' and are thus reliant on an agricultural product that needs little investment and can command high prices' (Taylor, 1997).

National governments in global society

So far, this section has focused on globalisation and crime. It has not considered how the policies of national governments may affect criminal activity within their national boundaries. This section closes by looking at this issue. It concludes that national governments can make a real difference even if they do operate in a global context.

Marketisation, crime and punishment While the development of a global economy and the decline in mass manufacturing may have been accompanied by a rise in the crime rate, we should not assume that such economic changes inevitably generate more crime. As Taylor recognises, we also need to take account of the policies of national governments. Currie (1997; 2003) takes up this theme and argues that in the USA the advent of governments in the 1980s and 1990s committed to the extension of market mechanisms and the reduction of public expenditure on welfare services resulted in *marketisation*, the creation of a market society. In a fully-fledged market society, market forces become the central mechanism for allocating goods and services. In addition, market values, in particular 'the pursuit of private gain become the organising principles for all areas of social life' (Currie, 2003).

For Currie, five interrelated mechanisms link a market society and crime: 'market society promotes crime by increasing inequality and concentrating economic deprivation…market society promotes crime by weakening the capacity of local communities for informal support, mutual provision and socialisation of the young…market society promotes crime by stressing and fragmenting the family…market society promotes crime by withdrawing public provision of basic services for those it has already stripped of livelihoods, economic security and informal communal support…market society promotes crime by magnifying a culture of Darwinian competition for status and dwindling resources, and by urging a level of consumption that it cannot fulfil for everyone through legitimate channels' (Currie, 2003).

Marketisation and violent crime Although no society can be said to be a fully-fledged market society, Currie argues that the USA comes closest and that this 'helps explain why homicide is so startlingly high in *one* advanced industrial society – the USA'. While advanced societies may all experience a similar process of globalisation, there remain significant differences in the political economies of different countries. Currie argues that societies where marketisation has gone furthest are the ones that 'are especially likely to breed high levels of violent crime' (Currie, 1997). In these societies, such as the USA, individuals are least protected from the inequities of the market and are most likely to resort to violence. By contrast, paternalistic societies like Japan and compassionate societies like those in Scandinavia are more egalitarian and individuals are much less likely to resort to violence.

9.3 Green crimes

We noted in Unit 1 that crimes in the sense of breaking the criminal law are not necessarily as damaging as certain 'non-criminal' activities. Examples were given of global warming, global pollution and the destruction of the world's wildlife. While these examples of green issues may not always be subject to the criminal law, they are all arguably extremely damaging. Awareness of this has prompted some criminologists 'to place crime within a broader context of social harm', to note the partial nature of a legal concept of crime and acknowledge that a range of harmful practices may be supported by the law (Muncie, 2001).

Globalisation and green issues

Let us briefly look at two cases which illustrate green issues. The first concerns a major industrial disaster at Bhopal in India in 1984. Here a poisonous gas, methyl isocyanate, leaked from the Union Carbide plant, with dire health consequences for local people. At least 20,000 people were injured and 10,000 may have died as a direct result of exposure to the fumes. The parent company in the USA blamed its Indian subsidiary and escaped prosecution after persuading the Indian government to accept a very low settlement of $470 million for all victims. Whether this case illustrates a green crime or corporate negligence is debateable. What is not debateable, however, is that the disaster entailed massive social and environmental harm.

The second case does concern a crime, in this case an infraction of a regulation relating to protected species. Here, expensive shoes and handbags made from the skins of the caiman alligator were illegally produced and imported to Italy. 'Overall, the illegal trade in caiman alligators results in an estimated one million animals being killed each year for the shoes and bags of affluent, fashion-conscious Westerners' (Hughes & Langan 2001).

Both these cases serve to illustrate how green issues (and crimes) do not respect national boundaries. This is indeed typically the case. For, to give two further examples, 'polluted air-currents know no boundaries and smugglers of toxic waste respect none' (South, 1998). Green issues have global implications.

Green issues and criminology

Green issues have only recently gained a place on the

criminological agenda. Their arrival arises from our greater sensitivity to the fact that 'negligence, violations and crimes for which corporations and states are responsible have led to great increases in pollution-related health harms as well as threats to the very sustainability of the planet' (South, 1998). As the examples of the disaster in Bhopal and the destruction of caiman alligators illustrate, corporations often act irresponsibly and/or criminally towards the environment.

The same is true of governments. Indeed in some cases governments may resort to 'terrorist methods' when confronted by environmental groups. A notorious case was the sinking of the Greenpeace flag ship in Auckland harbour. The explosion, which was carried out by the French secret service, killed a member of the crew. Authorised by the French government, this action was provoked by the use of the ship in protests against French nuclear tests in the Pacific. This is by no means an exceptional case 'of state-sponsored acts of violence and intimidation against environmental activists or groups' (South, 1998).

Despite the complicity of government in environmentally damaging acts and the vested interests of corporations to exploit natural resources, there has over the last two decades been a proliferation of environmental legislation and more resources put into regulation. This leads some to seek to break the law and circumvent the regulations. Here is an example.

Toxic waste The tightening of regulations in relation to the disposal of toxic waste has generated a profitable trade in the disposal and dumping of hazardous waste. This trade has taken different forms. In the first case it has taken a global form. Here, toxic waste considered unsuitable for landfill in Western countries is shipped to poor countries that do not have such tight regulations and need the foreign currency. In one example, toxic waste was illegally moved from the USA to Northern Europe and then shipped on to Benin in West Africa, where it was unloaded by soldiers before being driven north and dumped on the border. The second case also entails cross-border dumping but this time between neighbouring countries in Europe. Here, some Dutch entrepreneurs used fake documentation

activity20 green crime

Item A *EU green crime proposals*

In 2007, the European Commission published proposals to combat environmental crime – from casual fly-tipping by individuals to crimes committed by nation states. The proposals are mainly concerned with the enforcement of existing laws – providing standard guidelines across the European Union and encouraging cooperation across national borders. At first, member states resisted these proposals, but eventually agreed to them.

The Commission wants more prosecutions for green crimes, higher fines and more prison sentences. At present, says Samantha Jayaram of the UK Environment Agency, it is 'rare for councils to prosecute' and prison sentences are 'very rare'.

According to the EU justice commissioner Franco Frattini, rules on corporate liability are necessary because companies commit '73% of green crime cases. It is not enough to prosecute managers; it is very important that companies pay fines'.

Source: www.euro-correspondent.com, 6.12.2008

Item B *Fighting green crime*

Deforestation by soybean farmers in the Amazon rainforest in Brazil.

According to a report by Brazil's Catholic Land Commission, at least 260 environmental activists face the threat of murder because of their fight against a coalition of loggers, farmers and cattle ranchers. In September 2008, government figures showed that deforestation in the Amazon (most of it illegal) had risen by 64% over the previous 12 months. Opposing illegal logging is extremely dangerous – environmental activists attempting to protect the rainforest have been killed by gunmen employed by the loggers, farmers and ranchers who are rapidly deforesting the Amazon.

Source: Phillips, 2008

question

How do Items A and B illustrate the problems of combating green crime?

to cross the border and dump toxic waste on a Belgian dumping site with the connivance of the corrupt executive manager of the site. The third case is more local – in a particular town – and relied on bribing security guards. Here, a landfill site designated for non-toxic waste was being used for more dangerous waste. The dumping took place at night while the security guards 'looked the other way' (South, 1998).

9.4 State and human rights crimes

While states define what counts as crime within their own territories, they are also subject to international laws and conventions covering a range of actions, for example, torture. They can thus be said to commit crimes when they break these laws and conventions. In Unit 4.6, we distinguished two types of white-collar crime: occupational crime, committed by individuals at the expense of the organisation and corporate crime, committed by individuals on behalf of the organisation. In a similar way, we can distinguish offences, such as bribery, committed by politicians and state officials for their own advantage and offences, such as torture, committed by politicians and state officials on behalf of the state. While in practice it may be difficult to distinguish these two types, the focus in this section will be on the latter. What is noticeable, however, is that in both cases there is often a reluctance to characterise the activities of politicians and state officials as crimes. Bribery is often depicted as an issue involving the standards of public life, while torture is often seen as a human rights issue.

State crime and criminology

Is it appropriate for criminologists to see so-called state crimes as criminal activity? To address this question, we shall focus in particular on the state's use of force. The state claims a monopoly on the legitimate use of force. State agencies such as the police and military can thus legitimately use force when it is defined by politicians and state officials as being in the public interest. This applies, for example, in wars and situations where public order needs to be maintained. The use of force, however, is viewed very differently when it is perpetrated by individuals who are seen as terrorists. In both cases violence is being used, but in one case the violence is seen as legitimate and in the other case as illegitimate (McLaughlin, 2001).

The above account assumes that the violence exerted by state officials is legitimate and that of so-called terrorists illegitimate. The definition of what is legitimate and illegitimate violence, however, is hotly contested. Those labelled terrorists may see themselves as freedom fighters and indeed consider the state to be engaged in terrorism. While, therefore, the Israeli state may see those resisting their occupation of Gaza as terrorists, many of the Arab people who live in Gaza see Israel as a terrorist state. What is more, these labels may shift over time, with people labelled at one time as terrorists later forming internationally recognised legitimate governments. The clearest example is the transformation in South Africa of the African National Congress from terrorist group to legitimate government, and Nelson Mandela from dangerous terrorist to a highly respected statesman (Croall, 1998).

It is sometimes argued that the behaviour of terrorists is distinct from that of (most) states since terrorists use terror for political ends and often target innocent civilians. The attacks on the World Trade Center in New York and the Pentagon in Washington on September 11, 2001 and the London bombings on July 7, 2005, for example, are cases in point. This behaviour is often seen as typical of 'terrorist groups' and 'rogue states'. However, states with which we identify and to which we belong sometimes engage in similar behaviour. The British state, for example, used saturation bombing during the Second World War on the German city of Dresden. This is by no means a unique case, with atom bombs being used by the allies during the Second World War on the Japanese cities of Hiroshima and Nagasaki and saturation bombing being used by the USA in the Vietnam and Gulf Wars. In all these examples innocent civilians were targeted. As such, under international laws and conventions, they constituted war crimes. We are deluding ourselves if we assume that terrorism and war crimes are only committed by others. While we may not have been tried for war crimes, that reflects the fact that we were on the victorious side rather than the fact that we did not commit such crimes.

War crimes, along with other violent state activities – including torture and genocide – have only recently appeared on the criminological agenda. What has placed them on the agenda are two factors. First, the growth of the international human rights movement has sensitised us to such gross violations of human rights. Second, the growth of victimology within criminology has sensitised us to the plight of victims (Cohen, 1996).

Since the adoption of the Universal Declaration of Human Rights by the United Nations in 1948, the use of force by states has been covered by international laws and conventions. Such statutes define war crimes and outlaw the use of torture and genocide in no uncertain terms. While states have a vested interest in not defining their own actions as criminal, that is not a good reason to exclude state crimes from our agenda. This point is reinforced when we place the study of crime within a wider context of social harm. The extent of victimisation from state violence is extensive and in many cases far outweighs much of what is normally considered to be crime. Even crimes such as bribery committed by politicians and state officials for their own personal gain may entail widespread victimisation since they can erode trust in the democratic process (Cohen, 1996).

Extent of state and human rights crimes

Since state crimes are not normally seen as crimes, there are no official statistics or victim surveys that enable us to estimate how extensive they are. Like white-collar crimes, they are often invisible and indeed they are often deliberately hidden from public scrutiny. While it is impossible to provide a reliable estimate of the extent of state crimes, reports such as those of Amnesty International and Liberty reveal massive human rights abuses across the world.

In the 20th century genocides and mass political killings include: 'the Turkish genocide of at least a million Armenians; the Holocaust against six million Jews and hundreds of thousands of political opponents, gypsies and others; the millions killed under Stalin's regime; the tribal and religious massacres in Burundi, Benal and Paraguay; the mass political killings in East Timor and Uganda; the "autogenocide" in Cambodia; the "ethnic cleansing" in Bosnia; the death squads and disappearances in Argentina, Guatemala and El Salvador' (Cohen, 1996).

While genocides and mass political killings are clearly more characteristic of some regimes than others, we should not assume that the British state is immune from gross human rights violations. Torture has been used by the army in the current war in Iraq, as it was earlier in Northern Ireland, and the British state has colluded with the USA in 'extraordinary rendition', whereby suspected terrorists are transferred from one country to another country where torture is practised.

The arms industry Since state crimes are often deliberately hidden, we often only hear about them through particular scandals that come to light. A case in point is the Matrix Churchill case in 1992. Three executives from the firm were prosecuted for illegally exporting arms-making equipment to Iraq, a country which had been subject to an arms embargo. The destination for the export was falsely documented as Jordan and the declared purpose of the equipment was misrepresented. The case collapsed when it emerged that one of the executives had been working for the intelligence services and that government ministers had encouraged the export. Although the official guidelines which expressly discouraged such exports had not changed, the rules had been 'quietly' relaxed. This emerged in spite of the fact that ministers tried to hush things up by refusing to release essential papers for the defence through the issue of public immunity certificates. In this particular case, 'no government ministers were prosecuted' and indeed 'none resigned' (Croall, 1998).

Understanding state crimes

While it is tempting to believe that those state officials who commit the most extreme violence, such as war crimes and genocide, are psychologically disordered – sadists or psychopaths – we need to place their activities in context. Individuals are trained to play particular roles, and in the case of the police and the military to obey orders and, if necessary, inflict pain or even kill with professional detachment. 'To many torturers, terrorists or war criminals, horrific acts become accepted as an almost routine part of their role, as necessary to defeat an assumed enemy' (Croall, 1998). Countering terrorism and fighting wars often

entails learning to see the enemy as barely human. In addition, when individuals are ordered to commit horrific acts, they often put normal principles on hold and see it as their duty to obey.

Spiral of denial All too often people are reluctant to admit that horrific acts are being committed. Cohen explains this in terms of a *spiral of denial*. Initially the state denies that torture is taking place or that there was a massacre ('It doesn't happen here'). Confronted, however, by photographic evidence and mass graves, the government changes tack and uses a series of euphemisms to re-describe what is/was happening as 'self-defence' and 'collateral damage' ('If it does, it's something else'). The final step in the spiral is to justify what happened in terms of protecting national security or as part of the war against terrorism ('Even if it's what you say it is, it is justified') (Cohen, 1996).

Techniques of neutralisation In Unit 4.5, we identified five *techniques of neutralisation* that young people may use to justify committing delinquent acts. These techniques are also employed by people when they acknowledge that something serious happened but refuse to characterise it as a war crime or as a massacre or as morally wrong.

- *Denial of injury* – They exaggerate, they don't feel it.
- *Denial of victim* – They started it, they are terrorists.
- *Denial of responsibility* – I was following orders, only doing my duty, just a cog in the machine.
- *Condemnation of the condemners* – The whole world is picking on us, it's worse elsewhere, they are condemning us only because of their anti-semitism/their hostility to Islam/their racism.
- *Appeal to higher loyalty* – The appeal to the nation, the sacred mission, the higher cause, whether the purity of Islam, Zionism, or the defence of the free world (Cohen, 1996).

Finally, it is helpful to note the contribution that strain theory, outlined in Unit 4.3, can make to an understanding of many forms of state crime. State agencies often experience conflicting goals. Chambliss (1995), for example, points out that the activities of the Central Intelligence Agency often broke international laws and conventions because of the priority given to ridding the world of communism. And earlier we demonstrated how the British government's wish to protect the arms industry and maximise export revenues entailed flouting any human rights concerns and indeed its own official guidance (Croall, 1998).

key terms

Spiral of denial A series of denials about the occurrence and/or seriousness of immoral acts, ending with a justification for such acts.

Techniques of neutralisation A series of denials of and justifications for immoral acts which seek to neutralise the harm caused by such acts.

summary

1. Globalisation provides new opportunities for organised crime and corporate crime.
2. Transnational criminals usually form loose-knit, flexible networks rather than hierarchically structured organisations.
3. Transnational criminals tend to operate in a glocal system – they maintain strong local links while operating in a global context.
4. Critical criminologists identify the following changes in advanced society which they see as shaping crime in recent years.
   - The development of a global economy
   - The decline of mass manufacturing
   - Free market policies
5. Although a strong case can be made for the influence of globalisation on crime, the policies of national governments also affect criminal activity within their national boundaries.
6. Damaging the environment is increasingly seen as criminal behaviour even if it does not break the criminal law.
7. Green crimes often have global consequences.
8. Over the past 20 years, there has been a rapid increase in laws designed to protect the environment.
9. In recent years, increasing attention has been given to state crimes, particularly human rights abuses.
10. It is not possible to provide a reliable estimate of state crimes.
11. The lines between terrorists and freedom fighters and between legitimate state violence and state human rights crimes are becoming increasingly blurred.
12. State crimes are often justified by a spiral of denial and techniques of neutralisation.

activity21 a state human rights crime

Jimmy Carter, a former US president, accuses the state of Israel of human rights crimes in Gaza.

The world is witnessing a terrible human rights crime in Gaza, where a million and a half human beings are being imprisoned with almost no access to the outside world. An entire population is being brutally punished.

This gross mistreatment of the Palestinians in Gaza was escalated dramatically by Israel, with United States backing, after political candidates representing Hamas won a majority of seats in the Palestinian Authority parliament in 2006. The election was unanimously judged to be honest and fair by all international observers.

Economic sanctions and restrictions on the supply of water, food, electricity and fuel are causing extreme hardship among the innocent people in Gaza, about one million of whom are refugees. Israeli bombs and missiles periodically strike the area, causing high casualties among both militants and innocent women and children. I condemn the firing of rockets into Israel by Hamas militants in Gaza as abominable acts of terrorism. Despite this, it is time for strong voices in Europe, the USA, Israel and elsewhere to speak out and condemn the human rights tragedy that has befallen the Palestinian people.

Source: Carter, 2008

A Palestinian woman is helped from her house after an Israeli air strike on Gaza City, January 2, 2009.

question

1 On the basis of Jimmy Carter's statement, is Israel guilty of state human rights crimes in Gaza?

2 Are Hamas militants guilty of human rights crimes for firing rockets into Israel?

Unit 10 *Ethnicity and crime*

keyissues

1 Are some ethnic groups more likely to commit crimes than others?

2 Are some ethnic groups more likely to be victims than other groups?

3 Is the criminal justice system biased?

10.1 The ethnicity and crime debate

Questions of ethnicity and gender were barely looked at by sociologists of crime and deviance until the 1970s. The primary focus was on class. Since the 1970s, sociologists have recognised the need to examine ethnicity and gender. This unit focuses on the ethnicity and crime debate. Issues relating to gender and crime are examined in the following unit.

In the early phase of post-war migration, there was a widespread assumption that members of ethnic minority groups were no more likely to be offenders or victims than the majority White group. It was also assumed that the criminal justice system treated all ethnic groups fairly. Indeed, according to a major investigation into police-immigrant relations in 1972, 'Black people were more law abiding than the general population' and there was little evidence of racist attacks against Black and Asian immigrants (Layton-Henry, 1992). During the following ten years, however, relations between the police and the Black community deteriorated and evidence mounted of increasing racist attacks.

Two reports published in November 1981 signalled the onset of official concerns. The Scarman Report (1981) into the Brixton disorders emphasised how the riots were essentially an outburst of anger and resentment by young African Caribbeans against perceived harassment by the police. And a Home Office report into racial attacks revealed that South Asians were 50 times, and African-Caribbeans 36 times, more likely to be the victims of racially motivated attacks than Whites. There was growing evidence that Black and Asian people were increasingly involved with the criminal justice system.

Two issues in particular have given rise to concern – the racist violence and harassment experienced by ethnic minority groups and the criminalisation of Black people.

Criminalisation The issue which initially attracted most attention concerned the criminalisation of Black people. At the end of the criminal justice process, 'Black people are about six times as likely to be in prison as White people or South Asians' (Smith, 1997). Two broad explanations have been put forward for this. The first sees Black people as disproportionately criminal. This explanation tended to be adopted by the police and other criminal justice agencies and reproduced in the media (Hall et al., 1978). The second sees the criminal justice system as inherently racist and discriminating against Black people. This explanation has received some support from radical sociologists (Gilroy, 1983). Until the 1990s, the ethnicity and crime debate was primarily concerned with this issue.

Victimisation More recently, attention has turned to another question. The murder of Stephen Lawrence, a Black teenager, and the failure of the criminal justice system to convict those responsible, led to an official inquiry, the Macpherson Report in 1999. The report found serious failings with the police investigation into this racially motivated murder. It not only challenged the dominant picture of the criminal justice system as unbiased, but also raised the profile of another question. Are ethnic minority groups more likely to be victimised than the White majority ethnic group?

10.2 Ethnicity and offending

To discover whether there are differences between ethnic groups in rates of offending, we can turn to three sources – official statistics, victim surveys, and self-report studies.

Official statistics

Table 2 presents the official statistics detailing the ethnic groups at different stages of the criminal justice system.

The table indicates that in 2006/07, Black ethnic groups were particularly over-represented at different stages of the criminal justice system. While they comprised only 2.8% of the population, they made up 9.6% of arrests, 6.4% of cautions and 11.0% of the prison population. Asian groups, by comparison, were slightly over-represented. Comprising 4.7% of the population, they made up 5.3% of arrests, 4.4% of cautions and 2.8% of the prison population. In contrast to these ethnic minority groups, White ethnic groups were under-represented – they were less likely to be arrested, cautioned or sent to prison.

While the official statistics point to ethnic differences at different stages of the criminal justice system, they do not demonstrate that there are ethnic differences in rates of offending. The higher arrest rate of Black ethnic groups could reflect the fact that these groups are more likely to be targeted by the police. Similarly, the higher rate of imprisonment could reflect the fact that these groups are more severely sentenced by the courts.

Victim surveys

At first sight victim studies, such as the British Crime Survey, provide a more effective way of discovering whether there are ethnic differences in rates of offending, since they include questions asking victims about the

Table 2 Ethnic groups at different stages of the criminal justice process, England and Wales, 2006/07

	Ethnicity					
	White	Black	Asian	Other	Unknown/not recorded	Total
Population (aged 10 and over)	91.3%	2.8%	4.7%	1.2%	0.0%	100.0%
Stops and searches	72.3%	15.9%	8.1%	1.5%	2.1%	100.0%
Arrests	83.1%	9.6%	5.3%	1.3%	0.7%	100.0%
Cautions	81.3%	6.4%	4.4%	1.2%	6.6%	100.0%
Youth offencers	87.6%	6.2%	3.2%	0.3%	2.7%	100.0%
Tried at Crown Court	75.2%	13.2%	7.7%	3.9%	0.0%	100.0%
Prison population	81.5%	11.0%	6.0%	1.1%	0.4%	100.0%

Source: Ministry of Justice, 2008

ethnic identity of offenders. Unfortunately, victims are usually only aware of offenders when it comes to personal crimes, which account for only 20% of all crimes. These surveys show that, in many cases, both offenders and victims come from the same ethnic group. An analysis of the 1988 and 1992 British Crime Surveys (Mayhew et al., 1993) revealed that 88% of White victims of violence identified the offenders as White. In the majority of violent offences against ethnic minority groups, the offenders were also identified as White (51% in the case of Black victims and 62% in the case of Asian victims). This is to be expected since the general population is overwhelmingly White. Once account has been taken of White offenders, a majority of Black victims of violence identified Black offenders (42%) and the majority of Asian victims identified Asian offenders (19%).

Mugging The offence that has given rise to most controversy has been 'mugging'. Although this term is a criminal label that has no formal legal standing, it has been taken up widely since its arrival from the USA in 1972. It has been used by the police and the BCS to refer to robbery and some thefts from the person. Victim surveys suggest that Black ethnic groups are significantly more likely to commit this offence than other ethnic groups. Mayhew et al. (1993) point to 42% of muggings being committed by Black offenders in the early 1990s, while Clancy et al. (2001) point to a slightly lower figure of 31% in the late 1990s. BCS figures are similar to police data on the ethnicity of those arrested for robbery and therefore suggest that the Black over-representation amongst muggers indicates a higher Black offending rate (Clancy et al., 2001).

A word of caution is in order, however. 'The effects of stereotyping and prejudice may lead White victims sometimes to say that offences committed against them have been committed by Black people, even when they are not sure who was involved' (Bowling & Phillips, 2002). What is more, mugging constitutes only a small proportion of crime – only 2.8% of offences recorded by the BCS. While Black ethnic groups may have a higher offending rate for this crime, victim surveys do not point to significant over-representation of Black or other ethnic minority groups among offenders for other crimes.

Self-report studies

In contrast to both the official statistics, which measure the outcomes of the actions of criminal justice agencies, and victim surveys, which are only able to reveal the ethnic identity of offenders for a small proportion of crime, self-report studies address the question of offending directly. Self-report studies ask people whether they have been engaged in criminal and disorderly behaviour.

The major study conducted in Britain which expressly pays attention to the question of ethnicity is the Home Office study, *Young People and Crime* (Graham & Bowling, 1995). Based on a large sample of young people, 'this study found that White and Black respondents had very similar rates of offending (44% and 43% respectively), while Asian respondents – Indians (30%), Pakistanis (28%) and Bangladeshis (13%) – had significantly lower rates' (Phillips & Bowling, 2002).

This study challenges the widespread view that the rate of offending of Black ethnic groups is higher than that of White ethnic groups. And it supports the suggestion that the rate of offending of Asian groups is somewhat lower. However, we cannot infer that this study reveals the true rate of offending. Self-report studies rely on the honesty of respondents and exclude from their sample people in institutions who may be more involved in offending. They also underplay the more serious offences.

Evaluation

The evidence from the three sources on the extent and nature of offending by different ethnic groups is inconclusive. The sources of data are all flawed in some way, with self-report studies pointing in one direction and arrest data in the other (Bowling & Phillips, 2002).

However, there are two exceptions to this. Homicide statistics, which are more reliable than other official statistics, do 'indicate that a disproportionate number of homicides involve people from ethnic minorities [especially African Caribbeans] as both victims and suspects' (Bowling & Phillips, 2002). And victim reports do point to the greater involvement of African Caribbeans in robbery. While homicide and robbery represent only a small proportion of recorded crime, the data for these offences suggests somewhat higher rates of offending by African Caribbeans (Phillips & Bowling, 2002).

10.3 Racism and the criminal justice system

Some researchers argue that the greater likelihood for ethnic minority groups, particularly Black ethnic groups, to be criminalised (arrested and imprisoned, for example) reflects their greater involvement in crime. Other researchers argue that ethnic differences in criminalisation stem from institutional racism within the criminal justice system. This view received support from the Macpherson Report.

The Macpherson Report

Institutional racism The 1999 Macpherson Report on the police investigation into the murder of Stephen Lawrence concluded that 'institutional racism' in the police force was widespread. The Macpherson Report agreed with the earlier Report of Lord Scarman into the 1981 Brixton disorders that the police do not 'knowingly as a matter of policy, discriminate against Black people' (Scarman, 1981). However, it did not accept Scarman's view that 'institutional racism does not exist in Britain' (Scarman, 1981).

For Macpherson, the concept of institutional racism does not imply that the policies of organisations are racist. The term instead is defined as: 'the collective failure of an organisation to provide an appropriate and professional service to people because of their colour, culture or ethnic origin. It can be seen or detected in processes, attitudes and behaviour which amount to discrimination through unwitting prejudice, ignorance, thoughtlessness and racist stereotyping' (Macpherson, 1999).

The Macpherson Report gives official recognition to the fact that the police in particular, and the criminal justice system in general, are biased against minority ethnic groups.

Policing For Macpherson, the failure of the police investigation into the murder of Stephen Lawrence was not due to acts of discrimination by individual officers acting out their personal prejudices. Instead, it stemmed from the occupational culture of the police. In an occupation that may entail danger, great emphasis is placed on teamwork, with jokes and banter being used to cement solidarity. A number of studies have discovered that derogatory stereotypes about ethnic minority groups are prevalent among police officers, the vast majority of whom are White (Smith & Gray, 1995; Holdaway, 1996; Graef, 1990). Jokes and banter often take a racist form and reinforce a negative

perception of Black and Asian people.

While we cannot assume that such racism leads to discriminatory policing, it can do so. A case in point is Dwayne Brooks, Stephen Lawrence's companion on the night of his murder. As a Black young man at the scene of a knifing, he was regarded by the police as a suspect rather than a witness. In seeking to protect society from crime and disorder, the police identify certain groups as more likely to mean 'trouble'. Black young men and, more recently, Muslim young men are often viewed in this way. As a result, their actions are more likely to be regarded with suspicion (Kalra, 2003).

Stop and search The Macpherson Report identified the use of stop and search powers by the police as a key factor in contributing to poor relations between the police and ethnic minority groups. In 1998/99, Black people were six times and Asians twice as likely to be stopped and searched as Whites. The police have considerable discretion in the use of these powers, which can be used on the basis of 'reasonable suspicion'. At the time of the inquiry, the BCS revealed that ethnic differences in the likelihood of being stopped and searched could not be accounted for by other factors such as age or social class. This suggests that discrimination may be responsible.

The Macpherson Report's judgement on the use of stop and search powers by the police states: 'we are clear that the perception and experience of the minority communities that discrimination is a major element in the stop and search problem is correct' (Macpherson, 1999). In the immediate aftermath of the report, the use of stop and search powers fell and, at the same time, the ethnic differences declined. In addition, the 2000 BCS indicates that the ethnic differences in foot stops, as opposed to car stops, could now be accounted for by factors other than ethnicity – for example, by social class (Clancy et al., 2001). While this suggests that ethnic discrimination may have fallen, the official statistics in Activity 18 indicate that the fall may have been short-lived.

Arrests Figure 2 shows ethnic differences in arrest rates. Black people are approximately six times and Asians approximately twice as likely to be arrested as Whites.

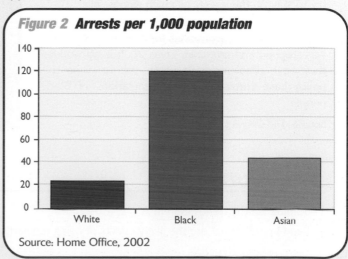

Figure 2 Arrests per 1,000 population

Source: Home Office, 2002

Most arrests result from the police responding to reports from the public. However, a significant minority are due to the police targeting particular ethnic minority groups through their use of stop and search powers (Phillips & Bowling, 2002).

Once arrested, and in contrast to other ethnic groups, Blacks are less likely to admit the offence. As a result, they are less likely to escape with a caution and more likely to face formal action (Home Office, 2002). Black juveniles are less likely than other groups to have their cases referred to multi-agency panels and thus more likely to go to court. This holds true even when 'admission of the offence' has been taken into account (Phillips & Bowling, 2002).

activity22 stop and search

Item A Stop and search statistics

Stop and search in Brixton, South London

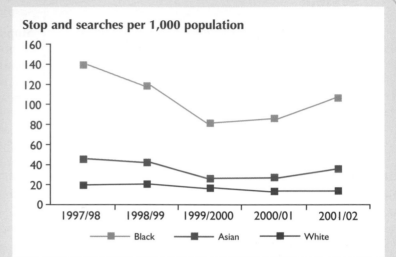

Stop and searches per 1,000 population

Source: Home Office, 2002

Item B 'It makes you feel stigmatised.'

Wesley Walters-Stephenson is a race relations trainer for the police. He is an African Caribbean.

'How many times have I been stopped and searched? It happens so often. I become defensive when I am stopped because I am weary of being pulled up and it makes you feel stigmatised, it makes you feel like a criminal. It can happen any time and I try to stay off the streets as much as possible.

My worst experience was when I got my shoulder busted and went unconscious for a short while after I was stopped and searched. I was 26. It is no wonder they have problems with youth culture when the police have criminalised two generations of Black people.'

Source: *The Guardian*, 8.11.2002

Wesley Walters-Stephenson

questions

1 Summarise the trends in Item A.

2 Read Item B. What are the likely effects of being regularly stopped and searched?

Prosecution Before a case goes to court, the Crown Prosecution Service (CPS) decides whether to proceed with a prosecution. It does so when it believes that there is a 'realistic prospect of conviction' and that it is in the public interest to do so. The CPS is more likely to terminate cases that involve ethnic minority groups. This suggests that the police may, as a result of holding negative stereotypes, put forward cases against ethnic minorities where the evidence is weak (Phillips & Bowling, 2002).

Once the decision to prosecute has been made, the next step is to decide whether to remand a defendant in custody or grant bail. Ethnic minorities are more likely to be remanded before and during a trial 'partly because they have an increased risk of being "of no fixed abode", a key criterion on which courts refuse bail' (Phillips & Bowling, 2002). Those remanded in custody are more likely to be given a custodial sentence if found guilty.

There is a greater likelihood of defendants from ethnic minority groups pleading not guilty and electing for trial in a Crown Court rather than a Magistrates' Court. If found guilty, they are likely to face a more serious sentence than they would if they had entered a guilty plea or opted for trial in a Magistrates' Court.

Ethnic minority defendants are more likely to be acquitted than White defendants (Home Office, 2002). This finding reinforces the suggestion above that cases involving ethnic minorities are more likely to be brought forward by the police where the evidence is weak. It also suggests that the CPS still allows 'a disproportionate number of weak cases against ethnic minorities to go to trial' (Denman, 2001).

Sentencing and imprisonment

Sentencing The most significant study on ethnic differences in sentencing was conducted in five Crown Courts in the West Midlands in 1989. All male ethnic minority defendants found guilty were compared to an equivalent sample of male White defendants. After taking the seriousness of the offence and previous convictions into account, the study revealed that Black men were 5% more likely to be given a custodial sentence. What is more, for defendants who pleaded not guilty and were sent to prison, Asian men were given sentences nine months longer and Black men three months longer than Whites (Hood, 1992). Sentencing is a clear example of discrimination against ethnic minority groups.

Imprisonment In comparison with other ethnic groups, Black people have significantly higher rates of imprisonment. This is illustrated in Figure 3. Some of the reasons for this difference have already been mentioned. Further reasons are given in the following section.

Evaluation

The evidence clearly points to racial discrimination in the criminal justice system. However, an important question still remains. Does discrimination wholly account for the greater criminalisation of ethnic minority groups? The two

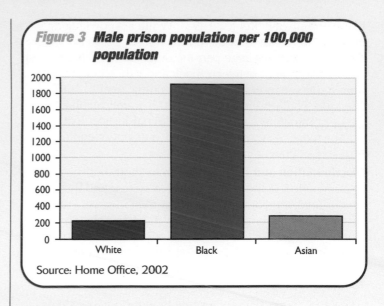

Figure 3 **Male prison population per 100,000 population**

Source: Home Office, 2002

most recent overviews that have looked at this question reach somewhat different conclusions.

Evidence of bias The first review acknowledges 'evidence of bias' against Black people at various stages of the criminal justice system – in the use of stop and search powers, in the decision to prosecute juvenile offenders, and in sentencing by the Crown Courts (Smith, 1997). Such bias does not demonstrate, however, that the criminal justice system is institutionally racist. For bias is not evident at all stages in the criminal justice system. What is more, if the criminal justice system were institutionally racist, it is difficult to understand why Black people are much more likely to be criminalised than Asians. The extent of the disproportionate imprisonment of Black people is, in this view, too great to be explained by racial discrimination in the criminal justice system.

Discrimination A more recent review is more sympathetic to the view that discrimination in the criminal justice system has a cumulative effect on Black people and helps to explain their over-representation in the prison population. 'It is not necessary for there to be discrimination at each and every stage in the process in order for the over-representation of Black people in prison to be the result of cumulative discrimination' (Bowling & Phillips, 2002).

The criminal justice system can still be racist even though Black people are treated more harshly than Asians. This may reflect the fact that Black people are more likely to be viewed with suspicion, itself a result of contrasting stereotypes held of Black (violent and dangerous) and Asian people (passive and traditional).

Despite the fact that the two most recent overviews reach somewhat different conclusions, they agree that the available evidence is not able to demonstrate whether the over-representation of Black people in prison is better explained in terms of their higher rate of offending or discrimination by the criminal justice system. There is now widespread agreement among sociologists that we need to move beyond the 'either/or of racist criminal justice vs.

Black criminality' (Reiner, 1993). While acknowledging bias at various stages of the criminal justice system, Smith emphasises that 'in large part the difference in rate of arrest and imprisonment between Black and White people arises from a difference in the rate of offending' (Smith, 1997). Similarly, Phillips and Bowling (2002) – after highlighting the discriminatory nature of the criminal justice system – acknowledge 'somewhat "elevated" rates of offending by African Caribbeans'.

Discrimination and criminalisation In short, both discrimination in the criminal justice system and the greater involvement of young Black men in street crime contribute to the criminalisation of Black people (Hudson, 1993). The two are linked – 'discrimination on the one hand, and Black crime on the other, reinforce and feed off one another in a vicious cycle of amplification' (Reiner, 1993).

Lea and Young (1982) illustrate how this vicious circle develops. For there to be policing by consent, a community must act as a source of information to the police so that they can 'catch and/or deter individual lawbreakers'. As unemployment generates an increasing crime rate in inner cities, however, the police begin to adopt a more aggressive policing policy and turn to operations which involve the random stopping of 'suspicious' youth. This inevitably results in large numbers of innocent people being stopped and searched. Once this happens, the community 'begins to become alienated from the police'. It 'comes to see any attempt at an arrest by officers as a symbolic attack on the community' and ceases to provide the police with any information which can help them identify individual offenders. Faced with this situation, the police adopt an even more aggressive policing policy and so the vicious circle continues. In this context, 'whatever racist sentiments exist within the police force are reinforced' (Lea & Young, 1982; Pilkington, 2003).

10.4 Ethnicity and victimisation

Racist incidents

Although racist violence and harassment is by no means new, mounting evidence indicates the scale of the problem in Britain. The police recorded 23,049 racist incidents in 1998/9, a massive increase since 1988 (4,383 incidents) when records of such incidents were first collected. The police statistics – though they cover the majority of the most serious cases – represent the tip of an iceberg if we include all racially motivated crimes. The 2000 British Crime Survey discovered, for example, 280,000 racially motivated offences in 1999. If we also include 'forms of racially insulting and threatening behaviour which are not seen as criminal events in themselves', the extent of racist victimisation becomes even more evident (Modood et al., 1997). The Policy Studies Institute Survey provides an estimate of such low-level racist harassment in 1994. It concludes 'that over a quarter of a million people were subjected to some form of racial harassment in a 12-month period' (Modood et al., 1997).

While all ethnic groups face the risk of being the victim of racist harassment, the risk is significantly greater for members of ethnic minority groups. In 1999, for example, 'the annual risk of being the victim of a racially motivated offence was 0.3% for White respondents, 2.2% for Black groups, 3.6% for Indians and 4.2% for Bangladeshis and Pakistanis' (Clancy et al., 2001). The consequences of such racist harassment are extremely damaging. A range of studies confirms how they can create a climate of continual insecurity for victims and their families (Chahal & Julienne, 1999). Such everyday harassment provides the backdrop to racist violence. The murder of Black teenager Stephen Lawrence at a bus stop by five White youths in 1993 is the most notorious example.

The Macpherson Report considered the reluctance of the police to acknowledge the existence of racially motivated offences and to protect ethnic minority groups from victimisation to be a serious failing. Its conclusion outlined a series of recommendations related to the handling of racist incidents. A plethora of activity has followed. A code of practice on the reporting and recording of racist incidents has been produced by the Home Office (2000); the Association of Chief Police Officers (ACPO, 2000) has produced a guide to identifying and combating hate crime; and Her Majesty's Inspectorate of Constabulary has produced a succession of reports on community and race relations (HMIC, 2001). Whether significant progress has been made in the handling of racist incidents remains to be seen.

Victimisation and fear of crime

Ethnic minority groups also face a higher risk of a range of 'household crimes' such as burglary and theft (Clancy et al., 2001). The same applies to violent crime, although in this case, ethnic minority groups are much more likely to see these incidents as racially motivated.

The 2000 British Crime Survey points out that a significant proportion of the increased risk of victimisation faced by ethnic minority groups is due to factors such as area of residence and age. However, even with regard to these factors, racial discrimination may still play a part in increasing the risk of victimisation – it can influence the area in which people choose to live. And finally, the increased victimisation faced by ethnic minorities is reflected in their increased fear of crime.

summary

1. The ethnicity and crime debate has addressed two key questions:
   - Why are some ethnic groups, especially Black groups, more likely to be criminalised?
   - Are some ethnic groups more likely to be victimised than others?

2. We cannot reach a definite conclusion as to whether there are ethnic differences in the rate of offending. For specific offences, such as mugging, there is some evidence of a higher rate of offending by Black ethnic groups.

3. There is clear evidence of racial discrimination at various stages of the criminal justice system.

4. It is likely that ethnic differences in rates of offending and a discriminatory criminal justice system combine to produce ethnic differences in criminalisation.

5. Ethnic minority groups face a higher risk of victimisation and suffer disproportionately from racially motivated offences. As a result, they are more likely to express fear of crime than other groups.

Unit 11 | Gender and crime

keyissues

1 Why are there gender differences in crime?

2 Is there a gender bias in the criminal justice system?

11.1 The gender and crime debate

Official statistics indicate that men are much more likely to commit crime than women. For example, in 2002, over 80% of known offenders were men (Home Office, 2003). This ratio is found in other Western countries and has remained remarkably similar over time.

In the past, sociologists paid little attention to these marked gender differences. They tended to take them for granted. Instead, they focused on why some men rather than other men were more likely to commit crime or become labelled as criminals.

Things began to change in the 1970s. Feminists, such as Carol Smart (1977), challenged what they saw as the male dominance of the subject. They opened up new lines of inquiry into women and crime and asked a new set of questions.

- Why do women commit fewer crimes than men?
- Why are women more likely to conform to social norms than men?
- Is there anything distinctive about women's experience as offenders and as victims of crime?
- Are women treated differently than men by the criminal justice system?

Today, there is widespread agreement that the sociology of crime and deviance must take account of gender. This means examining both women and crime *and* men and crime. And this also means asking a new set of questions about men – for example, what is the relationship between crime and masculinity?

11.2 Gender and offending

In 2002, over 481,000 people in England and Wales were cautioned for, or found guilty of, criminal offences. Just over four-fifths were men (*Social Trends*, 2004). These figures are drawn from official statistics based on police and court records. As outlined in Unit 2, there are a number of problems with the reliability and validity of official statistics.

Self-report studies provide an alternative source of information for gender differences in offending. For example, the 1998/9 Youth Lifestyles Survey, based on 4,849 12 to 30-year-olds, found that males were two-and-a-half times more likely to have offended in the last year than females (Home Office, 2003). However, there are also problems with self-report studies (see pages 138-139).

Despite these problems, all sources of data point in the same direction. As a result, there is now general agreement that:

- Significantly more men than women commit crime.
- Men are more likely to commit serious offences.
- Men are more likely to re-offend (Heidensohn, 2002).

Sex role theory

Sex role theory argues that boys and girls are socialised differently and, as a result, boys are more likely to become delinquent. There are a number of versions of this theory.

Edwin Sutherland According to Sutherland (1949), there are two main gender differences in the socialisation process. First, girls are more closely supervised and more strictly controlled. Second, boys are more likely to be encouraged to take risks and to be tough and aggressive. As a result, boys have more opportunity and more inclination to commit crime.

Talcott Parsons According to Parsons (1955), there are clearly defined gender roles in the modern nuclear family. The father performs the instrumental role of leader and provider, the mother performs the expressive role of giving

activity23 gender and offending

Offenders found guilty or cautioned, 2002

England & Wales					Rates per 10,000 population
	10-15	16-24	25-34	35 and over	All aged 10 and over (thousands)
Males					
Theft and handling stolen goods	86	183	104	17	131.5
Drug offences	18	159	62	9	84.1
Violence against the person	31	77	32	9	51.8
Burglary	29	49	21	2	30.4
Criminal damage	13	18	7	2	12.5
Robbery	6	14	4	0	7.2
Sexual offences	3	4	3	2	5.0
Other offences	11	102	59	12	69.0
All offences	196	606	292	53	391.5
Females					
Theft and handling stolen goods	51	67	32	6	50.1
Drug offences	2	15	9	1	9.8
Violence against the person	11	12	5	1	9.5
Burglary	3	3	1	0	2.1
Criminal damage	2	2	1	0	1.6
Robbery	1	1	0	0	0.9
Sexual offences	0	0	0	0	0.1
Other offences	3	20	13	2	14.4
All offences	74	119	61	12	88.6

Source: *Social Trends*, 2004

Shoplifting – according to official statistics, a typical female offence

questions

1 Summarise the data in the table.

2 Briefly outline the problems with official crime statistics.

---

emotional support and socialising children. These gender roles are rooted in biology since women give birth to and nurse children.

While girls usually have a readily available female role model at home – their mother – boys have less access to a male role model. Largely socialised by their mother, they tend to reject any behaviour seen as feminine and to compulsively pursue masculinity. There is an emphasis on toughness and aggression which can encourage anti-social behaviour and delinquency.

Albert Cohen According to Cohen (1955), socialisation can be a difficult process for boys. Without a readily available male role model, they can experience anxiety about their identity as young *men*. One solution to this is the all-male peer group or street gang. In these social contexts, aspects of masculinity can be expressed and rewarded. Being tough, taking risks and breaking rules can help to confirm a masculine identity. But, they can also encourage delinquent behaviour.

Evaluation Sex role theory is an early sociological theory which attempted to explain gender differences in crime. It has the advantage of explaining these differences in terms of learned behaviour rather than earlier theories which looked for explanations in biological differences between males and females. However, something of this earlier approach remains in the work of Talcott Parsons. He sees women as biologically adapted to a nurturing and caring role. As a result, they are mainly responsible for socialising children.

Feminist writers criticise sex role theory for failing to consider gender differences in power – in particular, the power that men have over women. This view is considered in the following section.

11.3 Feminist perspectives

Feminist perspectives start from the view that society is patriarchal. It follows that the behaviour of women can only be understood in the context of male dominance. In terms of women and crime, this viewpoint leads to new questions and new answers. The research examined in this section combines feminist insights with control theory.

Female crime as rational

Pat Carlen (1990) argues that women's crimes are largely 'the crimes of the powerless'. Many women who commit crimes are powerless in various ways. They often live in poverty with little power to change their situation. As children, many have been harshly supervised, and sometimes abused by their fathers. And as adults, they have often lived under the dominance of male partners who, in some cases, used violence in an attempt to assert control.

Carlen (1988) conducted in-depth interviews with 39 working-class women aged 15-46 convicted of a range of offences. She draws on control theory, arguing that people turn to crime if the advantages outweigh the disadvantages. For the women Carlen interviewed, crime appeared as a rational choice. Their experience of low-paid work and unemployment had not led to the standard of living and lifestyle they had hoped for. And their experience of family life, both as children and adults, had been unhappy and unfulfilling.

Unrewarded in the family and in the workplace and with little power to change their situation by legitimate means, they saw crime as a rational alternative. And the crimes they typically committed were seen as a rational choice. In Carlen's words, 'Property crime was *chosen* because certain types (eg, shoplifting and cheque fraud) were seen to be "easy"'.

Evaluation Carlen's sample of 39 women is too small to generalise from. However, her research suggests that conformity to social norms tends to break down when the rewards for doing so are largely absent. But, as the next section indicates, it may be much more difficult for women than men to deviate from society's norms.

Conformity and control

According to Frances Heidensohn (1996, 2002), the most striking thing about women's behaviour is their conformity to social norms. Drawing on control theory, she argues that women have more to lose than men if they deviate from norms. And drawing on feminism, she argues that in a male-dominated society, the control of women by men discourages deviance from norms.

Home and family Women still have the primary responsibility for raising children and domestic work. Their commitment to raising children and to family life also involves a commitment to conformity – to the traditional mother-housewife role and to socialising children in terms of society's norms and values. From the point of view of control theory, women have more to lose than men by deviating from social norms.

Women have been socialised to conform. Girls are more strictly supervised than boys, given less freedom and expected to perform more household duties. And these controls, duties and expectations continue into adult life. As adults, women are not only controlled by their childhood socialisation but also by their male partners. Women who challenge their traditional roles are often brought into line by men's financial and physical power. According to Heidensohn, wife-battering is an 'assertion of patriarchal authority'.

Women's socialisation and domestic responsibilities plus the controls imposed on them by men discourage deviance from social norms. Their lives are centred on the private sphere of the home and they have less freedom to go out. As a result, they have less inclination, less time and fewer opportunities to commit crime.

Beyond the home Outside the home, women's freedom to come and go as they please and to deviate from social norms is limited in various ways. For example, women are often reluctant to go out after dark, particularly in inner-city areas, for fear of attack or rape by men. And they are less likely to deviate from norms of respectability for fear of being labelled a slag or a bitch.

At work, men are more likely than women to be in control – in managerial and supervisory roles. And surveys indicate that sexual harassment is common in the workplace. This is a further indication of male power and control as it is often experienced as intimidating by women.

Both inside and outside the home, there is pressure for women to conform – pressure which is reinforced by male power.

Evaluation Heidensohn's combination of a feminist perspective with control theory provides an explanation for women's conformity to social norms and for their low crime rate. However, critics have made the following points. First, it presents women as passive, as simply accepting their situation (Naffine, 1987). The feminist movement from the 1960s onwards suggests a rather different picture. Second, Heidensohn makes sweeping generalisations about women and men. In doing so, she fails to recognise the differences between women, and the differences between men (Walklate, 2003).

11.4 Crime and masculinities

Research into gender and crime over the last 25 years has been mainly concerned with women and crime. Feminists focused on women, and men enter the picture in terms of their control over women.

Researchers now recognise that there is another side to the gender issue – men and masculinity. Why are men more likely to commit crime than women? Is there a relationship between male crime and masculinity?

Men, masculinities and crime

James Messerschmidt (1993) has presented the most influential and comprehensive view of the relationship between masculinity and crime.

Accomplishing masculinity Messerschmidt starts from the position that gender identity is a vital part of the individual's sense of self. It is something that people accomplish – they are continuously constructing, expressing and presenting themselves as masculine or feminine. And, in the case of males, crime can be a resource for accomplishing masculinity. It can be used in the construction of masculinity so that men can express their masculinity both to themselves and to others.

Masculinities Messerschmidt identifies a number of different masculinities which are shaped by social class, ethnicity, age and sexual orientation. Men's position in society provides differential access to power and resources which leads to different constructions and expressions of masculinity. And this, in turn, leads to different types of crime.

Messerschmidt refers to the dominant form of masculinity as *hegemonic masculinity*. It is the 'idealised' form which is 'defined through work in the paid-labour market, the subordination of women, heterosexism and the driven and uncontrollable sexuality of men'. This is the form of masculinity that most men seek to accomplish. However, for various reasons, some men are unable to, or do not wish to, accomplish this dominant form.

Messerschmidt calls the alternatives to hegemonic masculinity *subordinated masculinities*. They include masculinities which develop in some ethnic minority and lower-class groups, and homosexual masculinity.

Crime, masculinities and youth Young middle-class White males are usually able to demonstrate some of the characteristics of hegemonic masculinity through success at school and college. However, this comes at a price – subordination to teachers. Some assert their masculinity outside school through vandalism, petty theft and heavy drinking.

White working-class young men are less likely to be successful in education. They sometimes resist school and construct their masculinity around physical aggression, anti-social behaviour, delinquency and, in some cases, violence towards gays and members of ethnic minority groups.

Lower working-class young men from ethnic minority groups with little expectation of educational success or secure employment sometimes assert their masculinity in street gangs. With little chance of accomplishing hegemonic masculinity by legitimate means, they are more likely to turn to robbery and serious property crime.

Social class and masculinities Even middle-class males who have the resources to accomplish hegemonic masculinity use crime to express masculinity. Messerschmidt argues that white-collar and corporate crime are not simply a means for profiting the individual or the organisation. They are also a means of accomplishing hegemonic masculinity – as a successful breadwinner and as an aggressive, risk-taking male.

Working-class crime in the workplace can also be seen as a means of accomplishing masculinity. Workers sometimes resist the authority of management by theft and industrial sabotage.

Ethnicity and masculinities Messerschmidt uses the example of African Americans to illustrate a subordinated masculinity. Lower-class African-American males often lack the resources to accomplish hegemonic masculinity. The pimp and the hustler – long-established roles in African-American subculture – offer an alternative subordinated masculinity.

The pimp dominates a string of prostitutes and lives off their earnings. With his 'pimp walk', soft-top Cadillac, diamond rings, gold chains, and prowess with and power over women, the pimp demonstrates a highly visible alternative masculinity to himself and others.

Evaluation Messerschmidt has provided a sophisticated analysis of the relationship between masculinities, age, class, ethnicity and crime. His focus on accomplishing masculinity is an original explanation of the high level of male crime. However, there are a number of criticisms of his research.

● First, it over-predicts crime (Jones, 1998). For example, pimps are the exception rather than the rule in low-income African-American areas. And why do only a minority of men from all social classes and ethnic groups feel the need to assert their masculinity through crime?

● Second, the claim that hegemonic masculinity is the ideal which all men aspire to is questionable. It can be seen as little more than a popular stereotype. Masculinities may be considerably more complex and diverse than Messerschmidt claims.

● Third, Messerschmidt uses the idea of masculinity to explain practically every crime that men commit – theft, burglary, rape, domestic violence, joy-riding, white-collar and corporate crime. According to Richard Collier (1998), this stretches the explanatory power of the concept of masculinity much too far.

● Fourth, there is an element of tautology in Messerschmidt's argument – in other words, his argument tends to be circular. Masculinity explains male crimes. How do we know? Because males have committed those crimes.

key terms

Hegemonic masculinity The dominant and ideal form of masculinity which most men seek to accomplish.
Subordinated masculinities Less desirable forms of masculinity which some men seek to accomplish because they lack the resources required for hegemonic masculinity.

Masculinity and crime in late modern society

A crisis of masculinity Late modern societies have seen an economic transformation. There has been a rapid decline in manufacturing industry and a rise in service industries. This has resulted in a fall in unskilled and semi-skilled manual jobs and a rise in working-class male unemployment.

These changes have been particularly unsettling for men who, in the past, were able to express their masculinity through physical labour. In addition, unemployment and intermittent employment mean they can no longer accomplish their masculinity through full-time work and support for their families. This can lead to a crisis of masculinity (Campbell, 1993).

According to Jock Young (1999), this crisis is particularly acute for young men who have never had a job and have little prospect of getting one. They are 'cast adrift' and are not even suitable marriage material.

Some respond by creating subcultures of machismo which glorify an exaggerated form of masculinity – toughness, aggression, sexual prowess, and respect for manhood backed up by physical strength and, in some cases, by guns. This can be seen in gangsta rap where women are portrayed as whores, bitches and sex objects to be exploited, where pimping, hustling and gun law are expressions of masculinity, and men earn respect by defending their reputation with violence.

The night-time economy In recent years there has been a massive expansion in the night-time leisure economies of many towns and cities in Britain. Local authorities, anxious to regenerate their communities through attracting private investment to the inner cities, have adopted increasingly liberal attitudes towards alcohol and entertainment licensing. Night clubs have mushroomed, with large numbers of young people flocking to them.

A two-year research project studied this development (Hobbs et al., 2003). The researchers used both participant observation and interviews with bouncers, police, council staff, night-club managers, licensees and other key players in order to understand how the night-club economy worked. To facilitate access, three of the project team trained as bouncers and one of the research assistants worked underground as a bouncer.

According to Dick Hobbs, 'The night time economy is currently an unplanned largely unregulated zone where alcohol-related violence and disorder is rife'. Any control that does exist is mainly in the hands of bouncers who fill the void left by the police. The activities of these men (only 7% are women) are not effectively regulated and order is maintained by frequent threat or use of violence. While being a hard man has always been a source of status in many working-class communities, in the night-time economy it becomes a means of earning a living as a bouncer. What is more, being a bouncer provides opportunities for engaging in lucrative criminal activities. These include protection rackets, drug dealing, and importing duty-free cigarettes and alcohol and selling them at cut-price to clubs and pubs. With the loss of many working-class jobs, these men assert their masculinity through being hard, working as bouncers and, in many cases, getting involved in criminal activities.

Joy-riding A study of crime and riots in the early 1990s on two deprived council estates in Newcastle-upon-Tyne and Oxford points to the pleasures gained by working-class young men asserting their masculinity through joy-riding (Campbell, 1993). High unemployment on these estates meant that many young men could not look forward to a secure job that would enable them to support a family. They asserted their masculinity by manufacturing excitement through joy-riding and ram raiding. Brought up in a consumer society where high performance cars are associated with power and status, they drove stolen cars at speed around local estates and in some cases smashed them into shops to gain entry. This often led to a car chase with the police which added to the excitement.

Evaluation The case studies examined above relate to specific contexts. As a result, we cannot generalise from these studies. However, they do suggest that some working-class men turn to crime to accomplish masculinity. While research on masculinities and crime indicates there is a link between the two, it has yet to demonstrate that most, let alone all, male crime can be explained in these terms.

11.5 Gender and the criminal justice system

Is there a gender bias in the criminal justice system? Are women and men treated differently by the police and the courts? There are two schools of thought on this issue.

The chivalry thesis Chivalry means treating others, especially women, with courtesy, sympathy and respect. The chivalry thesis states that women are treated more leniently than men by the criminal justice system. Male chivalry means that the police are less likely to charge women and the courts will tend to give women lighter sentences, even when they have committed the same offences as men.

Double deviance This argument states that women are treated more harshly by the criminal justice system. This is because they are doubly deviant – they have deviated from social norms by breaking the law and deviated from gender norms which state how women should behave.

Many women feel they have been treated harshly by the criminal justice system. They see it as a male-dominated institution and feel their treatment has been unsympathetic and unjust (Heidensohn, 2002).

The evidence

Official statistics reveal the following.

- After arrest, women are more likely than men to be cautioned rather than charged.
- They are less likely than men to be remanded in custody or committed for trial.
- Women offenders are more likely than men to be discharged or given a community sentence and less likely to be fined or sentenced to prison.
- Women sent to prison receive shorter sentences than men (Home Office, 2003).

At first sight, these figures suggest that the criminal justice system treats women more leniently. They appear to

activity24 subordinated masculinities

Item A **Gangsta rap**

Gang members in Los Angeles

Tupac Shakur

The rapper Tupac Shakur died from gunshot wounds at the age of 25. He now sells more CDs dead than alive. He often used to pose with guns and had THUG LIFE tattooed on his stomach.

Gangsta rap reflects the violence of low-income ghetto areas. Rappers boast about using guns to defend their reputation, to settle scores and to avenge murdered 'homies' (friends from the neighbourhood). One rapper, Ice Cube, refers to himself as a 'natural born killer' and states:

> 'When I grab my sawnoff (shotgun)
> Niggas get hauled off.'

Women are often referred to as 'hoes' (whores) and bitches. Rappers boast about their sexual exploits and their prowess with women.

When work is mentioned, it is usually pimping, hustling, dealing in dope and the rewards they bring.

Source: in part from Light, 1998

Item B **Bouncers**

Bouncers need to present themselves as hyper-masculine. This form of masculinity has the following characteristics: toughness, autonomy, vitality, power, dominance, respect, honour, pride, and of course violence. Body size and shape are accentuated, and stance, clothing, facial expression and general demeanour are often tailored to display the mental and physical toughness required.

A licensee of a pub gives the following description of a bouncer. 'I already knew Jimmy for a few years. I knew he did the doors at some of the pubs in town so I just asked him to call in. I just picked a time when I knew some of the local lads would be in. We talked for about five minutes and you can hear them go quiet then start talking about him. After a few minutes, he just walked over and said 'all right' to them, and that he was working here now. They didn't say a fucking word. They knew who he was obviously, everyone knows Jimmy don't they? It's not like you can miss him. And that's it. I gave him twenty quid that first time, and fifteen quid a week after that. He gave me his mobile number to "phone if there's any bother" and he comes in every now and then. With someone like Jimmy doing that, I don't need a bouncer on at all really. I'm still here all the time and I keep a pickaxe handle behind the bar.'

Source: Hobbs et al., 2003

Bouncer outside the Chunnel club in London

questions

1 How do Items A and B illustrate subordinated masculinities?

2 Suggest reasons why these masculinities are developed by men from particular social groups.

---

provide support for the chivalry thesis. Matters are not that simple, however. To compare like with like, we need to take into account the seriousness of the offence and differences in offending history. The higher cautioning rate for women and the lower likelihood of being remanded in custody or sent for trial mainly reflect differences in the type of offence and past offences (Home Office, 2003). Women's offences tend to be less serious and women are less likely to have a criminal record. This suggests that there is no systematic bias for or against women.

Sentencing The evidence on sentencing is conflicting. Farrington and Morris (1983) examined sentencing in Cambridge City Magistrates' Court over a one-year period. They found that men and women received similar sentences, once relevant factors such as the seriousness of the offence and the offender's previous record were taken into account. By contrast, Hood's (1992) study of sentencing in Crown Courts in the West Midlands found that women were treated much more leniently, even when relevant factors were taken into account. A review of a range of studies on sentencing found that, on the whole, women and men received similar treatment. However, there is some evidence of women being treated more leniently, including avoiding imprisonment where men would not (Cavadino & Dignan, 2002).

There is evidence that courts treat some women differently than other women. This appears to be based on the view that the primary role of women is as a mother. On the basis of interviews with Scottish sheriffs (judges), Carlen (1983) concludes that women who are considered good mothers are unlikely to be imprisoned. Such leniency towards some women was accompanied by harshness towards others. Women who were not considered good mothers and whose children were in care received harsher sentences, including imprisonment.

Evaluation It is not possible to reach a definite conclusion about gender bias in the criminal justice system. There are clearly differences in the likelihood of men and women being sent for trial and placed in custody. However, many but not all of these differences disappear when the severity of the offence and the offender's record are taken into

account. In addition, there is evidence that some women are treated more harshly than others on the basis of how well they are judged to have performed their role as mothers.

11.6 Gender and victimisation

Victim surveys consistently show that men are more likely to be the victim of violent crime than women. The British Crime Survey 2002/03 reveals that 5.3% of adult males and 2.9% of adult females had been the victim of at least one violent crime in the preceding twelve months (Home Office, 2003). The type of violent crime men and women experience tends to differ. Men are more likely to be the victims of violent attacks by strangers and other men in

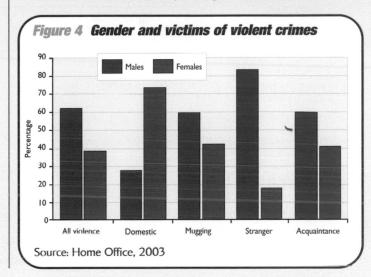

Figure 4 Gender and victims of violent crimes

Source: Home Office, 2003

summary

1. Available sources of data indicate that:
   - Significantly more men than women commit crime.
   - Men are more likely to commit serious offences.
   - Men are more likely to re-offend.
2. Sex role theory argues that boys and girls are socialised differently and, as a result, boys are more likely to become delinquent.
3. Feminists argue that the behaviour of women can only be understood in the context of male dominance.
4. Pat Carlen argues that women's crimes are largely 'crimes of the powerless'. She draws on control theory, arguing that working-class women turn to crime when the advantages appear to outweigh the disadvantages.
5. According to Frances Heidensohn, the most striking thing about women's behaviour is their conformity to social norms. She explains this in terms of their socialisation and control over their behaviour by men. As a result, women have less inclination, time and opportunity for crime.
6. James Messerschmidt argues that male crime can be seen as an expression and assertion of masculinity.
7. He distinguishes between hegemonic masculinity – the ideal which most men strive for – and subordinate masculinities –

constructed by men who lack the resources to accomplish the dominant form.
8. Masculinities are shaped by class, ethnicity, age and sexual orientation. Different masculinities lead to different forms of crime.
9. A number of researchers argue that there is a 'crisis of masculinity' in late modern society. This is due to the decline in manufacturing and the resulting loss of many unskilled and semi-skilled jobs. As a result, some men have turned to crime in order to assert their masculinity.
10. At first sight, it appears that men and women are treated differently by the criminal justice system. However, when the seriousness of offences and the history of offending are taken into account, most of these differences disappear.
11. There is evidence that some women are treated more leniently than others on the basis of how well they are judged to have performed their role as mothers.
12. Men are more likely to be the victims of violent crime. Women are more likely to be the victims of domestic violence and sexual violence.
13. Woman tend to express more fear of violent crime than men. This places constraints on their behaviour.

public spaces. Women, on the other hand, are more likely to know their attacker and to be victimised at home. The British Crime Survey 2002/03 reveals that 73% of domestic violence incidents were against women. In the case of homicide, 46% of female victims were killed by current or former partners compared to only 5% of males. Women are also more likely to be the victims of sexual violence. According to the British Crime Survey 2000, around one woman in 20 has been raped since the age of 16, with strangers accounting for only 8% of those rapes (Home Office, 2003).

Feminism and women's victimisation Feminists have highlighted the extent and seriousness of crimes such as rape and domestic violence. These crimes, which usually involve women as victims, are seen to reflect male power in a patriarchal society. They differ from most other crimes since they often continue over long periods of time. Male violence against women is not limited to the home – it also occurs at work and in public places.

Women tend to express more fear of violent crime than men, despite the fact that they are less likely to be victims. This can place constraints on women's lives. They may avoid going out after dark for fear of being attacked. And they may take measures to dress and behave in ways that prevent them being seen as provocative by men (Stanko, 1994).

Unit 12 Age and crime

keyissues

1 What is the relationship between age and offending?

2 What explanations have been given for this relationship?

12.1 Sources of data

Data from official statistics and self-report studies indicates that most offences are committed by young people – by teenagers and by adults in their early 20s. This section looks at the evidence.

Official statistics In 2002, over 481,000 people in England and Wales were sentenced in court or cautioned by the police for an offence. Compared to other age groups, young people offended most – the highest rate for males was at age 19, for females at age 15. Theft was the most common crime committed by young people, followed by drug offences, violence against the person and burglary (*Social Trends*, 2004).

Official statistics from various Western societies show a similar *age-crime curve*. Offending rises steeply from ages 10 to 18, declines sharply to around age 24, followed by a long, slow decline through the remaining age groups. This generalisation applies to different historical periods and different social groups – for example, males, females and ethnic minorities (Smith, 2002). Table 3 shows the age-crime curve for England and Wales in 2002.

Self-report studies Self-report studies of crime ask people whether they have committed a series of offences. They are usually based on a self-completed questionnaire or an interview. Respondents are presented with a list of offences and asked which they have committed over a period of time – for example, during the past 12 months or during their lifetime.

Self-report studies present a similar picture to official statistics of the relationship between age and offending. They mirror the age-crime curve shown by convictions and cautions.

Evaluation – official statistics As outlined in Unit 2, official statistics provide information on only a small proportion of offenders. For example, there were nearly 5.9 million recorded crimes in England and Wales in 2002/03. This compares with only 481,000 people convicted or cautioned. The proportion of known offenders becomes even smaller when a comparison is made with British Crime Survey data. According to one estimate, only 3% of BCS crimes resulted in an offender being convicted or cautioned (Barclay & Tavares, 1999).

We cannot assume that all offenders are similar to this small proportion of known offenders. In other words, we cannot generalise from such a small, and probably unrepresentative, sample.

The information provided by official statistics may exaggerate the proportion of young offenders. Young people are more likely to offend in groups and in public – they are more visible and more likely to be apprehended. And the crimes they tend to commit – for example, vehicle theft – are more likely to be reported to the police. By comparison, white-collar crimes, which a higher proportion of older people may well commit, are less visible and less likely to be reported.

Table 3 Offenders found guilty or cautioned

England and Wales				Rates per 10,000 population
Age group	**10-15**	**16-24**	**25-35**	**35 and over**	**All aged 10 and over (thousands)**
Males	196	606	292	53	391.5
Females	74	119	61	12	88.6

Source: *Social Trends*, 2004

Evaluation – self-report studies Research indicates that most people are prepared to admit to offences – even serious ones – when asked to take part in a confidential self-report study. And, in direct comparisons with individuals' official records, self-report studies reveal far more offences (Smith, 2002).

However, the results of self-report studies must be approached with caution. Traditionally, they have focused on male juvenile delinquency – the criminal behaviour of young men. And the lists of crimes presented in self-report studies tend to reflect those typically committed by young males – in particular, 'street crime'. They tend to omit 'hidden crimes' and adult crimes, such as domestic violence and child abuse, crimes which are likely to be spread more evenly across age groups. And they are unlikely to include fraud, often committed by middle-aged men. As a result, self-report studies provide only a partial view of crime. And this may lead to a distorted picture of the age-crime curve.

key term

Age-crime curve A curve showing the relationship between age and offending.

12.2 Explaining the age-crime curve

Control theory

Control theory – sometimes known as social control theory – has been used to explain the age-crime curve. It was outlined on pages 168-169. To recap, control theory argues that what stops people from committing crime are the strong social bonds which join us together – for example, the bonds with family, friends and work colleagues. Effective social bonds mean that we have too much to lose by committing crime. To do so would risk losing the good opinion of significant others – those who matter to us (Hirschi, 1969).

Control theory provides the following explanation for the age-crime curve. Most children have strong bonds with their parents. Most adults have strong bonds with their partners, children, friends and work colleagues. However, many adolescents and young adults loosen the bonds with their parents and have yet to form relatively permanent adult relationships and commitments. As a result, their behaviour is less likely to be constrained by social bonds and they are more likely to deviate from conventional norms and values and become involved in crime (Sampson & Laub, 1990).

Evaluation There is evidence to support this view. Regular offenders who formed a stable relationship with a partner in young adulthood were more likely to stop offending than those who did not (Quinton et al., 1993). Similarly, offenders who found a steady job were more likely to stop offending (Sampson & Laub, 1990). In both cases, the former offenders were making commitments and establishing bonds.

Judging from both police recorded crime figures and from victim studies, the crime rate rose significantly for most of the second half of the 20th century. During this time, the gap between childhood and adulthood widened. The period of compulsory education lengthened and growing numbers of young people continued their education beyond the minimum school leaving age. Full-time employment was postponed and people married at a later age. As a result, the traditional bonds created by marriage and work were not established until later in life. This may help to explain the rising crime rate from the 1950s to the mid-1990s (Rutter & Smith, 1995). However, it fails to explain the apparent decline in the crime rate indicated by the British Crime Survey from the mid-1990s onwards.

According to control theory, adolescence and young adulthood provide a window of opportunity for many young people to turn to crime. During this period, they are largely free from the constraints of both childhood and adulthood. But, why should they express this freedom in crime rather than other activities? Control theory fails to provide a satisfactory answer.

Independence and status

Adolescence is a period of transition from childhood to adulthood. It is a time when young people seek independence from their parents and look for status and respect as developing adults. Often, both independence and respect are in short supply – in many ways, young people remain dependent on their parents and they are not yet able to claim the status of fully-fledged adults.

A solution to the dependency problem is to seek out or create situations in which to express independence, freedom and autonomy. A solution to the status problem is to seek respect in the eyes of the peer group – those in a similar situation to themselves.

But, how does this argument help to explain the age-crime curve? Independence can be seen as freedom from constraints. In this respect, deviant and criminal activities – which reject the constraints of conventional society – can be seen as an expression and indication of independence. And, in the context of the peer group, these activities can bring the status and respect which the adult world largely denies young people (Caspi & Moffit, 1995).

Albert Cohen's (1955) subcultural theory of working-class delinquency provides an extreme example of this process (see page 151). Many of these young men do badly at school and fail to acquire the skills and qualifications needed for success. Defined as failures by the wider society, they experience status frustration – they are frustrated with their low status as 'losers'. Add this to the problems of young people in general, and their sense of status frustration is particularly acute.

According to Cohen, their creation of a delinquent

subculture can be seen as a solution to the problems they share. The 'successful' delinquent gains respect and admiration from his peers. And it allows him to hit back at a society which has denied him the opportunity to succeed and branded him as a failure.

summary

1. Data from official statistics and self-report studies indicates that most offences are committed by young people. There are problems with both sources of data.

2. Official statistics provide information on only a small proportion of offenders. And the crimes young people typically commit are more likely to be reported to the police.

3. Self-report studies reveal far more offences when compared to an individual's police record. However, they tend to list offences typically committed by young people and omit those which are likely to be spread more evenly across the age group.

4. Control theory argues that young people are more likely to offend because they have loosened the bonds with their parents and have yet to form relatively permanent adult relationships and commitments. Without strong bonds to constrain their behaviour, they are more likely to deviate from conventional norms and values.

5. Some researchers have seen young people's high rate of offending as a response to their desire for independence and status.

As the age-crime curve shows, most young offenders stop their criminal activity as they grow older. When they really become independent and adopt adult status, they no longer need the 'gestures of independence' of their youth (Smith, 2002).

activity 25
the age-crime curve

Conviction rates for different age groups

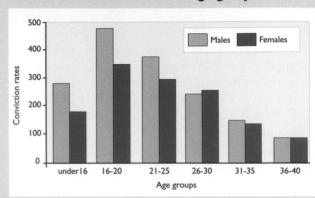

Source: Soothill et al., 2002

questions

1 What does the bar chart show?

2 Why is this pattern called the age-crime curve?

Unit 13 Location

key issues

1 What is the spatial distribution of offenders?

2 What is the spatial distribution of offences?

3 What explanations have been given for these distributions?

Offenders tend to be concentrated in particular areas. They are likely to live in particular places in towns and cities. In other words, the spatial distribution of offenders is not random.

The same applies to offences. Crimes tend to occur in particular areas. Again, the spatial distribution of offences is not random.

This unit looks at environmental criminology. It is concerned with mapping the spatial distribution of offenders and offences, and with explanations for these distributions.

13.1 The Chicago School

During the 1920s, a group of sociologists based in Chicago, who later became known as the Chicago School, argued that the growth of cities produced distinctive neighbourhoods, each with its own characteristic lifestyle. Clifford Shaw and Henry McKay (1942) applied this perspective to the study of delinquency.

They divided the city of Chicago into five zones, drawn at two-mile intervals, radiating outwards in concentric circles from the central business district (CBD). They then mapped the residences of male delinquents. Figure 5 shows the delinquency rates for boys aged 10 to 16 living in each zone from 1927 to 1933. For example, 9.8% of boys in zone 1 were charged with criminal offences during this period. The rates steadily declined from zone 1 to zone 5. Shaw and McKay found similar patterns in Chicago from 1900 to 1906 and from 1917 to 1923.

Zone 1 has the highest rate of delinquents. It is characterised by a high population turnover and *cultural heterogeneity* – a mixture of different cultures. Newcomers

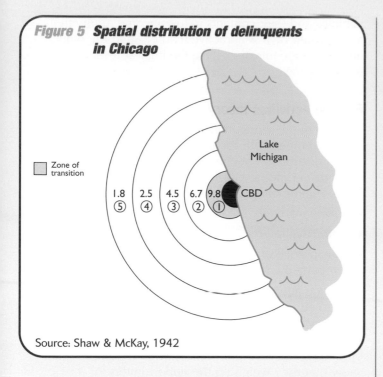

Figure 5 Spatial distribution of delinquents in Chicago

Zone of transition

Lake Michigan

1.8 ⑤   2.5 ④   4.5 ③   6.7 ②   9.8 ①   CBD

Source: Shaw & McKay, 1942

to the city usually begin their urban life in zone 1 – they often have little money and zone 1 provides the cheapest accommodation. And they come from a variety of cultural backgrounds – in the case of Chicago, Black and White rural migrants from the southern states and immigrants from various European countries such as Ireland, Italy, Greece and Poland. Zone 1 is a *zone of transition* – many migrants move out to higher income areas once they have become established, so making room for new arrivals. As a result, zone 1 has a shifting population.

Social disorganisation A high rate of population turnover plus cultural heterogeneity result in *social disorganisation*. There is a lack of social cohesion, little sense of community and weak social controls. Controls such as gossip, public disapproval and public surveillance are not strong enough to prevent the development of deviant norms and criminal behaviour.

Evaluation Shaw and McKay's methods were applied to a number of American cities and produced largely similar results. Where results were different, they tended to confirm Shaw and McKay's conclusions. For example, Bernard Lander's (1962) study of Baltimore found a high proportion of offenders in areas of shifting population in zone 1. However, there were also areas of stable population within zone 1 where the proportion of offenders was relatively low. Since both types of area were low income, this suggests that the level of population stability was a major factor accounting for the level of offenders.

Shaw and McKay note that the rate of delinquents corresponds closely to economic factors. Income rises steadily from zone 1 to zone 5. Rates of delinquents decline steadily from the inner-city slums to the tree-lined suburbs. A part of their explanation echoes Merton's views.

Shaw and McKay argue that crime in low-income areas 'may be regarded as one of the means employed by people to acquire, or attempt to acquire, the economic and social values generally idealised in our culture, which persons in other circumstances acquire by conventional means'.

key terms

Cultural heterogeneity An area with people from a number of different cultural backgrounds.
Zone of transition An area with a shifting population – people moving in and out.
Social disorganisation A low level of social cohesion and weak social controls.

13.2 Area offender rates in Britain

Croydon Research on area offender rates in Britain has not supported the neat and tidy zonal pattern found in many American cities. For example, a study of Croydon by Terence Morris (1957) suggested that area offender rates reflected local authority housing policies. Concentrations of delinquents were found on estates where the local council had housed high numbers of so-called 'problem families', some of whom already had members with a history of delinquent behaviour.

Sheffield Research in Sheffield also failed to reflect American findings. A study by Bottoms, Mawby and Xanthos (1989) looked at two council estates – Stonewall and Gardenia – separated by a main road. Recorded offender rates for Gardenia were 300% higher than those for Stonewall. Both estates were built in the 1920s. Each had a stable population of 2500 to 3000, with 60% of adults in both areas having lived in the same residence for 10 years or more. And there was little or no difference between the estates in terms of social factors such as class, ethnicity, age, gender, income and employment levels.

The researchers offered the following explanation for the differences in offender rates between Stonewall and Gardenia. Sometime in the 1940s, Gardenia 'tipped' – started a downward spiral towards a high crime area. This appears to have influenced the council's housing policy. Those with severe housing needs and various other social problems were allocated to Gardenia – the very people most at risk of crime. Gardenia developed a negative reputation which resulted in some residents leaving and others refusing to move on to the estate.

Evaluation The Sheffield study is important for three main reasons (Bottoms & Wiles, 2002).

● Since the two estates are almost identical in terms of social class, it challenges those who argue that offender rates on the local level simply reflect the link between class and offending on the national level.

● Shaw and McKay's explanation based on high population turnover and cultural heterogeneity does not apply to the Sheffield estates.

- The operation of the local housing market is a key factor in explaining area offender rates in Sheffield.

13.3 Area offence rates

So far this unit has focused on area offender rates – the rate of *offenders* living in a particular area. This section looks at area offence rates – the rate of *offences* in a particular area.

In traditional cities, offences tend to be clustered in and around the city centre. For example, in Sheffield in 1966, 24% of offences occurred within a half mile radius of the city centre – which made up only 3% of the city's total land area. Typical city-centre offences include theft of and from cars, theft from the person and violence and vandalism in public places. This pattern can change with the development of shopping malls and entertainment complexes away from the city centre. For example, the building of the Meadowhall shopping mall on the outskirts of Sheffield was a factor in reducing city-centre offences from 24% in 1966 to 10% in 1995 (Wiles & Costello, 2000).

In residential districts, offence rates tend to be highest in low-income, inner-city areas and in high-income neighbourhoods in cities which are close to areas with high offending rates. According to the 2002/03 British Crime Survey, the highest levels of burglary, vehicle-related crime and violent crime occur in low-income council estates with a high proportion of elderly, lone parent and unemployed residents; in multi-ethnic, low-income areas; and in town and city areas which house well-off professional singles and couples.

The following explanations have been suggested for the spatial distribution of offences.

Opportunity theory

Opportunity theory, as its name suggests, is concerned with the opportunities for crime. It focuses on *target attractiveness* and *accessibility* (Clarke, 1995).

Target attractiveness In terms of property, a target is attractive if its monetary value is high and if it can be easily transported and sold. Obviously, a laptop in the back seat of a car is a more attractive target than a bag of groceries.

Accessibility A target is accessible if it can be seen, if physical access is easy and the chances of being observed are low.

On its own, opportunity theory cannot account for the spatial distribution of offences. For example, the highest level of vehicle-related crime is in low-income multi-ethnic neighbourhoods where 21% of vehicle-owning households are victims of this crime. The rate for professionals living in towns and cities is 16%, while the rate for wealthy home-owning areas is only 8% (British Crime Survey, 2002/03). In terms of target attractiveness,

vehicles and their contents in low-income multi-ethnic areas would be less attractive than those in the other areas. Despite this, they have the highest level of vehicle-related crime.

Routine activities theory

Because of the shortcomings of opportunity theory, it is often combined with *routine activities* theory to explain the spatial distribution of offences. Routine activities theory states that crimes are likely to occur in particular places because three things tend to come together in those places:

- Likely offenders
- Attractive targets
- An absence of 'capable guardians' – for example, the property owners (Cohen & Felson, 1979).

Routine activities theory, as its name suggests, is concerned with the routine, everyday activities of those who may be involved with crimes – the possible offenders, the possible victims and the possible observers. For example, studies of convicted burglars show that they weigh up the opportunities for a successful crime. But, they also base their decisions on their routine activities and the knowledge they gain from those activities.

For example, their everyday movements are centred on their residential area, place of work, the shopping and entertainment centres they frequent and the routes they travel to and from these places. These are the places offenders are familiar with *and* the places where they tend to commit offences (Wright & Decker, 1994). This brings together explanations of the spatial distribution of offences and offenders.

> ## key terms
>
> **Target attractiveness** The attractiveness of a possible target for crime – for example, its monetary value.
> **Target accessibility** A target is accessible if it can be seen, access to it is easy and the chances of being observed are low.
> **Routine activities** A person's normal, everyday activities.

13.4 Explaining the spatial distribution of offenders and offences

So far, the spatial distributions of offenders and offences have been examined separately. This section looks at the relationship between them.

Most offences occur within a short distance from the offender's home. For example, a study in Sheffield found that, on average, offenders travelled only 1.93 miles from their home to commit a crime (Wiles & Costello, 2000). A number of studies suggest that this is related to offenders' routine activities and their normal use of space.

Cognitive maps

Patricia and Paul Brantingham (1984) argue that we have *cognitive maps* inside our heads which outline our perception of the geography of our local area. These maps contain the places we are familiar with – for example, home, work or school, shops and places of entertainment. They also include our routes to and from these places.

The Brantinghams suggest that most offenders will commit crimes in areas they are familiar with – that is, in areas which are clearly shown on their cognitive maps. Figure 6 illustrates this idea. It shows the suggested relationship between offenders' awareness of space, opportunities for crime, and areas where offences occur.

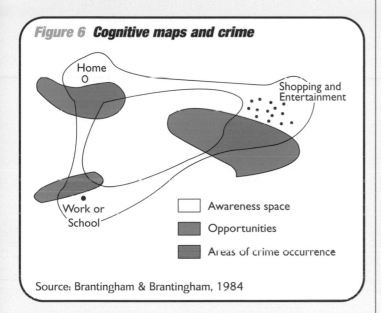

Figure 6 Cognitive maps and crime

Home

Shopping and Entertainment

Work or School

☐ Awareness space

■ Opportunities

■ Areas of crime occurrence

Source: Brantingham & Brantingham, 1984

Evidence There is some evidence to support the connection between familiarity, cognitive maps and offence location. A study of convicted burglars in Pennsylvania showed that most of their offences were committed near their regular routes to work and recreation (Rengert & Wasilchick, 2000). Research in Oklahoma City, which is divided into Black and White areas, showed that most offenders committed their crimes within their own ethnic group area – that is, in places they were familiar with (Carter & Hill, 1979).

A study in Sheffield by Wiles and Costello (2000) categorised neighbourhoods in terms of high, medium or low offence rates and offender rates. High offender and high offence rates were found in the same area – there were no cases of high offender rates and low offence rates in the same neighbourhood. This can be explained in terms of the routine activities of the offenders and their familiarity with their own neighbourhoods.

There were a few cases of low offender rates and high offence rates. This usually occurred in high-income neighbourhoods close to areas regularly used by offenders – for example, adjacent to their own neighbourhood, shopping or entertainment area.

13.5 Further explanations

Why do some areas have high offender and offence rates? Part of the explanation has been given in the previous section. Offenders tend to commit crimes in areas with which they are familiar. But why are offenders often clustered in the same area? Many of these areas are low-income, inner-city neighbourhoods. The common-sense answer is poverty breeds crime. But, as the Sheffield study of Stonewall and Gardenia indicates, this is not necessarily so. Both were low-income council estates, but the recorded offender rates for Gardenia were 300% higher than those of Stonewall. The reason given earlier was the council's policy of housing so-called 'problem families' in Gardenia. But how does a neighbourhood 'tip' into an area with high levels of offenders and offences?

Social disorganisation One explanation has already been examined – Shaw and McKay's theory of social disorganisation. To briefly recap – high population turnover and cultural heterogeneity lead to social disorganisation which results in weak social controls. These controls are not strong enough to prevent the development of criminal behaviour. This explanation may fit the development of certain American cities but does not fit British examples. As noted earlier, it does not explain the difference in offender rates between Stonewall and Gardenia in Sheffield. Both estates had both stable populations and culturally homogeneous populations.

'Broken windows' As noted in an earlier unit (see page 169), Wilson and Kelling (2003) provide the following explanation for *tipping* – the downward spiral of certain neighbourhoods. Informal social controls are essential for crime prevention. They are likely to break down when buildings are left in a state of disrepair – for example, with broken windows – and when disorderly and anti-social behaviour is left unchallenged. In this situation, graffiti spreads, noise levels increase, vandalism grows and more windows get broken. Failure to do anything about these developments tips a neighbourhood into decline – property values plummet, law-abiding members of the community are afraid to go out, many leave the neighbourhood, informal social controls break down and crime and disorder become widespread. (For further discussion of Wilson and Kelling, see pages 169-170.)

Spiral decay Wesley Skogan's (1990) analysis of the 'spiral decay of American neighbourhoods' echoes many of the points made by Wilson and Kelling. Skogan identifies two types of disorder – physical disorder, such as dilapidated buildings, broken streetlights and litter, and social disorder such as drinking on the street and prostitution. These two types of disorder tend to occur together. They have the following effects.

- Undermining neighbourliness – residents were less willing to help each other and take part in activities which reduce crime, such as keeping a watch on each other's houses when they were on holiday.

- Increasing concerns about safety – people were fearful

of going out, especially at night. This weakens social controls such as public surveillance.

- The area becomes stigmatised as a 'bad neighbourhood', property values decline, and those who can afford to do so move out.

- As a result of the 'spiral of decay' produced by disorder, the informal social controls which tend to prevent crime are weakened.

Evaluation The processes described by the 'broken windows' and 'spiral decay' arguments may well be an important part of tipping a neighbourhood into a high-crime area. But how do they begin in the first place? For example, how does the disorder which generates the spiral of decay start? The following study provides possible answers.

A three-stage process A study of juvenile offender rates in different areas of Los Angeles from 1950-1970 examined the changes that occurred in low-rate offender areas which later became high-rate offender areas (Schuerman & Kobrin, 1986). This study is important because it looks at changes over time – this may help to establish what causes what.

The researchers identified a three-stage process which, they argue, led to the development of high-rate offender areas.

- First, there were changes in land use – for example, an increase in apartment buildings and in renting as opposed to owner occupation.

- Second, there were changes in the size and make-up of the population – for example, a decline in population size and an increase in the proportion of unrelated individuals – more single people and fewer families.

- Third, there were changes in the economic status of the population – for example, an increase in the proportion of unskilled and unemployed workers.

Conclusion

Local, national and global Location studies of offender and offence rates are based on local areas. As such, they take little account of wider social and economic changes. Although they add to our understanding of crime, they are limited. Clearly, national and global changes will impact on local areas. A fuller understanding of local areas therefore requires an analysis which incorporates these wider changes. For example, the decline in manufacturing in Western societies has led to a reduction in the demand for manual labour and to high unemployment rates in certain urban areas (Bottoms & Wiles, 2002).

Methodology Studies of the distribution of offender and offence rates are based on data from police recorded crime and victim studies conducted in local areas. The validity of both types of data is questionable. As outlined earlier, police recording practices and priorities for investigation vary from area to area (see pages 132-133). For example, burglary may be a priority in one area, drug dealing in another. Similarly, the willingness of the public to report crimes to the police or to participate in victim surveys may also vary from one area to another.

key term

Tipping The process by which an area moves from a low to a high offender and offence rate.

summary

1. Environmental criminology looks at the spatial distribution of offences and offenders.

2. Shaw and McKay claimed that delinquents were concentrated in zones of transition in American cities. They argued that this was due to high population turnover and cultural heterogeneity which led to social disorganisation. This, in turn, weakened informal social controls.

3. Area offender rates in British cities do not reflect the American pattern. Research indicates that the housing of so-called 'problem families' on particular estates by local councils can result in a concentration of offenders.

4. In traditional cities, offences tend to be clustered in and around the city centre. 'Out-of-town' shopping malls and entertainment centres can change this pattern.

5. In residential districts, offences tend to be highest in low-income, inner-city areas, and in high-income neighbourhoods close to areas with high offending rates.

6. Opportunity theory states that targets with high attractiveness and high accessibility are likely to be selected by offenders.

7. Routine activity theory states that the spatial distribution of offences is linked to the routine activities of offenders.

Offenders tend to commit crimes in areas they are familiar with.

8. The Brantinghams argue that we have cognitive maps of the areas we are familiar with. To some extent, these maps guide offenders' selection of places to commit offences.

9. Wilson and Kelling argue that a neighbourhood 'tips' when buildings are left in disrepair and anti-social behaviour is unchallenged. Informal social controls break down and crime becomes widespread.

10. Skogan argues that physical and social disorder undermine neighbourliness, increase concerns about safety and stigmatise the neighbourhood. This weakens informal social controls.

11. A longitudinal study in Los Angeles suggests a three-stage process leading to tipping.
    - A change in land use
    - A change in the size and make-up of the population
    - A change in the economic status of the population.

12. Critics argue that location studies of offender and offence rates should incorporate wider social and economic factors.

13. The validity of the data on which location studies are based is questionable.

activity26 neighbourhoods and crime

Item A Neighbourhoods and offence rates

The bar chart looks at the percentage of household victims of burglary, vehicle-related crime and violent crime in different types of residential neighbourhoods in England and Wales. The data is drawn from the 2002/03 British Crime Survey. The types of neighbourhood are defined in the box on the right.

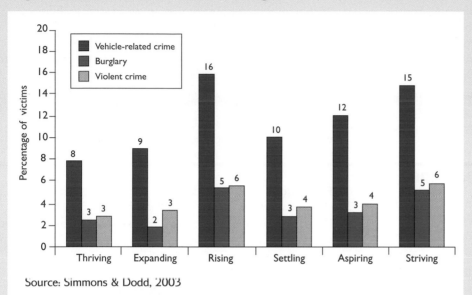

Source: Simmons & Dodd, 2003

Item B Type of neighbourhood

Thriving – wealthy, affluent home-owning areas. Commuters and prosperous older people.

Expanding – affluent working couples and families with mortgages, plus homeowners.

Rising – well-off professional singles and couples, living in town and city areas.

Settling – established home-owning areas, skilled workers.

Aspiring – mature communities, new homeowners and multi-ethnic areas.

Striving – council estates with elderly, lone parent or unemployed residents. Multi-ethnic, low-income areas.

questions

1 Briefly summarise the data in the bar chart.

2 Suggest reasons why different types of neighbourhood have different offence rates.

Unit 14 Social control, crime reduction and social policy

keyissues

1 What are the main approaches to crime reduction?

2 What are the crime policies of British governments since 1945?

The idea of social control was introduced on page 130. Various aspects of social control have been examined throughout this chapter in the context of theories of crime and deviance – for example, in terms of right realism (see pages 168-170). This unit looks at methods of social control with specific reference to crime reduction.

The terms crime reduction and crime prevention are often used interchangeably. However, the term crime reduction is now more popular and will be used in this unit.

14.1 Approaches to crime reduction

There are three main approaches to crime reduction – 1) structural or societal, 2) individual, 3) situational (Pease, 2002).

Structural/societal approaches These approaches see the basic causes of crime in society. For example, crime is generated by inequalities in income and wealth, or by inequalities of opportunity. Crime reduction therefore involves changes in society.

Individual approaches These approaches see particular individuals as prone to crime. Crime reduction therefore involves changing the behaviour of those at risk of starting a criminal career, or ending the criminal career of those with a history of lawbreaking.

Situational approaches These approaches seek to reduce the opportunities for crime by changing the settings in which crime occurs. Examples include surveillance – for instance, CCTV – and target hardening – for instance, steering locks on cars.

Evaluation No one approach provides a solution to the 'crime problem'. Crime is extremely varied – it ranges from vandalism to fraud, from domestic violence to street robbery. It is unlikely that one approach will provide an across-the-board reduction in this variety of crime (Pease, 2002).

A number of researchers recognise this point. For example, Jock Young (1992) argues for both a reduction in social inequality on a national level, and intervention on the local level by various agencies in order to reduce crime.

Finally, classifications of approaches to crime reduction provide only a rough framework. Some approaches don't fit neatly into a particular category, others overlap two or three categories.

14.2 Structural/societal approaches

Many of the sociological theories of crime examined in this chapter suggest that crime reduction involves major changes in society. The following examples illustrate this approach.

Strain theory Robert K. Merton's strain theory argues that the social structure prevents equal opportunity (see pages 150-151). It states that those at the bottom of the class structure are less likely to acquire the skills and qualifications needed to reach the top. As a result, some turn to crime in order to obtain the material rewards which are highly valued in Western society. The solution suggested by strain theory is the removal of barriers which prevent equal opportunity.

Subcultural theory Albert Cohen's subcultural theory starts from a similar position (see page 151). As a result of their position in society, many young working-class males do badly at school and fail to acquire the skills and qualifications needed for success. As a result of this failure, they experience status frustration. One way out of this situation is to develop a delinquent subculture in terms of which they can gain status and respect. As with Merton, the solution suggested by subcultural theory is the removal of barriers which prevent equal opportunity.

Marxist approaches From a traditional Marxist perspective, crime is systematically generated by the structure of capitalist society. The solution to crime is a classless society – communism – free from exploitation, oppression, conflicts of interest and inequalities of income and wealth. In terms of Marxist theory, people would then work for the common good, and crime as we know it would largely disappear.

Evaluation Apart from general statements about reducing social inequality and increasing equality of opportunity, strain theory and subcultural theory offer few if any practical proposals for achieving these aims. And, apart from predicting the eventual overthrow of capitalism, traditional Marxism offers little in the way of practical

solutions to the reduction of crime.

Left realism Unlike the theories outlined so far, left realism argues for both change on the societal level and for practical steps to reduce crime. In this respect, it claims to 'take crime seriously' (Young, 1986).

Jock Young (1999) sees relative deprivation as the major cause of crime in late modern society (see pages 172-173). Relative deprivation is generated by a society which is seen as blatantly unfair and unjust, in which inequalities of income and wealth are becoming greater, and in which equality of opportunity is blocked by barriers of class, race, gender and age. Young calls for a society in which rewards are based on talent and merit, and in which citizens become increasingly involved in the democratic process on both national and local levels. He hopes that this will lead to a society which will be seen as just and fair. If so, this will result in a reduction in relative deprivation, and to a reduction in the crime which relative deprivation generates.

Evaluation Jock Young provides a general outline of the way forward for late modern society, but gives little indication of how to get there. However, left realism does suggest practical solutions for crime reduction for the here and now (see pages 172-175).

14.3 Individual approaches

A variety of different approaches are examined under this broad heading. Their aim is to change the behaviour of individuals who are seen to be particularly at risk of crime. Although these have been termed individual approaches, they also refer to the groups to which at-risk individuals belong – for example, low-income groups in inner-city areas.

Early intervention

Early intervention programmes intervene in the lives of children, particularly children from disadvantaged groups. Their aim is to improve children's chances of success. The programmes assume that if children are caught young enough, then their chances of success at school and in later life can be improved. And their risks of turning to crime can be reduced.

There is some evidence that early intervention programmes can help to reduce the crime rate. The following programmes appear to have been particularly successful.

Pregnant mothers were seen in their homes by health visitors during their pregnancy and for two years after the birth of their child. Fifteen years later, their children had less than half the number of arrests compared with the children of a comparable sample of mothers who received no visits (Olds et al., 1997).

The Perry pre-school enrichment programme aimed to give children from low-income families a head start when they began school. Parents were encouraged to 'enrich' their children's lives with books, toys and educational activities. By the age of 27, the children who participated in the programme had been arrested only half as often as a sample of similar age and background (Schweinhart et al., 1993).

Evaluation There is evidence that some early intervention programmes appear to reduce crime. However, there is evidence that others appear to have little or no effect. In the USA in the 1960s, there was a massive programme of early intervention in low-income, inner-city areas. Known as Operation Head Start, it was designed to provide pre-school children with the skills, aptitudes and motivation to succeed in the school system.

Head Start assumed that enrichment in the early years would open doors and provide greater opportunities in the later years. Although crime reduction was not the major aim, it was assumed that young people who went through the programme would have less reason to turn to crime.

In terms of improving educational performance, Operation Head Start appeared to have, at best, short-term and limited success. Children in the programme sometimes made short-term gains when they began school but soon fell back to the level of their peers (Jensen, 1973). In terms of crime reduction, it is difficult to estimate the programme's effect. However, James Q. Wilson (1975) believes it had little or no effect. He notes that in the USA during the early 1960s:

> A great array of programmes aimed at the young, the poor and the deprived were mounted. Crime soared. It did not just increase a little; it rose at a faster rate and to higher levels than at any time since the 1930s, and, in some categories, to higher levels than any experienced in this century (Wilson, 1975).

Wilson also applies his comments to later intervention – programmes designed for older people. For example, Operation Head Start was accompanied by programmes for unemployed young people which attempted to provide 'work experience' and instil 'work habits' and 'work incentives'. In general, the evidence suggests that the later in life the intervention, the less likely it is to produce the desired effects (Pease, 2002).

Imprisonment

The responses of the criminal justice system to people who have broken the law can be seen as an attempt to change individual behaviour. Prison and the various alternatives to prison are obvious examples. Prison provides *incapacitation* – it prevents those inside from committing crimes on the outside. So, as long as habitual criminals remain behind bars, the crimes they would probably commit on the outside will be halted.

Apart from incapacitation, do prisons deter those who have already embarked on a career of crime? In other words, does the threat of future imprisonment make them change their behaviour and stop committing crimes? Or, do prisons *reform* those inside? One of the stated aims of the Prison Service is to rehabilitate offenders – to change them into law-abiding citizens who are ready to take up a

normal life on release. Many prisons have programmes which seek to improve educational and work skills and promote law-abiding behaviour after release (Prison Service, 2001).

Available evidence suggests that imprisonment neither deters nor rehabilitates many of those who have broken the law. In Britain during the early 1980s, prison expenditure rose by 85% and courts were encouraged to hand out longer sentences. By the late 1980s, Britain's rate of imprisonment was the highest in Europe. Yet the rate of recorded crime continued to grow rapidly. And nearly half of adult prisoners and around two-thirds of young prisoners were re-convicted within two years of release (McLaughlin & Muncie, 2001).

Prisons do not appear to be effective in terms of either *deterrence* or *rehabilitation*. Programmes designed to rehabilitate prisoners seem to have little or no effect. Those who participate in these programmes usually re-offend as often as those who do not participate (von Hirsch, 1976).

In view of this, some researchers argue that the main contribution of prison to crime reduction is incapacitation. For example, James Q. Wilson (1983) argues that the most active criminals should be removed from circulation and given long sentences. In his view, this will have a major impact on crime reduction.

The evidence suggests that incapacitation is not particularly effective. From 1987 to 1995, the USA increased its prison population by 124% and during that time there was a 2% increase in crime. Over the same period, Denmark increased its prison population by 7% and had a 3% increase in crime. As frequently noted in this chapter, any measurement of crime must be treated with extreme caution. However, available evidence suggests that the use of imprisonment to reduce the crime rate has not been very successful (Young, 1999).

key terms

Incapacitation Making someone incapable of doing something. In this case, using imprisonment to prevent offenders from committing crimes during their length of stay.
Deterrence Discouraging or preventing a person from doing something for fear of the consequences. In this case, using prison as a deterrent for lawbreaking.
Rehabilitation Restoring someone to a normal life. In this case, restoring offenders to law-abiding citizens.

Community sentences

In recent years there have been growing demands for alternatives to prison. This has been accompanied by a rise in *community sentencing* which involves the punishment, rehabilitation, treatment or supervision of offenders in the community (Hughes, 2001). Community sentences include:

- Community rehabilitation orders – the offender is supervised by a probation officer and may be required to take part in various programmes.

- Community punishment order – the offender is required to perform unpaid work for the benefit of the community under the supervision of a probation officer.

- Curfew orders – the offender is required to remain at a particular location during fixed times for up to six months (Raynor, 2002).

By the end of the 1990s, around 50% of all youth sentences in England and Wales were community-based. In 2002, 33% of all offenders were given community sentences and 25% were given prison sentences (*Social Trends*, 2004).

How effective are community sentences in reducing crime? In particular, how do they compare with prisons in terms of re-offending? A review of the evidence indicates that they are at least as effective as imprisonment (Brownlee, 1998). Although this isn't particularly impressive, some researchers argue that, given the dehumanising effects of prison, community sentencing is much more preferable.

It would be wrong to dismiss community sentencing on the basis of the overall re-offending rate. Research indicates that certain types of community-based programmes can reduce re-offending by up to 20%. The more effective programmes are 'highly structured, they make clear and explicit demands' on the offender, they are well resourced and supervised by trained staff (Raynor, 2002).

14.4 Situational approaches

Situational approaches to crime reduction are concerned with changing aspects of the environment to:

- increase the chances of detection when committing a crime

- increase the chances of failure when committing a crime.

Together, these measures increase the risks and reduce the rewards of crime. In theory, this should deter people from breaking the law.

Many offences are 'crimes of opportunity'. For example, if a car is left unlocked, it presents a far better opportunity for theft than a locked car with a steering column lock. Situational approaches to crime reduction seek to reduce the opportunities for crime.

Examples of situational approaches

Target hardening This refers to reducing the physical opportunities for crime. Examples include more secure doors and windows, toughened-glass screens in banks and building societies separating staff and customers, steering column locks on vehicles, entryphones to buildings, and gated communities which provide barriers to outsiders.

Surveillance This refers to various means of observing people's behaviour. It ranges from closed circuit television (CCTV) whereby cameras keep watch on city streets, malls and shops, to improvements in street lighting which increase the chance of people being seen in the dark.

The effectiveness of situational approaches

There have been many evaluations of situational approaches. Most techniques appear to result in crime reduction. The following examples indicate the effect of surveillance (Clarke, 2003).

- Vandalism is considerably reduced on buses with conductors.

- Public telephones in pubs and launderettes suffer almost no vandalism compared to those in kiosks.

- Car parks with attendants have lower rates of auto-crime.

- Apartment blocks with CCTV or doormen have fewer burglaries.

Informal social control At first sight, it seems obvious why situational approaches often work. However, a closer look suggests that the reasons are not so obvious. For example, gated communities appear to reduce crime because they present barriers to entry. But they also make residents feel safer and encourage a sense of community. Because of this, people tend to spend more time on the street, and are more likely to get to know each other. As a result, they are more likely to identify strangers and question their presence on the estate. Informal social controls such as gossip, public opinion, parental control and public surveillance tend to develop. And these controls can lead to a reduction in crime.

Similarly, street lighting appears to work because it increases surveillance in the dark. *But* it also reduces the amount of crime in daylight. Again, this suggests an increase in community solidarity and informal social control (Painter & Farrington, 1999).

Evaluation Situational approaches to crime reduction may not be as successful as they appear. In particular, they may result in *displacement* in the place, type, method and time of the offence. For example, target hardening and surveillance may simply move crime from one area to another, or from a protected to an unprotected building. Offenders may select alternative types of crime, use different methods and/or choose different times.

Research indicates that if displacement does occur, it is fairly limited. And some studies suggest the opposite of displacement – that crime reduction sometimes extends beyond the area where situational measures have been introduced (Pease, 2002).

key terms

Community sentencing Punishment, rehabilitation, treatment or supervision of offenders in the community rather than in prison.

Displacement Removing something from one place to another. In this case, changing the place, type, method and/or type of crime without changing the extent of crime.

activity27 situational approaches

Item A Gated communities

This picture shows the entrance to a gated community in Memphis, Tennessee. The houses and apartments are rented. Residents use a swipe card to enter the estate. The owners have an office at the entrance which arranges access for visitors. The office provides a number of facilities for residents – computers, faxes and a library of DVDs and videos, all at no charge. Alongside the office are tennis courts, an outdoor swimming pool and a gym – all available free to residents and their friends.

Item B Decoy vehicles

Vehicles can be adapted in various ways to detect anyone entering them illegally. Methods include tracking or camera systems, or physical restraints which prevent intruders from leaving the vehicle.

Specially adapted decoy vehicles were used in Stockton-on-Tees in an attempt to reduce vehicle theft. The result was a small reduction. The vehicles were then withdrawn. However, it was widely publicised that the initiative was still in operation. This time the reduction in vehicle theft was much greater.

Source: Sallybanks, 2000

questions

1 In what ways might gated communities reduce crime?

2 Use the idea of informal social control to explain the results of the decoy vehicle initiative in Item B.

Broken windows and informal social control

In a famous article entitled 'Broken windows: The police and neighbourhood safety' first published in 1982, James Q. Wilson and George L. Kelling (2003) argue that informal social control is the key to crime reduction. They claim that disorder and anti-social behaviour – 'incivility' – are closely linked to crime. For example, if a window is broken and left unrepaired, the remaining windows in the building will soon be broken. If nothing is done, it appears that nobody cares, and 'untended property becomes fair game for fun and plunder'. Similarly, 'untended behaviour' – that is behaviour which is not checked, challenged and controlled – can become increasingly anti-social. Incivilities such as rudeness, excessive noise and vandalism become common. This leads to a breakdown in community controls and produces a situation in which crime can flourish.

According to Wilson and Kelling, the main job of the police is to halt this downward spiral of disorder and maintain informal social controls in communities. In other words, their main job is to maintain order. This involves enforcing rules of orderly behaviour and doing this in partnership with people in the neighbourhood. For example, noisy teenagers should be told to keep quiet, begging should be forbidden, and drunks and addicts should be prevented from sleeping or lying down on the street.

James Q. Wilson (1983) argues that most police work occurs after crime has been committed and reported. Reducing crime therefore involves preventing crime in the first place. And this means maintaining 'orderly neighbourhoods'. Some neighbourhoods are beyond repair – the best the police can do is attempt to deal with crimes which have been committed by responding to calls and trying to catch offenders. They are not very good at this – most crimes remain unsolved. Other neighbourhoods are 'stable and serene' – they do not even need foot patrols. Where the police can make a difference is in neighbourhoods at the 'tipping point' – where public order is deteriorating but can be restored (see also pages 169-170 and 203-204).

Evaluation Wilson and Kelling's argument is based on evidence which indicates that policing has only limited effects on the crime rate. Rather than concentrate on crimes which have already occurred, the police should focus on strengthening the informal social controls which prevent disorder.

But do disorder and incivility lead to rising crime? As noted earlier (see page 170), a study of 196 neighbourhoods in Chicago suggests that as neighbourhoods became poorer there was an increase in both disorder and crime. In other words, it was economic disadvantage rather than disorder as such which led to a rise in crime (Sampson & Raudenbush, 1999).

Zero-tolerance policing

Wilson and Kelling's views suggest that the police should clamp down on a wide range of behaviour which is not necessarily criminal and take so-called 'petty offences' seriously. In other words, there should be zero-tolerance of all anti-social behaviour.

In 1994, William J. Bratton was appointed police commissioner for New York City. He introduced a policy of zero-tolerance policing. This meant that the police clamped down on all types of crime, however petty and insignificant. No longer did they turn a blind eye to people riding bikes on the sidewalk, urinating in public, small-time drug dealers, graffiti, beggars and street prostitution. In Bratton's words, 'If you don't stop the small offenders, it emboldens the really bad guys. It creates an atmosphere of lawlessness.' Within two years of the introduction of zero-tolerance, homicides in New York City were halved and robberies dropped by a third (Chaudhary & Walker, 1996).

So-called zero-tolerance policing in New York was not a get-tough policy imposed by the police on unsuspecting neighbourhoods. According to Commissioner Bratton, it involved a partnership with local communities and took account of their concerns and priorities (Young, 1999).

Evaluation Does zero-tolerance policing work? Certainly the results from New York City are impressive. But were they due to zero-tolerance policing or to other factors?

From 1993 to 1996 the crime rate declined in 17 out of the 25 largest cities in the USA. In some of these cities there had been no change in policing policy and in some cases there had been a reduction in the number of police officers. Some cities specifically adopted a less aggressive policing policy – for example, Los Angeles after the riots – and they too saw a reduction in crime. In addition, the crime rate in New York had started to decline before the appointment of Commissioner Bratton and zero-tolerance policing (Young, 1999).

At a minimum, this suggests that differing police methods do not necessarily have a marked effect on the crime rate. If this is the case, how else can the overall reduction in crime during this period be explained?

From 1990 to 1993, there was a crime wave in the USA. This coincided with an economic recession and high unemployment. From 1994 to 1996, 10.5 million new jobs were created in the USA. In addition, there was a marked decline in the crack-cocaine epidemic. Factors such as these, rather than zero-tolerance policing, may provide a better explanation for the decline in crime in New York City (Chaudhary & Walker, 1996).

Conclusion

It is difficult to evaluate the various approaches and strategies to crime reduction. First, the reliability and validity of crime statistics are questionable. As a result, any measurement of the effectiveness of crime reduction strategies must also be questionable. Second, many of the approaches to crime reduction are directed towards particular crimes – for example, street crime – and particular groups, for example, the working class. In view of the variety of both crime and of groups in society, it is unlikely that any single approach can provide a solution to the 'problem of crime'. Third, there are many factors which affect the crime rate. It is extremely difficult to isolate a particular factor and say with any degree of certainty that it is responsible for a reduction in crime.

14.5 Social policy and crime

Social policy refers to government policy on a range of social issues – for example, education, the family and health. This section looks at the crime policies of British governments from 1945 onwards. It also considers their relationship to sociological theories of crime.

1945-1979

Elected in 1945, the Labour Party set the early post-war agenda for dealing with crime. Crime reduction meant the reduction of social inequality. In this respect, Labour policy reflected sociological theories which see the roots of crime within the structure of society – the structural/societal approaches outlined in Section 14.2. In practice, this meant dealing with poverty, unemployment and educational failure, and reducing inequalities in income, wealth and opportunity. In terms of offenders, the focus was on treatment and rehabilitation rather than imprisonment and punishment (McLaughlin & Muncie, 2001).

From 1945-1959, crime was not a major political issue. It was hardly mentioned in the manifestos or election campaigns of the main political parties (Downes & Morgan, 2002).

Things started to change in the 1960s. The recorded crime rate rose rapidly during these years, particularly the rate for young offenders. Crime was becoming a political issue. So much so that by 1979, the Conservatives were talking about a 'law and order crisis'.

Conservative policy, 1979-1997

The Conservative Party won the 1979 election and remained in power for the next 18 years. Crime was a major issue in the election campaign. Labour maintained its traditional policy of dealing with 'the social deprivation which allows crime to flourish'. The Conservatives rejected this approach. They promised to restore the 'rule of law' with a 'war on crime'. Criminals rather than society were to blame for the rocketing crime rate. And they had been allowed to get away with it because of the 'soft' policies of Labour governments.

The emphasis now was on apprehending and punishing criminals. Muggers, burglars and hooligans were to blame for rising crime. They, not society, were responsible for their criminal behaviour. As a result, they deserved to be punished. Money was pumped into the criminal justice system. During the first half of the 1980s, expenditure on the police force rose by 40%. Courts were encouraged to give tougher sentences in an effort to deter offenders. Expenditure on prisons rose by 85% in the first half of the 1980s. And by 1988, the rate of imprisonment in Britain was the highest in Europe. Despite the Conservative policy of getting tough on crime, the rate of recorded crime continued to grow rapidly (McLaughlin & Muncie, 2001).

In line with their rejection of structural/societal approaches to crime reduction, the Conservatives looked to situational approaches such as target hardening and surveillance. Crime control was not just the responsibility of government – it was also the duty of every citizen and local community. Individuals must make their homes more secure and take action to protect their neighbourhoods with schemes like Neighbourhood Watch.

Labour policy, 1997-2008

In the 1980s, the Conservative's catch-phrase was 'Labour's soft on crime'. In the 1990s, the soundbite of Tony Blair's Labour Party was 'Tough on crime and tough on the causes of crime'.

Tough on crime Labour, like the Conservatives before them, argued that offenders should be held responsible for their criminal acts and be given their just deserts – that is be punished in relation to the seriousness of their crimes. The criminal justice system should 'come down hard' on persistent offenders. One of the results of this policy has been a further increase in the prison population. In Great Britain in 2007, there were nearly 87,000 people in prison, 82% higher than in 1980 (*Social Trends*, 2008).

In 2001, Tony Blair set out Labour's crime policy for his second term in office. 'We will take further action to focus on the 100,000 most persistent offenders. They are responsible for half of all crime.' As part of this response, Labour has favoured a zero-tolerance policy – clamping down on petty criminals, drunkenness, vandalism and a range of anti-social behaviour in order to prevent the development of environments in which more serious crime can flourish. This can be seen from the introduction of ASBOs – Anti-social Behaviour Orders – which can result in curfews for young people and banning them from certain areas. Failure to comply with an ASBO is a criminal offence.

To a large extent, Labour has seen crime reduction as 'a local problem requiring local solutions' (Cook, 2001). A *multi-agency approach* has been encouraged. This involves various local authority agencies – for example, social services, health, housing and criminal justice agencies – working together to combat crime. Wherever possible, local people should participate in this process (Cook, 2001).

Tough on the causes of crime When Labour came to power in 1997, they offered a 'Third Way' in politics – neither the traditional left-wing policies of 'old' Labour, nor the right-wing policies of the Conservatives. The Third Way sought new directions and new solutions to old and new problems.

Much of this was influenced by one of Britain's leading sociologists, Anthony Giddens, who has been described as Tony Blair's favourite guru. Giddens' *The Third Way: The Renewal of Social Democracy* was published in 1998.

Giddens saw *social exclusion* as the main threat to social order and social solidarity. Society would tend to fracture and disintegrate if groups became excluded from the mainstream. For example, if the poor or ethnic minorities were detached from the wider society, they would not feel part of the national community.

Social Exclusion Unit Giddens' Third Way is reflected in Labour's social policy. In their first year of government, Labour set up the Social Exclusion Unit to find solutions to the problem of exclusion. The Unit is directly responsible to the Cabinet and it attempts to ensure that all policies – health, education, poverty, crime, urban renewal – are part of a coordinated strategy to deal with social exclusion (MacGregor, 2001).

Poverty Living in poverty means exclusion from many of the activities that most people take for granted. The largest group in poverty are low-paid workers and their dependent children. Labour's policy to reduce poverty has focused on this group. It has introduced the following:

- A minimum wage
- The Working Families Tax Credit to top up the wages of low-paid workers
- A significant increase in Child Benefit allowances
- The National Childcare Strategy which provides money for the development of childcare centres
- The Sure Start programme which provides health and support services for low-income families with children under four (Donnison, 2001; Page, 2002).

Unemployment Labour's New Deal, introduced in 1998, was part of their programme for social inclusion. The New Deal offered education and training for young people between the ages of 18 and 24 who had been out of work for more than six months. It was later extended to older people.

The New Deal provided personal advisors who offered direction and support to the unemployed, guiding them through the various options – academic courses, vocational training, self-employment, or voluntary work.

The New Deal emphasised the duties of citizenship. It was the duty of unemployed people to take up work and training opportunities. If they didn't, their benefits might be withheld until they did.

Education Shortly after their election in 1997, Labour promised to 'overcome economic and social disadvantage and make equality of opportunity a reality' (DfEE, 1997).

The focus was reaching out to the excluded and providing them with opportunities to enter mainstream society. This involved finding new ways of motivating young people in deprived inner-city areas and of improving 'underachieving schools'. For example, Education Action Zones were set up in urban areas which had low levels of educational attainment.

Crime and social exclusion In terms of Labour's policy, crime is generated by social exclusion. Crime reduction in the long term can only result from policies of social inclusion. This means opening doors and providing opportunities, particularly for those at the bottom of the class system. In practice, this means reducing poverty, reducing unemployment and reducing educational failure. The aim is to give the excluded opportunities to enter mainstream society and to encourage them to do so.

Labour's assessment and future policy In 2007, the Home Office published *Cutting Crime: A new partnership 2008-11* in which it assessed progress in the fight against crime and outlined policy proposals for the future. It gave Labour an excellent report noting that crime had fallen by around a third since they came to power in 1997. It then outlined Labour's policy proposals for further crime reduction. They include the following.

- An 'end-to-end approach' to crime reduction which involves 1) 'early intervention' at a young age to prevent offending as soon as possible 2) 'situational prevention' to reduce opportunities for committing crime 3) 'enforcement' – ensuring that crime is detected and that the penalty is appropriate to both the offender and the offence 4) 'reducing re-offending' – managing known offenders to prevent future re-offending.

- A focus on organised crime. In 2006, the Serious Organised Crime Agency was launched to combat organised crime.

- 'Reaching out' to the 2-3% of the population in 'deep and persistent exclusion' in order to bring them into the mainstream.

In 2009, the Labour Party prioritised the fight against violent crime with the following proposals.

- Tougher sentences for knife crime
- New controls on deactivated firearms
- Portable weapon scanners for police
- Targeted action to tackle gang crime
- Education to turn young people away from crime (www.labour.org.uk).

Evaluation In terms of crime reduction, has Labour's policy worked? According to the British Crime Survey, crime in England and Wales has been steadily falling since 1995. Whether this has anything to do with Labour's policies of crime reduction and social inclusion is difficult to say.

summary

1. There are three main approaches to crime reduction – a) structural/societal, b) individual, c) situational.

2. Structural/societal approaches see the basic causes of crime in society – for example, crime is generated by social inequality. Crime reduction therefore involves changes in society.

3. Individual approaches aim to change the behaviour of those seen to be at risk of crime.

4. There is some evidence that early intervention can reduce the risk of crime in later life. However, there is also evidence that it has little or no effect.

5. Evidence indicates that prison as a means of rehabilitation or deterrence has little effect. Some argue that the main value of prison is incapacitation. However, this appears to have little effect on the crime rate.

6. In terms of re-offending, community sentences are little different from imprisonment. However, certain types of community-based programmes can reduce re-offending by up to 20%.

7. Situational approaches seek to reduce the opportunities for crime by changing the settings in which crime occurs. Examples include target hardening and surveillance.

8. There is evidence that most situational approaches have some success, particularly if they lead to the strengthening of informal social control.

9. Wilson and Kelling see informal social control as the key to crime reduction. Disorder and anti-social behaviour lead to a breakdown in informal controls which allows crime to flourish. The main job of the police is to maintain order.

10. Zero-tolerance policing may be a successful method of crime reduction. However, the evidence is not clear-cut. Many other factors may account for a reduction in crime.

11. After 1945, crime reduction for the Labour Party meant a reduction in social inequality.

12. Conservative policy from 1979 to 1997 tended to blame the offender rather than society. Offenders must be given the punishment they deserve. Despite a rapidly growing prison population, the crime rate grew rapidly.

13. Like the Conservatives, Labour claimed to be 'tough on crime'. They favoured a zero-tolerance policy and argued that offenders should be punished in relation to the seriousness of their crime.

14. Labour saw social exclusion as the main cause of crime. Their policies were designed to reduce exclusion, provide equality of opportunity, and so reduce crime.

15. This view has been criticised. For example, some sociologists argue that inequality of opportunity cannot be significantly reduced until economic inequalities are reduced.

Traditional Labour policy for tackling the causes of crime was based on a structural/societal approach. It was concerned with reducing social inequalities by redistributing income and wealth from the top to the bottom. More recently, Labour has been primarily concerned with reducing inequality of opportunity rather than redistribution. Many sociologists argue that inequality of opportunity cannot be significantly reduced unless economic inequalities are reduced. And this is particularly true when the gap in wealth and income between top and bottom is widening as it has under New Labour (Paxton & Dixon, 2004).

Labour's emphasis on social inclusion and increasing opportunity as a means for dealing with the causes of crime has been strongly criticised. For many sociologists, the target should be economic inequalities. In David Marquand's (1998) words, 'No project for social inclusion will work unless it captures some of the winners' gains and redirects them to the losers'.

Can social exclusion be seen as *the* cause of crime? What about the white-collar crimes of the socially included? In Dee Cook's (2001) words, 'It is unclear how tackling social exclusion would reduce racially motivated crime, domestic violence or white-collar crimes such as embezzlement, fraud, pollution and tax evasion'.

activity28 *Labour and crime*

Item A **Tony Blair**

Tony Blair in the House of Commons

'If you are tolerant of small crimes, and I mean vandalism and the graffiti at the end of the street, you create an environment in which pretty soon the drug dealers move in, and then after that the violent people with their knives and their guns and all the rest of it, and the community is wrecked.'

Item B **A critical view**

In 2001, Tony Blair outlined Labour's crime policy for his second term in office.

> 'We will take further action to focus on the 100,000 most persistent offenders. They are responsible for half of all crime. They are the core of the crime problem in this country. Half are under 21, nearly two-thirds are hard drug users, three quarters are out of work and more than a third were in care as children. Half have no qualifications at all and 45% are excluded from school.'

Jock Young makes the following comments on this statement.

'Let us note that these figures are as hypothetical as they are politically convenient. They ignore the fact that a large proportion of young people commit crime, that only a few are caught, and that generalisation about their background from these few is grossly unreliable. Further, that the number of crimes committed is based on police interviews with apprehended young offenders, who are encouraged to exaggerate in order to boost the clear-up figures; and that even given this, only one-quarter of offences are cleared up, so that for four million uncleared offences we do not have the faintest idea of the identity of the offenders. Furthermore, that for youth offences such as burglary and robbery the clear-up rate is even lower, 18% and 13% respectively, and the culprits even more unknown and indescribable.'

Source: Young, 2002

questions

1 Critically assess Tony Blair's claim in Item A.

2 One of the main problems with developing policies to fight crime is that governments know very little about the majority of lawbreakers. Discuss with reference to Item B.

Unit 15 *Suicide*

keyissues

1 What are the main sociological studies of suicide?
2 What methodologies do they use?
3 What are the strengths and weaknesses of each methodological approach?

Suicide is examined to illustrate various methodological approaches in Chapter 4 (see pages 229-230 and 235-237). This unit looks at suicide in more detail. For convenience, some of the material in Chapter 4 will also be covered here.

15.1 Durkheim's study of suicide

Published in 1897, Emile Durkheim's *Suicide: A Study in Sociology* was the first major sociological study of suicide. Keen to establish the value of a sociological approach, Durkheim chose suicide, a highly personal act, which seemed more suited to a psychological rather than a sociological explanation. If he could show that suicide was linked to society, rather than simply to individual psychology, then the value of sociology would be established.

The suicide rate

The suicide rate is the number of people who kill themselves in a particular society, or in a group within a society, in a given period of time. Durkheim based his research on the rate of suicide per million inhabitants in different European countries. The statistics revealed a number of patterns.

- First, suicide rates varied between different countries (see Table 4). For example, they were generally higher in Protestant countries than Catholic countries.
- Second, when suicide rates across Europe rose and fell, the differences between countries generally remained (see Table 4).
- Third, the rise and fall in suicide rates appeared to be related to social factors. For example, the rates rose during periods of economic recession and, more surprisingly, during periods of economic prosperity. And they fell during times of war and political upheaval.
- Fourth, there were variations in the suicide rate between different groups within the same society. For example, the unmarried and the childless had higher rates than the married and those with children.

Explaining suicide rates

Suicide and society According to Durkheim, patterns in suicide rates could not be explained in terms of the psychology of individuals. Instead, the answer lay in society – in the relationship *between* individuals and society and, in particular, the degree to which they were integrated into social groups and the degree to which they were regulated by society.

Integration In a strongly integrated society, individuals are bound together by shared norms and values. The level of integration can be measured by the strength and number of relationships between individuals. In a strongly integrated society, people have powerful duties and obligations to each other. Levels of integration vary between societies and between groups within society.

Regulation Similarly, regulation varies between societies and groups within society. Regulation refers to the control which society has over its members – to the degree to which society regulates their behaviour.

Without regulation, people's desires are limitless. Society places limits on their desires by defining specific goals and the means of obtaining them.

Social order Durkheim, like all functionalists, was concerned with the following questions. How was society held together? How was social order maintained? What constituted a 'healthy' society? Durkheim's answer was appropriate levels of integration and regulation.

Too little integration and regulation would result in social disorder. The norms and values which bound individuals together and the regulations which controlled their behaviour would be weakened. Society would become unbalanced. The results would be 'pathological' or harmful to society.

Durkheim believed that this was happening in modern society. And the rise in suicide rates in European countries was one indication of this trend.

Too much integration and regulation was also harmful to society. If norms and values are too strong, they would prevent the innovation and change necessary for a healthy society.

Types of suicide

Durkheim identified four types of suicide, each of which is

Table 4	**Rates of suicide per million inhabitants in European countries**		
Country	**1866-70**	**1871-75**	**1874-78**
Italy	30	35	38
Austria	78	94	130
Saxony	293	267	334

Source: Durkheim, 1970

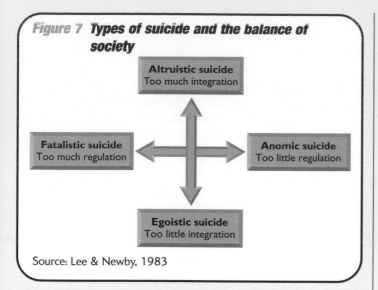

Figure 7 **Types of suicide and the balance of society**

- Altruistic suicide
  Too much integration
- Fatalistic suicide
  Too much regulation
- Anomic suicide
  Too little regulation
- Egoistic suicide
  Too little integration

Source: Lee & Newby, 1983

related to the level of integration or the level of regulation in society.

- *Altruistic suicide* occurs when the level of integration is too strong.
- *Egoistic suicide* occurs when the level of integration is too weak.
- *Fatalistic suicide* occurs when the level of regulation is too strong.
- *Anomic suicide* occurs when the level of regulation is too weak.

The relationship between types of suicide and levels of integration and regulation is illustrated in Figure 7.

Altruistic suicide Altruism means acting unselfishly, directed by a concern for others even if this is harmful to oneself. Altruistic suicide occurs when individuals are so strongly integrated into society that they take their own lives out of a sense of duty. They are so powerfully committed to the norms and values of society that they make the ultimate sacrifice.

Altruistic suicide can be seen in traditional Hindu India where a wife would throw herself on to her husband's funeral pyre and burn to death. It can also be seen in some nomadic hunting and gathering bands who followed the seasonal movements of game. Those who were too old and frail to travel stayed behind and died for the benefit of the group. In traditional Inuit (Eskimo) society, the elderly died in the snow as the band moved on in order to survive.

According to Durkheim, altruistic suicide is rare in modern societies. However, it does occur. For example, in the Second World War, Japanese kamikaze pilots flew planes packed with explosives on to the decks of American warships. They committed suicide for the benefit of their countrymen.

Fatalistic suicide Fatalism is a belief that nothing can be done to change the situation. Fatalistic suicide is characteristic of societies where there is too much regulation, too much control of individuals. Slavery is an example of excessive regulation – often there was little or nothing slaves could do to change their situation. Suicide

offered an escape. Durkheim argued that this accounts for the high rate of suicide which occurred when people's hopes and desires were crushed by 'oppressive discipline'.

Egoistic suicide The word ego refers to the self. Egoistic suicide occurs when there is too little integration, when the individual increasingly stands alone. It results from a weakening of the ties which bind individuals to social groups.

Durkheim saw egoistic suicide as characteristic of societies which were making the transition to modernity. These societies have an 'excess of individualism' – people tend to think primarily of themselves, they are less concerned with their duties and obligations to others, and with the opinions of others. The lower their level of integration with social groups, the more likely they will be to commit suicide. They have fewer obligations to others. And there is less moral pressure from others to prevent them from taking their own life.

Durkheim provides the following evidence to support his views. Unmarried people have the highest rate of suicide, followed by married people without children. And the more children married people have, the less likely they are to commit suicide. Thus, the larger the family group, the higher the level of social integration and the less vulnerable people are to suicide.

Protestant countries have a higher rate of suicide than Catholic countries. According to Durkheim, the Catholic religion integrates its members more strongly into a religious community.

The suicide rate falls during times of war and political upheaval. At times like these, the level of integration in society increases as people draw together to focus on a common cause.

In Durkheim's words, when the level of integration is low, 'The individual yields to the slightest shock of circumstances because the state of society has made him ready prey to suicide'.

Anomic suicide Like egoistic suicide, anomic suicide mainly occurs in modern societies. It results from a lack of regulation of people's desires and expectations.

Modern societies are characterised by rapid social change which disrupts the norms governing behaviour. The result is a situation of anomie or normlessness. There is no ceiling on people's desires, no limits to their expectations. Without norms to govern what people can reasonably expect from life, desires are uncontrolled and can never be satisfied. Living in a moral vacuum without sufficient regulation, people are more vulnerable to suicide.

Anomie is particularly acute in times of rapid economic change – in times of 'boom' and 'bust', prosperity and recession. This leads to changes in people's circumstances which further disrupt the norms governing their behaviour. Durkheim found that suicide rates rose with rapid upturns and downturns in the economy.

Conclusion Durkheim claimed that both suicide rates and types of suicide were shaped by social factors – by the levels of integration and regulation in society. He concluded that, 'There is therefore, for each people [society], a collective force of a definite amount of energy, impelling men to self-destruction'.

key terms

Altruistic suicide A type of suicide that occurs when individuals are so strongly integrated into society that they take their own lives out of a sense of duty.
Egoistic suicide A type of suicide that occurs when there is little integration in society, when the ties that bind individuals into social groups are very weak.
Fatalistic suicide A type of suicide that occurs when individuals are so strongly regulated that they can see no way out of their situation other than suicide.
Anomic suicide A type of suicide that results from a lack of regulation of people's desires and expectations.

Durkheim's methodology

Social facts In *The Rules of the Sociological Method*, Durkheim outlined the rules that sociologists should follow in order for sociology to become a science. In his words, 'The first and most fundamental rule is: Consider social facts as things'. Social facts include the norms, values and institutions of society (see pages 229-230).

Social facts exist outside individuals – they are over and above them. However, they become part of them via the socialisation process during which they learn society's norms and values. Norms and values are shared, they are not simply personal beliefs. Because of this, Durkheim argued that 'collective ways of acting and thinking have a reality outside the individuals'. As such, they are social facts and can be studied 'objectively as external things'.

Just as the behaviour of matter is directed by external forces, so the behaviour of human beings is directed by external forces – by social facts. In view of this, human behaviour can be studied using the methodology of natural sciences. And in this way, sociology can become a science.

The social facts of suicide Suicide rates are social facts. And they are determined by other social facts – by levels of integration and regulation in society. These are 'real, living, active forces which, because of the way they determine the individual, prove their independence from him'.

Durkheim found correlations between suicide rates and a range of social facts. He claimed that these correlations indicated causal relationships. For example, an individual's religion, marital status, family size and age can all be used as measures of their level of integration in society. And in each case, the lower the level of integration, the higher the rate of suicide. In Durkheim's words, 'suicide varies inversely with the degree of integration of the social groups of which the individual is a part'.

Durkheim then provided an explanation for this relationship. People are social beings – they have been socialised to participate in society. The lower their level of integration, the less they can do this. Isolated from others, their lives lack meaning and purpose. In Durkheim's words, 'The individual alone is not a sufficient end for his activity. He is too little'. As a result, the individual is vulnerable to suicide.

activity29 classifying suicide

Item A Types of suicide

Death from poison – living alone in a one-room attic

A Baltimore banker who has lost all his money in a recession blows himself up.

A Japanese servant, pretending to be his master, cuts out his entrails and throws them at the enemy, so allowing his master to escape.

Haitians kill themselves and their children to escape from the cruelty of their Spanish masters.

Item B Problems of classification

Suicide bombings can be categorised as an extreme form of political protest. They appear to fit into Durkheim's category of altruistic suicide – acts by people who are so highly integrated into a group that they are prepared to sacrifice their own lives to further its cause. The hopelessness experienced by some might also give ground for interpreting these suicides as fatalistic – the actions of people who feel trapped in a repressive regime, which is how Palestinians would undoubtedly describe the state of Israel. Alternatively, their suicides could also be described as anomic – the result of living in a society undergoing dramatic and disorientating social change. They could be egoistic, if the desire for reward in Paradise is the bombers' highest motivation.

Source: Swale, 2004

A Palestinian suicide bomber

questions

1. a) Match each of the pictures in Item A with one of Durkheim's four types of suicide – altruistic, egoistic, fatalistic and anomic.

   b) Give reasons for your answers.

2. a) How does Item B challenge Durkheim's classification of suicide?

   b) Choose one of the pictures from Item A and suggest how it might fit into more than one of Durkheim's suicide types.

A science of society Durkheim believed that his research on suicide showed that scientific methodology was appropriate for the study of human society. In his view, he had followed the procedures of the natural sciences and his results showed that 'real laws are discoverable' in the social world, just as they are in the natural world.

Realism or positivism Durkheim's methodology is sometimes described as positivist. Positivists believe that sociology should adopt the methodology of the natural

sciences and focus only on directly observable facts. At first sight, this is exactly what Durkheim does. He identifies observable social facts and correlates them with other observable social facts.

However, Durkheim goes further. He identifies other social facts which cannot be directly observed. He refers to these as social currents. They cannot be observed and measured in the same way as social facts such as family size and religious beliefs. But they are just as real and they have just as much power over people's behaviour.

Social currents flow through society. In his study of suicide, Durkheim identified four social currents – altruism, fatalism, egoism and anomie. Durkheim's methodology 'involved searching for the invisible underlying causes of the relationships between things that are observed' (Taylor, 1988). In terms of his study of suicide, this meant identifying social currents which were the underlying causes of various types of suicide.

This is a realist rather than a positivist approach. Realists argue that the causes of many of the things we observe lie in underlying structures and processes which cannot be directly observed. From a realist viewpoint, both the natural and social sciences operate in much the same way. In this sense, Durkheim's methodology can be seen as scientific.

Evaluation of Durkheim's research

Many sociologists have enormous respect for Durkheim's study of suicide. However, both his general approach and specific aspects of his research have been criticised.

Suicide statistics Durkheim's study was based on official statistics of suicide. Critics argue that he paid insufficient attention to both their reliability and validity.

Suicide statistics are reliable if coroners – the officials who decide the cause of death – reach the same conclusions. However, one coroner might give a verdict of suicide when the evidence suggests that a person probably took their own life. Another coroner might want more conclusive evidence – for example, a suicide note. Differences in suicide rates between two towns may simply reflect the views of different coroners. The reliability of suicide statistics is therefore questionable (Taylor, 1988).

Statistics are valid if they represent a true and accurate measurement. Coroners have to decide whether a death is a suicide, an accident, or due to natural causes. This can be a difficult judgement. If coroners cannot reach a decision, they give an 'open verdict'. Such verdicts do not form part of the suicide statistics. For these reasons, the validity of suicide statistics is questionable.

The positivist response Positivists accept that much of Durkheim's work is scientific. He quantified a number of social facts. His statistical analysis revealed correlations between them and indicated cause and effect relationships. However, they part company with Durkheim on two main counts.

First, Durkheim sometimes failed to provide an operational definition of social facts – that is a definition which could provide quantifiable data. For example, without an operational definition of social integration, this aspect of Durkheim's theory could not be tested and shown to be true or false (Gibbs & Martin, 1964).

Second, positivists reject Durkheim's realist approach. In particular, they reject his view that causes can be found in underlying structures and processes that cannot be directly observed and measured. From a positivist viewpoint,

Durkheim's use of unobservable social currents to explain suicide rates is unacceptable and unscientific.

Further criticisms of Durkheim's methodology are examined in the following sections.

15.2 Suicide – an interpretivist view

The meanings of suicide

From an interpretivist perspective, people act in terms of meanings. Sociologists must therefore interpret the meanings which direct action in order to understand human behaviour.

In *The Social Meanings of Suicide* (1967), Jack Douglas argues that the first step in studying suicide is to interpret how individuals who commit suicide define and give meaning to their action.

Step 1 Douglas admits that this is easier said than done. He suggests the following ways of discovering the meanings which victims give to acts of suicide.

- An analysis of suicide notes if available
- An examination of diaries if kept
- Interviews with those who knew the victim – for example, family and friends
- Building up a biography of the victim
- Analysing the events which immediately preceded the suicide
- Interviews with those who have survived suicide attempts.

According to Douglas, this first step is essential in order to classify suicides into types. He rejects Durkheim's approach, arguing that he imposes definitions on suicides. The resulting classification into types may have little or nothing to do with the meanings that suicide victims give to their actions.

Step 2 The next step is to look for patterns of meaning which are common to a number of suicides. Only if these are found is it possible to classify suicides into different types. Using this method, Douglas claims that the most common types of suicide include the following. In each case, he argues that this is how victims give meaning to their action.

- **Revenge suicide** is seen as an act of revenge against those who have wronged the victim – for example, to make a former lover feel guilty.

- **A search for help suicide** is seen as a 'cry for help' when all else has failed.

- **Escape suicide** is seen as an escape from a life which has become unbearable.

- **Repentance suicide** is seen as an act of repentance, a means of expressing sorrow for wrongdoing and an attempt to put it right.

- **Self-punishment suicide** is seen as a way of punishing oneself for misdeeds – a self-imposed penalty.

Step 3 The third step is to link these patterns of meaning with the wider beliefs of the culture. For example, in Western culture, suicide is seen as an act of desperation when all else fails. In other cultures it is expected and accepted in certain situations – for example, the suicide of the elderly in nomadic hunting and gathering bands.

Apart from making a few suggestions, Douglas doesn't take Step 3 any further.

Suicide statistics Douglas criticises Durkheim for largely accepting the reliability and validity of official statistics on suicide. He argues that suicide statistics are the result of negotiated meanings and a complex series of social interactions. For example, the family and friends of the victim may do their best to conceal his or her death as suicide. And this, in turn, may influence the coroner to deliver a verdict of accidental death or death by natural causes.

Successful concealment is most likely when the suicide victim is highly integrated into a social group. Friends and family will be concerned to protect the deceased's reputation and standing in the community. As a result, correlations which indicate a relationship between low suicide rates and high integration may simply reflect a link between successful concealment and high integration.

Douglas maintains that an examination of the negotiated meanings which accompany a suicide death are essential for an understanding of suicide statistics. And this, he argues, is what Durkheim failed to do.

Evaluation Jack Douglas offers an alternative view of suicide. It is an act which is defined and given meaning by the victim, their family, friends and acquaintances, and the officials whose job it is to make a judgement on the cause of death. And suicide statistics are socially constructed from these definitions and meanings, and from the negotiations of those involved.

However, as Steve Taylor (1988) argues, there is a contradiction in Douglas' work. At times, Douglas suggests that it is possible for the researcher to discover whether a death really was suicide. If so, it should be possible to produce valid suicide statistics and a valid suicide rate. And from this, it should be possible to discover the causes of suicide.

At other times, Douglas implies that suicide is nothing more than the meanings given to particular deaths. If so, there are no such things as real, objective suicide acts or suicide rates. The job of the sociologist is simply to discover the meanings which people use to define suicide. And there is no reality beyond these meanings.

Discovering suicide

In *Discovering Suicide* (1978), J. Maxwell Atkinson takes the interpretivist position to its extreme. He states quite categorically that suicide is simply a meaning and there is no reality beyond that meaning. This is sometimes known as a *phenomenological* approach. It argues that the phenomenon, the 'thing' being studied, must be studied in its own right. In this case, suicide is nothing more than a meaning and must be treated as such. Suicide statistics are not right or wrong, they simply are. And the job of the sociologist is to discover the meanings used to define suicide and to find out how those meanings are constructed. In Atkinson's words, the question which should direct a sociological investigation of suicide is 'How do deaths get categorised as suicide?'

Research methods Atkinson's research examined the ways in which coroners and coroner's officers classified deaths. It was based on observations of inquests, interviews with coroners in three different towns, an examination of a coroner's records and observations of a coroner's officer at work. Atkinson claims that his findings show that coroners have a 'common-sense theory' of suicide. If the facts fit the theory, then a verdict of suicide is likely.

Primary cues According to Atkinson, coroners begin by looking for 'primary cues' which appear to indicate suicide. They include the following.

- The existence of suicide notes and/or reports of threats of suicide.
- The type of death – 'typical suicide deaths' include gassing, hanging, drowning and drug overdose. Road deaths are unlikely to be seen as suicides.
- The place and circumstances of death – an individual found shot to death in a car parked on a deserted country lane is more likely to be seen as a suicide victim than somebody who shot themselves while climbing over a fence on a pheasant shoot. And gassing is more likely to be seen as suicide if windows and doors have been sealed.

Secondary cues These include the life history of the deceased. According to Atkinson, coroners have a picture of a 'typical suicide biography'. It includes the following.

- A history of mental illness, particularly of depression
- A disturbed childhood
- A recent loss – a divorce or death of a loved one
- Few, if any, friends
- Financial difficulties
- Problems at work.

Categorising suicide According to Atkinson, if the circumstances of death and the life history of the deceased fit the 'typical suicide death' and the 'typical suicide biography' then a verdict of suicide is likely.

Coroners' common-sense theory of suicide contains an explanation of suicide. For example, if the deceased is friendless, has a history of depression and financial difficulties, then they may feel that life is not worth living and commit suicide. In some respects, this is similar to the theories of suicide put forward by sociologists. For example, Durkheim's socially isolated individual fits neatly into the coroners' theory.

According to Atkinson, this comes as no surprise. Sociologists are simply uncovering the meanings used by coroners to reach a verdict of suicide. Since social isolation is seen by coroners as a reason for suicide, then suicide statistics will contain a high proportion of socially isolated individuals.

Evaluation Atkinson's work is a valuable contribution to the study of suicide. He has indicated how coroners see and define particular deaths as suicide. And he has provided evidence to support his claims. However, there are two main criticisms of his research.

First, how come coroners appear to share the same common-sense theories of suicide? Where do the meanings they use to define suicide come from? Atkinson fails to answer these questions. For example, it could be argued that coroners' theories are derived from ideas about suicide in the wider culture.

Second, as Barry Hindess (1973) argues, if suicide statistics are simply based on the interpretations of coroners, then research findings are simply based on the interpretations of sociologists. In terms of Atkinson's logic, the interpretations of coroners are neither right nor wrong, they just are, and the same applies to the interpretations of sociologists.

According to Hindess, this means that there is no 'possibility of an objective knowledge of society'. If this is the case, sociologists may as well pack up and go home.

15.3 Suicide – a realist approach

This section looks at the work of the British sociologist Steve Taylor (1982, 1988). Taylor draws on both Durkheim's realist perspective and the interpretivist approaches of Douglas and Atkinson.

Like Durkheim, Taylor adopts a realist perspective. He argues that sociologists should look for the 'underlying, unobservable structures and causal processes' which lie behind suicide acts. However, he parts company from Durkheim, claiming that 'official suicide rates are a most inappropriate source of data for sociological research'.

Taylor agrees with Douglas that the case study – studies of particular suicide acts – is the most appropriate research method for studying suicide. He argues that suicide cannot be understood 'without reference to the actor's intentions' and their immediate social situations. And this means examining individual cases. However, he parts company with Douglas' implication and Atkinson's claim that suicide is simply a social construction – a meaning which develops from social interaction. People do kill themselves. And it is the sociologist's job to explain their actions.

*activity*30 *interpreting suicide*

Item A **Terminal illness**

A young man jumps to his death suffering from an incurable disease.

Item B **Salvation**

A young woman burns to death praying for forgiveness for her sins.

Item C *Reasons for suicide*

A young man killed himself because his bride of four months wanted a divorce so she could marry his brother. He left a message to his wife which began, 'I used to love you, but I die hating you and my brother too'. The day before he died, he said to his wife and brother, 'I can do you more harm dead than alive'.

Source: Douglas, 1967

Item D *Contemplating suicide*

Item E *Homeless, friendless, deserted*

The Maniac Father and The Convict Brother Are Gone – The Poor Girl, Homeless, Friendless, Deserted, Destitute and Gin Mad, Commits Self Murder.

questions

1 Which of Douglas' types of suicide do Items A, B and C illustrate?
2 How does Item D illustrate 'typical suicide deaths'?
3 How does Item E indicate a 'typical suicide biography'?

Persons under trains

Around five people a month die under London Transport trains. London Transport keeps records of each case and files them under 'People under Trains'. Taylor (1982) studied 32 cases, 17 of which resulted in a verdict of suicide. He attended inquests in coroner's courts in order to discover how these verdicts were reached. His evidence shows that coroners focused on the following aspects of the deceased.

State of mind Coroners call one or two witnesses who knew the dead person. If they indicate that the deceased was depressed, anxious or withdrawn, this was seen as a possible reason for suicide. In general, the closer the witness to the deceased, the more likely they were to resist a suggestion of suicide. For example, one witness insisted that his brother had nothing 'preying on his mind'.

Mental and physical health Coroners tend to see suicide as a result of mental or physical illness. There were eight cases where people had been patients in mental hospitals – seven were recorded as suicides. There were two cases of severe physical illness – both were recorded as suicides.

Social problems Coroners looked for social problems –

marital difficulties, failing careers, financial problems. On their own, these were not seen as sufficient causes for suicide. However, combined with negative states of mind or serious illness, they may well be seen as a reason for suicide.

Life history Coroners looked for evidence of a broken home, a failure to form lasting relationships, drug taking and crime. Again, on their own, these were not sufficient for a suicide verdict.

Conclusion Taylor argues that coroners attempt to reconstruct a suicide biography on the basis of their beliefs about the likely causes of suicide. If the deceased fits, then a verdict of suicide is likely.

However, Taylor rejects Atkinson's view that suicide is nothing more than a social construction based on coroners' definitions and meanings. Instead, he argues that these meanings produce a systematic bias in official statistics. As a result, deaths officially defined as suicides are an unrepresentative sample. We should therefore be highly sceptical of the reliability and validity of suicide rates. In view of this, sociologists should look to alternative sources of data for studying suicide.

A realist theory of suicide

Steve Taylor (1982) developed a theory of suicide based on case studies. Using a range of specific cases from a variety of sources, he attempted to discover the underlying causes of suicide.

Defining suicide acts The main sociological studies of suicide have focused on 'genuine' and 'successful' suicides – on people who actually killed themselves. Taylor argues for a broader definition. He notes that the vast majority of suicides fall between two extremes.

● At one extreme are people who are determined to die and make every effort to kill themselves.

● At the other extreme are those who make suicidal gestures and ensure there is little chance of death.

Suicide acts are not simply aimed at death. For example, they may be designed to communicate the person's feelings to others with a real possibility of survival.

Taylor argues that a wider definition of suicide is needed in order to explain the broad spectrum of suicidal behaviour. He therefore defines a suicide act as 'any deliberate act of self-damage, or potential self-damage, where the individual cannot be sure of survival' (Taylor, 1988).

Taylor's realist theory argues that the *underlying* motivation for suicidal behaviour arises from imbalances in individuals' sense of their own identity and in their relationships with others.

Certainty and uncertainty Taylor argues that for an individual to lead a normal life – that is without thoughts of suicide – they require a balance between certainty and uncertainty about themselves and the world around them. Certainty is about stability and the predictability of events, uncertainty is about change and the unexpected. Taylor hypothesises that suicide is more likely in situations of complete certainty and complete uncertainty.

Submissive suicides/certainty suicides Taylor uses the term *submissive suicide* to refer to suicide acts where the individual feels they know everything worth knowing. They are *certain* about the future – there is no hope, no light at the end of the tunnel. In one sense they are already dead, life is already over.

Suicide acts which stem from certainty are wholehearted, determined attempts to die. The individual is 'embracing death from a firm conviction that nothing further remains in life'. For example, a 62-year-old woman with a terminal illness said, 'I'm through, I'm whipped. I can't take it any longer. I will not die a lingering death'. And an elderly widower who committed suicide to rejoin his dead wife felt that without her he *was* dead.

Thanatation/uncertainty suicide Uncertainty suicides, which Taylor calls *Thanatation*, are the opposite end of the spectrum from submissive suicides. The individual is tortured by uncertainty – about themselves, their identity, what others think about them and the meaning of their existence. They feel that it's impossible to go on living until this uncertainty is resolved. The individual demands an answer from suicide to reveal whether they are intended to go on living.

Suicide acts which stem from complete uncertainty are a gamble with life. For example, the poet Sylvia Plath deliberately drove her car off the road knowing it *might* kill her. She survived and felt validated, qualified to live – she felt really alive. Similarly, the novelist Graham Greene felt exhilarated when he survived a game of Russian roulette – 'I remember an extraordinary sense of jubilation, as if carnival lights had been switched on in a dark drab street'.

Ectopia and inner-directed suicides Thanatation and submissive suicide result from a state of mind which Taylor calls ectopic. It involves a psychological detachment or moral insulation from the feelings, opinions and actions of others. Sylvia Plath described her sense of detachment as being trapped in a bell jar. In a famous case study of suicide, Ellen West says, 'I feel excluded from all real life. I sit in a glass ball'.

In cases of submissive suicide, this detachment means that others cannot dissuade the individual from what they already know – they cannot shake their certainty. And in Thanatation, detachment means that others cannot tell the individual what they want to know – they cannot remove their uncertainty. Detachment means that Thanatation and submissive suicide are inner-directed acts. They are private and self-contained since those concerned have no sense of attachment to others.

Taylor argues that suicide acts result from 'a *combination* of detachment from others *and* uncertainty about one's existence, *or* a certainty that one's life is over'.

Symphysis and other-directed suicides In situations which Taylor calls symphysic, suicide acts are directed by an overriding attachment to others. The individual has no real existence apart from others, requiring their love and respect as a basis for their sense of self.

Suicide acts directed by symphysic situations are other-directed – they are a communication to somebody. There are two types – appeal suicides and sacrifice suicides.

Appeal suicides These are a cry for help to those to whom they are strongly attached. *Appeal suicides* are accompanied by considerable uncertainty – the individual has serious doubts about the significance of their existence to others. Appeal suicides are often preceded by warnings, threats and pleas. To end the uncertainty, the individual gambles with their life.

Appeal suicide is illustrated by the following case study. A 19-year-old girl was having an affair with a married man. When he returned to his pregnant wife, she became very distressed and took an overdose of barbiturates. She wandered out on to the street and was taken to hospital. Later, when asked if she intended to kill herself, she said, 'I don't know. Not really I suppose, but I couldn't see any other way of getting through to him.'

Sacrifice suicides Like appeal suicides, *sacrifice suicides* are directed by a powerful attachment to others. However in this case, there is no uncertainty. The individual is certain that they have no alternative to suicide – they are therefore determined to kill themselves. They have either done something which makes it impossible to live with a person to whom they are deeply attached. Or, the other person has done something to them which completely destroys the relationship.

Taylor illustrates sacrifice suicide with the example, given in Activity 30, of the young man whose wife of four months wanted a divorce so that she could marry his brother. He loved and trusted both his wife and his brother. He saw no way of repairing his relationships with either of them. In his words, left in a note, 'I sentence myself to die for having been fool enough to ever have loved anyone as contemptible as my wife has proven to be'.

Conclusion and evaluation

Steve Taylor has taken a realist approach which seeks to reveal the 'underlying rules of suicidal action'. He tries to show how a wide and complex variety of suicide acts result from four 'general states of meaning' – a sense of certainty or uncertainty and a sense of attachment to others or detachment from others. The four possible combinations of these states of meaning result in four types of suicide – Thanatation, submissive, appeal and sacrifice. This is shown in Figure 8.

Evaluation Taylor's theory has the advantage of covering both completed and attempted suicide. It includes the contribution of others to the suicide act and the communication to others of the intention to commit suicide. His theory is comprehensive in the sense that it claims to cover all types of suicide.

Taylor identifies two main problems with his research (Taylor, personal communication, 2004). First, case studies do not provide a representative sample of suicide acts. Second, he fails to develop his theory to include the wider society. To move to the societal level of causality, Taylor needs to ask what kinds of society produce high levels of certainty and uncertainty, attachment and detachment. Including the wider society would complete his theoretical model.

Despite these problems, Taylor has produced an elegant and original theory.

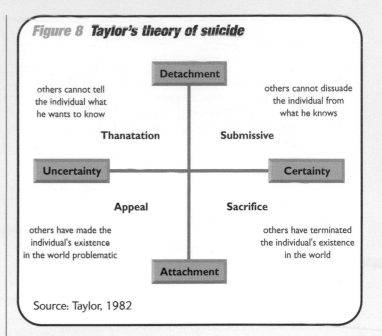

Figure 8 Taylor's theory of suicide

Source: Taylor, 1982

key terms

Submissive suicide A type of suicide that arises from certainty and detachment. The individual is certain that there is no hope for the future.

Thanatation A type of suicide that arises from uncertainty and detachment. The individual demands an answer from suicide to resolve their uncertainty.

Appeal suicide A type of suicide that arises from uncertainty and attachment. The individual has serious doubts about the significance of their life to others.

Sacrifice suicide A type of suicide that arises from certainty and attachment. A deep attachment has been broken and the individual is certain that they cannot live with this situation.

summary

1. On the basis of official statistics, Emile Durkheim found that suicide rates varied between different countries, between different groups within the same country and over time.

2. Durkheim identified four types of suicide, each of which is related to the level of integration or the level of regulation in society.
   - Altruistic suicide occurs when the level of integration is too strong.
   - Egoistic suicide occurs when the level of integration is too weak.
   - Fatalistic suicide occurs when the level of regulation is too strong.
   - Anomic suicide occurs when the level of regulation is too weak.

3. Durkheim claimed that both suicide rates and types of suicide were shaped by social facts – by the levels of integration and regulation in society.

4. Durkheim's methodology is usually seen as a realist approach. He looked for the invisible underlying causes of the relationships between the things he observed.

5. Critics argue that Durkheim paid insufficient attention to the validity and reliability of official statistics.

6. Positivists reject the realist view that causes can be found in underlying structures and processes that cannot be directly observed and measured.

7. From an interpretivist viewpoint, Jack Douglas argues that the first step in studying suicide is to interpret how individuals who commit suicide define and give meaning to their action.

8. Douglas argues that this is essential in order to classify suicides into types.

9. Douglas sees suicide statistics as the result of negotiated meanings within a complex series of social interactions.

10. J. Maxwell Atkinson states that suicide is simply a meaning and there is no reality beyond that meaning.

11. His research indicates that coroners have pictures of a 'typical suicide death' and a 'typical suicide biography'. The closer the death and the life history of the deceased to these pictures, the greater the likelihood of a suicide verdict.

12. Barry Hindess argues that the logic of Atkinson's methodology means that there is no 'possibility of an objective knowledge of society'.

13. Steve Taylor adopts a realist perspective, arguing that sociologists should look for the 'underlying, unobservable structures and causal processes' which lie behind suicide acts.

14. Taylor agrees with Douglas that the case study is the most appropriate research method for studying suicide.

15. Taylor's theory argues that the underlying motivation for suicide acts arises from imbalances in individuals' sense of their own identity (too much certainty or too much uncertainty) and in their relationships with other (too much attachment to, or too much detachment from, others).

16. Taylor identifies two main problems with his research.
   - Case studies do not provide a representative sample of suicide acts.
   - He fails to develop his theory to include the wider society – for example, what kinds of society produce high levels of certainty or uncertainty.

4 Methodology

Introduction

Methodology refers to the whole research process – to the methods used to collect data, to the analysis of the data, and to the theories which underlie both.

At its simplest, methodology refers to research methods such as interviews and questionnaires. What are their strengths and weaknesses, how good is the data they produce? These questions were examined in *Sociology in Focus for AQA AS Level*.

At the other extreme, methodology deals with philosophical questions such as the nature of knowledge. How can we say that one statement is true and another false? How can we 'know' anything? This chapter examines some of the attempts to answer such questions.

The scientific method - one view of methodology

chaptersummary

▶ **Unit 1** looks at ways of assessing the validity and reliability of research data.

▶ **Unit 2** examines various views of science and their application to sociological research.

▶ **Unit 3** looks at interpretivist methodology.

▶ **Unit 4** looks at postmodernist methodology.

▶ **Unit 5** looks at feminist methodology.

▶ **Unit 6** considers the relationship between values and sociological research.

▶ **Unit 7** examines the relationship between sociology and social policy.

Unit 1 Assessing research findings

keyissues

1 How valid and reliable are research findings?

2 Do researchers affect the data they collect?

3 What are the advantages of combining various research methods and types of data?

Sociological research methods were outlined and evaluated in *Sociology in Focus for AQA AS Level*. This unit takes a more general view of the research process. It asks how good are research findings and how do we know?

1.1 Quantitative and qualitative methods and data

Quantitative data is data in a numerical form – in the form of numbers. Official statistics are an obvious example. Questionnaires and structured interviews are the usual research methods used to obtain quantitative data. Their responses can often be fairly easily translated into numbers.

Some researchers argue that unless human behaviour is expressed in numerical terms, it cannot be accurately measured. Without accurate measurement conclusions will be based on impressions and as such will be little more than unsupported opinion.

Qualitative data covers a range of material from the descriptions of social life provided by participant observation and unstructured interviews to information from written sources such as diaries, autobiographies and novels. Some researchers argue that qualitative data provides greater depth, a richer and more detailed picture of social life. It is more likely to capture the subtleties, nuances and shades of meaning than the numerical data provided by quantitative methods.

Use of the contrast quantitative/qualitative implies either/or and better/worse – that researchers use and favour either one or other type of data. In practice, most researchers use both kinds of data, recognising their strengths and weaknesses and seeing them as suited to different purposes. For example, the findings of a small-scale participant observation study can form the basis for a questionnaire used in a large-scale social survey. And, as we shall see shortly, quantitative and qualitative data can be used together as 1) a means of checking the other and 2) building up a more complete picture of social life.

1.2 Validity and reliability

Validity refers to the accuracy of a description or measurement. Data is valid if it gives a true picture of a way of life or an accurate measurement of something. For example, official statistics on crime are valid if they provide an accurate measurement of the extent of crime.

Some researchers argue that qualitative data with its depth and richness is more likely than quantitative data to provide a valid picture of social life. However, methods used to collect qualitative data, such as participant observation, rely heavily on the interpretive skills of the researcher. It is therefore difficult to assess the validity of the data they produce. Possible ways of doing this will be examined shortly.

Reliability Research methods and data are reliable when different researchers using the same methods obtain similar results. For example, if the same questionnaire and the same sampling procedure produce similar results when used by different researchers, then the methods and the data are reliable. A reliable method allows studies to be replicated, that is repeated.

1.3 Triangulation

Triangulation is a term used to describe various ways of assessing the validity and reliability of research methods and data (Denzin, 1970). It looks at the topic under investigation from different angles and vantage points. Triangulation can take various forms. These include:

1 Investigator triangulation This involves the use of different researchers, for example, different observers and interviewers. The aim is to check for observer and interviewer bias by, for example, using interviewers from different social backgrounds.

2 Data triangulation This involves collecting data at different times from different people in different places. It can also involve combining primary and secondary data. Data triangulation serves as a cross-check for validity. It can also serve as a means of assessing researchers' interpretations and conclusions.

3 Methodological triangulation This takes two forms. 'Within-method' triangulation uses a variety of techniques within the same method, for example open and closed questions within a questionnaire. Asking similar questions in a variety of ways can check on the validity of the answers and the reliability of the method. 'Between-method' triangulation refers to the combination of a number of research methods, for example questionnaires, unstructured interviews and participant observation. The

data produced by each method can be checked by comparing it with the data produced by the other methods.

The idea of triangulation is illustrated by the following quotation from *Belfast in the 30s: An oral history* (quoted in Macdonald & Tipton, 1993).

'In the first place we carried out ... "investigator triangulation". That is, each transcript was checked by two or three researchers to ensure that it said what people had meant to say. In the second place, we systematically did a cross-method triangulation, in that every piece of oral evidence that could be, was checked against a range of written sources: newspapers, parliamentary reports, documents etc. Finally, there was a considerable amount of data triangulation possible within the oral sources themselves' (Munck & Rolston, 1987).

1.4 Reflexivity

A White male middle-class researcher – and most of them are – will tend to see the social world he studies through White male middle-class eyes. And, to some extent, he will be seen by those he studies in terms of his social identity which will influence the way they respond to him. In these respects social research is *reflexive* – it reflects and is shaped by the researcher.

As a researcher, our findings will be coloured by our social background, our experiences and our culture. What we see and how we interpret it will be influenced by the fact that we are social beings. Social research involves social relationships. To some extent those being studied will be influenced by the presence of the researcher.

The idea of reflexivity also refers to a recognition, an awareness, that research is reflexive. This awareness means that, as researchers, we should be critical of ourselves, our research and our findings. We should examine ourselves in order to discover to what extent our findings reflect our own beliefs and values. We should question whether our presence affects the actions of those we study. This critical awareness will help us get nearer to our goal – a valid picture of social reality. (The influence of values on research is examined in Unit 6.)

Assessing validity How do sociologists attempt to minimise their influence on research? How do they try to ensure the validity of their data? Some of the ways of assessing research findings have been discussed under the heading of triangulation. Some others will now be examined.

Asking the researched In his study of an Italian American gang in Boston, William Whyte (1955) discussed his findings with Doc, the leader of the gang. Doc assessed Whyte's interpretation of the gang's behaviour from an insider's viewpoint.

Playing the part Aaron Cicourel (1976) spent four years studying probation officers in California. Part of this time was spent as an unpaid probation officer. His aim was to discover the meanings used by probation officers to define young people as delinquent. Cicourel claimed that by learning to play the part of a probation officer, he was able to identify the same young people as delinquents as his full time colleagues. This provided support for his interpretation of the meanings that *they* used to define delinquency.

Presenting the data In *The Social Organisation of Juvenile Justice*, the published report of his findings, Cicourel presents lengthy extracts from conversations between probation officers and juveniles along with detailed descriptions of their interaction. Although this presentation is selective – it represents only a small part of his field notes – it gives others some opportunity to assess Cicourel's interpretation of the data.

Comparing results Researchers often compare their findings with those of others who have conducted similar research. This comparison encourages them to question their results and to assess to what extent their findings reflect their research methods and their own beliefs and values.

Critical self-awareness None of the above methods is foolproof but they do encourage a critical self-awareness which can only assist the quest for validity. Recognising the reflexive nature of social research is an important step forward. (Units 4, 5 and 6 develop this point.)

Dialogic research

Awareness of reflexivity has led some sociologists to examine the relationship between researchers and those they research. They argue that this relationship is unequal. The researcher directs operations, decides what's important, what questions to ask, who to ask, and who to observe – when, where and for how long. The voices of the researched can be lost in this process, and so can the validity of the research findings. A possible solution to this problem is *dialogic research*.

Dialogic research involves a dialogue between researcher and researched. It is about the researcher letting go of power and inviting the researched to set the agenda, to decide what's important and how to express it (Puwar, 2001).

Phil Cohen's (1996-97) research on youth in East London provides an example of the dialogic method. Some of the young people were given cameras and tape recorders and asked to record their social world in their own way. As a result, the researched also became the researchers.

activity1 triangulation

Carolyn Hoyle's research examined how the police dealt with domestic violence. She used a variety of methods – 'interviews with police officers and victims, observation of officers on duty, and examination of official records were all used to understand the police response to incidents of domestic violence'.

She interviewed victims *after* she had interviewed police officers 'partly to ensure that the police officers had given me an accurate version of the incident and of the wishes of the victims'. She used semi-structured interviews which produced 'quantitative data and qualitative descriptions'.

In discussions with the researcher and talking amongst themselves, police officers sometimes trivialised domestic violence. Dealing with 'domestics' was more trouble than it was worth, it was exasperating because they were 'so griefy'. These comments may reflect the 'canteen culture' of police stations where officers get things off their chests and put on a show of bravado. But, when asked about specific incidents, their replies contradicted these comments. They said they listened carefully to both sides in the dispute and had done their best to deal sympathetically and effectively with the situation. These claims were supported by Carolyn Hoyle's direct observation of officers dealing with domestic violence.

Source: Hoyle, 2000

Canteen culture

question

1   In what ways can Hoyle's research be seen as an example of triangulation?
2   With reference to Hoyle's research, outline the advantages of triangulation.

Dialogic research offers an opportunity to capture people's outlook, priorities, hopes and anxieties with a minimum of intrusion by the 'official' researcher. This concern is often reflected in feminist research – see pages 241-243.

1.5 Methodological pluralism

Methodological pluralism is similar to triangulation and can serve a similar purpose. However, its aim is not so much as a means of checking validity and reliability but rather to build up a fuller picture of social life by combining different research methods and different types of data. It recognises that each method and type of data has its particular strengths and weaknesses. Combined they are seen to produce a more comprehensive and rounder picture of social reality. And their combination can also provide new insights and new directions for research.

Some of the strengths of methodological pluralism can be seen from Eileen Barker's (1984) study of the Moonies – the Unification Church. She conducted in-depth interviews, each lasting 6-8 hours, with a number of Moonies. The interviews dealt with their background, why they became a Moonie, their life in the church and the meaning of religion as they saw it. Barker also lived as a participant observer in several centres with the Moonies at various times during the six years of her research. This enabled her to gain the trust of many members of the church, resulting in information which would not have been given to an outsider. Two years after the start of her research, she constructed a large (41-page) questionnaire based on her findings from interviews and observation. This provided

key terms

Quantitative data Numerical data – data in the form of numbers.

Qualitative data All types of data that are not in the form of numbers.

Validity Data is valid if it presents a true and accurate description or measurement.

Reliability Data is reliable when different researchers using the same methods obtain the same results, ie the same description or measurement.

Triangulation Using different researchers and/or combining different research methods and different types of data in order to check the validity and reliability of findings.

Reflexivity The idea that the findings of social research are shaped by the researcher – by their beliefs and values, by their meanings and interpretations, and by the relationships they develop with research participants.

Dialogic research Research that involves a dialogue between researcher and researched, that allows those being studied to directly participate in the research process.

Methodological pluralism Combining different research methods and different kinds of data in order to build up a fuller picture of social life.

information from a larger sample and was intended to reveal 'social patterns, trends and tendencies and gain a more reliable understanding of regularities between variables - of "what goes with what"'.

Barker claims that combining different methods of investigation gave her a much fuller picture than any one method or data source could have provided.

summary

1. Many researchers use both quantitative and qualitative data, while recognising the strengths and weaknesses of each.

2. Triangulation provides a way of assessing the validity and reliability of research findings. It takes three main forms:
   - Investigator triangulation
   - Data triangulation
   - Methodological triangulation.

3. Social research is reflexive – to some extent it reflects and is shaped by the researcher. This can seriously affect the validity of research findings.

4. Dialogic research may improve the validity of research findings. It offers research participants the opportunity to take part in the direction of the research – to set the agenda, to decide what's important and even conduct their own research. This allows the voices of the researched to be heard.

5. Apart from triangulation and an awareness of reflexivity, there are various ways of assessing the validity of research findings. They include:
   - Asking research participants if the researcher has got it right
   - Playing the part – successfully acting out the role of those being studied
   - Presenting the data – providing sufficient data for others to make a judgement about its validity
   - Comparing research findings with the results of similar studies.

6. Methodological pluralism combines different research methods and different kinds of data with the aim of producing a more detailed, in-depth and comprehensive picture of social life.

Unit 2 *Sociology and science*

keyissues

1 What is science? What are scientific methods?

2 Are the methods and assumptions of the natural sciences appropriate to the study of human behaviour?

Sociology is often referred to as a *social science*. Whether or not it can be seen as a scientific discipline is one of the major debates within the subject. The founding fathers of sociology in the 19th century were, however, in no doubt. By following the rules and logic of the scientific method, sociology could discover the laws underlying the development of human society. And, in this respect, it was a science just like the *natural sciences* of physics and chemistry which seek to discover the laws underlying the behaviour of matter.

2.1 Auguste Comte – positivism

Auguste Comte (1798-1857) is credited with inventing the term sociology. He argued that sociology should be based on the methodology of the natural sciences. This would result in a 'positive science of society' which would reveal the 'invariable laws' which governed the evolution of human society. Comte's approach is known as *positivism*.

Comte insisted that only directly observable 'facts' were acceptable as evidence in his science of society. Anything that couldn't be directly measured, such as subjective meanings and purposes, was ruled out. The facts of society must be objectively measured and quantified, that is, put into a numerical form. It would then be possible to identify cause and effect relationships and discover the laws underlying social evolution.

2.2 Emile Durkheim – the rules of sociological method

Social facts In *The Rules of Sociological Method*, first published in 1895, Durkheim outlined the logic and methods to be followed for sociology to become a science of society. The starting point, 'the first and most fundamental rule is: Consider social facts as things'. *Social facts* are the institutions, beliefs and values of society. As things, social facts can be treated in the same way as the objects, events and processes of the natural world. They can be objectively measured, quantified and subjected to statistical analysis. Correlations can be drawn between social facts, cause and effect relationships established and theories developed to explain those relationships. In this way 'real laws are discoverable' in the social world as in the natural world.

But how can social facts be treated as things? Aren't

beliefs, for example, part of human consciousness? And aren't human beings, because they have consciousness, fundamentally different from the inanimate objects which make up the natural world? In view of this, is natural science methodology appropriate for the study of human behaviour?

External reality Durkheim accepted that social facts form part of our consciousness – they have to for society to exist. Without shared norms and values, for example, society could not operate. But, although they are a part of us, social facts also exist outside of us. In Durkheim's words, 'collective ways of acting and thinking have a reality outside the individuals'. Members of society do not simply act in terms of their particular psychology and personal beliefs. Instead they are directed to act by social facts, by values and beliefs which are over and above the individual and part of the wider society. In this respect social facts 'have a reality outside the individuals' and can therefore be studied 'objectively as external things'.

Thus just as matter is constrained to act by natural forces, so human beings are constrained to act by social forces. Given this, social facts can be studied using the methodology of the natural sciences.

The social facts of suicide Durkheim's *Suicide: A Study in Sociology* was published in 1897. This study exemplified his rules of sociological method. Durkheim argued that the causes of suicide rates (the number of suicides per million of the population) are to be found in society, *not* in the psychology of individuals. Suicide rates are social facts. They are also a product of social facts, of 'real, living, active forces which, because of the way they determine the individual, prove their independence from him'.

Statistical evidence Durkheim examined official statistics on suicide from a number of European countries (see Activity 2, Item A, page 233). He found that 1) suicide rates within each country were fairly constant over a number of years and 2) there were significant differences in the rates both between societies and between social groups within the same society.

Correlation and analysis Durkheim found correlations between suicide rates and a wide range of social facts. For example, he found statistical relationships between suicide rates and religion, location, age and family situation. Some of these are illustrated in the following table. In each of the pairs, the group on the left had a higher suicide rate than the group on the right.

Protestants	–	Catholics
City dwellers	–	Rural dwellers
Older adults	–	Younger adults
Unmarried	–	Married
Married without children	–	Married with children

Causation Having established correlations between social facts, Durkheim's next task was to see if he could discover causal connections. He argued that variations in suicide rates were caused by variations in levels of social integration that is the extent to which individuals are part of a wider social group. In the case of the examples given above, the groups on the left have lower levels of social integration than the groups on the right. For example, older adults are less socially integrated than younger adults because their children have grown up and left home, many of their friends and relatives have died, and if they have retired from work they may well have lost touch with their workmates. Using examples such as this, Durkheim claimed that 'suicide varies inversely with the degree of integration of the social groups of which the individual forms a part' – that is, the higher an individual's social integration the less likely they are to take their own life.

Theory and explanation Durkheim's final task was to explain why suicide rates vary with levels of social integration. Part of his explanation runs as follows. As members of society, people are social beings – they have been socialised to play a part in society. The greater their social isolation the less they can participate in society. Their lives lack meaning and purpose unless they are shared with others. In Durkheim's words, 'The individual alone is not a sufficient end for his activity. He is too little.' In a situation of social isolation, 'the individual yields to the slightest shock of circumstance because the state of society has made him ready prey to suicide'.

Durkheim doesn't claim to explain all aspects of suicide. For example, he does not explain why only a small minority of socially isolated individuals commit suicide. He sees this as the job of the psychologist because it concerns individual behaviour rather than social facts.

Durkheim believed that his research on suicide proved that scientific methodology was appropriate for the study of society, because it had shown that 'real laws are discoverable'. (For further discussion of Durkheim's study of suicide see pages 214-218. For a broader discussion of Durkheim's view of society, see pages 262-265).

2.3 Karl Popper – deduction and falsification

Induction vs. deduction Durkheim argued that theories should come from evidence, from gathering data, from describing, classifying and analysing social facts. It is from this process that theories are generated. This is known as an *inductive* approach.

A *deductive* approach reverses this process. It begins with a theory and uses data to test that theory. This is the approach advocated by Karl Popper. From his viewpoint it is the only way science can proceed.

Falsification According to Popper, rather than looking for evidence to confirm their theories, scientists should do their best to disprove or falsify them. This is the distinguishing characteristic of science – the development of theories which can be tested against evidence and be capable of *falsification*.

This means that theories must be constructed in such a way that falsification is possible. Popper argues that Marx's theory of history fails in this respect – it cannot be falsified and is therefore non-scientific. In particular, it fails to specify precisely what has to happen before the proletarian revolution occurs in capitalist society. And when the revolution does not happen, Marxists simply push its coming further and further into the future, thus preventing the possibility of falsification.

Popper rejects the search for laws governing the evolution of human society, which he sees as a 'unique historical process' (1959). However, he sees no reason why the methodology of the natural sciences cannot be applied to the social sciences. Theories of human behaviour which are open to the possibility of falsification can be developed.

Theories that survive falsification tests, however, are not necessarily true. They have simply not been falsified. The following oft-quoted example illustrates this point. 'All swans are white' is a scientific statement because it can be falsified. But, however many times it is confirmed by observation, it cannot be accepted as true because the very next swan might be black, red, blue or yellow. In this respect, there are no absolute truths in science.

Sociology and falsification Despite Popper's claim to the contrary, there are real problems in applying his model of scientific methodology to the study of human society. In the closed system of the laboratory where variables such as matter, temperature and pressure can be controlled, it may be possible to falsify a theory. However, human societies are open systems which means it is impossible to control variables. Because of this, it is difficult to see how a theory can be falsified.

2.4 Thomas Kuhn – normal science

For Durkheim, science consists of accumulating evidence and developing theories from that evidence. For Popper, science consists of creating testable theories and attempting to falsify them. For Thomas Kuhn *normal science* – the vast majority of work which is called science – differs from both these views. Kuhn's *The Structure of Scientific Revolutions* (1962) argues that the way science has developed bears little relationship to conventional views of the scientific method.

Paradigms According to Kuhn, most of the time scientists are busily preoccupied with 'normal science'. Normal science operates within a *paradigm*. A paradigm is a framework of concepts and theories which states how the natural world operates. It identifies appropriate methods for studying that world and specifies what questions to ask and how to answer them. A paradigm is shared by members of the scientific community. It shapes the way they see the world they study.

In some respects paradigms are like blinkers – they place limits on inquiry, they erect barriers to alternative views, they restrict the scientific imagination. This is because normal science operates within the confines of a paradigm – developing and refining it but not challenging it. For example, until the 16th century Western astronomy was based on the theory of terracentricity – the idea that planets and the sun move around the earth. It is perfectly possible to confirm this idea with observations and measurements. And it is also possible to ignore or explain away contradictory evidence which might challenge it. So committed are scientists to the existing paradigm that they operate within it rather than attempting to falsify it.

Scientific revolutions Kuhn rejects the conventional view which sees science as a progressive accumulation of knowledge based on the testing and proving and disproving of hypotheses. Change does occur, but only when one paradigm is replaced by another. Kuhn calls this process a *scientific revolution* – it is sudden and revolutionary as a whole way of thinking about the world is swept away within a relatively short period of time. An example is the replacement of Newton's paradigm in physics with Einstein's. Once a new paradigm is established, normal science resumes and any real change has to wait until the next scientific revolution.

Scientific revolutions occur when evidence accumulates which cannot be explained in terms of the existing paradigm. This evidence accumulates to the point where it cannot be ignored, dismissed as an anomaly or as the result of incorrect observation and measurement. This happened with the Copernican revolution in astronomy in the 16th century. Copernicus stated that the sun, not the earth was the centre of the universe and that the planets orbited the sun. This view of the universe appeared to make sense of observations that could not be explained in terms of the previous paradigm.

Kuhn's view of paradigms and scientific revolutions has been criticised as a distortion of the history of science. For example, Lakatos (1970) rejects the view that normal science is dominated by a single paradigm. Instead, he sees the development of science as a history of constantly competing paradigms.

Sociology and paradigms In terms of Kuhn's view of science it has been argued that sociology is in a pre-paradigmatic and therefore pre-scientific situation. There is a range of competing sociological perspectives and there is little indication that this variety will develop into a single paradigm which will be acceptable to the sociological community. However, in terms of Lakatos' view, this does not disqualify sociology from being a science. In fact, sociology's history of competing perspectives largely accords with his view of the history of science.

2.5 The realist approach to science

The *realist* view of science, while accepting that there are basic differences between the social and natural worlds, maintains that a social science is possible. It argues that events in both the social and natural worlds are produced by underlying structures and mechanisms. According to Roy Bhaskar, the essential task of realism is to uncover and explain these structures and mechanisms (Bhaskar, 1978).

Open and closed systems Andrew Sayer (1992) distinguishes between open and closed systems as arenas of study. The laboratory is the prime example of a *closed system*. Sciences like physics and chemistry have the advantage of being able to create closed systems in which conditions can be fixed and variables controlled. This allows them to reveal 'more clearly the operation of mechanisms' (Sayer, 1992).

However, a large body of scientific research takes place within *open systems* where it is not possible to control variables. Meteorology is an example of a natural science where closed systems are rare. As a result, it is unable to predict the weather with any degree of accuracy, as daily weather forecasts indicate. However, it is able to offer an explanation of the weather after the event in terms of underlying mechanisms. In much the same way, geology is able to provide explanations for the occurrence of oil deposits. However, geologists' attempts to predict its presence have only limited success as the billions of dollars spent on unsuccessful oil exploration show.

One of the most famous non-predictive explanations is the theory of evolution, which specifies mechanisms such as natural selection and mutation which are seen to underlie the evolutionary process. But, because evolution takes place within an open system it is not possible to predict its future.

Human behaviour takes place in open systems. Because of this it is not possible to predict its course with any degree of accuracy. There is no way of controlling all the variables which affect human action. However, from a realist viewpoint, this does not rule out a social science. It is still possible to explain human behaviour in terms of underlying structures and mechanisms, just as

The landlord-tenant structure

Source: Sayer, 1992

meteorologists, geologists and evolutionary biologists explain behaviour in the natural world.

Structures, mechanisms and consciousness From a realist point of view, human behaviour operates within structures. Sayer (1992) defines structures as 'sets of internally related objects and practices'. He gives the following example using the landlord-tenant relation. The diagram illustrates the necessary relations for its existence. In Sayer's words, 'The landlord-tenant relation itself presupposes the existence of private property, rent, the production of economic surplus and so on; together they form a structure'. There are of course structures within structures. For example, the landlord-tenant structure forms part of the wider class structure in capitalist society.

Structures constrain human behaviour, they place limits on human action. However, this does not mean that human beings are simply directed by structural constraints. In the open system which is human society, they have varying degrees of freedom to direct their own actions. Realists include consciousness as part of the explanation for behaviour. They accept the interpretivist view of social reality as socially constructed. And they also accept the Marxist view of false consciousness – that socially constructed meanings can distort reality (Blaikie, 1993).

Mechanisms operate within structures. It is part of the scientist's job to identify these mechanisms and explain how they work. And in this respect the social scientist's job is the same as the natural scientist's. So just as an evolutionary biologist identifies mechanisms such as natural selection to account for biological change, so a sociologist identifies mechanisms such as the class struggle to account for social change.

Realism, sociology and science From a realist viewpoint, events in both the natural and social worlds are produced by structures and mechanisms. Given this, social science is based on the same principles as natural science. Both are concerned with the identification and explanation of structures and mechanisms.

2.6 Sociology and science – conclusion

Objectivity The traditional picture of a scientist is of a rational, logical researcher who collects and explains 'facts'. In terms of the research process, he or she is objective, value-free and unbiased. The 'facts' are undistorted and uncontaminated – they are not coloured by the beliefs, experiences and values of the researcher.

Unit 1 has argued that, as far as sociology is concerned, this view of the researcher and the research process is a myth. Whether this disqualifies sociology as a science is a matter of opinion. Researchers in the natural sciences are also influenced by their beliefs and values. Kuhn's view of science suggests that the concepts and theories which make up paradigms are, in part, articles of faith – they include many of the common-sense beliefs of the time, for example, the belief that the earth is the centre of the universe.

These points are developed in Unit 6, Sociology,

methodology and values, which asks:

● Is an objective, value-free sociology possible?
● And, is it desirable?

Natural and social science The natural and social sciences study different things. The natural sciences study matter which behaves in a predictable manner in a given situation. Matter simply reacts to a particular stimulus. There is no need for the natural scientist to interpret meanings and motives and discover beliefs and values in order to explain the behaviour of matter.

The same is not true for sociologists. Human beings define situations and act accordingly. They give meanings to events and act in terms of those meanings. And the beliefs and values they hold direct their behaviour. In view of this, sociologists have to discover definitions, meanings, beliefs and values in order to understand human action.

This has led many sociologists to argue that natural science methods are not suitable for the study of human behaviour. Interpreting meanings is very different from observing inanimate objects. And if sociology is seen as a science, then it is a very different science from the likes of physics and chemistry.

These points are developed in the next two units – Unit 3 Interpretivist methodology and Unit 4 Postmodernist methodology.

Views of science There are many views of science and scientific methods. As a result, there are many views about the relationship between sociology and science, and about the appropriateness of applying the assumptions and methods of the natural sciences to the study of human behaviour.

key terms

Positivism In Comte's view, a method of study based on directly observable facts, objectively measured, from which it is possible to identify cause and effect relationships and discover laws underlying social evolution.

Social facts In Durkheim's view, the institutions, beliefs and values of society, which although they exist within individuals also exist outside of them and direct their behaviour.

Inductive approach Developing theories from evidence.

Deductive approach Beginning with a theory and using evidence to test that theory.

Falsification The process of testing a theory against evidence and showing the theory to be false.

Normal science Science which operates within an established paradigm.

Paradigm A framework of concepts and theories which states how the natural world operates.

Scientific revolution The overthrow of an established paradigm by a new paradigm.

Realist approach Assumes that events in both the natural and social worlds are produced by underlying structures and mechanisms.

Closed system A system in which all the variables can be controlled.

Open system A system in which it is not possible to control all the variables.

summary

1. Comte believed that sociology should be based on the methodology of the natural sciences.

2. Durkheim argued that social facts have a reality outside individuals. Social facts can therefore be studied as 'things'. This means that the methodology of the natural sciences can be used to study human society.

3. Durkheim argued that his study of suicide supported this view. He claimed to have discovered cause and effect relationships between social facts.

4. According to Popper, science is based on the development of theories which can be tested against evidence and be capable of falsification. It is difficult to see how sociology can fit this view of science. Human societies are open systems which means that it is impossible to control variables. Because of this, it is difficult to see how a theory can be falsified.

5. According to Kuhn, 'normal science' operates within a paradigm. A scientific revolution occurs when the existing paradigm is overthrown by a new paradigm.

6. Sociology has a range of competing perspectives rather than a single paradigm. In terms of Kuhn's view of science, it is in a pre-paradigmatic and, therefore, pre-scientific situation.

7. From a realist viewpoint, events in both the social and natural worlds are produced by underlying structures and mechanisms. In view of this, there is no reason why sociology cannot be a science.

8. Human society is an open system. So is the world in which natural sciences such as meteorology and geology operate. Again, there is no reason why sociology cannot be a science.

9. In view of the differences between the natural world and the social world, many researchers argue that natural science methodology is inappropriate for the study of human society.

activity2 views of science

Item A Suicide statistics

Rate of suicides per million inhabitants in European countries

| | Period | | | Numerical position in the | | |
	1866-70	1871-75	1874-78	1st period	2nd period	3rd period
Italy	30	35	38	1	1	1
Belgium	66	69	78	2	3	4
England	67	66	69	3	2	2
Norway	76	73	71	4	4	3
Austria	78	94	130	5	7	7
Sweden	85	81	91	6	5	5
Bavaria	90	91	100	7	6	6
France	135	150	160	8	9	9
Prussia	142	134	152	9	8	8
Denmark	277	258	255	10	10	10
Saxony	293	267	334	11	11	11

Source: Durkheim, 1970 (originally published in 1897)

Item B An open system

Man-made pollution and climatic change are threatening the survival of the world's great whales. Nine years after commercial whaling was banned, the effects of global industrialisation now pose as great a threat to the world's largest mammals as the huge factory whaling fleets of the past. The hazards are outlined in scientific papers submitted to the International Whaling Commission. The authors argue that chemical pollution, ozone depletion and global warming are hindering the recovery of whale populations hunted almost to extinction in the 60s and 70s.

A separate report by biologist Dr Kevin Brown, commissioned by the London-based Environmental Investigation Agency, estimates that at least 150,000 man-made chemicals, increasing by 2,000 a year, are dumped in the oceans. He warns that damage to marine life caused by global warming and a thinning ozone layer could worsen the effects of chemicals through complex interactions which scientists are unable to predict.

'There are vast gaps in our knowledge ... but I wouldn't be surprised if there is a spiralling effect and whale numbers start crashing,' said Dr Brown, of Durham University.

His fears are echoed by Dr Mark Simmonds, of the University of Greenwich, who points out that six mass deaths of seals and dolphins have been recorded since 1987 – all in highly contaminated waters such as the North Sea – compared with only four over the previous eight decades.

Although viruses were the immediate cause of death, he argues that pollution must have played a major role.

Source: *The Observer*, 28.5.1995

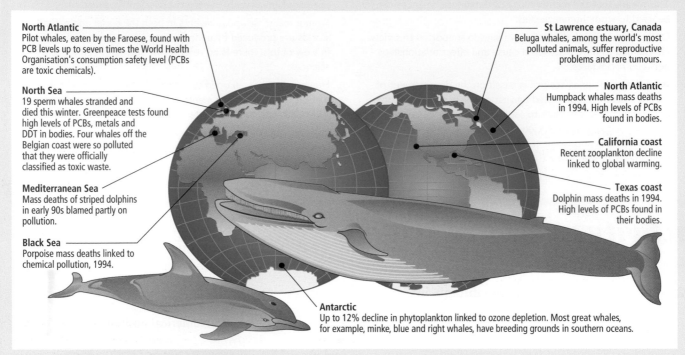

North Atlantic
Pilot whales, eaten by the Faroese, found with PCB levels up to seven times the World Health Organisation's consumption safety level (PCBs are toxic chemicals).

North Sea
19 sperm whales stranded and died this winter. Greenpeace tests found high levels of PCBs, metals and DDT in bodies. Four whales off the Belgian coast were so polluted that they were officially classified as toxic waste.

Mediterranean Sea
Mass deaths of striped dolphins in early 90s blamed partly on pollution.

Black Sea
Porpoise mass deaths linked to chemical pollution, 1994.

St Lawrence estuary, Canada
Beluga whales, among the world's most polluted animals, suffer reproductive problems and rare tumours.

North Atlantic
Humpback whales mass deaths in 1994. High levels of PCBs found in bodies.

California coast
Recent zooplankton decline linked to global warming.

Texas coast
Dolphin mass deaths in 1994. High levels of PCBs found in their bodies.

Antarctic
Up to 12% decline in phytoplankton linked to ozone depletion. Most great whales, for example, minke, blue and right whales, have breeding grounds in southern oceans.

questions

1 Durkheim claimed that 'each society is predisposed to contribute a definite quota of voluntary deaths'.
   a) What support for this statement is provided by Item A?
   b) Use Item A to support Durkheim's claim that a science of society is possible.

2 Use Item B to support the realist view that:
   a) both the social and natural sciences operate in open systems
   b) conclusive verification or falsification are not possible in open systems
   c) in view of this, there are basic similarities between the methodologies of the natural and social sciences.

Unit 3 Interpretivist methodology

keyissues

1 How significant are meanings for understanding social action?

2 What are the similarities and differences between the main interpretivist perspectives?

Interpretivist sociology covers a range of theoretical perspectives which see fundamental differences between the natural and social worlds. From an interpretivist perspective, the social world is essentially a world of meaning. Human beings construct their own social reality.

Their actions are directed by meanings, their experience is based on meanings. Any understanding of human action must therefore involve an understanding of those meanings. And for many researchers, this means employing methodologies which are very different from those used in the natural sciences.

3.1 Max Weber – social action

Social action Max Weber (1864-1920) defined sociology as 'a science which attempts the interpretive understanding of social action in order thereby to arrive at a causal explanation of its course and effects' (1964). Social action is action which involves other members of society. It is based on meanings in the minds of social actors which direct their actions. Weber was particularly concerned with motives – the intentions and purposes which direct social actors to achieve certain goals.

Verstehen Motives are an important part of any explanation of social action. Weber's method of interpreting motives is known as *verstehen* which roughly translates as empathetic understanding. Researchers put themselves in the place of social actors and attempt to see the world through their eyes. The problem of course is whether verstehen produces a true picture of the actor's world view. Weber's solution to this problem will be examined shortly.

The Protestant ethic Weber's methodology can be illustrated with his most famous work, *The Protestant Ethic and the Spirit of Capitalism* (see also pages 28, 30-31). Weber was interested in the meanings and motives - the 'spirit of capitalism' – which, he believed, led to the rise of capitalism. On the basis of a wide range of historical documents, he claimed that they developed from early forms of Protestantism which preceded capitalism. Weber identified a Protestant work ethic in terms of which work became a 'calling' which must be pursued with a single mind. Making money is an indication of success in one's calling, it shows that a person has not lost favour in God's sight. Weber argues that the Protestant work ethic is a major cause of the rise of capitalism.

The comparative method How does Weber know that his interpretation of motives – in this case the Protestant work ethic – is correct? His answer is to use the *comparative method* which compares different societies and different groups within the same society. In the absence of a laboratory in which variables can be manipulated and controlled, Weber attempts to find 'natural' laboratories which allow the influence of variables to be measured.

If Weber's interpretation of the Protestant work ethic is correct, then Protestants should have spearheaded the rise of capitalism. He produces evidence which indicates that early capitalism developed within predominantly Protestant rather than Catholic societies, and within those societies the 'business leaders and owners of capital are overwhelmingly Protestant'. From this, Weber claims that his interpretation of the motives of social actors is validated. (For further discussion of Weber's methodology, see pages 265-268.)

3.2 Herbert Blumer – symbolic interactionism

Weber investigated meanings on a wide canvas, often drawing on information from across the world and from different time periods. Symbolic interactionists tend to focus on meanings in the context of small-scale interaction situations. From this point of view, the meanings which direct action are developed and negotiated during the process of social interaction. The job of the sociologist is to discover these meanings.

Discovering meaning Herbert Blumer (1962) has developed a methodology for the study of social interaction. The first step is for researchers to immerse themselves in interaction situations, to observe and interpret the actions of others and attempt to see the world through their eyes. In Blumer's words, this involves 'feeling one's way inside the experience of the actor' in order to 'catch the process of interpretation through which they construct their action'. Blumer is refreshingly honest when discussing how this might be achieved. 'It is a tough job requiring a high order of careful and honest probing, creative yet disciplined imagination, resourcefulness and flexibility in study, pondering over what one is finding, and constant readiness to test and recast one's views and images of the area.'

Structure and meaning Symbolic interactionists accept that to some extent social interaction is structured. Meanings are not constantly reinvented, social interaction is often routine and repetitive rather than creative and spontaneous. But this does not mean that negotiation and interpretation aren't still important aspects of interaction. Nor does it mean that human action is shaped by the structures and mechanisms of the social system, as some sociologists would argue.

Blumer gives the example of family structure and industrialisation to illustrate this point. It has been claimed that industrialisation leads to the replacement of extended families by nuclear families. Blumer objects to this view which tends to see human action as a product of structures and mechanisms. Where in the equation are the meanings people give to family life, where are the interpretations they place on industrialisation? Without these meanings and interpretations sociologists have little chance of grasping social reality.

Blumer argues that the research process must be as systematic, rigorous and objective as possible. Equally important, however, are qualities such as sensitivity and sympathy. Both the tone and substance of Blumer's methodology are a long way from many of the views of science outlined in previous sections. (For further discussion of Blumer's methodology, see pages 279-280.)

3.3 Phenomenology

Phenomenological perspectives take the logic of a social reality to its furthest point. They argue that as human beings our only reality consists of meanings. The job of the sociologist is to discover these meanings and nothing more – for the logic of this argument states there is nothing more to discover. The methodology that results from this view will now be examined using the example of suicide.

Discovering suicide In *Discovering Suicide*, J. Maxwell Atkinson's basic question is 'How do deaths get categorised as suicide?' When he has answered this question he can go no further because suicide is simply a meaning and has no reality beyond this. Classifications of suicide are not right or wrong, they just are. For example, there is no such thing as a 'real' or objective suicide rate waiting to be discovered. The official statistics are the rate, full stop.

Atkinson's research attempts to discover the meanings used by coroners to classify deaths as suicide. He held discussions with coroners, attended inquests, observed a coroner's officer at work and analysed a coroner's records. He argues that coroners have a 'commonsense theory of suicide' which they use to both classify and explain deaths as suicide. In terms of this theory, the following evidence is seen as relevant for reaching a verdict.

1 Whether suicide threats have been made or suicide notes left.

2 The type of death – hanging, gassing and drug overdose are seen as typical suicide deaths.

3 The location of death – death by gunshot at home is more likely to be seen as suicide than in the countryside where it may well be interpreted as a hunting accident.

activity3 suicide

Item A Suicide in 1870

SUICIDE OF TWO LOVERS BY LEAPING OVER THE TAFFRAIL OF THE AMERICAN PASSENGER SHIP "BLOOMENTHORPE" ON THE PASSAGE TO SAN LUIS.

DISTRESSING SUICIDE AFTER WARWICK RACES.

Item B Retired coroner

During the Second World War it was something of an understanding that you didn't bring in suicide verdicts unless you really had to. 'Bad for National Morale' – and of course I think most people felt responsible for keeping morale up. I think with suicide at that time we felt it was a kind of 'defeatism', defeatism in the face of the enemy, and that was a cardinal sin, letting the side down, you know. So when there was a verdict of suicide, lots of coroners couldn't resist reading a sermon about moral cowardice. I expect I did.

Source: Langley, 1988

Item C No more suicides

Suicide has been officially abolished in the Irish Republic – not because people have stopped taking their own lives, but because coroners are forbidden to say that they did.

A decision by the High Court in Dublin last April means that verdicts of suicide cannot be brought in by coroners. As a result, the Republic has officially had a nil suicide rate since then.

This situation came about when relatives of a person recorded as having committed suicide challenged the coroner's verdict. The law has always prevented coroners from apportioning blame: verdicts on road accident victims, for example, could not say who was to blame.

The High Court ruled that this prohibition extended to suicide: coroners could not blame victims for their own deaths either.

Source: *The Guardian*, 4.11.1985

questions

1 Use Items A, B and C to support a phenomenological view.

2 Do you believe there is a 'real', 'objective' suicide rate? Give reasons for your answer.

4 The biography of the deceased – a recent divorce, the death of a close friend or relative, a history of depression, problems at work, financial difficulties, lack of friends are seen as typical reasons for suicide.

The closer the deceased fits this commonsense theory of suicide, the more likely his or her death will be defined as suicide. In Atkinson's words, coroners 'are engaged in analysing features of the deaths and of the biographies of the deceased according to a variety of taken-for-granted assumptions about what constitutes a "typical suicide", "a typical suicide biography", and so on'.

Having uncovered to his satisfaction the meanings used to classify deaths as suicide, Atkinson's research is finished. There are no more questions to ask.

Causation As outlined in a previous section, Durkheim's research on suicide was concerned with causation, in particular with the causes of variations in suicide rates. Phenomenologists see this as a pointless and misguided exercise. Suicides are not objective 'social facts' with causes that can be explained, they are meanings. To try and discover the 'causes' of suicide will simply result in uncovering the meanings used to classify a death as suicide. Thus it comes as no surprise that the 'typical suicide biography' – the friendless, divorced loner – is very similar to Durkheim's socially isolated individual. Suicides, like any other aspect of social reality, are simply constructions of meaning.

Conclusion Phenomenology rejects the entire scientific enterprise as it is normally understood. It is a distortion of social reality to treat it as 'social facts', as 'things'. There are no 'structures' or 'mechanisms' operating in human society. There are no objective facts with causes which can be explained. There are only meanings to be uncovered and understood.

3.4 Two sociologies?

It is sometimes argued that there are 'two sociologies' (Halfpenny, 1984). The first is based on 'scientific methodology', using 'hard' quantitative data and concerned with discovering causal relationships. This approach is sometimes labelled 'positivism'. The second is based on 'interpretivist methodology', using 'soft' qualitative data and concerned with understanding the meanings which make up social reality. This approach is sometimes labelled 'interpretivism', sometimes 'phenomenology'.

Supporting the distinction Some sociologists find this distinction between the two sociologies useful. They claim that there is a tendency for some researchers to adopt a positivist view and see the methods of the natural sciences as the most effective way of acquiring knowledge. And they see a real distinction between this group and those who adopt an interpretivist approach.

Those who support this distinction also claim to detect a tendency for positivists to favour certain research methods, for example survey research based on questionnaires, and certain forms of data, for example quantitative data. On the other hand, those who adopt an interpretivist approach are said to favour methods such as participant observation and unstructured interviews which are seen to produce rich, in-depth qualitative data.

These differences are seen to reflect the aims of the 'two sociologies'. Positivism aims to discover cause and effect relationships. This requires quantitative data so that the strength of relationships between variables can be measured. Interpretivism aims to understand human action. This requires rich, qualitative data in order to discover the meanings which lie behind action.

Opposing the distinction Ray Pawson (1989) rejects this view of the 'two sociologies'. He argues that it gives a false

key terms

Interpretivist sociology A range of theoretical perspectives which emphasise the importance of meanings for understanding human action.

Verstehen A term used by Weber for interpreting motives. Roughly translated it means empathetic understanding – that is, attempting to understand motives by putting yourself in the actor's place.

Comparative method Comparing different societies, and different groups within the same society.

Phenomenology A view which states that phenomena – things or events – must be studied in their own right, not as representing something else. Thus, meanings must be studied as meanings – they have no other reality.

summary

1. Interpretivist perspectives emphasise the importance of meanings for understanding social action.

2. However, there are important differences between interpretivist perspectives. Some look for causal explanations of social action, others seek only to discover the meanings used to construct social reality.

3. Some sociologists make a distinction between two sociologies – positivism and interpretivism. They argue that these sociologies differ in terms of theory and methodology.

4. Other sociologists argue that this distinction is false. They see sociology as far more varied in terms of theory and methodology than the idea of two sociologies suggests.

picture of the relationship between theory, research methods and the actual practice of doing sociology.

Pawson describes the idea of 'two sociologies' as a 'methodological myth'.

In other words, the two sociologies don't exist. Instead, there is a whole range of different views, different assumptions and different methodologies. As previous sections have shown, there are various views of science and its application to the study of human society. And sociologists who are primarily concerned with meanings use a variety of research methods and types of data and often start from different theoretical perspectives. This variety cannot be reduced to 'two sociologies'.

Unit 4 *Postmodernist methodology*

keyissues

1   How does postmodernism challenge sociological research methodology?

2   What alternatives does it offer?

The challenge

Postmodernists directly challenge the entire basis of research methodology in the social sciences. They reject the whole idea of collecting data to support or reject hypotheses or theories. They question the possibility of making any definite statements about social reality. They reject the idea that there is an objective reality 'out there' waiting to be discovered. They argue that the 'facts' and 'knowledge' that fill sociological research reports and textbooks are nothing of the sort. They are simply sociologists' constructions of reality rather than a valid description and analysis of the social world 'out there'.

The following discussion of postmodernist methodology is largely based on Mats Alvesson's excellent book *Postmodernism and Social Research* (2002).

A postmodernist view of reality

From a postmodernist perspective, any description, analysis, view or picture of the social world is simply one view amongst many. And this applies to sociologists as much as anybody else.

Nothing is certain – everything is tentative, doubtful, indeterminate. Take yourself. In one sense you are one person, in another sense you are lots of people. In one sense you have one identity, in another sense you are made up of multiple identities. In various situations you adopt different identities, see things in different ways, operate with different meanings. What you see or say in one situation may contradict what you see or say in another situation.

This applies both to the sociologist and those who participate in his or her research. Nothing is fixed, everything is fluid; nothing is whole, everything is fragmented; there is no single reality, only multiple realities.

Objectivity and research

Sociologists aim to be objective, to present the social world of those they are studying as it really is, to give us the 'facts'. Many sociologists accept that complete objectivity is an ideal that is unattainable. However, they do their best to get there. And they believe their research reports are a lot better than the view of the person in the street.

From a postmodernist view, research reports are not objective. Instead, they are constructions which are designed to persuade, to give the impression of rational, analytic thinking, and to convince the reader that the researcher's view is 'the truth'. And often, the persuasion works. In the words of Mats Alvesson (2002),

'This is made possible through the skilful denial of any relevance of the pre-structured understanding of the researcher, his or her class, gender, nationality, his or her paradigmatic, theoretical and political preferences and biases, the vocabularies employed, the dynamics of the research process, the expectations and more or less politically skilled operations of the informants, the more or less arbitrary decisions about informants, the selective presentation of evidence and rhetorical tricks and conventions of writing.'

Sociologists are a bit like conjurers. They deceive, they play tricks, they create illusions. For example, they skilfully present an illusion of objectivity where none exists.

Sociological categories

Think of the following terms – culture, subculture, norm, value, social class, ethnicity, social structure, social status, social role. These are all categories used by sociologists to order, organise and make sense of the social world. According to postmodernists, the social world is forced into these categories, wedged into these pigeonholes. In this respect, the social world becomes a construction built by sociologists. In this way, researchers impose their own order and framework on the social world.

From a postmodernist viewpoint, the social world is ambiguous rather than clear-cut, fluid rather than fixed, open rather than closed. It cannot be rammed into fixed, predetermined categories.

Is there any alternative to researchers imposing their reality on the social world? Do they have to make sense of human action by using pre-set categories?

Categories as problematic A starting point is to see all categories as problematic, to be aware that they create order where none may exist, that they impose a particular view of reality, that they structure the social world in a particular way.

Defamiliarisation This offers the possibility of getting away from a sociological construction of the social world. *Defamiliarisation* means looking at the familiar in new and novel ways. Instead of assuming human action is natural, rational, patterned, ordered, the observer should try and see it from other viewpoints – as exotic, random, irrational, contradictory, arbitrary, crazy. For example, look back on your schooldays and family life and try and look at them in a fresh and novel way – for instance, as an alien from another planet or somebody from the distant past or future.

Multiple interpretations

Postmodernists are particularly scathing and dismissive of *metanarratives* – literally 'big stories' such as Marxism and functionalism which offer a single explanation, a single perspective on social reality. Metanarratives have their own set of categories, their own vocabulary (or jargon), they are based on particular values, they define the social world in a particular way, and they wrap it all up in a neat, tidy, rigid framework. A metanarrative is a total package into which all social reality can be accommodated.

But if you buy into one metanarrative, that's all you get. All your research will be coloured by it. What you look for, how you interpret it, will be guided by the big story you believe.

From a postmodernist viewpoint, there are multiple, if not infinite, interpretations of the social world. Who is to say which is 'right' or the 'best'?

Where does this take us? Some would say nowhere – what's the point of doing research if it's no better or worse than any other view – for example, no better or worse than the view of the journalist, novelist, comedian, child, grandparent, Christian, Muslim or Jew?

For some, there is a halfway house. Sociologists should be more humble. They should accept the idea of *multiple interpretations*. They should look at the social world from different vantage points, in terms of different perspectives. And they should allow other voices to be heard in their research publications, particularly the voices of those they are researching.

Evaluation

Much of what postmodernists have to say about sociological methodology is negative. Taken to its extreme, it suggests that sociological research is a waste of time. Worse, it can be seen as an illusion which distorts the social world and deceives the audience.

But have postmodernists got it right? Using their arguments, there's no way of judging whether they're right or wrong. The voice of postmodernism is simply one voice amongst many – neither better nor worse.

Despite this criticism, postmodernism has made sociologists more aware of the problems and pitfalls of research. It has made many researchers more sensitive, more questioning and more humble. Mats Alvesson (2002) presents the following evaluation. Postmodernism 'offers a challenge and an inspiration to revise and make qualitative research more sophisticated and creative. This is not bad, and a strong reason for taking it seriously. But not too seriously.'

key terms

Defamiliarisation Looking at the familiar in new and novel ways.

Metanarratives Big stories or pictures of how the world works. Grand theories produced by the natural and social sciences.

Multiple interpretations Looking at the social world from different vantage points and in terms of different perspectives.

summary

1. From a postmodernist perspective, any description or analysis of the social world is simply one view among many.

2. As a result, it is not possible to make any definite statements about social reality. Sociological research is not, and cannot be, objective.

3. Researchers impose their own order and framework on the social world by using pre-set categories.

4. Researchers should regard all categories as problematic. And they should defamiliarise themselves from the social world in order to open their eyes to a variety of interpretations.

5. Postmodernists reject metanarratives, arguing they should be replaced by multiple interpretations of the social world.

6. Using their own arguments, there is no way of judging whether postmodernists are right or wrong.

7. Postmodernism has made sociologists more aware of the problems and pitfalls of research. And it has encouraged them to be more creative and innovative.

activity4 postmodernism and research

Item A The research process – a simple version

1. Collection of data

2. Production of a wealth of information eg, writing up observations and transcribing interviews

3. Structuring the data, reducing mess

4. Analysis and further reduction of material

5. Creating an order and logic to the report

6. Producing a text

Source: Alvesson, 2002

Item B The research process – a complex version

2. During the research
Use of particular research methods
Interaction between researcher and research participants
Presentation of self, impression management
Bias, meanings, interpretations, feelings

3. Broad-brushed selection of research data
Reconstruction and ordering of data

5. Interpretation and analysis of data

1. Researcher brings to research their:
Expectations, understandings, assumptions
Culture, gender, ethnicity, nationality, class, age
Values, attitudes, meanings, political and religious beliefs
Identities, personal experiences
Theoretical background and categories

4. Fine-tuned selection of data
Further reconstruction and ordering

6. Producing a text
Following conventions of a research report
Writing skills
Skills of persuasion

Source: Alvesson, 2002

Item C Body ritual among the Nacirema

The Nacirema spend a large part of the day in ritual activity. The focus of this activity is the human body. The basic belief underlying their rituals is that the human body is ugly and has a natural tendency to debility and disease. Every household has a shrine where the body rituals take place.

The focal point of the shrine is a box or chest which contains many charms and magical potions. Beneath the charm-box is a small font where they perform the daily mouth ceremony. The Nacirema have a horror of and fascination with the mouth. Were it not for the rituals of the mouth, they believe that their teeth would fall out, their gums bleed, their friends desert them and their lovers reject them.

Once or twice a year, the Nacirema seek out a holy-mouth-man. The ceremony involves almost unbelievable ritual torture. The power of the holy-mouth-man is evident from the fact that his clients return year after year, despite the fact that their teeth continue to decay.

Source: Miner, 1965

questions

1 Research is not as simple and straightforward as it seems. Comment on this statement from a postmodernist view with some reference to Items A and B.

2 Item B is an adapted extract from an article by Horace Miner, an American anthropologist. Nacirema is American spelt backwards.

a) How is this description an example of defamiliarisation?

b) Do you find it useful?

c) Write a brief defamiliarised description of an aspect of everyday behaviour.

Unit 5 *Feminist methodology*

keyissues

1 What is feminist methodology?

2 What contribution has it made to sociology?

Over the past 30 years 'women's studies' has become a major growth industry. In university bookshops, shelves are stacked with books about women and their place in history and society. And most of these books are written by women.

What does this mean? Clearly it means that women are seen as more important than before. The growth of women's studies can be seen as a reflection of the rise of feminism and changes in perceptions of women's roles in Western society. There is little doubt that social change and the changes in values which accompany it influence choices about what to study. For many feminists, however, the effects of these changes are a lot more fundamental than simply choice of subject matter.

5.1 Feminism – the weak thesis

Ray Pawson (1992) distinguishes between the 'weak thesis' and the 'strong thesis' of feminist methods. In terms of the 'weak thesis', research methods in sociology are essentially sound. The problem is that in practice they are shot through with sexism. The solution is to purge them of sexism. Margrit Eichler's *Non-Sexist Research Methods* (1988) is an example of this approach. She identifies major areas of sexism which infuse the research process. These include:

Androcentricity This means viewing the world from a traditional male perspective, with its assumptions of male dominance and superiority – for example – seeing women as passive objects rather than active subjects. As a result, women are largely 'invisible' – in Sheila Rowbotham's (1973) words, they are 'hidden from history'.

Overgeneralisation Many studies deal only with men but present their findings as though they applied to both men and women. For example, until recently social mobility

studies in Britain were based solely on men. Since women's social status was seen to derive from the status of their husbands, there seemed little point in looking at women in their own right. Their class position could be simply 'read off' from the position of their husband.

Research methods

According to Eichler, the sexist assumptions outlined above are found in all aspects of the research process. This can be seen from her examples of questions taken from questionnaires. The first is an example of a sex specific term when talking about people in general.

● If someone wanted to make a speech in your community claiming that Blacks are inferior, should he be allowed to speak or not?

The next question reflects common assumptions about male dominance.

● Is it acceptable for women to hold important political offices in state and national government? Yes/No.

The solution is to reformulate the questions in a non-sexist way.

Eichler's argument suggests reform rather than radical change. Research methods, in and of themselves, are not sexist. Once researchers learn to use them in a non-sexist way, then the problem will be solved.

5.2 Feminism – the strong thesis

The changes advocated by the strong thesis are more fundamental. Something of their flavour is provided by Ann Oakley's article 'Interviewing Women: A Contradiction in Terms' (1981).

Feminist interviewing

Oakley (1981) argues that the standard approach to interviewing has the following characteristics. '(a) its status as a mechanical instrument of data-collection; (b) its function as a specialised form of conversation in which one person asks the questions and another gives the answers; (c) its characterisation of interviewees as essentially passive individuals and (d) its reduction of interviewers to a question asking and rapport-promoting role'.

Oakley sees this approach as clinical, manipulative, exploitive and hierarchical. The interviewer 'uses' the respondent for 'his' purposes, controlling the content and direction of the interview. The relationship is unequal – the interviewer takes and the respondent gives. A feminist methodology would replace this by a non-hierarchical relationship, with the researcher giving as well as receiving. For example, an interviewer must 'be prepared to invest his or her personal identity in the relationship' which means honesty, sincerity, understanding and compassion between equals. It means that both parties have a say in the content and direction of the interview. Only with this personal involvement will 'people come to know each other and admit others into their lives'.

This example argues for a change in research methods – a new type of interviewing – rather than simply cleansing existing methods of sexism. It argues that research techniques are so imbued with male assumptions and practices that they must be radically changed. These changes are not only morally correct, they will also result in better data.

One reaction to Oakley's views is summed up by Ray Pawson's (1992) query, 'What's new?'. There is a long tradition of interviewing which emphasises sensitivity and non-directive approaches. Whether Oakley's views are significantly different from this is questionable.

Gender politics and methodology

Some feminists argue that the 'women's struggle' and feminist methodology are inseparable. 'Malestream' sociology is so saturated with assumptions of male dominance that a feminist alternative is required. Maria Mies (1993) provides an example of this approach. She argues that a feminist methodology must have the following features.

1 **Conscious partiality** The idea of so-called value free research has to be replaced by conscious partiality, which in practise means that female researchers must positively identify with the women they study.

2 **View from below** This replaces the 'view from above', with its assumptions of male dominance, which supports the existing power structure. Researchers must take the 'view from below' because it is more likely to reflect women's experiences and more likely to empower women in their struggle for liberation.

3 **Action research** Rather than being a detached spectator, a dispassionate observer, the researcher should actively participate in the struggle for women's liberation.

4 **Changing the status quo** From this involvement in their own emancipation, both researchers and the women they study will develop a better understanding of their situation. This is based on the idea, 'If you want to know a thing, you must change it'. Only by challenging and changing patriarchy will its true nature be revealed.

5 **Raising consciousness** Both researchers and the researched must raise their consciousness – become aware of their oppression. In particular, it is the job of the researcher to give women the means to gain insight into and change their situation.

6 **Individual and social history** Part of the process of raising consciousness requires a study of women's individual and social history. This will allow women to reclaim their history from its appropriation by men.

7 **Collectivising experience** Women must collectivise their experience and join together and cooperate in their struggle for liberation. They must overcome the individualism, competitiveness and careerism which characterise the male world.

In terms of these propositions, Maria Mies is claiming that valid knowledge can only emerge from the struggles waged by the oppressed against their oppressors. The journey to truth involves just the opposite of value freedom. In Mies' case it requires a wholehearted commitment to women's liberation.

Mies' views are not new. Marxists have produced similar arguments for the liberation of the working class, as have African Americans for Black liberation in the USA. Whatever the virtues of this point of view, it is unlikely to offer a recipe for sociology as a whole since there is more to human society than oppressors and oppressed.

5.3 The primacy of experience

A number of feminists have argued that the only way to know something is to experience it. Given this, it is crucial for feminist research to capture the experience of women and to express it as directly as possible with a minimum of reinterpretation on the part of the researcher.

Too often researchers see the experience of others in terms of their own values and preconceptions. In particular, they force this experience into theoretical frameworks and categories which only serve to distort it. This argument was put forcibly by Kaluzynska (1980) when she rejected the whole Marxist debate about domestic labour – whether it was 'productive' or 'non-productive', whether it created 'surplus value', whether it was 'alienating' and so on. She objects to the imposition of concepts which, she argues, distort the experience of housework. In her words, 'Why did we have to get to grips with value theory to appreciate what a drag housework was?'

There are, however, problems with giving primacy to personal experience. It makes the assumption that if we dig hard enough and deep enough we'll get to the 'real thing' – the direct experience of others. But, as the section on reflexivity indicated, recording the experience of others will always to some degree be coloured by the values and theoretical concepts of the researcher.

5.4 Postmodern feminism

Women as a category

Feminism is not a single perspective. In its early days, things were fairly simple. Women were the oppressed, men were the oppressors, the target was patriarchy, the aim to liberate women. There was a tendency to see women as a single, undifferentiated category. Groups of women objected to this approach – for example, Black women and lesbian women. OK, they were women, but, they argued, their experiences and social situation distinguished them from women in general. As a result, many of the generalisations about women did not apply, or only partly applied, to them.

Postmodern feminism takes this argument a step further. It rejects the standard feminist metanarrative ('grand story') of women as a homogeneous, undifferentiated category, faced with an oppressive patriarchal system. And it even rejects categories which subdivide the category 'women', such as Black women, lesbian women and working-class women. Instead, postmodern feminists emphasise diversity and variation. They argue that researchers should be open to this diversity rather than approaching it with pre-set, preconceived categories.

Evaluation This approach has been criticised by a number of feminists. Breaking down or rejecting the category 'women' prevents the possibility of making generalisations which apply to most or all women. It also blunts the force of feminist protest and threatens the unity of women as a group. Emphasising variation and uniqueness may lead to 'divide and conquer', so serving male dominance (Alvesson, 2002).

The research process

Research as a construct Postmodern feminists favour interpretivist research methods such as participant observation. They are particularly aware that the results of research are a social construct – they are largely constructed by the researcher from fieldnotes which document their observations. This awareness leads them to revisit, reopen and reinterpret their fieldnotes. As Sara Delamont (2003) states,

> 'fieldnotes are not a closed, completed, final text: rather, they are indeterminate, subject to reading, rereading, coding, recording, interpreting, reinterpreting.'

This is in line with the postmodernist view that there are multiple interpretations of any observation.

Multiple voices As outlined in Unit 4, postmodernists argue that researchers should allow the voices of those they research to be heard. Again, in Sara Delamont's (2003) words, this means 'the text will reproduce the actors' own perspectives and experiences. This may include extended biographical and autobiographical accounts, extended dialogues between the researcher and informants, and other "documents of life". Typically, there is an emphasis on the kinds of narratives or stories through which social actors construct their own and others' experiences.'

Reflexity The researcher's own voice should be heard loud and clear, expressing her or his thoughts and feelings about the research. This will be a reflexive voice, reflecting on the research process, the author's interpretations, emotions and relationships with the research participants. This reflects the researcher's awareness that they are a part of the social world they are researching, that the results of their research may say as much, if not more, about them as about the research participants they are studying.

Presenting research Postmodernists' focus on multiple identities and multiple interpretations is reflected in their writing styles. Descriptions of social action and social scenes vary from 'cold' to 'hot', from dispassionate to passionate, from clinical to evocative. There is a mix of styles from poetic to descriptive, from the researcher's words to those of the research participants. The intention is to allow the reader to move through a variety of interpretations and observe from a variety of standpoints (Delamont, 2003).

key terms

Androcentricity A male-centred view of the world which assumes male superiority and dominance.

Overgeneralisation Generalising further than the evidence allows. For example, generalising from a male sample to both males and females.

Conscious partiality Positively identifying with and favouring a particular group.

Multiple voices Many voices. In this case, it refers to the view that many voices should be heard in the research report.

summary

1. There are a number of feminist methodologies.
2. The 'weak thesis' states that androcentricity and overgeneralisation are found in all aspects of the research process.
3. Research methods, in and of themselves, are not sexist. Once researchers learn to use them in a non-sexist way, the problem will be solved.
4. The 'strong thesis' states that feminism requires its own research methods – for example, feminist interviewing.
5. Some feminists see the women's struggle and feminist methodology as inseparable. The feminist researcher should be consciously partial and actively participate in women's liberation.
6. Postmodern feminism rejects pre-set, pre-determined categories. It emphasises diversity and variation.
7. It argues that there are multiple interpretations of any observation and that this should be reflected by multiple voices in research reports.

Conclusion

Sociology used to be a male subject, run by males and concerned with males. Women were largely absent from sociology departments and in a minority among research participants. When sociologists studied workers, they usually studied male workers. When they studied social mobility, it was men who went up and down the class system – women didn't even make it into the supposedly representative sample. And women's concerns and issues were unlikely to be heard and researched.

Thanks in large part to feminists, women now feature in every area of sociology – as workers, members of ethnic minorities, as voters, as students, as mothers and housewives, as participants in the class system and as members of religious organisations. Women are no longer invisible.

The research process has been largely cleansed of sexism. Researchers are increasingly aware that sexism will produce invalid results.

Feminists have been in the forefront of recent developments in methodology. Many have argued that sociology is not, should not and cannot be value free. They have emphasised the importance of capturing the experience of research participants and of expressing that experience directly. They have argued that emotion has an important part to play in the research process. And they have opened up, questioned, and presented alternatives to, established research methodology.

activity5 feminism and methodology

Item A Sexist questionnaires

A study of the lifestyles of adolescent girls and boys included sets of questions about the roles they might identify with (Murdock & Phelps, 1973). Both girls and boys were given a list of roles to choose from, which included 'good pupil', 'rebel', 'good friend' and 'pop fan'. Boys were given a separate list which included 'sports fan' and 'natural leader'. Girls were also given their own list with roles such as 'homemaker' and 'fashion follower'. The girls had no opportunity of choosing from the boys' options and the boys' had no opportunity of choosing from the girls' options.

Source: Jones 1974

Item B Woman-to-woman

Janet Finch describes herself as a feminist sociologist. She conducted two studies based on in-depth interviews in which all the interviewees were women – 1) clergyman's wives and 2) women who used and ran preschool playgroups. She talked to the women in their own homes about marriage, motherhood and childbearing.

She preferred a woman-to-woman discussion in an informal setting 'on both methodological and political grounds'. In her view 1) it works better and 2) it's morally better. Finch found that she gained their trust because she was a woman and because, as a feminist, she treated them as equals. Sharing their gender, both parties shared a subordinate position in society and, as a result, were likely to identify with each other. And, in an equal relationship, the interviewees felt they could talk freely. The women welcomed the interviews and were enthusiastic during the discussions.

As a feminist sociologist, Finch was 'on the side' of the women she studied. In her words, this 'inevitably means an emotional as well as an intellectual commitment to promoting their interests'. Does this bias her research? No more than any other research, since, in her view, 'all social science knowledge is intrinsically political in character'.

Source: Finch, 1993

questions

1 a) How can the questions in Item A be seen as sexist?
   b) How might the results of this study simply reproduce traditional gender stereotypes?
2 a) In what ways does Janet Finch's woman-to-woman interviewing style reflect Ann Oakley's 'feminist interviewing'?
   b) What are the advantages of this style of interviewing?

Unit 6 *Sociology, methodology and values*

keyissues

1 Is an objective, value-free sociology possible?

2 Is it desirable?

What we see, the questions we ask and the way we interpret data are influenced by a range of social and personal factors. They include our class, gender, ethnicity, nationality, culture and our personalities, experiences and life histories. These points will now be developed, focusing on the influence of values on social research.

Values are strongly held beliefs about what is right and wrong, what is good and bad, what is worth fighting for and fighting against, what is worth having and not having, who is worthy of respect and support and who is not.

Can the research process in particular and sociology in general be *value free*? And, going one step further, is a value-free sociology desirable?

The founding fathers of sociology believed that an objective, value-free science of society was both possible and desirable. Despite their many differences, not least in terms of personal values, Comte, Marx and Durkheim each believed his work to be uncontaminated by value judgements. Today's sociologists are a lot less certain. A brief look at the debate about values and the study of deviance illustrates this.

6.1 Values and the study of deviance

In an article entitled 'Whose Side Are We On?' the American sociologist Howard Becker (1970) argues that it is impossible to conduct research 'uncontaminated by personal and political sympathies'. Becker's sympathies lie with the underdog, those who have been labelled deviant. He is critical of the agents of social control who, in his eyes, create deviance by selectively applying labels to the poor and powerless (see page 159). Becker argues that not only the research process but the theories which lie behind it – in his case interactionism – are infused with value judgements. From his standpoint 'interactionist theories look (and are) rather left'.

Like Becker, the American sociologist Alvin Gouldner (1975) believes that a value-free sociology is impossible. However, his values are a lot further to the left than Becker's. From his standpoint, Gouldner accuses the interactionists of adopting a 'bland liberal position' (liberalism advocates reform within the existing structure rather than radical social change). A more radical position would lead to a critical examination of the relationship between deviance and the unequal distribution of power in society.

Gouldner pictures Becker and his interactionist

colleagues as White middle-class liberals who 'get their kicks' from a 'titillated attraction to the underdog's exotic difference'. Their sympathies result in no more than mild criticism of the agents of social control. Their bland liberalism prevents a radical critique of the structure of social inequality which creates deviance.

Gouldner argues that values underlie every sociological perspective. And these values influence the way sociologists picture and explain the social world.

Functionalism has often been seen as reflecting a conservative position which advocates the maintenance of the status quo – the way things are. In doing so, it is seen to justify existing social structures. With its view that order, stability and consensus are essential for the smooth running of society and its emphasis on the positive functions of social institutions, it implies that radical change is harmful to society.

Alvin Gouldner (1971) argues that in terms of the logic of functionalism, 'only "evil" – social disorder, tension or conflict – can come from efforts to remove the domination of man by man or make fundamental changes in the character of authority'.

Marxism The values which underlie Marxism are plain for all to see. Marx was committed to socialism. His vision of communism is utopian – a perfect society. He looked forward to an egalitarian society free from the evils of capitalism – free from oppression, exploitation and alienation, with wealth and power shared by all rather than concentrated in the hands of the few. And it is partly in terms of this vision that Marxists see capitalist society. For example, J.C. Kincaid's (1973) solution to poverty states, 'Poverty cannot be abolished in a capitalist society but only in a socialist society under workers' control, in which human needs and not profits determine the allocation of resources'. Marxism replaces the functionalist commitment to the status quo with a commitment to revolutionary change.

6.2 Sociological theory and values

Feminism The previous unit looked at feminist methodology and made the point that most feminist researchers argue that sociology is not, should not, and cannot be value free.

Many feminists wear their hearts and values on their sleeves. They place a high value on gender equality. They regard the present system of patriarchy as unjust and oppressive. They identify with the women they study and seek to empower them in their struggle for liberation. Patriarchy is wrong – the injustices of the system must be spelt out as a first step to overthrowing it.

Feminist research is directed by values which define what is right and wrong and what should be done.

6.3 The question of relativism

If we accept that to some degree value judgements underlie all sociological perspectives, where does this leave the search for 'truth'? Since all perspectives are value based it can be argued that there is no way – apart from our own value judgements – of deciding whether one is superior to another. Some would agree with this argument. They would take a *relativist* position, seeing all knowledge as relative. In terms of this view, there is no such thing as objective knowledge since everything is seen through the lens of our values and culture.

Others argue that just because a perspective is based on values does not necessarily negate its insights and its findings. Taking a relativist view is like dismissing the research findings of Greenpeace and the nuclear industry simply because of the differing values and vested interests of those organisations. And since any view of society can only be partial, differing perspectives in sociology may add breadth to that view. It is this breadth that allows Melvin Tumin (1967) to make the following statement about social stratification. 'The evidence regarding the mixed outcomes of stratification strongly suggests the examination of alternatives. The evidence regarding the possibilities of social growth under conditions of more equal rewarding is such that the exploration of alternatives seems eminently worthwhile.' And here Tumin is referring to evidence produced from a variety of sociological perspectives.

Views of reality

At one extreme, there is the position that objectivity and value freedom are possible. At the other extreme, all knowledge is seen as relative and there is no way of deciding between opposing views of reality. The most radical version of relativism rejects any possibility of objective knowledge, seeing in its place only subjective experience. In this respect, there is no reality outside human perception. What we see is what there is and there is nothing else.

Few, if any, sociologists accept this position – if they did there would be little point in doing sociology. Here is an elegant rejection of relativism by Julia O'Connell Davidson and Derek Layder (1994).

'But the idea that there is no reality separate from the conceptual systems employed by people to grasp it accords quite ludicrous powers to human thought (Trigg, 1989). A tree that falls in a forest falls regardless of whether a person is there to witness and conceptualise the event, children in Somalia die of starvation regardless of whether the governments of the Western world believe that they are providing adequate aid. Many people in Britain and the United States fondly imagine that they live in a meritocratic, post-racist, post-sexist society, but this does not mean that a working-class child or a Black child or a female child is truly blessed with the same chances of obtaining wealth and social power as the middle-class, White, male child. Of course one person's freedom fighter is another person's terrorist. And of course you can never know with absolute certainty that another person understands what you say in exactly the same way that you understand it. And of course language, concepts and beliefs affect our perception of social reality. But this does not mean that there really is no solid world out there separate from human beings' concepts and beliefs. In practice, as King Canute is purported to have discovered, the object world has a nasty habit of intruding no matter what people may believe about it.'

key terms

Value-free research Research that is free from the values of the researcher. Research that is objective.

Relativism The idea that there can be no objective, value-free knowledge.

summary

1. There is evidence to suggest that values underlie every aspect of the sociological enterprise from the gathering of data to the construction of theories.

2. It can be argued that feminism, functionalism, Marxism and other theories are, at least in part, value based.

3. A relativist position states that an objective, value-free sociology is impossible. Carried to its extreme, this means that there is no way of judging whether research findings are valid or invalid.

4. Many sociologists, while accepting that a value-free sociology is not possible, still retain the ideal of objectivity. This means that research which is rigorous, systematic and reflexive is better than research which is sloppy, unsystematic and uncritical.

activity6 thinking about values

Item A *Taking sides*

To have values or not to have values: the question is always with us. When sociologists undertake to study problems that have relevance to the world we live in, they find themselves caught in a crossfire. Some urge them not to take sides, to be neutral and do research that is technically correct and value free. Others tell them their work is shallow and useless if it does not express a deep commitment to a value position.

This dilemma, which seems so painful to so many, actually does not exist; for one of its horns is imaginary. For it to exist, one would have to assume, as some apparently do, that it is indeed possible to do research that is uncontaminated by personal and political sympathies. I propose to argue that it is not possible and, therefore that the question is not whether we should take sides, since we inevitably will, but rather on whose side we are on.

Source: Becker, 1970

Item B *Better ways of conducting research*

Social researchers draw on their everyday knowledge and on their political and moral values in the process of research; they use them to set the research agenda and to design classification systems; they use their social, as well as professional, skills to obtain information; they employ their knowledge as members of society and their political values to analyse and interpret their findings. But accepting this inevitable and indissoluble link between scientific and everyday thinking and between social theories and moral and political values does not make critical investigation impossible. As Geerz (1973, p30) comments in relation to ethnographic and anthropological work:

'I have never been impressed by the argument that, as complete objectivity is impossible ... one might as well let one's sentiments run loose. As Robert Solow has remarked, that is like saying that as a perfectly aseptic (germ free) environment is impossible, one might as well conduct surgery in a sewer.'

Research that is rigorous and reflexive produces knowledge that is more objective than research which is sloppy and uncritical. Researchers who, as well as being technically competent, consider the impact of their own gender, 'racialised' and class identity upon the research process and who understand that research is itself a form of social interaction will produce a more reliable picture of the social world. In short, there are better and worse ways of conducting research.

Source: O'Connell Davidson & Layder, 1994

Item C *The value of money – a Blackfoot view*

One day White men came into our camp to buy our land for dollar bills and put us on reservations with other Indians.

When the White chief had laid all of his money down on the ground and shown how much he would give all of us for signing a treaty with him, our chief took a handful of clay and made a ball of it and put it on the fire and cooked it. And it did not crack. Then he said to the White chief:

'Now, give me some of your money; we will put the money on the fire and the clay alongside of it, and whichever burns the quickest is the cheapest.'

The White chief said:

'My money will burn the quickest, because it is made of paper; so we can't do that.'

Our chief then reached down into his belt pocket and took out a little buckskin bag of sand, and he handed it to the White chief, and said: 'Give me your money. I will count the money, while you count the grains of sand. Whichever can be counted the quickest will be the cheapest.'

The White chief took the sand and poured it out into the palm of his hand, and as he looked at it, he said:

'I would not live long enough to count this, but you can count the money quickly.'

'Then,' our chief said, 'our land is more valuable than your money. It will last forever. It will not even perish by the flames of fire. As long as the sun shines and the waters flow, this land will be here to give life to men and animals. We cannot sell the lives of men and animals; therefore we cannot sell this land. It was put here for us by the Great Spirit, and we cannot sell it because it does not belong to us. You can count your money and burn it within the nod of a buffalo's head, but only the Great Spirit can count the grains of sand and the blades of grass on these plains. As a present to you, we will give you anything we have that you can take with you; but the land, never.'

Source: Long Lance, 1956

Blackfoot Indians performing a religious ceremony

Item D **King Canute**

King Canute ordering the waves to go back

questions

1   Do you agree with Becker's view in Item A? Give reasons for your answer.
2   'There are better and worse ways of conducting research.' Discuss with reference to Item B.
3   It is useful to look at social life from a variety of standpoints and vantage points. Discuss with some reference to Item C.
4   How does the cartoon in Item D support O'Connell Davidson and Layder's rejection of relativism? (See page 246.)

Unit 7 *Sociology and social policy*

key issues

1   What is the relationship between sociology and social policy?

2   To what extent has sociology influenced governments in recent years?

Social policy refers to government policy on a range of social issues – for example, education, the family and poverty. Have sociologists a contribution to make? After all, they study these areas. Should they be consulted by government and join the working parties which shape social policy? Or, should they stand apart from government, criticising social policy and developing alternatives to existing policy?

7.1 The founding fathers

Many of the founding fathers believed that sociology had a central part to play in society – in reforming social institutions, solving social problems and improving the human condition.

Auguste Comte (1798-1857) Comte saw sociology as a practical subject. It shouldn't remain in the universities, it should be applied to the wider society. Comte believed in order and progress – he saw sociology providing the ideas to reinforce social order and direct social progress. In his words, the purpose of sociology is 'to know, in order to predict, in order to control'.

Emile Durkheim (1858-1917) Like Comte, Durkheim focused on the question of order in society. He was concerned with the political upheaval and civil unrest which he believed resulted from industrialisation and a breakdown of value consensus. He saw sociology as providing ways of restoring order and strengthening the integration of society.

Durkheim believed that sociology pointed to a need for a new moral order in industrial society, whereby people would be bound together by a sense of duty and obligation to the community as a whole.

Karl Marx (1818-1883) Where Durkheim saw sociologists working with governments to improve existing societies, Marx looked forward to the overthrow of governments and their replacement with communist societies.

Marx hoped that his work would inspire and direct working-class movements in capitalist societies. However, it was only after his death that his ideas shaped history. For example, Lenin's interpretation of Marxism provided a practical framework for the establishment of a communist state after the Russian Revolution of 1917.

Sociologists today Today's sociologists tend to be a lot less ambitious than the founding fathers. Many feel that sociology can make important contributions to social policy. However, they tend to see these contributions as limited to specific areas such as family policy or education policy. They are unlikely to see sociological ideas or research findings reforming society as a whole, as Durkheim hoped, or spearheading revolutionary change as Marx anticipated.

7.2 Shaping social policy

Before looking in detail at the relationship between sociology and social policy, it is important to have some indication of the factors which shape social policy.

David Donnison, one of the UK's leading experts on poverty, makes the following points about how social policy is shaped.

'As in all debates about important issues of social policy, the questions posed and the concepts used in debates about poverty are shaped partly by changing circumstances and growing knowledge, but also by the changing political agendas of the societies concerned.' (Donnison, 2001)

Changing circumstances Societies change. To some extent social policy is shaped by changes in society. This is illustrated by the following example.

The aftermath of a war often brings changes. People have made great sacrifices, their lives have been disrupted and they are often not prepared to accept their old status – they want something better. This can be seen in the expansion of social services after the First World War (1914-1918) when the then Prime Minister, Lloyd George, promised the troops 'homes fit for heroes'.

During the Second World War (1939-1945) a committee chaired by Sir William Beveridge produced the famous *Beveridge Report on Social Insurance and Allied Services*. Published in 1942, it became an immediate bestseller. Popular support for its principles was widespread both at home and among the troops abroad. Its recommendations appeared to embody the very things being fought for – democracy, freedom and equality.

The Beveridge Report's recommendations were put into effect by a series of Acts from 1944 to 1948. Together they created the modern welfare state in the UK.

Growing knowledge Social policy is also shaped by a growth in knowledge. The following evidence illustrates this point.

During the 19th century, the dominant view of poverty saw it resulting from some form of character defect – the poor lacked moral fibre, they were work-shy, lazy and idle. In other words, the poor were to blame for their poverty (Page, 2001).

In 1899, Seebohm Rowntree conducted a systematic study of poverty in York. In terms of his definition of poverty – insufficient food, fuel and clothing to maintain good health – 28% of York's population were poor. In many cases, there was no evidence of individual blame. In some cases, the breadwinner's wages were simply too low to keep the family out of poverty. And in other cases, people were too old or sick to work.

Research such as this influenced governments. For example, Liberal governments in the early 1900s were increasingly likely to see poverty as a social rather than an individual problem, and as a problem for which the state should accept some responsibility. This view is reflected in their social policies. For example, the 1908 Old Age Pensions Act provided pensions for those over 70. And the 1911 National Insurance Act provided sickness benefit to all manual workers and other workers below a certain income level.

Changing political agendas This is the third major influence on social policy identified by Donnison (2001).

Different political parties have different political agendas which shape their social policies. For example, the Labour Party has traditionally been the main supporter of social welfare policies. And political agendas change. For example, the policies of New Labour in the 2000s are very different from those of Labour of 20 years ago.

To what extent does sociology influence the thinking of political parties in general and their social policies in particular? This is a difficult question to answer. An attempt will be made in Section 7.3 with reference to Tony Blair's Labour governments.

It is probably safe to say that governments listen to sociologists when it suits them and when sociological theories and research findings fit their politics. This can be seen from the Conservative governments of Margaret Thatcher (1979-1990) and John Major (1990-1997). Mrs Thatcher had no time for sociology. However, she was influenced by New Right thinkers who included sociologists like David Marsland in the UK and Charles Murray in the USA.

The New Right blamed the welfare state for creating what they saw as a dependency culture whereby those at the bottom of the class structure became dependent on welfare benefits. As a result, so the argument goes, they lost the will to work, self-reliance, initiative and individual responsibility. The Thatcher and Major governments attempted to end this 'culture of dependency' by reducing welfare benefits and introducing measures such as the Job Seekers' Allowance and the Child Support Agency (Page, 2001).

New questions David Donnison (2001) claims that 'major shifts in policy often come about, not when the old questions are finally answered, but when new questions are asked'. He gives the following example to illustrate this.

For years the question had been: Does the death penalty deter people from killing each other? Researchers researched, politicians debated and the death penalty remained in force. Around 1963, a new question was increasingly heard: Is the death penalty acceptable in a civilised society? And two years later the death penalty was abolished. A new question had led to a new policy.

Does sociology ask new questions which influence government policy? The short answer is sometimes. The following provides an example.

Rowntree's study of poverty in York, discussed earlier, was largely based on the idea of *absolute poverty*. People were defined as poor if they were unable to meet basic needs such as adequate food and shelter. In terms of this concept, it appeared that, by the 1960s, poverty was a small and dwindling problem. Then, two British sociologists, Brian Abel-Smith and Peter Townsend, developed a new concept – *relative poverty* – which led to new questions.

Relative poverty was defined as the inability to afford an acceptable standard of living and a reasonable style of life. The idea of basic needs was extended to include things that most people would see as reasonable – for example, an annual holiday and Christmas presents for the children. In terms of relative poverty, 7.5 million people, that is 14.2% of the population, were now defined as poor – a massive jump from previous estimates (Abel-Smith & Townsend, 1965). Earlier studies had seen the elderly as the largest group in poverty. This now changed to the low paid with dependent children (see Activity 7). And this suggested a change in social policy – direct more resources to the low paid with young children.

From the 1960s onwards, sociologists have used the concept of relative poverty. This concept leads to new questions and new answers. Governments have increasingly seen poverty in relative terms and reflected this view in their policies.

7.3 Sociology, social policy and New Labour

The influence of sociology on government can probably be seen most clearly in Tony Blair's New Labour – both in the general philosophy of the party and in its social policy.

When New Labour came to power in 1997, they offered a *Third Way* in politics – neither the traditional left-wing policies of 'old' Labour, nor the right-wing policies of the Conservatives. The Third Way sought new directions and new solutions to old and new problems.

Much of this was influenced by one of Britain's leading sociologists, Anthony Giddens, who has been described as Tony Blair's favourite guru. Giddens' *The Third Way: The Renewal of Social Democracy* was published in 1998.

Giddens and the Third Way

In *The Third Way*, Giddens stressed the importance of social solidarity and social cohesion. He argued that a strong society needed active citizens who were concerned not just about their rights but also their duties and obligations to the community.

Giddens called for a renewal of civil society. He saw it as the job of government to promote this renewal. Community-based organisations who have a sense of civic duty should be encouraged. This would strengthen social integration.

Giddens saw *social exclusion* as the main threat to social order and social solidarity. Society would tend to fracture and disintegrate if groups became excluded from the mainstream. For example, if the poor or ethnic minorities were detached from the wider society, they would not feel part of the national community.

What can governments do to prevent social exclusion? In the case of the poor, for example, exclusion can be prevented by raising welfare benefits, improving public services – especially health and education – and providing opportunities to move out of poverty. Without measures such as these, the poor would be excluded from mainstream society and social solidarity would be threatened (Giddens, 1998, 2000; Bennett, 2001).

New Labour and the Third Way

Social Exclusion Unit Giddens' Third Way is reflected in New Labour's social policy. In their first year of government, Labour set up the Social Exclusion Unit to find solutions to the problem of exclusion. The Unit is directly responsible to the Cabinet and it attempts to ensure that all policies – health, education, poverty, crime, urban renewal – are part of a coordinated strategy to deal with social exclusion (MacGregor, 2001).

Poverty Living in poverty means exclusion from many of the activities that most people take for granted. The largest group in poverty are low-paid workers and their dependent children. Labour's policy to reduce poverty has focused on this group. It has introduced the following:

- A minimum wage
- The Working Families Tax Credit to top up the wages of low-paid workers
- A significant increase in Child Benefit allowances
- The National Childcare Strategy which provides money for the development of childcare centres
- The Sure Start programme which provides health and support services for low-income families with children under four (Donnison, 2001; Page, 2002).

Unemployment Labour's New Deal, introduced in 1998,

was part of their programme for social inclusion. The New Deal offered education and training for young people between the ages of 18 and 24 who had been out of work for more than six months. It was later extended to older people.

The New Deal provided personal advisors who offered direction and support to the unemployed, guiding them through the various options – academic courses, vocational training, self-employment, or voluntary work.

The New Deal emphasised the duties of citizenship. It was the duty of unemployed people to take up work and training opportunities. If they didn't, their benefits might be withheld until they did.

Education Shortly after their election in 1997, Labour promised to 'overcome economic and social disadvantage and make equality of opportunity a reality' (*Excellence in Schools*, 1997).

The focus was reaching out to the excluded and providing them with opportunities to enter mainstream society. This involved finding new ways of motivating young people in deprived inner-city areas and of improving 'underachieving schools'. For example, Education Action Zones were set up in urban areas which had low levels of educational attainment.

Citizenship Labour has made the teaching of citizenship a compulsory part of the secondary school curriculum. One of the aims is to encourage 'active citizenship' – to develop young people who are public-spirited, who recognise their social responsibilities and who translate this into action in their local communities (Chitty, 2002).

Labour under Gordon Brown The Labour Party under Gordon Brown has continued the social policies of the Blair years. There has been a particular focus on equality of opportunity – on providing a framework which gives 'every child the chance to unlock their talent' and move up the social scale. To this end, Sure Start has been expanded to nearly 3,000 children's centres in 2008, with an additional 500 planned for 2010. The aim is to draw children from disadvantaged areas into mainstream society by giving them the skills to become upwardly mobile.

Sociologists have shown that social mobility has ground to a halt during the Labour years. Partly to address this situation, Labour put forward proposals in 2008 for an Equality Act which they claimed would 'promote fairness and equality of opportunity' and 'tackle disadvantage and discrimination' (labour.org.uk, 2009).

Conclusion There is plenty of evidence here to suggest that sociology has had an important influence on Labour's social policy. However, this is only one perspective in sociology, and to some extent, only one person – Anthony Giddens. Other sociologists are critical of both the perspective and the person. For example, Stuart Hall has criticised *The Third Way* for attempting to smooth over basic contradictions and conflicts in society. And Angela McRobbie accuses both Giddens and New Labour of giving insufficient attention to the situation of women in society (Bennett, 2001).

Conclusion

It is not possible to establish with any certainty the relationship between sociology and social policy. The following points can be made.

- Sociology has some influence on social policy. However, it varies from government to government. As noted earlier, sociology was out of favour during the Conservative governments of Margaret Thatcher and John Major. However, in the person of Anthony Giddens, it has had a significant influence on Tony Blair and New Labour.

- Governments tend to select particular perspectives within sociology when forming social policy. They are rarely influenced by radical perspectives.

- Sociology provides a range of ideas and evidence which can inform social policy. Sociologists often sit on government committees and working parties which develop social policy. Some are employed by pressure groups such as the Low Pay Unit and the Child Poverty Action Group.

- People with a background in sociology are often employed by government departments. For example, the Home Office, which carries out its own research, sometimes employs people with qualifications in sociology.

- Some sociologists see themselves as problem raisers rather than problem solvers. They should be critical, they should identify problems, they should open governments' eyes rather than helping to solve problems which governments have identified and selected as deserving of solution.

- Other sociologists see sociology simply as an academic subject. Their job is to conduct research and present their findings, not to apply their research skills to solving problems defined by government. In fact, standing apart from government is a virtue – it helps sociologists to maintain their independence.

- Sociology is only one of many influences on social policy.

key terms

Social policy Government policy on social issues – for example, education, the family and social inequality.

Absolute poverty The inability to meet basic needs such as adequate food and shelter.

Relative poverty The inability to afford an acceptable standard of living and a reasonable style of life.

Third Way A new direction in politics which differs from traditional left-wing and right-wing policies.

Social exclusion Exclusion from the mainstream of society.

summary

1. Many of the founding fathers believed that sociology had an important part to play in changing society for the better.

2. According to David Donnison, social policy is shaped by a variety of factors. These include:
   - Changing circumstances in society
   - A growth in knowledge
   - Changing political agendas.

3. The influence of sociology on social policy varies from government to government. For example, the Conservative governments of the 1980s and 1990s had no time for sociology. However, Tony Blair's Labour governments were strongly influenced by Anthony Giddens' writings.

4. New Labour's concern with social exclusion reflects Giddens' view that social exclusion is the main threat to social solidarity and social order.

activity7 sociology and social policy

Item A Two views of poverty

Rowntree conducted three studies of poverty in York – in 1899, 1936 and 1950. Based mainly on a concept of absolute poverty, they indicated a steady reduction in poverty. The table compares Rowntree's 1950 study with a study by Abel-Smith and Townsend in 1960 based on a concept of relative poverty.

Percentage of those in poverty Rowntree 1950	Cause of poverty	Percentage of those in poverty Abel-Smith and Townsend 1960
4.2	Inadequate wages and/or large families	40
68.1	Old age	33
6.4	Fatherless families	10
21.3	Sickness	10
0	Unemployment	7
1.5	Percentage of sample population in poverty	14.2

(Wages are adequate or not depending on the number of dependent family members who require support.)

Source: Coates & Silburn, 1970

Item C Equality of opportunity

In his address to the Labour Party Conference in 2008, Gordon Brown made the following statement.

'For me fairness ... isn't levelling down but empowering people to aspire and reach even higher. And to take advantage of the global economy, I want to unleash a new wave of social mobility across the country.'

Source: labour.org.uk, 2009

Gordon Brown addressing the Labour Party Conference in 2008

Item B Tony Blair on social policy

- 'For too long, the demand for rights from the state was separated from the duties of citizenship and the imperative for mutual responsibility on the part of individuals and institutions.'

- 'A key challenge of progressive politics is to use the state as an enabling force, protecting effective communities and voluntary organisations and encouraging their growth to tackle new needs, in partnership as appropriate.'

- 'Our historic aim will be for ours to be the first generation to end child poverty, and it will take a generation.'

- 'The sight of a rough-sleeper bedding down for the night in a shop doorway or on a park bench is one of the most potent symbols of social exclusion in Britain today.'

Source: May et al., 2001

questions

1. Read Item A. How might an acceptance of the idea of relative poverty change government social policy?

2. Judging from the quotes in Item B, what influence has Anthony Giddens had on Tony Blair's social policy?

3. How does Gordon Brown's statement in Item C fit with the policies of the Blair years?

5 Sociological theory

Introduction

Throughout your sociology course, you have been examining specific topics with the help of sociological theories. You may have considered, for example, functionalist theories of education and the family, or Marxist theories of power and religion. Whilst these theories certainly do have a lot to say about such specific issues, they are in fact much more general theories about the nature of society, individuals, and the relationship between the two. The aim of this chapter is to explore these general theories in more depth, and to evaluate their contribution to our understanding of the nature and development of human societies and the individuals who comprise them.

chaptersummary

▶ **Unit 1** outlines the nature of sociological theory and the ways in which sociological theories can be evaluated.

▶ **Unit 2** discusses the origins of sociological theory and the work of three major 19th century theorists.

▶ **Unit 3** examines the establishment of three major

schools of sociological theory which emerged during the first half of the 20th century.

▶ **Unit 4** looks at the ideas of structure and action in sociological theory.

▶ **Unit 5** examines two recent challenges to sociological theory.

Unit 1 What is sociological theory?

keyissues

1 What is sociological theory?
2 How can sociological theories be evaluated?

The topics you have looked at so far have been viewed from a number of different perspectives – for example, Marxism, functionalism and symbolic interactionism. These, together with several others, are sociological theories, and they are fundamental to the whole discipline of sociology. Before we go on to examine what the various sociological theories say, it will be helpful to explain what a sociological theory actually is. There are essentially two elements to this – sociological theories as *models* and sociological theories as *propositions*.

1.1 Sociological theories as models

If we try to create a model of something, we attempt to create a representation of it. The sorts of models with which most of us are familiar are models of objects such as boats or aircraft. When we make models of such objects,

we attempt to represent their main features in such a way that they are recognisable, without actually building another whole boat or aircraft. Inevitably, when we build such a model, we emphasise some features of the real object at the expense of the others – one model of the *Queen Elizabeth 2* (QE2) might have a particularly realistic passenger deck, whilst another a very realistic funnel. When we see a good model of the QE2, we recognise it as a model of the QE2, but do not mistake it for the real thing. We can also recognise two different models as being equally good models, even though each has different strengths and weaknesses.

Sociologists do something rather similar when they attempt to represent society. In creating models of society they attempt to represent its important features. Just as with building a model ship, some features of society are inevitably emphasised at the expense of others. So, for example, Marxism places particular emphasis on the conflicts in society whilst functionalists tend to emphasise the degree of consensus in society. Neither gives a complete representation of society, but each draws attention to some of its important features.

A difficulty with this view of sociological theories as

models concerns how we can choose between them. Although sociological theories can often be directly compared with features of the society they represent, and judgements made about their accuracy, sometimes this is not the case. Some theories are rather like a hall of mirrors at a seaside resort. A hall of mirrors is a collection of distorting mirrors, some of which make you appear very thin, some very fat and others which grossly distort the proportions of your body. Of course, we know that our bodies are being distorted by these mirrors because we have seen our reflections in ordinary mirrors.

Similarly, sociological theories can function like a hall of mirrors. Each provides a different representation of society. But, since we do not know which mirror gives the true representation, it is very difficult, if not impossible, for us to select the most accurate image. For this reason, choosing between competing sociological theories can be one of the most challenging, but also one of the most interesting, tasks facing the sociologist.

1.2 Sociological theories as propositions

Although it might be difficult to choose which competing sociological theory gives us the best representation of society, it is important that we try to find ways of doing so. If we did not, and simply decided to regard each theory as a different but equally valid representation of society, we would face some serious difficulties.

The idea that competing theories are merely different but equally valid views is often called *relativism*. The chief difficulty with relativism is that it can lead to conclusions which are logically impossible. This is sometimes referred to as the problem of incoherence. Consider the following example of a relativist argument: 'the feminist claim that the most fundamental divisions in society are those of gender is a different but equally valid argument as the Marxist claim that the most fundamental divisions in society are those of class'.

The problem is this – the most fundamental divisions in society cannot be *both* those of class and gender. One must be, by definition, more fundamental than the other. We could claim the following: 'divisions of class and gender are equally fundamental'. In so doing, however, we would in fact be contradicting both claims in the original argument, because each insists that one division is more fundamental than the other. This shows us that when we are faced with contradictory theories – theories which cannot both be right – we must reject either one or both of the theories.

The question is, therefore, on what basis should we reject or accept any given sociological theory? To begin to see the answer to this, it is important to notice that sociological theories – like other types of theory – usually contain within them what we might call *propositions*. Essentially, a proposition is any statement which purports to say something which is true. Both of the theories we considered above purported to say something which was

truthful – that gender was the most fundamental division in society and that class was the most fundamental division in society. Both theories therefore contained propositions. There are basically two ways in which we can evaluate propositions.

Logical evaluation The first of these we could call *logical evaluation*. This concerns the internal validity of the argument we are examining. Do the various elements of the theory fit together in a logically coherent way, or do they contradict each other? We have already examined one example of logical evaluation. We saw that to simultaneously accept the different claims of Marxists and feminists about which divisions in society are the most fundamental is simply illogical. It should therefore be rejected before we even begin to examine the available evidence.

Sometimes a theory might be perfectly logical, but contradicted by some piece of evidence. Consider the following example:

All sociologists vote Labour.
Basil is a sociologist.
Therefore, Basil votes Labour.

Logically, the conclusion, 'Therefore, Basil votes Labour' follows from the premises of this argument. It may well be, however, that each statement within the argument is untrue – not all sociologists vote Labour and Basil could be an accountant who votes for the Natural Law Party.

Similarly, some or all of the elements of an argument could be perfectly true, but the argument itself is logically flawed. Consider the following:

The first professor of sociology was French.
Durkheim was the first professor of sociology.
Therefore, Durkheim wrote a book called *Suicide*.

Each one of these statements is perfectly true, but taken together the conclusion simply does not follow from what went before. In fact, logically, this 'argument' is nonsense, even though each of its elements is perfectly true.

These examples show us is that it is just as important to pay attention to the form of an argument as it is to the truth of its various elements. Clearly, however, the logical validity of any particular sociological argument is not the only criterion by which it should be evaluated.

Empirical evaluation As well as a theory's logical validity, we should also be concerned about the truth of the specific propositions it contains. If we cannot accept on logical grounds the argument that Marxism and feminism present equally valid views of which are the most fundamental social divisions, then we are still left with the need to decide which divisions are in fact most fundamental. Somewhat obviously, we need to do this by comparing the various claims being made with the social reality they are purporting to describe. This task we can call *empirical evaluation*.

As you will have seen in the chapter on methodology, sociologists have devised many ingenious methods of gathering data about social phenomena. Let us take just one to illustrate the example we are considering. Imagine we decide to try to settle the dispute between Marxists and feminists by conducting a series of interviews with a carefully selected sample of individuals. Imagine we ask working-class women which group they feel they have most in common with – working-class men, or upper-class women. If the majority choose upper-class women, then we might conclude that the feminist theory is the most accurate, in that gender is being identified by the respondents as the most important variable. If the majority choose the working-class men, then we would perhaps conclude that the Marxist point of view is the most accurate, since class has been identified as the most important variable.

Whilst at first sight this appears to be a straightforward way of settling disputes between theories, there is in fact a serious problem with it. Marxists, faced with the evidence that most people regard gender as the most important division in society, could easily argue that this result has arisen from the *false consciousness* of the respondents. In other words, those people interviewed falsely believed gender to be most important because such a belief serves the interests of the capitalist ruling class. Marxists might therefore argue that in reality it is class which is most important, even though people do not generally recognise this.

This last example illustrates a very important point about the relationship between sociological theories and empirical evidence. Whilst theories certainly make statements about the real world which they claim to be true, they also often contain their own standards by which these statements should be evaluated. In other words, some piece of empirical evidence might be accepted as valid by supporters of one theory, but not by supporters of another. What this means is that sociological theories cannot always be straightforwardly tested by obtaining empirical evidence, as the validity and relevance of this evidence may always be challenged by supporters of the theory in question.

We have tried in this section to show that sociological theories need to be evaluated both logically and empirically, but that the latter may not always be straightforward because there exists a complex relationship between theories and empirical evidence. We now turn to a consideration of the origins of sociological theory in the ideas of the Enlightenment, and the writings of Karl Marx, Emile Durkheim and Max Weber.

key terms

Model A representation of something.
Proposition A statement which claims to be true.
Relativism In this context, the view that theories are different but equally valid.
Logical evaluation Evaluating a theory to see if its logic is sound. For example, do its propositions contradict each other?
Empirical evaluation Evaluating a theory in terms of evidence. For example, does the evidence support the theory?
False consciousness A false or distorted view of the world.

activity1 life of Galileo

Brecht wrote *Life of Galileo* in 1938. Galileo was a 17th century scientist whose discoveries challenged the Ptolemaic model of the universe which placed the earth at the centre of the universe, a view supported by the Church. Galileo's discoveries also challenged the ideas of the ancient Greek philosopher Aristotle which were still influential. In this extract from Scene 4, Galileo is trying to persuade court scholars of the significance of his discoveries.

GALILEO *at the telescope:* As your highness no doubt realises, we astronomers have been running into great difficulties in our calculations for some while. We have been using a very ancient system which is apparently consistent with our philosophy but not, alas, with the facts. Would you gentlemen care to start by observing these satellites of Jupiter, the Medician stars?

ANDREA (the housekeeper's son) *indicating the stool by the telescope:* Kindly sit here.

PHILOSOPHER: Thank you, my boy. I fear things are not quite so simple. Mr Galileo, before turning to your famous tube, I wonder if we might have the pleasure of a disputation?

Galileo displays his telescope to Florentine nobles.

Its subject to be: Can such planets exist?

MATHEMATICIAN: A formal dispute.

GALILEO: I was thinking you could just look through the telescope and convince yourselves.

ANDREA: This way, please.

MATHEMATICIAN: Of course, of course. I take it you are

familiar with the opinion of the ancients that there can be no stars which turn round centres other than the earth, nor any which lack support in the sky?

GALILEO: I am.

PHILOSOPHER: Moreover, quite apart from the very possibility of such stars, which our mathematicians – *he turns towards the mathematician* – would appear to doubt, I would like in all humility to pose the philosophical question: are such stars necessary? The universe of the divine Aristotle, with the mystical music of its spheres and its crystal vaults, the orbits of its heavenly bodies, the slanting angle of the sun's course, the secrets of the moon tables, the starry richness catalogued in the southern hemisphere and the transparent structure of the celestial globe add up to an edifice of such exquisite proportions that we should think twice before disrupting its harmony.

GALILEO: How about your highness now taking a look at his impossible and unnecessary stars through this telescope?

MATHEMATICIAN: One might be tempted to answer that, if your tube shows something which cannot be there, it cannot be an entirely reliable tube, wouldn't you say?

GALILEO: What d'you mean by that?

MATHEMATICIAN: It would be rather more appropriate, Mr Galileo, if you were to name your reasons for assuming that there could be free-floating stars moving about in the highest sphere of the unalterable heavens.

PHILOSOPHER: Your reasons, Mr Galileo, your reasons.

GALILEO: My reasons! When a single glance at the stars themselves and my own notes makes the phenomenon evident? Sir, your disputation is becoming absurd.

MATHEMATICIAN: If one could be sure of not over-exciting you, one might say that what is in your tube and what is in the skies is not necessarily the same thing.

PHILOSOPHER: That couldn't be more courteously put.

FEDERZONI: They think we painted the Medician stars on the lens.

GALILEO: Are you saying I'm a fraud?

PHILOSOPHER: How could we? In his highness's presence too.

MATHEMATICIAN: Let's not beat about the bush. Sooner or later Mr Galileo will have to reconcile himself to the facts. Those Jupiter satellites of his would penetrate the crystal spheres. It is as simple as that.

FEDERZONI: You'll be surprised: the crystal spheres don't exist.

PHILOSOPHER: Any textbook will tell you that they do, my good man.

FEDERZONI: Right, then let's have new textbooks.

PHILOSOPHER: Your highness, my distinguished colleague and I are supported by none less than the divine Aristotle himself.

GALILEO *almost obsequiously*: Gentlemen, to believe in the authority of Aristotle is one thing, tangible facts are another. You are saying that according to Aristotle there are crystal spheres up there, so certain motions just cannot take place because the stars would penetrate them. But suppose those motions could be established? Mightn't that suggest to you that those crystal spheres don't exist? Gentlemen, in all humility I ask you to go by the evidence of your eyes.

MATHEMATICIAN: My dear Galileo, I may strike you as very old-fashioned, but I'm in the habit of reading Aristotle now and again, and there, I can assure you, I trust the evidence of my eyes.

GALILEO: I am used to seeing the gentlemen of the various faculties shutting their eyes to every fact and pretending that nothing has happened. I produce my observations and everyone laughs. I offer my telescope so they can see for themselves, and everyone quotes Aristotle.

FEDERZONI: The fellow has no telescope.

MATHEMATICIAN: That's just it.

PHILOSOPHER *grandly*: If Aristotle is going to be dragged in the mud – that's to say an authority recognised not only by every classical scientist but also by the chief fathers of the church – then any prolonging of this discussion is in my view a waste of time.

Source: B. Brecht, *Life of Galileo*, 1980

questions

1 a) What reasons does Galileo give for believing his model of the universe?

   b) What reasons do the court scholars give for rejecting this model?

2 When sociologists evaluate theories, are they likely to draw upon the type of evidence Galileo uses or the type of evidence the court scholars use? Give reasons for your answer.

summary

1. There are two essential elements to sociological theories – models and propositions.

2. Theories can be evaluated in two ways – logical evaluation and empirical evaluation.

3. These types of evaluation are necessary to avoid relativism.

Without them, it is not possible to decide between competing theories.

4. Empirical evaluation is problematic because people may have a false consciousness. As a result, evidence based on their statements may not be valid.

Unit 2 *Classical sociology and the advent of modernity*

keyissues

1 What are the origins of sociological theory?

2 How significant is the work of Marx, Durkheim and Weber to the development of sociological theory?

Modernity Sociology, as a distinct form of enquiry, emerged in the 19th century in the wake of 'the so-called "twin revolutions" – the Industrial Revolution of England (and later elsewhere) which occurred roughly between 1780 and 1840 and the Democratic Revolutions of the United States of America in 1776 and France in 1789' (Lee & Newby, 1983). These revolutions signalled a radical transformation in society and the advent of *modernity*. Although the early sociologists characterised the transformation in different ways, they recognised that the modern world – which they saw emerging in their lifetimes – represented a significant break from the past.

There is now widespread agreement over the major features of modernity. They can be grouped under three headings – the economic, the political, and the cultural. Economically, modernity involves the dominance of industrial capitalism; politically, it involves the consolidation of the nation-state and, typically, liberal democracy; culturally it involves a stress on reason as opposed to tradition (Jones, 1993).

Responses to modernity The dramatic changes which occurred in North America and Northern Europe in the second half of the 18th century and the first half of the 19th century generated very different political responses. For liberals, the changes were welcome. Individuals are naturally rational and should be free to pursue their own interests. The removal of traditional restraints and the emergence of governments which guaranteed the rights of individuals were therefore seen as progressive developments. For socialists, the changes were not unwelcome, but were seen as not going far enough. Human beings are naturally communal and their interests can, therefore, only be met collectively. This necessitates the replacement of capitalism, which divides people, by socialism which enables people to cooperate. In contrast to these two optimistic responses to social change, conservatives exhibited horror. Human beings are naturally members of a social organism – unequal but dependent on each other. The revolutions, in their disregard for tradition and their rupture of the natural order, were seen as dangerous developments.

Liberalism, socialism and conservatism have all influenced the development of sociology. Much 19th century sociology took up the conservative concern with the threat to social order and much subsequent sociology

has involved a debate with the ghost of Marx, exhibiting in the process the influence of socialism (Zeitlin, 1971). Liberalism, however, was the most significant in the emergence of sociology as a distinct form of enquiry, because this was the dominant political philosophy of the Enlightenment.

2.1 The Enlightenment

The Enlightenment refers to 'a period in European intellectual history which spans the time from roughly the first quarter to the last quarter of the 18th century. Geographically centred in France, but with important outposts in most of the major European states, the "Enlightenment" is composed of the ideas and writings of a fairly heterogeneous group, who are often called by their French name *philosophes*' (Hamilton, 1992).

Whatever differences there were between the philosophes, they recognised that they were engaged on a common project. This is evident in their cooperative enterprise – the publication over 20 years of the *Encyclopédie*. This work reflected two shared principles – confidence in the ability of human reason to provide an understanding of the world, and faith in the ability of human beings to use this understanding to improve the world.

The radical nature of these two principles should not be underestimated. They constituted a direct challenge to the traditional conception of the world propagated by the Roman Church. Reason was no longer seen as subservient to divine revelation as interpreted through the teachings of the Roman Church. And history was no longer seen as 'synonymous with God working his purpose out' (Smart, 1992). Instead, stress was placed on the power of human reason to create knowledge, which in turn can be used to improve the human condition. In the process, the Enlightenment brought about a cultural change in what constitutes knowledge and what the purpose of knowledge is. A distinctly modern conception of knowledge was born.

The Enlightenment philosophes systematically developed and popularised among influential members of society ideas which had been originally formulated in an earlier era. Scientific discoveries in the 16th and 17th centuries challenged the traditional religious world view which placed the earth at the centre of the universe. The problem of deciding what constituted the truth was therefore raised in an acute form. Philosophers in the 17th century grappled with this question and came up with two broad answers.

For the *rationalists*, true knowledge was logically deduced from a few basic premises which could not be doubted. Descartes, for example, concluded that however much he doubted, he could be sure of one thing, 'cogito ergo sum' (I think therefore I am). This constituted for him a firm foundation for knowledge. For the *empiricists*, true knowledge was induced from, that is derived from observations. Berkeley, for example, concluded that 'esse est percipi' (to exist is to be perceived). This constituted for him a firm foundation for knowledge.

Although the rationalists and empiricists (and indeed many of the Enlightenment philosophes) continued to believe in a God, the basis of knowledge was no longer seen as the word of God (as interpreted through the Church) but reason or sensory observation. What the Enlightenment philosophes did was to synthesise these two traditions. 'An understanding or knowledge of natural and social reality was deemed to depend upon a unity of reason and observation, made possible by the practice of scientific methods of inquiry' (Smart, 1992).

Indeed, when 18th century writers talk of the power of human reason they 'meant the scientific method: the deductive reasoning of the mathematical sciences and the inductive, empirical reasoning of the sciences of nature' (Dunthorne, 1991).

The 17th century also witnessed a dispute between the 'ancients' and the 'moderns' over the respective merits of the works of classical antiquity and the more recent thinking of an emerging modern Europe. The view of the 'moderns' that knowledge had grown over time eventually gained ascendancy and paved the way for the Enlightenment to argue that there existed a more general process of social development and that knowledge could be used to promote further progress.

The Enlightenment belief that science was a force for enlightenment and progress generated tremendous optimism. The success of the natural sciences encouraged a belief 'that in the struggle of man against nature the balance of power was shifting in favour of man' (Gay, 1973). Science would enable human beings to gain mastery over nature. And the application of the scientific method to social arrangements would justify the reform of social institutions. In both cases, the result would be the enhancement of human freedom.

The emergence of a sociological perspective can be detected in the Enlightenment. 'For the first time, man could "dare to know" about the social arrangements under which he lived, rather than have them presented to him through the obscuring haze of a religious ideology. By knowing about these social arrangements, their operation would become clear, and thus open to change' (Hamilton, 1992). The philosophes tended not to have a clearly worked out model of society, however. Wedded to the notion that individuals are essentially rational and self sufficient, society was seen as a collection of individuals. It was therefore left to later writers in the 19th century to develop more coherent models of society and to give birth to sociology as a distinct form of enquiry. What is significant is that these writers built on the cultural change which the Enlightenment brought in ways of thinking about society. It is to the work of the three who above all others have established the principal frames of reference of modern sociology – Marx, Durkheim and Weber – that we now turn.

key terms

Rationalists They believed that true knowledge was logically deduced from a few basic premises or statements which were clearly true.

Empiricists They believed that true knowledge was derived from observations – from empirical evidence that could be directly observed.

activity2 the individual and society

Item A *A medieval model of the individual and society*

Society, like the human body, is an organism composed of different members. Each member has its own function – prayer or defence or merchandise or tilling the soil. Each must receive a means suited to its station and must claim no more. Within classes there must be equality. If one takes into his hand the living of two, his neighbour will go short. Between classes there must be inequality, or otherwise a class cannot perform its function or enjoy its rights.

Source: Tawney, 1936

Item B *The view of a 16th century writer*

God made all the parts of the body for the soul and with the soul to serve him and all the subjects in the kingdom to serve their King and with their King to serve him. If the head of the body ache, will not the heart be greatly grieved and every part feel his part of the pain of it. And if a King in his world be displeased then the heart of his kingdom (the hearts of his subjects) will have a feeling of it.

Nicholas Bretton, a 16th century writer

Item C *The rise of individualism*

The transformations which ushered in modernity tore the individual free from their stable moorings in traditions and structures. Since these were believed to be divinely ordained, they were held not to be subject to fundamental change. One's status, rank and position in the 'great chain of being' – the secular and divine order of things – overshadowed any sense that one was a sovereign individual. The birth of the 'sovereign individual' represented a significant break with the past.

The sovereign individual – the idea that the individual is the centre of the universe, that all things can be traced back to the individual, that the individual sets things in motion, makes the world go round and is the motor of social action and change – was a new idea which only gradually emerged.

Many major movements in Western thought and culture contributed to the emergence of this new conception: the Reformation and Protestantism, which set the individual conscience free from the religious institutions of the Church and exposed it directly to the eye of God; Renaissance humanism, which placed Man at the centre of the universe; the scientific revolutions, which endowed Man with the faculty and capacities to inquire into, investigate and unravel the mysteries of Nature; and the Enlightenment, centred on the image of rational, scientific Man, freed from dogma and intolerance, before whom the whole of human history was laid out for understanding and mastery.

Source: Hall, 1992

Item D An Enlightenment model of the individual and society

Man was born free, and he is everywhere in chains. Those who think themselves the masters of others are indeed greater slaves than they. How did this transformation come about? I do not know. How can it be made legitimate? That question I believe I can answer... The social order is a sacred right which serves as a basis for all other rights. And as it is not a natural right, it must be one founded on covenants – binding agreements. The problem is to determine what those covenants are.

'How to find a form of association which will defend the person and goods of each member with the collective force of all, and under which each individual, while uniting himself with the others, obeys no one but himself, and remains as free as before?' This is the fundamental problem to which the social contract holds the solution.

Whichever way we look at it, we always return to the same conclusion: namely that the social pact establishes equality among the citizens in that they all pledge themselves under the same conditions and must all enjoy the same rights.

Source: Rousseau, 1968

Item E Sir Isaac Newton

William Blake's painting (dated 1795) of the scientist Sir Isaac Newton. Blake portrays him as a godlike figure drawing on a chart beside his underwater grotto.

questions

1 Read Items A and B. How do they portray the relation between the individual and society?

2 Read Item C. How does the relation between the individual and society change with the rise of modernity?

3 Read Item D. How does this Enlightenment model of society differ from that presented in Items A and B?

4 Briefly comment on the painting of Sir Isaac Newton in the light of Items A to D.

2.2 Karl Marx (1818-1883)

Marx did not see himself as a sociologist, but his ideas have been extremely influential within sociology and have in fact formed the basis for a distinct sociological perspective. This perspective is characterised by three central features. First, the starting point for analysing society should always be the material conditions of production – the way people organise the production of goods and services. Second, the motor of social change is class conflict and it is such conflict which propels society forward from one production system to another. Third, the conditions which will enable the working class to replace the modern oppressive productive system by a classless system can be scientifically identified. Marx's support for a scientific approach and his view that this approach can help society to progress indicate his debt to the Enlightenment.

The materialist conception of history

For Marx, the first priority of human beings is to ensure physical survival by producing the means of subsistence. Unless the provision of food and shelter is met, no other activity is possible. Hence, according to Marx, the way society organises its production is the most fundamental aspect of human existence and it is from this that all other aspects of human activity develop. Thus ideas, which other writers such as Hegel had seen as fundamental for social life, are ultimately dependent upon the way people organise the production of their means of subsistence.

The economic base and social superstructure

In developing his materialist conception of history, Marx distinguished between the *base* and *superstructure* of society. The base consists of the *forces of production* (the tools and machinery, the knowledge and the raw materials which people use in order to produce goods and services) and the *relations of production* (the social relationships between people involved in the production process).

Those parts of the forces of production which can be legally owned, for example land in feudal society and factories in capitalist society, are known as the *means of production*.

Together, the forces and relations of production define the way a society organises its production of goods or services, or *mode of production*. The economic base or dominant mode of production is the bedrock of society and all other social institutions and processes develop from it and are ultimately dependent upon it. As Marx put it, the economic base is 'the real foundation on which legal and political superstructures arise and to which definite forms of social consciousness correspond. The mode of production of material life determines the general character of the social, political and spiritual processes of life' (Bottomore & Rubel, 1961).

Let us take an example of one mode of production, feudalism. In societies where this was the dominant mode of production, land was the chief means of production so that ownership of land put the lords in a position of dominance over the serfs who had to work the land in order to survive. Since the serfs did not own the land, they were forced to hand over a proportion of what they produced as tithes to the lords. The rest of the social structure reflected the economic subordination of the serfs to the lords. The legal system obliged serfs to provide military service for their lords and the church justified their exploitation.

Class and social change

Marx was less concerned to offer a description of any particular mode of production than to put forward an account of how it changes and is eventually replaced by another. He distinguished four main modes of production

which have succeeded each other. In chronological order they are primitive communism, ancient society, feudalism and capitalism. Apart from primitive communism where people only produce enough to subsist and there is no surplus for a particular group to appropriate, each mode of production is characterised by a particular set of class relations.

Those who own the means of production exploit the labour of those who do not own the means of production. In ancient society masters exploited the labour of slaves whom they owned; in feudal society the lords exploited the labour of serfs who were tied to the land; and in capitalist society the bourgeoisie exploit the labour power of the proletariat who are forced to work for them in order to survive. In each case exploitation leads to *class conflict* and the eventual replacement of each mode of production.

Class conflict leads to the overthrow of a mode of production because of underlying contradictions which develop within the mode of production between the forces of production and relations of production. The forces of production develop as people discover new ways of mastering nature and generating wealth. There comes a point, however, when their full potential is held back by the existing relations of production. It is then that the conditions are conducive for the class who own the new means of production to rise up and overthrow the old mode of production.

This process can be illustrated by the transition from feudalism to capitalism. Within feudalism, the discovery of new sources of power, such as steam, allowed human beings to master nature more effectively. For this potential to be realised, however, it was essential that people were no longer tied to the land but free to work for those who owned the new sources of power. These were the conditions which encouraged the bourgeoisie to unite and overthrow the feudal relations of production and establish a new mode of production. In Marx's words, 'With the change of the economic foundation the entire immense superstructure is more or less rapidly transformed' (Bottomore & Rubel, 1961). Thus the bourgeoisie oust the feudal aristocracy from political power and the culture is transformed as concepts such as freedom replace the dominant concepts of feudalism such as loyalty. The resolution of old contradictions, however, does not mean an end to contradictions. Contradictions develop within the new mode of production – the contradictions of capitalism will eventually lead to its replacement by communism.

The transition from capitalism to communism

Marx's primary concern was to analyse capitalism and identify the conditions which will bring about its downfall. Capitalism can be defined in terms of two interrelated features: a) the production of goods and services is primarily geared to the search for profits which accrue to those people who own the means of production and b) the process is organised in terms of a market in which commodities, including labour power itself, are bought and sold. As a consequence, capitalism is characterised by two classes – those who own the means of production (the bourgeoisie) and those who do not own the means of production (the proletariat) who are therefore forced to sell their labour power and work for the bourgeoisie.

The relation between these classes is, on the surface, less exploitive than in a feudal society in which people were obliged, for example, to hand over a definite amount of produce to the lord of the manor or to work unpaid on the lord's land. In a capitalist society, workers hire out their energies and skills, in order to produce the goods and services which are eventually sold on the market, in exchange for wages. The exchange, however, is not a fair one. The wages invariably represent less in terms of value than the value realised through the sale of the products of proletarian labour and the difference between the two, which Marx called *surplus value*, is appropriated by the bourgeoisie as profit. For Marx, the relation between the bourgeoisie and proletariat is clearly one of exploitation, and has, as a consequence, the increasing *alienation* of the proletariat.

Alienation 'In what does this alienation consist?' Marx asked. 'First, that the work is external to the worker, that it is not a part of his nature, that consequently he does not fulfil himself in his work but denies himself, has a feeling of misery, not of wellbeing, does not develop freely a physical and mental energy, but is physically exhausted and mentally debased. The worker, therefore, feels himself at home during his leisure, whereas at work he feels homeless. His work is not voluntary but imposed, forced labour. It is not the satisfaction of a need, but only a means for satisfying other needs. Its alien character is clearly shown by the fact that as soon as there is no physical or other compulsion, it is avoided like the plague. Finally, the alienated character of work for the worker appears in the fact that it is not his work but work for someone else, that in work he does not belong to himself but to another person' (Bottomore & Rubel, 1961).

Crisis and contradiction As capitalism develops, Marx argued, so the conditions for its downfall and replacement become more apparent. Driven by the need to maintain the rate of profit, the bourgeoisie adopts increasingly sophisticated technology, thus creating the possibility for the population as a whole to enjoy a high standard of living and for its members to fulfil themselves. Such an outcome is, however, not possible so long as the bourgeoisie continues to appropriate surplus value for itself. In Marx's terms, the relations of production in a capitalist society prevent the promise of shared material abundance, which the developing forces of production point to, from being fully realised. What is more, the existence of a fundamental imbalance between production and consumption results in periodic crises when the market is unable to absorb all the goods and services which have been produced.

The bourgeoisie, of course, responds to such crises by seeking new markets around the world, thus encouraging in the process European colonial expansion. Economic crises, however, recur and invariably result in bankruptcies. In order to counteract these tendencies to overproduction, capital becomes more concentrated, thus making it increasingly possible for production to be centrally coordinated and orientated to people's needs. However, such an outcome is again not possible so long as the bourgeoisie compete with each other to make profits. For these possibilities to be realised, the revolutionary action of the proletariat is needed.

Class polarisation At first the proletariat's resistance to bourgeois domination is only sporadic. Members are not united but struggle among each other as well as against the bourgeoisie. Over time, however, a combination of circumstances promotes the *class consciousness* of the proletariat. The development of capitalism tends to mean the demise of classes characteristic of the former pre-industrial society – landowners and serfs – and therefore the emergence of a more simplified class structure as the last vestiges of the previous class structure disappear. The existence of a particularly vulnerable and unorganised sector of the labour force, which can be tapped during a boom but disposed of during a slump, described by Marx as 'a reserve army of labour,' tends to mean that wages remain around subsistence levels. As a result, the relative disparity in wealth between the bourgeoisie and proletariat increases. The introduction of machinery tends to mean the erosion of traditional craft skills and the elimination of skill divisions within the proletariat.

In short, a process of *class polarisation* occurs, in which the proletariat, less divided and subject to increasing relative poverty, face a clearly distinct bourgeoisie. As they live through the economic crises of capitalism with their attendant increases in unemployment and decreases in wages and as they work concentrated together in large factories, so members of the proletariat communicate to each other their increasing dissatisfaction with bourgeois exploitation. They organise themselves to begin with on a local level, and later on a national level, to improve their wages and conditions until, finally, they are strong enough to oust the bourgeoisie and set up a new society. In the process, they transform themselves from a mere category of people who happen to share the same conditions, to a group of people who, realising they share the same conditions, organise to change them. In Marx's terms, they make the transition from a *class in itself* to a *class for itself*.

Revolutionary change The bourgeoisie of course does attempt to prevent the proletariat from making this transition from a class in itself to a class for itself. Although its power rests ultimately on ownership of the means of production, such economic dominance is translated into political dominance with the result that the bourgeoisie becomes a ruling class. The state, considered by Marx to be 'the executive committee for managing the common affairs of the whole bourgeoisie' represents the interests of the class as a whole, managing its common affairs in two major ways. The first relies on its control of the means of coercion and involves being repressive. Examples here include legislation inhibiting the formation of trade unions and the use of the army to quash strikes. The second depends on the dissemination of beliefs and values throughout society and involves propagating *ideologies* which purport to show the justice and necessity of bourgeois domination. Particularly because, as Marx put it, 'the ideas of the ruling class are, in every age, the ruling ideas: ie the class which is the dominant material force in society is at the same time its dominant intellectual force' (Bottomore & Rubel, 1961). As a result, the development of class consciousness may be delayed.

Ultimately, Marx argued, the proletariat will see through the fog of bourgeois ideology and become revolutionary. For the revolution is inevitable. Marx went even further claiming that the proletarian revolution will be unique. Whereas past revolutions have been made by a minority for the benefit of a minority, the proletariat's revolution will be made by the majority for the benefit of the majority. This will enable a classless society to be formed in which the ideals put forward during the French Revolution will be fully realised – freedom will replace oppression; fulfilment alienation; equality inequality; fraternity self-interest. Such a society Marx called *communism*.

Evaluation

Economic determinism While it is indisputable that Marx saw economic factors as crucial in any analysis of society, it is unlikely that he ever believed, as some argue, that all social development is caused by economic changes. His famous statement, 'Men make history but not under circumstances of their own choosing' suggests rather that Marx believed human beings can have an influence on the outcome of events, but that this freedom of action is constrained by the limits set by the development of the economy. Whether Marx placed an undue emphasis on economic factors still remains a contentious issue, however.

Social change The opening line of the *Communist Manifesto*, written by Marx and Engels, states that 'the history of hitherto existing society is the history of class struggle'. This suggestion that history has an overall direction and that it is governed by a dynamic principle – the class struggle – is questioned by many contemporary sociologists. What's more, there is some dispute as to whether it's possible to talk of class divisions prior to the advent of capitalism. And whether other social divisions in modern societies are at least as significant as class.

The transition to communism Capitalist societies have not developed in the direction Marx anticipated. Although the 20th century has witnessed the establishment of communist states following revolutions, these have occurred in non-capitalist societies and have failed to fulfil Marx's vision of freedom and equality. What's more, the collapse of communist regions in Eastern Europe since 1989 has led some commentators to argue that Marx's ideas are no longer relevant. Needless to say, Marxists believe that they

can explain why capitalist societies have remained resistant to revolution, why communist regimes have collapsed, and why Marx's ideas remain as significant today as they ever were.

key terms

Forces of production The tools, machinery, raw materials and knowledge used to produce goods and services.

Relations of production The social relationships between people involved in the production process – for example, the relationships between employers and employees.

Means of production Those parts of the forces of production that can be legally owned – for example, factories in capitalist society.

Mode of production The forces and relations of production – the economic base of society. The way a society organises its production of goods and services.

Superstructure All other aspects of society – for example, the political and legal systems.

Class conflict The conflict of interest between the two major classes in society – those who own the means of production and those who do not.

Surplus value The difference between the costs of labour and the wealth received from that labour by those who own the means of production. In capitalist society, surplus value is the profits received by the bourgeoisie.

Alienation An alienated worker is cut off from their work, unfulfilled at work, is forced to work, and works for somebody else.

Class consciousness This occurs when the subject class, for example the proletariat, become fully aware of the truth about their situation.

Class polarisation This occurs when the gap in income and wealth between the ruling and subject classes grows steadily wider.

Class in itself People who share the same class position but are not aware of their true situation. They are blinded by false consciousness.

Class for itself People who share the same class position, are aware of their true situation, and organise to change it.

Ideology From a Marxist position, false beliefs and ideas – for example, justifications for the domination of the bourgeoisie.

Communism A classless society in which the means of production are communally owned and people are equal, free from oppression, and fulfilled as human beings.

2.3 Emile Durkheim (1858-1917)

Although the word 'sociology' and many of the discipline's founding principles had been established by Auguste Comte (1798-1857), it was Emile Durkheim who finally established sociology as a serious and respectable academic discipline. In particular, it was Durkheim who first offered a formal statement of 'sociological method' in his book *The Rules of Sociological Method* (1964; first published in 1895). Although, as we shall see, Durkheim's approach to the study of society can be subjected to a number of criticisms, its influence on sociology to this day should not be underestimated.

activity3 class and ideology

Item A Clement Attlee, Labour Prime Minister, 1945

Now a new Parliament must be elected. The choice is between that same Conservative Party which stands for private enterprise, private profit and private interests and the Labour Party which demands that in peacetime as in war the interests of the whole people should come before that of a section.

Item B Harold Macmillan, Conservative Prime Minister, 1959

This election has shown that the class war is obsolete.

Item C Harold Wilson, Labour Prime Minister, 1964

Let us be understanding. Let us not condemn them too harshly. For remember that these are men who were sure at birth that they were ordained by providence to rule over their fellow citizens and to find themselves rudely deprived of the powers that they exercised cannot have been easy for them.

Item D Ted Heath, Conservative Prime Minister, 1970

Our purpose is not to divide but to unite and where there are differences to bring reconciliation; to create one nation.

Item E Margaret Thatcher, Conservative Prime Minister, 1988

In the world in which we now live, divisions into class are outmoded and meaningless. We are all working people who basically want the same things.

Item F John Major, Conservative Prime Minister, 1992

I believe that in the next ten years we will have to continue to make changes that will genuinely produce across the whole of this country a genuinely classless society in which people can rise to whatever level that their own abilities and their own good fortune may take them from wherever they started.

Item G Tony Blair, Labour Prime Minister, 1999

I look forward to a new Britain... based not on privilege, class or background but on equal worth of all people.

Item H Gordon Brown, Prime Minister, 2007

I stand for a Britain where everyone should rise as far as their talents can take them.

Item I Your Country Needs You

"YOUR COUNTRY NEEDS **YOU**"

questions

1 Read items A to H. What similarities can you detect in these statements by post-war British Prime Ministers. How would Marx account for these similarities?

2 Look at Item I. How does this poster illustrate a similar ideology to that in Items A to H?

Durkheim's methodology – the study of 'social facts'

Durkheim's central methodological principle, first outlined in his *The Rules of Sociological Method*, was as follows: 'Consider social facts as things'. To understand what Durkheim meant by this, and to appreciate its significance, we need to begin by defining his concept of 'the social fact'. For Durkheim, *social facts* are characterised by two things: first, they must be *external* to the individual, and second, they must *exercise constraint* over the individual. Some examples will help to clarify what is meant by this.

A very obvious example (when we think about it) of a social fact is language. Let us see how language fulfils Durkheim's two criteria. First, language is external to individuals. Although it is perfectly true that it is internal to us in the sense that we all possess an individual knowledge of the language(s) which we speak, it is external to us in the sense that the language we speak was in existence before any one of us was born, and will continue to be in existence after each of us has died. Language is not an individual characteristic or creation. It is shared by and produced by the social group. As such, it is external to the individual.

Second, although we might not feel that language exercises a constraint over us, a moment's reflection will reveal that it certainly does. If we wish to say something to another speaker of the same language as us, we really have no choice but to use certain words as opposed to others. It is thus no use my using the word 'cheval' if I want to talk to a fellow English speaker about a horse – I have little choice but to use the word 'horse', if I want to be understood.

Perhaps Durkheim's best known example of a social fact can be seen in his analysis of suicide. In his book, *Suicide: A Study in Sociology* (1970; first published in 1897), Durkheim shows how the apparently highly individual act of suicide can be analysed as a social fact. First suicide, or rather the suicide rate, can be shown to be external to individuals by the fact that the suicide rate varies between different social groups, and that this variation remains fairly constant over time. For example, Durkheim noticed that suicide rates were consistently lower in Catholic countries than they were in Protestant countries and that this difference remained stable over relatively long periods of time. Suicide rates thus seemed to be products of social groups, rather than of individuals. Second, the suicide rate could be seen as constraining because the probability that any individual would commit suicide could be shown to vary according to which social groups they belong.

Of course, Durkheim does not claim that the social fact of the suicide rate will tell us which members of a social group will commit suicide. This, he argued, was the proper province of the psychologist. The job of the sociologist was first to identify social facts – such as the suicide rates of various social groups – and second to explain them. (For further discussion of Durkheim's view of social facts, see pages 229-230; for his study of suicide, see pages 214-218 and 229-230).

Cause and function

One of the more important arguments advanced by Durkheim in *The Rules of Sociological Method* was that in explaining social facts it is necessary to distinguish between their causes and their *social functions*. To understand what Durkheim meant by social functions we must consider his so-called 'organismic analogy' – the idea that societies are like living organisms.

To see how this analogy works consider the following example. If I take a living organism, say a dog, each of its parts – its legs, its tail, its liver, its heart and so on – can be seen to make a contribution to the dog's overall functioning. However, if I were to take any one of these parts in isolation, say its tail, it would 'do' very little, and I would be unable to see how it makes a contribution to the overall functioning of the dog. It only makes sense, as it were, in relation to all the other parts which go to make up the dog. Even if I took all the individual parts of a dog, and placed them in a box, I still would not have something we could meaningfully call 'a dog', which barked and wagged its tail. All I would have would be a pile of lifeless limbs and organs. Similarly, Durkheim argued that only by examining the contribution which each of a society's parts makes to its overall functioning can we arrive at a complete understanding of these parts. This approach is sometimes known as *holism*, and can be summed up in the phrase: *the whole is greater than the sum of its parts*.

For Durkheim, the study of any social fact's functions must be different from the study of its causes. This is because unless we were to say that a particular social fact was the result of deliberate intentions, its cause cannot be the same as its functional effects. The reason for this is obvious – since functional effects occur only *after* a phenomenon has come into existence, they cannot have caused that phenomenon to come into existence in the first place. Durkheim therefore claimed that the causes of social facts should be sought in other social facts which had

occurred at an earlier point in time. If, however, we wish to explain why a social fact persists over time, we should seek to discover the contribution it makes to the overall working of society, in short, its *function*.

The division of labour

Moral regulation At the centre of Durkheim's work is a concern with morality. Morality can be seen as a classic example of a social fact. Moral codes are external to individuals in the sense that they are properties of social groups, and they are constraining over individuals in that they plainly influence our behaviour. But for Durkheim morality is also central to his understanding of how social order is possible.

At the centre of Durkheim's analysis, as with most social theorists, are a set of assumptions about 'human nature'. For Durkheim, following the philosopher Rousseau, human beings possess an innate tendency towards limitless desire. If these desires remain unchecked then, Durkheim argued, human beings could never be happy, because their desires would always outstrip their ability to satisfy them. At the same time, such limitless desires would pose an obvious threat to social order. Durkheim thus argued that human happiness, social order and social solidarity could only be achieved by the regulation of human desires to within attainable limits. It is for this reason that morality – the social fact responsible for the regulation of individual desires – was so central to Durkheim's whole approach.

Social solidarity In his first major work, *The Division of Labour in Society* (1933; first published 1893) Durkheim set out to show how, as societies developed from simple, small-scale pre-literate forms, to modern, complex and industrial forms, the basis of moral regulation, and hence of social solidarity, also underwent change. In the former type of society, Durkheim argued that social order was achieved by what he termed *mechanical solidarity*. In such societies, the extent to which different individuals perform different tasks – the *division of labour* – was very limited. Therefore, since most people shared a common set of interests and problems, a single set of moral rules to guide them was sufficient. The source of such moral regulation was religious, and Durkheim assumed that members of such societies shared a common commitment to the authority of their religion which provided appropriate moral limits in any situation they were likely to face. This he called the 'conscience collective', which roughly translates as the 'collective conscience'.

The basis of the mechanical solidarity of small-scale societies is *similarity* – the division of labour is limited and there is little role differentiation. As the division of labour becomes increasingly specialised and complex, *mechanical solidarity* is replaced by *organic solidarity*. This organic solidarity is based on *difference*. The different and specialised parts of the division of labour work together to maintain the social unit. Specialised occupational roles are interdependent – they need each other.

Anomie As societies became more complex, however, Durkheim argued that the ability of a single source of moral authority to regulate the increasingly divergent lives of society's members was gradually weakened. So much so that modern societies, which are characterised by a very highly developed division of labour, faced a chronic state of crisis as far as moral regulation was concerned. Durkheim called this lack of moral regulation *anomie*, and this is closely linked to his belief in the growth of excessive individualism – people come to see themselves first and foremost as individuals rather than as members of social groups.

Although Durkheim regarded anomie as a very significant feature of modern societies, he maintained that it could be overcome by the development of strong occupational associations which would become the source of moral regulation for their members. For example, they would regulate terms and conditions of employment and wages and salaries. These associations, Durkheim argued, would overcome the problems posed by modern societies in two main ways. First, they would counter the modern trend towards individualism by integrating their members into a social group. Second, they would set limits on the rewards which members of society could expect to receive, and hence would serve to limit desires to within attainable bounds.

Evaluation

Although there can be little doubt about Durkheim's enormous influence on the development of sociology, we need to take account of a number of criticisms of his work.

Anomie and human nature It can be argued that Durkheim's view of human nature is unrealistically pessimistic. In many ways, his argument that human beings need to be morally regulated by society is the direct opposite of Marx's view that human nature is in fact corrupted by the social relations of production in capitalist societies.

Determinism It is sometimes said that Durkheim's approach represents an extreme form of *determinism*. That is, human actions are explained purely by the effects of external forces acting upon the individual. It has been argued that this can be seen in his analysis of suicide – apparently one of the most individual choices a human being can ever make. Durkheim claims that the suicide rate is, in fact, nothing more than a product of social forces over which individuals have absolutely no control. Many sociologists, most notably perhaps symbolic interactionists whose ideas we consider later in this chapter, have argued that this presents an inaccurate picture of human action. Instead, they argue that although social forces perhaps influence individual choices, they do not determine them in a straightforward way. Human beings, they argue, possess freedom of choice, and so can always resist the influences of social forces if they so choose.

Power and inequality Durkheim was extremely concerned about the consequences of the increasingly specialised division of labour – the inequalities which it entails and the anomie it generates. However, it is sometimes argued that he failed to grasp the extent to which modern capitalist societies are composed of groups with fundamentally opposing interests. Marx considered capitalist societies to be characterised by irresolvable class conflicts. Durkheim regarded such conflicts as did occur to be temporary anomalies which could be overcome by the development of new forms of moral regulation. At no time, however, does he consider that the moral regulations which are central to all forms of social solidarity might be ideologies – that is, sets of beliefs which portray a false picture of reality and justify fundamentally unjust power relations.

Whilst each of these criticisms might be convincing to some sociologists, it is important to note that we cannot settle any of them simply by appealing to available evidence. Each point of view presented reflects, in large measure, simply different ways of 'seeing' society. To return to our earlier analogy, each is viewing society in a different distorting mirror. They do, nevertheless, sensitise us to possible weaknesses in Durkheim's approach. We shall return to some of these later in the chapter when we consider the development of functionalism after Durkheim.

> ## key terms
>
> *Social facts* Aspects of society which are external to the individual and constrain their behaviour.
> *Holism* A view which states that the whole is greater than the sum of its parts.
> *Function/social function* The contribution made by a social fact to the operation of society as a whole.
> *Mechanical solidarity* A form of moral regulation based on shared values. The 'collective conscience' which unites members of society.
> *Organic solidarity* A form of solidarity based on the interdependence of a specialised division of labour.
> *Anomie* A lack of moral regulation, normlessness.

2.4 Max Weber (1864-1920)

Durkheim's approach to the study of society rested firmly upon his assumption of the effects of external and constraining social facts on individual behaviour. Max Weber emphasised the importance of taking into account the points of view of social actors, and the meanings which they attribute to their own behaviour and that of others. For this reason, Weber is often regarded as the founding father of *interpretivist sociology*, or of the *social action approach* within sociology.

Meaning and the concept of verstehen

As we saw in the previous section, Durkheim regarded the proper task of sociology to be the identification of relationships between social facts. It is often argued, however, that this approach ignores the *meaningful* nature of human conduct. Let us examine what is meant by this.

activity4 the case of Robinson Crusoe

Item A Shipwrecked

In 1719, the novelist Daniel Defoe published a classic story about a man on his own, called Robinson Crusoe. Crusoe went out from England to make his fortune and had many adventures before being shipwrecked on a desert island. He was the only survivor of the wreck, and though he managed to salvage many things from it and to make himself some sort of life on the island, he survived entirely alone until he discovered a single footprint in the sand. This was the mark of a native whom he discovered and named 'Friday' (after the day on which he found him) and made him his servant. Crusoe was finally rescued and taken home.

Item B Family

'Born in the city of York, of a good family, though not of that country, my father being a foreigner of Bremen, who first settled at Hull. He got a good estate by merchandise, and leaving off his trade lived afterwards at York, from whence he married my mother from a very good family in that country.'

Item C Education

'My father had given me a competent share of learning, as far as house education and a county free-school generally goes, and designed me for the law. Being the third son of the family and not bred to any trade, my head began to be filled with early rambling thoughts.'

Item D Religion

'I frequently sat down with thankfulness and admired the hand of God's providence, which had thus spread my table in the wilderness. These reflections made me very sensible of the goodness of Providence to me and very thankful for my present condition.'

Item E Power

'In a little time I began to speak to him and to teach him how to speak to me; and first I made him know his name should be Friday, which was the day I saved his life. I likewise taught him to say Master, and then let him know that was to be my name.'

Robinson Crusoe pictured in the first edition, 1719

Item F A social being

Robinson Crusoe was indeed a unique individual, making his way in the world by his own efforts, 'master of all he surveys', as the poem puts it. But this is very different from saying that he can be understood and explained in individual terms. We can't fully explain who he is, where he comes from, what he thinks and does, how he behaves, by looking at him simply as an individual. This is the problem with individualist types of explanation.

Source: Hall, 1993

questions

1   What social facts influenced Robinson Crusoe?

2   Is there an argument for combining social and individual explanations to understand Robinson Crusoe's behaviour?

If we are concerned to identify what it is that distinguishes human beings from either animals or inanimate objects, then perhaps the most crucial difference is that human beings are capable of intentional action. We do things on purpose, in order to reach some goal, and usually we have some choice both about the goal and the means we select to achieve it. For example, if asked why you are reading this chapter, you will probably answer with reference to some goal – to enable you to pass an examination in sociology, perhaps. You will also, presumably, have some choice about both the goal and the means you have selected to achieve it – you could always decide not to take the examination, and you could always choose to read another book. It is for this reason that

Weber would say that your action is meaningful. It is not merely the product of the operation of external forces over which you have no control, but is the result of your own interpretations of the world around you and of the conscious choices you make about your future.

Weber thus emphasised that it is not enough merely to note statistical correlations between social facts as Durkheim had done – although Weber certainly believed that such correlations were an important starting point for sociological analysis. He insisted, in addition, that explanations of human action should be grasped on the level of meaning. Whilst, methodologically, it may not be difficult to explore the meanings of actors' conduct when one has the opportunity to interview them – although

Weber did not himself practice this kind of sociological investigation – obvious difficulties are faced when one is dealing with social events which took place in the past. Since Weber's own preoccupation was with the origins of modern capitalism, he had himself to overcome this difficulty. The events he was concerned with had taken place several centuries before he was born. His solution was the method of *verstehen*.

Verstehen can be translated from the German as broadly meaning 'empathetic understanding'. In simple terms, one attempts to imagine how the world would have looked from the point of view of the actors whose actions one wishes to understand, even where such a point of view is quite alien to one's own. The classic example of the application of verstehen can be found in Weber's account of the behaviour of early Calvinists in *The Protestant Ethic and the Spirit of Capitalism* (1958). (For further discussion of Weber's methodology, see pages 234-235; for his study of Protestantism and capitalism, see pages 28, 30-31.)

The ideal type

Before we move on to consider the ways in which Weber categorised social action, it will be helpful to explain his concept of the *ideal type*. Ideal types are generalisations which help researchers to organise and classify their findings. Rarely, if ever, are they found in their pure form, but they provide us with a set of categories through which we can make sense of our observations. For example, Weber produced an ideal type of a bureaucracy. He lists six 'ideal' characteristics of bureaucracies, but it is unlikely that any actual bureaucratic organisation will possess all six characteristics in pure form. We can nevertheless identify it as a bureaucracy, because it comes closer to the ideal typical bureaucracy than to any other form of organisation.

Types of action

Both the concept of verstehen, and Weber's use of ideal types can be seen in his four-fold categorisation of types of action. These categories of action begin from the assumptions of verstehen in that they adopt the point of view of the actor. They are ideal types in that they are theoretically pure forms to which real instances of action only ever approximate.

Instrumentally rational action In this type of 'purely' rational action, the actor assesses both their goals and the means by which these should be achieved. For example, if it is my goal to win a marathon, then it would be *instrumentally rational* for me to undergo a strict regime of training and dieting prior to the race. By contrast, it would not be rational, in relation to this goal, for me to spend the weeks prior to the race indulging in an almost incessant orgy of drinking, smoking and over-eating. However, it would still be instrumentally rational for me to decide that the costs (in terms of pain and suffering) of dieting and training were not worth the benefit of winning the marathon. Under these circumstances, I would simply reject the goal of winning the marathon, thus making my

over-indulgent behaviour rational in terms of my revised goal of gaining as much immediate pleasure as possible.

Value-rational action This type of rational action is similar to instrumentally rational action in that means are judged to be rational if they are thought to be successful in reaching the goal towards which they are directed. However, in this case, the goals cannot be abandoned even if they are immensely difficult to achieve. For example, a devoutly religious person who believed that they would only enjoy salvation if they lived a life of celibacy would, if acting in accordance with *value-rationality*, accept a life of celibacy no matter how difficult this might prove. To reject the goal as being simply too difficult to achieve, however, would be an example of instrumentally rational action.

Traditional action This form of action does not involve the assessment of either goals or means. Instead, it is performed simply because tradition dictates that it should be. Although Weber felt that *traditional action* had declined in significance in modern societies, which he believed were characterised increasingly by rational action, examples of traditional conduct can still be found. In Britain, for example, it is still usual to celebrate Christmas by, among other things, purchasing and decorating a Christmas tree. The majority of people who engage in this behaviour, however, can give no reason for doing so other than the fact that it is 'traditional'.

Affective action This final form of action can best be expressed as being a result of emotion. Again, Weber felt that this type of action was becoming less significant in modern societies, but examples can still be found. Someone hearing the news that a close relative had been killed in an accident might burst into tears out of grief. Or, a wife discovering her husband's infidelity might assault him out of anger. No well thought out goals are involved in such actions. And since the circumstances are by definition novel, the actions can clearly not be described as traditional. They are the direct result of the unusual emotional state of the actor.

Rationalisation and disenchantment

Weber argued that modern societies are characterised increasingly by a process of *rationalisation*. As the term suggests, this means that the world is increasingly governed by rationality, in which traditional and affective forms of action are replaced by predominantly rational forms. Organisations increasingly adopt a bureaucratic form and legitimate authority is predominantly rational legal. Corresponding to this was a trend towards what is usually translated from the German as *disenchantment*, although a more literal translation of Weber would be *the driving out of magic from things*. This can be seen partly as *secularisation*, but is in fact broader than this and includes the progressive removal of non-rational elements from all spheres of life. Weber was fearful that in the process warmth and humanity might be driven out of social life – the very things which give meaning to human existence (see pages 30-31 and 68).

Evaluation

Psychologism Whilst Durkheim has often been accused of ignoring the role of psychological factors in human behaviour, it has sometimes been said that Weber over-emphasises the role of such factors. This criticism has two aspects to it. First, it has been suggested that in using the method of verstehen, Weber is forced to go beyond available evidence and attribute motives to social actors without any means of verifying them. Taken to its extreme, this could reduce sociological enquiry to little more than guesswork. Second, it can be argued that, in giving such weight to individual motives, Weber underestimates the power of external social forces to constrain and determine behaviour.

Ambiguity Although Weber makes a great effort to be clear about exactly what he means by the ideal type, it can nevertheless be argued that the concept can lead to certain ambiguities, particularly when applied to types of action. Percy Cohen points out, for example, that many forms of traditional action may also conform to one or other type of rationality (Cohen, 1968). For instance, when people in small-scale non-literate societies give gifts to the village headman, they do so both because it is traditional *and* because they hope to receive some benefits as a result. Similarly, whilst an outburst of rage might appear to be purely affective, it could be seen, from the point of view of a psychoanalyst, as rational in that it could have been motivated by an unconscious desire to reduce one's level of stress.

Conclusion

In this unit, we have considered some of the most important early influences on the development of sociological theory. Although each has been subjected to criticism, the ideas we have discussed have had an enduring influence on the ways in which sociologists seek to understand human societies. In the unit which follows, we turn our attention to the ways in which these founding theorists' ideas have been developed by later generations of social theorists.

key terms

Verstehen Empathetic understanding. A method used to interpret the meanings and motives which guide action.
Ideal type A classification of something into 'pure' types – for example, Weber's types of action.
Instrumentally rational action Action in which both goals and the means to attain them are rationally assessed.
Value-rational action The goals are fixed and the means are rationally assessed.
Traditional action Both goals and means are fixed by tradition.
Affective action Action is directed by emotion, with no clearly defined goals.
Rationalisation A process by which the world is increasingly governed by rational thought and action.
Disenchantment The removal of religion, 'magic', warmth and humanity in an increasingly rational world.
Secularisation A process by which religion loses its power and influence in society.

summary

1. Sociology has its roots in the Enlightenment. It reflected two key aspects of Enlightenment thought.
   - The ability of human reason to provide an understanding of the world.
   - A belief that this understanding can be used to improve the world.
2. Marx saw the material conditions of production – the way people organise the production of goods and services – as the starting point for the analysis of society.
3. The mode of production largely shapes the rest of society – that is the superstructure, which includes political and legal systems, religion, and so on.
4. Apart from primitive communism, all societies have a dominant ruling class which exploits a subordinate subject class. The power of the ruling class derives from their ownership and control of the means of production.
5. Class conflict provides the motor for social change. It propels society forward from one production system to another.
6. There is increasing alienation and class polarisation in capitalist society. This will promote class consciousness and help to unite the proletariat. This, in turn, will eventually lead to the overthrow of capitalism and its replacement by communism.
7. Marx has been criticised for:
   - What some see as economic determinism
   - Overestimating the importance of class in directing social change

- Failing to predict the development of capitalist societies.
8. Durkheim saw sociology as the study of social facts. Social facts are external to the individual and constrain individual behaviour.
9. In explaining social facts, it is necessary to distinguish between their causes and their functions. Causes should be sought in other social facts which occurred at an earlier point in time. In order to explain why a social fact persists over time, we need to discover its function – the contribution it makes to society.
10. Durkheim's work focused on moral regulation and its contribution to social solidarity and social order.
11. He distinguished between two types of solidarity – mechanical solidarity based on common values and a limited division of labour, and organic solidarity based on a specialised division of labour.
12. Durkheim saw anomie – a lack of moral regulation – as characteristic of modern society.
13. Durkheim has had an enormous influence on the development of sociology. However, he has been criticised for:
    - Over-emphasising human beings' need for moral regulation
    - Determinism – external forces shaping behaviour
    - A failure to appreciate the significance of conflict in society – particularly class conflict.
14. Weber argued that in order to understand and explain

behaviour, it is essential to discover the meanings which social actors give both to their own actions and the actions of others.

15. To discover these meanings, Weber used the method of verstehen – empathetic understanding.

16. Using this method, Weber identified four types of action. They are ideal types.
    ● Instrumentally rational action
    ● Value-rational action
    ● Traditional action
    ● Affective action.

17. Weber saw a process of rationalisation occurring in modern societies – action is increasingly rational rather than traditional or affective. Related to this is a trend towards disenchantment.

18. Like Marx and Durkheim, Weber has had a lasting and significant influence on sociology. However, his approach has been criticised for:
    ● Attributing motives and meanings to social actors without sufficient means of verifying them
    ● Underestimating the power of external social forces to direct behaviour
    ● Failing to recognise that certain forms of behaviour can be directed by two or more of the types of social action he identifies.

activity5 disenchantment

Item A   Modernity and religion

Modernity is the transition from fate to choice. At the same time, it dissolves the commitments and loyalties that once lay behind our choices. Technical reason has made us masters of matching means to ends. But it has left us inarticulate as to why we should choose one end rather than another. The values that once led us to regard one as intrinsically better than another – and which gave such weight to words like good and bad – have disintegrated, along with the communities and religious traditions in which we learned them. Now we choose because it is what we want; or it works for us; or it feels right to me. Once we have dismantled a world in which larger virtues held sway, what is left are success and self-expression, the key values of an individualistic culture.

Max Weber delivered the famous prophetic warning that the cloak of material prosperity might eventually become an iron cage. It was already becoming an end in itself, and other values were left, in his words, 'like the ghost of dead religious beliefs'. Once capitalism consumed its religious foundations, he feared the consequences.

In the past, disadvantaged groups could find in religion what Karl Marx called 'the feeling of a heartless world'. A purely economic order offers no such consolations. A culture of success places little value on the unsuccessful.

The erosion of those bonds of loyalty and love which religion supported has left us increasingly alone in an impersonal economic and social system. Emile Durkheim was the first to give this condition a name. He called it anomie: the situation in which individuals have lost their moorings in a collective order. It is the heavy price we pay for our loss of communities of faith.

Source: Sachs, 1990

Item B   Pictures of modernity

The shopping mall – a temple to materialism and consumerism

Former church, now Cottiers Bar and Restaurant, Glasgow

Item C   The logical song

When I was young, it seemed that life was so wonderful,
A miracle, oh it was beautiful, magical.
And all the birds in the trees, well they'd be singing so happily,
Joyfully, playfully watching me.
But then they sent me away to teach me how to be sensible,
Logical, responsible, practical.
And they showed me a world where I could be so dependable,
Clinical, intellectual, cynical.

Source: *Breakfast in America* by Supertramp, 1979, words and music by Roger Hodgson

questions

1 How do Items A, B and C illustrate Weber's belief that rationalisation is resulting in disenchantment?

2 Judging from Item A, what similarities and differences are there between Weber's picture of modernity and those of Marx and Durkheim?

Unit 3 *The establishment of sociological theory*

keyissues

1   What are the main assumptions of functionalism, Marxism and symbolic interactionism?

2   How significant are these perspectives for the development of sociological theory?

There has never been one model of society on which all sociologists are agreed. In this unit we shall be considering three competing models which have their origins in the work of Marx, Durkheim and Weber. The three models which we shall consider – functionalism, Marxism and symbolic interactionism – each make very different assumptions about the nature of human beings and the societies which they inhabit. Although these are not the only models which have emerged in sociology, and some sociologists straddle different models, they are nevertheless three of the most significant in the development of sociology as a discipline. This is evident both in this book, where continual references are made to these models, and in any of the major textbooks in sociology. Although, as we shall see in later sections, matters are now more complex than a consideration of these three models suggests, they do nonetheless form the basis of the modern discipline.

3.1 Functionalism

During the first half of the 20th century, functionalism became the dominant theoretical perspective in sociology. Functionalism has its origins in the work of such 19th century social theorists as Auguste Comte and Herbert Spencer, but owes most to the work of Emile Durkheim. Functionalism was subsequently adopted by sociologists, but much of its early impact was through the work of British social anthropologists such as Bronislaw Malinowski and A. R. Radcliffe-Brown.

Social systems Although the views of functionalist sociologists differ in detail, they share in common a concern with studying societies as *systems*. The idea that a society is a system has a number of implications, which are central to functionalist analysis. First, is the assumption that societies should be studied as wholes, rather than as collections of independent parts. As we saw in Durkheim's work, just as a living organism is more than merely the sum of its constituent parts, so societies need to be treated as entities in their own right with, as it were, a life of their own.

Second, and following from this, is the assumption that the parts of society need to be understood in terms of the contribution which they make to the functioning of the whole. If, for example, we were to be interested in central

heating systems, we could only understand the role of, say, the radiators, in relation to the system as a whole. On their own radiators do very little, and had we never seen one as part of a functioning central heating system, we would stand little chance of figuring out what they are for. In exactly the same way, functionalists assume that we can only understand the role of the constituent parts of societies in terms of their contribution to the functioning of the society as a whole.

Third is the assumption that parts of societies perform a primarily positive function in relation to the overall functioning of the society. Just as we would not expect to find parts of central heating systems which either perform no function whatsoever, or actually impair the overall performance of the system, so functionalists would not expect to find parts of societies which either do not contribute to, or actually impair their overall functioning. This means that functionalist analysis tends to search for positive functions of social institutions, whilst either denying or seriously underplaying, their negative or disruptive aspects.

Although by the 1950s, functionalism had become the dominant theoretical perspective in sociology, this dominance was not to last. From this time onwards, functionalism was subjected to a range of criticisms which ultimately led to its widespread rejection. Nevertheless, the influence of functionalism on modern sociological theory remains substantial.

Talcott Parsons (1902-1979)

Although Parsons' work is often criticised for what some see as its rather dry and obscure style, it represents the fullest and most systematic statement of functionalist theory available. For Parsons, as with Durkheim before him, the central problem for all social theory was, in the name of the 17th century philosopher Thomas Hobbes, the 'Hobbesian problem of order'. Hobbes believed that human beings were driven by passions which, if left unrestrained, would lead to social chaos, or a 'war of all against all'. The problem, therefore, was how to explain the fact that this state of affairs does not routinely occur in human societies. Indeed, human societies are, for most of the time, rather orderly and peaceful places. Hobbes' solution to this problem was to assume that, driven ultimately by the need for self-preservation, people voluntarily agree to restrain their passions and submit to the sovereign authority of the state.

As we saw in the discussion of Durkheim's work, he offered the rather different solution that social order is maintained by a shared commitment to a common morality. This, essentially, was Parsons' solution too.

The social system and its functional prerequisites

It was suggested in the introduction to this unit that the assumption that societies are systems is fundamental to functionalist theory. This assumption is made most explicitly in the work of Parsons – indeed, his major statement of functionalist theory is presented in a book entitled *The Social System* (Parsons, 1951). For Parsons, any social system inevitably faces four problems, which must be solved if the system is to survive. Parsons calls these four problems *functional prerequisites*, and they are as follows: adaptation, goal attainment, integration and pattern maintenance or latency.

Adaptation The first, *adaptation*, refers to the need for any social system to adapt to its environment. In even the most simple societies, some mechanism must exist whereby food and shelter are obtained. This could involve, for example, hunting and gathering and the production of simple shelters against the elements. Such activities might strike us as straightforward in comparison with the complex arrangements which exist in our own societies for converting the raw materials of the natural environment into produced goods for consumption and use. They do nevertheless require social organisation, and crucially for Parsons, normative regulation. Whilst in simple societies this might be achieved by the existence of customs and norms, in advanced industrial societies it tends to be achieved by legally regulated economies.

Goal attainment The second of Parsons' functional prerequisites is *goal attainment*. This refers to the need for societies to set goals towards which the activities of their members and institutions are directed. In simple societies, this might revolve around the need to obtain sufficient food, whilst in societies such as our own, it involves more complex economic goals such as seeking profit. In modern societies, goal attainment is fundamentally the responsibility of the political system, which establishes a legal and economic framework which regulates and directs the pursuit of such goals.

Integration The third functional prerequisite is *integration*. This refers to the need to maintain cohesion within the social system and to deal effectively with deviance which threatens the overall stability of the system. Whilst in simple societies this function would be fulfilled largely as a result of what Weber called traditional authority, in modern complex societies it is performed largely by the legal system – what Weber called rational-legal authority.

Pattern maintenance The final functional prerequisite is *pattern maintenance*, or *latency*. This refers to the need to maintain the pattern of value commitments amongst a society's members. Crucial to this is the process of socialisation which takes place within institutions such as the family and the education system. Socialisation serves to internalise a society's values into the personalities of individual actors.

This framework allowed Parsons to classify all the parts of any given society into one of these four categories, and in doing so, to claim that each contributes in at least one of these four ways to the overall functioning of that society.

Social evolution and equilibrium

It is sometimes said that functionalism in general, and Parsons' theory in particular, emphasise social stability to such an extent that they are in danger of failing to account for social change. We shall return to this charge in our evaluation of functionalism. For the present, it is important to note that Parsons does not ignore the issue of social change, but in fact makes its explanation a central part of his general theory.

Equilibrium An important element of Parsons' analysis of social systems is that they exist in a state of equilibrium. Equilibrium is best defined as 'balance', and in relation to social systems, refers to the ways in which the four subsystems are interrelated. This means, for Parsons, that a change in one part of a social system tends to produce changes elsewhere in the social system such that the system, overall, returns to a state of equilibrium. Social systems are therefore regarded as self-regulating, always tending to return to a state of equilibrium, albeit a changed one. In this way, Parsons explains social change as a dynamic and functionally necessary response to disturbances within the system. Although, for Parsons, social systems tend towards a state of equilibrium, a perfect equilibrium is never attained – instead, societies are thought to exist in a state of 'moving equilibrium'.

Social evolution A second aspect of Parsons' approach to social change is his notion of *social evolution*. Heavily influenced by such 19th century social evolutionists as Herbert Spencer, Parsons believed that all social systems are involved in an evolutionary development from more simple to more complex forms. The central concept used by Parsons to explain the patterns of social evolution is *structural differentiation*. This refers to the tendency of social institutions to become more specialised. Thus, for example, prior to the industrial revolution, the household used to be not only a domestic space, but also a place where goods were produced. After the industrial revolution, factories replaced the household as a site of production and the household came to fulfil the more specialised role as a site of domestic activity only.

This trend carries with it its own problems, however, which modern societies must solve. In particular, the development of increasingly specialised roles and institutions requires the development of an increasingly broad and general set of values capable of regulating a wider range of activities. In modern industrial societies, such values include a belief in universalism and in achievement – universal society-wide standards of achievement are applied to everyone and form the basis for allocating people to roles and fixing their rewards. Such general values are capable of regulating a very wide range of specialised activities in our societies.

Robert K. Merton

Parsons' work represents the height of functionalist theorising in sociology, and is the most systematic and abstract of functionalist approaches. Parsons' desire to explain all aspects of all societies from within a single theoretical framework has led to his theory being described as a grand theory. One functionalist sociologist who attempted to refine functionalist analysis, but at the same time rejected the highly abstract approach developed by Parsons, was Robert K. Merton.

Merton's modification of functionalist theory begins with a critique of the notion – fundamental to Parsons' model – that societies exhibit 'functional unity'. This is the idea that all parts of a society are interconnected such that all parts of the system work together for the benefit of the whole, and that a change in one part of the system will necessarily produce change elsewhere. Merton suggests that whilst this may sometimes be the case, one cannot assume that it will be in advance. Rather, the degree to which parts of the social system are interconnected is a matter which should be empirically investigated in each case. Indeed, Merton suggests that in modern highly differentiated societies, a relatively high degree of *functional autonomy* will exist within parts of the social system. In other words, some parts will operate as largely independent units.

Merton also challenges the idea of 'universal functionalism', that is, the idea that all parts of the social system fulfil some positive function. Again, as with the issue of functional unity, Merton suggests that whether or not a particular part of the social system fulfils a positive function is a matter for investigation and is not something which can be assumed in advance. For Merton, any part of the system might be either functional, dysfunctional or non-functional. In other words, its contribution to the social system may be positive, negative or non-existent.

Finally, Merton challenges what he terms the 'postulate of indispensability' – the assumption that the institutions or roles which actually exist within a society are the only ones which could meet that society's functional prerequisites. In other words, he challenges the assumption made by many functionalists that social institutions and roles exist by necessity and are therefore inevitable parts of that society. Instead, Merton argues that the same functional needs could just as well be met by different institutions and roles which are functionally equivalent.

These specific criticisms of grand theory advanced by Merton led him to suggest that social theorists should abandon their search for over-arching theoretical systems which specify the nature and functions of social institutions in advance. Instead, they should concentrate upon developing more concrete theories grounded in empirical evidence, which address specific social phenomena rather than entire social systems. Such theories were called by Merton, *theories of the middle range*.

Evaluation

Teleology Despite Durkheim's early caution about confusing the cause of a phenomenon with its functions, this charge can be levelled at later functionalist theorists. In particular, functionalist theories may be accused of being *teleological*. A theory is said to be teleological if it explains a phenomenon's causes in terms of its effects. Thus if functionalists argue that the cause of social stratification is to allocate the most able individuals to the most important positions in society, then their argument is teleological – it explains causes in terms of effects. This can lead to some very strange explanations. For example, if it is argued that the family exists because it has the effect of stabilising adult personalities and of accomplishing the primary socialisation of children, then it seems difficult to avoid the assumption that this is because someone sat down and invented the family for this purpose. Of course this would be absurd. As we have seen, however, functionalist explanations tend to be of this type, and so can be criticised on the logical grounds that they confuse cause and effect.

Value consensus A second criticism which can be levelled at functionalist theory is that it over-emphasises the degree of value consensus – agreement about values – in societies. As Merton's critique of functionalism suggests, it can be argued that the degree of value consensus in a society is an empirical matter which cannot be presumed in advance. At the very least, it seems difficult to avoid the conclusion that the degree of value consensus which exists will undergo change over time, and will vary between different social groups. In addition, it has been suggested there is no reason to assume that even if a high degree of value consensus exists, it will necessarily promote social solidarity. Collective commitment to an ethic of individualism, for example, may produce exactly the opposite effect.

Conflict A third criticism of functionalism is that in its concentration on social order and value consensus, it largely ignores the existence of coercion and conflict in society. For example, David Lockwood has pointed out that Parsons' emphasis on social order and value consensus ignores the fact that competition for scarce resources, an inherent feature of modern societies, will inevitably lead to conflict over scarce resources.

key terms

Functional prerequisites Requirements which must be met and problems which must be solved in order for the social system to survive.

Adaptation The need for the social system to adapt to its environment.

Goal attainment The need for society to set goals for its members and institutions.

Integration The need to maintain order and stability in society, and to deal with deviance.

Pattern maintenance The need for value consensus and commitment to those values.

Structural differentiation The tendency for social institutions, such as the family and religion, to become more specialised in terms of their functions.

Functional autonomy The idea that some parts of society operate as largely independent units.

Teleology Explaining the causes of something in terms of its effects.

activity6 functions and dysfunctions

Item A

Street party in Jubilee Drive, Liverpool, to celebrate the Queen's Silver Jubilee

Item B

Anti-capitalist riot, London, 2000

Item D

Domestic violence

Item C

Glastonbury music festival

questions

1 From a functionalist view, which activities in Items A to D would be seen as functional and which as dysfunctional?

2 Explain your answers in terms of functionalist theory.

3.2 Marxism

Although Marxism has a long ancestry, it did not grow to prominence within sociology until the 1960s. That decade saw a range of social movements which challenged the dominant social order and made the functionalist picture of a social system based on value consensus seem less plausible. In this context, Marxism gained converts with its picture of society as inherently riven by social conflict.

Marxism, as a sociological perspective, does not slavishly follow Marx in every particular but rather accepts three of his central beliefs – a belief that in some sense the economy is of primary importance, that class conflict is consequently central, and that ultimately this will result in a more desirable form of society. Where modern Marxists part company with Marx is over the question of whether it is possible to identify the conditions which will entail the demise of capitalism. Marx himself was somewhat vague on this issue, but a number of his followers adopted an economic determinist position whereby economic crises were seen as inevitably dooming capitalism to extinction.

The Marxists we shall be examining in this section reject this position. Impressed by the capacity of capitalism to survive crises, they pay particular attention to the role of the superstructure in maintaining it. We shall look at two very different versions of Marxism – *humanist Marxism* and *structuralist Marxism*. The first develops Marx's early work and adopts as its starting point the assumption that human beings are able to transform their environment. The second develops Marx's later work and adopts as its starting point the assumption that human beings are the product of structures.

Humanist Marxism

Gramsci Gramsci's central contribution to Marxism is his development of Marx's ideas on ideology through a theory of *hegemony* (1971). The bourgeoisie, he argues, seek to maintain their domination not only by using the state to coerce people but also, increasingly, by propagating ideologies, through the institutions of civil society such as the churches, in order to win people's consent. For the bourgeoisie to be ideologically dominant, or hegemonic, these ideologies need to be tied into the popular culture of the subordinate classes.

The extent to which such hegemony is achieved varies over time but it is unlikely ever to be complete. There are two reasons for this. First, the bourgeoisie are often divided and frequently need to forge alliances with other groups in order to constitute a *power bloc* and control the state. Second, the proletariat has a *dual consciousness*, one part of which reflects the ideas of the bourgeoisie and the other part of which reflects their everyday experience. The need to create a power bloc inhibits the propagation of a coherent ideology, while the existence of dual consciousness means that workers will at least partially see through bourgeois ideology.

For Gramsci a proletarian revolution will *not* inevitably result from economic crises. What is needed is for the proletariat to make alliances with other groups and for Marxists to win the hearts and minds of the subordinate classes by connecting Marxist ideas to popular culture. Gramsci is optimistic that in the struggle for hegemony, people will eventually be persuaded of the need for revolution. The stress Gramsci places on popular culture as the site in which ideologies compete has been taken up in cultural studies where youth subcultural styles are seen on the one hand as indicative of resistance to domination and on the other hand as an opportunity for marketing a new fashion, for general consumption and profit.

Critical theory What distinguishes critical theory is its attempt to identify what is distinctively human and to use this as a yardstick from which to criticise existing society. We shall look at two examples here – the Frankfurt School, and its three main figures, Adorno, Horkheimer and Marcuse, and the chief heir to that inheritance, Habermas.

The Frankfurt School For the Frankfurt School there are two attributes which distinguish human beings from animals – the ability, which Marx highlighted, to transform the environment, and the ability, which the Enlightenment stressed, to make rational decisions about our lives. Capitalist societies do not allow human beings to exercise their creativity and reason and thus deserve criticism for being oppressive and irrational. The Frankfurt School agrees with Gramsci that particular attention needs to be paid to ideology which is increasingly integrating people into the capitalist system. Two phenomena are highlighted as crucial here – the growth of *instrumental reason* which is seen as the dominant way of thinking in capitalist societies and the development of *mass culture*.

The stress on instrumental reason is reminiscent of Weber's emphasis on rationalisation as a central feature of modernity. It is a way of looking at the world which 'is concerned with discovering how to do things, not what should be done' (Craib, 1984). According to the Frankfurt School, the search for the most efficient means to achieve ends not only generates an uncritical attitude towards the ends pursued in capitalist societies, but also encourages us to treat people as means rather than ends in themselves. Reason does not, as the Enlightenment hoped, liberate people in capitalist societies but instead becomes a mechanism for oppressing people.

People's acceptance of instrumental reason is explained by the Frankfurt School in terms of the development of mass culture. Not only is culture now an industry, but developments in technology have meant that through various media such as newspapers it reaches the mass of the population. Adorno and Horkheimer use the term 'culture industry' to refer to the products and processes of mass culture. Such an industry does not meet people's true needs but instead produces and satisfies false needs. Our true need – to make collective rational choices about our lives – is denied and instead we are encouraged as individuals to choose which standardised products to consume. We are discouraged in the process from thinking beyond the confines of the moment. Art or high culture is different because it embodies ideals which cannot be met within capitalist societies and therefore provides us with a vision of an alternative society. This function of art, however, is increasingly lost as the culture industry turns it into another cultural commodity. While at one stage, the music of Mozart provided a vision of a harmonious world at odds with existing disorder, now it has become incorporated into mass culture. The culture industry claims that the world is already harmonious so that the critical function of art now only resides at the margins, in the work of those who challenge this supposed harmony, such as the music of Schoenberg.

Such an analysis leads the Frankfurt School to a very pessimistic conclusion. Hegemony in contemporary capitalist societies now seems almost complete. People are dominated not only at work but also in their leisure. What's more, there seem to be few signs of resistance. Although Marcuse recognises that there are a few marginal groups such as ethnic minorities who are not fully integrated into the system, the overriding picture is of society as a mass of isolated individuals who are manipulated by big business. There seems to be no way out.

Habermas Habermas' starting point is different from that of the Frankfurt School. For Habermas, what distinguishes human beings is not only their ability to transform the environment but also language – the ability to use signs to communicate with each other. This has far reaching consequences. According to Habermas, when one person talks to another, that person implicitly claims that what is said is intelligible, true, justified and sincere. For there to be rational communication, speakers need to be able to defend all four claims. This presumes various conditions, ie that 'there are no external constraints preventing participants from assessing evidence and argument, and in which each participant has an equal and open chance of entering the discussion' (Giddens, 1985). Circumstances where these conditions are met Habermas calls an *ideal speech situation*. And it is this which provides him with a yardstick against which to measure existing social arrangements.

Social evolution has witnessed increasing possibilities for rational communication and at the same time the emergence of legally sanctioned institutions such as state bureaucracies and markets. In a complex society, it is not always possible for communication to settle competing claims. Instead, power and money become major mechanisms for routinely settling issues ranging from an individual's welfare entitlement to the price of bananas. A problem arises, however, when power and money 'penetrate into areas of everyday life and practice which require communicative action' (Layder, 1994). According to Habermas, this has happened with politics. Whereas politics should involve discussion and debate over what are desirable ends, increasingly it has become simply a question of who can run the economy best. In other words, communicative rationality has been displaced by instrumental rationality. Unlike the Frankfurt School, Habermas does see the glimmering of a way out, for he does not see capitalism as a stable system.

Habermas identifies four types of crisis through which the system moves. In early capitalism *economic crises* present the main problem. According to Habermas, the state reacts to economic crises by accepting an increasing level of responsibility for the management of the economy through such familiar strategies as the protection of home markets and promotion of public sector production. Such action, however, generates a *rationality crisis*. Government intervention in the economy requires heavy borrowing but

this creates inflation and disrupts the normal working of the market. Government intervention ceases for a time but the shift between interventionist and laissez-faire (non-interventionist) approaches to the management of the economy makes the state appear to be acting in an irrational manner. This leads to a *legitimation crisis*. The state finds it increasingly difficult to reconcile the conflicting demands placed upon it. The switch from an interventionist to a laissez-faire approach means that people's expectations of improved welfare cannot be met. At this stage the state loses its legitimacy. This in turns leads to a *motivation crisis*. Increased state power, coupled with the seeming irrelevance of which political party forms the government, undermine people's motivation for participating in the system at all.

There is a way out, however. For new social movements may emerge, such as the environmentalist and women's movements, to challenge instrumental rationality and inject back into politics a concern with values. Although critical theory questions the link which Marx saw between the rise of the proletariat and the advent of a free society, its search for 'an emancipatory alternative to the existing order' indicates its continuing commitment to the Enlightenment ideal (Bronner & Kellner, 1989).

Structuralist Marxism

For structuralist Marxism, the notion that we are the authors of our actions is mistaken. Rather we are the products of underlying structures. Despite its opposition to humanistic Marxism on this issue, there is agreement that economic determinism needs to be rejected. This is clear(ish) in the work of Althusser.

According to Althusser, societies – which he labels social formations – comprise three levels: the economic, the political and the ideological. Although the economy is 'determinant in the last instance', the political and ideological levels are not mere reflections of the economy but have 'relative autonomy' – a degree of independence – and do have effects on the economy.

To clarify what this means, it is helpful to think of an analogy – a three storey building comprising a shop on the ground floor, offices on the second and living quarters on the third. It does not make sense to say 'that the first and second floors are caused by the ground floor, even though they rest upon it' (Craib, 1984). If we assume that the building is one enterprise, the office work which goes on on the first floor is obviously dependent upon the kind of trading conducted in the shop, but work relationships there may well develop in a quite different way. Similarly, if the owners live on the second floor their style of life is influenced by the nature of the business, but their family life has its own dynamics. The economy, in short, does set limits on the political and ideological levels but the latter are not completely dependent upon the former. What's more these levels affect the economy. Returning to our example, new information systems in the office may increase turnover in the shop, while a family bust up might force the business to close down. The interaction, in short, between the three levels is extremely complex.

Althusser's rejection of economic determinism is further apparent when he argues that different types of society can be distinguished according to the dominance of the different levels. What he means by this is that in the operation of a society, one particular level may become more important than the others. It is, however, the economic level which determines which of the levels is dominant at any particular time. 'It is as if the economic level hands over its power to one of the other levels, or keeps it to itself, for the duration of that type of society' (Craib, 1984). Two examples illustrate this. Under feudalism, the landlords have to ensure that serfs hand over the surplus which they have produced. To do this, they are reliant on the state forcing the serfs to do so, or the church persuading them to do so. In this mode of production, the political and ideological levels are thus dominant. Under capitalism, by contrast, the bourgeoisie automatically receive the surplus produced by the proletariat. In this mode of production, the economic level is dominant.

Although this is the case, Althusser recognises that capitalist relations of production depend upon a number of conditions being fulfilled which cannot be guaranteed purely at the economic level. Workers need, for example, to be trained in the appropriate skills and persuaded to accept their role. For Althusser (1971), it is above all the state which ensures that these conditions are met and that 'the reproduction of the relations of production' occurs. It does this in two ways – through 'repressive state apparatuses' such as the army and the police which coerce people and through 'ideological state apparatuses' such as education and the mass media which ensure that people are socialised to fill their allotted places in the relations of production. We may think that we are the authors of our own actions but, in fact, we are the products of pre-existing structures which map out our lives for us. Capitalism can be overthrown, but this will depend not upon people changing their consciousness, but rather upon contradictions at different levels coming together to reinforce each other. Althusser calls this process *overdetermination*. This is when capitalism is most vulnerable to revolution, as in the case of the Russian Revolution in 1917.

Evaluation

What is most striking when looking at Marxism are the different approaches within it. We need really to evaluate each separately. Nonetheless, there is some agreement that central to the analysis of modern society are the concepts of capitalism and class. The main concerns of Marxism are twofold: 1) to account for the unexpected stability of capitalism and 2) to identify the factors likely to lead to the demise of capitalism. While Marxists agree that the economy is in some sense fundamental and that class conflict is therefore central, in practice they often pay particular attention to the superstructure (the state and ideology) and acknowledge the importance of social movements not based on class.

They therefore often find themselves on the horns of a dilemma. If they attempt to do justice to the complexity of the world and question, for example, the link between the proletariat and the demise of capitalism, aren't they abandoning Marxism? If they attempt to do justice to the complexity of the world and see, for example, the economy as only determinant in the last instance, aren't they putting forward a theory which is 'unfalsifiable' and in Karl Popper's view as unscientific as the belief that God is all powerful? (For Popper's views on falsification and science, see page 230.)

key terms

Humanist Marxism Assumes that human beings can transform their environment and influence social change.
Structuralist Marxism Assumes that human behaviour is largely shaped by the structure of society and that human beings are a product of structures.
Hegemony Domination through ideology.
Dual consciousness The view that proletarian consciousness is shaped by the dominant ideology and everyday experience.
Instrumental reason The use of reason to discover the most efficient means to achieve ends.
Mass culture A culture based on false needs which is transmitted through the media to the mass of the population.
Overdetermination When contradictions at different levels of society – the economic, political and ideological – come together and reinforce each other.

activity7 a crisis of hegemony?

Item A The Handsworth 'mugging'

In March 1973, two boys were found guilty of robbing and inflicting grievous bodily harm on a man in Handsworth, Birmingham. The boys had stolen a total of 30p, some keys and five cigarettes. They had also returned to attack the victim two hours after the initial incident. Each boy received a ten-year sentence. A third boy, the 'ringleader', according to the judge on the case, was found guilty of attempted murder and robbery with regard to the same victim. He was given a 20 year sentence. All three sentences were extremely long and, arguably, harsh for the type of crimes committed.

Item B Press headline, 17 August, 1972

'As Crimes of Violence Escalate, a Word Common in The United States Enters the British Headlines: Mugging. To our Police, it's a frightening new strain of crime.'

Source: *Daily Mirror*

Item C Press editorial, 13 October, 1972

WHAT ARE the British people most concerned about today? Wages? Prices? Immigration? Pornography? People are talking about all these things. But the Sun believes there is another issue which has everyone deeply worried and angry: VIOLENCE IN OUR STREETS... Nothing could be more utterly against our way of life, based on a common sense regard for law and order ... If punitive jail sentences help to stop the violence – and nothing else has done – then they will not only prove to be the only way. They will, regrettably, be the RIGHT way. And the judges will have the backing of the public.

Source: *The Sun*

Item D A judge's view

Mugging is becoming more and more prevalent, certainly in London. As a result, decent citizens are afraid to use the Underground late at night, and indeed are afraid to use the underpasses for fear of mugging. We are told that in America people are even afraid to walk in the streets late at night for fear of mugging. This is an offence for which deterrent sentences should be passed.

Source: Judge Alexander Karmel, QC

Item E A politician's view

In my view it is absolutely essential to stop this rising tide of mugging in our cities. I have seen what happens in America where muggings are rife. It is absolutely horrifying to know that in all the big American cities, coast to coast, there are areas where people dare not go out after dark. I am extremely anxious that such a situation should never come to Britain.

Source: Birmingham MP, Mrs Jill Knight, quoted in the *Birmingham Evening Mail*, 20.8.1972

Item F Social conflict – Northern Ireland, 1972

In 1972, the IRA stepped up its bombing campaign and tens of thousands of Catholics took part in civil rights marches. On 30 January 1972, soldiers opened fire on an illegal march in Derry killing 13 and injuring 29. On 22 February, seven people were killed in an IRA attack on the 16th Parachute Brigade at Aldershot. On 28 March, 100,000 Protestants marched against direct rule from Westminster.

The Bogside, Derry, 1972. Rioting Catholic youths flee from a gas canister fired by British troops.

Item G Social conflict – the miners' strike, 1972

In 1972, striking miners attempted to create a power crisis. In February they clashed with police as they tried to prevent trucks taking coke from the West Midland Gas Board coke depot in Birmingham. At Longannet, near Edinburgh, 2,000 miners fought with police to prevent deliveries of oil to the power station. Most power stations were working well below capacity and 12 were completely shut down by fuel shortages. The government called a state of emergency.

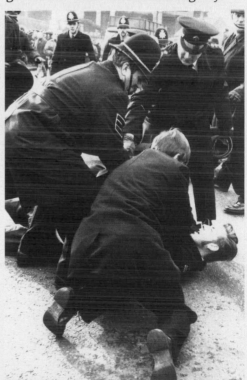

Striking miners face 500 police at West Midlands Gas Board coke depot, 1972.

questions

1 Read Items A to E. What common themes appear in the reactions from the press, the judiciary and the politician?

2 Look at Items F and G. How might they indicate a crisis in hegemony?

3 Why did the state respond to this crisis by focusing attention on the seemingly trivial issue of 'mugging'?

3.3 Symbolic interactionism

Although, as we have seen, there are significant differences between functionalist and Marxist theories of society, both emphasise the ways in which individual behaviour and consciousness are shaped by external forces in society. In their own ways, therefore, both may be regarded to some extent as *deterministic* theories, in which little scope is allowed for individuals to shape their own destinies by the exercise of their free will. Symbolic interactionists, by contrast, emphasise the ways in which society is actively shaped by the conscious and deliberate actions of its members. For this reason, symbolic interactionism is usually regarded as a *social action theory*, whilst functionalism and Marxism are regarded as *structural* theories.

Although a wide range of intellectual influences on the development of symbolic interactionism may be traced – including especially the work of such 18th century Scottish moralists as Adam Ferguson, John Millar and Adam Smith, and in the 19th century, Charles Darwin's theory of evolution. Perhaps the greatest influence was the late 19th century American philosophy of 'pragmatism' developed by such men as John Dewey, William James and Charles Pierce.

At the heart of pragmatism, as with symbolic interactionism, was a concern with 'meaning'. For pragmatists, the meaning of an object was not intrinsic to that object, but depended upon the ways in which human beings behaved towards it. So, for example, there is nothing about a chair which intrinsically gives it its significance as something we sit upon – this significance derives entirely from the fact that this is indeed how human beings behave towards chairs. It would be entirely possible for us to treat chairs as objects of worship, as places for our pet canaries to perch, or as virtually anything else. And if we were to do so, the meaning of 'chair' would be quite different, even though the physical nature of the object remains unchanged. It is this pragmatist concern with the ways in which human beings actively make their environments meaningful that forms the starting point of symbolic interactionism.

George Herbert Mead

One of the most significant figures in the development of the symbolic interactionist tradition was the American philosopher and social psychologist, George Herbert Mead. Mead taught at the University of Chicago from 1893 until his death in 1931, and founded what, because of its continued association with the university and the city, became known as the 'Chicago School' of symbolic interactionism. During his lifetime Mead published very little, most of his work being published after his death on the basis of lecture notes and fragmentary manuscripts. Probably his most significant book from the point of view of symbolic interactionism is *Mind, Self and Society*, first published in 1934.

Human conduct versus animal behaviour What is the difference between the behaviour of animals and that of human beings? Mead's answer to this question gives us the clue to the whole approach of symbolic interactionism. For Mead, following the ideas of behaviourists such as John B. Watson, animal behaviour could be accounted for in terms of responses to stimuli. Such responses may either be directly instinctual, such as a cat's response to a physical threat, or learned, as was demonstrated by Ivan Pavlov in his famous experiments where he 'conditioned' a dog to salivate whenever a bell was rung, by repeatedly associating the sound of the bell with the arrival of food. Whilst Mead agreed that such processes could account for certain aspects of human behaviour, he argued that most needed to be characterised in a qualitatively different way.

To see Mead's point, consider the following situation. If I walk up to a dog belonging to one of my students and deliver a hefty kick to its rear end, its behaviour will be predictable. It will probably bark, turn around and snap at my ankles. It would do the same whoever was to deliver the kick, and under whatever circumstances. Of course, following Pavlov's principle, it is possible that if I repeat this often enough, the dog will come to associate my presence with being kicked, and will begin to bark and snap at my ankles even when I do not kick it. But even so, its behaviour remains predictable. Now, imagine that instead of kicking the dog, I kick its owner, my student. How will the student respond? An initial response might be to say that he will kick me back, but a moment's reflection reveals that things are not so straightforward as at first they might seem. Will the student kick me back? He may, but this will depend upon how he has interpreted my kick. For example, he may interpret it as simply an act of gratuitous violence, in which case he would probably feel quite justified in returning the kick. However, there are a good many other ways in which my behaviour could be interpreted. He might judge that it was the result of mental instability on my part, in which case returning the kick begins to seem not merely inappropriate, but even callous – in our society, at least, assaulting the mentally ill is generally frowned upon. He might judge that my kick was merely an over-enthusiastic attempt to explain the principles of symbolic interactionism, in which case he might consider a verbal remonstration sufficient, as at least I had intended no harm.

The point is that how the student reacts will depend upon how he interprets my behaviour, or, in other words, what *meaning* he attributes to it. For Mead, this ability involves the distinctively human capacity to put oneself in the place of others, and to see oneself from the point of view of others. This he calls *role-taking*. In assessing how to respond to my kick, my student has to imagine the situation from my point of view – in short, he has to 'take my role'.

The self In an attempt to understand this distinctively human ability to take the role of others, Mead developed the concept of the *self*. For Mead, the self is viewed as having two elements which he terms the *I* and the *Me*. To understand the distinction which Mead is making, consider the following example. Imagine that, in the course of a particularly dull lecture, you become aware of an impulse to leave the room and go for coffee. This impulse originates from the part of your personality which Mead calls the *I*. It is spontaneous and, as it were, uncensored.

However, although such impulses may be common enough, they are in fact rarely acted upon. This is because as soon as you become aware of such a desire, you cannot avoid imagining what sort of response your walking out of the lecture would provoke in those around you, and especially the lecturer! This 'imagining' of the likely responses of others originates from the part of the personality which Mead calls the *Me*. This is the internalised points of view of other people, and acts as a sort of censor of the *I's* plans.

Crucial to Mead's notion of the self, was the fact that it can only emerge as the result of social interaction. We have to learn the points of view of specific other people (*significant others* in Mead's terminology) and of society in general (for Mead, the *generalised other*). Mead identified two principal stages by which the child acquires a social self. The first he calls the *play stage*. This phase, which begins as soon as the child starts to use language, is exemplified by the tendency of young children to pretend to be someone else. For example, children will play 'doctors and nurses' or 'teachers', or pretend to be their father or mother chastising a younger sibling. Mead argues that, in doing this, children learn to see themselves from the point of view of significant others. The second stage is termed by Mead the *game stage*. This phase is exemplified by the playing of team games, in which the child has to see himself not only from the point of view of specific individuals, but of entire groups. For example, although the members of the opposing team in a game of football all have individual points of view, a player must be able to imagine himself from the collective point of view of that team, ie as their opponent. It is this process which, in Mead's view, completes the development of the social self because it leads to the ability to view oneself from the generalised point of view of one's society.

The significance of Mead's work Although Mead's work has important implications for both philosophy and social psychology, its importance to sociological theory lies principally in his view of human beings as socially self-conscious. They are not the mindless products of external social norms over which they have no control. Potentially, therefore, Mead's theory has the ability to explain how social order is maintained – by the fact that human beings possess an internalised representation of the point of view of their fellow members of society. At the same time, Mead also recognises that human beings act self-consciously in possibly unpredictable ways.

Herbert Blumer

After Mead's death in 1931, the tradition which he had helped to establish at the University of Chicago was continued by the sociologist Herbert Blumer. Indeed, although his work clearly owed an immense amount to Mead's influence, it was in fact Blumer who coined the term *symbolic interactionism*. Perhaps Blumer's greatest contribution to the development of symbolic interactionism was his working out of some of the major implications of symbolic interactionist theory for how sociologists should study society.

Blumer's critique of variable analysis As we have seen, a major assumption of a number of sociological approaches is that human behaviour can be understood in terms of the influences of external causes which are amenable to measurement. A classic example of this is Durkheim's study of suicide, in which a society's suicide rate is correlated with certain other features of that society, such as the degree of integration or regulation which prevails. Such explanations take the form, variable X (say a low level of integration) produces variable Y (say a high suicide rate). Individual consciousness as such is deliberately ignored in such explanations.

For Blumer, this was unacceptable. First of all, he emphasises the fact that variables are in fact creations of sociologists, and can usually only be identified and measured if the sociologist makes some quite arbitrary and groundless assumptions. Consider the example of social class. Imagine that a sociologist wishes to demonstrate a relationship between being working class and experiencing relatively poor health. Before this can even be meaningful, the sociologist must define and operationalise 'social class'. She may define social class in terms of occupation and classify her sample accordingly. Next she must define and operationalise the second variable, 'relatively poor health'. She may choose to use the incidence of longstanding illness. Finally, she must examine the relationship between the two variables – does being working class increase one's risk of experiencing poor health? The crucial point for Blumer, however, is that the answer to the sociologist's question will depend almost entirely on how the variables have been defined and operationalised. They could, quite legitimately, have been defined and operationalised quite differently, and this would inevitably have produced a different answer to the question being addressed.

Second, and most importantly for Blumer, is the fact that even if social class does influence health, the process by which this occurs needs to be examined. Following Mead's theoretical lead, Blumer emphasises the fact that human behaviour does not result from the blind operation of external social forces (or, in other words, variables). Instead, behaviour (or *conduct*) results from how a social actor interprets or attributes meaning to a situation. Thus, to continue the same example, the central question would be, what meanings do people attach to their class position, and how do these meanings contribute to subsequent conduct which either promotes, or damages, their health? Crucial for Blumer, as for Mead, is the fact these meanings are not inevitable and pre-determined, but will change over time and vary between individuals.

Blumer therefore uses symbolic interactionist theory to challenge certain other sociological approaches on methodological grounds. In Blumer's view it is simply not legitimate to see human behaviour as resulting from the operation of measurable variables. Instead, individual actions need to be examined from the point of view of the actor's interpretation of the situation in which they find themselves. It is for this reason that symbolic interactionists have tended to rely upon such qualitative research techniques as participant observation in an attempt to discover these meanings. (See page 235 for further discussion of Blumer's methodology.)

Erving Goffman – the dramaturgical analogy

All the world's a stage,
And all the men and women merely players:
They have their exits and their entrances;
And one man in his time plays many parts.

(*As You Like It*, Act II, Scene VII, Shakespeare)

Impression management Erving Goffman (1959), the most influential symbolic interactionist, uses a *dramaturgical analogy* – society as drama – to illuminate social interaction and explore 'the way in which the individual in ordinary work situations presents himself and his activity to others, the ways in which he guides and controls the impression they form of him'. Goffman argues that in everyday social interaction individuals are not only constantly expressing themselves to others, but also are trying to create certain impressions of themselves in the mind of an audience. This process of *impression management* is central to behaviour, as social actors attempt to control the impressions others have of them.

Goffman pays most attention to the non-verbal aspects of interpersonal communication and this is illustrated by the example he quotes from his research into rural life in the Shetland Islands. The crofter's wife, when serving local dishes to tourists, would check on the stated feelings of liking the food by watching how quickly the tourists ate the food and how eagerly it was consumed. In social interaction, we constantly watch for these non-verbal 'signs given off' as the ways in which a person's true feelings might be revealed. We do not always take things at face value, but we check the whole performance for any discrepancies, and for signs of the underlying motivations of the performer.

Performance The idea of *performance* is very important to Goffman's analysis. It refers to any activity of a participant in a social interaction which influences other participants. When playing a part, the individual is implicitly asking the others in an interaction to believe in their performance. And to achieve this, the social actor must create the appropriate impression. For example, some teachers take the view that it is important to get the upper hand in a new class – starting out tough and letting the students know who's boss. Any bumbling around or signs of weakness will not create the desired impression and the performance

will fail, endangering future performances before that class. Goffman recognises that we can believe in the roles we play, or perform them with no real conviction. Deluding an audience may be out of self-interest, or it may be because the audience demands to be deluded. An illustration of the latter is the way doctors may give placebos (something which will have no medical effect) to hypochondriacal patients in the knowledge that there is nothing wrong with them, but simply because they demand treatment.

To be effective, performances need to be cohesive and sustained. Some of the techniques used to confirm an impression are considered next.

Front and regions Social actors employ the equivalent of theatrical 'props' to assist in the creation of a particular impression or definition of a situation. Anything which is intentionally or unintentionally used to enhance the effectiveness of a performance, Goffman refers to as 'front'. Furniture, decor and specialised equipment may be used to create the right setting for a performance and these are allied to the personal 'front' of clothing, speech, facial expressions and body language in order to create a cohesive impression, consistent with the role being expressed. The budding young executive, keen to create an impression of dynamism, will go in for 'power dressing' and is likely to develop the leisure interests and activities associated with that image. Many of the 'props' we carry or utilise have an apparently practical purpose, but their real value lies in the way they contribute to creating a desired impression. Solicitors' case papers are usually tied with ribbon, ostensibly to prevent the contents from falling out, but the social impact is one of setting aside legal papers from other kinds of material, inferring a special and superior status to them and to the person carrying them.

Just as a theatre has a 'frontstage' where the performance takes place, and a 'backstage' where actors can relax out of their roles, so there are separate 'regions' in social interactions. A 'region' is any area which is bounded to some degree by barriers to perception. Performances take place in a 'front region' whilst in the 'back region', a performance can be knowingly contradicted by out-of-role behaviour. In a school or college, the classroom, corridors, dining areas, etc form the 'front region' for adults performing the role of teacher and for younger people presenting the role of student. However, both teachers and students can relax from their respective roles in either the staff room, or in areas where teachers tend not to visit. Even in these 'back regions' however, a performance of a different kind has to be maintained as colleagues or friends now form a different audience to the 'frontstage' one. So the 'back region' for one performance becomes the 'front region' for another.

When performances fail Goffman notes that sometimes discrepancies appear in our performances which affect the audience's impressions of us. Sometimes an individual fails to maintain their expressive control, the mask slips and the whole performance can be jeopardised in the same way as a jarringly wrong note can spoil an entire concert.

Goffman suggests that examining occasions when this happens tells us a great deal about the nature of performances. For example, an audience, or part of an audience, sometimes colludes with a role player to cover up or ignore discrepancies in a performance and this illustrates the way social actors can work in 'teams', helping to maintain expressive control. Sometimes, however, discrepant behaviour can be more damaging to attempted impression management, culminating in embarrassment and even retirement from that role.

Role distance Goffman creates a strongly humanistic version of social role. The roles we perform in social interaction are not scripted for us by society, but are actively created and defined by our performances. Individuals often distance themselves from the role they are occupying by making communications out of character with the role, thus showing themselves to be more than the role being performed. Elements of the individual's self, made up from other roles they occupy, may appear in the performance of a role, and it is this which allows for spontaneity and creativity in a performance. In acting out the role of teacher for example, an individual may allow other roles – of parent, 'ordinary person' or friend – to enter their performance. Similarly, a civil servant, even when turning down a request because it doesn't fit the rules, may show a 'human face', to indicate that they are more than the role they are performing. We are not programmed into a role, straight-jacketing our behaviour, but through the use of *role distance*, actively create the roles we occupy.

Roles and power Analogies in sociology have to be used with care. It is one thing to point to apparent similarities between social behaviour and acting on a stage, and another to suggest that the two are identical. Goffman recognises the limitations of the dramaturgical analogy, pointing out that the stage presents activity which is imaginary and rehearsed, whilst social behaviour is real and frequently unplanned. Furthermore, in social life the audience often takes a very much more active role than it does in the theatre. For Goffman, therefore, the dramatic analogy is only a framework with which to begin to understand behaviour and many parts of his analysis, for example the idea of role distance, go much further.

Unlike some of the early symbolic interactionists, Goffman does pay specific attention to the ways in which inequalities in power are played out in face-to-face interaction. Without attempting to analyse the structural location and causes of inequality, Goffman nevertheless identifies the way hierarchies create problems of self-respect and opportunity. In *Asylums*, a study of the experience of inmates in a mental hospital, Goffman (1968) explores the problem posed for individual social actors by the imposition on them of a complete regime in a 'total institution' – an institution, such as a prison or mental hospital, in which inmates live, eat and sleep. Even in this, the most extreme case of apparent powerlessness, the individual is still capable of employing strategies which ensure that some self-determination can be retained. Inmates who fool the staff to get extra food or cigarettes are

maintaining their sense of self-determination. In this respect, Goffman's work carries the important message that power is not merely the creation of a hierarchy of positions in society, but the constant acting out in face-to-face interaction of that inequality.

Whilst Goffman rejects the structural view that the individual is what their place in an organisation defines them to be, he does not, unlike some of the early symbolic interactionists, ignore the effect of external constraints. The individual's self does not arise solely out of their interaction with others, but within the context of the limitations imposed by social institutions. The self constantly moves between the limitations of external society and the needs of inner individuality. Goffman concludes that, 'it is against something that the self can emerge'. That 'something' is society. From this, it can be seen that Goffman is acknowledging the impact on our individuality of external social constraints. Our individual 'self' is created in the context of hierarchical organisations which, although they do not rigorously define the way we are, play a part in forging our individuality.

Evaluation

As noted above, symbolic interactionism has a number of strengths. First, it moves away from the deterministic assumptions of much sociological theory, and emphasises the conscious involvement of the actor in social life. Second, it recognises that human conduct is meaningful, and hence that a grasp of actors' meanings and interpretations is essential to an understanding of their actions.

Equally, however, symbolic interactionism can be criticised. The most fundamental and persistent difficulty is its tendency to ignore the influence of social structures. It is possible to acknowledge Blumer's criticisms of variable analysis whilst still recognising that an individual's

---

key terms

Role-taking Putting oneself in the place of others and seeing oneself from the point of view of others.

Self In Mead's view, the self consists of two elements, the *I* and the *Me*.

Significant others Specific other people who matter to the individual.

Generalised other Society in general.

Play stage The first stage in which a child acquires a social self. Involves seeing themselves from the point of view of significant others.

Game stage The second stage in this process, where they see themselves from the point of view of groups rather than just individuals.

Dramaturgical analogy Seeing a similarity between society and drama, and using this to illuminate social interaction.

Impression management The attempt by social actors to shape and control the impressions others have of them.

Performance Any activity of a participant in social interaction which influences other participants.

Role distance Distancing ourselves from the roles we are playing.

economic position (their class, however this is defined) will affect their behaviour whether they recognise it or not. Poverty, for example, would seem to be real enough, and its effects will be obvious whether or not an actor defines himself as poor. A second, and related, criticism is that symbolic interactionism exaggerates the extent to which human actors do in fact consciously interpret their environments. It may be argued that whilst self-conscious interpretation does occur, this tends to be only when some unusual situation is encountered. For most of the time, human beings seem to act as though on 'automatic pilot', or merely out of habit. The notion of habit seems closer to the view of action advanced by systems and structural theorists than to that advanced by symbolic interactionists.

summary

1. Functionalists argue that societies should be studied as systems – as wholes made up of interconnected parts.

2. The function of any part is the contribution it makes to society as a whole.

3. Talcott Parsons identifies four functional prerequisites which must be met if the social system is to survive – adaptation, goal attainment, integration and pattern maintenance.

4. Parsons explained social change in two ways.
   - As a response to disturbances in the system in order to restore it to equilibrium.
   - In terms of social evolution. As societies evolve, institutions become increasingly specialised – a process known as social differentiation.

5. Robert Merton questions the assumption that all parts of the social system are closely interconnected and work together for the benefit of the whole.

6. Merton argues that:
   - Some parts may have functional autonomy – they may operate as largely independent units.
   - Any part of society may be functional, non-functional or dysfunctional.

7. Criticisms of functionalism include the following.
   - Its theories are teleological – it tends to explain the causes of parts of society in terms of their effects or functions.
   - It overestimates the degree of value consensus in society.
   - Its focus on social order and value consensus downplays the importance of conflict in society.

8. There are two main versions of modern Marxism – humanist Marxism and structuralist Marxism.

9. Gramsci's humanist Marxism argues that the proletariat have a dual consciousness which means they will partially see through bourgeois ideology.

10. According to the Frankfurt School, instrumental reason and mass culture produce and satisfy false needs. Hegemony in capitalist societies is now almost complete.

11. Habermas sees capitalism as an unstable system which moves through a series of crises. He sees hope for the future in the emergence of new social movements which challenge instrumental rationality.

12. According to Althusser's structuralist Marxism, capitalism can be overthrown when contradictions at different levels of society – the economic, political and ideological – come together and reinforce each other.

13. The central concern for modern Marxism is to explain the unexpected stability of capitalism and to identify factors that will lead to its downfall.

14. Symbolic interactionism focuses on small-scale interaction situations and the meanings which direct action.

15. According to Mead, people react to others in terms of the meanings they give to the actions of others. This involves role-taking.

16. The self emerges from social interaction. The child acquires a social self as they pass through the play stage and the game stage.

17. Mead sees human beings as socially self-conscious – they do not simply behave in terms of social norms.

18. Blumer criticises variable analysis, arguing that it sees human beings as shaped by forces beyond their control. This ignores how social actors define and give meaning to their situation. And it fails to discover the meanings which direct action.

19. Goffman uses a dramaturgical analogy to interpret social action. Just like actors in a play, people in society are seen to create performances by the skilful use of impression management.

20. Social actors are seen as creative – negotiating the meanings which direct their actions and adapting and developing the roles they play.

21. Goffman accepts that there is an external society which can constrain human behaviour. However, there is still plenty of room for people to express their creativity and individuality.

22. Critics of symbolic interactionism argue that:
   - It largely ignores the influence of social structures on human behaviour.
   - It exaggerates the extent to which people consciously interpret their situation – often they act out of habit with little thought.

activity8 defining the situation

Henderson Dores is out with his girlfriend, Irene Stein. They are trying to locate his car after spending the evening in a restaurant. It is central New York, just after midnight and Henderson has just noticed three men coming towards them. Irene is searching in her handbag for a tissue and has noticed nothing.

Henderson looked round again in what he hoped was an unconcerned natural way. The figures – dark, lithe-looking – had crossed to their side of the street with what looked like more urgency.

Jesus Christ, Henderson thought, they say it happens to everybody sooner or later – like a car crash or a burglary.

He felt a surging panic begin to overwhelm him. It's only when you haven't got any money that they kill you. Or pour petrol over you and set you alight. Or rape you. Gang-sodomise you. They were only ten yards away.

'RUN!' Henderson screamed, simultaneously flinging away the umbrella and giving Irene a mighty push. His hand closed around his wallet, fat with credit cards and dollars.

'You can have it, you bastards!' he yelled at the muggers and with all his strength bowled his wallet in their direction. He saw it fly open and notes and cards shower out, then he turned and ran.

Henderson races off, pursued by two of the men who eventually catch up with him.

'OK,' he bellowed in mingled rage and terror as he was hauled to a stop, 'Kill me, kill me, I don't care!'

Both his hands were firmly gripped. 'Sir,' a quiet voice came. 'Relax, please, sir. We have your wallet and your money here.'

Later, Henderson was able to reconstruct what happened. The three men were returning theatre-goers who had been surprised by Henderson suddenly throwing his girlfriend to the ground, throwing his wallet at them and running off in panic-stricken flight!

Source: Boyd, 1999

questions

1 Make a list of the ways in which meanings are transmitted in the situation described above.

2 How does this extract illustrate the view of one symbolic interactionist, W. I. Thomas, that 'if men define situations as real, they are real in their consequences'?

Unit 4 *Structure and action in sociology*

keyissues

1 What are the main assumptions of structuralism, ethnomethodology and structuration theory?

2 How have they seen the relationship between structure and action?

Although functionalism, Marxism and symbolic interactionism have been central to the establishment of sociology as a discipline, alternative approaches have developed. In this unit, we shall look at three which present very different ways of looking at the relation between 'structure' and 'action'.

4.1 Structuralism

As the name implies, *structuralism* is concerned with structures. It has been an influential way of looking at the world, not only in sociology and the social sciences, but also in the arts, literary studies and history. The origins of structuralism lie in linguistics – the study of language – and in particular in the work of a Swiss linguist, Ferdinand de Saussure. In order to understand how structuralism has been of relevance as a sociological theory, it will be helpful to begin by considering the distinctive approach adopted by Saussure to the study of language.

Ferdinand de Saussure

Central to Saussure's analysis of language, and indeed to structuralism in general, is the observation that it is possible to study a language in two dimensions. First, we can study what individual people actually write and say. If a person utters a sentence like 'elephants are bigger than apples' we can pay attention to the meaning of this particular utterance, consider its truth, their reasons for saying it and so on. This dimension of language – the dimension of what people actually write and say – is called the *diachronic*. Contrasted with this, however, is the fact that it is only possible for anyone to utter this sentence, or indeed any other, because there are *rules* which go to make up the language which is being spoken. Most obviously, there are rules governing the relationship between words and things (or what Saussure calls *signifiers* and *signifieds*). In English, the word elephant (the signifier) is attached by convention to the large animals with trunks which are indigenous to Africa and India. Of course, there is no absolute reason why we should call them elephants (the word itself is quite arbitrary), but once the convention is established we must use it if we are to make sense.

Second, there are rules of grammar. In English, for example, there are particular rules governing tenses. So the sentence 'elephants were bigger than apples' has a different meaning from our original sentence, 'elephants are bigger than apples', by virtue of the grammatical rules governing past and present tenses. Saussure's point is that we can also study language in this way – as a system of rules governing what we can and cannot say. This second dimension, which concerns itself with the structure of language itself, is called the *synchronic*.

This distinction between the diachronic and the synchronic is fundamental not only to structuralist linguistics, but to the whole structuralist approach. To see how the distinction works, let us consider an example of human activity. Let us take lunch. When we have a meal, we are most likely to be concerned with its diachronic dimension – that is, what we are actually going to eat, and in what order. Imagine we go into a restaurant. Our order may well look something like this. We begin with soup of the day; we then move on to roast chicken, with potatoes, carrots and peas, and finally we choose strawberries and cream followed by coffee and mints. However, as with uttering individual sentences, this meal as it appears in the diachronic dimension depends upon rules which exist in the synchronic. First there are rules, often specific to cultures, about what we can and cannot eat. It is not generally permitted in our culture, for example, to eat parrots, whilst chickens are perfectly acceptable. Second, there are rules about what we can eat together from the same plate, and in what order – the grammatical rules of eating in fact. In our culture, for example, it is not really permissible to begin a meal with dessert and coffee, or to round it off with a bowl of soup. What is clear from this example, as with the example of language, is that the diachronic dimension – the element of action – depends upon the synchronic dimension – the element of structure. It is this concern with the synchronic, or structural elements of human activity, which is characteristic of structuralism.

Claude Lévi-Strauss

As you will by now have noticed, many of the sociological theorists considered in this chapter could be called structuralist. Certainly, Durkheim's concern with social facts, or Marx's emphasis on the underlying logic of capitalism, could win them the label of structuralist. However, the theorist who did most to formulate the implications of the structuralist approach for the social sciences was the Belgian anthropologist Claude Lévi-Strauss. Lévi-Strauss was concerned to apply structuralist methods to the analysis of human culture. One of his most famous analyses was of myths.

Myths exist in all societies. Although, superficially, the myths which different societies possess are quite different from each other, Lévi-Strauss' analysis emphasises that this is only so when considered in a diachronic sense. When viewed synchronically, he argues that myths possess certain common structural features. One can, according to Lévi-

Strauss, and indeed he spends much time attempting to demonstrate this, place a large number of myths (theoretically all myths) alongside each other, and detect a common set of underlying rules which govern their structure. Lévi-Strauss attempts to explain this deep structure in terms of fundamental properties of the human mind. The underlying structure of culture, he says, is ultimately produced by the biologically determined structures of the human brain.

Oppositions Here is a brief illustration of Lévi-Strauss' approach. Myths are based on *oppositions*. Typical oppositions are good/evil; male/female; life/death; night/day; land/sea. For example, these and many other oppositions are found in the creation myth in *Genesis* which tells the story of the creation of the world, of life, and of human beings.

Many of these oppositions cause unwelcome contradictions for human beings. For example, death contradicts life. Myths can resolve this contradiction by stating that death is not a necessary consequence of life. They can introduce a new possibility, a new form of existence which is neither life nor death. Thus myths often contain 'mythical beings' such as angels, ghosts and other supernatural creatures who are neither alive nor dead as we normally understand these terms. In this way, myths mediate between the opposition of life and death, they resolve the contradiction.

Lévi-Strauss argues that all myths have the same basic structure – opposition and mediation or, put another way, contradiction and resolution. Only when this structure is revealed are we in a position to interpret the function of myths. In Lévi-Strauss' (1965) words, 'the purpose of myth is to provide a logical model capable of overcoming a contradiction'.

Semiotics

Derived from the theoretical basis of structuralism, *semiotics*, or the study of signs, was developed most famously in the work of Roland Barthes. Semiotic analysis concentrates upon the central structuralist principle that the relationship between signifier and signified is arbitrary, and hence determined only by convention and applied according to rules. For example, consider a red rose. A red rose can be considered a signifier, in the sense that it has a meaning beyond its mere physical existence as a flower. We know this from the fact that if a man gives a bunch of red roses to a woman, she will interpret this in a quite different way than if he had given her a bunch of daffodils. Red roses, in our culture, signify love, whilst daffodils do not. There is no necessary reason for this – it could just as easily be the other way round. The task of semiotics is to interpret the meanings of signs in our culture.

Barthes was also heavily influenced by Marxism, and one of his central tasks was to analyse the deep ideological meanings of signs in modern popular culture. He argued that very often such signs, whilst appearing on the surface trivial enough, betray deeper ideological 'myths', which are often invisible to ordinary people and can only be seen when subjected to semiological analysis. One of Barthes' own examples will serve to illustrate this point. The example is of a Black soldier saluting the French flag on the cover of the magazine *Paris Match*. At face value, this is just what it appears to be – a Black soldier saluting the French flag. However, at a deeper level, Barthes argues, this picture signifies a strongly ideological message, namely, 'that France is a great Empire, that all her sons, without colour discrimination, faithfully serve under her flag, and that there is no better answer to the detractors of an alleged colonialism than the zeal shown by this Negro in serving his so-called oppressors' (Barthes, 1973). In other words, this seemingly straightforward picture of a Black soldier saluting the flag contains a hidden justification of French imperialism and a denial of racial discrimination.

As with other structuralist writers, Barthes' approach rests upon his analysis of the synchronic dimension, and specifically upon the systems of rules which govern the relationship between signifiers and that which they signify. It is only in relation to these systems of rules, which link certain signs with deeper ideological meanings, that the specific products (that is the diachronic dimension) of popular culture can be understood.

Evaluation

There can be no doubt that structuralism provides a powerful method for the analysis of virtually any aspect of human culture. More specifically, it has encouraged sociologists to recognise that 'what appears to us as solid, normal or natural, is in fact the end result of a process of production from some form of underlying structure' (Marshall, 1994). It has nevertheless been subject to criticisms.

One is that in reducing the diachronic to the synchronic – or, interpreting actual utterances, myths, pictures or whatever in terms of underlying systems of rules – we are in danger of losing the uniqueness and subtlety of actual human action. Subtle differences in meaning between myths, for example, are in danger of being lost sight of in the eagerness of the structuralist to find some underlying pattern which all myths have in common.

Second, it can be argued that structuralism has an inevitable difficulty in explaining change. If particular instances of action are to be explained with reference to some underlying structure, then it is difficult to see how changes in that structure are to be explained.

Despite these criticisms, as we shall see, the insights of structuralism have nevertheless been important in shaping modern sociological theory.

4.2 Ethnomethodology

Ethnomethodology is an approach to sociological theorising developed during the 1960s by the American writer, Harold Garfinkel. Ethnomethodology can be seen largely as a reaction to the highly structural and systematic theorising in sociology which reached its climax with the work of Garfinkel's teacher, Talcott Parsons.

activity9 semiotics

Item A

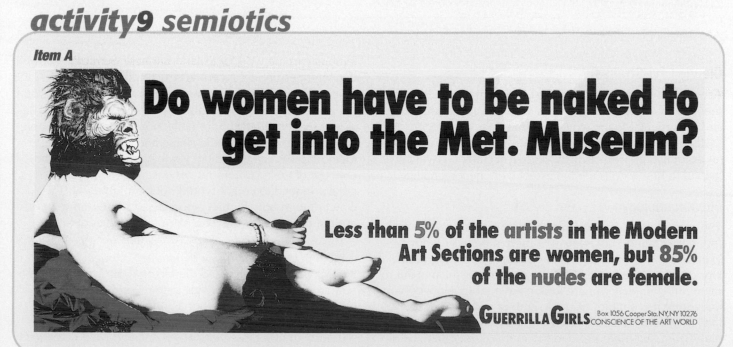

Do women have to be naked to get into the Met. Museum?

Less than 5% of the artists in the Modern Art Sections are women, but 85% of the nudes are female.

GUERRILLA GIRLS Box 1056 Cooper Sta. NY, NY 10276 CONSCIENCE OF THE ART WORLD

Item B

First World War poster

Item C

Second World War poster

question

Interpret the ideological significance of Items A, B and C.

The philosophical underpinnings of ethnomethodology lie in a branch of European philosophy known as phenomenology, and in particular in the work of Edmund Husserl (1859-1938) and Alfred Schutz (1899-1959). Before we undertake an examination of ethnomethodology, therefore, it will be helpful to briefly consider the essence of phenomenology.

Phenomenology

The central point of phenomenology, first outlined by its founder Edmund Husserl, is that human beings do not experience the world at first hand, but rather interpret the world through their senses in a way which is meaningful to them. Imagine that you are looking at a table. How do you know that it is a table? At first sight, of course, that sounds like an absurd question, but a moment's thought reveals that it is in fact more profound than it seems. What you are in fact looking at is not intrinsically a table, but a solid

object of a certain shape and size. You only call it a table because you know about tables – in other words, because you possess the category of table in your mind, and when you see objects of a certain shape and size, you place them into this category. Had you never encountered the concept of table you would not describe the object as a table – indeed to you, it would not be a table. It is this concern with how human actors make sense of the world around them that is at the centre of phenomenology.

This fundamental concern was applied specifically to the subject matter of sociology by Husserl's student, Alfred Schutz. Schutz emphasised the fact that the ways in which human beings classify objects in the world is not an individual process, but rather a collective process. The categories we use are not peculiar to ourselves, but are shared with other members of our society. Such categories are called by Schutz *typifications*.

Typification refers to any shared concept – golf ball, democracy, Church, armchair, etc – and forms the basis of communication. Collectively, Schutz says that our typifications build up into what he calls a stock of 'commonsense knowledge'. Of course, one consequence of this notion is that there is no guarantee that any two individuals will perceive the world in the same way, as there may always be differences in the typifications which they adopt as a result of different experiences of life. Yet Schutz argues that, in order for communication to be possible at all, we must assume that the typifications which we adopt are shared with others. We thus get by in the social world by creating and sustaining a sort of illusion of shared understanding.

Harold Garfinkel and ethnomethodology

An approximate meaning of the term 'ethnomethodology' is 'the methods used by people'. Specifically, it refers to the study of the methods which social actors (or 'members' as ethnomethodologists usually refer to them) use to make sense of their social world. It thus begins from the phenomenological assumption that the world does not present itself with an already meaningful and clearly demarcated order. Rather this order is actively constructed through the activities of members. Ethnomethodology seeks to understand how they do this.

The documentary method For Garfinkel, members employ the *documentary method* to make sense of and account for the social world which they inhabit. The documentary method involves taking certain aspects of a situation from an infinite number which could have been selected, defining them in a particular way, and then using this definition to provide evidence for some underlying pattern. New situations are then themselves interpreted in relation to this underlying pattern.

An example of this is Atkinson's study of the practices of coroners (see pages 219-220 and 235-237). The underlying pattern here was the coroner's commonsense view of what constituted a suicide, and on this basis individual deaths were deemed either to be or not to be suicides. However, the very act of classifying deaths itself gives further support to the belief in the existence of an underlying pattern. Identifying particular examples of the pattern and the belief in the existence of the pattern itself are therefore mutually reinforcing. This mutual reinforcement was termed by Garfinkel *reflexivity*, and he felt that this was an essential element of social life. Members constantly seek to explain events in terms of underlying patterns, and use these explanations to justify and reinforce their initial belief in the existence of the underlying patterns. There is no reason to believe, however, that these patterns refer in any direct way to some external social reality.

Indexicality A central part of Garfinkel's analysis was the observation that members make interpretations of situations on the basis of context. Two members, acting in precisely the same way, may be subject to quite different interpretations depending upon the contexts of their actions. For example, if the action concerned is telling an off-colour joke, then if it is performed by a comedian in a night club it is likely to elicit a different interpretation than if it is told by a nun in a convent. This is what Garfinkel meant by *indexicality* – the meaning of the action in each case is not derived from intrinsic features of the action, but rather from the social contexts in which it takes place.

Rules and social order Parsons and many other sociologists assumed that rules were simply learned in the process of socialisation and were capable of guiding conduct in most situations. Garfinkel emphasises that it is the assumption of the existence of rules, rather than rules themselves, which is responsible for the maintenance of social order. Garfinkel illustrates this with reference to a simple game. His point is that even in a simple game, where the rules are written down in an unambiguous fashion, it is easy to find what he calls 'monsters', or possibilities not covered by the rules. Here is his illustration of how easy it is to find such monsters in even the simplest of games.

> Say we are going to propose a game of ticktacktoe. Two persons play ticktacktoe. Any two persons? When, today? Tomorrow? Do we have to be in sight of each other? Can we play by mail? Can one player be dead? (cited in Heritage, 1984).

The point of this illustration is that we assume that our activities are guided by clearly understood rules. However, in reality this is not the case. The extent to which the maintenance of social order is based upon such fragile assumptions is illustrated in Garfinkel's so-called 'breaching experiments'. Here, he asked his students to go into familiar situations and behave in unexpected ways. For example, some went into a department store and started to haggle over the price of goods, while others went home to their families and behaved like lodgers. In each case, the behaviour could not be easily accounted for, and produced reactions such as confusion and anger. What these experiments illustrate is that social order is in fact very fragile and only maintained by the mutual assumptions of members.

Ethnomethodology and sociology

As well as being a radically different approach to understanding social order, ethnomethodology also offers a general critique of sociological theory. Garfinkel argued that 'man' is usually represented by sociology as a 'cultural dope' – that is someone who unthinkingly and compliantly acts out the norms of their society. In contrast, ethnomethodology regards the individual as a skilled member of society, who is constantly engaged in interpreting and giving meaning to situations, and maintaining a sense of social order. For Garfinkel, then, social order is not an objective pre-given determinant of human action, but rather is the active accomplishment of members.

Ethnomethodologists have argued that conventional sociology employs very similar procedures to members living their everyday lives. Specifically, just as members employ the documentary method to identify and justify underlying patterns, so do professional sociologists. Social class is one example. Because sociologists assume that there is an underlying pattern of social class relationships, particular instances of behaviour – such as voting patterns, educational achievements and so on – are interpreted in the light of this underlying pattern. This interpretation, in turn, gives further support for the existence of the underlying pattern. For ethnomethodologists, however, this would just be another example of a mutually reinforcing fiction. The realities of sociologists, therefore, are seen as just as 'constructed' as those of any other members.

Evaluation

There can be no doubt that ethnomethodology constituted a radical critique of conventional sociology. Its emphasis upon interpretation and social order as the active accomplishment of members did indeed offer a new way of looking at social order. It can nevertheless be subjected to various criticisms.

First, Alvin Gouldner has accused ethnomethodology of being preoccupied with trivia. In concentrating upon the mundane elements of everyday life, it ignores the wider inequalities in power and wealth which prevail in modern societies. Even granting Garfinkel's emphasis on the active construction of social reality by members, he seems to

ignore the ways in which different groups in society might find it easier than others to have their view of reality adopted by the majority.

Second, ethnomethodology's critique of mainstream sociology could very easily be directed back on itself. Surely, if all other actors – including sociologists – employ the documentary method, then why should ethnomethodologists themselves be exempt? If they are not, then ethnomethodology becomes just another self-reinforcing account of an ultimately unknowable social world.

*activity***10** *ethnomethodology*

Item A *An experiment in counselling*

In an experiment conducted in a university department of psychiatry, students were invited to take part in what was described as a new form of psychotherapy. Students were told to summarise a personal problem, and then ask the counsellor a series of questions which could be answered either 'yes' or 'no'. The counsellor sat in an adjoining room, and communicated with the student by intercom. Unknown to the students, the 'counsellor' was not who they claimed to be, and the answers were randomly divided in a predetermined sequence between 'yes' and 'no'. Despite the fact that the answers were completely random, and indeed that some contradicted previous answers, the students felt that the advice received was helpful and sensible.

Source: Garfinkel, 1967.

questions

1   Read Item A. In what ways does this experiment demonstrate the documentary method?

2   Item B is a picture of a streaker. How does this statement illustrate Garfinkel's concept of indexicality?

Item B *A streaker*

4.3 The unification of structure and action

As we have seen in this chapter, sociological theories tend to come closer to one of two general approaches – one which emphasises social structure, and the other which emphasises social action. It would be wrong to say that any theory in sociology completely ignores either structure or action, but it would be fair to say that whilst Marxists, functionalists and structuralists tend to emphasise the role of social structures, Weber, symbolic interactionists and ethnomethodologists tend to emphasise the creative and interpretivist nature of social action. This tendency for sociological theories to emphasise one aspect at the expense of the other has led some writers on sociological theory to suggest that structure and action represent alternative ways of looking at society which cannot be brought together. In this section, we shall consider one influential approach to this problem, that of the British sociologist Anthony Giddens.

Anthony Giddens and the theory of structuration

The duality of structure At the centre of Giddens' concern to overcome the division between structural and action approaches within sociology is his concept of the *duality of structure*. In simple terms, action (or 'agency' as he usually calls it) and structure are just two ways of looking at the same thing. For Giddens, structures are produced by social action, and it is only through social action that they are maintained over time. However, at the same time, it is only by the existence of structures that actions are made possible. Let us take the example of speech and language to illustrate this.

Language can be regarded as a structure. It is a set of rules for communication which exists independently of any particular individual who uses it. It therefore exerts constraint over individual language users (like Durkheim's social facts) in that if I wish to say something, I am obliged to use certain words in a certain order – if I want to be understood, that is. However, language (the structure) only exists because people use it correctly when they speak and write – in other words, through action. Indeed, it is only because people speak and write according to the rules of their language, that the language continues to exist. This should not be taken to imply that languages are simply reproduced by the act of speaking and writing, however. Although this will usually be the case, it is quite possible for new words to be introduced, old ones to be forgotten, and even new grammatical rules to enter the language as a result of the ways in which people write and speak. Thus for Giddens, although structure clearly influences action, action may also independently influence structure.

Structure, rules and resources Giddens identifies two important elements of structure: *rules* and *resources*. Rules refer to the range of regulatory principles which influence action. They could refer to unwritten rules such as how one proposes marriage, or to laws regulating how one is to drive a motor car. The second element of structure for Giddens is *resources*. Giddens identifies both *allocative* and *authoritative* resources. Allocative resources refer broadly to what Marx identified as the 'forces of production', whilst authoritative resources refer to the distribution of social power. For Giddens, each of these elements of structure may be reproduced through the agency of social actors, but equally they may be transformed by social actors.

Agency and the reproduction of structures Although Giddens allows the possibility that structures can be transformed through *agency*, he also seeks to explain their reproduction. According to Giddens, much human action is 'mundane', and draws upon stocks of shared commonsense knowledge which is routinely applied with little conscious thought. Agents draw upon their knowledge of rules, and make use of available resources to accomplish their goals. Giddens, in fact, suggests that human beings have an innate desire for predictability in their social lives. He believes that we share a basic need for what he calls 'ontological security'– a confidence that the world is in fact as it appears to be. This tends to produce social stability and persistence rather than social change.

Reflexity Although Giddens does emphasise the degree to which structures are reproduced through human agency, he also allows the possibility that they may change. Drawing on the insights of writers such as Goffman, Giddens points out that actors do not merely react to external stimuli, but engage in the 'reflexive monitoring of action'. This means that they can reflect upon their own actions and their consequences, and have the ability to choose new courses of action. However, Giddens acknowledges that structures do not only change as a result of deliberate actions by actors, but can change as the result of the unintended consequences of actions. For example, the decision by sufficient numbers of actors to visit a particular holiday resort may produce major changes in the local economy which no one intended, but which nevertheless resulted from these actions.

Evaluation

There can be no doubt that Giddens' work represents a major attempt to solve an apparently intractable problem in sociological theory – the relationship between structure and agency. Whilst Giddens' theory of structuration does indeed appear to offer a way out of this theoretical cul-de-sac, his work has nevertheless been subjected to criticism.

Margaret Archer has criticised Giddens for failing to give sufficient attention to the extent to which structures themselves influence the degree to which they can be changed through agency. She emphasises the fact that actors cannot simply change the world as they wish, and that very often structures will constrain action and systematically frustrate the transformative efforts of actors.

On a different theme, Ian Craib has argued that Giddens' model of the personality is in fact rather confused, and rests upon certain basic misunderstandings of psychoanalytic theory. Specifically, Craib suggests that the important notion of ontological security – an inborn desire for predictability – is based upon a 'fundamentally oversimplified notion of the individual' (Craib, 1992).

key terms

Duality of structure Action and structure are two ways of looking at the same thing. Structures are produced by action and action maintains structure.
Agency Giddens' term for social action.
Reflexivity As used by Giddens, the ability of human beings to monitor and reflect on their own actions, and to choose new courses of action.

summary

1. Structuralism is concerned with the structures which underlie behaviour.

2. Lévi-Strauss applied structuralism to the study of culture. He argued that all myths have the same basic structure – opposition and resolution.

3. Barthes applied structuralism to the study of signs – semiotics. He claimed that 'deep' ideological meanings lie beneath the relatively trivial surface appearance of signs.

4. Phenomenology is concerned with how human actors make sense of the world around them. It argues that actors use typications – shared concepts – to build up a stock of 'commonsense knowledge'.

5. Ethnomethodology argues that members of society actively construct meanings and impose them on the world. This gives a sense of meaningful order.

6. According to Garfinkel, people use the documentary method to make sense of the world. This involves creating underlying patterns of meaning and imposing them on events and situations in order to make sense of them.

7. The meaning of an action is derived from the context in which it takes place, not from the intrinsic or essential features of the action.

8. According to Garfinkel, social order is maintained because members of society assume that rules exist. It is this assumption, rather than the rules themselves, which creates social order. In reality, social order is very fragile.

9. Ethnomethodology has been criticised for ignoring inequalities of wealth and power in the wider society, and for not considering the possibility that the powerful may impose their meanings on others.

10. According to Giddens, structure and action are two ways of looking at the same thing. Structures are produced by social action, and it is only through social action that structures are maintained over time.

11. Human behaviour is not completely determined by structures. Human beings are reflexive – they can reflect on their own actions and choose new courses of action.

12. Giddens' theory of structuration offers a way out of the opposition between structural and social action approaches.

13. Critics argue that Giddens fails to recognise the power that structures have to shape and constrain action. Actors cannot simply change the world as they choose.

Unit 5 Challenges to sociological theory

keyissues

1 What are the main assumptions of globalisation and postmodernism?

2 How do they challenge more traditional sociological theories?

New approaches are constantly emerging which challenge the conventional wisdom of sociologists. Feminism, for example, questioned the male bias of the discipline and opened up new areas for investigation (see pages 241-243). In this unit we shall look at two recent approaches which challenge the taken-for-granted assumptions of many sociologists.

5.1 Globalisation

At various stages in this chapter we have talked about society and indeed, if pushed to define the subject matter of sociology, many sociologists would say 'modern society'. Society, in turn, is often visualised as a social system with distinct boundaries separating it from other social systems. And this 'society' is usually equated with the nation-state. This is not surprising. For it reflects the 19th century origins of sociology when 'nation-states become supreme because they won at war, were economically successful and, subsequently, achieved a significant degree of legitimacy in the eyes of their populations and other states' (Held, 1992).

Beyond the nation-state There are two problems with picturing the subject matter of sociology in this way. First, human behaviour has never been explicable purely in terms of particular societies or nation-states. The influence of major religions, patterns of trade and indeed war and conquest extend well beyond the boundaries of nation-states.

Second, we live in a 'shrinking' world. In this context, human behaviour is increasingly influenced by global forces. While *globalisation*, in the sense of the growing interconnectedness of societies, has always been a feature of modernity, a number of theorists have suggested that in the last two decades we have entered a qualitatively new phase of globalisation. One of its main features has been described as 'time-space compression', in recognition of the fact that our lives are increasingly, and remarkably quickly, influenced by distant events. David Harvey puts it well: 'As space appears to shrink to a "global" village of telecommunications and a "spaceship earth" of economic and ecological interdependencies – to use just two familiar and everyday images – and as time horizons shorten to the point where the present is all there is, so we have to learn to cope with an overwhelming sense of compression of our spatial and temporal words' (Harvey, 1989).

Let us take each of these images of globalisation in turn. The Live Aid movement of the mid-1980s provides a good example of the way the world 'has come to seem like a village' (Tester, 1995). The movement, founded by the singer Bob Geldof, emerged in order to raise money to relieve an appalling famine in Ethiopia. It culminated in a day-long concert, held at venues in Britain and America 3,000 miles apart but linked by satellite into one programme. The mass media was central. For it was television which allowed people in Britain and America to become aware in their living rooms of a famine miles away, and it was television which broadcast the concert around the world.

A dramatic illustration of our ecological interdependence on 'spaceship earth' was the explosion in 1986 at the Chernobyl nuclear power station in the former Soviet Republic of Ukraine. The consequences were not foreseeable but were felt as far away as Cumbria. The explosion provides an example of the way globalisation is producing what Ulrich Beck (1992) calls a 'risk society', in which the survival of the planet is threatened by technological developments. While natural hazards such as floods, hurricanes and volcanoes threatened people in the past, the risk environment which now confronts us 'is structured mainly by humanly created risks' (Giddens, 1990).

Opposing tendencies While there is widespread agreement that we are in a period of increasing globalisation, there is no agreement about what has brought it about, or what it will lead to. Indeed some aspects of globalisation appear contradictory.

In Giddens' (1990) words, globalisation does not bring about 'a generalised set of changes acting in a uniform direction, but consists of mutually opposed tendencies'. Here are some examples of these opposed tendencies.

- **First, cultural homogenisation versus differentiation**. Globalisation encourages *cultural homogenisation* – a uniform global culture. We can now drink Coca-Cola at McDonald's, wear trainers and watch Hollywood films on television across the world. At the same time, there is a fascination with difference so that ethnic food, dress and music are also available around the world.

- **Second, old identities versus new identities**. Globalisation makes us increasingly aware of cultural differences. For some, this may be experienced as a threat to the familiar certainties of the past. Racism and religious fundamentalism are examples. They can be seen as defensive reactions which attempt to preserve or recreate a perceived past. For others, however, an awareness of other cultures may be interpreted as an opportunity to construct new identities which fuse different cultural traditions.

- **Third, centralisation versus decentralisation**. Globalisation enables organisations to develop which transcend national boundaries. Transnational corporations and the European Union are examples. At the same time, it generates a powerful decentralising force as communities seek to control their own fate. Hence the resurgence of nationalism in Eastern Europe with the break up of the Soviet Union.

The effects of globalisation are not only complex but there is also an unevenness with which globalisation has been experienced across space and time. It has quickened recently, but its consequences are not uniform across the globe. 'In the latest form of globalisation, it is still the images, artefacts and identities of Western modernity, produced by the cultural industries of "Western" societies (including Japan) which dominate the global networks' (Hall, 1992).

Evaluation The concept of globalisation does capture an important phenomenon and it does challenge the idea of society as a well-bounded system. While this means that we need to be highly sceptical of sociological theories which visualise societies as discrete social systems, it does not mean that we should abandon the idea of society. For societies can still exist within the framework of a global society. They are still recognised as societies by their members. And their boundaries are sufficiently clear for sociologists to recognise and study them as social units.

key terms

Globalisation The process by which societies become increasingly interconnected.
Cultural homogenisation The process by which cultures become increasingly similar.
Cultural differentiation The process by which aspects of one culture enter another.

activity11 globalisation

Item A Global products and global icons

Beijing, China

A Russian poster for Daywatch

A Japanese poster for Jurassic Park

Item B Global risks – the world's fish

Last month a fleet's annual quota of fish was caught in eight minutes. The sea cannot stand it.

The world's fisheries are hurtling towards commercial extinction as hi-tech supertrawlers become ever more efficient at hoovering up their prey. The oceans, covering 70% of the globe, should – and could – adequately meet the needs of humanity without unbalancing the marine ecosystem. But greed, rather than commonsense or conservation, is driving exploitation of the seas.

Last month, the United Nations Food and Agriculture Organisation (FAO) warned 9 of the world's 17 major fishing grounds had been devastated by over-fishing, with four more under serious threat. The global fish catch, which rose five-fold between 1950 and 1989, has now levelled out at around 100 million tonnes a year.

Nobody knows for sure what effect chronic over-fishing will have on other marine wildlife. Just as worrying is the effect on the human beings who rely on fish to stay alive. But, for the developing world, the disappearance of commercial fisheries would spell disaster. In Asia alone, a billion people rely on fish as their main source of animal protein. And apart from the spectre of starvation, a fishing crash would cost an enormous number of jobs.

Source: *The Observer*, 2.4.1995

Danish industrial fishing vessel, North Sea

Item C Global risks – Chernobyl

In 1986, the nuclear power station at Chernobyl in the Ukraine exploded. It provided a stark lesson about the huge sum which a single major nuclear accident can cost the world.

Nine years after the radioactive cloud released from Chernobyl passed over Wales, long-suffering farmers 1,500 miles from the scene of the accident still face controls on their sheep flocks.

In the Ukraine and Belarus, which took the brunt of the radiation, 1.3 million hectares of land is contaminated, and estimates put the final clean-up bill at between £1.25 billion and £3.75 billion.

This figure includes resettlement of 2.5 million refugees living on contaminated land, medical treatment for victims, and the clean-up of the plant and surrounding irradiated countryside.

The trouble is that no matter how we generate energy, we create problems. The burning of coal, gas and oil plays havoc with our atmosphere, just as surely as the abuse of nuclear power devastates the ground.

It is an issue that transcends national borders. Global economic growth needs global energy planning. We do not have that, and there are precious few signs we will ever get it. The human mind seems almost incapable of dealing with the time scales and geography which are required when dealing with nuclear power. Yet we must face up to the issues. The alternative is short-term manoeuvring, and long-term disaster.

Source: *The Observer*, 30.4.1995

Radiation check, Chernobyl

questions

1 How do the pictures in Item A illustrate globalisation?

2 How do Items B and C suggest that we live in a global 'risk society'?

3 Globalisation requires institutions for global government. Discuss with reference to Items B and C.

5.2 Postmodernism

Postmodernism as theory

Postmodernism is a new way of looking at the world. It questions all the key ideas of the Enlightenment. It rejects the view that it is possible to build either a natural or social science on the basis of observable facts. It argues that there is no objective or indisputable way of distinguishing truth from falsity. It sees no firm foundation for knowledge. And it rejects the Enlightenment belief that human beings are capable of achieving a rational understanding of social reality and can use this understanding to create a more rational and just society.

As such, postmodernism is a direct challenge to sociology.

Postmodernity and postmodern society

Postmodernists believe that we are now living in a new era – postmodernity – and a new form of society – postmodern society. This represents a clear break from the previous era – modernity – and the previous form of society – modern society.

Before examining postmodernist theory in more detail, here is a short sketch of how postmodernists see postmodern society.

A diversity of images and values Postmodern society is dominated by new information and communication technologies which bring the world into our homes and into our consciousness. Websites, emails, chat rooms, computer games, DVDs, CDs, and terrestrial, satellite and cable TV bombard us with sounds, symbols and images from across the globe. They expose us to an increasingly diverse range of ideas and values, many of which have little connection with our present or past lives. This can cut us off from our past, make our present seem rootless and unstable, and our future unpredictable.

This myriad of diverse images and values is constantly changing. New lifestyles come and go, new styles of music and fashion and new types of food and drink are regularly appearing. Everything appears fluid – nothing seems permanent and solid. The mainstream culture of modern society is replaced by the fleeting, unstable, fragmented culture of postmodern society.

Postmodern identities In modern societies, people's identities were usually drawn from their class, gender, occupation and ethnic group. In postmodern society, people have more opportunity to construct their own identities and more options to choose from. For example, a woman can be heterosexual, bisexual or lesbian, a business executive and a mother, she can be British, a Sikh *and* a member of Greenpeace. And her lifestyle and consumption patterns can reflect her chosen identity. Brand-name goods such as Gucci and Dolce & Gabbana can be used as statements of her identity.

With all the choices on offer, it is fairly easy for people to change their identities, or to have several identities which they put on and take off depending on their social situation. As a result, postmodern identities are more unstable and fragile. They offer choice, but they don't always provide a firm and lasting foundation.

Loss of faith Exposure to increasingly diverse beliefs, values and lifestyles can lead to a relativist point of view. Nothing is right or wrong, everything is relative. A single truth is replaced by many truths and there is no objective way of choosing between them. Certainty is replaced with uncertainty and there is a loss of faith in rational thinking.

As a result, people are increasingly turning to a range of alternatives in their search for answers and solutions to problems – New Age religions, traditional healers and alternative therapists.

Postmodernity has seen a loss of faith in science and technology. The threat of weapons of mass destruction, the negative side effects of drugs used to treat physical and psychological problems, global warming and the destruction of the environment caused by pollution, all point to science and technology gone wrong.

Views of reality Some postmodernists claim that our view of reality is largely shaped by the flood of images from the media. These images become as, if not more, real and significant than the things we directly experience in everyday life. For example, the death of Princess Diana resulted in an outpouring of grief across the world – but, for the vast majority, she existed only through the media. The 'unreal' becomes 'real' when a death, a divorce, or a marriage in a soap opera glues millions to the screen and forms a topic of conversation the following day. And, as its name suggests, reality TV brings 'real' people into everybody's homes and lives.

Evaluation Many of these observations of postmodern society are accepted, to a degree, by mainstream sociologists. However, they usually see them as aspects of late modernity rather than postmodernity.

Many sociologists are critical of the picture of society presented by postmodernists. For example, Greg Philo and David Miller (2001) make the following points.

- The claim that people are no longer able to make judgements of right and wrong about different views of the world and different ideologies is incorrect. The vast majority of people would still condemn the fascist ideology of Nazi Germany and the slaughter of millions of Jews, gypsies and gays in Nazi death camps.

- People are well aware that there is a reality beyond the images broadcast by the media. They recognise that media messages are often one-sided, partial and distorted.

- Many people are not free to construct their own identities, choose their own consumption patterns and select their own lifestyles. For example, people living in poverty simply don't have the money to buy Gucci sunglasses or Jean Paul Gaultier fragrance.

Having briefly outlined and assessed the postmodernist view of contemporary society, we now turn to the work of two of the most influential postmodernist writers – Jean-Francois Lyotard and Jean Baudrillard.

Lyotard – a crisis in knowledge

Knowledge in the modern era meant science. Philosophers were, however, unable to agree upon the foundations for such knowledge. Science therefore needed to be justified in terms of a grand story or *metanarrative*. For the Enlightenment, science was justified on the grounds that it would lead to human emancipation and freedom. In view of the contribution of science in creating, for example, weapons of indiscriminate mass destruction, people are now sceptical towards this metanarrative and the status of science has consequently been questioned. And what is true of this metanarrative is true of others. None can be 'objectively' proved or rejected and so we need to be sceptical towards all metanarratives. Hence, Lyotard defines the condition of postmodernity as 'incredulity towards metanarratives' (Lyotard, 1992).

This is not to say that knowledge is unimportant. We live in a post-industrial society where, in fact, it is central. Knowledge has, however, fragmented into a series of 'language games' where the rules governing what counts as knowledge differ. The central concern is 'performativity', whether the information produced is efficient and saleable rather than of intrinsic value or serving some human purpose.

Lyotard welcomes the downfall of metanarratives and the emergence of a plurality of language games. Grand stories, with their privileged truth, rode roughshod over many groups and, in the case of Marxism, led to totalitarianism. In the postmodern era, there is a chance to hear the voices of diverse groups previously on the margins, such as women and ethnic minorities.

Baudrillard – a crisis in representation

Baudrillard agrees with Lyotard that we now live in a post-industrial society. His emphasis, however, is different and centres on the production and consumption of signs. Baudrillard's view is that although at one stage signs were a 'reflection of a basic reality' they now often 'bear no relation to any reality whatsoever' (Poster, 1988). Such signs are known as *simulations* and are characteristic of the images we see on our television screens, when stories and items that have no meaningful or logical connection to each other are juxtaposed.

Baudrillard argues that news reporting often involves simulation. For example, business fraud is reported as shocking and scandalous to conceal the fact that is widespread. Sometimes simulations can be experienced as more real than reality. This is the 'hyperreal' where, for example, people write to characters in soap operas. John Storey gives a good example : 'The riots, following the acquittal of the four Los Angeles police officers captured on video physically assaulting the black motorist Rodney King, were headlined in two British newspapers as "LA Lawless", and in another as "LA War"; the story anchored not by historical reference to similar disturbances in Watts Los Angeles in 1965, or to the implications of the words – "No justice, no peace" – chanted by demonstrators during the riots. The editors chose instead to locate the story within the fictional world of the American television series *LA Law*. Baudrillard calls this "The dissolution of TV into life, the dissolution of life into TV" '(Storey, 1993).

Baudrillard is in two minds about his response to this situation where image and reality can no longer be distinguished. At times, he suggests that we live in a society where we are able to construct our own identities in the process of consumption. Clothes and other items of consumption are not only material objects but also are signs which have meaning. By picking and mixing appropriate images we can distinguish ourselves from others. At other times, he suggests the best we can do is to enjoy the meaningless spectacle produced for us and delight in the sensuous pleasure which images can offer us.

Postmodern theory and social change

The work of Lyotard, Baudrillard and other postmodern theorists has been stimulating in raising new questions about social change. Are we witnessing a shift to a new postmodern culture? Have Lyotard and Baudrillard correctly identified the central features of this new culture? Is it true that people increasingly find general theories implausible and are sceptical towards the old political philosophies of liberalism, socialism and social democracy? Do we live in an era where media images are so pervasive that we find it increasingly difficult to distinguish what is real? Does the advent of a postmodern culture signify a shift towards a new social condition of postmodernity? Is it true that we now live in a post-industrial society? Is this a society which allows an increasing diversity of lifestyles to flourish? Is it one where we have much greater freedom to construct our own individual and collective identities, or one which witnesses an increasing fragmentation of our identities? These questions, which were initially raised by postmodern theorists, are central to much contemporary sociology and have stimulated other theorists, including Marxists such as Jameson and Harvey, to develop their theories in order to account for the fact that we are clearly living through an era of massive social change (Thompson, 1992).

Postmodernism and the Enlightenment

The challenge which postmodernism poses for sociological theory results from its rejection of the Enlightenment 'project' – the promise, which underpinned the emergence of sociology, that human beings could use their reason to produce knowledge of the social world and on that basis promote human progress. Postmodernists have put three central arguments forward.

Anti-foundationalism The first argument is known as *anti-foundationalism*. The search by philosophers for indisputable foundations to knowledge has been a failure. There are no general criteria which enable us to distinguish truth and falsity. We therefore have to accept that different communities will use different criteria to distinguish truth and falsity. What's more these communities will look at the world differently. For we are the subjects of language and other sign systems and can't step outside them to discover what things really mean. In short, there is absolutely nothing to guarantee what is true or what things mean.

Anti-totalisation The second argument is known as *anti-totalisation*. In view of the fact that there are no indisputable foundations to knowledge or firm bases to meaning, it is extremely arrogant of us to put forward general theories which pretend to reveal *the* truth or *the* meaning of things. We need to abandon attempts to produce theories which seek to depict the structure and dynamics of society as a whole and tolerate the coexistence of a diversity of more limited theories.

Anti-utopianism The third argument is known as *anti-utopianism*. In practice, knowledge has not produced the utopia of human freedom and emancipation, but has been used by some to impose one truth and one meaning on others. Knowledge has not so much provided us with the power to do things that we could not otherwise do, as allowed some groups to exert power over others.

These arguments cannot be dismissed lightly. First, we cannot attain certainty over questions of truth and meaning. Second, general theories which claim to reveal the inevitable development of society are flawed. There is no justification for believing that history has a purpose, or that we can predict the future. Third, knowledge has often been used by Western societies to dominate others. (For an outline of postmodernist methodology, see pages 238-240.)

Evaluation

The Enlightenment project, and with it the possibility of sociological theory, cannot be so easily dismissed.

- First, the fact that there are no indispensable foundations to knowledge and meaning does not mean that there are no general criteria of truth and that there is not a connection between sign systems and the world. To assume otherwise is to fall into the trap of relativism. Presumably, the postmodern theorists believe that what they say is meaningful and true or otherwise they would not bother to write books.

- Second, the fact that different societies have different ideas and beliefs of what is true and what things mean does not mean that we should abandon the search for general theories which seek to explain these differences. Indeed, somewhat inconsistently, postmodern theorists do provide such general theories.

• Third, the fact that reason has been used to dominate people does not mean that it did not play a progressive role in the past in combating 'the relative blinkeredness and backwardness of the epoch of pre-modernity' (McClennan, 1992), and that we should abandon the Enlightenment ideal that knowledge might further human emancipation. The arguments of postmodernist theories which challenge the very possibility of sociological theory are unconvincing.

key terms

Metanarrative A grand story or theory which explains and justifies something – for example, scientific theories, political ideologies and religions are seen by postmodernists as metanarratives.
Simulations Signs and images which have no relationship to reality.
Anti-foundationalism The argument that there are no clear, indisputable foundations to knowledge.
Anti-totalisation The argument that there are no general theories which reveal and explain the truth or the meaning of things.
Anti-utopianism The argument that knowledge has not been used to create a utopia – a perfect society. Instead, it has been used by some to exert power over others.

summary

1. Traditionally, the main unit for study in sociology has been the society – a social system with distinct boundaries which separates it from other social systems.

2. Globalisation challenges this view. Societies are becoming increasingly interconnected and cultures increasingly similar.

3. Some sociologists see opposing tendencies in the process of globalisation. They include:
   • Cultural homogenisation versus cultural differentiation
   • Old identities versus new identities
   • Centralisation versus decentralisation.

4. While recognising the impact of globalisation, sociologists have not abandoned the idea of society. The boundaries of societies are sufficiently distinct for them to be studied as social units.

5. Postmodernism rejects the key ideas of the Enlightenment – in particular, the view that it is possible to build a natural or social science on the basis of observable facts.

6. According to postmodernists, postmodern society has the following characteristics.
   • A diversity of images, values and lifestyles
   • Opportunities for people to construct their own identities
   • A loss of faith in rational thinking and in science and technology

   • Views of reality which are largely shaped by the media.

7. Lyotard argues that postmodern society is characterised by the downfall of metanarratives. Knowledge is judged in terms of performativity – whether it is efficient and saleable.

8. Baudrillard argues that members of postmodern society see the world in terms of simulations – images which bear no relation to reality.

9. Postmodernists reject Enlightenment ideas on the basis of three main arguments.
   • Anti-foundationalism
   • Anti-totalisation
   • Anti-utopianism.

10. Criticisms of postmodernism include the following.
   • To claim that there are no foundations to knowledge leads to relativism. In terms of their own argument, postmodernists' views are no better than anybody else's.
   • Just because different societies have different versions of the truth does not mean that their beliefs cannot be studied and explained.
   • Just because rational thinking has been used to dominate people does not mean it cannot be used to free them.

activity 12 postmodern society

Item A Detached identities

The more social life is influenced by the global marketing of styles, places and images, by international travel, and by globally networked media images and communications systems, the more identities become detached – disembedded – from specific times, places, histories and traditions, and appear 'free-floating'. We are confronted by a range of different identities, each appealing to us, or rather to different parts of ourselves, from which it seems possible to choose. It is the spread of consumerism, whether as reality or dream, which has contributed to this 'cultural supermarket' effect.

Source: Hall, 1992

Item B I am me

Salima Dhalla: I don't know how to start to describe myself. I feel identity-less but very unique. On paper I'm 'Asian' but in my head I'm a cocky little person with lots of hopes and ambitions.

My parents are East African, their parents are Indian, I was born in Wales. I went to a White middle-class girls' private school and I have brown skin, short Western hair, Western clothes, Eastern name, Western friends. So I guess I'm in an identity wasteland. Now I will only agree to being *me*.

Source: Kassam, 1997

Item C A shrinking world

Item D Norman and Norma

Norman on Tuesdays   *Norma on Wednesdays*

Norman Horton enjoyed his new hobby of line dancing so much that he decided to go twice a week – once as a man and once as a woman. Mr Horton, aged 58, would set off on Tuesday nights in open neck shirt, trousers and stetson. But on Wednesdays he transformed himself into Norma, with a frilly blouse, short skirt, gold tights and high heels. A former paratrooper and military policeman, he has been cross-dressing since the age of 12. 'My wife doesn't mind me cross-dressing as long as I don't do it too often and keep it under control.'

Source: *The Guardian*, 17.4.1998

Item E Bodybuilders

The top three in the women's bodybuilding world championship, 2002

Item F Panjabi MC

Panjabi MC. His music is a fusion of bhangra and hip hop.

Item G   Growing up in poverty

questions

1 What does Stuart Hall in Item A mean by 'detached identities'?

2 What support do Items B to F provide for the view of postmodern society given by Stuart Hall in Item A and described in the preceding text?

3 What criticism of this view of postmodern society is suggested by Item G?

References

Abdelhadi, M. (2003). *The Islamic revival in Egypt.* news.bbc.co.uk.

Abel-Smith, B. & Townsend, P. (1965). *The poor and the poorest.* London: G. Bell & Sons.

Abercrombie, N. (1996). *Television and society.* Cambridge: Polity.

Abercrombie, N., Hill, N. & Turner, B.S. (1980). *The dominant ideology thesis.* London: Allen & Unwin.

ACPO (Association of Chief Police Officers) (2000). *A guide to identifying and combating hate crime.* London: ACPO.

Agyeman, L. (2003). *End of year report: BSC and ITC research 2003.* London: Broadcasting Standards Commission & Independent Television Commission.

Ahmed, L. (2000). Women and gender in Islam: Historical roots of a modern debate. In L. Woodhead & P. Heelas (Eds.), *Religion in modern times: An interpretive anthology.* Oxford: Blackwell.

Allan, J., Livingstone, S. & Reiner, R. (1997).The changing generic location of crime in film. *Journal of Communication, 47,* 4, 1-13.

Allan, S. (1999). *News culture.* Buckingham: Open University Press.

Allport, G.W. & Postman, L. (1947). *The psychology of rumour.* New York: H. Holt & Company.

Althusser, L. (1971). *Lenin and philosophy and other essays.* London: New Left Books.

Alvesson, M. (2002). *Postmodernism and social research.* Buckingham: Open University Press.

Ammerman, N.T. (2003). Re-awakening a sleeping giant: Christian fundamentalists in late twentieth-century US society. In G. ter Haar & J.J. Busuttil (Eds.), *The freedom to do God's will: Religious fundamentalism and social change.* London: Routledge.

Amnesty International (2006). *Undermining freedom of expression in China: The role of Yahoo!, Microsoft and Google.* London: Amnesty International UK.

Ang, I. (1985). *Watching 'Dallas': Soap opera and the melodramatic imagination.* London: Methuen.

An-Na'im, A. (1999). Political Islam in national politics and international relations. In P.L.Berger (Ed.), *The desecularisation of the world.* Washington, D.C.: Ethics and Public Policy Center.

An-Na'im, A. (2003). Islamic fundamentalism and social change: Neither the 'end of history' nor a 'clash of civilisations'. In G. ter Haar & J.J. Busuttil (Eds.), *The freedom to do God's will: Religious fundamentalism and social change.* London: Routledge.

Annual abstract of statistics (2004). London: TSO.

Atkinson, J.M. (1978). *Discovering suicide.* London: Macmillan.

Bagdikian, B. (2004). *The new media monopoly.* Boston: Beacon Press.

Barclay, G. & Tavares, C. (1999). *Digest 4: Information on the criminal justice system in England and Wales.* London: HMSO.

Barker, C. (1999). *Television, globalisation and cultural identities.* Buckingham: Open University Press.

Barker, E. (1983). New Religious Movements in Britain: The context and the membership. *Social Compass, XXX/1,* 33-48.

Barker, E. (1984). *The making of a Moonie.* Oxford: Blackwell.

Barker, E. (1999). New Religious Movements: Their incidence and significance. In B. Wilson & J. Cresswell (Eds.), *New Religious Movements: Challenge and response.* London: Sage.

Barnes, C. (1992). *Disabling imagery and the media.* London: Ryburn Press.

Barthes, R. (1973). *Mythologies.* London: Paladin.

Bauman, Z. (1992). *Intimations of postmodernity.* London: Routledge.

Beck, U. (1992). *Risk society: Towards a new modernity.* London: Sage.

Becker, H.S. (1963). *Outsiders: Studies in the sociology of deviance.* London: Macmillan.

Becker, H.S. (1970). Whose side are we on? In H.S. Becker, *Sociological work.* New Brunswick: Transaction Books.

Beckford, J.A. (1975). *The trumpet of prophecy: A sociological study of Jehovah's Witnesses.* Oxford: Blackwell.

Beckford, J.A. (2003). Religion: Consensus and conflict. *Sociology Review,* November.

Bellah, R.N. (1967). Civic religion in America. In R. Richey & D. Jones (Eds.), *American civic religion.* New York: Harper & Row.

Bennett, A. (2001). Local interpretations of global music. In N. Abercrombie & A. Warde (Eds.), *The contemporary British society reader.* Cambridge: Polity Press.

Bennett, T. (2001). Sociology and government. In P. Hamilton & K. Thompson (Eds.), *The uses of sociology.* Oxford: Blackwell.

Berger, P. (1970). *A rumour of angels: Modern society and the rediscovery of the supernatural.* London: Allen Lane.

Berger, P. (1973). *The social reality of religion.* Harmondsworth: Penguin.

Berger, P., Berger, B. & Kellner, H. (1974). *The homeless mind.* Harmondsworth: Penguin.

Berger, P.L. & Luckmann, T. (1967). *The social construction of reality.* London: Allen Lane, The Penguin Press.

Berger, P.L. (1999). The desecularisation of the world: A global overview. In P.L.Berger (Ed.), *The desecularisation of the world.* Washington, D.C.: Ethics and Public Policy Center.

Berkeley, G. & Robinson, H. (1999). *Principles of human knowledge and three dialogues.* Oxford: Oxford Paperbacks

Bernstein, A. (2002). Representation, identity and the media. In C. Newbold, O.Boyd-Barrett & H. van Den Bulck (Eds.), *The media book.* London: Arnold.

Bhaskar, R. (1978). *A realist theory of science* (2nd ed.). Hassocks: Harvester.

Birnbaum, N. (1955). Monarchs and sociologists: A reply to Professor Shils and Mr Young. *Sociological Review,* July.

Blaikie, N. (1993). *Approaches to social enquiry.* Oxford: Polity Press.

Blumer, H. (1962). Society as symbolic interaction. In A.M. Rose (Ed.), *Human behaviour and social processes.* London: Routledge.

Blumer, H. (1969). *Symbolic interactionism: Perspective on method.* Englewood Cliffs: Prentice Hall.

Bordua, D. (1962). A critique of sociological interpretations of gang delinquency. In M.E. Wolfgang, L. Savitz & N. Johnston (Eds.), *The sociology of crime and delinquency.* New York: John Wiley & Sons.

Bottomley, A. & Coleman, C. (1981). *Understanding crime rates.* Farnborough: Saxon House.

Bottomore, T. & Rubel, M. (1961). *Karl Marx: Selected writings.* Harmondsworth: Penguin.

Bottoms, A.E. & Wiles, P. (2002). Environmental criminology. In M. Maguire, R. Morgan and R. Reiner (Eds.), *The Oxford handbook of criminology* (3rd ed.). Oxford: Oxford University Press.

Bottoms, A.E., Mawby, R.I. & Xanthos, P. (1989). A tale of two cities. In D. Downes (Ed.), *Crime and the city.* London: Macmillan.

Bourgois, P. (1995). *In search of respect.* Cambridge: Cambridge University Press.

Bowling, B. & Phillips, C. (2002). *Racism, crime and justice.* London: Longman.

Box, S. (1983). *Power, crime and mystification.* London: Tavistock.

Boyd, W. (1999). *Stars and bars.* Harmondsworth: Penguin.

Brantingham, P. J. & Brantingham, P.L. (1984). *Patterns of crime.* New York: Macmillan.

Brecht, B. (1980). *Life of Galileo.* London: Methuen Drama.

Brierley, P. (2000). *Religious trends.* London: Christian Research Association.

British Crime Survey (BCS) see Simmons & Dodd (2003).

British Social Attitudes Survey 2001-02 – see Park, A. (Ed.), 2001.

Bronner, S.E. & Kellner, D.M. (Eds.) (1989). *Critical theory and society.* New York: Routledge.

Brown, D. (1975). *Bury my heart at Wounded Knee.* London: Pan Books.

Brownlee, I. (1998). *Community punishment: A critical introduction.* Harlow: Longman.

Bruce, S. (1995). *Religion in modern Britain.* Oxford: Oxford University Press.

Bruce, S. (2001). *Fundamentalism.* Oxford: Polity Press.

Bruce, S. (2002). *God is dead: Secularisation in the West.* Oxford: Blackwell.

Brunsdon, C., Johnson, C., Moseley, R. & Wheatley, H. (2001). Factual entertainment on British television. *European Journal of Cultural Studies, 4.*

Brusco, E. E. (1995). *The reformation of machismo: Evangelical conversion and gender in Colombia.* Austin: University of Texas Press.

Bryant, A. (1953). *The story of England: Makers of the realm.* London: Collins.

Bulsara, A. (2005). *Depictions of people with disabilities in the British media,* www.media-diversity.org.

Burton, G. (2005). *Media and society: Critical perspectives.* Maidenhead: Open University Press.

Butsch, R. (1995). Ralph, Fred, Archie and Homer: Why television keeps recreating the white male working-class buffoons. In G. Dines & J. Humez (Eds.), *Gender, race and class in media.* London: Sage.

Campbell, B. (1993). *Goliath: Britain's dangerous places.* London: Macmillan.

Cantril, H. (1940). *The invasion from Mars: A study in the psychology of panic.* New York: Harper & Row.

Carlen, P. (1983). *Women's imprisonment.* London: Routledge.

Carlen, P. (1988). *Women, crime and poverty.* Buckingham: Open University Press.

Carlen, P. (1990). *Alternatives to women's imprisonment.* Buckingham: Open University Press.

Carrabine, E., Cox, P., Lee, M. & South, N. (2002). *Crime in modern Britain.* Oxford: Oxford University Press.

Carter, J. (2008). A human rights claim. *The Guardian,* 8 May.

Carter, R.L. & Hill, K.Q. (1979). *The criminal's image of the city.* New York: Pergamon Press.

Caspi, A. & Moffit, T. (1995). The continuity of maladaptive behaviour: From description to understanding in the study of anti-social behaviour. In D. Cicchetti & D. Cohen (Eds.) *Developmental psychology.* New York: Wiley.

Castells, M. (1983). *The city and the grass roots: A cross-cultural theory of urban social movements.* London: Edward Arnold.

Castells, M. (1996). *The rise of the network society.* Oxford: Blackwell.

Cavadino, M. & Dignan, J. (2002). *The penal system* (3rd ed.). London: Sage.

Chahal, K. & Julienne, L. (1999). *'We can't all be white!' Racist victimisation in the UK.* York: York Publishing Services.

Chambliss, W (1995). State organised crime. In N. Passas (Ed.) *Organised crime.* Aldershot: Dartmouth.

Chambliss, W. (1969). *Crime and the legal process.* New York: McGraw-Hill.

Chaudhary, V. & Walker, M. (1996). The petty crime war. *The Guardian,* 21 November.

Chibnall, S. (1977). *Law and order news.* London: Tavistock.

Chitty, C. (2002). *Understanding schools and schooling.* London: RoutledgeFalmer.

Cicourel, A.V. (1976). *The social organisation of juvenile justice.* London: Heinemann.

Clancy, A., Hough, M., Aust, R. & Kershaw, C. (2001). *Crime, policing and justice: The experience of ethnic minorities: Findings from the 2000 British Crime Survey, Home Office Research Study 223.* London: Home Office.

Clarke, R.V.G. (1995). Situational crime prevention. In M. Tonry & D. Farrington (Eds.), *Building a safer society.* Chicago: University of Chicago Press.

Clarke, R.V.G. (2003). 'Situational' crime prevention: Theory and practice. In E. McLaughlin, J. Muncie & G. Hughes (Eds.), *Criminological perspectives: Essential readings* (2nd ed.). London: Sage.

Clinard, M. (1974). *Sociology and deviant behaviour* (4th ed.). New York: Holt, Rinehart and Winston.

Cloward, R. & Ohlin, L. (1961). *Delinquency and opportunity.* Glencoe: The Free Press.

Coates, K. & Silburn, R. (1970). *Poverty: The forgotten Englishmen.* Harmondsworth: Penguin.

Cohen, A. (1955). *Delinquent boys.* Glencoe: The Free Press.

Cohen, L.E. & Felson, M. (1979). Social change and crime rates: A routine activities approach. *American Sociological Review, 44,* 588-608

Cohen, P. (1968). *Modern social theory.* London: Heinemann.

Cohen, R. & Kennedy, P. (2007). *Global sociology.* Basingstoke: Palgrave.

Cohen, S. (1987). *Folk devils and moral panics* (2nd ed.). Oxford: Blackwell.

Cohen, S. (1996). Human rights and crimes of the state: The culture of denial. In J. Muncie, E. McLaughlin & M. Langan (Eds.). *Criminological perspectives.* London: Sage.

Cohen, S. (2003). Human rights and crimes of the state: The culture of denial. In E. McLaughlin, J. Muncie & G. Hughes (Eds.), *Criminological perspectives: Essential readings* (2nd ed.). London: Sage.

Cohn, N. (1957). *The pursuit of the millennium.* London: Secker and Warburg.

Cole, W.O. (Ed.) (1991). *Moral issues in six religions.* Oxford: Heinemann.

Coleman, C. & Moynihan, J. (1996). *Understanding crime data.* Buckingham: Open University Press.

Collier, R. (1998). *Masculinities, crime and criminology.* London: Sage.

Collins, R. & Murroni, C. (1996). *New media, new politics.* Oxford: Polity Press.

Cook, D. (2001). Safe and sound? Crime, disorder and community safety policies. In M. May, R. Page & E. Brunsdon (Eds.), *Understanding social problems: Issues in social policy.* Oxford: Blackwell.

Cook, G. (2000). *European values survey.* Gordon Cook Foundation.

Coote, A. & Campbell, B. (1982). *Sweet freedom.* London: Pan.

Cottle, S. (Ed.) (2000). *Ethnic minorities and the media.* Buckingham: Open University Press.

Cowan, R. (2004). Police failing to tackle domestic abuse. *The Guardian,* 19 February.

Craib, I. (1984). *Modern social theory.* London: Harvester Wheatsheaf.

Craib, I. (1992). *Anthony Giddens.* London: Routledge.

Crawford, A., Jones, T., Woodhouse, T. & Young, J. (1990). *Second Islington Crime Survey.* London: Middlesex Polytechnic.

Critcher, C. (2003). *Moral panics and the media.* Buckingham: Open University Press.

Croall, H. (1998). *Crime and society in Britain.* Harlow: Longman.

Croall, H. (2001). *Understanding white collar crime.* Buckingham: Open University Press.

Croteau, D. & Hoynes, W. (1997). *Media/society.* London: Forge Pine Press.

Cullen, W.D. (1990). *The public inquiry into the Piper Alpha disaster.* London: The Stationery Office.

Cumberbatch, G., Woods, S. & Maguire, A. (1995). *Crime in the news.* Birmingham: Aston University.

Curran, J. & Seaton, J. (1997). *Power without responsibility.* London: Routledge.

Currie, E. (1997). Market, crime and community: Towards a mid-range theory of post-industrial violence. *Theoretical Criminology, vol 1, no 2.*

Currie, E. (2003). Social crime prevention strategies in a market society. In J. Muncie, E. McLaughlin & G. Hughes (Eds.), *Criminological perspectives.* London: Sage.

Daniels, T. (1996). Programmes for Black audiences. In J. Corner & S. Harvey (Eds.), *Television times.* London: Arnold.

Davidman, L. (1991). *Tradition in a rootless world: Women turn to orthodox Judaism.* Berkeley: University of California Press.

Davie, G. (1994). *Religion in Britain since 1945: Believing without belonging.* Oxford: Blackwell.

Davie, G. (2002). *Europe: The exceptional case.* London: Darton, Longman and Todd.

Davie, G. (2007). *The sociology of religion.* London: Sage.

Davies, N. (1994). Dirty business: Red light for Blue Squad. *The Guardian,* 29 November.

Davis, K. (1961). Prostitution. In R. Merton & R. Nisbet (Eds.), *Contemporary social problems.* New York: The Free Press.

Davis, M. (1990). *City of quartz: Excavating the future in Los Angeles.* London: Verso.

Delamont, S. (2003). *Feminist sociology.* London: Sage.

Denman, S. (2001). The *Denman report – Race discrimination in the Crown Prosecution Service.* London: Crown Prosecution Service.

Denzin, N.K. (1970). *The research act in sociology.* London: Butterworths.

Devereux, E. (2003). *Understanding the media.* London: Sage.

DfEE (1997). *Excellence in schools.* (Cmnd 3861). London: HMSO.

Dobash, R.E., Schlesinger, P., Dobash, R. & Weaver, C. (1998). Crimewatch UK. In M. Fishman & G. Cavender (Eds.), *Entertaining crime.* New York: Aldine De Gruyter.

Dobson, A. (1992). Ideology. *Politics Review, 1,* 4.

Dodd, K. & Dodd, P. (1992). From the East End to EastEnders. In D. Strinati & S. Wagg (Eds.), *Come on down: Popular media culture.* London: Routledge.

Donnison, D. (2001). The changing face of poverty. In M. May, R. Page & E. Brunsdon (Eds.), *Understanding social problems: Issues in social policy.* Oxford: Blackwell.

Dorn, N., Levi, M. & King, L. (2005). *Literature review on upper level drug trafficking.* London: Home Office, RDS OLR 22/05.

Douglas, J. D. (1967). *The social meanings of suicide.* New York: Princeton

Downes, D. & Morgan, M. (2002). The skeletons in the cupboard: The politics of law and order at the turn of the millennium. In M. Maguire, R. Morgan & R. Reiner (Eds.), *The Oxford handbook of criminology* (3rd ed.). Oxford: Oxford University Press.

Downes, D. & Rock, P. (2003). *Understanding deviance* (4th ed.). Oxford: Clarendon Press.

Downton, J. (1979). *Sacred journeys: The conversion of young Americans to the Divine Light Mission.* New York: Columbia University Press.

Dunthorne, H. (1991). *The enlightenment.* London: The Historical Association.

Durkheim, E. (1933). *The division of labour in society.* New York: The Free Press.

Durkheim, E. (1964). *The rules of sociological method.* New York: The Free Press.

Durkheim, E. (1968). *The elementary forms of the religious life.* London: Allen & Unwin.

Durkheim, E. (1970). *Suicide: A study in sociology.* London: Routledge & Kegan Paul.

Ehrenreich, B. (1995). The silenced majority: Why the average working person has disappeared from American media and culture. In G. Dines & J. Humez (Eds.), *Gender, race and class in media.* London: Sage.

Eichler, M. et al., (1988). *Non-sexist research methods.* London: Allen & Unwin.

Eisenstadt, S.N. (1967). The Protestant Ethic Thesis in analytical and comparative context. *Diogenes, 59.*

Eldridge, J. (1995). *Getting the message: News, truth and power.* London: Routledge.

Eldridge, J., Kitzinger, J. & Williams, K. (1997). *The mass media and power in modern Britain.* Oxford: Oxford University Press.

Eysenck, H.J. (1987). Personality theory and the problem of criminology. In B. McGurk, D. Thornton & M. Williams (Eds.), *Applying psychology to imprisonment.* London: HMSO.

Farnworth, M., Thornberry, T., Krohn, M. & Lizotte. A. (1994). Measurement in the study of class and delinquency: Integrating theory and research. *Journal of Research in Crime and Delinquency, 31,* 32-61.

Farrington, D. & Morris, A. (1983). Sex, sentencing and reconviction. *British Journal of Criminology, 23.*

Ferguson, M. (1983). *Forever feminine.* London: Heinemann.

Finch, J. (1993). 'It's great to have someone to talk to': Ethics and politics of interviewing women. In M. Hammersley (Ed.), *Social research: Philosophy, politics and practice.* London: Sage.

Fiske, J. (1987). *Television culture.* London: Methuen.

Fowler, D. (1997). Secularisation in the English context. *Independent Saturday Magazine,* December 6.

Franklin, B. (1997). *Newszak and news media.* London: Arnold.

Franklin, J.H. & Starr, I. (Eds.) (1967). *The Negro in 20th century America.* New York: Vintage.

Freeden, M. (2003). *Ideology: A very short introduction.* Oxford: Oxford University Press.

Furner, B. (2005). How are we looking? *The Guardian.*

Furseth, I. & Repstad, P. (2006). *An introduction to the sociology of religion.* Burlington, VT: Ashgate.

Gabor, T. (1994). *Everybody does it.* Toronto: University of Toronto Press.

Garfinkel, H. (1967). *Studies in ethnomethodology.* Englewood Cliffs, NJ: Prentice Hall.

Gauntlett, D. (2002). *Media, gender and identity.* London: Routledge.

Gay, P. (1973). *The enlightenment: An interpretation Vol 2: The science of freedom.* London: Wildwood House.

Geerz, C. (Ed.) (1973). *The interpretation of cultures.* New York: Basic Books.

Gibbs, J. & Martin, W. (1964). *Status integration and suicide.* Oregon: University of Oregon Press.

Giddens, A. (1991). *Modernity and self-identity: Self and society in the late modern age.* Cambridge: Polity Press.

Giddens, A. (1998). *The Third Way: The renewal of social democracy.* Cambridge: Polity Press.

Giddens, A. (2000). *The Third Way and its critics.* Cambridge: Polity Press.

Giddens, A. (2001). *Sociology* (4th ed.). Cambridge: Polity Press.

Gilbert, G.M. (1951). Stereotype persistence and change among college students. *Journal of Abnormal and Social Psychology, 46,* 245-254.

Gillespie, M. (1995). *Television, ethnicity and cultural change.* London: Routledge.

Gillespie, M. (2002). *From comic Asians to Asian comics.* London: BFI.

Gilroy, P. (1983). Police and thieves. In Centre for Contemporary Cultural Studies *The empire strikes back.* London: Hutchinson.

Glasgow University Media Group (1982). *Really bad news.* London: Writers & Readers.

Glasgow Media Group (1997). *Ethnic minorities in television advertising.* Glasgow: GMG.

Glock, C.Y. (1964). The role of relative deprivation in the origin and evolution of religious groups. In R. Lee & M. Marty (Eds.), *Religion and social conflict.* Berkeley, CA: University of California Press.

Glover, D. (1985). The sociology of the mass media. In M. Haralambos (Ed.), *Sociology: New Directions.* Ormskirk: Causeway Press.

Goffman, E. (1959). *The presentation of self in everyday life.* Harmondsworth: Penguin.

Goffman, E. (1968). *Asylums.* Harmondsworth: Penguin.

Golding, P. & Middleton, S. (1982). *Images of welfare: Press and public attitudes to poverty.* Oxford: Blackwell.

Goode, E. & Ben-Yehuda, N. (1994). *Moral panics: The social construction of deviance.* Oxford: Blackwell.

Gorman, L. & McLean, D. (2003). *Media and society in the twentieth century.* Oxford: Blackwell.

Gottfredson, M. & Hirschi, T. (1990). *General theory of crime.* Stanford: Stanford University Press.

Gouldner, A.W. (1971). *The coming crisis of Western sociology.* London: Heinemann.

Gouldner, A.W. (1975). *For sociology.* Harmondsworth: Penguin.

Graber, D.A., Bimber, B. Bennett, W.L., Davis, R. & Norris, P. (2004). The Internet and politics: Emerging perspectives. In N. Nissenbaum & M.E. Price (Eds.), *Academy and the Internet.* New York: Peter Lang.

Graef, R. (1990). *Talking blues.* London: Fontana.

Graham, J. & Bowling, B. (1995). *Young people and crime, Home Office Research Study,145.* London: Home Office.

Gramsci, A. (1971). *Selections from the Prison Notebooks: Notebooks of Antonio Gramsci.* London: Lawrence & Wishart.

Greenslade, R. (1993). Sky is not the limit. *New Statesman and Society,* 10 September.

Gross, L. (1995). Out of the mainstream: Sexual minorities and the mass media. In G. Dines & J. Humez (Eds.), *Gender, race and class in media.* London: Sage.

Habermas, J. (1992). Further reflections on the public sphere. In C. Calhoun (Ed.), *Habermas and the public sphere.* Cambridge, MA: MIT Press.

Hadaway, C.K. & Marler, P.L. (1999). *Did you really go to church this week? Behind the poll data.* www.religion-online.org

Hadden, J.K. (2003). *The Religious Movements Page.* http://religiousmovements.lib.virginia.edu/cultsect/concult.htm

Halfpenny, P. (1984). *Principles of method.* York: Longman.

Hall, S. (1992). The question of cultural identity. In S. Hall et al. (Eds.), *Modernity and its futures.* Cambridge: Polity.

Hall, S. (1993). The idea of the social. *In Open University, D103. Society and social science: A Foundation Course, Block 2 Social structure and social divisions.* Buckingham: Open University Press.

Hall, S. (1995). The whites of their eyes. In G. Dines & J. Humez (Eds.), *Gender, race and class in media.* London: Sage.

Hall, S. (1997). The spectacle of the 'other'. In S. Hall (Ed.), *Representation: Cultural representations and signifying practices.* London: Sage.

Hall, S., Critcher, C., Jefferson, T., Clarke, J. & Roberts, B. (1978). *Policing the crisis.* London: Macmillan.

Hallsworth, S. (1994). Understanding new social movements. *Sociology Review,* September.

Hamilton, M. (2001). *The sociology of religion: Theoretical and comparative perspectives.* London: Routledge.

Hamilton, P. (1992). The enlightenment and the birth of social science. In S. Hall & B Gieben (Eds.), *Formations of modernity.* Cambridge: Polity.

Hanson, S. (1997). The secularisation thesis: Talking at cross purposes. *Journal of Contemporary Religion, 12,* 2.

Haralambos, M. & Jones, R. (2006). *Critical thinking for OCR AS level.* Harlow: Pearson Education.

Haralambos, M. (1995). *Right on: From blues to soul in Black America.* Ormskirk: Causeway Press.

Harris, M. (1984). The strange saga of the Video Bill. *New Society,* 26 April, 140-142.

Harvey, D. (1989). *The condition of postmodernity.* Oxford: Blackwell.

Heelas, P. & Woodhead, L. (2003). The Kendal Project: Testing the 'spiritual revolution thesis'. *Sociology Review,* November.

Heelas, P. & Woodhead, L. (2005). *The spiritual revolution: Why religion is giving way to spirituality.* Oxford: Blackwell.

Heelas, P. (1996). *The New Age Movement: The celebration of the self and the sacralisation of modernity.* Oxford: Blackwell.

Heelas, P. (1998). Introduction. In P. Heelas (Ed.), *Religion, modernity and postmodernity.* Oxford: Blackwell.

Heelas, P. (2000). Religion and postmodern difference. In Woodhead & Heelas (Eds.), *Religion in modern times.* Oxford: Blackwell.

Heidensohn, F. (1996). *Women and crime* (2nd ed.). London: Macmillan.

Heidensohn, F. (2002). Gender and crime. In M. Maguire et al. (Eds.), *The Oxford handbook of criminology* (3rd ed.). Oxford: Oxford University Press.

Heilbut, T. (1971). *The gospel sound.* New York: Simon & Schuster.

Held, D. (1992). The development of the modern state. In S. Hall & B. Gieben (Eds.), *Formations of modernity.* Cambridge: Polity.

Herberg, W. (1960). *Protestant-Catholic-Jew: An essay in American religious sociology.* Chicago: University of Chicago Press.

Herbert, D. (2001). Representing Islam: The 'Islamisation' of Egyptian society, 1970-2000. In G. Beckerlegge (Ed.), *From sacred text to internet.* Milton Keynes: Open University Press.

Heritage, J. (1984). *Garfinkel and ethnomethodology.* Cambridge: Polity Press.

Herman, E. & Chomsky, N. (1988). *The political economy of the mass media.* New York: Pantheon Books.

Hetherington, A. (1985). *News, newspapers and television.* London: Macmillan.

Heywood, A. (2002). *Politics* (2nd ed.). Basingstoke: Palgrave.

Higson, A. (1998). National identity and the media. In A. Briggs & P. Cobley (Eds.), *The media: An introduction.* Harlow: Longman.

Hindess, B. (1973). *The use of official statistics in sociology: A critique of positivism.* London: Macmillan.

Hirschi, T. (1969). *Causes of delinquency.* Berkeley CA: University of California Press.

HMIC (Her Majesty's Inspectorate of Constabulary) (2001). *Winning the race: Embracing diversity.* London: Home Office.

Hobbs, D. & Dunningham, C. (1998). Glocal organised crime: Context and pretext. In V. Ruggerio, N. South & I. Taylor (Eds.), *The new European criminology.* London: Routledge.

Hobbes, T. & Gaskin, J. (1998). *Leviathan.* Oxford: Oxford Paperbacks.

Hobbs, D., Hadfield, P., Lister, S. & Winlow, S. (2003). *Bouncers.* Oxford: Oxford University Press.

Holdaway, S. (1988). *Crime and deviance.* London: Macmillan.

Holdaway, S. (1996). *The racialisation of British policing.* London: Macmillan.

Holden, A. (2002). Witnessing the future? Millenarianism and postmodernity. *Sociology Review,* February.

Home Office (2000). *Code of practice on reporting and recording racist incidents.* London: Home Office.

Home Office (2002). *Statistics on race and the criminal justice system.* London: Home Office.

Home Office (2003). *Statistics on women and the criminal justice system.* London: Home Office.

Home Office (2007). *Cutting crime: A new partnership 2008-2011.* London: Home Office.

Hood, R. (1992). *Race and sentencing.* Oxford: Clarendon Press.

House of Lords (2008). *The ownership of the news.* London: The Stationery Office.

Hoyle, C. (2000). Being 'a nosy bloody cow': Ethical and methodological issues in researching domestic violence. In R.D. King & E. Wincup (Eds.), *Doing research on crime and justice.* Oxford: Oxford University Press.

Hudson, B. (1993). Racism and criminology: Concepts and controversies. In D. Cook & B. Hudson (Eds.), *Racism and criminology.* London: Sage.

Hughes, G. & Langan, M. (2001). Good or bad business?: Exploring corporate and organised crime. In J. Muncie & E. McLaughlin (Eds.), *The problem of crime* (2nd ed.). London: Sage.

Hughes, G. (1998). Constructions of disability. In E. Saraga (Ed.), *Embodying the social: Constructions of difference.* London: Routledge.

Hughes, G. (2000). What are the futures of crime control? *Sociology Review,* 9.

Hughes, G. (2001). The competing logics of community sanctions: Welfare, rehabilitation and restorative justice. In McLaughlin, E. & Muncie, J. (Eds.), *Controlling crime* (2nd ed.). London: Sage.

Hunt, S. (1992). *Religion in Western society.* Basingstoke: Palgrave.

Iannucci, A. (1995). Play your card right. *The Guardian,* May 2.

IMF (2004). *About the International Monetary Fund.* www.imf.org

Irwin, A. & Michael, M. (2003). *Science, social theory and public knowledge.* Maidenhead: Open University Press.

James, O. (2003). So George, how do you feel about your mom and dad? *The Guardian,* 2 September.

Jarvis, J. (2005). Chaos spreads from the web to the streets. *The Guardian,* 14 November.

Jenkins, J. (1987). *Contemporary moral issues.* Oxford: Heinemann Educational.

Jensen, A.R. (1973). *Educational differences.* London: Methuen.

Jones, I. (1974). *A critique of Murdock and Phelps' 'Mass media and the secondary school'.* Unpublished dissertation. School of Education, University of Leicester.

Jones, K. (1998). Death of a Princess. *Sociology Review,* September.

Jones, P. (1993). *Studying society: Sociological theories and research practices.* London: Collins Educational.

Jones, S. (1998). *Criminology.* London: Butterworth.

Jones, T., McLean, B. & Young, J. (1986). *The Islington Crime Survey.* Aldershot: Gower.

Judah, J.S. (1974). *Hare Krishna and the counter culture.* New York: John Wiley.

Kalra,V. (2003). Police lore and community disorder: Diversity in the criminal justice system. In D. Mason (Ed.), *Explaining ethnic differences.* Bristol: The Policy Press.

Kaluzynska, E. (1980). Wiping the floor with theory. *Feminist Review no. 7.*

Karlins, M., Coffman, T.L. & Walters, G. (1969). On the fading of social stereotypes: Studies in three generations of college students. *Journal of Personality and Social Psychology, 13,* 1-16.

Kassam, N. (1997). *Telling it like it is.* London: Women's Press.

Katz, D. & Braly, K.W. (1933). Racial stereotypes of 100 college students. *Journal of Abnormal and Social Psychology, 28,* 280-290.

Katz, E. & Lazarsfeld, P. (1955). *Personal influence.* New York: The Free Press.

Kendall, D. (2005). *Framing class.* Lenham: Rowman & Littlefield.

Kerr, J. (1994). *Understanding football hooliganism.* Buckingham: Open University Press.

Kershaw, C., Nicholas, S. & Walker, A. (2009). *Crime in England and Wales, 2007-08.* London: Home Office.

Khasala, K. (1986). New religious movements turn to worldly success. *Journal for the Scientific Study of Religion, 25,* 233-247.

Kincaid, J.C. (1973). *Poverty and equality in Britain.* Harmondsworth: Penguin.

Knorr-Cetina, K. (2005). The fabrication of facts: Towards a microsociology of scientific knowledge. In N. Stehr & V. Meja (Eds.), *Society and knowledge* (2nd ed.). Brunswick, NJ: Transaction.

Kuhn, T.S. (1962). *The structure of scientific revolutions.* Chicago: University of Chicago Press.

Lakatos, I. (1970). Falsification and the methodology of scientific research programmes. In I. Lakatos & A. Musgrave (Eds.), *Criticism and the growth of knowledge.* Cambridge: Cambridge University Press.

Lander, B. (1962). An ecological analysis of Baltimore. In M.E. Wolfgang, L. Savitz & N. Johnston (Eds.), *The sociology of crime and delinquency.* New York: John Wiley & Sons.

Langley, P. (1988). *Discovering sociology.* Ormskirk: Causeway Press.

Law, I. (1997). *Privilege and silence: 'Race' in the British news during the general election campaign, 1997.* Leeds: University of Leeds.

Layder, D. (1994). *Understanding social theory.* London: Sage

Layton-Henry, Z. (1992). *The politics of immigration.* Oxford: Blackwell.

Lea, J. & Young, J. (1982). The riots in Britain: Urban violence and political marginalisation. In D. Cowell, T. Jones & J. Young (Eds.), *Policing the riots.* London: Junction Books.

Lea, J. & Young, J. (1993). *What is to be done about law and order?* (2nd ed.). London: Pluto Press.

Lederman. L. (2008). What we'll find inside the atom. *Newsweek,* 15 September.

Lee, D. & Newby, H. (1983). *The problem of sociology.* London: Hutchinson.

Lemert, E.M. (1972). *Human deviance, social problems and social control* (2nd ed.). Englewood Cliffs NJ: Prentice Hall.

Levi, M. (1993). *The investigation, prosecution and trial of serious fraud, Research Study, 14.* London: Royal Commission on Criminal Justice.

Levi, M. (2007). Organised crime and terrorism. In M. Maguire, R. Morgan & R. Reiner (Eds.), *The Oxford handbook of criminology* (4th ed.). Oxford: Oxford University Press.

Lévi-Strauss, C. (1965). The structural study of myth. In W.A. Lessa & E.Z. Vogt (Eds.), *Reader in comparative religion* (2nd ed.). New York: Harper & Row.

Light, A. (Ed.) (1997). *Tupac Ama Ru Shakur, 1971-1996.* London: Plexus.

Lippmann, W. (1922). *Public Opinion.* New York: Harcourt Brace

Livingstone, S. (2004). The challenge of changing audiences: Or, what is the audience researcher to do in the Internet age? *European Journal of Communication, 19,* 75-86.

Llana, S.M. (2007). Wealth gospel propels poor Guatemalans. *Christian Science Monitor,* 17 December.

Loader, I. & Sparks, R. (2007). Contemporary landscapes of crime, order and control: Governance, risk and globalisation. In M. Maguire, R. Morgan & R. Reiner (Eds.), *The Oxford handbook of criminology* (4th ed.). Oxford: Oxford University Press.

Lombroso, C. (1876). *L'uomo delinquente.* Milan: Hoepli.

Long Lance, Chief Buffalo Child. (1956). *Long Lance.* London: Corgi.

Longley, C. (1986). Robin Hood and liberation theology. *The Times,* 27 January.

Luckmann, T. (1970). *The invisible religion: The problem of religion in modern society.* New York: Macmillan.

Lyon, D. (2000). *Jesus in Disneyland: Religion in postmodern times.* Cambridge: Polity Press.

Lyotard, J.F. (1984). *The postmodern condition.* Manchester: Manchester University Press.

Lyotard, J.F. (1992). Abandoning the metanarratives of modernity. In S. Hall et al. (Eds.), *Modernity and its futures.* Cambridge: Polity.

Macdonald, K. & Tipton, D. (1993). Using documents. In N. Gilbert (Ed.), *Researching social life.* London: Sage.

MacGregor, S. (2001). The problematic community. In M. May, R. Page & E. Brunsdon (Eds.), *Understanding social problems: Issues in social policy.* Oxford: Blackwell.

Macpherson, W. (1999). *The Stephen Lawrence Inquiry.* London: HMSO.

Maduro, O. (1982). *Religion and social conflicts.* New York: Orbis.

Maguire, M. (2002). Crime statistics. In M. Maguire et al. (Eds.), *The Oxford handbook of criminology* (3rd ed.). Oxford: Oxford University Press.

Malinowski, B. (1954). *Magic, science and religion and other essays.* New York: Anchor Books.

Mandel, E. (1984). *Delightful murder: A social history of the crime story.* London: Pluto.

Marcuse, H. (1964). *One dimensional man.* London: Routledge & Kegan Paul.

Marquand, D. (1998). *The unprincipled society: New demands and old politics.* London: Fontana.

Marsh, D. (1985). Power and Politics. In M. Haralambos (Ed.), *Developments in Sociology, vol 1.* Ormskirk: Causeway Press.

Marshall, G. (Ed.) (1994). *The concise Oxford dictionary of sociology.* Oxford: Oxford University Press.

Martin, B. (2003). The Pentecostal gender paradox. In R.K. Fenn (Ed.), *The Blackwell companion to the sociology of religion.* Oxford: Blackwell.

Martin, D. (1969). *The religious and the secular.* London: Routledge & Kegan Paul.

Martin, D. (2002). *Pentecostalism: The world their parish.* Oxford: Blackwell.

Matza, D. & Sykes, G.M. (1961). Juvenile delinquency and subterranean values. *American Sociological Review, 26,* 5.

Matza, D. (1964). *Delinquency and drift.* London: Wiley.

Mauer, M. (1997). *Intended and unintended consequences: State racial disparities in imprisonment.* Washington DC: The Sentencing Project.

May, M., Page, R. & Brunsdon, E. (2001). Social problems in social policy: An introduction. In M. May, R. Page & E. Brunsdon (Eds.), *Understanding social problems: Issues in social policy.* Oxford: Blackwell.

Mayhew, P., Aye Maung, N. & Mirrlees-Black, C. (1993). *The 1992 British Crime Survey, Home Office Research Study, 132.* London: HMSO.

Mayhew, P., Mirrlees-Black, C. & Aye Maung, N. (1994). *Trends in crime: Findings from the 1994 British Crime Survey, Home Office Research and Statistics Department Research Findings, 18.* London: HMSO.

McClennan, G. (1992). The Enlightenment project revisited. In S. Hall et al. (Eds.), *Modernity and its futures.* Cambridge: Polity.

McCullagh, C. (2002). *Media power.* Basingstoke: Palgrave.

McGuire, M. (1981). *Religion: The social context.* New York: Orbis.

McGuire, M. (2003). Ritual healing in suburban America. In S.J. Sutcliffe (Ed.), *Children of the New Age: A history of spiritual practices.* London: Routledge.

McLaughlin, E. & Muncie, J. (2001). Introduction. In McLaughlin, E. & Muncie, J. (Eds.), *Controlling crime* (2nd ed.). London: Sage.

McLaughlin, E. (2001). Political violence, terrorism and crimes of the state. In J. Muncie & E. McLaughlin (Eds.), *The problem of crime.* London: Sage.

McNair, B. (1996). *News and journalism in the UK.* London: Routledge.

McQuail, D., Blumler, J. & Brown, R. (1972). The television audience: A revised perspective. In D. McQuail (Ed.), *Sociology of mass communication.* Harmondsworth: Penguin.

McQueen, D. (1998). *Television: A media student's guide.* London: Arnold.

McRobbie, A. (1999). *In the culture society: Art, fashion and popular music.* London: Routledge.

Mead, G.H. (1967). *Mind, self and society.* Chicago: Chicago University Press

Media Awareness Network (2005). *Representations of gays and lesbians on television.* www.media-awareness.ca

Merton, R.K. (1968). Social structure and anomie. In R.K. Merton, *Social theory and social structure.* New York: The Free Press.

Messerschmidt, J. (1993). *Masculinities and crime.* Lanham: Rowman & Littlefield.

Mies, M. (1993). Towards a methodology for feminist research. In M. Hammersley (Ed.), *Social research: Philosophy, politics and practice.* London: Sage.

Miliband, R. (1973). *The state in capitalist society.* London: Quartet Books.

Miller, C.C. (2008). *How Obama's internet campaign changed politics.* bits.blogs.nytimes.com.

Miller, W.B. (1958). Lower class culture as a generating milieu of gang delinquency, *Journal of Social Issues,14.*

Millett, K. (1970). *Sexual politics.* New York: Doubleday.

Miner, M. (1965). Body ritual among the Nacirema. In W.A. Lessa & E.Z Vogt (Eds.), *Reader in comparative religion: An anthropological approach* (2nd ed.). New York: Harper & Row.

Modood, T., Berthoud, R. Lakey, J., Nazroo, J., Smith, P., Virdee, S. & Beishon, S. (1997). *Ethnic minorities in Britain.* London: Policy Studies Institute.

Morgan, C. (1997). Vicars inflate attendance figures. *The Sunday Times,* 1 June.

Morris, T.P. (1957). *The criminal area: A study in social ecology.* London: Routledge & Kegan Paul.

Mossberger, K., Tolbert, C.J. & McNeal, R.S. (2008). *Digital citizenship: The internet, society and participation.* Cambridge, MA: MIT.

Mulvey, L. (1975). Visual pleasure and narrative cinema. *Screen, 16,* 3.

Muncie, J. (1987). Much ado about nothing? The sociology of moral panics, *Social Studies Review, 3.*

Muncie, J. (1996). The construction and deconstruction of crime. In J. Muncie & E. McLaughlin (Eds.), *The problem of crime.* London: Sage.

Muncie, J. (1999). *Youth and crime.* London: Sage.

Muncie, J. (2001). The construction and deconstruction of crime. In J. Muncie & E. McLaughlin (Eds.), *The problem of crime.* London: Sage.

Munck, R. & Rolston, W. (1987). *Belfast in the 30s: An oral history.* Belfast: Blackstaff Press.

Murdock, G. & Golding, P. (2005). Culture, communications and political economy. In J. Curran & Michael Gurevitch (Eds.), *Mass media and society* (4th ed.). London: Hodder Arnold.

Murdock, G. (1992). Embedded persuasions: The fall and rise of integrated advertising. In D. Strinati & S. Wagg (Eds.), *Come on down: Popular media culture.* London: Routledge.

Murray, C. (1990). *The emerging British underclass.* London: Institute of Economic Affairs.

Murray, C. (1996). *Charles Murray and the underclass: The developing debate.* London: Institute of Economic Affairs.

Naffine, N. (1987). *Female crime.* Sydney: Allen & Unwin.

Negrine, R. (1994). *Politics and the mass media in Britain.* London: Routledge.

Neil, A. (1996). *Full disclosure.* London: Macmillan.

Nelson, G.K. (1986). Religion. In M. Haralambos (Ed.), *Developments in Sociology, Volume 2,* Ormskirk: Causeway Press.

Newbold, C., Boyd-Barrett, O. & Van Den Bulk, H. (Eds.) (2002). *The Media Book.* London: Arnold.

Niebuhr, H.R. (1929). *The social sources of denominationalism.* New York: World Publishing.

Nightingale, C. (1993). *On the edge.* New York: Basic Books.

O'Connell Davidson & Layder, D. (1994). *Methods, sex and madness.* London: Routledge.

O'Toole, R. (1984). *Religion: Classic sociological approaches.* Toronto: McGraw-Hill.

Oakley, A. (1981). Interviewing women: A contradiction in terms. In H. Roberts (Ed.), *Doing feminist research.* London: Routledge.

Ofcom (2008). Social networking: A quantitative and qualitative research report into attitudes, behaviours and use. *Ofcom.org.uk,* 2 April.

Olds, D.L. et al. (1997). Long-term effects of home visitation on material life course and child abuse and neglect: Fifteen year follow-up of a randomised trial. *Journal of the American Medical Association, 278,* 637-643.

Page, R. (2001). The exploration of social problems in the field of social policy. In M. May, R. Page & E. Brunsdon (Eds.), *Understanding social problems: Issues in social policy.* Oxford: Blackwell.

Page, R.M. (2002). New Labour and the welfare state. In M. Holborn (Ed.), *Developments in Sociology, Volume 18.* Ormskirk: Causeway Press.

Painter, K. & Farrington, D. (1999). Street lighting and crime: Diffusion of benefits in the Stoke-on-Trent Project. In K. Painter & D. Farrington (Eds.), *Surveillance of public space: CCTV, street lighting and crime prevention.* Monsey, NY: Criminal Justice Press.

Parsons, G. (2002). *Perspectives on civil religion*. Milton Keynes: Open University and Aldershot: Ashgate Publishing.

Parsons, T. (1951). *The social system*. New York: Free Press.

Parsons, T. (1955). The American family: Its relations to personality and social structure. In T. Parsons & R. Bales (Eds.), *Family, socialisation and interaction process*. New York: The Free Press.

Parsons, T. (1965). Religious perspectives in sociology and social psychology. In W.A. Lessa & E.Z. Vogt (Eds.), *Reader in comparative religion: An anthropological approach* (2nd ed.). New York: Harper & Row.

Pawson, R. (1989). Methodology. In M. Haralambos (Ed.), *Developments in sociology, Volume 5*. Ormskirk: Causeway Press.

Pawson, R. (1992). Feminist methodology. In M. Haralambos (Ed.), *Developments in sociology, Volume 8*. Ormskirk: Causeway Press.

Pawson, R. (1995). Methods of content/document/media analysis. In M. Haralambos (Ed.), *Developments in sociology, Volume 11*. Ormskirk: Causeway Press.

Paxton, W. & Dixon, M. (2004). *The state of the nation: An audit of injustice in the UK*. London: Institute for Public Policy Research.

Peake, S. (2002). *The Guardian media guide 2003*. London: Atlantic Books.

Pearson, G. (1983). *Hooligan: A history of respectable fears*. London: Macmillan.

Pease, K. (2002). Crime reduction. In M. Maguire et al. (Eds.), *The Oxford handbook of criminology* (3rd ed.). Oxford: Oxford University Press.

Phillips, C. & Bowling, B. (2002). Racism, ethnicity and criminal justice. In M. Maguire et al. (Eds.), *The Oxford handbook of criminology* (3rd ed.). Oxford: Oxford University Press.

Phillips, T. (2008). Hundreds of Brazil's eco-warriors at risk of assassination. *The Guardian*, 22 December.

Philo, G. & Miller, D. (2002). Circuits of communication and power: Recent developments in media sociology. In M. Holborn (Ed.), *Developments in Sociology, Vol. 18*. Ormskirk: Causeway Press.

Philo, G. & Miller, D. (Eds.) (2001). *Market killing: What the free market does and what social scientists can do about it*. Harlow: Longman.

Philo, G. (1993). Getting the message: Audience research in the Glasgow University Media Group. In J. Eldridge (Ed.), *Getting the message: News truth and power*. London: Routledge.

Pilkington, A. (2003). *Racial disadvantage and ethnic diversity in Britain*. London: Palgrave.

Plommer, L. (2009). I want Baghdad to feel like home again. *The Guardian*, 15 January.

Plummer, K. (1979). Misunderstanding labelling perspectives. In D. Downes & P. Rock (Eds.), *Deviant interpretations*. Oxford: M. Robertson.

Popper, K.R. (1959). *The logic of scientific discovery*. London: Hutchinson.

Popper, K.R. (2002). The poverty of historicism. London: Routledge

Poster, M. (Ed.) (1988). *Jean Baudrillard: Selected writings*. Cambridge: Polity.

Puwar, N. (2001). Problematising, seeing, listening and telling: Reflections on the research enterprise. In M. Haralambos (Ed.), *Developments in Sociology, Volume 17*. Ormskirk: Causeway.

Quinton, D., Pickles, A., Maughan, B., Rutter, M. (1993). Partners and peers and pathways: Assortative pairing and continuities in conduct disorder. *Development and psychopathology, 5*, 763-783.

Randerson, J. (2007). *Social networking sites don't deepen friendships*. www.Guardian.co.uk, 10 September.

Rawlinson, P. (2005). Understanding organised crime. In C. Hale, K. Hayward, A. Wahidin & E. Wincup (Eds.), *Criminology*. Oxford: Oxford University Press.

Raynor, P. (2002). Community penalties: Probation, punishment and 'what works'. In M. Maguire, R. Morgan & R. Reiner (Eds.), *The Oxford handbook of criminology* (3rd ed.). Oxford: Oxford University Press.

Raynsford, J. (2003). *Blogging: The new journalism*. www.journalism.co.uk.

Reiner, R. (1993). Race, crime and justice: Models of interpretation. In L. Gelsthorpe (Ed.), *Minority ethnic groups in the criminal justice system*. Cambridge: Institute of Criminology.

Reiner, R. (1994). Policing and the police. In M. Maguire et al. (Eds.), *The Oxford handbook of criminology* (1st ed.). Oxford: Oxford University Press.

Reiner, R. (2002). Media made criminality. In M. Maguire et al. (Eds.), *The Oxford handbook of criminology* (3rd ed.). Oxford: Oxford University Press.

Reiner, R., Livingstone, S. & Allen, J. (2000). No more happy endings? The media and popular concern about crime since the Second World War. In T. Hope & R. Sparks (Eds.), *Crime, risk and insecurity*. London: Routledge.

Rengert, G. & Wasilchick, J. (2000). *Suburban burglary: A tale of two suburbs* (2nd ed.). Springfield, Ill: Charles C. Thomas.

Richardson, J. (2005). *Youth and culture for OCR*. Ormskirk: Causeway Press.

Robertson, R. (1970). *The sociological interpretation of religion*. Oxford: Blackwell.

Rock, P. (1979). Sociology of crime. In D. Downes & P. Rock (Eds.), *Deviant interpretations*. Oxford: M. Robertson.

Roper, L. (2003). *Disability in media*. www.mediaed.org.uk

Ross, K. (1996). *Black and White media*. Cambridge: Polity Press.

Rousseau, J. (1968). *The social contract*. Harmondsworth: Penguin Books.

Rowbotham, S. (1973). *Woman's consciousness: Man's world*. Harmondsworth: Penguin.

Rutter, M. & Smith, D (Eds.) (1985). *Psychosocial disorders in young people: Time trends and their causes*. Chichester: Wiley.

Sachs, J. (1990). The persistence of faith. *The Listener*, 15 November.

Sallybanks, J. (2000). Assessing the police use of decoy vehicles. *Police Research Series, 137*. London: Home Office.

Sampson, R. & Laub, J. (1990). Crime and deviance over the life course: The salience of adult social bonds. *American Sociological Review, 55*, 609-627.

Sampson, R. & Raudenbush, S. (1999). Systematic social observation of public spaces: A new look at disorder in urban neighbourhoods. *American Journal of Sociology*.

Saunders, D. (2001). Bush's Christian guru Marvin Olasky aims to reshape America. *Toronto Globe & Mail*, 13 January.

Sayer, A. (1992). *Method in social science: A realist approach*. London: Routledge.

Scarman, L. (1981). *The Scarman Report: The Brixton disorders*. London: HMSO.

Schlesinger, P. (1991). *Media, state and nation*. London: Sage.

Schudson, M. (2000). The sociology of news production revisited – again. In J. Curran & M. Gurevitch (Eds.), *Mass media and society*. London: Arnold.

Schuerman, L. & Kobrin, S. (1986). Community careers in crime. In A.J. Reiss & M. Tonry (Eds.), *Communities and crime*. Chicago: University of Chicago Press.

Shaw, C.R. & McKay, H.D. (1942). *Juvenile delinquency and urban areas*. Chicago: University of Chicago Press.

Simmons, J. & Dodd, T. (2003). *Crime in England and Wales 2002/2003*. London: ONS.

Sklair, L. (2003). Globalisation, capitalism and power. In M. Holborn (Ed.), *Developments in Sociology, Vol. 19*. Ormskirk: Causeway Press.

Skogan, W.G. (1990). *Disorder and decline: Crime and the spiral of decay in American neighbourhoods*. New York: The Free Press.

Smart, B. (1992). *Modern conditions, postmodern controversies*. London: Routledge.

Smart, C. (1977). *Women, crime and criminology*. London: Routledge.

Smith, D. & Gray, J. (1995). *Police and people in London*. Aldershot: Gower.

Smith, D. (1997). Ethnic origins, crime and criminal justice. In M. Maguire, R. Morgan & R. Reiner (Eds.), *The Oxford handbook of criminology* (2nd ed.). Oxford: Oxford University Press.

Smith, D. (2002). Crime and the life course. In M. Maguire, R. Morgan, & R. Reiner (Eds.), *The Oxford handbook of criminology* (3rd ed.). Oxford: Oxford University Press

Soothill, K., Francis, B. & Fligelstone, R. (2002). Patterns of offending behaviour: A new approach. *Home Office research findings, 171*. London: Home Office

Solomos, J. & Back, L. (1996). *Racism and society*. London: Macmillan.

South, N. (1998). Corporate and state crimes against the environment: Foundations for a green perspective in European criminology. In V. Ruggerio, N. South & I. Taylor (Eds.), *The new European criminology*. London: Routledge.

Sparks, R. & Hood, R. (1970). *Key issues in Criminology*. London: Weidenfeld.

Sparks, C. (2007). *Globalisation, development and the mass media*. London: Sage.

Stanko, E. (1994). Challenging the problem of men's individual violence. In T. Newburn & E. Stanko (Eds.), *Just boys doing business?* London: Routledge.

Stark, R. & Bainbridge, W.S. (1985). *The future of religion*. Berkeley, CA: University of California Press.

Stark, R. & Bainbridge, W.S. (1987). *A theory of religion*. New York: Lang.

Starrett, G. (1998). *Putting Islam to work: Education, politics and religious transformation in Egypt*. Berkeley CA: University of California Press.

Stone, D. (1976). The human potential movement. In C.Y. Glock & R.N. Bellah (Eds.), *The consciousness reformation*. Berkeley, CA: University of California Press.

Storey, J. (1993). *An introductory guide of cultural theory and popular culture*. London: Harvester Wheatsheaf.

Strange, S. (1996). *Casino capitalism*. Oxford: Blackwell.

Strinati, D. (1992). Postmodernism and popular culture. *Sociology Review*, April.

Sutcliffe, S.J. (2003). *Children of the New Age: A history of spiritual practices*. London: Routledge.

Sutherland, E. (1949). *White collar crime*. New York: Holt, Rinehart & Winston.

Sutton, P. W. & Vertigans, S. (2005). *Resurgent Islam: A sociological approach*. Cambridge: Polity.

Swale, J. (2000). Women's role in religion. *Sociology Review*, April.

Swale, J. (2004). Suicide: A synoptic approach, *Sociology Review*, 12.

Schweinhart, L.J., Barnes, H.V. & Weikart, D.P. (1993). *Significant benefits: The High Scope Perry preschool study through age 27*. Ypsilanti, Michigan: High Scope Press.

Sykes, G.M. & Matza, D. (1962). Techniques of neutralisation: A theory of delinquency. In M.E. Wolfgang, L. Savitz & N. Johnston (Eds.), *The sociology of crime and delinquency*. New York: John Wiley & Sons.

Taheri, A. (1987). *Holy terror: The inside story of Islamic terrorism*. London: Sphere.

Tawney, R.H. (1938). *Religion and the rise of capitalism*. Harmondsworth: Penguin.

Taylor, I. (1997). The political economy of crime. In M. Maguire, R. Morgan & R. Reiner (Eds.), *The Oxford handbook of criminology* (2nd ed.). Oxford: Oxford University Press.

Taylor, I., Walton, P. & Young, J. (1973). *The new criminology*. London: Routledge.

Taylor, S. (1982). *Durkheim and the study of suicide*. London: Macmillan.

Taylor, S. (1988). *Suicide*. London: Longman.

Tester, K. (1995). Postmodernism. In M. Haralambos (Ed.), *Developments in sociology, Vol 11*. Ormskirk: Causeway Press.

Thompson, K. (1992). Social pluralism and postmodernity. In S. Hall et al. (Eds.), *Modernity and its futures*. Cambridge: Polity.

Trigg, R. (1989). *Reality at risk: A defence of realism in philosophy and the sciences*. New York: Harvester Wheatsheaf.

Troeltsch, E. (1931). *The social teachings of the Christian Churches*. London: Allen & Unwin.

Tuchman, G. (1978). *Making news*. New York: The Free Press.

Tuchman, G. (1981). The symbolic annihilation of women by the mass media. In S. Cohen & J. Young (Eds.), *The manufacture of news*. London: Constable.

Tumin, M. (1967). *Social stratification: The forms and functions of social inequality*. Englewood Cliffs: Prentice Hall.

Tunstall, J. (1983). *The media in Britain*. London: Constable.

Utley, R.M. (1963). *The last days of the Sioux nation*. New Haven: Yale University Press.

Van der Wurff, R. & Lauf, E. (Eds.) (2006). *Print and online: Newspapers in Europe, a comparative analysis in 16 countries*. Amsterdam: Het Spinhuis.

Van Dijk, T. (1991). *Racism and the press*. London: Routledge.

von Hirsch, A. (1976). Giving criminals their just deserts. *Civil Liberties Review, 3*, 23-35.

von Leyden, J. (2008). *Ad wars: The internet election*. www.Channel4.com/news.

Wagner, M. (2008). *Obama election: Ushering in the first internet presidency*. www.Adsensetrick.com.

Walklate, S. (2003). *Understanding criminology: Current theoretical debates* (2nd ed.). Buckingham: Open University Press.

Wallis, R. & Bruce, S. (1989). Religion: The British contribution. *British Journal of Sociology, 40*, 3.

Wallis, R. (1974). Ideology, authority and the development of cultic movements. *Social Research, 41*, 299-327.

Wallis, R. (1975). Scientology: Therapeutic cult to religious sect. *Sociology, 9*, 89-100.

Wallis, R. (1984). *The elementary forms of the new religious life*. London: Routledge & Kegan Paul.

Wallis, R. (1985). The sociology of the New Religions. *Social Studies Review*, September.

Weber, M. (1958). *The Protestant ethic and the spirit of capitalism*. New York: Charles Scribner's Sons.

Weber, M. (1963). *The sociology of religion*. Boston, MA: Beacon Press.

Weber, M. (1964). *The theory of social and economic organisations*. New York: The Free Press.

White, D. (1950). The 'gatekeeper': A case study in the selection of news. *Journalism Quarterly, 2*.

Whyte, W.F. (1955). *Street corner society* (2nd ed.). Chicago: University of Chicago Press.

Wiles, P. & Costello, A. (2000). *The 'road to nowhere': The evidence for travelling criminals. Home Office Research Study, 207*. London: Home Office.

Williams, K. (2003). *Understanding media theory*. London: Arnold.

Williams, K.M. (1981). *The Rastafarians*. London: Ward Lock Educational.

Williams, P. and Dickinson, J. (1993). Fear of crime: Read all about it? *British Journal of Criminology, 33*.

Wilson, B.R. (1966). *Religion and secular society*. London: C.A. Watts.

Wilson, B.R. (1970). *Religious sects*. London: Weidenfeld & Nicolson.

Wilson, B.R. (1976). *Contemporary transformations of religion*. London: Oxford University Press.

Wilson, B.R. (1982). *Religion in sociological perspective*. Oxford: Oxford University Press.

Wilson, J. & Kelling, G. (2003). Broken windows: The police and neighbourhood safety. In E. McLaughlin et al. (Eds.), *Criminological perspectives* (2nd ed.). London: Sage.

Wilson, J.Q. & Hernstein, R. (1985). *Crime and human nature*. New York: Simon & Schuster.

Wilson, J.Q. (1975). *Thinking about crime*. New York: Basic Books.

Wilson, J.Q. (1983). *Thinking about crime* (2nd ed.). New York: Basic Books.

Winant, H. (1994). Racial formation and identity. In A. Rattansi & S. Westwood (Eds.), *Racism, modernity and identity*. Cambridge: Polity Press.

Winlow, S. (2001). *Badfellas: Crime, violence and new masculinities.* London: Macmillan.

Woodhead, L. & Heelas, P. (Eds.) (2000). *Religion in modern times: An interpretive anthology.* Oxford: Blackwell.

Woodiwiss, M. (1993). Crime's global reach. In F. Pearce & M. Woodiwiss (Eds.), *Toxic capitalism: Corporations, crime and the chemical industry.* Aldershot: Ashgate.

Wright, R.T. & Decker, S.H. (1994). *Burglars on the job: Street life and residential break-ins.* Boston, MA: Northeastern University Press.

Yeo, A. (1988). Is there anybody out there? *Midweek,* 28 July.

Yinger, M. (1970). *The scientific study of religion.* London: Routledge.

York, M. (1995). *The emerging network: A sociology of the New Age and Neo-Pagan networks.* Lanham, MD: Rowman & Littlefield.

Young, J. (1971). *The drugtakers.* London: Paladin.

Young, J. (1986). The failure of criminology: The need for a radical realism. In R. Matthews & J. Young (Eds.), *Confronting crime.* London: Sage.

Young, J. (1992). Ten points of realism. In J. Young & R. Matthews (Eds.), *Rethinking criminology: The realist debate.* London: Sage.

Young, J. (1997). Left realist criminology. In M. Maguire et al. (Eds.), *The Oxford handbook of criminology* (2nd ed.). Oxford: Oxford University Press.

Young, J. (1999). *The exclusive society: Social exclusion, crime and difference in late modernity.* London: Sage.

Young, J. (2002). Crime and social exclusion. In M. Maguire et al. (Eds.), *The Oxford handbook of criminology* (3rd ed.). Oxford: Oxford University Press.

Younge, G. (2008). Greed has pushed political credibility and financial trust into freefall. *The Guardian,* 22 December.

Zeitlin, I. (1971). *Ideology and social theory.* Glencoe Illinois: The Free Press.

Author index

Subject index

Text acknowledgements

We are grateful to the following for permission to reproduce copyright material:

A&C Black Publishers Ltd and Suhrkamp Verlag for an extract from *Life of Galileo (Leben des Galilei)* by Brecht, B., copyright © 1986, A&C Black Publishers Ltd and Suhrkamp Verlag; Beacon Press, Boston for a chart from *The New Media Monopoly* by Bagdikian, B., copyright © 2004 by Ben Bagdikian, reprinted by permission of Beacon Press, Boston; Berghahn Books Ltd for an extract from "From Comic Asians to Asian Comics: Goodness Gracious Me TV Comedy and Ethnicity" by Gillespie, M., published in *Group Identities on French and British Television* eds Scriven, M. & E. Roberts copyright © Berghahn Books Ltd; Birmingham Post for an extract from Birmingham MP, Mrs Jill Knight, quoted in the *Birmingham Evening Mail*, 20 August 1972, reproduced with permission; Blackwell Publishing Ltd for the table "Religious beliefs" adapted from *God is dead: Secularisation in the West* by Bruce, S., copyright © 2002, reproduced with permission of Blackwell Publishing Ltd; Cengage Learning Services Limited for the figure "Types of suicide and the balance of society" adapted from *The Problem of Sociology* by Newby, H., and Lee, D., copyright © Cengage Learning Services Limited 1983; Christian Research Association for the table "Membership of Religious Groups (UK, Thousands)" adapted from Religious Trends by Brierley, P., 2000, reproduced with permission; The Christian Science Monitor for an extract from "Wealth gospel propels poor Guatemalens" by Miller Llana, S., reproduced with permission from the December 17, 2007 issue of *The Christian Science Monitor* (www.csmonitor.com) copyright © 2007 The Christian Science Monitor; Emissaries of Divine Light for an extract from http://emissaries.org/, reproduced with permission; Euro Correspondent for an extract adapted from "EU green crime proposals" www.euro-correspondent.com 6 December 2008, granted with permission; The Express for the headline "Yobs Plot War" *The Star* during European Championship in 1988 and an extract from "Harry is 'out of control" *The Sunday Express* 20 July 2003 copyright © The Express 1988, 2003; Greenpeace for an extract about GM crops from wwwgreenpeace.org.uk; Guardian News & Media Ltd for extracts adapted from "No more suicides" *The Guardian*, 4 November 1985; "The real scroungers" *The Observer*, 23 October 1988; The chart "Mad dogs and Englishmen" *The Guardian* 23 January 1991; Quote by Newburn, T., Policy Studies Institute *The Guardian* 26 November 1993; "Global risks - the world's fish" *The Observer*, 5 April 1995; "Global risks – Chernobyl" *The Observer*, 30 April 1995; "Play your card right" by Iannucci, A., *The Guardian* 2 May 1995; the chart and text "An open system" *The Observer*, 28 May 1995; Line dancing "Hoedown showdown as Norman changes to Norma" by Wilson, J., *The Guardian*, 17 April 1998; "Argument rages over Sarah's law" by Hall, S., *The Guardian* 13 December 2001; "Police accused of failure over racism" by Carter, H., *The Guardian*, 8 November 2002; "Police failing to tackle domestic abuse" by Cowan, R., *The Guardian*, 19 February 2004; "Freedom in Farsi" *The Guardian* 20 December 2004; "Dispatches" *The Guardian* 28 November 2005; "Comment and Debate: Greed has pushed political credibility and financial trust into freefall" by Younge, G., *The Guardian*, 22 December 2008; and "Hundreds of Brazil's eco-warriors at risk of assassination" by Phillips, T., *The Guardian*, 22 December 2008 copyright © Guardian News & Media Ltd 1985, 1988, 1991, 1993, 1994, 1998, 2001, 2002, 2004, 2005, 2008; Hodder & Stoughton Ltd for the book cover *A Most Wanted Man* by Le Carré, J., 2008, reproduced with permission; Holt McDougal for an extract from "The Ghost Dance" adapted from *Bury my heart at Wounded Knee*, by Brown, D., copyright © 1975. Used by permission of Holt McDougal, a division of Houghton Mifflin Harcourt publishing company; The Home Office for "Crimes recorded by the police, England and Wales 1920-2007/08" adapted from Home Office, 2001; "Annual Abstract of Statistics, 2004"; "Conviction rates for different age groups" from *Patterns of offending behaviour: A New Approach*, Home Office Research Findings 171, 2002 and an extract adapted from "Applying psychology to imprisonment" by Eysenck, 1987, edited by McGurk, B., Thornton, D., & Williams, M.; and "Assessing the police use of decoy vehicles" from *Police Research Series 137*, 2000 Crown copyright © 1987, 2000, 2002, 2004; The Independent for extracts adapted from *The Independent* 26 November 1993 and "Secularisation in the English context" by Fowler, D., *The Independent* 6 December 1997, copyright © The Independent 1993, 1997; International Atomic Energy Agency for the figure 'Chernobyl', IAEA Bulletin, Vol. 28, No. 3 (1986) copyright © International Atomic Energy Agency, 1986; The Labour Party for quotations by Clement Atlee, Harold Wilson, Tony Blair from his speech to Labour party conference, 1999 and 2001 speech; and Gordon Brown's speeches at the Labour Party Conference, 2007 and September 2008, reproduced with permission; Macmillan for a figure from *Durkheim and the Study of Suicide* by Taylor, S., published 1982, St. Martin's Press, reproduced with permission of Palgrave Macmillan; The Margaret Thatcher Archive Trust for 2 quotations by Lady Margaret Thatcher, granted by kind permission of The Margaret Thatcher Archive Trust; Mirrorpix for the headlines "Plague of the Euro yob: Dutch go top of the Thug's table" *The Mirror* on 17 August 1972; "Mugging, To our Police, it's a frightening new strain of crime" *The Mirror* 30 March 1988; and "We trap internet child sex sicko - Shocking Internet peril that all concerned parents should be aware of" *The People* 20 July 2003 copyright © Mirrorpix 1972, 1988, 2003; Music Sales Limited for the lyric reproduction of "Breakfast In America" words & music by Rick Davies & Roger Hodgson copyright © 1979 Almo Music Corporation, USA/Delicate Music, USA, Universal Music Publishing Limited. Used by Permission of Music Sales Limited. All Rights Reserved. International Copyright Secured; NI Syndication Ltd for extracts adapted from press editorial *The Sun* 13 October 1972; "Robin Hood and Liberation Theology" by Longley, C., *The Times* 27 January 1986; headlines "Euro hoolies league" and "World War III" *The Sun* 1988; an extract and the image 'Burn your video nasties' *The Sun* 26 November 1993; headline "The terrifying violence that shames Britain" *Today* 28 September 1994; and the front page 'The Sun backs Blair" *The Sun* 18 March 1997 copyright © NI Syndication Ltd 1972, 1986, 1988, 1993, 1994, 1997; Office for National Statistics for "The BCS and police recorded crime"; "Worry about crime and newspaper readership" and "Neighbourhoods and offence rates" adapted from "Crime in England and Wales 2002/2003" by Simmons & Dodd; "BCS crime estimates, England and Wales 1981-2007/08 published in *Social Trends* 2002, 2004; the tables "Highest qualifications of school leavers" published in *Social Trends* 1972, 1986 by Census, Labour Force Survey and Office for National Statistics; "Representation of ethnic groups at different stages of the criminal justice process, 2000/01"; "Stop and search statistics" 2002; "Arrests per 1,000 population" 2002; "Male prison population per 100,000 population" 2002; "offenders found guilty or cautioned 2002" published in *Social Trends* 2004; and "Gender and victims of crime" 2003, Crown copyright © 2008; Open University Press for 2 figures adapted from *Postmodernism and Social Research* by Alvesson, M., 2002. Reproduced with the kind permission of Open University Press. All rights reserved; Palgrave Macmillan for extracts from *Policing the Crisis*, by Hall et al copyright © 1978, Palgrave Macmillan; Pew Research Center for 2 figures from "Internet Overtakes Newspapers As News Outlet", 23 December 2008, The Pew Research Center For The People & The Press, www.people-press.org, reproduced with permission; Philip Allan Updates for the graph "The timing of the revolution" adapted from *The Kendal Project: Testing 'The Spiritual Revolution Thesis'* by Heelas, P., *Sociology Review*, 13 (2) Nov 2003; 2 figures adapted from "Much ado about nothing? The sociology of moral panics", Muncie, J., *Social Studies Review 3*, 1987; an extract adapted from "Suicide a synoptic approach" by Swale *Sociology Review*, 12 2004, and extracts from *The sociology of the New Religions* by Wallis, R., September 1985, reproduced by permission of Philip Allan Updates; Princeton University Press for an extract from *The Invasion from Mars* by Cantril, H., copyright © 1940 Princeton University Press, 1968 renewed PUP, Preface copyright © 1966 by Hadley Cantril. Reprinted by permission of Princeton University Press; Project Syndicate for an extract from "A Human Rights Crime: The World must stop standing idle while the people of Gaza are treated with such cruelty" by Carter, J., *The Guardian*, 8 May 2008 copyright © Project Syndicate; Regime Change Iran for the website web blog header and The Blogspere Support logo copyright © Regime Change Iran http://regimechangeiran.com; Sage Publications for extracts adapted from "Scientology: Therapeutic Cult to Religious Sect" by Wallis, R., published in *Sociology Vol 9, 1*, pp 89-100, 1 January 1975, copyright © 1975; and *The problem of crime* edited by Muncie, J. & McLaughlin, E., 1996. Reproduced by permission of SAGE Publications, London, Los Angeles, New Delhi and Singapore, copyright © Sage Publications, 1975, 1996; The Sentencing Project for a table adapted from *Intended and Unintended Consequences: State Racial Disparities in Imprisonment* by Mauer, M., 1997 reproduced with permission; Shambhala International and artist Cynthia Moku for a screenshot and extract about Shambhala from www.shambhala.org, reproduced with permission; Richard Silburn for a table adapted from *Poverty: The Forgotten Englishman* by Coates & Silburn, 1973 copyright © Richard Silburn and Ken Coates, reproduced with permission; Solo Syndication for extracts from "How to sweep these beggars from our streets" by Marsland, D., *The Daily Mail* 30 May 1994; "Heat on ministers as violent crimes go up by 20pc" by Butler, J., *The Daily Mail* 26 May 2003; "Murdered by a savage out on bail" *The Daily Mail* 6 May 2004; "Financial adviser accused of murdering his client" *The Daily Mail* 14 May 2004; "Terror of 'SAS' rapist" by Levy, A., *The Daily Mail* 18 May 2004; "Thugs target the famous" *The Daily Mail* 24 May 2004 and the headlines "In a coma, the lawyer attacked by teen gang" by Kelly, T., *The Daily Mail* 21 June 2005; "This proud father came to Britain for a better life. He died in the street, one more victim of our yob culture" by Finney, S., *The Daily Mail* 30 June 2005; and "Louts destroy another family" by Wilkes, D., *The Daily Mail* 4 July 2005 copyright © The Daily Mail 1994, 2003, 2004, 2005; Spirituality & Health Media, LLC for the front cover of *Spirituality & Health Magazine* May/June 2008, reproduced with permission; The Stationery Office for extracts from House of Lords 2008, *The ownership of the news* Crown copyright © 2008; Taylor and Francis Books UK for the chart 'The Landlord-tenant structure' published in *Methods in Social Science: A Realist Approach* by Sayer, A., 1992; an extract from *Power, Crime and Mystification* by Box, S., 1983; and a table from *Suicide: a Study in Sociology* by Durkheim, E., 1970 copyright © Taylor and Francis Books UK; University of Chicago Press for an extract adapted from "Spatial distribution of delinquents in Chicago" in *Juvenile delinquency and urban areas* by Shaw & McKay copyright © 1942 University of Chicago Press, permission conveyed through Copyright Clearance Center, Inc; Watch Tower Bible and Tract Society of Pennsylvania for material about Jehovah's Witnesses and The Watch Tower, reproduced with permission; Waveland Press, Inc., for an extract from *Religion: The Social Context 5/e* by McGuire, M. B.; Long Grove, IL, reprinted by permission of Waveland Press, Inc., 2002 (reissued 2008). All rights reserved; and Yale University Press for an extract adapted from *The Last days of the Sioux Nation* by Utley, R.M., 1963 copyright © Yale University Press.

In some instances we have been unable to trace the owners of copyright material and we would appreciate any information that would enable us to do so.